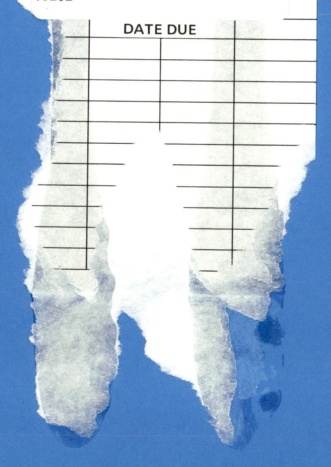

WORLD ENCYCLOPEDIA OF POLITICAL SYSTEMS AND PARTIES

Fourth Edition

Volume II

(Haiti to Norway)

Neil Schlager and Jayne Weisblatt, Editors
Orlando J. Pérez, Consulting Editor

An imprint of Infobase Publishing

World Encyclopedia of Political Systems and Parties, Fourth Edition

Facts On File, Inc.
An imprint of Infobase Publishing
132 West 31st Street
New York NY 10001

Library of Congress Cataloging-in-Publication Data
World encyclopedia of political systems and parties—4th ed. / edited by
  Neil Schlager and Jayne Weisblatt ; consulting editor, Orlando J. Pérez.
    p. cm.
  Includes Index
  ISBN 0-8160-5953-5
  1. Political parties—Encyclopedias. 2. Comparative government—
    Encyclopedias. I. Delury, George E. II. Schlager, Neil, 1966–
    JF2011.W67 2006
      324.203—dc22   2005028118

Facts On File books are available at special discounts when purchased in bulk quantities for businesses, associations, institutions, or sales promotions. Please call our Special Sales Department in New York at (212) 967-8800 or (800) 322-8755.

You can find Facts On File on the World Wide Web at
http://www.factsonfile.com

Text design by Erika K. Arroyo
Cover design by Dorothy Preston
Illustrations by Dale Williams

Printed in the United States of America

VB FOF 10 9 8 7 6 5 4 3 2 1

This book is printed on acid-free paper.

Contents

Volume II

Volume III

List of Acronyms and Abbreviations

AAFU–see Anti-Communist and Anti-Imperialist Front of Ukraine

AAPO–see All-Amhara People's Organization (Ethiopia)

ABVP–see All-India Students Organization

AC–see Action for Change (Mauritania)

ACDP–see African Christian Democratic Party (South Africa)

ACLM–see Antigua Caribbean Liberation Movement (Antigua and Barbuda)

AD–see Alleanza Democratica (Italy)

AD–see Democratic Action (Venezuela)

AD–see Democratic Alliance (Guatemala)

ADA–see Democratic Alliance of Angola

ADEMA–see Alliance for Democracy in Mali-The African Party for Solidarity and Justice

ADERE–see Democratic and Republican Alliance (Gabon)

ADFL–see Alliance of Democratic Forces for Liberation of Congo/Zaire (D. Rep. Congo)

ADIK–see Fighting Democratic Movement (Cyprus)

ADM-19–see M-19 Democratic Alliance (Colombia)

ADP–see Alliance for Democracy and Progress (Benin)

ADP–see Alliance for Democracy and Progress (Central African Republic)

ADP–see Alliance for Democracy and Progress (Central African Republic)

ADP–see Arab Democratic Party (Israel)

ADP–see Assembly of People's Deputies (Burkina Faso)

ADR–see Action Committee for Democracy and Pension Justice (Luxembourg)

ADS–see Alternative for Democracy and Socialism (France)

ADSR–see Alliance of Democrats of the Slovak Republic

AEEM–see Association of Pupils and Students of Mali

AEPA–see All-Ethiopian Peasants Association

AETU–see All-Ethiopian Trade Union

AFC–see Alliance of Forces of Change (Niger)

AFD–see Alliance For Democracy (Nigeria)

AFD–see Alliance of Free Democrats (Hungary)

AFKM–see Congress Party for the Independence of Madagascar

AFKM-Renewal–see Congress Party for Madagascar Independence-Renewal Party

AFL–see Armed Forces of Liberia

AFL-CIO–see American Federation of Labor-Congress of Industrial Organizations (U.S.A.)

AFORD–see Alliance for Democracy (Malawi)

AFPF–see Armed Forces Pension Fund (Turkey)

AFPFL–see Anti-Fascist People's Freedom League (Myanmar)

AFRC–see Armed Forces Revolutionary Council (Sierra Leone)

Agaleu–see Ecologist Parties (Belgium)

AGP–see Assam Peoples Council (India)

AIADMK–see All-India Anna-Dravida Munnetra Kazhagam

AICC–see All-India Congress Committee

AICP–see All-India Communist Party

AID–see Agency for International Development (U.S.A.)

AKAR–see People's Justice Movement (Malaysia)

AKEL–see Progressive Party of the Working People (Cyprus)

AKPML–see Workers' Communist Party Marxist-Leninist (Norway)

AL–see Awami League (Bangladesh)

AL–see Awami League (Pakistan)

AL–see Liberal Alliance (Nicaragua)

ALEBA–see Luxembourg Association of Bank Staffs

ALF–see Arab Liberation Front (Palestinian Authority)

ALN–see National Liberation Army (Algeria)

ALO–see Austrian Alternative List

ALP–see Antigua Labour Party (Antigua and Barbuda)

ALP–see Australian Labor Party

AMAL–see Detachments of the Lebanese Resistance

AMP–see Association for Muslim Professionals (Singapore)

AMS–see Islamic Salvation Army (Algeria)

AMU–see African Mineworker's Union (Zambia)

AMU–see Arab Maghreb Union (Libya)

ANAGAN–see National Association of Ranchers (Panama)

ANAPO–see National Popular Alliance (Colombia)

AN–see Alleanza Nationale (Italy)

ANC–see African National Congress (South Africa)

ANC–see Conservative National Action (Nicaragua)

AND–see National Democratic Group (Andorra)

AND–see Nationalist Democratic Action (Bolivia)

ANDDS-Zaman Lahiya–see Nigerian Alliance for Democracy and Social Progress-Zaman Lahiya (Niger)

ANDI–see National Association of Industrialists (Colombia)

ANDM–see Amhara National Democratic Movement (Ethiopia)

ANL–see National Liberating Alliance (Brazil)

ANM–see Armenian National Movement

ANO–see Alliance of a New Citizen (Slovakia)

ANP–see Alliance for New Politics (Philippines)

ANPP–see All Nigeria People's Party

AOV and UNIE 55+–see General Union of the Elderly (Netherlands)

AP–see Popular Action (Peru)

AP–see Popular Alliance (Spain)

AP5–see Popular Alliance 5 (Guatemala)

APAI–see Israel Workers Party

APC–see All People's Congress (Sierra Leone)

APC–see Popular Conservative Alliance (Nicaragua)

APED–see Alliance for Ecology and Democracy (France)

APEDE–see Panamanian Association of Business Executives

APGA–see All Progressive Grand Alliance (Nigeria)

APK–see Worker Party Communists (Sweden)

APMU–see All-Popular Movement of Ukraine

APNI or AP–see Alliance Party of Northern Ireland

APP–see All People's Party (Nigeria)

APRA–see American Popular Revolutionary Alliance (Peru)

APRC–see Alliance for Patriotic Reorientation and Construction (Gambia)

APRE–see Ecuadorian Popular Revolutionary Action

APU–see United Peoples Alliance (Portugal)

ARD–see Alliance for the Restoration of Democracy (Pakistan)

ARD–see Democratic Resistance Alliance (D. Rep. Congo)

AREMA–see Vanguard of the Malagasy Revolution (Madagascar)

ARENA–see National Renovating Alliance (Brazil)

ARENA–see Nationalist Republican Alliance (El Salvador)

AREV–see Red and Green Alternative (France)

ARF–see Armenian Revolutionary Federation

ARLN–see Revolutionary Army of Liberation of Northern Niger

ARMM–see Autonomous Region of Muslim Mindanao (Philippines)

ARP–see Anti-Revolutionary Party (Netherlands)

ASD–see Dominican Social Alliance Party

ASDT–see Timorese Social-Democratic Association (Timor Leste)

ASEAN–see Association of Southeast Asian Nations

ASI–see Federation of Labor (Iceland)

ASIS–see Alliance of Small Island States (Maldives)

ASP–see Afro-Shirazi Party (Tanzania)

ASU–see Arab Socialist Union (Egypt)

ASU–see Arab Socialist Union (Libya)

ATC–see Association of Rural Workers (Nicaragua)

ATLU–see Antigua Trades Labour Union (Antigua and Barbuda)

AV/MRDN–see And Jeff: Revolutionary Movement for the New Democracy (Senegal)

AWARE–see Association of Women for Action and Research (Singapore)

AWS–see Solidarity Electoral Action (Poland)

AYD–see Alliance of Young Democrats (Hungary)

AZADHO–see Zairian Association for the Defense of Human Rights (D. Rep. Congo)

BAKSAL-see Bangladesh Krishak Sramik Awami
　　League
BAM-see Botswana Alliance Movement
BAMCEF-see All-India Backward and Minority
　　Communities Employees Federation
BBB-see Bulgarian Business Bloc
BCP-see Basotho Congress Party (Lesotho)
BCP-see Botswana Congress Party
BDF-see Botswana Defense Force
BDG-see Gabonese Democratic Group
BDH-see Peace and Democracy Movement (Cyprus)
BDP-see Bahamian Democratic Party
BDP-see Botswana Democratic Party
BDS-see Senegalese Democratic Bloc
BE-see Left Bloc (Portugal)
BIP-see Citizen's Initiative Parliament (Austria)
BIS-see Social Democratic Institutional Block
　　(Dominican Rep.)
BITU-see Bustamante Industrial Trade Union
　　(Jamaica)
BJP-see Bhanatiya Jawata Party (India)
BKU-see Bhanasiya Kisan Union, Punjab (India)
BKU-see Bhanatiya Kisan Union, Uttar Pradesh
　　(India)
BLDP-see Buddhist Liberal Democratic Party
　　(Cambodia)
BLP-see Barbados Labour Party
BLP-see Botswana Labour Party
BN-see National Front (Malaysia)
BNA Act-see British North America Act (Canada)
BNF-see Botswana National Front
BNG-see Galician Nationalist Bloc (Spain)
BNP-see Bangladesh National Party
BNP-see Basotho National Party (Lesotho)
BNP-see British National Party (UK of Great Britain)
BPC-see Basic People's Congress (Libya)
BPF-see Belarusian Popular Front "Adrazennie"
BPP-see Bechuanaland People's Party (Botswana)
BPP-see Botswana Peoples Party
BPU-see Botswana Progressive Union
BQ-see Bloc Quebecois (Canada)
BRA-see Bougainville Revolutionary Army (Papua
　　New Guinea)
BSB-see Burkina Socialist Bloc
BSP-see Bhutan Samas Party (Party of Society's
　　Maturity) (India)
BSP-see Bulgarian Socialist Party
BSPP-see Burma Socialist Program Party (Myanmar)
BWF-see Botswana Workers Front
C-see Center Party (Sweden)
C90-see Change 90 (Peru)
CA-see Canadian Alliance

CAC-see Argentine Chamber of Commerce
CACIF-see Coordinating Committee of Commercial,
　　Industrial, and Financial Associations
　　(Guatemala)
CADE-see Annual Conference of Business Executives
　　(Panama)
CAFPDE-see Council of Alternative Forces for Peace
　　and Democracy (Ethiopia)
CAFTA-see Central American Free Trade Agreement
CAN-see Authentic Nationalist Central (Guatemala)
CAP-see Convention for a Progressive Alternative
　　(France)
CASC-see Autonomous Confederation of Christian
　　Syndicates (Dominican Rep.)
CAUS-see Council for Union Action and Unity
　　(Nicaragua)
CC-see Canarian Coalition (Spain)
CC-see Christian Way (Nicaragua)
CCD-see Christian Democratic Center (Italy)
CCD-see Democratic Constituent Congress (Peru)
CCE-see Central Elections Council (El Salvador)
CCF-see Co-operative Commonwealth Federation
　　(Canada)
CCM-see Concerned Citizens Movement (Saint
　　Kitts)
CCM-see Revolutionary Party (Tanzania)
CCOOs-see Worker's Commissions (Spain)
CCP-see Chinese Communist Party
CD-see Center Democrats (Denmark)
CD-see Center Democrats (Netherlands)
CD-see Democratic Change (Panama)
CD-see Democratic Coordination (Nicaragua)
CDA-see Christian Democratic Appeal (Netherlands)
CdIA-see Camp des Iles Autonomous (Comoros)
CDJ-see Congress for Democracy and Justice
　　(Gabon)
CDP-see Congress for Democracy and Progress
　　(Burkina Faso)
CDP-see Convention of Democrats and Patriots
　　(Senegal)
CDPA-see Democratic Convention of African People
　　(Togo)
CDPP-see Christian Democratic People's Party
　　(Hungary)
CDRs-see Committees for the Defense of the
　　Revolution (Ghana)
CDRs-see Committees of the Defense of the
　　Revolution (Burkina Faso)
CDS-see Center of Social Democrats (France)
CDS-see Party of the Social Democratic Center
　　(Portugal)
CDS-see Social Democratic Center (Angola)

CDS-see Social Democratic Center (Spain)
CDS-see Social Democratic Center Party (Portugal)
CDS-Rahama-see Democratic and Social ConventionRahama (Niger)
CDT-see Democratic Labor Confederation (Morocco)
CDU-see Unified Democratic Coalition (Portugal)
CDU-see Union of Christian Democrats (Italy)
CDU-see United Democratic Center (El Salvador)
CDU-see United Democratic Coalition (Portugal)
CDU/CSU-see Christian Democrats (Germany)
CEA -see Argentine Episcopal Conference
CEC-see Central Executive Committee (Singapore)
CEFTA-see Central European Free Trade Agreement
CEMAC-see Economic and Monetary Community of Central Africa (Central African Republic)
CEMC-see Central Election Management Committee (South Korea)
CEN-see National Executive Committee (Mexico)
CEN-see National Executive Committee (Venezuela)
CES-see Convergence Ecology Solidarity (France)
CETU-see Confederation of Ethiopian Trade Unions
CFD-see Coordination of Democratic Forces (Burkina Faso)
CFN-see Coordination of New Forces (Togo)
CFP-see Concentration of Popular Forces (Ecuador)
CG-see Galician Centrist (Spain)
CGEM-see General Economic Confederation of Morocco
CGT-see General Confederation of Labor (Argentina)
CGT-see General Confederation of Labor (France)
CGT-see General Confederation of Workers (Nicaragua)
CGTI-see Independent General Workers Confederation (Nicaragua)
CGTP-see General Central of Workers of Panama
CGUP-see Guatemalan Committee of Patriotic Unity
CHAUSTA-see Movement for Justice and Prosperity (Tanzania)
CHU-see Christian-Historical Union (Netherlands)
CIA-see U.S. Central Intelligence Agency
CIDOB-see Indigenous Confederation of the East, Chaco, and Amazonia of Bolivia
CIPRODEH-see Center for the Investigation and Promotion of Human Rights (Honduras)
CIS-see Commonwealth of Independent States
CiU-see Convergence and Union (Spain)
CLA-see Caprivi Liberation Army (Namibia)
CLC-see Canadian Labor Congress
CLR-see Convention of Reformist Liberals (Gabon)
CLSTP-see Liberation Committee of Sao Tome and Principe
CM-see Council of Ministers (Cuba)

CMC-see Central Military Commission (China)
CMEA or COMECON-see Council for Mutual Economic Assistance (Vietnam)
CMLN-see Military Committee of National Liberation (Mali)
CMRPN-see Military Committee of Redressment for National Progress (Burkina Faso)
CMS-see Supreme Military Council (Niger)
CMSS-see Czech-Moravian Party of the Center (Czech Rep.)
CN-see National Convention (CAR)
CNC-see National Peasant Confederation (Mexico)
CND-see National Development Council (Rwanda)
CNDF-see Congress of National Democratic Forces (Ukraine)
CNE-see National Electoral Council (Venezuela)
CNI-see National Center of Independents and Peasants (France)
CNID-see National Congress of Democratic Initiative (Mali)
CNIR-see Inter-Regional National Council (France)
CNJ-see National Council of the Judiciary (El Salvador)
CNOP-see National Federation of Popular Organizations (Mexico)
CNR-see National Council of Revolution (Burkina Faso)
CNRM-see National Council of Maubere Resistance (Timor Leste)
CNS-see National Unity Commission (Rwanda)
CNS-see Sovereign National Council (Chad)
CNT-see National Workers Federation (Mexico)
CNTP-see National Worker's Central of Panama
CNU-see Cameroon National Union
COAS-see Chief of Army Staff (Pakistan)
COB-see Confederation of Bolivian Workers
COD-see Coalition of Democratic Opposition (Togo)
CoD-see Congress of Democrats (Namibia)
CODE-see Democratic Coordinator (Peru)
CODEH-see Committee for the Defense of Human Rights in Honduras
COFADEH-see Committee of the Families of the Detained and Disappeared in Honduras
COMELEC-see Commission on Elections (Philippines)
CONAIE-see Confederation of Indigenous Nationalities of Ecuador
CONAPRODEH-see National Commission for the Protection of Human Rights (Honduras)
CONCAMIN-see Confederation of Industrial Chambers (Mexico)
CONCANACO-see Confederation of National Chambers of Commerce (Mexico)

CONCLAT-see National Coordination of the Working Class (Brazil)

CONDEPA-see Conscience of the Fatherland (Bolivia)

CONEP-see National Council of Private Enterprise (Panama)

CONFENIAE-see Confederation of Indigenous Nationalities of the Amazon (Ecuador)

COPCON-see Continental Operations Command (Portugal)

COPE-see Committee on Political Education (U.S.A.)

COPEI-see Christian Social Party (Venezuela)

COSATU-see Congress of South African Trade Unions

COSEP-see Superior Council of Private Enterprise (Nicaragua)

COSU-see Coordination of the United Senegalese Opposition

COTU-see Central Organization of Trade Unions (Kenya)

CP-see Popular Coalition (Spain)

CPBM-see Communist Party of Bohemia and Moravia (Czech Rep.)

CPC-see Central People's Committee (North Korea)

CPC-see Conservative Party of Canada

CPCC-see Chinese People's Consultative Conference

CPD-see Citizens for Democracy (Guatemala)

CPDM-see Cameroon People's Democratic Movement

CPI-see Communist Party of India

CPIB-see Coordinator of the Indigenous Peoples of Beni (Bolivia)

CPM-see Communist Party of India (Marxist)

CPM-see Communist Party of Moldavia (Moldova)

CPML-see Communist Party of India

CPN-see Communist Party of the Netherlands

CPP-see Cambodian People's Party

CPP-see Communist Party of the Philippines

CPP-see Convention People's Party (Ghana)

CPRF-see Communist Party of the Russian Federation

CPSA-see Conservative Party (South Africa)

CPSU-see Communist Party of the Soviet Union (Tajikistan)

CPSU-see Communist Party of the Soviet Union (Turkmenistan)

CPT-see Communist Party of Tajikistan

CPT-see Communist Party of Turkmenistan

CPT-see Permanent Congress of Workers (Nicaragua)

CPU-see Communist Party of Ukraine

CPUz-see Communist Party of Uzbekistan

CRA-see Argentine Rural Confederations

CRA-see Coordination of Armed Resistance (Niger)

CRC-see Convention for the Renewal of the Comoros

CRM-see Citizens Rights Movement (Israel)

CRN-see Council of National Reconciliation (Mali)

CROC-see Revolutionary Federation of Workers and Peasants (Mexico)

CRP-see Circle for Renewal and Progress (Gabon)

CS-see Council of State (Cuba)

CSE-see Supreme Electoral Council (Nicaragua)

CSL-see Czech People's Party

CSN-see Council of National Health (Niger)

CSP-see Council of Health of the People (Burkina Faso)

CSR-see Congress for the Second Republic (Malawi)

CSS-see Czech Socialist Party

CSSD-see Czech Social Democratic Party

CST-see Higher Transitional Council (Chad)

CST-see Sandinista Workers Confederation (Nicaragua)

CSTC-see Trade Union Confederation of Colombian Workers

CSU-see Christian Social Union (Germany)

CSUTCB-see United Syndical Confederation of Bolivian Peasant Workers

CSV-see Christian Social People's Party (Luxembourg)

CTC-see Confederation of Colombian Workers

CTM-see Confederation of Mexican Workers

CTN-see Social-Christian Nicaraguan Worker's Confederation

CTP-see Republican Turkish Party (Cyprus)

CTRP-see Confederation of Workers of the Republic of Panama

CTSP-see Transition Committee for the Health of the People (Mali)

CTV-see Confederation of Venezuelan Workers

CU-see Center Democrats (Netherlands)

CUAS-see Chief of Army Staff (Pakistan)

CUE-see Civic United Front (Tanzania)

CUG-see Citizen's Union of Georgia

CUS-see Confederation of Labor Unification (Nicaragua)

CUT-see Central Union of Workers (Brazil)

CVP-see Christian Democratic Parties (Belgium)

CVP-see Christian Democratic People's Party of Switzerland

CVP-see Civic United Front (Tanzania)

CWC-see Ceylon Workers Congress (Sri Lanka)

CWC-see Congress Working Committee (India)

CYL-see Congress Youth League (South Africa)

D66-see Democrats 66 (Netherlands)
DA-see Democratic Alliance (South Africa)
DA-see Democratic Alternative (Macedonia)
DAC-see Democratic Action Congress (Trinidad & Tobago)
DAP-see Democratic Action Party (Malaysia)
DC-see Christian Democracy (Spain)
DC-see Christian Democratic Party (Italy)
DC-see Democratic Arrangement (Dominican Rep.)
DC-see Democratic Center (Croatia)
DC-see Democratic Convergence (Guatemala)
DC-see Deputy Commissioner (Pakistan)
DCG-see Christian Democrats (Guatemala)
DDCs-see District Development Councils (Sri Lanka)
DDLP-see Dominican Democratic Labor Party (Dominica)
DEMOS-see Democratic Opposition of Slovenia
DEMYC-see Democratic Youth Community of Europe
DEPOS-see Democratic Movement of Serbia
DF-see Danish People's Party
DFLP-see Democratic Front for the Liberation of Palestine
DFP-see Democratic Freedom Party (Dominica)
DFPE-see Democratic Front for Peace and Equality (Israel)
DIKKI-see Democratic Social Movement (Greece)
DIKO-see Democratic Party (Cyprus)
DISK-see Confederation of Revolutionary Workers' Unions (Turkey)
DISY-see Democratic Rally (Cyprus)
DJAMA-see Masses (Guinea)
DJP-see Democratic Justice Party (South Korea)
DL-see Liberal Democracy (France)
DLBM-see Democratic League of Bosniaks in Macedonia
DLECG-see Democratic List for a European Montenegro (Serbia and Montenegro)
DLF-see Liberal People's Party (Norway)
DLP-see Democratic Labour Party (Barbados)
DLP-see Democratic Left Party (Turkey)
DLP-see Democratic Liberal Party (South Korea)
DLP-see Dominican Labour Party (Dominica)
DM-see District Minister (Sri Lanka)
DMC-see Democratic Movement for Change (Israel)
DMK-see Dravidian Progressive Federation-Dravida Munnetra Kazhagam (India)
DMLP-see Democratic Movement for the Liberation of Eritrea
DMOs-see Democratic Mass Organizations (Tanzania)

DN-see National Directorate (Nicaragua)
DNA-see Labor Party (Norway)
DOLA-see Department of Local Administration (Thailand)
DOP-see Declaration of Principles (Israel)
DP-see Democratic Party (Cyprus)
DP-see Democratic Party (Kenya)
DP-see Democratic Party (Luxembourg)
DP-see Democratic Party (Seychelles)
DP-see Democratic Party (Tanzania)
DP-see Democratic Party (Turkey)
DP-see Democratic Party (Uganda)
DP-see Democratic Party (Zimbabwe)
DP-see Popular Democracy (Ecuador)
DPA-see Albanian Democratic Party (Macedonia)
DPJ-see Democratic Party of Japan
DPP-see Democratic People's Party (Turkey)
DPP-see Democratic Progressive Party (Taiwan)
DPS-see Movement for Rights and Freedoms (Bulgaria)
DPSCG-see Democratic Party of Socialists of Montenegro (Serbia & Montenegro)
DPSM-see Democratic Party of Serbs in Macedonia
DPT-see Democratic Party of Tajikistan
DPT-see Democratic Party of Turkey
DPT-see Democratic Party of Turkmenistan
DPTM-see Democratic Party of Turks in Macedonia
DPU-see Democratic Party of Ukraine
DRC-see Democratic Republic of Congo
DRP-see Democratic Republican Party (South Korea)
DRY-see Democratic Republic of Yemen
DS-see Democratic Party (Serbia & Montenegro)
DS-see Democratic Party (Slovakia)
DS-see Socialist Democracy (Spain)
DSS-see Democratic Party of Serbia
DTA-see Democratic Turnhalle Alliance (Namibia)
DUI-see Democratic Union for Integration (Macedonia)
DUP-see Democratic Unionist Party (Northern Ireland)
DUP-see Democratic Unionist Party (Sudan)
DUS-see Democratic Union of Slovakia
DVU-see German People's Union (Germany)
DZJ-see Pensions for Secure Living (Czech Rep.)
DZMH-see Democratic Union of Magyars in Croatia
EA-see Basque Solidarity (Spain)
Ecolo-see Ecologist Parties (Belgium)
ECOMOG-see Economic Community of West African States Cease-Fire Monitoring Group
ECOWAS-see Economic Community of West African States
ECZ-see Church of Christ in Zaire (D. Rep. Congo)

EDI–see United Democrats (Cyprus)
EDP–see Erk "Will" Democratic Party (Uzbekistan)
EDU–see European Democratic Union
EE–see Basque Left (Spain)
EEA–see European Economic Agreement
EEC–see European Economic Community
EGLE–see Every Ghanian Living Everywhere
EGP–see Guerrilla Army of the Poor (Guatemala)
EL–see Euroleft Coalition (Bulgaria)
ELF–see Eritrean Liberation Front
EMU–see Economic and Monetary Union
ENIP–see Estonian National Independence Party
EOP–see Executive Office of the President (U.S.A.)
EP–see European Parliament
EPDP–see Eelam People's Democratic Party (Sri Lanka)
EPLF–see Eritrean People's Liberation Front
EPP–see Evangelical People's Party (Netherlands)
EPRDF–see Ethiopian Peoples' Revolutionary Democratic Front
EPRLF–see Eelam Peoples' Revolutionary Liberation Front (Sri Lanka)
EPS–see Sandinista Popular Army (Nicaragua)
ERC–see Catalonian Republican Left (Spain)
ERTU–see Egyptian Radio and Television Union
ESNS–see Coexistence (Slovakia)
ET–see Ethics and Transparency (Nicaragua)
ETA–see Basque Nation and Liberty (Spain)
ETDF–see East Timor Defence Force
ETP–see Enlightened Turkey Party
EU–see European Union
EVP–see Protestant People's Party (Switzerland)
FAA–see Angolan Armed Forces
FACA–see Armed Forces of the Central African Republic
FALINTIL–see National Armed Liberation Forces of East Timor (Timor Leste)
FAR–see African Forum for Reconstruction (Gabon)
FAR–see Front of Associations for Renewal (Togo)
FAR–see Rebel Armed Forces (Guatemala)
FAR–see Republic Action Federation (Chad)
FAR–see Royal Armed Forces (Morocco)
FARC–see Revolutionary Armed Forces of Colombia
FARD–see Action Front for Renewal and Development (Benin)
FATAs–see Federally Administered Tribal Areas (Pakistan)
FAZ–see Armed Forces of Zaire (D. Rep. Congo)
FBP–see Progressive Citizen's Party (Liechtenstein)
FC–see Civic Forum (CAR)
FC–see Federal Capital (Pakistan)
FCC–see Federal Communications Commission (U.S.A.)

FCD–see Civic Democratic Front (Guatemala)
FD–see Democratic Force (France)
FDA–see Angolan Democratic Forum
FDCs–see Forces Defence Committees (Ghana)
FDF–see French-Speaking Democratic Front (Belgium)
FDIC–see Front for the Defense of Constitutional Institutions (Morocco)
FDN–see National Democratic Front (Mexico)
FDNG–see New Guatemalan Democratic Front
FDN-Mountounchi–see Nigerian Democratic Front-Mountounchi (Niger)
FDP–see Democratic and Patriotic Forces (Rep. of Congo)
FDP–see Free Democratic Party (Germany)
FDP–see Radical Democratic Party of Switzerland
FDR–see Democratic Front of Renewal (Niger)
FDU–see United Democratic Forces (Rep. of Congo)
FEDECAFE–see National Federation of Coffee Growers (Colombia)
FEDECAMAS–see Federation of Chambers of Commerce (Venezuela)
FEDEMU–see Federal Democratic Movement of Uganda
FENALCO–see National Federation of Merchants (Colombia)
FESE–see Federation of Secondary Students of Ecuador
FEUE–see Federation of University Students of Ecuador
FEUU–see Federation of Uruguayan University Students
FF–see Front of Democratic Forces (Djibouti)
FFD–see Front of the Democratic Forces (Morocco)
FFS–see Socialist Forces Front (Algeria)
FI–see Forward Italy
FIDA–see Palestinian Democratic Union Party
FIM–see Independent Clean Government Front (Peru)
FIS–see Islamic Salvation Front (Algeria)
FL–see Free List Party (Liechtenstein)
FLAA–see Liberation Front of Air and Azaouad (Niger)
FLAM–see African Liberation Forces of Mauritania
FLC–see Congolese Liberation Front (Central African Republic)
FLEC–see Front for the Liberation of the Cabinda Enclave (Angola)
FLING–see Front for the Liberation and Independence of Guinea
FLN–see National Liberation Front (Algeria)
FLOSY–see Front for the Liberation of Occupied South Yemen
FLQ–see Quebec Liberation Front (Canada)
FLT–see Liberation Front of Tamoust (Niger)
FMG–see Federal Military Government (Nigeria)
FMLN–see Farabundo Marti National Liberation Front (El Salvador)

FN–see National Front (Belgium)

FN–see National Front (France)

FN–see National Front (Spain)

FNC–see Federal National Council (United Arab Emirates)

FNDR–see National Front for the Defense of the Revolution (Madagascar)

FNJ–see National Front for Justice (Comoros)

FNLA–see National Front for the Liberation of Angola

FNM–see Free National Movement (Bahamas)

FNP–see National Progressive Force (Dominican Rep.)

FNR–see National Reconstruction Front (Ecuador)

FNT–see National Worker's Front (Nicaragua)

FNTC–see National Front of Workers and Peasants (Peru)

FO–see Worker's Force (France)

FODEM–Democratic Forum for Modernity (Central African Republic)

FORD–see Forum for Restoration of Democracy (Tanzania)

FORD–see Forum for Restoration of Democracy-Kenya-Asili

FP–see Federal Party (Sri Lanka)

FP–see Felicity Party (Turkey)

FP–see Liberal Party (Sweden)

FP–see National Solidarity (Madagascar)

FP–see Patriotic Front (D. Rep. Congo)

FP–see Popular Front (Burkina Faso)

FP–see Progress Party (Denmark)

FP–see Progressive Federation (Spain)

FPD–see Free Democrats (Germany)

FPD–see Front for Democracy (Angola)

FPI–see Ivorian Popular Front (Ivory Coast)

FPLS–see Patriotic Front of Liberation of the Sahara (Niger)

FPO–see Freedom Party (of Austria) or Freedomites

FPP–see Patriotic Front for Progress (Central African Republic)

FPR–see Rwanda Patriotic Front

FPT–see Ivorian Popular Front (Ivory Coast)

FRA–see Afarist Radical Front (Ecuador)

FRAP–see Popular Action Front (Chile)

FRD–see Forum for the Restoration of Democracy (Comoros)

FRDD–see Front for the Restoration and Defense of Democracy (Niger)

FRDE–see Front for the Restoration of Right and Equality (Djibouti)

Frelimo–see Front for the Liberation of Mozambique

FREPAP–see Popular Agrarian Front of Peru

Frepaso–see Front for a Country in Solidarity (Argentina)

FRETILIN–see Revolutionary Front for an Independent East Timor (Timor Leste)

FRG–see Guatemalan Republican Front

FRN–see Front for National Reconstruction (Haiti)

FRODEBU–see Burundi Democratic Front

FROLINAT–see Chad National Liberation Front

FRP–see Free Republic Party (Turkey)

FRUD–see Front for the Restoration of Unity and Democracy (Djibouti)

FSB–see Bolivian Socialist Falange

FSB–see Federal Security Council (Russia)

FSLN–see Sandinista National Liberation Front (Nicaragua)

FSN–see National Salvation Front (Romania)

FSTMB–see Bolivian Mineworkers Syndical Federation

FSTSE–see Federation of Unions of Workers in the Service of the State (Mexico)

FTC–see Federal Trade Commission (U.S.A.)

FUDR–see United Front for Democracy and the Republic (Burkina Faso)

FULRO–see United Front for the Struggle of Oppressed Races (Vietnam)

FUN–see National Unity Front (Guatemala)

FUNCINPEC–see National United Front for an Independent, Neutral, Peaceful and Cooperative Cambodia

FUR–see United Revolutionary Front (Guatemala)

FUSA–see United Front for the Salvation of Angola

FUT–see Unitary Workers Front (Ecuador)

GA–see Green Alternatives (Austria)

GAD–see Action Group for Democracy (Dominican Rep.)

GAD–see Grand Alliance for Democracy (Philippines)

GANA–see Grand National Alliance (Guatemala)

GAO–see General Accounting Office (U.S.A.)

GAP–see Guyana Action Party

GAWU–see Guyana Agricultural Workers Union

GCP–see Great Consolidated People's Party (Ghana)

GDF–see Guyanese Defense Force

GDK Azat–see Freedom Civil Movement of Kazakhstan "Azat"

GDP–see Guyana Democratic Party

GE–see Ecological Generation (France)

GGG–see Good and Green Georgetown (Guyana)

GIA–see Armed Islamic Group (Algeria)

GL–see Green Left (Netherlands)

GMMLU–see Grenada Manual and Mental Labourer's Union

GN–see National Guard (Nicaragua)

GNP–see Gross National Product
GPA–see General Peace Agreement (Mozambique)
GPC–see General People's Congress (Libya)
GPC–see General People's Congress (Yemen)
GPRA–see Provisional Government of the Republic of Algeria
GPS–see Green Party of Switzerland
GPV–see Reformed Political Association (Netherlands)
GRCs–see Group Representation Constituencies (Singapore)
GST–see Goods and Service Tax
GULP–see Grenada United Labour Party
GUP–see Grand Unity Party (Turkey)
GURN–see Government of Unity and National Reconciliation (Angola)
GURN–see Government of Unity and National Reconciliation (Palestinian Authority)
GWU–see General Workers' Union (Malta)
GYLA–see Georgian Young Lawyer's Association
HAMAS–see Movement for an Islamic Society (Algeria)
HB–see United People (Spain)
HBP–see People's Unity Party (Uzbekistan)
HCR–see High Council of the Republic (Togo)
HCR-PT–see High Council of the Republic-Transitional Parliament (D. Rep. Congo)
HD–see Grand National Party (South Korea)
HDF–see Hungarian Democratic Forum
HDP–see People's Democratic Party (Uzbekistan)
HDSS–see Croatian Democratic Peasants Party
HDZ–see Croatian Democratic Union
HDZ–see Croatian Democratic Union (Bosnia and Hercegovina)
HDZ–see Movement for Democracy (Slovakia)
HFP/PFH–see Humanist Feminist Party (Belgium)
HNS–see Croatian People's Party
HOS–see Croatian Defense Forces
HSD-SMS–see Movement for Autonomous Democracy of Moravia and Silesia (Czech Rep.)
HSLS–see Croatian Social Liberal Party
HSP–see Croatian Party of Rights
HSP–see Hungarian Socialist Party
HSS–see Croatian Peasant Party
HSU–see Croatian Party of Pensioners
HZ–see Farmer's Movement (Slovakia)
HZDS–see Movement for a Democratic Slovakia
I–see India National Congress
IAC–see Industrial Arbitration Court (Singapore)
IAF–see Islamic Action Front (Jordan)
ICJ–see International Court of Justice
ICP–see Indochinese Communist Party (Vietnam)

ICRDGE–see International Center for the Reformation and Development of the Georgian Economy
ICV–see Catalonia Green Initiative (Spain)
ID–see Democratic Left Party (Ecuador)
ID–see Independent Democrats (South Africa)
IDF–see Israeli Defense Force
IDH-RH–see Institute for Research, Documentation and Human Rights (Dominican Rep.)
IDN–see National Democratic Initiative (Andorra)
IDS–see Istrian Democratic Assembly (Croatia)
IEC–see Independent Electoral Commission (South Africa)
IEPES–see Institute of Political, Economic and Social Studies (Mexico)
IFE–see Federal Electoral Institute (Mexico)
IFES–see International Foundation for Election Systems
IFLB–see Islamic Front for the Liberation of Bahrain
IFLRY–see International Federation of Liberal & Radical Youth
IFP–see Independence Freedom Party (Botswana)
IFP–see Inkatha Freedom Party (South Africa)
IGNU–see Interim Government of National Unity (Liberia)
IKL–see People's Patriotic League (Finland)
ILO–see International Labor Organization
IMF–see International Monetary Fund
IMRO-DPMNU–see Internal Macedonian Revolutionary Organization-Democratic Party of Macedonian National Unity
INCRA–see National Institute for Colonization and Agrarian Reform (Brazil)
INF–see National Front of Iran
INLA–see Irish National Liberation Party (Northern Ireland)
INM–see Imbokodvo National Movement (Swaziland)
INPFL–see Independent National Patriotic Front of Liberia
INTU–see Indian National Trade Union Congress
IP–see Independence Party (Iceland)
IP–see Independence Party (Morocco)
IPD–see Impulse to Progress and Democracy (Benin)
IRA–see Provincial Irish Republican Army (Northern Ireland)
IRP–see Islamic Renaissance Party (Uzbekistan)
IRPT–see Islamic Renaissance Party of Tajikistan
IRSP–see Irish Republican Socialist Party (Northern Ireland)
ISP–see Independent Smallholders' Party (Hungary)
ITFY–see International Tribunal for the Former Yugoslavia (Serbia and Montenegro)

IU–see United Left (Bolivia)
IU–see United Left (Peru)
IU–see United Left (Spain)
IWSG–see Industry Will Save Georgia
IZG–see Independent Zimbabwe Group
JADP–see Jordanian Arab Democratic Party
JAPBP–see Jordanian Arab Progressive Ba'th Party
JASBP–see Jordanian Arab Socialist Ba'th Party
JCP–see Japan Communist Party
JCP–see Jordanian Communist Party
JD–see People's Party (India)
JDP–see Justice and Development Party (Turkey)
JDPUP–see Jordanian Democratic Popular Unity Party
JHU–see Sinhala National Heritage (Sri Lanka)
JI–see Islamic Assembly (Bangladesh)
JI–see Islamic Assembly (Pakistan)
JJSO–see Juvenile Justice System Ordinance (Pakistan)
JLP–see Jamaica Labour Party
JNE–see National Board of Elections (Peru)
JP–see Jatiya Party (Bangladesh)
JP–see Justice Party (Turkey)
JRM–see Society of Combatant Clergy (Iran)
JRV–see Polling Places (Nicaragua)
JRV–see Vote Receiving Commitees (Ecuador)
JSC–see Judicial Service Commission (Sri Lanka)
JSDS–see Jewish State, Democratic State (Israel)
JTI–see Islamic Assembly (Student Wing) (Pakistan)
JUDP–see Jordanian United Democratic Party
JUI–see Conference of ULEMA of Islam (Pakistan)
JUP–see Conference of ULEMA of Pakistan
JUP-N–see Conference of Ulema of Pakistan
JVP–see People's Liberation Front (Sri Lanka)
KADU–see Kenya African Democratic Union
KAMPI–see Supporters of the Free Philippines
KANU–see Kenya African National Union
KAU–see Kenyan African Union
KBL–see New Society Movement (Philippines)
KCIA–see Korean Central Intelligence Agency (South Korea)
KD–see Christian Democrats (Sweden)
KDH–see Christian Democratic Movement (Slovakia)
KDS–see Christian Democratic Party (Czech Rep.)
KDU–see Christian Democratic Union (Czech Rep.)
KF–see Conservative People's Party (Denmark)
KF–see Cooperative Movement (Sweden)
KFDC–see Kurdish Freedom and Democracy Congress (Turkey)
KISOS–see Movement of Social Democrats (Cyprus)
KKE–see Communist Party of Greece
KMT–see Nationalist Party (Taiwan)

KNDP–see Kamerun National Democratic Party (Cameroon)
KNUT–see Kenya National Union of Teachers
KOP–see Movement of Ecologists and Environmentalists (Cyprus)
KPA–see Korean People's Army (North Korea)
KPB–see Party of Communists of Belarus
KPC–see Kurdistan People's Congress (Turkey)
KPD–see Communists (Germany)
KPK–see Communist Party of Kazakhstan
KPL–see Communist Party of Luxembourg
KPO–see Communist Party (Austria)
KPRP–see Kampuchean People's Revolutionary Party (Cambodia)
KPU–see Kenya People's Union
KRF–see Christian People's Party (Denmark)
KrF–see Christian People's Party (Norway)
KRO–see Congress of Russian Communities
KRRS–see Karnataka State Farmers' Association (India)
KSCM–see Communist Party of Bohemia and Moravia-Left Bloc (Czech Rep.)
KSOOR–see "Republic" Coordinating Council of Public Associations (Kazakhstan)
KSP–see Farmer's and Worker's Party (Bangladesh)
KSS–see Communist Party of Slovakia
KTPI–see Indonesian Party of High Ideals (Suriname)
KUP–see Catholic People's Party (Netherlands)
KWP–see Korean Workers' Party (North Korea)
KWP–see Kurdistan Workers' Party (Turkey)
LA–see Leftist Alliance (Finland)
LAA–see Local Administration Bill (Zambia)
LABAN–see People's Force (Philippines)
LAKAS–see People's Power-National Christian Muslim Democrats (Philippines)
LAMMP–see Fight of the Free Filipino Masses Party
LAOS–see Populist Orthodox Rally (Greece)
LAP–see Liberian Action Party (Liberia)
LCD–see Lesotho Congress for Democracy
LCP–see Lebanese Communist Party
LCR–see Revolutionary Communist League (France)
LCR–see The Radical-Cause (Venezuela)
LCS–see League of Communists of Yugoslavia (Slovenia)
LCs–see Local Councils (Uganda)
LD/MPT–see Democratic League/Popular Labor Movement (Senegal)
LDLP–see Lithuanian Democratic Labor Party
LDP–see Democratic Filipino Struggle
LDP–see Liberal Democratic Party (Japan)
LDP–see Liberal Democratic Party (Macedonia)
LDP–see Liberal Democratic Party (Malaysia)

LDPR–see Liberal Democratic Party of Russia

LDS–see Liberal Democracy of Slovenia

LdU–see Alliance of Independents (Switzerland)

LF–see Liberal Forum (Austria)

LFO–see Legal Framework Order (Pakistan)

LG–see Latvia's Way

LIBRE–see Liberal Republican Party (Panama)

LIPAD–see Patriotic League for Development (Burkina Faso)

LIPE–see Guinean League for the Protection of the Environment

LKDS–see Farmer's Union/Christian Democratic Union/Latgale/Democratic Party Coalition (Latvia)

LLA–see Lesotho Liberation Army

LMI–see Liberation Movement of Iran

LN–see Liveable Netherlands

LN–see Northern League (Italy)

LNNK–see Latvian National Conservative Party and Green Party

LNTG–see Liberian National Transitional Government

LO–see Norwegian Trades Union Federation

LO–see Swedish Confederation of Trade Unions

LOPPE–see Law of Political Organizations and Electoral Processes (Mexico)

LP–see Labor Party (Saint Kitts)

LP–see Liberal Party (Philippines)

LPAI–see African People's League for Independence (Djibouti)

LPF–see List Pim Fortuyn (Netherlands)

LPP–see Law of Popular Participation (Bolivia)

LPP–see Liberia People's Party

LPR–see League of Polish Families

LPRP–see Lao People's Revolutionary Party (Laos)

LRF–see National Farmer's Association (Sweden)

LS–see Liberal Party of Croatia

LSAP–see Socialist Workers' Party (Luxembourg)

LSP–see Latvian Socialist Party

LSP–see Liberal Socialist Party (Egypt)

LSSP–see Ceylon Equal Society Party (Sri Lanka)

LSSP–see Lanka Sama Samajaya Party (Sri Lanka)

LSU–see Liberal Social Union (Czech Rep.)

LTTE–see Liberation Tigers of Tamil Eelam (Sri Lanka)

LU–see Liberal Union (Andorra)

LUP–see Liberian Unification Party

M–see Moderate Party (Sweden)

MA–see Melanesian Alliance (Papua New Guinea)

MAC–see Christian Authentic Movement (El Salvador)

MAFREMO–see Malawi Freedom Movement

MAG–see Monitor Action Group (Namibia)

MAKI–see Israel Communist Party

MAKINA–see Movement for Dignified Democracy (Tanzania)

MAPAM–see United Workers Party (Israel)

MAS–see Movement toward Socialism (Venezuela)

MAS–see Movement toward Socialism-People's Political Instrument for Sovereignty (Bolivia)

MAS–see Solidarity Action Movement (Guatemala)

MAUDR–see Angolan Democratic Unity Movement for Reconstruction

MBL–see Movement for a Free Bolivia

MBPM–see Maurice Bishop Patriotic Movement (Grenada)

MBR-200–see Revolutionary Bolivarian Movement (Venezuela)

MCA–see Malayan Chinese Association

MCDDI–see Congolese Movement for Democracy and Comprehensive Development (Rep. of Congo)

MCP–see Malawi Congress Party

MCPC–see Central African People's Liberation Movement

MCs–see Municipal Councils (Sri Lanka)

MDA–see Movement for Democracy in Algeria

MDB–see Brazilian Democratic Movement

MDC–see Citizen's Movement (France)

MDC–see Malawi Development Corporation

MDD–see Movement for Democracy and Development (Central African Republic)

MDJT–see Movement for Democracy and Justice in Chad

MDN–see National Democratic Movement (Guatemala)

MDP–see Democratic Popular Movement (Senegal)

MDP–see Malawi Democratic Party

MDP–see Maldivian Democratic Party

MDP–see Movement for Democracy and Progress (Cameroon)

MDP–see Movement for the Defense of the Republic (Cameroon)

MDP–see Portuguese Democratic Movement

MDR–see Democratic Republican Movement (Rwanda)

MDREC–see Movement for Democracy, Renaissance and Revolution in Central Africa

MDS–see Democratic and Social Movement (Morocco)

MDS–see Movement of Social Democrats (Tunisia)

MDU–see Malawi Democratic Union

MEA–see Malta Employers' Association

MEI–see Independent Ecology Movement (France)

MEIMAD-see Jewish State, Democratic State (Israel)

MELS-see Marxist-Engels Leninist Stalinist Movement of Botswana

MEP-see People's Electoral Movement (Venezuela)

MESAN-see Movement of Social Evolution in Black Africa (Central African Rep.)

MFA-see Armed Forces Movement (Portugal)

MFDC-see Movement of Democratic Forces of Casamance (Senegal)

MFP-see Marematlou Freedom Party (Lesotho)

MGR-see M.G. Ramachaudran (India)

MHRA-see Mauritanian Human Rights Association

MIC-see Malayan Indian Congress

MILF-see Moro Islamic Liberation Front (Philippines)

MINUGUA-see UN Verification Mission (Guatemala)

MIP-see Pachakutik Indigenous Movement (Bolivia)

MIR-see Movement of the Revolutionary Left (Bolivia)

MIRT-see Movement for the Islamic Revival of Tajikistan

MISK-see Confederation of Nationalist Labor Unions (Turkey)

MJP-see Movement for Justice and Peace (Ivory Coast)

MK-see Member of Knesset (Israel)

MKDH-see Hungarian Christian Democratic Movement (Slovakia)

ML-see Liberty Movement (Peru)

ML-see Muslim League (Pakistan)

MLA-see Martial Law Administrator (Pakistan)

MLN-see National Liberation Movement (Guatemala)

MLN-see National Liberation Movement (Uruguay)

MLP-see Mauritian Labor Party

MLPC-see Central African People's Liberation Movement

MLSTP-see Liberation Movement of Sao Tome and Principe

MMA-see United Council of Action (Pakistan)

MMD-see Movement for Multiparty Democracy (Zambia)

MMM-see Mauritanian Militant Movement

MMP-see Mixed-Member Proportion (New Zealand)

MNDP-see Malawi National Democratic Party

MNLF-see Moro National Liberation Front (Philippines)

MNPP-see New Country Movement (Ecuador)

MNR-see Mozambique National Resistance

MNR-see National Movement of Revolution (Republic of Congo)

MNR-see National Revolutionary Movement (El Salvador)

MNR-see Nationalist Revolutionary Movement (Bolivia)

MNR/Renamo-see Mozambique National Resistance

MNSD-see National Movement for Solidarity and Democracy (Cameroon)

MNSD-Nassara-see National Movement for a Society of Development-Nassara (Niger)

MNU-see Movement for National Unity (Saint Vincent and the Grenadines)

Modin-see Movement for Dignity and National Independence (Argentina)

MOJA-see Movement for Justice in Africa (Liberia)

MOLIRENA-see Liberal National Republican Movement (Panama)

MOPOCO-see Colorado Popular Movement (Paraguay)

MORENA-see National Renovation Movement (Panama)

MORENA-B-see Movement for National Regeneration-Woodcutters (Gabon)

MOTION-see Movement for Social Transformation (Trinidad & Tobago)

MOVERS-see Movement for Responsible Public Service (Philippines)

MP-see Green Ecology Party (Sweden)

MP-see Member of Parliament

MP-see Millat Party (Pakistan)

MP-see Motherland Party (Turkey)

MP-see Popular Movement (Morocco)

MPCI-see Ivory Coast Patriotic Movement

MPD-see Democratic Popular Movement (Ecuador)

MpD-see Movement for Democracy (Cape Verde)

MPE-see Papa Egoró Movement (Panama)

MPF-see Movement for France

MPIGO-see Ivorian Popular Movement of the Great West

MPLA-PT-see Popular Liberation Movement of Angola-Labor Party

MPQ-see Movement for the Beloved Fatherland (Paraguay)

MPR-see Patriotic Movement for Renewal (Mali)

MPR-see Popular Movement of the Revolution (D. Rep. Congo)

MPRP-see Mongolian People's Revolutionary Party

MPs-see Members of Parliament

MPS-see Patriotic Salvation Movement (Chad)

MQM-see United National Movement (Pakistan)

MQM-A-see Mutahida Qaumi Movement (Altaf) (Pakistan)

MQM–H-see Mutahida Qaumi Movement (Haqiqi) (Pakistan)

MR-see Reform Movement (Guatemala)

MRD-see Movement for the Restoration of Democracy (Pakistan)

MRG-see Left Radical Movement (France)

MRM-see Assembly of Combatant Clerics (Iran)

MRND-see National Revolutionary Movement for Development (Rwanda)

MRNDD-see National Republican Movement for Democracy and Development (Rwanda)

MRP-see Popular Republican Movement (France)

MRS-see Sandinista Renovation Movement (Nicaragua)

MRS-see Senegalese Republican Movement

MRTA-see Tupac Amaru Revolutionary Movement (Peru)

MRTKL-see Tupak Katari Revolutionary Liberation Movement (Bolivia)

MSC-see Social Christian Movement (Ecuador)

MSI-see Italian Social Movement

MSL-see Liberal Salvation Movement (Nicaragua)

MSM-see Mauritian Socialist Movement

MSN-see National Salvation Movement (Colombia)

MSP-see Movement for a Peaceful Society (Algeria)

MST-see Landless Peoples' Movement (Brazil)

MTD-see Togolese Movement for Democracy

MTDP-see National Revival Democratic Party (Uzbekistan)

MTI-see Islamic Tendency Movement (Tunisia)

MUN-see Mission of National Unity (Panama)

MUZ-see Mine Workers Union of Zambia

MVR-see Fifth Republic Movement (Venezuela)

MYP-see Malawi Young Pioneers

NA-see National Alliance Party (Pakistan)

NA-see New Alliance (Slovakia)

NABR-see National Alliance for Belizean Rights

NAF-see Norwegian Employers' Association

NAFTA-see North American Free Trade Agreement

NAP-see National Awami Party (Bangladesh)

NAP-see Nationalist Action Party (Turkey)

NAP-see New Aspiration Party (Thailand)

NAPP-see National Awami Party Pakistan

NAR-see National Alliance for Reconstruction (Trinidad and Tobago)

NATO-see North Atlantic Treaty Organization

NBM-see New Beginnings Movement (Jamaica)

NCC-see Our Common Cause (Benin)

NCCR-see National Convention for Constitutional Reform (Tanzania)

NCF-see Nordic Youth Center Association

NCGUB-see National Coalition Government Union of Burma (Myanmar)

NCMPs-see Non-Constituency Members of Parliament (Singapore)

NCNC-see National Council of Nigeria and the Cameroons (Nigeria)

NCNP-see National Council for New Politics (South Korea)

NCP-see National Conservative Party (Finland)

NCP-see National Constitutional Party (Jordan)

NCP-see National Convention Party (Ghana)

NCP-see Nepalese Congress Party

ND-see New Democracy (Andorra)

ND-see New Democracy (Greece)

NDA-see National Democratic Alliance (Sudan)

NDA-see National Democratic Assembly (Israel)

NDC-see National Defense Commission (North Korea)

NDC-see National Democratic Congress (Grenada)

NDC-see National Democratic Convention (Ghana)

NDF-see Namibian Defense Force

NDF-see New Democratic Front (Botswana)

NDM-see National Democratic Movement (Jamaica)

NDP-see National Democratic Party (Antigua and Barbuda)

NDP-see National Democratic Party (Barbados)

NDP-see National Democratic Party (Egypt)

NDP-see National Democratic Party (Georgia)

NDP-see National Democratic Party (Macedonia)

NDP-see National Democratic Party (Saint Vincent and the Grenadines)

NDP-see National Development Party (Trinidad and Tobago)

NDP-see Nationalist Democracy Party (Turkey)

NDP-see New Democratic Party (Canada)

NDP-see New Democratic Party (South Korea)

NDP-see New Democratic Party (Suriname)

NDP-see New Development Policy (Malaysia)

NDP Zheltoksan-see December National Democratic Party (Kazakhstan)

NDPL-see National Democratic Party of Liberia

NDRP-see New Democratic Republican Party (South Korea)

NDS-see National Democratic Party (Slovakia)

NDS-see People's Democratic Party (Serbia and Montenegro)

NDU-see National Democratic Union (Argentina)

NEC-see National Election Commission (Nigeria)

NEO-see New Horizons (Cyprus)

NEP-see New Economic Policy (Malaysia)

NERP-see New Economic Recovery Program (Zambia)

NESC–see National Economic and Social Council (Ireland)
NFD–see New Democratic Force (Colombia)
NFP–see New Frontier Party (Japan)
NFR–see New Republican Force (Bolivia)
NFSL–see National Front for the Salvation of Libya
NGOs–see Non-Governmental Organizations
NHI–see New Croat Initiative (Bosnia and Herzegovina)
NIF–see National Islamic Front (Sudan)
NIO–see Northern Ireland Office
NIUP–see Northern Ireland Unionist Party
NJAC–see National Joint Action Committee (Trinidad and Tobago)
NJM–see New Jewel Movement (Grenada)
NKK–see People's Congress of Kazakhstan
NKP–see Communist Party of Norway
NKP–see New Korea Party (South Korea)
NLC–see National Labour Congress (Nigeria)
NLD–see National League for Democracy (Myanmar)
NLD–see National League for Democracy (Tanzania)
NLF–see National Liberation Front (Yemen)
NLM–see National Labour Movement (Saint Lucia)
NLP–see Nationalist Labor Party (Turkey)
NM–see New Majority (Peru)
NMPs–see Nominated Members of Parliament (Singapore)
NNDP–see Nigerian National Democratic Party
NNLC–see Ngwane National Liberatory Congress (Swaziland)
NNP–see New National Party (Grenada)
NORAID–see Irish Northern Aid Committee (Northern Ireland)
NP–see National Party (South Africa)
NPA–see New People's Army (Philippines)
NPC–see National People's Coalition (Philippines)
NPC–see National People's Congress (China)
NPC–see Northern People's Congress (Nigeria)
NPD–see National Democratic Party (Germany)
NPF–see National Policy Forum (UK of Great Britain)
NPFL–see National Patriotic Front of Liberia
NPH–see New Party Harbinger (Japan)
NPP–see National Patriotic Party (Liberia)
NPP–see National People's Party (Pakistan)
NPP–see New Patriotic Party (Ghana)
NPS–see Suriname National Party
NPUP–see National Progressive Unionist Party (Egypt)
NRA–see National Reconstruction Alliance (Tanzania)
NRA–see National Resistance Army (Uganda)

NRB–see National Reconstruction Bureau (Pakistan)
NRC–see National Republican Convention (Nigeria)
NRC–see National Resistance Council (Uganda)
NRC–see Nuclear Regulatory Commission (U.S.A.)
NRM–see National Resistance Movement (D. Rep. Congo)
NRM–see National Resistance Movement (Uganda)
NRP–see National Reconciliation Party (Gambia)
NRP–see National Reform Party (Ghana)
NRP–see National Religious Party (Israel)
NRP–see Nevis Reform Party (Saint Kitts)
NRP–see Nevis Reformation Party (Saint Kitts)
NSC–see National Security Council (Tunisia)
NSC–see National Security Council (U.S.A.)
NSP–see National Salvation Party (Turkey)
NSP–see National Solidarity Party (Singapore)
NSS–see Nature Society of Singapore
NTC–see National Transition Council (Algeria)
NTC–see National Transitional Council (Central African Republic)
NTP–see New Turkey Party
NU–see Rise of Islamic Scholars (Indonesia)
NUCD–see National Union for Christian Democrats (Philippines)
NUP–see National Union Party (Sudan)
NUP–see National Unity Party (Myanmar)
NUPRG–see New Ulster Political Research Group (Northern Ireland)
NVU–see Dutch People's Union (Netherlands)
NWFP–see Northwest Frontier Province (Pakistan)
NWU–see National Workers' Union (Jamaica)
NYM–see Nigerian Youth Movement
NZLP–see New Zealand Labour Party
OAAB–see Austrian Association of Workers and Employees
OAPEC–see Organization of Arab Petroleum Exporting Countries
OAS–see Organization of American States
OAU–see Organization of African Unity
OBB–see Austrian Farmer's Association
OBCs–see Backward Castes (India)
ODA–see Civic Democratic Alliance (Czech Rep.)
ODP/MT–see Organization for Popular Democracy/ Labor Movement (Burkina Faso)
ODS–see Civic Democratic Party (Czech Rep.)
ODU–see Civic Democratic Union (Slovakia)
OECD–see Organization for Economic Cooperation and Development
OEK–see Palau National Congress
OHR–see Our Home Is Russia
OIRA–see Official Irish Republican Army (Northern Ireland)

OLF-see Oromo (Ethiopia)

OMB-see Office of Management and Budget (U.S.A.)

OMUG-see Organizations for the Exploitation of the Gambia River (Guinea-Bissau)

OMUS-see Organizations for the Exploitation of the Senegal River (Guinea-Bissau)

ONA-JPU-see Uruguayan National Organization of Retirees' and Pensioners' Associations

ONM-see National Organization of Veterans (Algeria)

ONR-see Organization for National Reconstruction (Trinidad and Tobago)

ONUSAL-see United Nations Observer Mission in El Salvador

OPC-see Ovambolamo People's Congress (Namibia)

OPDO-see Oromo People's Democratic Organization (Ethiopia)

OPEC-see Organization of Petroleum Exporting Countries

OPG-see Official Parliamentary Group (Pakistan)

OPL-see Lavalas Political Organization (Haiti)

OPL-see Organization of the Struggling People (Haiti)

OPP-see Organ of People's Power (Cuba)

OPRM-see United Party of Romas in Macedonia

ORA-see Organization of Armed Resistance (Niger)

ORPA-see Armed People's Organization (Guatemala)

OSCE-see Organization for Security and Cooperation in Europe

OUP-see Official Unionist Party (Northern Ireland)

OW-see Austrian People's Party

OWB-see Austrian Economic Association

OYAK-see Army Mutual Assistance Foundation (Turkey)

PA-see Arnulfista Party (Panama)

PA-see Palestinian Authority

PA-see People's Alliance (Iceland)

PA-see People's Alliance (Sri Lanka)

PAC-see Civilian Self-Defense Patrol (Guatemala)

PACIA-see Angolan Party of African Identity Conservative

PACs-see Political Action Committees (U.S.A.)

PAGS-see Socialist Vanguard Party (Algeria)

PAI-see African Independence Party (Senegal)

PAI-see Angolan Independent Party

PAICV-see African Party for the Independence of Cape Verde

PAIGC-see African Party for the Independence of Guinea and Cape Verde (Guinea-Bissau)

PAIS-see Open Politics for the Social Country (Argentina)

PAJOCA-see Party of the Alliance of Youth, Workers, and Farmers of Angola

PAL-see Angolan Liberal Party

PAL-see Progressive Alliance of Liberia

PALA-see Labor Party (Panama)

PALI-see Neo-Liberal Party (Nicaragua)

PALIPEHUTU-see Party for the Liberation of the Hutu People (Burundi)

PALU-see United Lumumbist Party (D. Rep. Congo)

PAM-see Peoples Action Movement (Saint Kitts)

PAMSCAD-see Program of Action to Mitigate the Costs of Adjustment (Ghana)

PAMUC-see United Coastal Movement Party (Nicaragua)

PAN-see National Action Party (Mexico)

PAN-see National Advancement Party (Guatemala)

PAN-see National Mandate Party (Indonesia)

PAP-see People's Action Party (Papua New Guinea)

PAP-see People's Action Party (Sierra Leone)

PARENA-see Party for National Renewal (Mali)

PARM-see Authentic Party of the Mexican Revolution

PAS-see Pan-Malaysian Islamic Party

PASOC-see Socialist Action Party (Spain)

PASOK-see Pan-Hellenic Socialist Movement (Greece)

PAT-see Pakistani Awami Tehreek

PATAs-see Provincially Administered Tribal Areas (Pakistan)

PAV-see Public Against Violence (Slovakia)

PAVN-see People's Army of Vietnam

PBB-see Crescent Star Party (Indonesia)

PBDS-see Sarawak Dayak People's Party (Malaysia)

PBR-see Reform Star Party (Indonesia)

PBS-see United Sabah Party (Malaysia)

PC-see Carlist Party (Spain)

PC-see Center Alliance Party (Poland)

PC-see Conservative Party (Ecuador)

PC-see Conservative Party (Nicaragua)

PC-see Progressive Conservative Party of Canada

PCB-see Belgian Communist Party

PCB-see Bolivian Communist Party

PCB-see Brazilian Communist Party

PCB-see Communist Party of Benin

PCC-see Colombian Communist Party

PCC-see Cuban Communist Party

PCD-see Democratic Conservative Party (Nicaragua)

PCD-see Liberal Democratic Party (Angola)

PCD-see Party for the Democratic Convergence (Cape Verde)

PcdeN-see Nicaraguan Communist Party

PcdoB-see Communist Party of Brazil

PCE-see Spanish Communist Party

PCF-see French Communist Party

PCI-see Italian Communist Party

PCL-see Plenary of Legislative Commissions (Ecuador)

PCM-see Communist Party of Mexico

PCML-see Maoist Marxist-Leninist Communist Party (Ecuador)

PCMR-see Presidential Council for Minority Rights (Singapore)

PCN-see Conservative Party of Nicaragua

PCN-see Party of National Reconciliation (El Salvador)

PCO-see provisional constitution order (Pakistan)

PCP-see Communist Party (Paraguay)

PCP-see Palestine Communist Party

PCP/PEV-see Portuguese Communist Party/Green Ecologist Party

PCS-see San Marino Communist Party

PCT-see Congolese Workers' Party (Republic of Congo)

PCT-see Tunisian Communist Party

PCV-see Venezuelan Communist Party

PD-see Democrat Party (Indonesia)

PD-see Democratic Party (Ecuador)

PD-see Democratic Party (Romania)

PD-see Democratic Party (Timor Leste)

PDA-see Angolan Democratic Party

PdA-see Swiss Labor Party

PDB-see Democratic Bolivian Party

PDB-see Party of German-Speaking Belgians

PDC-see Christian Democrat Party (Argentina)

PDC-see Christian Democrat Party (Honduras)

PDC-see Christian Democratic Party (Brazil)

PDC-see Christian Democratic Party (Burundi)

PDC-see Christian Democratic Party (Chile)

PDC-see Christian Democratic Party (El Salvador)

PDC-see Christian Democratic Party (Panama)

PDC-see Christian Democratic Party (Paraguay)

PDC-see Christian Democratic Party (Rwanda)

PDC-see Peace and Development Council (Myanmar)

PDCI-see Democratic Party of Ivory Coast

PDCN-see Democratic Party of National Cooperation (Guatemala)

PDCS-see Christian Democratic Party (San Marino)

PDCs-see People's Defence Committees (Ghana)

PDGE-see Democratic Party of Equatorial Guinea

PDG-see Gabonese Democratic Party

PDG-RDA-see Democratic Party of Guinea-African Democratic Assembly

PDI-see Democratic Independence Party (Morocco)

PDI-see Institutional Democratic Party (Dominican Rep.)

PDI-P-see Indonesian Democracy Party-Struggle

PDI-P-see Indonesian Democracy Party-Struggle

PDL-see Liberal Democratic Party (Spain)

PDLA-see Angolan Democratic Liberal Party

PDM-see Mexican Democrat Party

PDM-see People's Democratic Movement (Papua New Guinea)

PDOIS-see People's Democratic Organization for Independence and Socialism (Gambia)

PDP-see Filipino Democratic Party

PDP-see Moral Force Party (Thailand)

PDP-see Pakistan Democratic Party

PDP-see Party for Democracy and Progress (Burkina Faso)

PDP-see Party for Democracy and Progress (Tanzania)

PDP-see Party for Democratic Progress (Bosnia and Herzegovina)

PDP-see Party for Democratic Progress (Bosnia and Herzegovina)

PDP-see Party for Democratic Prosperity (Macedonia)

PDP–see People's Democracy Party (Turkey)

PDP-see People's Democratic Party (Nigeria)

PDP-see People's Democratic Party (Sudan)

PDP-see Popular Democratic Party (Spain)

PDP-see Progressive Democratic Party (Argentina)

PDP-ANA-see Democratic Party for Progress-Angolan National Alliance

PDPA-see Angolan Democratic Party for Peace

PDPAM-see Party for Democratic Prosperity of Albanians in Macedonia

PDRU-see Party of Democratic Rebirth of Ukraine

PDRY-see People's Democratic Republic of Yemen

PDS-see Democratic Party of the Left (Italy)

PDS-see Democratic Social Party (Brazil)

PDS-see Party of Democratic Socialism (Germany)

PDS-see Prosperous Peace Party (Indonesia)

PDS-see Senegalese Democratic Party

PDSH-see Democratic Party of Albania

PDSR-see Social Democratic Party of Romania

PDT-see Democratic Labor Party (Brazil)

PDT-see Democratic Worker's Party (Brazil)

PdvA-see Party of Labor (Belgium)

PEC-see Provisional Electoral Council (Haiti)

PEN-see National Encounter Party (Paraguay)

PeP–see Peace Party (Turkey)

PEV-see Green Ecologist Party (Portugal)

PF-see Patriotic Front (Zimbabwe)

PFB-see Popular Front in Bahrain

PFDJ-see Popular Front for Democracy and Justice (Eritrea)

PFE-see Spanish Feminist Party

PFL-see Party of the Liberal Front (Brazil)

PFLOAG-see Popular Front for the Liberation of Oman and the Arab Gulf (Bahrain)

PFLOAG-see Popular Front for the Liberation of Oman and the Arab Gulf (United Arab Emirates)

PFLP-see Popular Front for the Liberation of Palestine

PGP-see Gabonese Progress Party

PGP-see Guinea Progress Party (Guinea)

PGS-see Alliance of Primorje-Gorski Kotar (Croatia)

PGT-LN-see Guatemalan Labour Party-National Leadership Nucleus

PH-see Humanist Party (Spain)

PID-see Democratic Institutionalist Party (Guatemala)

PIL-see Public Interest Litigation (India)

PIM-see Multiethnic Indigenous Party (Nicaragua)

PINU-see Party of Innovation and Unity (Honduras)

PIP-see Puerto Rican Independence Party

PiS-see Law and Justice (Poland)

PIT-see Independence and Labor Party (Senegal)

PIT-see Ivorian Workers Party (Ivory Coast)

PIT-CNT-see Interunion Workers' Assembly-National Workers Convention (Uruguay)

PJ-see First Justice (Venezuela)

PJD-see Justice and Development Party (Morocco)

PKB-see National Awakening Party (Indonesia)

PKMAP-see National Peoples' Pathan Brotherhood Party (Pakistan)

PKMS-see Singapore National Malay Organization

PKPB-see Concern for the Nation Functional Party (Indonesia)

PKPI-see Justice and Unity Party of Indonesia

PKS-see Prosperous Justice Party (Indonesia)

PL-see Liberal Party (Brazil)

PL-see Liberal Party (Panama)

PL-see Liberal Party (Paraguay)

PL-see Liberal Party (Rwanda)

PL-see Liberal Party (Spain)

PL-see Liberty Party (Ecuador)

PLA-see Authentic Liberal Party (Panama)

PLA-see People's Liberation Army (China)

PLAN-see People's Liberation Army of Namibia

PLB-see Communist Party (Belgium)

PLC-see Liberal Constitutionalist Party (Nicaragua)

PLD-see Dominican Liberation Party (Dominican Rep.)

PLD-see Liberal Democratic Party (Central African Republic)

PLE-see "The Structure" Liberal Party (Dominican Rep.)

PLH-see Honduras Liberal Party

PLI-see Independent Liberal Party (Nicaragua)

PLIUN-see Liberal Party of National Unity (Nicaragua)

PLJ-see Liberty and Justice Party (Bolivia)

PLM-see Progressive Labour Movement (Antigua and Barbuda)

PLN-see Liberal Nationalist Party (Nicaragua)

PLN-see National Liberal Party (Panama)

PLN-see National Liberation Party (Costa Rica)

PLO-see Palestine Liberation Organization

PLO-see Palestine Liberation Organization (Israel)

PLOTE-see People's Liberation Party of Tamil Eelam (Sri Lanka)

PLP-see Peace and Liberation Party (Sierra Leone)

PLP-see People's Labor Party (Turkey)

PLP-see People's Liberation Party (Senegal)

PLP-see Progressive Labour Party (Saint Lucia)

PLP-see Progressive Liberal Party (Bahamas)

PLP-see Progressive List for Peace (Israel)

PLR-see Liberal Radical Party (Paraguay)

PLRA-see Liberal Radical Authentic Party (Paraguay)

PLRE-see Radical Liberal Party (Ecuador)

PLS-see Liberal Party (Switzerland)

PLT-see Liberal Teete Party (Paraguay)

PMAC-see Ethiopian Provisional Military Administrative Council (Eritrea)

PMC-see Military-Peasant Pact (Bolivia)

PMDB-see Party of the Brazilian Democratic Movement

PML-see Pakistan Muslim League

PML-N-see Pakistan Muslim League-N (Pakistan)

PML-Q-see Pakistan Muslim League Quaid-e-Azam Group

PMP-see Party of the Filipino Masses

PMT-see Mexican Workers' Party

PMXD-see Mauritian Party of Xavier Duval

PN-see National Project (Nicaragua)

PNA-see Pakistan National Alliance (Pakistan)

PNBK-see Freedom Bull National Party (Indonesia)

PNC-see National Conservative Party (Nicaragua)

PNC-see Palestinian National Council

PNC-see People's National Congress (Guyana)

PNC-see People's National Convention Party (Ghana)

PND-see National Democratic Party (Djibouti)

PND-see National Democratic Party (Morocco)

PNDA-see Angolan National Democratic Party

PNDC-see Provisional National Defense Council (Ghana)

PNDS-Tarayya-see Nigerian Party for Democracy and Social Progress-Tarayya (Niger)

PNEA-see Angolan National Geological Party
PNEK-see Party of People's Unity of Kazakhstan
PNH-see National Party of Honduras
PNIM-see Indonesian National Party Marhaenisme
PNL-see National Liberty Party (Romania)
PNM-see People's National Movement (Trinidad and Tobago)
PNP-see New Progressive Party (Puerto Rico)
PNP-see Pakistan National Party
PNP-see Peoples National Party (Jamaica)
PNR-see National Renewal Party (Guatemala)
PNR-see National Revolutionary Party (Mexico)
PNU-see Basque Nationalist Party (Spain)
PNV-see No Sellout Platform (Guatemala)
PNV-see Platform Ninety (Guatemala)
PNVC-see National Party of Veterans and Civilians (Dominican Rep.)
POC-see Joint Opposition Party (Eq. Guinea)
POEs-see Party-Owned Enterprises (Taiwan)
POLA-see Political Spring (Greece)
PoP–see Populist Party (Turkey)
PP-see Patriotic Party (Guatemala)
PP-see People's Party (Portugal)
PP-see Pioneers' Party (Indonesia)
PP-see Popular Party (Brazil)
PP-see Popular Party (Spain)
PP-see Progressive Party (Brazil)
PP-see Progressive Party (Iceland)
PP-see Prosperity Party (Turkey)
PPA-see Public Prosecutions Administration (South Korea)
PPB-see Brazilian Progressive Party
PPB-see Progressive Reform Party (Brazil)
PPBB-see United Traditional Bumiputra Party (Malaysia)
PPC-see Christian People's Party (Dominican Rep.)
PPC-see Popular Christian Party (Peru)
PPD-see Djibouti People's Party
PPD-see Doctrinaire Panamenista Party
PPD-see Party for Democracy (Chile)
PPD-see Popular Democratic Party (Puerto Rico)
PPDF-see Popular Party for French Democracy
PPDI-see Indonesian Democratic Vanguard Party
PPDK-see United Democratic Nationhood Party (Indonesia)
PPE-see Papa Egoro Party (Panama)
PPI-see Italian People's Party
PPM-see Party of the People of Mauritania
PPN-see Niger Progressive Party
PPN-RDA-see Niger Progressive Party-African Democratic Rally
PPOs-see Primary Party Organizations (Kazakhstan)

PPP-see Pakistan People's Party
PPP-see Palestine People's Party
PPP-see People's Political Party (Saint Vincent and the Grenadines)
PPP-see People's Power Party (Philippines)
PPP-see People's Progress Party (Papua New Guinea)
PPP-see People's Progressive Party (Gambia)
PPP-see People's Progressive Party (Guyana)
PPP-see People's Progressive Party (Saint Lucia)
PPP-see People's Progressive Party of Malaysia
PPP-see United Development Party (Indonesia)
PPPP-see Pakistan People's Party Parliamentarians
PPR-see Progressive Republican Party (Brazil)
PPS-see Popular Socialist Party (Brazil)
PPS-see Popular Socialist Party (Mexico)
PPS-see Progress and Socialist Party (Morocco)
PPSC-see Popular Social Christian Party (Nicaragua)
PPT-see Country for All (Venezuela)
PPT-see Fatherland for Everyone (Venezuela)
PPT-see People's Party of Tajikistan
PQ-see Democratic Quisqueyan Party (Dominican Rep.)
PQ-see Parti Quebecois (Canada)
PR-see Proportional Representation
PR-see Revolutionary Party (Guatemala)
PRB-see Party of the Rebirth of Benin
PRC-see Central African Republican Party
PRC-see Civic Renewal Party (Panama)
PRC-see Communist Refoundation Party (Italy)
PRC-see Cuban Revolutionary Party
PRD-see Democratic Reformist Party (Spain)
PRD-see Democratic Renewal Party (Angola)
PRD-see Democratic Renewal Party (Benin)
PRD-see Dominican Revolutionary Party (Dominican Rep.)
PRD-see Party of Democratic Renewal (Djibouti)
PRD-see Party of the Democratic Revolution (Mexico)
PRD-see Revolutionary Democratic Party (Panama)
PRDS-see Social and Democratic Republican Party (Mauritania)
PRE-see Roldosista Party of Ecuador
Pref-see Reformist Party (Dominican Rep.)
PRF-see Revolutionary Febrerist Party (Paraguay)
PRI-see Independent Revolutionary Party (Dominican Rep.)
PRI-see Institutional Revolutionary Party (Mexico)
PRI-see Italian Republican Party
PRIAN-see National Action Institutional Renewal party (Ecuador)
PRL-see Liberal Parties (Belgium)

PRLPN-Nakowa-see Republican Party for the Liberty and Progress of Niger-Nakowa

PRM-see Party of Greater Romania

PRN-see National Republican Party (Costa Rica)

PRN-see Nicaraguan Resistance Party

PRN-see Party of National Reconstruction (Brazil)

PRP-see Party of Renewal and Progress (Morocco)

PRP-see Party of Renovation and Progress (Guinea)

PRP-see Popular Revolutionary Party (D. Rep. Congo)

PRP-see Progressive Republican Party (Turkey)

PRPB-see Popular Revolutionary Party of Benin

PRS-see Radical Socialist Party (France)

PRS-see Social Renewal Party (Angola)

PRS-see Social Renovation Party (Guinea-Bissau)

PRSC-see Reformist Social Christian Party (Dominican Rep.)

PRSD-see Social Democratic Radical Party (Chile)

PRT-see Revolutionary Party of the Workers (Mexico)

PS-see Brazilian Socialist Party

PS-see Portuguese Socialist Party

PS-see Socialist Parties (Belgium)

PS-see Socialist Party (Bolivia)

PS-see Socialist Party (Chile)

PS-see Socialist Party (France)

PS-see Socialist Party (Senegal)

PS-see Solidarity Party (Ecuador)

PS-see Solidarity Party (Panama)

PSB-see Burkina Socialist Party

PSC-see Christian Democratic Parties (Belgium)

PSC-see Social Christian Party (Ecuador)

PSC-see Social Christian Party (Guatemala)

PSC-see Socialist Party of Catalonia (Spain)

PSCN-see Social Christian Party (Nicaragua)

PSD-see Democratic Socialist Party (Central African Rep.)

PSD-see Democratic Socialist Party (Central African Republic)

PSD-see Social Democratic Party (Angola)

PSD-see Social Democratic Party (Benin)

PSD-see Social Democratic Party (Brazil)

PSD-see Social Democratic Party (France)

PSD-see Social Democratic Party (Guatemala)

PSD-see Social Democratic Party (Guinea-Bissau)

PSD-see Social Democratic Party (Portugal)

PSD-see Social Democratic Party (Rwanda)

PSD-see Social-Democratic Party (Timor Leste)

PSDA-see Angolan Social Democratic Party

PSDB-see Brazilian Social Democratic Party

PSDN-Alheri-see Niger Social-Democratic Party-Alheri

PSDR-see Social Democratic Party of Romania

PSE-see Basque Socialist Party (Spain)

PSI-see Italian Socialist Party

PSL-see Polish People's Party

PSM-see Monegasque Socialist Party (Monaco)

PSN-see Nicaraguan Socialist Party

PSN-see Party of National Solidarity (Guatemala)

PSNI-see Police Service of Northern Ireland

PSOC-see Social Conservatism Party (Nicaragua)

PSOE-see Spanish Socialist Workers' Party

PSP-see Pacifist Socialist Party (Netherlands)

PSP-see Patriotic Society Party (Ecuador)

PSP-see Popular Socialist Party (Cuba)

PSP-see Progressive Socialist Party (Lebanon)

PSs-see Regional Councils (Sri Lanka)

PSS-see San Marino Socialist Party

PSSH-see Socialist Party of Albania

PSUM-see Unified Socialist Party of Mexico

PT-see Workers' Party (Brazil)

PTA-see Angolan Labor Party

PTB-see Brazilian Labor Party

PTB-see Brazilian Worker's Party

PTD-see Dominican Worker's Party

PTP-see Togolese Progressive Party

PU-see Unionist Party (Guatemala)

PUD-see Democratic Unification Party (Honduras)

PUDEMO-see People's United Democratic Movement (Swaziland)

PUN-see National Unity Party (Central African Republic)

PUND-Salama-see Party for National Unity and Development-Salama (Niger)

PUNR-see Romanian National Unity Party

PUNT-see National Workers' Party (Eq. Guinea)

PUP-see Party of Unity and Progress (Guinea)

PUP-see People's United Party (Belize)

PUP-see Popular Unity Party (Tunisia)

PUP-see Progressive Unionist Party (Northern Ireland)

PUR-see Republican Union (Ecuador)

PUSC-see Social Christian Unity (Costa Rica)

PUU-see Party of Liberty and Progress (Belgium)

PvdA-see Labor Party (Netherlands)

PVE-see Spanish Green Party

PW-see Walloon Party (Belgium)

PWP-see Peasants and Workers Party (India)

PYO-see Progressive Youth Organization (Guyana)

RAAN-see Northern Atlantic Autonomous Region (Nicaragua)

RAAS-see Southern Atlantic Autonomous Region (Nicaragua)

RAKAH-see New Communist List (Israel)

RATZ–see Citizens Right Movement (Israel)
RC–see Communist Refoundation (Italy)
RCC–see Revolutionary Command Council (Ecuador)
RCC–see Revolutionary Command Council (Iran)
RCC–see Revolutionary Command Council (Libya)
RCD–see Congolese Rally for Democracy (D. Rep. Congo)
RCD–see Rally for Culture and Democracy (Algeria)
RCs–see Resistance Committees (Uganda)
RDA–see African Democratic Assembly (Burkina Faso)
RDA–see African Democratic Rally (Ivory Coast)
RDC–see Central African Democratic Assembly (Central African Republic)
RDL–see Rally of Liberal Democrats (Benin)
RDP–see Rally for Democracy and Progress (Chad)
RDP–see Rally for Democracy and Progress (Gabon)
RDP–see Reformist Democracy Party (Turkey)
RDP–see Reunification and Democracy Party (South Korea)
RDR–see Rally of Republicans (Ivory Coast)
Renamo–see Mozambique National Resistance
RF–see Republican Front (Ivory Coast)
RGB-MB–see Guinea-Bissau Resistance-Bah Fatah Movement
RMC–see Revolutionary Military Council (Grenada)
RN–see National Renovation (Chile)
RNB–see National Woodcutters Rally (Gabon)
RND–see National Democratic Assembly (Senegal)
RND–see National Democratic Rally (Algeria)
RND–see National Rally for Development (Comoros)
RNDP–see National Assembly for Democracy and Progress (Chad)
RNI–see National Assembly of Independents (Morocco)
ROAD–see Citizens' Movement for Democratic Action (Poland)
ROAR–see Rise, Organize, and Rebuild (Guyana)
RP–see Republic Party (Trinidad and Tobago)
RP–see Republican People's Party (Turkey)
RPF–see Rally for the French People
RPF–see Rwandan Patriotic Front
RPF-SEE–see Reformational Political Federation (Netherlands)
RPG–see Assembly of the Guinean People
RPI–see Republican Party of India
RPM–see Rally for Mali
RPO–see Constitutional Offensive Party (Germany)
RPP–see Popular Rally for Progress (Djibouti)
RPP–see Radical Political Party (Netherlands)
RPP–see Republican People's Party (Turkey)

RPR–see Rally for the French Republic
RPSD–see Rally for Social Democracy (Madagascar)
RPT–see Rally of Togolese People
RSF–see Rhodesian Security Forces
RSFSR–see Russian Soviet Federated Socialist Republic
RSP–see Socialist Progressive Rally (Tunisia)
RSS–see Agrarian Party of Slovakia
RSS–see National Volunteer Organization (India)
RUC–see Royal Ulster Constabulary (Northern Ireland)
RUF–see Revolutionary Front (Sierra Leone)
RV–see Radical Liberals (Denmark)
RV–see Red Electoral Alliance (Norway)
S–see Janata Dal (India)
S–see Self-Defense of the Polish Republic
S/SAP–see Social Democratic Party (Sweden)
SAC–see Cabinet of the State Administration Council (North Korea)
SACP–see South Africa Communist Party
SAD–see Shiromani Akali Party (India)
SADC–see Southern African Development Council (Zimbabwe)
SADCC–see South African Development Coordination Conference (Malawi)
SADF–see South African Defense Force
SAP–see Social Action Party (Thailand)
SAP–see Structural Adjustment Program
SAPP–see Sabah Development Party (Malaysia)
SAR–see Special Administrative Region (China)
SBIH–see Party for Bosnia-Herzegovina
SBPF–see Sind-Baluch Pakhtoun Front (Pakistan)
SD–see Social Democrats (Denmark)
SDA–see Party of Democratic Action (Bosnia and Hercegovina)
SDA–see Sindh National Alliance (Pakistan)
SDA–see Singapore Democratic Alliance
SDA–see Social Democratic Alliance (Iceland)
SDF–see Social Democratic Front (Cameroon)
SDK–see Slovak Democratic Coalition
SDKU–see Slovak Democratic Coalition and Christian Union
SDL–see Party of the Democratic Left (Slovakia)
SDLP–see Social Democratic and Labour Party (Northern Ireland)
SDP–see Singapore Democratic Party
SDP–see Social Democracy Party (Turkey)
SDP–see Social Democratic Party (Bahamas)
SDP–see Social Democratic Party (Bosnia and Herzegovina)
SDP–see Social Democratic Party (Botswana)
SDP–see Social Democratic Party (Finland)
SDP–see Social Democratic Party (Iceland)

SDP-see Social Democratic Party (Japan)
SDP-see Social Democratic Party (Nigeria)
SDP-see Social Democratic Party (United Kingdom)
SDP-see Social Democratic Party of Croatia
SDPP-see Social Democrat Populist Party (Turkey)
SdRP-see Social-Democratic Party of Poland
SDS-see Serb Democratic Party (Bosnia and Hercegovina)
SDS-see Union of Democratic Forces (Bulgaria)
SDSS-see Independent Democratic Serbian Party (Croatia)
SDSS-see Social Democrat Party of Slovakia
SDSS-see Social Democratic Party of Slovenia
SDU-see Social Democratic Union (Bosnia and Herzegovina)
SDUM-see Social Democratic Union of Macedonia
SEC-see Securities and Exchange Commission (U.S.A.)
SED-see Socialist Unity Party of Germany
SEPDF-see Southern Ethiopian Peoples' Democratic Front
SF-see Sinn Fein (Northern Ireland)
SF-see Socialist People's Party (Denmark)
SFRY-see Socialist Federal Republic of Yugoslavia
SGP-see State Reform Party (Netherlands)
SHAS-see Sephardi Torah Guardians (Israel)
SIP-see Industrial Union of Panama
SJKH-see National Council for New Politics (South Korea)
SJP-see Samajwadi Janata Party (India)
SKD-see Slovenian Christian Democrats
SKDL-see Finnish People's Democratic League
SKNLP-see St. Kilts & Nevis Labour Party
SKOI-see Standing Conference of the Civic Institute (Slovakia)
SKP-see Finnish Communist Party
SLD-see Democratic Left Alliance (Poland)
SLFP-see Sri Lanka Freedom Party
SLP-see Socialist Labor Party (Egypt)
SLP-see St. Lucia Labour Party
SLPP-see Sierra Leone People's Party
SLS-see Serbian Liberal Party
SLS-see Slovene People's Party
SMC-see Single Member Constituencies (Singapore)
SMK-see Hungarian Coalition (Slovakia)
SMP-see Sipah-I-Muhamund (Pakistan)
SMS-see Great Council of Sinhalese (Sri Lanka)
SNAP-see Sarawak National Action Party (Malaysia)
SNC-see Supreme National Council (Cambodia)
SNE-see National Education Union (Morocco)
SNF-see Sindh National Front (Pakistan)

SNP-see Scottish National Party (UK of Great Britain)
SNP-see Seychelles National Party
SNS-see Slovak National Party
SNSD-see Party of Independent Social Democrats (Bosnia and Herzegovina)
SNTVs-see Single Nontransferable Votes (Taiwan)
SODEP-see Social Democracy Party (Turkey)
SOP-see Party of Civic Understanding (Slovakia)
SP-see Center Party (Norway)
SP-see Samajwadi (Socialist) Party (India)
SP-see Samata Party (India)
SP-see Socialist Parties (Belgium)
SP-see Socialist Party (Netherlands)
SPA-see Supreme People's Assembly (North Korea)
SPD-see Social Democrats (Germany)
SPDC-see State Peace and Development Council (Myanmar)
SPK-see Socialist Party of Kazakhstan
SPLM-see Sudan People's Liberation Movement
SPO-see Serbian Renewal Movement
SPO-see Social Democratic Party (Austria)
SPP-see Singapore People's Party
SPPF-see Seychelles People's Progressive Front
SPRS-see Socialist Party of Republika Sprska (Bosnia and Herzegovina)
SPS-see Social-Democratic Party of Switzerland
SPS-see Socialist Party of Serbia
SPU-see Socialist Party of Ukraine
SPZ-see Slovak Party of Entrepreneurs and Traders
SRA-see Argentine Rural Society
SRP-see Serb Radical Party (Bosnia and Herzegovina)
SRS-see Serbian Radical Party
SRV-see Socialist Republic of Vietnam
SSIM-see Southern Sudan Independence Movement
SSP-see Sipah-i-Sahaba (Pakistan)
SSR-see Uzbek Soviet Socialist Republic
SSU-see Sudan Socialist Union
STV-see Single Transferable Vote (Ireland)
SUPP-see Sarawak United People's Party (Malaysia)
SV-see Socialist Left Party (Norway)
SVLP-see St. Vincent Labour Party
SVP-see Swiss People's Party/Democratic Center Union
SWAPO-see South West Africa People's Organization of Namibia
SWAPO-see Southwest Africa People's Organization
SWATF-see South West Africa Territorial Force (Namibia)
SYN-See Coalition of the Left of Movements and Ecology (Greece)
SZ-see Green Party (Czech Rep.)
SZS-see Green Party in Slovakia

TADEA–see Tanzania Democratic Alliance Party

TAIP–see Taiwan Independence Party

TAMI–see Movement for Jewish Tradition (Israel)

TANU–see Tanganyikan African National Union

TAWU–see Grenada Technical and Allied Workers Union

TB–see Fatherland and Freedom (Latvia)

TC–see Tamil Congress (Sri Lanka)

TDP–see Telegu Desam Party (India)

TELO–see Tamil Eelam Liberation Organization (Sri Lanka)

TEU–see Maastricht Treaty of European Union

TGC–see Constitutional Tribunal (Ecuador)

TGNA–see Turkish Grand National Assembly

THM–see Tapia House Movement (Trinidad and Tobago)

TI–see Struggle Movement (Pakistan)

TIM–see I Love Madagascar

TKP–see Communal Liberation Party (Cyprus)

TLP–see Tanzania Labour Party

TMC–see Tamil Maanila Congress (India)

TPEs–see Provisional Electoral Tribunals (Ecuador)

TPLF–see Tigray People's Liberation Front (Ethiopia)

TPP–see True Path Party (Turkey)

TPSL–see Social Democratic League of Workers and Small Farmers (Finland)

TRT–see Thais Love Thais (Thailand)

TSE–see Supreme Electoral Tribunal (Ecuador)

TSE–see Supreme Electoral Tribunal (El Salvador)

TSP–see National Harmony Party (Latvia)

TTPI–see United Nations Trust Territory of the Pacific (Marshall I.)

TTS–see Toamasina Tonga Saina (Madagascar)

TUC–see Trade Union Congress (Bahamas)

TUC–see Trade Union Congress (Zambia)

TUC–see Trade Unions Congress (Guyana)

TULF–see Tamil United Liberation Front (Sri Lanka)

TUSIAD–see Turkish Industrialists and Businessmen's Association

TVS–see Tamil Nadu Agriculturalists' Association (India)

TWP–see True Whig Party (Liberia)

UAL–see United Arab List (Israel)

UAP–see United Action Party (Botswana)

UBC–see Unified Buddhist Church (Vietnam)

UBP–see Party of National Unity (Cyprus)

UC–see Constitutional Union (Morocco)

UC–see Union Council (Pakistan)

UCC–see Center-Center Union (Chile)

UCD–see Union of the Democratic Center (Spain)

Ucede–see Union of the Democratic Center (Argentina)

UCN–see National Center Union (Guatemala)

UCN–see National Civic Union (Dominican Rep.)

UCR–see Radical Civic Union (Argentina)

UCRP–see Ukrainian Conservative Republican Party

UCS–see Civic Solidarity Union (Bolivia)

UCs–see Urban Councils (Sri Lanka)

UD–see Democratic Union (Guatemala)

UD–see Democratic Union (Morocco)

UD–see Democratic Union (Poland)

UD–see Democratic Unity Party (Dominican Rep.)

UDA–see Ulster Defense Association (Northern Ireland)

UDC–see Cameroon Democratic Union

UDD–see Djibouti Democratic Union

Udemo–see Democratic Union of Mozambique

UDF–see Union for French Democracy

UDF–see United Democratic Front (Botswana)

UDF–see United Democratic Front (Malawi)

UDF–see United Democratic Front (Namibia)

UDI–see Independent Democratic Union (Chile)

UDI–see Independent Democratic Union (Panama)

UDI–see Unilateral Declaration of Independence (Zimbabwe)

UDJED–see Democratic Union for Justice and Equality in Djibouti

UDLP–see United Dominica Labor Party (Dominica)

UDM–see United Democratic Movement (South Africa)

UDMR–see Democratic Union of Hungarians in Romania

UDN–see National Democratic Union (Brazil)

UDN–see National Democratic Union (El Salvador)

UDP–see Popular Unity Coalition (Bolivia)

UDP–see Ulster Democratic Party (Northern Ireland)

UDP–see United Democratic Party (Belize)

UDP–see United Democratic Party (Gambia)

UDP–see United Democratic Party (Tanzania)

UDP–see United Democratic Party (Zambia)

UDP-Amici–see Union for Democracy and Progress-Amici (Niger)

UDPD–see United People's Democratic Party (Tanzania)

UDPE–see Union of the Spanish People

UDPM–see Democratic Union of Malian People

UDPS–see Democratic Republic of Congo

UDPS–see Union for Democracy and Social Progress (D. Rep. Congo)

UDPS-Amana–see Union for Democracy and Social Progress-Amana (Niger)

UDR–see Ulster Defense Regiment (Northern Ireland)

UDS-R–see Senegalese Democratic Union

UDSG-see Gabonese Democratic and Social Union
UDT-see Timorese Democratic Union
UDU-see Unionist Democratic Union (Tunisia)
UDV-see Volta Democratic Union (Burkina Faso)
UF-see United Force (Guyana)
UFA-see United Farmers of Alberta (Canada)
UFC-see Union of Forces of Change (Togo)
UFD-see Union of Democratic Forces (Mauritania)
UFF-see Ulster Freedom Fighters (Northern Ireland)
UFM-see Uganda Freedom Movement
UFMD-see United Front for Multi-Party Democracy (Malawi)
UFPDP-Sawaba-see Union of Popular Forces for Democracy and Progress-Sawaba (Niger)
UFRI-see Union of Federalists and Independent Republicans (Democratic Republic of Congo)
UGEMA-see General Union of Algerian Muslim Students
UGM-see United Ghana Movement
UGT-see General Union of Workers (Spain)
UGTA-see General Union of Algerian Workers
UGTT-see General Union of Tunisian Workers
UIA-see Argentine Industrial Union
UIRP-see Uganda Islamic Revolutionary Party
UJD-see Union for Justice and Democracy (Togo)
UKIP-see United Kingdom Independence Party (UK of Great Britain)
UKUP-see United Kingdom Unionist Party (Northern Ireland)
ULCR-see Union of Reconstructed Communists (Burkina Faso)
ULD-see United Liberal Democrats (South Korea)
ULF-see United Labour Front (Trinidad and Tobago)
ULI-see Union of Independent Liberals (Togo)
ULIMO-see United Liberia Movement for Democracy
ULP-see United Labour Party (Saint Vincent and the Grenadines)
UM-see Union for Change Coalition (Guinea-Bissau)
UMA-see Union of the Arab Maghrib (North Africa)
UMD-see Union for Multiparty Democracy (Tanzania)
UML-see Nepal-Unified Marxist Leninists
UMNO-see United Malays National Organization
UMOA-see West African Monetary Union
UMT-see Moroccan Union of Labor
UNA-see Ukrainian National Assembly
UNACE-see National Union of Ethical Citizens (Paraguay)
UNAG-see National Farmer's and Cattleman's Association (Nicaragua)
UNAMO-see Mozambican National Union
UNAVEM-see UN Angola Verification Mission

UNC-see Uganda National Congress
UNC-see United National Congress (Trinidad and Tobago)
UND-see National Democratic Union (Monaco)
UNDC-see National Union for Democracy (Comoros)
UNDD-see National Union for Development and Democracy (Madagascar)
UNDD-see National Union for the Defense of Democracy (Burkina Faso)
UNDP-see National Union for Democracy and Progress (Cameroon)
UNDP-see United National Democratic Party (Antigua and Barbuda)
UNDR-see National Union for Democracy and Renewal (Chad)
UNE-see National Unity of Hope (Guatemala)
UNEC-see National Union of Education and Culture (Mali)
UNEEM-see National Union of Students and Pupils of Mali
UNFA-see National Union of Algerian Women
UNFP-see National Union of Popular Forces (Morocco)
UNFP-see United National Federal Party (Zimbabwe)
UNIDO-see United Democratic Opposition (Philippines)
UNIP-see United National Independence Party (Zambia)
UNITA-see National Union for the Total Independence of Angola
UNLDDA-see National Union for the Light of Democracy and Development in Angola
UNMIL-see United Nations Mission in Liberia
UNO-see Nicaraguan Opposition Union
UNOMOZ-see UN Operation Mozambique
UNP-see National Union for Prosperity (Guinea)
UNP-see United National Party (Sri Lanka)
UNPA-see National Union of Algerian Peasants
UNPP-see National People's Party (Sierra Leone)
UNPP-see United Nigeria People's Party
UNR-see Union for the New Republic (Guinea)
UNS-see Sinarquista National Union (Mexico)
UNSO-see United Sabah National Organization (Malaysia)
UNTAC-see United Nations Transitional Authority in Cambodia
UNTAET-see United Nations Transitional Administration in East Timor (Timor Leste)
UNTM-see National Union of Malian Workers
UNZA-see University of Zambia
UP-see Patriotic Union (Colombia)

UP-see Union of Labor (Poland)

UP-see Unity Party (Liberia)

UPADS-see Pan-African Union for Social Democracy (Republic of Congo)

UPC-see Ugandan People's Congress

UPC-see Union of Cameroon Populations

UPDM-see Uganda People's Democratic Movement

UPDP-see Ukrainian Peasant Democratic Party

UPDP-Shamuwa-see Union of Democratic and Progressive Patriots-Shamuwa (Niger)

UPFA-see United Peoples Freedom Alliance (Sri Lanka)

UPG-see Gabonese Peoples Union

UPG-see Union for the Progress of Guinea

UPKO-see United Pasokmomogun Kadazandusun Murut Organisation (Malaysia)

UPM-see Ugandan Patriotic Movement

UPM-see United Peoples Movement (Antigua and Barbuda)

UPN-see Navarrese Peoples' Union (Spain)

UPO-see Union of the People of Ordino (Andorra)

UPP-see Union for Peru

UPP-see Union for the Progress of Chile

UPP-see United Peoples Party (Liberia)

UPP-see United Progressive Party (Antigua and Barbuda)

UPR-see People's Union for the Republic (Central African Republic)

UPRONA-see Union for National Progress (Burundi)

UPT-see Unity Party of Turkey

UPV-see Volta Progressive Union (Burkina Faso)

URD-see Union for Democratic Renewal (Republic of Congo)

URD-see Union for Renewal and Democracy (Chad)

URNG-see Guatemalan National Revolutionary Unity

URP-see Ukrainian Republican Party

URS-see Social Reformist Union (Guatemala)

US-RDA-see Marxist Sudanese Union (Mali)

USC-see Cameroon Social Union

USC-see Ulster Special Constabulary (Northern Ireland)

USC-see Union for Gabonese Socialism

USDA-see Union Solidarity Development Association (Myanmar)

USFP-see Socialist Union of Popular Forces (Monaco)

USP-see United Socialist Party (Botswana)

USTC-see Central African Trade Union

UT-see United Togolese Committee

UTC-see Union of Colombian Workers

UTD-see Togolese Union for Democracy

UTJ-see United Torah Judaism (Israel)

UTM-see Mauritanian Workers' Union

UTO-see United Tajik Opposition

UUP-see Ulster Unionist Party (Northern Ireland)

UUUC-see United Ulster Unionist Council (Northern Ireland)

UVDB-see Union of Greens for the Development of Burkina

UVF-see Ulster Volunteer Force (Northern Ireland)

UW-see Freedom Union (Poland)

UWP-see United Workers Party (Dominica)

UWP-see United Workers' Party (Saint Lucia)

V-see Danish Liberal Party

V-see Left Party (Sweden)

VA-see Voter's Association (Finland)

VBC-see Vietnam Buddhist Church

VCP-see Vietnam Communist Party

VGO-see United Green Party of Austria

VHP-see Progressive Reform Party (Suriname)

VLD-see Liberal Parties (Belgium)

VP-see Virtue Party (Turkey)

VRD-see Democratic Republican Union (Venezuela)

VSI-see Federation of Employees (Iceland)

VU-see Fatherland Union (Liechtenstein)

VU-see People's Union (Belgium)

VVD-see People's Party for Freedom and Democracy (Netherlands)

WCPDM-see Women's Organization of Cameroon People's Democratic Movement

WDCs-see Worker's Defense Committees (Ghana)

WP-see Worker's Party (Singapore)

WP-see Worker's Party (Turkey)

WPA-see Working People's Alliance (Guyana)

WPO-see Women's Progressive Organization (Guyana)

WTO-World Trade Organization

WTP-see Progress of the Fatherland Party (Uzbekistan)

YAR-see Yemen Arab Republic

YATAMA-see Miskito Opposition Group (Nicaragua)

YB-see Flemish Bloc (Belgium)

YCPDM-see Youth Organization of Cameroon People's Democratic Movement

YSP-see Yemeni Socialist Party

ZANC-see Zambian African National Congress

ZANLA-see Zimbabwe African National Liberation Army

ZANU-see Zimbabwe African Nationalist Union

ZANU-N-see Zimbabwe African National Union-Ndongo

ZANU-PF-see Zimbabwe African National Patriotic Front

ZAPU-see Zimbabwe African People's Union
ZCTU-see Zambia Congress of Trade Unions
ZDC-see Zambia Democratic Congress
ZDP-see Zimbabwe Democratic Party
ZIPRA-see Zimbabwe People's Revolutionary Army
ZLA-see Zimbabwe Liberation Army
ZLSD-see United List of Social Democrats of Slovenia
ZNF-see Zimbabwe National Front

ZP-see Montenegrin Together for Changes Party (Serbia and Montenegro)
ZPA-see Zimbabwe People's Army
ZRC-see Zanzibar Revolutionary Council (Tanzania)
ZRS-see Worker's Association of Slovakia
ZS-see Agrarian Party (Czech Rep.)
ZUM-see Zimbabwe Unity Movement
ZUPO-see Zimbabwe United Peoples Organization

REPUBLIC OF HAITI
(République d'Haïti)

By Michel S. Laguerre, Ph.D.
Revised by Soeren Kern

Haiti, with a population of approximately 8.1 million in 2005, occupies one-third (27,750 square kilometers) of the island of Hispaniola. It shares the island with the Dominican Republic. Haiti's capital city is Port-au-Prince.

MODERN HISTORY

In 1986 the three-decade-old dictatorial regime headed first by François "Papa Doc" Duvalier and then by Jean Claude "Baby Doc" Duvalier collapsed under its own weight as a result of street unrest and the unwillingness of the U.S. administration to support the corrupt government. To manage the crisis, the Haitian military stepped in and established a National Council of Government headed by General Henri Namphy. This was the beginning of a turbulent period of political instability, with a succession of nine presidents and eight prime ministers between 1986 and 1996, each spending on average less than a year and half in office.

Following the proclamation of the new constitution of 1987, legislative elections were held to select the senators (Sénat) and representatives of the people (Chambre des Députés) in preparation for the 1990 presidential elections. The new president, Jean Bertrand Aristide, a Catholic priest, took the oath of office in February 1991. He was toppled in a military coup the following September. This coup, by unseating a popular president with a national mandate, was seen by the Haitian electorate and the Organization of American States (OAS) as a setback for the installation of democracy in Haiti. It brought about a major constitutional crisis for the nation and much human suffering among the pro-democratic forces and supporters of the fallen regime. From Venezuela, where he was given political asylum, the deposed president Aristide brought the seat of the exiled government to Washington, D.C., to be closer to the mainstream American political scene, the Haitian diaspora in America, and human rights activists and grassroots organizations that supported his administration.

In order to return Aristide to Haiti, much negotiation took place among his administration, the General Assembly of the United Nations, the general secretary of the OAS, the administrations of George H. W. Bush and Bill Clinton, and the powerbrokers of the Haitian armed forces. On July 3, 1993, President Aristide and General Raoul Cédras signed the Governors Island Accord that set in motion President Aristide's return to Haiti. Still unwilling to let Aristide in, the general staff of the Haitian armed forces changed their minds only after it became obvious that they were going to be willingly or unwillingly removed by U.S. marines. The U.S.-UN Occupation Forces landed in Port-au-Prince in September 1994, and, a month later, President Aristide ended his exile and was able to return to complete his mandate. Humiliated by the presence of foreign military forces in Haiti and demoralized by the exile of key players among the general staff of the army, many soldiers deserted their barracks, and some went into hiding. In 1995, preoccupied with the creation and training of the new civilian police force and under pressure from the populace to do away with the army, President Aristide disbanded the Haitian armed forces.

On December 17, 1995, René Garcia Préval was elected president with 88 percent of the vote. Préval appointed Rosny Smarth prime minister in March 1996. However, in June 1997 Smarth resigned his post, largely over the government's complicity in the electoral fraud committed during and after the April 6, 1997, partial Senate and local government elections. Eventually, in December 1998 Jacques Edouard Alexis was confirmed as prime minister.

This period was one of political gridlock, and the government was unable to organize the local and parliamentary elections due in late 1998. In early January 1999 Préval dismissed legislators whose terms had expired—the entire Chamber of Deputies and all but nine members of the Senate—and converted local elected officials into state employees. The president and prime minister then ruled by decree, establishing a cabinet composed almost entirely of partisans of the Lavalas Family (FL), a new political party created by former president Aristide in late 1996. Under pressure from a new political coalition called the Democratic Consultation Group (ESPACE), the government mandated the nine-member Provisional Electoral Council (CEP) to organize the overdue elections for the end of 1999. Following several delays, the first round of elections for local councils, municipal governments, town delegates, the Chamber of Deputies, and two-thirds of the Senate took place on May 21, 2000. The election drew the participation of a multitude of candidates from a wide array of political parties and a voter turnout of more than 60 percent.

Controversy ensued, however, when the CEP used a flawed methodology to determine the winners of the Senate races, thus avoiding runoff elections for eight seats and giving the FL a virtual sweep in the first round. The flawed vote count, combined with the CEP's failure to investigate alleged irregularities and fraud, undercut the credibility of that body. The CEP president fled Haiti, and two members eventually resigned rather than bow to government pressure to release the erroneous results. Nevertheless, on August 28, 2000 Haiti's new parliament, including the contested senators accorded victory under the flawed vote count, was convened.

The international community had sought to delay parliament's seating until the electoral problems could be rectified. When these efforts were rebuffed, Haiti's main bilateral donors moved to re-channel their assistance away from the government and announced they would not support or send observers to the November elections. Concurrently, most opposition parties regrouped in an alliance that became the Democratic Convergence. The Democratic Convergence asserted that the May elections were so fraudulent that they should be annulled and held again under a new CEP. Elections for president and nine senators took place on November 26, 2000. All major opposition parties boycotted these elections, in which voter participation was estimated at 5 percent. Jean-Bertrand Aristide emerged as the easy victor of these controversial elections, and the candidates of his FL party swept all contested Senate seats. On February 6, 2001, the Democratic Convergence named respected lawyer and human rights activist Gerard Gourgue as provisional president of their "alternative government." On February 7, 2001, Jean-Bertrand Aristide was inaugurated as president.

The political stalemate, however, continued, and OAS-mediated negotiations began in April 2001 to find a resolution, focusing on the possible makeup of a new electoral council, a timetable for new elections, and security for political parties. These negotiations were suspended in mid-July without a final agreement.

In January 2002 the OAS adopted Resolution 806 on Haiti that called for government action to address the political stalemate and growing political violence. It also authorized OAS establishment of a special mission in Haiti to support implementation of the steps called for in Resolution 806. The OAS special mission began operations in March 2002, working with the government on plans to strengthen Haiti's democratic institutions. Nevertheless, the climate of security deteriorated, and a rapidly weakening economy created risks of a humanitarian disaster. On September 4, 2002, the OAS adopted Resolution 822, which set a new course for resolving the crisis by committing the Haitian government to a series of steps leading to an improved climate of security for free and fair elections in 2003.

Protests and attacks on opposition demonstrations by government-supported gangs between November 2002 and February 2003 hardened attitudes on both sides. The opposition issued a public call for Aristide's removal and announced plans for a transitional government. In March 2003 a high-level joint delegation of the OAS and the Caribbean Community presented specific demands to President Aristide to restore public security and create confidence necessary to move toward elections.

Political instability grew throughout the fall of 2003, and government-sponsored repression of opposition protests reached a nadir when, on December 5, pro-government gangs entered Haiti's state university campus and broke the legs of the rector.

Following a meeting with Aristide at the Summit of the Americas in January 2004, Caribbean Community leaders proposed a plan to resolve the political crisis. Aristide stated that he accepted the plan at a meeting on January 31. However, when the plan remained unimplemented, a high-level international delegation came to Haiti on February 21 to obtain an agreement on a specific implementation timetable. Aristide agreed, but the opposition Democratic Platform group of political parties and the overall civil society sector expressed reservations.

Meanwhile, violence spread across the country, culminating on February 28, 2004, when a rebel group led by a former police chief, Guy Philippe, advanced to within 40 kilometers of the capital. As a result of the popular revolt, Aristide, on February 29, 2004, submitted his resignation as president of Haiti and flew on a chartered plane to the Central African Republic. Aristide and his supporters claimed that the action was essentially a coup d'etat organized by the U.S. and French governments.

Boniface Alexandre, president (chief justice) of Haiti's Supreme Court, assumed office as interim president in accordance with Haiti's constitution. On the recommendation from the Council of Elders, the president chose Gérard Latortue as interim prime minister.

The System of Government

Haiti in theory is a parliamentary republic. It has a bicameral legislature, and the prime minister is the most powerful member of the executive branch. In practice, these institutions remain extremely weak and in some cases do not function at all.

EXECUTIVE

The president of the republic is the head of state, while the government is headed by the prime minister. To be elected as president of Haiti, a person must be born in Haiti, must never have renounced his or her Haitian nationality, must own real estate or practice a profession, must have resided in Haiti for five consecutive years, and must have no criminal background. To become president a person must be 35 years old, and to become prime minister, 30 years old.

The functions of the president and the prime minister are spelled out in the following manner by the constitution: The president is elected for a five-year mandate beginning on the February 7th following the general elections and cannot be reelected at the end of his term in office. However, after an interim period of five years, the individual may serve an additional term. Under no circumstances can he or she be elected to a third term.

The powers of the president are multiple. The president is responsible for the implementation of constitutional norms, the maintenance of political stability, the functioning of state institutions, and the preservation of the internal and external security of the state. The individual must select a prime minister from among the majority party in parliament. If no party holds a majority of seats in parliament, the president has to confer with the president of the Senate and the speaker of the house in selecting a prime minister. The president has the right to dismiss the government after receiving a letter of resignation from the prime minister, promulgates laws voted by the two houses, and enforces judicial decisions. The president may pardon or commute sentences if he or she deems such a practice appropriate, appoints ambassadors, consuls, and special envoys to foreign countries, and receives letters of accreditation of ambassadors from foreign powers. The president also presides over the Council of Ministers.

There are also limitations to the powers of the president as set forth by the constitution. He or she must submit to the Senate its nominees for ambassadorial posts and to the National Assembly (Assemblée Nationale) its choice for prime minister and all international treaties, conventions, agreements, and peace treaties. Furthermore, the president must deliver the state of the nation address before parliament at the first annual meeting of that body.

The government is made up of the prime minister, ministers, and secretaries of state. The prime minister has the right to select the members the Council of Ministers and to appoint or dismiss government officials. The prime minister's primary role, however, is to run the government smoothly and enforce the laws. He may appear before the upper or lower house to defend the policies of the government. Also, the individual may serve both as prime minister and as minister in charge of a specific ministry; however, the prime minister cannot serve as a member of parliament. In the absence of the president, he or she may preside over the Council of Ministers. In addition to the ministers the prime minister is entitled to select, he or she may appoint secretaries of state to make the work of the government more efficient.

The primary role of a cabinet minister is to run his or her ministry efficiently, enforce laws, implement government policies, and cooperate with the prime minister. He or she may appoint government employees in his or her ministry. However, a minister cannot hold another job in the public sector. (An exception is made for those who teach in the public school system or at the university level.) Furthermore, a minister can be dismissed by the executive branch if he or she is censured by the Senate or the Chamber of Deputies.

LEGISLATURE

The legislature, which is formally known as the National Assembly (Assemblée Nationale) consists of two bodies: the Senate (Sénat) and the Chamber of Deputies (Chambre des Députés). The Senate, the upper house, is a 27-member body, with three senators for each of nine departments. The senators are elected for six-year terms, with one-third up for election every two years. The senators are elected by direct suffrage.

The Chamber of Deputies, or the lower house, has 83 members who are elected for four-year terms. The representatives begin their terms on the second Monday of January, which coincides with the beginning of the first session of parliament. The parliament holds two sessions, the first from the second Monday in January to the second Monday in May and the second from the second Monday in June to the second Monday in September.

The lower house may, with a two-thirds majority, initiate the process of impeachment of the president, the prime minister, or any of the ministers or secretaries of state. It can do so by simply convoking the accused before the Haute Cour de Justice (High Court of Justice, which is not to be confused with the Supreme Court) made up of the president of the Senate and the president and the vice president of the Supreme Court.

Unlike the Chamber of Deputies, which holds two annual sessions, the Senate is permanently in session. In the interim of the legislative sessions, it may adjourn, but it must put in place a permanent committee to handle current business. One-third of the Senate is replaced every two years. In addition to its legislative mission, the Senate has the duty to propose to the executive branch of government a list of potential Supreme Court justices and has the right to transform itself into a High Court of Justice to deal with specific legal problems under its jurisdiction.

The National Assembly is made up of the Senate and the Chamber of Deputies when they meet in a joint legislative session. These two bodies hold joint meetings to open and close each legislative session. The National Assembly administers the oath to the president of the republic, ratifies any decision to declare war

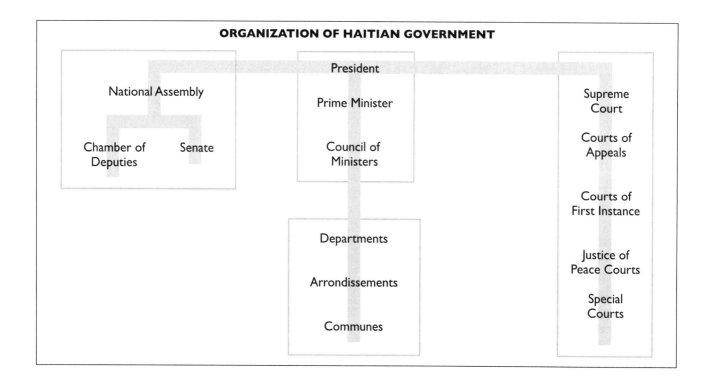

ORGANIZATION OF HAITIAN GOVERNMENT

President

National Assembly

Prime Minister

Supreme Court

Chamber of Deputies   Senate

Council of Ministers

Courts of Appeals

Courts of First Instance

Departments

Justice of Peace Courts

Arrondissements

Special Courts

Communes

before it can take effect, approves or rejects all international treaties and conventions, is an active player in the selection of the Permanent Electoral Council, and is provided at the opening of each session with a report on the government's activities. The National Assembly is headed by the president of the Senate, who serves as its president, and the president of the Chamber of Deputies, who serves as its vice president.

The main role of the legislature is to enact laws for the common good and the welfare of the state. Either house or the executive branch can introduce legislation. Each law or bill must be voted upon and adopted by a majority of legislators present before it can be sent to the executive branch for promulgation. The president reserves the right to veto any laws submitted to his office. The legislature has the legal right to impose disciplinary penalties or even expel members who have not lived up to their constitutional duties.

The number of districts is selected according to the electoral law developed by the Provisional Electoral Council (PEC). However, an electoral district is defined by the constitution as "a collective municipality" whose boundaries are set by the PEC. The last electoral law, issued in 1995, does not spell out how the number of districts is determined.

According to the constitution, any Haitian man or woman who has never renounced his or her Haitian nationality, owns real estate or practices a profession or a trade, and enjoys civil and political rights can be elected to serve in the Chamber of Deputies. He or she must be at least 25 years old and have resided for two consecutive years in the district he or she is to represent. The same requirements hold true for a person to be elected to the Senate; however, he or she must be at least 30 years old and have lived in the department he or she is to represent for at least four consecutive years. Contractors, concessionaires of the state in the operation of public services, and their representatives and agents are not eligible for membership in the legislature.

JUDICIARY

The mechanisms by which the judiciary functions in Haitian society are set up by the constitution. The judicial branch of government is composed of the following courts: Supreme Court (Cour de Cassation), courts of appeals, lower courts or courts of first instance (Tribunaux de Première Instance), peace courts, and special courts. The judges of the Supreme Court are appointed by the president of the republic from a list of candidates submitted by the Senate. Judges of the courts of appeals and lower courts are appointed by the president from a list submitted by the departmental assembly concerned, and judges of the peace courts are selected by the president from a list submitted by the communal assemblies. While the judges of the Supreme Court and the courts of appeals are appointed for 10-year terms, those of the lower courts are appointed for seven-year terms. Jurisdictions over civil, political, and commercial rights are usually handled by the lower courts and the courts of appeals, while the Supreme Court concentrates its attention on jurisdictional conflicts and the constitutionality of laws.

REGIONAL AND LOCAL GOVERNMENT

The department (département), the largest territorial division of the republic, is administered by a council of three members elected for four years. Haiti is divided into 10 such departments. The executive branch is represented in each department by a delegate and in each arrondissement by a vice delegate. The liaison between the executive branch and the department is made possible by the existence of the interdepartmental council that is made up of representatives designated by departmental assemblies.

Each department is further subdivided into arrondissements, and each arrondissement has one or more communes and communal sections under its jurisdiction. Any Haitian man or woman who enjoys civil and political rights, has no criminal background, and is at least 25 years old can be elected to serve on the communal section council if he or she has been living in the area for two consecutive years.

The communal section is the smallest administrative territorial entity. A council of three members, who are elected for four-year terms, administers it. These individuals can be reelected. The commune is administered by a municipal council headed by a president who functions as mayor, aided by a municipal assembly made up of representatives of the commune. These officers are elected for four-year terms and can be reelected thereafter.

The Electoral System

Suffrage is universal for all citizens over 18 years of age. Both houses of parliament are directly elected, with the members of the Senate serving six-year terms and the members of the Chamber of Deputies serving four-year terms. The president is also elected by popular vote; the term of office is five years. The prime minister is appointed by the president and approved by the Chamber of Deputies.

A former foreign minister and UN official, Prime Minister Gérard Latortue was appointed to the post in March 2004, and he proceeded to form a cabinet whose members had no political affiliations. Latortue and his caretaker government, backed by more than 6,700 United Nations peacekeepers, focused on setting conditions for elections in November 2005. However, with preparations for the elections in disarray, officials were likely to postpone the elections until 2006. Members of the interim government will not run in these elections.

The Party System

During the first six years of the Duvalier dictatorship, all political parties were banned. Not until the 1987 constitution were political parties officially sanctioned in Haiti. There are now many parties and coalitions in existence, with the primary one being the Lavalas Family, the party of former president Aristide. The next most influential party in terms of popularity with the electorate is the Democratic Convergence (Convergence Démocratique), a coalition of most leading opposition parties formed to protest the results of May 2000 legislative and local elections.

Major Political Parties

LAVALAS FAMILY

(Fanmi Lavalas; FL)

This is the party of former president Aristide. It was formed in 1996 after Aristide broke away from the Lavalas Political Organization to form his own grassroots party. The party dominated the elections in 2000, winning 73 of 83 seats in the Chamber of Deputies and 26 of 27 seats in the Senate. In advance of the next scheduled elections in late 2005 or 2006, a split appeared in the party, with one camp determined to boycott the elections and another in favor of participating. One of the party's most prominent members, Rene Preval, announced that he would run for president as an independent.

DEMOCRATIC CONVERGENCE

(Convergence Démocratique)

Democratic Convergence is a coalition of some 200 small political parties and groups, all opposed to the Lavalas Family party of Aristide. Democratic Convergence was formed in the aftermath of the May 2000 legislative and local elections; it received funding and organization assistance from the U.S. government. It is led by former Port-au-Prince mayor Evans Paul, a previous Aristide supporter. Paul announced his candidacy for the next presidential election, scheduled in either late 2005 or 2006.

Minor Political Parties

FRONT FOR NATIONAL RECONSTRUCTION

(Front de Reconstruction Nationale; FRN)

The FRN was founded in May 2004. It is run by former rebel leader Guy Phillipe, who played a major role in ousting Aristide. The FRN was previously called the Front de Résistance de l'Artibonite (Artibonite Resistance Front), which itself was once a street gang known as the Cannibal Army. The Cannibal Army helped lead the antigovernment rebellion in early 2004 by attacking the Gonaïves police station in January and killing police officers. Then in February, using the Dominican Republic as a staging ground, Phillipe and a larger force associated with the Cannibal Army launched a bloody incursion into Haiti aimed at toppling the government of Aristide. Phillipe was among the candidates determined to run in the next presidential elections.

ORGANIZATION OF THE STRUGGLING PEOPLE

(Organisation du Peuple en Lutte; OPL)

The OPL is the other party that emerged from the split in the Lavalas Political Organization in 1996; Aristide and his followers formed the FL, and those that remained formed the OPL. It was headed by Gérard Pierre-Charles until his death in 2004.

Other Political Forces

Following the ouster of Aristide in 2004, the security situation in the already dangerous country degenerated even further, with armed gangs in charge of much of the country. The international community provided some level of stability with the presence of nearly 7,000 UN troops stationed in the country. Another important political force is the large number of Haitian immigrants living outside the country; approximately 15 percent of all Haitians live abroad.

National Prospects

Haiti remains the least-developed country in the Western Hemisphere and one of the poorest in the world. Comparative social and economic indicators show Haiti falling behind other low-income developing countries (particularly in the hemisphere) since the 1980s. Haiti now ranks 150th of 175 countries in the UN's Human Development Index.

Although the July 2004 World Bank Donor's Conference pledged $1.085 billion through 2006, Haiti's most serious social problem, the huge wealth gap between the impoverished Creole-speaking black majority and the French-speaking mulattos, 1 percent of whom own nearly half the country's wealth, remains unaddressed. Furthermore, the country's infrastructure has almost completely collapsed, and drug-trafficking has corrupted both the judicial system and the police force.

In April 2004 the United Nations Security Council adopted Resolution 1542, which created the UN Stability Mission in Haiti (MINUSTAH). The mission numbers 6,700 troops and 1,622 civilian police. In October 2004 the UN mission, which is being led by Brazil, faced renewed political violence, this time guerrilla-style urban warfare operations by small groups of "Chimères"—violent gangs calling for Aristide's return to Haiti. Aristide's Lavalas Family party has refused to participate in the electoral council organizing the 2005 elections (likely to be postponed to 2006), although some members of the party broke from this position and vowed to participate in the elections. The political violence that has buffeted the country is likely to continue for the foreseeable future.

Further Reading

Dupuy, Alex. *Haiti in the New World Order: The Limits of the Democratic Revolution.* Boulder, Colo.: Westview Press, 1997.

Fatton, Robert, Jr. *Haiti's Predatory Republic: The Unending Transition to Democracy.* Boulder, Colo.: Lynne Rienner, 2002.

Laguerre, Michel S. *The Military and Society in Haiti.* Knoxville: University of Tennessee Press, 1993.

———. "National Security, Narcotics Control, and the Haitian Military." In *Security Problems and Policies in the Post–Cold War Caribbean.* Edited by Jorge Rodriguez Beruff and Humberto Garcia Muniz. London: Macmillan, 1996.

Rotberg, Robert I., ed. *Haiti Renewed: Political and Economic Prospects.* Washington, D.C.: Brookings Institution Press, 1997.

Stotzky, Irwin P. *Silencing the Guns in Haiti: The Promise of Deliberative Democracy.* Chicago: University of Chicago Press, 1997.

REPUBLIC OF HONDURAS
(República de Honduras)

By Kirk Bowman, Ph.D.

Honduras is a constitutional republic in Central America still attempting to consolidate a democratic government and a political culture. The country has been nominally democratic since 1982, but civilian control of the powerful armed forces is a recent success, and a consolidated full-fledged democracy is still an uncertain goal. While the country has a long history of instability with 14 written constitutions and limited experience with democratic rule, it did not experience the large-scale social upheaval and violence in the 1980s that occurred in neighboring El Salvador, Guatemala, and Nicaragua. Honduras is an extremely poor country, which, coupled with a highly unequal distribution of resources, leaves the vast majority of the citizenry struggling and many not meeting minimal nutrition and health requirements.

The country of nearly 7 million people has a land mass of 43,277 square miles, roughly the size of Tennessee. The vast majority of Hondurans live in the western half of the country, while the eastern Caribbean or Mosquito Coast region is sparsely populated. The country has a long northern coastline on the Caribbean and a small opening to the Pacific. Honduras shares a long border with Nicaragua to the south, the site of the U.S.-sponsored contra rebels who fought the Sandinista government in the 1980s. Guatemala is to the west and El Salvador to the southwest. Honduras is largely a Mestizo (mixed-race), Spanish-speaking, and Roman Catholic country, although a small indigenous population exists (7 percent) as well as a number of Garifuna (of African and Carib Indian descent) communities along the Caribbean (2 percent). Protestant churches are growing in number.

The System of Government

Honduras is a constitutional republic featuring a president and a unicameral legislature. The constitution dates from 1982, although it has been amended several times since then.

EXECUTIVE

Honduras features a presidential system where the chief of state is elected every four years by winning a simple majority of votes. The president must be native-born, at least 30 years old, and not an active member of the armed forces or a pastor or priest. Three vice presidents are elected concurrently with the president. If for any reason the president is unable to continue, the National Assembly selects one of the vice presidents to finish the president's term. The president appoints 14 ministers who form the cabinet.

In the 1994–98 term President Carlos Reina created two new ministries (the Public Ministry and the Ministry of Environment). The Public Ministry, which is the attorney general's office, is especially important as it coordinates and oversees the police once they

ORGANIZATION OF HONDURAN GOVERNMENT

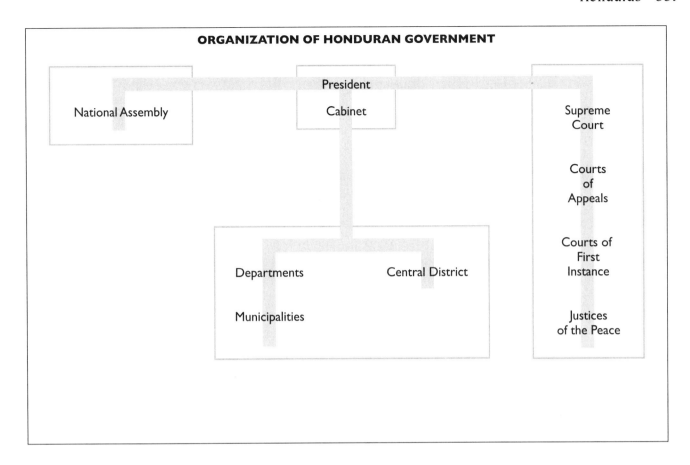

leave the jurisdiction of the military, a transition that is in process.

The president has veto power and can both call the Assembly into special session and extend a regular session; a two-thirds vote is required to overturn a veto. The president also has foreign policy and security responsibilities, although there are questions as to where de facto power resides since the military is largely autonomous. While the 1982 constitution gives the National Assembly the power to appoint many government officials, such as Supreme Court justices and the attorney general, in reality the Assembly generally rubber-stamps the wishes of the president (although over time the Assembly is showing greater signs of independence). The president oversees the government bureaucracy of some 70,000 state workers. Government jobs have long been a source of patronage; the civil service lacks professionalism with many positions changing with each election. The president also appoints governors for the country's 18 administrative departments (provinces or *departamentos*).

After decades of military rule, the road to elected executives began in 1980. Legislators were elected and were expected to choose a president, but instead they asked the military president, Policarpo Paz, to stay

on until 1982. Roberto Suazo Cordova of the Liberal Party won the 1981 presidential election. In the 1985 elections Suazo attempted to extend his term and the major parties were unable to select candidates; the military was called on to broker a solution. This solution, known as Option B, was to hold elections that were simultaneously primary and general elections. Multiple candidates for each party appeared on the ballot with the candidate receiving the most votes for each party becoming the nominee. Each party's nominee subsequently received all of the party's combined votes. The final results of the balloting gave 42.6 percent to Rafael Leonardo Callejas Romero of the National Party and 27.5 percent to the Liberal Party's José Azcona. However, because the total vote of the combined Liberal candidates was 51.5 percent, Azcona was declared the victor and assumed office in 1986.

Callejas Romero was victorious in the 1989 elections, and a peaceful electoral transfer of power from the Liberals to the Nationals occurred for the first time in Honduran history. Power was transferred back to the Liberal Party with the elections of November 1993, which were won by Carlos Roberto Reina Idiaquez, an attorney with a strong human rights record who ran on an anticorruption and antimilitary platform. Reina assumed office in January 1994.

The 1997 general elections were the fifth consecutive generally free and competitive elections since the return to democracy in the early 1980s. The Liberal Party candidate was Carlos Roberto Flores Facusse, the former president of the National Congress who had been defeated as the Liberal Party candidate in the presidential election of 1989. Flores studied engineering at Louisiana State University and is the owner of one of the country's leading newspapers. The National Party standard-bearer was Nora Gunera de Melgar, a former elementary schoolteacher and mayor of Tegucigalpa and the widow of a former president who took power in a military coup in 1975. The campaign was uneventful until early polls showed Flores with a large lead, and the National Party brought in U.S. campaign handler and strategist Dick Morris, who had previously caused a scandal as a consultant to President Bill Clinton. Morris was quick to employ negative campaign tactics, trying to make an issue of the fact that Flores's mother is of Palestinian descent and his wife is American. Melgar began to run ads emphasizing her "100 percent Honduran roots," and flyers and placards appeared denouncing the Middle Eastern business class in Honduras. Despite these ploys, Flores secured an impressive victory, receiving 52.8 percent of the vote compared with 42.7 percent for Melgar.

In 2001 the National Party ran dashing and charismatic candidate Ricardo Maduro. Maduro ran an efficient campaigned focused on fighting gangs and criminality, the number one problem in the country. Maduro, whose only son was kidnapped and murdered, personalized the crime issue and won the presidency with 52.2 percent of the vote.

LEGISLATURE

The National Assembly (Asamblea Nacional) is a unicameral legislature whose members serve four-year terms concurrently with the president. Congressional members are elected through proportional representation allocated among the 18 departments according to population with each department assured at least one representative. Each deputy is elected with a substitute (suplente) who may serve out any vacated office. There are 128 congressional deputies (diputados). The largest delegations represent the departments of Morazán (home of Tegucigalpa, the capital) and Cortés (the San Pedro Sula area).

Deputies must be Honduran by birth and over 21 years of age. Religious leaders, members of the military

and police forces, and public officials and their spouses and close relatives are barred from becoming deputies. Deputies enjoyed personal immunity from most legal and police action. This privilege became a source of national outrage. The immunity protected 20,000 government officials from prosecution and dozens that were implicated in serious crimes, including many national legislators. In 2004 the National Assembly voted unanimously to eliminate criminal immunity for its members.

The Assembly elects its own president and appoints a permanent commission of nine members that conducts congressional business when the legislature is not in session. The Assembly is in regular session from January 24 to October 31. Extraordinary sessions may be called by the president, by the permanent commission, or by a simple majority of members. These extraordinary sessions may only consider matters specifically stated in the convocatory decree.

The powers, duties, and responsibilities of the Assembly include the election of the nine Supreme Court justices and seven alternates, the commander in chief of the armed forces, the comptroller general, and other officials. In practice however, the legislature generally rubber-stamps the recommendations of the president, except in the case of the chief of the armed forces. Then it simply accepts the choice of the armed forces' executive council, although historic reforms of the military institution that would provide greater civilian control are currently under legislative review. The Assembly has the power to make peace and declare war and to approve or disapprove treaties made by the president. The Assembly receives the national budget from the president and has the power to make modifications before formal adoption.

To become law, a bill must pass three readings on three different days. An amendment to the constitution must receive a majority vote of the entire congress, not just of a quorum, in two different years.

The 2001 elections resulted in a congress comprised of 61 deputies from the National Party, 55 from the Liberal Party, 5 from the Democratic Unification Party, 4 from the Social Democratic Party, and 3 from the Christian Democratic Party.

JUDICIARY

The Honduran judiciary consists of a Supreme Court of Justice, courts of appeals, courts of first instance, and justices of the peace. The Supreme Court has both appellate and original jurisdiction and exercises judicial review in cases involving constitutional questions; it consists of nine justices and seven alternates who are selected by the National Assembly to serve four-year terms concurrent with the election cycle. This leaves the court highly politicized with judges often hand-picked by the president. The Supreme Court in turn selects all lower court judges and justices of the peace. These positions are often political rewards, and many of the justices of the peace are of questionable qualifications, often even lacking primary education.

The nine courts of appeals are three-judge panels that hear all appeals from lower courts. Appeal judges must be attorneys and at least 25 years of age. The 64 first-instance courts are trial courts that hear serious civil and criminal cases. Each department capital and municipalities of more than 4,000 inhabitants have two justices of the peace, and municipalities of fewer than 4,000 have one. Justices must be 21, live in the municipality that they serve, and be able to read and write.

While the constitution stipulates that the judiciary receive 3 percent of the total national budget, this is in practice never followed. The Honduran judiciary is underfunded, politicized, and of questionable effectiveness. Courageous judges have, for example, held trials of military officers for human rights abuses and other crimes, but often the police mock or threaten the judges and ignore orders to capture and imprison convicted soldiers. In addition, women's groups argue that the penal code, approved in 1996, is an affront to women. Articles 151 and 152 of the code provide that a man who rapes a girl between the ages of 14 and 18 can go free if he marries the victim and that government prosecutors are prevented from pressing rape charges if the rapist used nonviolent methods—such as drugs or taking advantage of a sleeping or unconscious woman—to commit the crime.

REGIONAL AND LOCAL GOVERNMENT

The nation's 18 departments are headed by presidentially appointed governors, who are essentially dignitaries. The 18 departments are divided into 297 municipalities. Each municipality (*municipalidad*) may contain more than one town within its boundaries and is similar to a county in the United States. Every municipality has an elected mayor and between 4 and 10 council members, depending on the population. In recent years there has been a movement toward decentralization and stronger local governments. Beginning with the 1993 elections municipal officials were elected on a separate ballot from the president and legislature (one vote per ballot). This allows ticket splitting and makes local officials responsible to the electorate. Additionally, this gives the smaller parties much greater opportunities to win local elections. Tegucigalpa, the capital and largest city, also now has an elected mayor and city council. Local governments are highly dependent on the central government for funding.

The Electoral System

The Honduran electoral system is based on universal suffrage (since 1956) for all citizens over the age of 18. Voting is compulsory for those between 18 and 60, though compliance is not enforced. Active members of the armed forces do not vote. The ballot is secret, and since voters merely make a single fingerprint mark on each colored ballot that features symbols of the parties, literacy is not necessary.

For the elections from 1981 through 1989, a single ballot included the name of a presidential candidate and ranked lists of that party's candidates for the National Assembly and the municipal council in the area. Voters cast a single ballot for an entire slate. Beginning in 1993 municipal officials were elected on a separate ballot that allowed ticket splitting between local and national candidates. The 128 seats of the legislature are divided proportionally by votes cast in each department. The president is elected by a simple majority, as are local mayors.

A National Election Tribunal (Tribunal National de Elecciones) was created under the 1981 electoral law. The tribunal is charged with registering all eligible citizens, regulating the registration process of political parties, and overseeing electoral rules. The tribunal is an independent, autonomous body that has a president chosen by the Supreme Court and one member chosen by each of the registered national parties. In anticipation of the 1997 elections, the tribunal proposed various changes to electoral rules. The most important was to make a separate ballot for the election of legislative deputies, a proposal that was formally adopted and that benefited the smaller parties. One electoral rule that helps maintain the status quo is that parties are given public campaign funds based on the number of votes received in the previous election.

The Party System
ORIGINS OF THE PARTIES

Among Central American countries, Honduras has the longest tradition of two dominant parties: the Liberals and the Nationals. The Liberal Party was formed in 1891 by one of the country's most successful presidents, Policarpo Bonilla. The National Party was originally a breakaway group of liberals led by Manuel Bonilla. Until 1948 the Nationals and the Liberals were the only official political parties in the country. For many years the two parties were aligned with rival North American banana companies, the Liberals with Cuyamel and the Nationals with United Fruit. The military has been strongly allied with the National Party. While Hondurans have shown displeasure with the corruption, nepotism, and policy failings of the principal parties, alternative parties have never captured a significant portion of the electorate.

THE PARTIES IN LAW

The constitution recognizes the role of legally inscribed political parties in providing for the effective participation of citizens in the political process. Parties are only recognized upon the presentation of petitions bearing the signature of a specified number of voters in each department. Registration traditionally has been difficult due to the challenges in collecting and authenticating the signatures. As would be expected, the two major parties have stopped all movement to more easily facilitate the registration of parties.

At present five parties are legally recognized: the two traditional rivals, the National Party and the Liberal Party; two parties formed in the 1970s, the Party of Innovation and Unity (PINU) and the Christian Democratic Party (PDC); and one party recognized in 1996, the Democratic Unification Party (PUD).

PARTY ORGANIZATION

With the exception of the newly formed Democratic Unification Party, all Honduran parties are national in scope. Even departments that are considered National or Liberal strongholds have swung back and forth between the two in national elections. There are no parties based solely in one region nor departments entirely in the hands of one or another party.

Political parties have grassroots organizations, student organizations, and dues-paying members with locally selected officials in each department. Many of these groups, in addition to political organization and indoctrination, maintain programs of political education and services such as dental and medical clinics and food distribution at the regional and municipal levels. Local party bosses, especially in the rural areas, are often powerful area chieftains (*caciques*) who still resort to violence to maintain their positions of power and dominance.

Party structures are highly centralized, and power has traditionally been centered in Tegucigalpa. With the rise of San Pedro Sula as the industrial center of the country, this city and the department of Cortés is beginning to challenge the old guard in the capital. The two major parties themselves are divided into bitter factions, and intraparty competition is as bitter and important as that between parties.

CAMPAIGNING

The limited size of the country and the concentration of the population in the western half permits personal campaigning by the candidates in all populated areas. The campaign begins a full two years before the national elections when the candidates start their quest for their party's nomination. Candidates visit towns, participate in parades, sponsor barbecues, kiss babies, speak to local groups, and try to garner support from the movers and shakers. Town officials and elites try to line up early behind a successful candidate in order to later receive patronage positions in the government or bureaucracy. The major parties hold national primaries to select their nominees to the presidency. These primaries often involve backroom deals where candidates withdraw and throw their support to another. For the 1993 elections the National Party's major factions struck a deal and only one candidate ran in the primaries. For the 1997 elections both the National Party and the Liberal Party primaries featured multiple candidates.

Honduran primaries are held almost a full year before the national election, resulting in a very long campaign season. The country is canvassed with flags, posters, balloons, billboards, wall paintings, hats, and television, radio, and newspaper advertisements featuring the colors and symbols of the parties and the names of the standard-bearer. Even the rocks along the sides of the highways are painted with National blue or Liberal red paint.

While the government provides campaign subsidies based on the number of votes received in the previous election, campaigns are very expensive and expenditures are not limited or reported. Campaign funds are provided by wealthy party members, individuals hoping for a patronage position, and merchants and industrialists who are said to hedge their bets by contributing to both major parties.

INDEPENDENT VOTERS

Formal party membership, in the sense of paying dues and carrying a membership card, covers a minority of registered voters. Family traditions and party loyalties are strong but declining. The use of a separate ballot to select national legislators produced a surprising amount of ticket splitting, resulting in the election of deputies from nontraditional parties, and may lead to a larger number of independent voters in the future.

Major Political Parties

HONDURAS LIBERAL PARTY

(Partido Liberal de Honduras; PLH)

HISTORY

The oldest political party in the country, the Liberal Party has its roots in the 1890s liberal movement of Policarpo Bonilla, whose presidential term (1894–99) marked one of the most successful eras in Honduran political history. During the first half of the 20th century, the Liberal Party was closely allied with Cuyamel, a North American banana company owned by Samuel Zemurray. Zemurray waged land wars against another U.S. company, United Fruit, which was aligned with the National Party. In 1929 Zemurray gave up the battle and sold Cuyamel to United Fruit, leaving the Liberals with a loss of support and on the political sidelines from 1933 to 1957.

In 1957, after years of dictatorship (Tiburcio Carías from 1933 to 1949), the Liberals regained power with Ramón Villeda Morales. While staunchly anti-Communist, Villeda was socially progressive, and his Liberal administration brought about a new labor code, began discussions on land reform, and started to modernize the country. When it became apparent that an even more progressive Liberal, Modesto Rodas Alvarado, would sweep the 1963 elections, the military engineered a coup.

The Liberals were not to regain power until the election of Suazo in 1981. A country doctor, Suazo was an incompetent and unpopular executive who attempted to maintain his power beyond his four-year term. In part due to Suazo's machinations, the Liberal Party was unable to select a candidate for the 1985 elections. The military intervened and brokered a plan whereby each party could run multiple candidates in the national election and the party that got the most total votes would win, making the president the candidate who obtained the most votes for said party. This ended in fiasco, with the winning candidate, the Liberal's José Azcona, garnering only 27.5 percent of the vote.

Azcona was forced to make a pact with the National Party in order to govern. Carlos Flores Facussé won the 1988 primary for the Liberals but was defeated in the 1989 elections. In 1993 Carlos Roberto Reina, of the progressive wing of the party, was the party's nominee and ran on a platform of moral revolution (anticorruption) and weakening the power and prerogatives of the military. Reina, an attorney, is a former chancellor of the university and justice on the Interamerican Human Rights Court. The Liberal Party won the 1993 elections in a landslide, and Reina was moderately successful in his attempts to rein in the military. Although there were various attempts on his life and both overt and subtle threats from the military high command, Reina was able to change military service from obligatory to voluntary and to pass a constitutional amendment to transfer the police from military to civilian control. While it is widely accepted that the Reina administration was cleaner than that of its National predecessor, some members in the administration were accused of corruption. On the economic front, the Reina administration was unable to ignite the moribund economy, and levels of poverty and unemployment remain critically high.

Flores returned as a party candidate in 1997, became the standard-bearer for the Liberals, and won the presidential elections. The party lost in 2001 but remained one of the two major parties.

MEMBERSHIP AND CONSTITUENCY

The PLH has a broad base of support throughout the country and strong support in urban areas. Claims of membership are highly suspect, but in open elections it has shown to be the dominant party in the country. The more centrist of the two major parties, the PLH traditionally has had a strong following among organized labor, the educated, and the young.

FINANCING

The government subsidizes campaigns based on the number of votes received in the previous election. Individual and business donations are not regulated and go unreported.

PROSPECTS

While the party continues to suffer from factionalization, its prospects are good to remain a major political force for some time. Its 2001 electoral defeat was only the second loss in six elections since electoral democracy was established in 1981. Ahead of the 2005 presidential elections, it nominated Manuel Zelaya as its candidate.

NATIONAL PARTY OF HONDURAS
(Partido Nacional de Honduras; PNH)

HISTORY

The National Party, one of two dominant parties in Honduras, was first formed in 1902 as a splinter group of the Liberal Party. It was the party of long-term president and dictator Tiburcio Carías A., who ruled the country with an iron fist from 1932 to 1949, and of his successors, Juan Manuel Gálvez and Julio Lozano. The PNH's candidate, Ramón Cruz, won the 1970 elections, but his weak and aimless administration was toppled by a military coup after only a year in office. The PNH has been an active collaborator in military governments and throughout the cold war was a right-wing, pro-military party with strong ties to the rural landed elite.

During the 1980s the party was a strong supporter of the militarization of Honduras and cooperation with the United States and U.S.-sponsored contras who used Honduran territory to wage war on the Nicaraguan Sandinistas. In the 1981 elections, which ended years of military rule, the PNH ran Ricardo Zúñiga, an unpopular member of the ultraright wing of the party, who fared poorly in the national elections. In the 1985 elections the PNH's candidate was Rafael Callejas, a young, U.S.-educated figure who was to put a new face on conservatism in the party. While Callejas won the largest number of votes in the national election, the unusual electoral format of this election gave the victory to the Liberals. Callejas won convincingly in 1989, giving the PNH its first victory in the new era of democracy. Callejas immediately adopted a series of neoliberal economic reforms and structural adjustment programs designed by international lending institutions. This caused widespread protest throughout the country. By the end of his term unprecedented charges of fraud and abuse were leveled against the administration and against Callejas's family and friends.

In the 1993 elections the party was taken over by the right wing, which launched the candidacy of Oswaldo Ramos. Ramos's charges that Reina, his presidential opponent, was a Communist, fell on deaf ears, and the party lost badly. A host of PNH officials, including Callejas, were indicted on charges of fraud.

Following years of infighting and corruption charges on Callejas and others, the PNH rebounded in the presidential election of 2001. Its candidate, Ricardo Maduro, waged an effective campaign and captured the presidency with 52.2 percent of the vote.

ORGANIZATION

The party is nominally run by a convention and executive committee. In practice, various factions battle to gain control. The party has national coverage and party organizations throughout the country. Power runs from the party center in Tegucigalpa out to the grass roots. Patronage and the hope of jobs with winning candidates remain the glue that holds the organization together.

MEMBERSHIP AND CONSTITUENCY

The PNH has traditionally been strong in rural areas and the less-developed departments. The party has a large membership, although it is believed that official membership claims are exaggerated.

FINANCING

The government subsidizes campaigns based on the number of votes received in the previous election. Individual and business donations are not regulated and are unreported.

PROSPECTS

Ricardo Maduro reinvigorated the party with his candidacy for president in 2001. Charismatic and an excellent campaigner, Maduro effectively used his personal story as a father grieving over the kidnapping and murder of his son to connect with the Honduran masses, who suffer widespread deprivation from the national epidemic of gangs and crime. After becoming president, Maduro continued to focus on this issue, often joining anti-gang units on arrests and neighborhood sweeps. This resulted in direct personal threats against the president by the organized gangs, which only added to his anticrime persona. In this regard, Maduro has transformed the pro-military image of the party into a pro–law enforcement image. For the 2005 presidential election, the PNH nominated Porfirio Lobo as its candidate.

Minor Political Parties

CHRISTIAN DEMOCRAT PARTY
(Partido Demócrata Cristiano; PDC)

The PDC was formed in 1980 and is a full member of the Christian Democrat International. The party has never won more than three seats in the National Assembly and in the 1993 elections won 1 percent of the vote and no seats. In 1997 the party recovered slightly, receiving 2.2 percent of the vote and gaining a single seat. In 2001 the party won three seats and 3.7 percent of the national legislative vote.

PARTY OF INNOVATION AND UNITY

(Partido de Inovación y Unidad; PINU)

The PINU was founded in 1970 and identifies itself as a social democratic party with links to the German Social Democratic Party (SPD). The PINU earned 1.5 percent of the presidential vote, 4.6 percent of the legislative vote, and four seats in the National Assembly in 2001.

DEMOCRATIC UNIFICATION PARTY

(Partido de Unificación Democrática; PUD)

The latest party to gain recognition from the National Election Tribunal is the PUD, which ran for the first time in the 1997 elections. The PUD's founder and presidential candidate was Matias Funes, a university professor and author. The PUD is the first recognized party of the Left. The PUD is antimilitary, advocates an anti-neoliberal economic policy, and supports humanist and progressive economic and social legislation. The PUD's support in the 1997 elections was a major surprise as the party earned a seat in congress and some municipal positions.

The PUD increased its electoral strength considerably by 2001, winning five seats in the National Assembly. As the minor parties pick up seats, their importance grows, since the two largest parties no longer win a majority of seats in the National Assembly, but only a plurality. Therefore, the ruling party is required to form coalitions on particular issues to gain passage of legislation.

Other Political Forces

THE MILITARY

The strongest alternative political force in the country remains the military. The Honduran military was first professionalized in 1954 with the establishment of the Francisco Morazán military academy. By 1956 the military unleashed its first coup. The military played an important role in writing the 1957 constitution, which granted the organization autonomy from elected presidents and freed the head of the armed forces from allegiance to elected officials. The military ruled almost continuously from 1963 to 1982.

In 1982, while power was ostensibly transferred to civilians, the real power in the country lay with the military and its commander in chief, Gustavo Álvarez. Military autonomy was also strengthened in the 1982 constitution. In the Honduran military, leaders are appointed from within—rubber-stamped by the Assembly—and the presidentially appointed defense minister only coordinates. Simultaneously, in the early 1980s the United States was using Honduras as a base for anti-Sandinista contras and sending the Honduran generals unprecedented levels of aid. Commander in Chief Álvarez was staunchly anti-left, and during his tenure human rights abuses increased dramatically. Battalion 3-16, an elite military unit with U.S. training, was responsible for the disappearance of many suspected leftists. The police, totally under military control, also participated in kidnappings, disappearances, and assassinations.

Álvarez was ousted by an internal military coup, and the worst of the human rights abuses disappeared. In January 1999 the constitution was amended to abolish the position of military commander in chief of the armed forces, thus codifying civilian authority over the military. Honduran armed forces have refocused toward combating transnational threats such as narcoterrorism and organized crime. In 2002 Honduras deployed troops to Iraq in support of Operation Iraqi Freedom; the troops were recalled in 2004.

The resolution of civil wars in El Salvador and Nicaragua, as well as budget cuts in all ministries, has reduced funding for the armed forces, causing the military to fall far below its authorized strength.

FOREIGN RELATIONS

Honduras worked toward implementation of a regional customs union by the end of 2004 in order to ease border controls and tariffs among Honduras, Guatemala, Nicaragua, and El Salvador. Honduras and Nicaragua had tense relations throughout 2000 and early 2001 due to a maritime boundary dispute off the Atlantic Coast. Relations have since improved, but animosity remains.

Discussion over the Central American Free Trade Agreement (CAFTA) are in process among the countries of Costa Rica, El Salvador, Guatemala, Honduras, and Nicaragua. By mid-2005 the agreement had been ratified by several of the governments, including those in Honduras and the United States.

National Prospects

Honduras is in the midst of the longest period of civilian rule in its history, with six presidents elected in relatively free elections since 1981. There is a strong two-party tradition, and the volatile Central American region appears to have found a permanent peace. However, all is not well for Honduras and Hondurans. The country is poor, its citizens undereducated and underfed, and its industry incapable of competing in the global market. The loss of life and infrastructure resulting from Hurricane Mitch in 1998 remains a devastating setback for the country. The sleaze of the Callejas administration reinforced the belief among the citizenry that politicians are corrupt.

Honduras has one of the most inegalitarian distributions of income in the world, which leads to episodes of violence, especially in the countryside. The end of the U.S.-sponsored Sandinista-contra war left thousands of contras and tens of thousands of weapons idle in Honduras. With massive poverty and unemployment and an oversupply of weapons and mercenaries in the country, crime has escalated out of control. The military and police seem unable and even unwilling to combat lawlessness; indeed, they are charged with masterminding the largest crime organizations. Due in part to U.S. pressure, electoral democracy will continue for some time. But the citizenry is becoming increasingly cynical of the promises of democracy, and perpetual crisis will continue as the norm.

Honduras's material and political challenges are compounded by the AIDS epidemic and the unprecedented increase in criminal gangs and crime. Honduras has one of the highest rates of HIV infection in the hemisphere and by some estimates as many as 100,000 gang members; one such gang carried out a massacre of 28 civilians on a bus in 2004. The economic potential of tourism and investment are seriously undermined by crime and disease. President Maduro made crime and the gangs his number one priority, leading some to assert that the demonization of gangs has led to human rights abuses.

Honduras has made progress in democratization, opening up the country to trade, privatizing state enterprises, and eliminating the immunity of government officials to prosecution for alleged crimes. Much more needs to be done.

Further Reading

Bowman, Kirk S. *Militarization, Democracy, and Development: The Perils of Praetorianism in Latin America.* University Park: Pennsylvania State University Press, 2002.

Euraque, Dar'o. *Reinterpreting the Banana Republic: Region and State in Honduras, 1870–1972.* Chapel Hill: University of North Carolina Press, 1996.

Merrill, Tim, ed. *Honduras: A Country Study.* Washington, D.C.: U.S. Government Printing Office, 1994.

Norsworthy, Kent, and Tom Barry, eds. *Inside Honduras.* Albuquerque: Interhemispheric Press, 1994.

Paz, Ernesto. "The Origin and Development of Political Parties in Honduras." In *Political Parties and Democracy in Central America.* Edited by Louis Goodman et al. Boulder, Colo.: Westview Press, 1992.

Peckenham, Nancy, and Annie Street, eds. *Honduras: Portrait of a Captive Nation.* New York: Praeger, 1985.

Rosenberg, Mark. "Democracy in Honduras: The Electoral and Political Reality." In *Elections and Democracy in Central America, Revisited.* Edited by Mitchell Seligson and John Booth. Chapel Hill: University of North Carolina Press, 1995.

Ruhl, J. Mark. "Doubting Democracy in Honduras." *Current History,* February 1997.

Schulz, Donald E., and Deborah Sundloff Schulz. *The United States, Honduras, and the Crisis in Central America.* Boulder, Colo.: Westview Press, 1994.

REPUBLIC OF HUNGARY

(Magyar Köztársaság)

By Jeffrey K. Hass, Ph.D.

Hungary lies in the middle of East-Central Europe, adjacent to traditional "Western Europe" on the west and to former Warsaw Pact members on the east, giving Hungary a prime geopolitical location.

Hungary's economy was viewed as the potential miracle of Eastern Europe until 1994. Before 1989 Hungary had the most Western-oriented economy of all East bloc countries, with stronger trade ties and with economic reforms—surprising for Soviet-sphere economies (the "New Economic Mechanism")—that allowed for some degree of private enterprise. However, rising external debt made economic reform, especially in the form of privatization and austerity programs, imperative. From 1990 to 1993 economic reforms included financial stabilization and mass privatization. But with the economic reforms came economic pain: an inflationary spike from price liberalization, rising unemployment, and some social backlash against the rising wealth of the former Communist elite (the *nomenklatura*) and some economic traders.

In 1994 this pain was translated into an electoral victory for the Hungarian Socialist Party, with slower economic change. Privatization essentially came to a halt, and the state budget and current account deficits rose sharply. In 1995 the Socialists reversed themselves and introduced an austerity package that reduced Hungary's debt and returned to mass privatization. The GDP began to grow in 1994 (2.9 percent) and 1995 (1.5 percent), and unemployment began to fall in 1995 (14 percent to 10 percent). Inflation was episodic, with spikes in 1991 and 1995. For the most part, however, the economy has been stable and foreign investment has increased in the 1990s and after 2000. Entry into the European Union may create some dislocation but generally should benefit Hungarian economic growth and post-Socialist adjustment.

Hungary has been one of the more promising countries of Eastern Europe to make the transition from a Communist polity and economy to democracy and market capitalism. While the transition has not been smooth—economic pain paved the way for the Socialists to return to power, and complexities or snags in legislation and procedure have made political institutions run less than smoothly—Hungary still exhibits successful institution building. While political actors regularly fight and coalitions and splits have occurred, there is little threat of political instability, and Socialists have not tried to turn back the clock on democracy or the free market.

The System of Government

Hungary's political system at the national level is split into three branches: the executive, headed by the president and the prime minister; the legislative, headed by the National Assembly; and the judiciary, headed by the Constitutional Court. The overall political system resembles that of Germany: the prime minister is the most important executive figure and,

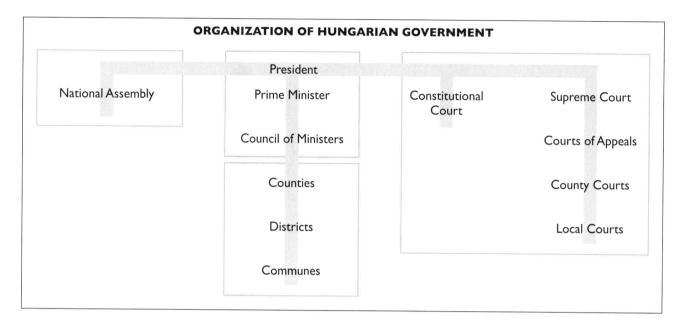

ORGANIZATION OF HUNGARIAN GOVERNMENT

while autonomous, the executive in the end answers to the legislature, where ultimate political sovereignty resides.

EXECUTIVE

The executive branch is headed by two figures, the president and the prime minister. The president is, as in much of Eastern Europe, a figurehead whose powers reside mostly in the realm of diplomacy and international affairs. The prime minister derives his or her power from heading the state bureaucracy. Both executives, however, are subjugated to the ultimate sovereignty of the National Assembly.

The president, considered in the constitution as the "head of state," is weak. Formally the job of the president is to represent the nation in the international arena and to guard democratic procedure, in essence putting the president above the executive branch and all other branches as well. However, commensurate with this responsibility, the president has few powers. Formally the president can conclude international treaties (which must then be approved by the National Assembly); announce parliamentary and local elections; petition the Assembly to undertake legislation or other actions; initiate a national referendum; appoint and dismiss the heads of the National Bank, universities, and the armed forces; and grant pardons and bestow citizenship. Most of these acts require the countersignature of the prime minister if they are to be legally valid.

The president also has two forms of a weak veto. First, he can send disagreeable legislation back to the Assembly for reconsideration, but the parliament can override this veto with a simple majority vote. Second, the president can refer legislation to the Constitutional Court, which must then rule on its constitutionality.

The president can be removed from office via impeachment if he has violated the constitution (e.g., having a conflict of interest between presidential responsibilities and personal interests, such as side employment) or some other law. A motion for impeachment may be introduced by no less than one-fifth of the members of the Assembly and requires a two-thirds majority for impeachment proceedings to begin. At that point the president is suspended from his duties, and the Constitutional Court is called on to rule whether the president did in fact violate the constitution or any other law; the Court then has the final say on the president's guilt. Should the president be found guilty, he must step down. In this case or in any other case when the president cannot execute his or her duties of office, the chain of command runs to the speaker of the National Assembly (who does not have the power to send legislation back to the parliament or to the Constitutional Court or dissolve the Assembly).

The president also has the power to dissolve the National Assembly, but only within strict bounds—either when the parliament has not approved a prime minister 40 days after the first candidate was nominated (e.g., soon after the prime minister resigned) or when the Assembly passes a no-confidence motion four times in the course of 12 months. To dissolve the parliament the president must request the opinions of the prime minister, the speaker of the National Assembly, and the parliamentary leaders of the represented parties. The president must be careful when dissolving the Assembly, however; if he tries to do so beyond these limits, then Assembly members can consider the president in violation of the constitution and motion for his impeachment.

The prime minister and his deputy ministers run the state bureaucracy and so have great potential power. Ministers do answer to the National Assembly: they must make reports when asked to do so, and ministerial power to rule by decree is very limited. All ministers except the prime minister are appointed and removed not by the parliament but only by the prime minister himself. The prime minister generally comes from the largest parliamentary party and must be approved by majority vote. The National Assembly also has some control over the prime minister through the vote of no confidence; in this way the prime minister can be removed from office.

However, two factors make it more difficult to remove a prime minister in Hungary than elsewhere. First, the prime minister comes from the largest party, and so it would take a major split between the prime minister and his own party before a no-confidence vote could come to pass; and a vote for no confidence cannot come to the floor unless it is brought up with a parallel nomination for another prime minister. This mechanism has made for more stable relations: Hungary does not suffer from as many no-confidence motions and successful votes as do other countries. However, this has not prevented conflict between the two branches, in particular between the prime minister and opposition parties or junior partners in the ruling coalition. (This happened to Jozsef Antall, who in 1992 found himself the target of criticism from the Independent Smallholders' Party, which was a junior member of the ruling coalition.)

Because the executive has two possible heads, conflict between them is a possibility, especially when one member is from the parliamentary opposition. This was the case in the early 1990s, when Antall and Arpad Goncz went head to head over executive prerogative. Goncz had come from the opposition Alliance of Free Democrats as president in a political pact with the Hungarian Democratic Forum, which as the senior member of the ruling coalition had put its own leader, Antall, in the office of prime minister.

A series of scandals emerged after 2002 involving past involvement with the Communist secret police.

New prime minister Peter Medgyessy, from the ruling alliance of Socialists and Alliance of Free Democrats, was accused of working for counterintelligence in the Interior Ministry. The chairman of the Alliance of Young Democrats (Fidesz) was also accused of links (through his father) to the secret police. In the end, the scandals remained confined to momentary newspaper headlines, and did not generate further accusations or investigations.

LEGISLATURE

The parliament, called the National Assembly (Orszag-gyules), is a unicameral body and is the most powerful branch of government in Hungary. This resulted from the legacy of Communism: the Communist opposition first came to power within the parliament (and was determined to maintain its power by locating sovereignty in the National Assembly), and politicians did not want to pave the way for potential dictatorship (which they overthrew in 1989).

The main powers of the National Assembly are passing legislation, defining policies, approving the budget and the government's programs, declaring war or a state of national emergency, calling a national referendum, approving and dismissing the prime minister, and dissolving local assemblies that have violated the law or constitution. Parliamentary approval is reached by simple majority or by two-thirds majority, depending on the situation. For a declaration of war or national emergency, for passing a motion on impeachment, and for altering the constitution, a two-thirds majority is required. In order for parliamentary actions to be binding, a quorum (one-half of delegates) must be present for voting.

Legislation may be initiated by the president, the prime minister, parliamentary committees, or by any member of the National Assembly. If a bill has been passed by a simple majority, the speaker signs it and sends it to the president, who has 15 days to sign it and promulgate it (5 days if the speaker has declared the bill an urgent act). Within this period the president may send the bill back to the National Assembly for reconsideration and then to the Constitutional Court. According to the constitution, if the bill is found unconstitutional, the president must send it back to the National Assembly.

The National Assembly, according to the constitution, is the supreme political body in Hungary. All other bodies are subordinate: local government is restrained by national legislation, and the executive branch must report its activities and results of policies to the parliament. Only the Constitutional Court is autonomous from the parliament, and then only in its proceedings; justices must be approved by the National Assembly before entering the bench. Further, the parliament has the power to dismiss the prime minister and government through a vote of no confidence.

PARLIAMENTARY ELECTIONS, 4/7/02 AND 4/21/02

Party	seats
FIDESZ-MDF	188
— Fidesz–Magyar Polgári Párt	(164)
— Magyar Demokrata Fórum	(24)
Magyar Szocialista Párt	178
Szabad Demokraták Szövetsége	20
Other parties (% less than 5%)	(0)

Source: www.electionworld.org

JUDICIARY

Since 1990 the Hungarian government has been committed to creating an independent judiciary that follows international norms and standards and is able to guarantee the rule of law in the country. Toward this goal the Hungarian government has created the Association of Hungarian Judges, has limited the power of the Ministry of Justice over the judiciary to administrative tasks alone, and has supported the power of the National Judges' Council to approve changes in personnel and judicial budgets. (For example, a judge may be appointed to a position by the Ministry of Justice only after such an appointment has been approved by the National Judges' Council; this helps reduce administrative and political pressure on the judicial branch.)

The Hungarian judicial system follows a continental procedure. This has two practical implications for the functioning of the judiciary. First, contrary to Anglo-American common-law tradition, the Hungarian courts do not follow precedent when deciding cases; instead, each case is decided on the basis of the facts of that case alone and on the relevant laws. Second, and related, the Hungarian courts do not have the power to interpret laws; they have only the power to decide legal outcomes based on the laws themselves. Even the Constitutional

Court does not have the power of interpretation, although it can judge the merits of laws.

The judicial hierarchy starts at the lowest level, county tribunals and local courts that oversee decisions in civil disputes and criminal cases. Appeals on rulings may be made up the judicial hierarchy to courts of appeals and then on to the Supreme Court, which is the final arbiter of civil disputes and criminal decisions. Further, courts do have the power to review the *actions* of local authorities. (The Constitutional Court has this power for the national government.) Thus, while the courts themselves cannot interpret the law, they can act as a safeguard against government abuse of the law.

The Constitutional Court stands outside the normal court system. While other courts are concerned with deciding conflicts between civil parties, deciding guilt in criminal cases, or ruling on appeals, the Constitutional Court instead is an overseeing court. Its purpose is to make sure that all branches and organs of government follow the rule of law and remain inside the bounds of power prescribed by law. Since 1990 the court has reviewed an immense number of laws, petitions, and other documents. They have included rulings on abortion and the death penalty (where the court found Hungary's law unconstitutional), on property distribution, on extending the statute of limitations for crimes committed in the Communist period (which the court ruled unconstitutional), and on the scope of presidential powers.

According to the constitution, the Constitutional Court consists of 11 justices who are nominated by a Nominating Committee (consisting of one member from each party represented in the National Assembly). The National Assembly as a whole must then approve by two-thirds vote each candidate for justice of the Constitutional Court.

REGIONAL AND LOCAL GOVERNMENT

At the local level Hungary is divided into 42 counties (*megyek*), with the capital city, Budapest, equivalent to a county, and each county is composed of districts and communities or communes. Local legislative assemblies are elected for four-year terms; local executives are headed by mayors. Powers of local government include disposing of local government property and funds, levying of local taxes, and passing and implementing of local legislation (which must not violate national laws or the constitution).

Local legislatures are chaired by the mayors. Powers and rights of the local government are constrained by national laws, which may be adopted only by two-thirds majority vote of the National Assembly.

The Electoral System

In Hungary the president is elected by the National Assembly to a five-year term and may repeat himself in office only once. When 30 days remain before the end of the current president's mandate, the speaker of the National Assembly proclaims the process of selecting a new president, which must be concluded not more than 30 days after the announcement. For a person to become a candidate, at least 50 members of the National Assembly must nominate him or her prior to the announcement of the election. On the day of voting, a candidate receiving two-thirds of all votes cast by parliamentarians is declared the winner. If no candidate receives the two-thirds majority, the voting process is repeated; if for a second time no candidate receives two-thirds of the vote, a third round is held, in which the two candidates with the most votes from the second round compete. Only a simple majority is required in the third round. The whole voting process is to take no more than three days, according to the constitution.

The first post-Communist president was Arpad Goncz of the Alliance of Free Democrats (SzDSz)—a party that was not in the post-1990 ruling coalition. Goncz received the position in spite of this because of a pact between the SzDSz and the Hungarian Democratic Forum (MDF): an SzDSz candidate would receive the presidential post (but not a position in the coalition) if the laws were changed so that a two-thirds majority would not be needed for passing legislation (thus making political life easier for the ruling coalition, which consisted of three parties and held only 59 percent of the vote). In 1995 Goncz was reelected by parliament, receiving 259 of the 335 votes cast. In 2000 Ferenc Mádl was selected as president, and in 2005 Laszlo Solyom won the post.

The National Assembly sits for a period of four years; only presidential dissolution of the parliament may interfere with this period. (Once the National Assembly is dissolved, new elections must occur within three months.) Parliamentary elections in Hungary are extraordinarily complicated owing to the electoral law. Because various parties wanted to safeguard their ability to enter or remain in the National Assembly, several mechanisms were included that have made the Hungarian electoral process difficult to understand; predicting an outcome and the implications of one's vote for different parties is almost impossible.

Delegates enter the National Assembly in one of three ways: through individual races, through local party lists, or through a "national list" based on "fragment votes." (This system is for all practical purposes the same as that in Estonia.) Of the 386 seats in the National Assembly, 176 are set aside for the individual races, 152 are set aside for local county lists (party-based races), and 58 are set aside for the national lists and fragment votes. The two figures of 152 and 58 are only a maximum and a minimum, however; less than 152 seats may be distributed through local party races depending on whether parties receive the necessary votes to garner a mandate, and those seats not determined through the local party races go to the national list. Each voter has two votes: one for a candidate in the individual races and one for a party in the county-level party races.

The individual race is straightforward. For a vote to be valid, more than 50 percent of registered voters must cast a ballot. To win in the first round, a candidate must receive a majority of votes cast; otherwise, a runoff is held between those candidates who received at least 15 percent of votes cast, or among the top three candidates if less than three received 15 percent or more. In the runoff, only 25 percent participation is required and, to win, one needs to receive only a plurality (i.e., the highest number of votes) rather than a majority.

The next path is through "county lists," races between parties at the level of the county (not the national level). Parties present lists of potential delegates, and voters cast their votes for a party. To have an opportunity to send candidates to the National Assembly, a party has to overcome a threshold of 5 percent. Each county has a number of mandates, depending on the population, and each mandate is a number of votes. A party can receive mandates at the county level, which are translated into Assembly seats. A party has to overcome the percentage barrier to have a chance to receive a mandate. For example, if in a certain county there are 10,000 votes per mandate and a party receives 30,000 votes, then that party receives three mandates; the first three candidates on the party list become members of the National Assembly.

Those mandates that are not filled are transferred to the national list, which is a minimum of 58 but can be augmented by unfilled county mandates. These national-level seats are distributed to the parties that receive overall more than 5 percent of votes cast nationally. Parties that do not cross the barrier do not get seats from this pool; and those that do cross the barrier receive a number of seats equal to the percentage of votes that party received of all votes cast for parties that break the 5 percent barrier.

One must note a slight caveat: once a delegate enters the parliament, he or she is not bound to party discipline and at worst can be dropped from the party list of candidates only in the *next* election. Hence, party strength cannot be based on number of seats alone. For example, the Hungarian Democratic Forum won 165 total seats in the 1990 elections; however, by 1994 the "formal" number of Forum delegates was 136. Of the original 165, 31 had left for other factions (Alliance of Young Democrats or other parties), and the Forum had gained two delegates from two other parties.

The Party System

ORIGINS OF THE PARTIES

Hungary's transition to democracy began with political negotiations between the embryonic Hungarian Democratic Forum (MDF)—the vehicle for rising democratic opposition under Communism—and the Hungarian Socialist Workers' Party (the ruling Communist Party). The initial steps in the direction of democracy were the revising of the existing constitution in 1989 and the setting of parliamentary elections for 1990. The electoral law was a result of political negotiations, allowing ruling parties to remain in politics but also giving challengers a chance to enter the parliament. The first post-Communist elections gave the most seats to the Democratic Forum and then to other left-leaning social democratic parties and right-leaning (but not nationalist or extremist) parties. After the 1990 elections a ruling coalition, headed by the Democratic Forum and with the support of the Independent Smallholders' Party (FKgP) and the Christian Democratic People's Party (CDPP), was established; while the president was chosen from the Alliance of Free Democrats (Arpad Goncz), the Democratic Forum managed to get its party leader, Jozsef Antall, approved as prime minister.

Governance in Hungary was made more difficult by several political factors. The first arose from tensions within the ruling coalition, especially between the Forum and the junior member, the FKgP. The FKgP pushed for land restitution, the return of land to previous owners taken by Communists. Forum members resisted and then wavered, since the ISP was adamant

on the issue and the Forum required ISP support to maintain a majority in the National Assembly. A second source of political instability came from tensions between the president and the prime minister. With the separation of powers between the two nominal heads of the executive left vague in the constitution, both actors tried to become the top player; only as disputes emerged did the Constitutional Court begin to delineate the boundaries of power (usually in favor of the prime minister).

The MDF-led government began with the best starting conditions of any former Communist country. Hungary had been tinkering with economic reform, and it had a polity relatively free from nationalist/ethnic or party strife. However, by 1992 Antall came under criticism from opposition parties, especially the Alliance of Free Democrats (SzDSz) and the new rising star, the Alliance of Young Democrats (Fidesz), for its inability to take advantage of such conditions and actually reform the economy. Land reform followed the FKgP's demands, which did not create a vibrant sector of independent farmers; privatization had bogged down, as the government could not decide among several plans, and what privatization did occur seemed to favor interconnected shareholding between directors of large firms; and the government did not have in place programs to address unemployment, social support, deficits, and inflation.

In 1994 the MDF-led government's inability to bring quick, effective reform and the pragmatic image propagated by the Socialists led to a victory of the Hungarian Socialist Party. While the MSzP achieved a parliamentary majority, it turned to the SzDSz (whose economic and political programs were similar) to form a coalition; the MSzP party leader, Gyula Horn, was approved as prime minister. In 1995 the MSzP decided to take action on Hungary's rising deficits and stagnating economy by privatizing state firms and by initiating a fiscal austerity program in order to bring in IMF funding. Such measures did not please the electorate, and the MSzP saw its popularity in polls drop.

In 1998 Fidesz took advantage of public anger over the rising crime rate and a series of government scandals to win a plurality of seats in the Assembly. It formed a government with the FKgP and the Democratic Forum. In 2002 the MSzP and SzDSz took back control of the Assembly, winning a combined 51 percent of the vote.

The Hungarian party scene is both stable and unstable. It is stable in that a small group of parties appear to have become constant players, but unstable in that this number will most likely be whittled down. Parties hold to set ideological positions only in a vague sense; tactics often determine what a party believes. Finally, party strength over the long haul is questionable for two reasons. First, parties do not exercise high discipline, and so members can leave and join parliamentary factions; this hurt the Alliance of Young Democrats, for example. Second, with the exception of the Hungarian Socialist Party, parties do not have strong grassroots divisions and do not try to mobilize social support; instead, they usually act like groups of political elites making an appeal to the populace from above.

Hungarian parties can be grouped along a traditional left-right continuum. However, certain points can be noted at the outset. For one thing, there are no true extremist parties in the National Assembly. While some parties hold to a more nationalist outlook or promote Christian principles, none take this rhetoric to an extreme, as is the case with Gheorghe Funar's party in Romania. Most parties are basically moderate.

Major Political Parties
HUNGARIAN SOCIALIST PARTY
(Magyar Szocialista Párt; MSzP)

The major party on the Left is the Hungarian Socialist Party. While the MSzP *organizationally* is a direct descendant of the Hungarian Workers' Socialist Party (i.e., the Communist Party), *ideologically* the MSzP has openly broken all links with the old Communist ideology. The MSzP has agreed that a market economy is desirable. Where the MSzP differs from other parties is that it supports a slower and more gradual transition that takes into account support for the social safety net (economic support for the population, especially those at risk of poverty) and support for social justice.

However, as 1995 showed, the Socialists realize that the requirements for economic health may contradict party ideology and take precedence. In 1995 the Socialist-led government backed away from a gradualist position and implemented an austerity package that helped lower budget and current account deficits and continued mass privatization of $3 billion worth of state assets. Finally, while the MSzP had a majority in the parliament after the 1994 elections, it preferred to build a larger ruling coalition that could embrace other like-minded parties in order to create a larger sense of political community and unity.

In the 1998 elections MSzP appeared to be headed toward victory, but Fidesz gained the most votes and seats in the National Assembly, leaving MSzP in second place. Laszlo Kovacs, one of the party's more popular leaders, became head of the MSzP parliamentary faction and set about remaking the party's image, in particular making ties and integration with Europe more central to its platform. (In this MSzP followed a line that other social democratic parties in West and East Europe have been doing, namely, a move toward the center-left.) The strategy had some success. While some politicians and elites on the Left have been critical of Kovacs's move toward the center, MSzP remains the single dominant left-leaning party and faces little competition from that side of the political spectrum; it can shore up support from the left and expand its political base. In 2002 MSzP gained the second-highest number of seats and put aside arguments with the SzDSz to form a left-of-center government. With approximately 35,000 members and continuing support from labor unions, MSzP remains one of the two most important parties in Hungary.

ALLIANCE OF FREE DEMOCRATS
(Szabad Demokratak Szovetsege; SzDSz)

The Alliance of Free Democrats initially emerged in the 1980s as a political group of many leading intellectuals disaffected with Communism. The Alliance was formally organized as a party in 1988 in opposition to the ruling Communist Party, and it aided with the transfer of power from the single-party Communist system in 1989. SzDSz supported pro-market reforms in the 1990s (turning away from the historical third way of "market Socialism" advocated for a time by Hungarian social scientists), and initially after 1989 it held to an anti-Communist line. This position, including support for such policies as compensating people who lost property in the Communist takeover, began to weaken in the party rhetoric, and SzDSz began to turn in a more liberal direction. Thus, despite its support for market reforms, SzDSz is not neoliberal party. Rather, SzDSz began to support mostly left-of-center policies, although it does not lean as far to the left as social democratic or Socialist parties. This made possible alliances and coalitions with the Hungarian Socialist Party, but this prospective tactic led to internal conflict when the issue came up in 1994. As a result of internal struggles, several leaders and members who wanted to pursue opposition to the Socialist Party switched their support to Fidesz. Regardless, relations between the Socialists and those remaining in SzDSz became strained in the second half of the 1990s, until the 2002 coalition.

SzDSz enjoys modest electoral support, counting on Hungary's emerging middle class of professionals and entrepreneurs, as well as intellectuals. This has not helped stop SzDSz's political fortunes from tumbling, partly because there was no new cohort of younger leaders ready to carry the party forward in its political development. Despite its small number of seats (20) and previous tensions with the Socialists, SzDSz entered into a ruling coalition with the Socialists after the 2002 elections.

CHRISTIAN DEMOCRATIC PEOPLE'S PARTY (CDPP)

(Keresztèny Demokrata Nèppàrt)

The Christian Democratic People's Party, one of the members of the 1990–94 ruling coalition, claims to support Christian values and support pro-market ideology and reforms. Based in Christian beliefs, the CDPP makes individual freedom a central tenet of its political program. The other basic elements of its program are a state led by Christian ideals, parliamentary democracy, and sovereignty of the people. While CDPP does support some form of social safety net, especially for those most likely to be hurt by economic transformation, it also staunchly supports private property, especially in the agricultural sector, where it believes small private farming should be the foundation. In the 1998 elections, support for the Christian Democrats dropped considerably—they did not gain any seats—and by 2002 they appeared to be a spent force. Part of this may be due to other parties (such as Fidesz) taking up positions close to Christian democracy but from a stronger position in employing more forceful rhetoric and in fielding more attractive party personalities.

ALLIANCE OF YOUNG DEMOCRATS

(Magyar Polgàri Pàrt; Fidesz)

The Alliance of Young Democrats was formed in 1992 by young intellectuals and "yuppie"-type political aspirants as a counter to other parties. The Fidesz, however, had difficulty finding a platform that both its elite and the population at large would support. The party has supported pro-market reforms, in particular, rapid privatization and a state economic role reduced to promoting private growth. Early on, the Fidesz was left-leaning and popular, enabling it to act as an effec-

tive opposition party against the MDF-dominated ruling coalition.

However, in preparation for the 1994 elections, party leaders tried to re-create the party's ideological platform, leading to a split between pro-market reformers (headed by Viktor Orban) and another group of reformers (headed by Gabor Fodor) who preferred a balance between market reforms and economic and social justice. After the split, in which Orban successfully gained control to define the party platform, Fodor and his followers abandoned the Fidesz for the SzDSz—both because the AFD platform was similar and because Orban had the reputation of being a strong-armed political leader who could not well accommodate different views. As a result of the split and defection, the Fidesz's star dimmed in the 1994 elections.

By 1998 and 2002 Fidesz's fortunes changed, mostly because Orban successfully changed the nature of the party. He replaced the party's initial liberal ideology with right-wing conservatism, more nationalism, and occasional Christian themes, tapping into the rising wave of right-wing nationalist sentiments that spread through segments of Eastern European populations toward the end of the 1990s. Fidesz's new popularity translated into 148 seats in 1998 and 164 in 2002. However, it has not been able to form a government, even in alliance with the Democratic Forum in 2002.

HUNGARIAN DEMOCRATIC FORUM

(Magyar Demokrata Fòrum; MDF)

MDP emerged as an informal opposition movement in 1987 that pursued nationalist rhetoric and stressed the possibility of a Hungarian third way between Socialism and capitalism (for a time popular among Hungarian academics).

The Democratic Forum was the winner of the 1990 parliamentary elections and the center of the ruling coalition from 1990 to 1994. MDF was the group most involved with Hungary's initial transition from Communism, acting as the major opposition to the Hungarian Socialist Workers' Party and forging the creation of parliamentary democratic politics through political negotiation with the Communists. The MDF has supported overall economic and political change, but not through reforms so radical that they would destabilize society and bring social catastrophe. MDF has supported Hungarian traditions and in this way has been democratic, nationalist, and Christian and has opposed all forms of extremism on the Left and Right. In fact, the

MDF supported the idea of gradualist market reform, although gradualism was softened somewhat in the debates with the Independent Smallholders over property compensation.

MDF policies in 1990–94 included slow privatization (privatizing 15 percent of state-owned enterprises), unemployment support and retraining, encouragement of small business, and promotion of foreign investment. Hence, the MDF tempered market reforms with policies of social support. In 1996, after a national convention to decide the party's ideological tone for the future, the MDF split in two—between those who wanted a turn to the right (pro-market reform, moderate nationalism, and ties with the smaller and more extremist Hungarian Truth and Life Party) and a more center-right group. The center-right members left the MDF, thus reducing the MDF presence in the National Assembly to 19 deputies, and formed the Hungarian Democratic People's Party. MDF has never been able to recover from the split, and MDF still has traits of being a "movement" rather than a structured political party. Because of this its electoral fortunes remain on the wane. (The Hungarian Democratic People's Party never did gain much popularity, and so it has not acted as harmful competition to MDF.)

Minor Political Parties

Other small parties litter the Hungarian political scene. Some parties, such as the Independent Smallholders' Party (Független Kisgazda Pàrt; FKgP), have lost what political clout they once had. In the 1990s FKgP tried to set itself up as the major opposition party, putting it in competition with Fidesz. FKgP championed land reform, including returning land taken by the Communists in the 1940s to its original owners or some other form of compensation. Otherwise, FKgP generally espouses values and ideology similar to the Christian Democrats. Because FKgP could not expand on its base of small farmers and strident anti-Communists, it has seen its political fortunes fall. It was also hurt by leader Joszef Torgyan's harsh rhetoric in opposition to post-Socialist reformers. As a sign of its collapse, the party received just 0.8 percent of the vote in 2002.

Three other minor parties are Hungarian Justice and Life Party, Center Party, and the Workers' Party. Hungarian Justice and Life was founded in 1993 when its leader was ejected from the Hungarian Democratic Forum. This party promotes xenophobic, nationalist rhetoric (sometimes with anti-Semitic sentiments). While it did not overcome the electoral barrier, it

has obtained a better showing than all other minor parties. This result reflects the nationalist wave that spread across Eastern Europe at the end of the 1990s, affecting Poland (e.g., Samoobrona) and Romania (Greater Romanian Party). The Center Party is a more recent phenomenon, emerging in the 2002 elections (although unable to overcome the electoral barrier) to try to capture the center of Hungarian politics. The Workers' Party is a marginal leftist group that caters to nostalgia for Communism and supports a Socialist-style welfare state. The Workers' Party has played a largely insignificant role in parliamentary politics, but it does shore up an important position in the political spectrum by catering to the radical Socialist Left.

Other Political Forces

One prop of the Communist regime was the armed forces, prepared and backed by Moscow to maintain the Communist Party in power. Since the collapse of Communism, however, the armed forces have remained passive and outside politics. Trade unions as well have not been powerful actors. This is due partly because of historical legacies: unions were co-opted and controlled by the Communist Party and rendered impotent, and they did not regain power after the collapse of Communism. The European Union likely will exert some force over Hungarian politics in the future. It already has led to relaxation of visa requirements vis-à-vis Western Europe, but uniformity with EU directives and policies on such matters as civil rights, economics (such as customs laws, monetary and budgetary policy, and the like), and others will increase with further integration into the European Union.

National Prospects

Relative to other former Communist countries, Hungary seems well on its way to creating a well-functioning democracy and market economy. The legacy of Socialist economic reforms made the transformation of the Hungarian economy, particularly the creation of a small entrepreneurial sector, much easier than elsewhere, and the return of Socialists to power did not bring populism and economic decline but the opposite: new economic reforms. Hungary's political system does not suffer from the problems faced elsewhere in the former Communist bloc: ethnic disputes (Romania), overly ambitious leaders holding levers of power (Belarus), institutional bias for one branch that can endanger democracy (Russia), or hatred for the past hindering cooperation in the present (Poland).

Hungary does have one particular problem, however, stemming from its electoral system. A "well-functioning democracy" (as currently understood in the West) fulfills three functions: political justice, chance for negotiations, and some degree of predictability (although not absolute). Voters must be able to have some idea of what outcome their voting will have; political participants must have the possibility to negotiate in order to avoid losses; and voting must bring some degree of justice and legitimacy. This three-way interaction presents the possibility of contradictions, which has happened in Hungary.

To ensure their own continued existence in politics, party elites negotiated an electoral system that, through individual races, county lists, and a national list, gives them opportunities to remain on the political scene. Such a negotiated electoral contract assuaged the worries of elites; however, the electoral system that resulted has run aground of the other two assumptions of democracy. The electoral system is thoroughly confusing, and so it is nearly impossible for the average (or above-average) Hungarian to figure out just what will happen if he or she and others vote a certain way. Further, such a system has unexpected consequences, making political justice difficult: if voters do not want a certain party to be represented, then that party has no fundamental right to representation, yet the system was created in part to make sure that parties have every chance of returning to the parliament.

However, this point aside, Hungary's future prospects appear brighter than those of many other Eastern European countries. The economy remains one of the more attractive to foreign investment, especially given privatization and an orientation both to exports and to integration with the European economy. Hungary's joining NATO in 1999 and its accession into the European Union in 2004 were two further links cementing relations with the West.

Also, given the absence of strong nationalist or ethnic feeling and the absence of popular and mass-mobilizing nationalist parties, Hungary does not suffer from internal political and ethnic strife, which has been problematic in other countries. Finally, Hungary appears to have turned away from the Communist past

in two senses. First, even the Hungarian Socialists have embraced market reforms, much more so than Socialist parties elsewhere; while the degree of the human face on capitalism differs from party to party, all appear to be in agreement on the need for a market economy. Second, Hungarian politicians appear not only to be playing by the rules (based on the idea of a rule of law) but also to be appealing to a sense of political community. While political criticism has been present and sometimes radical, for the most part Hungarian politics does not exhibit the same degree of polarization as seen in Russia, Romania, or Bulgaria.

Hungary has seen a rise in right-wing nationalism and even xenophobia and racism, but its impact on party politics has been more limited than in Romania, Russia, or Poland, where ethnic tensions persist and have become institutionalized in extreme parties (e.g., in Romania) or internal war (e.g., in Chechnya) or where intense anti-Communism has combined with conservative religious sentiments to create a potential divide within the country (e.g., in Poland). Closer to the outcome in Bulgaria, Hungarian parties have managed to contain the spread of right-wing extremism, racism, and xenophobia. (As well, Hungary's economic recovery has lessened tensions over economic resources.) Before the fall of Communism, Hungary was singled out as the bright star of the Eastern bloc, and, in the aftermath of 1989, despite bumps and obstacles on the road to reform, it remains a bright star.

Further Reading

Cox, Terry, and Andy Furlong, eds. *Hungary: The Politics of Transition.* London: Frank Cass, 1995.

Ehrlich, Éva, and Gábor Révész. *Hungary and Its Prospects: 1985-2005.* Translated by András Ottlick. Budapest: Akadémiai Kiadó, 1995.

Linz, Juan J., and Alfred Stepan. *Problems of Democratic Transition and Consolidation: Southern Europe, South America, and Post-Communist Europe.* Baltimore: Johns Hopkins University Press, 1996.

Oltay, Edith. "Toward the Rule of Law: Hungary." *RFE/RL Research Report,* July 3, 1992, 16–24.

Pataki, Judith. "Hungarian Government Midway through Its First Term." *RFE/RL Research Report,* June 12, 1992, 18–24.

Stark, David, and Lázló Bruszt. *Postsocialist Pathways.* New York: Cambridge University Press, 1998.

REPUBLIC OF ICELAND
(Lýðveldið Ísland)

By Ólafur Th. Hardarson, Ph.D.

Iceland is an island in the North Atlantic with some 300,000 inhabitants. The country was settled in the ninth and 10th centuries, mainly from Norway. The settlers founded a commonwealth without a king or executive power. Its central institution, which had legislative and judicial powers, was the Althingi, founded in 930. In 1262 the country came under rule by the Norwegian king. When Norway and Denmark united under the Danish Crown in 1380, Iceland became a Danish dependency. The Althingi gradually lost its legislative function, and in 1662 the Danish king obtained absolute power. In 1800 the Althingi was abolished, having functioned mainly as a judicial body for centuries. It was reestablished in 1845 as a consultative assembly to the Danish king.

In 1874 the king "gave" the Icelanders a constitution, which granted the Althingi legislative and financial powers, while the king retained an effective veto. Home rule in 1904 granted the Icelanders authority in most domestic affairs with the establishment of an Icelandic administration headed by a minister, responsible to the Althingi. Iceland became a sovereign state in 1918 but remained in a union with Denmark under the king until 1944, when it adopted its present republican constitution.

The System of Government

Iceland is a parliamentary republic and a unitary state. It has a unicameral parliament, the Althingi.

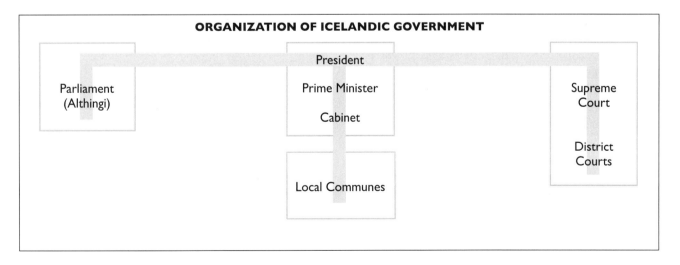

ORGANIZATION OF ICELANDIC GOVERNMENT

Parliament (Althingi)

President
Prime Minister
Cabinet

Supreme Court

District Courts

Local Communes

EXECUTIVE

The president (forseti), who is elected directly by the people every four years, has mainly ceremonial duties, while the executive power in fact belongs to the cabinet, which ususally represents a majority coalition of two or more parties and is led by the prime minister. The president can, however, play some political role if the bargaining process of a new coalition government becomes difficult, and has done so on a few occasions. According to the constitution, the president has the right to refuse to countersign a statute, which then shall go to a referendum. This clause had never been used and was widely considered to be a dead letter, when President Ólafur Ragnar Grímsson refused to sign a new (and very unpopular) media law in 2004, creating a major controversy in Icelandic politics. The government withdrew the new law without a referendum, announcing that the government would attempt to get an agreement on constitutional changes during the current electoral term.

LEGISLATURE

The Icelandic parliament, Althingi, was made a unicameral parliament in 1991, having previously been divided into an Upper Chamber and a Lower Chamber since 1874. The Althingi has 63 members, elected in a general election for a term of four years. During this period the Althingi can be dissolved at any given time, and a new election held. This is done by a decree of the president, acting upon the advice of the prime minister, who in practice dissolves the Althingi only with the approval of all coalition partners in the cabinet. Since 1944 there have been 18 general elections, with an average term of around 3½ years.

Formally, the Althingi is the most powerful institution in the Icelandic political system. It can make law on any subject it chooses (within the limits set by the constitution), it makes and breaks governments, it can make any changes it likes on the draft budget, and it elects a considerable number of people to various important boards and committees. In practice, however, the political parties are the most important units in the political system, and most policy decisions, as well as major decisions on government coalition formations, are taken by their parliamentary groups rather than the party organizations.

While the cabinet has increasingly played a major role in policy formation—in 2000-01, 91 percent of passed bills were government bills—the Althingi still retains considerable power vis-à-vis the administration. Government bills are scrutinized by the parliamentary groups of the government coalition before being presented to the assembly. Since Iceland became a founding member of the European Economic Area in 1994, an increasing part of legislation stems from Brussels.

JUDICIARY

The Icelandic court system consists of only two levels of courts, eight district courts (héradsdómur) and the Supreme Court (Haestiréttur). These courts have jurisdiction in both civil and criminal matters. The rules of procedure are largely based on Scandinavian and German principles.

The Supreme Court, established in 1920, can declare a statute unconstitutional and has done so on a few occasions. The judges are appointed for life by the president, acting upon the advice of the minister of justice.

Two special courts have a limited jurisdiction. The High Court of State (Landsdómur) can impeach cabinet ministers, but this court has not convened since it was established in 1905. The Labor Court (Félagsdómur) tries cases relating to laws on trade unions and employers' associations.

REGIONAL AND LOCAL GOVERNMENT

The functions and financial revenues of local governments are mainly decided by law. The basic units are communes (sveitarfélög), which elect their own councils (mainly by proportional representation using the d'Hondt formula). The local communes (101 in 2005) vary greatly in size: The capital Reykjavík has some 100,000 inhabitants, whereas the population in other communes varies from around 50 to 17,000. In recent years, the government has tried to unify communes voluntarily, in order to give local governments increased responsibilities, but with limited success so far. Nevertheless, unification by legislation has been ruled out, while in 1996 the responsibilities of local governments were greatly increased by handing over the running of the elementary schools to them. Current government proposals aim at reducing the number of local communes to 39.

The Electoral System

Important changes of the electoral system took place by a constitutional change in 1999 and subsequent changes in electoral law in 2000.

Since 1934 the constitution had contained a detailed description of the electoral system, including, among other matters, the boundaries and the number of MPs of individual constituencies. The system had been very slow in responding to population changes, despite constitutional amendments in 1942, 1959 and 1983. This resulted in a huge overrepresentation of the countryside. In 1999 the 67 percent of voters living in the urban southwestern areas elected only a minority of the MPs (31 out of 63). Due to a very complicated electoral system, however, the number of MPs for each party had been quite proportional to their national vote since the constitutional change of 1983.

The major aims of the 1999 changes were to reduce the overrepresentation of the countryside and to simplify the electoral system. Future improvements were also made easier as some important aspects of the electoral system are no longer subject to constitutional change.

The following aspects of the electoral system are now specified by the constitution: The number of MPs (63), proportionally elected for a four-year term, is unchanged. Instead of eight constituencies with constitutionally defined boundaries, the number of constituencies is reduced to six or seven: their exact number and boundaries are to be decided by law. Each constituency, however, shall have at least six seats, allocated on the basis of constituency results. Supplementary seats are to be allocated in order to make each party's number of seats proportional to the party's share of the national vote. However, a party now must obtain at least 5 percent of the national vote in order to obtain supplementary seats. Earlier, parties could obtain supplementary seats if they had at least one member elected in a constituency. After each election, the National Election Board shall calculate the number of registered voters per seat in each constituency (including supplementary seats). If this number turns out to be half or less compared to any other constituency, the National Election Board shall change the number of seats in these constituencies in order to decrease the discrepancy—except if a constituency is down to the minimum of six seats. Changes of constituency boundaries and allocation rules can now be amended by electoral law, but only by an increased majority of two-thirds in the Althingi. It should be noted, however, that a simple majority in the Althingi can, by law, reduce the number of seats in any constituency to six if it so chooses.

According to the electoral law passed in 2000, the number of constituencies shall be six. Three of these are in the urban Southwest: two Reykjavík constituencies, and the southwestern Reykjavík suburbs. The number of constituencies in the countryside is reduced from six to three: the Northwest, the Northeast, and the South. The boundaries are defined by law, except the boundaries between the two Reykjavík constituencies: when an election is called, the National Election Board shall draw those boundaries in such a way that the number of voters per seat in both constituencies is approximately equal.

The law also decides that 54 of the 63 seats shall be allocated on the basis of constituency results. The nine remaining seats are supplementary seats, fixed to particular constituencies. All six constituencies obtain nine constituency seats. The two Reykjavík constituencies and the Southwest Reykjavík suburbs each also obtain two supplementary seats, while each of the three constituencies in the countryside obtain one such seat.

The allocation rule in constituencies is changed. Before the 1987 election, the d'Hondt rule had been replaced by LR-Hare, in order to increase the possibility of small parties to obtain one of the four or five seats on offer in the regional constituencies, and thus reducing the need for supplementary seats. As all constituencies now contain nine constituency seats, this was no longer deemed necessary and the d'Hondt rule was adopted again. For the same reason only nine supplementary seats—instead of 13 before—are thought sufficient to secure proportionality between the parties. The allocation of the supplementary seats between the parties is based on the d'Hondt rule as before.

Those changes are quite important, as they greatly reduced malapportionment in the Icelandic electoral system. In the 2003 Althingi election, the majority of voters living in the urban Southwest for the first time elected the majority of MPs (33 out of 63). However, the three regional constituencies, containing around 38 percent of the voters, elected 48 percent of the MPs.

The voter can cast his or her vote only for a list. While changes in the rank order of candidates on the chosen list are allowed, the rules make it unlikely that such changes, even made by a substantial proportion of the voters, will alter the ranking. Elections take place on a Saturday by secret ballot. With many polling places in each constituency it is easy for the voters to get to the polls. The ballot papers are counted by constituencies. Registration is automatic, and suffrage is universal for adults 18 years of age or older. Absentee ballots can be cast in the eight-week period preceding polling day. Turnout in Althingi elections has been stable around 90 percent in recent decades.

If an elected member cannot attend Althingi sessions for at least two consecutive weeks, his place is taken (temporarily, if the member returns) by the next person on the party list. Thus, by-elections are unnecessary.

The president is elected by direct, simple majority vote for a four-year term. The first president, Sveinn Björnsson, was elected by the Althingi in 1944. In 1945 and 1949 Björnsson was the only candidate for nationwide direct election, so no actual election was held. When Björnsson died, in 1952, the Independence Party and the Progressive Party together supported one candidate, who was defeated by an Althingi member from the small Social Democratic Party, Ásgeir Ásgeirsson, who maintained that the people, not the parties, should choose the president. The political parties never again attempted to put up a candidate or take a stand in presidential elections. In 1968 the director of the National Museum, Kristján Eldjárn, was elected, and in 1980 the director of the Reykjavík Theater, Vigdís Finnbogadóttir, became the first popularly elected female head of state in the world. In 1996 a former leader of the left-socialist People's Alliance, Ólafur Ragnar Grímsson, somewhat surprisingly won the presidential race. His victory was thought clearly based on personal merit, rather than political grounds.

Until 2004 a sitting president wishing to be reelected had only been opposed once (in 1988), when Finnbogadóttir easily beat a candidate from a fringe political group. In the 2004 presidential election, two candidates opposing President Grímsson obtained jointly 14 percent of the valid votes. In addition, 21 percent of those turning up at the polling booths turned in a blank ballot, probably to protest the president's refusal to countersign a statute for the first time in the history of the republic. As of 2005 the prime minister was Halldór Ásgrímsson.

The Party System

ORIGINS OF THE PARTIES

In the 19th and early 20th centuries the question of Iceland's relationship with Denmark dominated Icelandic politics. The first political parties emerged at the turn of the 20th century, when home rule and control of the executive were in sight. Those cadre-style parties were mainly based on different attitudes toward tactics in the independence struggle.

The independence question was largely resolved in 1918, and in the 1916–30 period the party system was completely transformed. Economic and class-related issues became the focal point of politics, as four new parties emerged: the Social Democratic Party, the agrarian Progressive Party, the conservative Independence Party, and the Communist Party. The four-party format came to dominate Icelandic politics, but on occasions short-lived minor parties have entered the Althingi, especially since the 1970s. However, only one of those parties, the Women's Alliance, has survived more than two terms.

A major restructuring of the left wing of the Icelandic party system took place in the 1999 election. The old Social Democratic Party, the left socialist People's Alliance, the Women's Alliance, and the People's Movement formed a new social democratic party, the Social Democratic Alliance, which subsequently became the second largest party in Icelandic politics. The more traditional left socialists from the People's Alliance, however, joined hands with some environmentalists and some prominent members of the Women's Alliance and formed a new party, the Left-Greens, which had six members elected to the Althingi, thus carrying, on the left, the socialist banner in Icelandic politics and continuing the four-party format as the core of the Icelandic party system.

The left-right dimension is still by far the most important in Icelandic politics. While foreign policy also became a major cleavage after World War II, those issues are closely related to the left-right spectrum in the minds of voters. In the 2003 election study the voters ranked the five parties that won parliamentary seats from left to right (on a 0–10 scale) in the following manner: Left Greens (2.3), Social Democrats (4.1), Liberal Party (5.5), Progressive Party (6.0), Independence Party (8.3)

THE PARTIES IN LAW

The right of association, including the right to form political parties, is guaranteed in the constitution. There is no law on how political parties operate or on how they select candidates, and they do not have to disclose their finances. It is easy to get a list on the ballot: all that is needed is a formal recommendation by 100 to 380 registered voters.

PARTY ORGANIZATION

Since the 1930s the major parties have formally been mass parties organized on a regional basis. The local organizations elect representatives to the party's constituency council and to the party convention. The party convention elects a central national council and usually also the party leader. The institutionalization of the Icelandic parties has, however, probably always been weaker than among their counterparts in Northern

Europe. Criteria for membership have been unclear, as membership fees have rarely been collected on a regular basis and membership files have been inaccurate. The parliamentary groups have been much stronger than the party organizations regarding policy making, and the position of the leadership is quite strong. Party conferences tend to confirm decisions made by the leadership. Usually that leadership is reelected, although challenges to the leadership, usually by a competing leadership group, have been successful at times.

Since the 1970s primary elections have been the major method of selecting candidates. Many of these primaries have been open, that is, not confined to party members, as clearly indicated by the fact that on several occasions the number of people taking part in a party's primary in a constituency has greatly exceeded the party's number of votes in the following Althingi elections. Some primaries, formally confined to party members, have also in fact been open, due to the unclear membership criteria of the parties and the fact that at times people have been able to join the party at the primary polling place. The primaries have clearly weakened party organizations and undermined party cohesiveness.

CAMPAIGNING

Election campaigns are waged to a large extent on a national level through the mass media. In an increasingly competitive and nonpartisan media market, candidates from all parties present their views in articles in the national newspapers and take part in discussion programs on television and radio. The impact of local party papers and rallies has decreased. On the other hand, political advertisements have come to play a major role.

While the parties are not required by law to reveal anything concerning their income and expenditures, only the Independence Party refuses to give any information on party finances. The information the other parties present is, however, often incomplete and can be misleading. Nevertheless it is clear that membership fees have rarely been strictly collected. Instead, the parties have relied on lotteries and financial support from individuals, interest groups, and firms—some companies are known to donate to all parties. But this kind of fund-raising by the parties has become relatively less important in recent years, as public grants are now the main source of party income, at least in most cases. State support has greatly increased and is proportionally (per vote) much higher than in neighboring countries. The main reasons for increasing party

expenditure are more professional and expensive election campaigns, including extensive political advertising in newspapers, on radio, and—most important—on television since 1987.

INDEPENDENT VOTERS

Since the early 1970s electoral volatility has been high. The gains and losses of parties in elections are often quite large. In the elections of 1987, 1991, 1995, and 2003 around one-third of the voters claimed to have switched parties between elections. The number of voters claiming no party sympathy whatsoever increased from 19 percent in 1983 to 29 percent in 1999, but dropped again to 27 percent in 2003.

ALTHINGI ELECTION RESULTS, 1987–2003 (PERCENTAGES OF TOTAL VALID VOTES AND NUMBERS OF ELECTED MEMBERS)

	1995	1999	2003
Independence Party (IP)	37.1 (25)	40.7 (26)	33.7 (22)
Progressive Party (PP)	23.2 (15)	18.4 (12)	17.7 (12)
Social Democratic Alliance (SDA)	26.8 (17)	31.0 (20)	—
Left Greens	9.1 (6)	8.8 (5)	—
Liberal Party	4.2 (2)	7.4 (4)	—
Social Democratic Party (SDP)	11.4 (7)	—	—
People's Alliance (PA)	14.3 (9)	—	—
Women's Alliance	4.9 (3)	—	—
People's Movement	7.1 (4)	—	—
Citizen's Party	—	—	—
Others	1.9 (0)	0.8 (0)	1.5 (0)
Total Number of Seats	63	63	63
Total Valid Votes	165,043	165,727	183,172
Percent Turnout	87.4%	84.1%	87.7%

Major Political Parties

INDEPENDENCE PARTY (IP)

(Sjálfstaedisflokkurinn)

The Independence Party (IP) was founded in 1929 with a merger of the Conservative Party (founded 1924) and the Liberal Party (founded 1926). Partly because of Iceland's unusually high degree of ethnic, religious, and linguistic homogeneity, the IP was able to unite the right-of-center opponents of the SDP and the agrarian PP in one party, which has remained the largest party in the country from its foundation, usually polling around 40 percent of the votes. However, in the 1930s the IP's strength among the electorate was not reflected in seats held in the Althingi and the party spent most of its first years in opposition. After a change in the electoral system in 1942, the IP became "the natural party of government" with all of its leaders serving as prime ministers: Ólafur Thors (1942, 1944–47, 1949, 1953–56, 1959–63), Bjarni Benediktsson (1963–70), Jóhann Hafstein (1970–71), Geir Hallgrímsson (1974–78), Thorsteinn Pálsson (1987–88), and Davíd Oddsson (1991–2004).

A serious schism emerged in the party in 1980, when the deputy leader, Gunnar Thoroddsen, supported by a few IP members of the Althingi, formed a coalition government with the PP and the PA, leaving the bulk of the party, including party leader Hallgrímsson, in opposition. Thoroddsen and his supporters remained in the party, however; and in 1983 Thoroddsen left politics, while his supporters were all reelected as Althingi members for the IP.

The IP split in 1987, when a popular patronage politician, Albert Gudmundsson, formed the Citizen's Party just before an Althingi election. Gudmundsson had been forced to resign as a minister, due to tax evasion while serving as minister of finance. The election results were a disaster for the IP, as the party polled only 27.2 percent of the votes, whereas the new Citizen's Party had seven members elected to the Althingi. During the next term, however, Gudmundsson left politics for an ambassadorial post in Paris, the Citizen's Party disintegrated, and the IP recovered its previous electoral strength in 1991.

The IP has emphasized that it is a party of independent individuals without strong party discipline, but it has been the best-organized party in Iceland in terms of electoral machinery and national coverage. The party has generally combined strong leadership with a notable tolerance in party discipline. Individual IP members of Althingi have—without sanctions—voted against their government on crucial issues (such as Icelandic membership in the European Economic Area in 1993), refused to support a government headed by their party (in 1944), and even formed a coalition government strongly opposed by their party (in 1980).

Separate organizations for women and youth are affiliated to the IP. Separate associations for working-class members have also been organized. The party is a member of the European Democratic Union (EDU) and associated with the Nordic conservative parties. The women's organization is affiliated with the Nordic Association of Conservative Women while the youth organization is a member of the Democrat Youth Community of Europe (DEMYC), European Young Conservatives, International Young Democrat Union, and Nordic Conservative Youth.

In domestic policy, the IP has combined elements from liberalism and conservatism and emphasized nationalism and opposition to class conflict. In the 1930s, while the party was in opposition, the emphasis in party policy was clearly directed toward economic liberalism and private initiative. After the war the IP became more pragmatic, as the party accepted the welfare state and participated in governments that greatly increased government involvement in the unstable and overpoliticized economy. The IP has quite successfully avoided an anti–working-class image.

In the 1960s a coalition government of the IP and the SDP abolished strict import controls and introduced free trade as the main principle of external economic policy. Iceland acceded to the General Agreement on Tariffs and Trade and joined the European Free Trade Association, and the government also opened for foreign investment in power-intensive industry. Since the 1980s the IP has emphasized further liberalization of the economy, following international trends as the other parties have also done to varying degrees. But the IP has been cautious in its approach, for instance, supporting active government involvement in the bargaining process in the labor market, successfully trying to maintain economic stability. In a coalition government with the SDP in 1991–95, the IP resisted SDP demands for liberalizing agricultural imports. While Iceland joined the European Economic Area during that coalition, the IP opposes an application for Icelandic membership of the European Union.

In security policy the IP has been the most consistent supporter of Icelandic membership in NATO and of the NATO base in Keflavík. Since 1995 the IP has, along with its coalition partner the PP, carried out a further liberalization of the economy. Most important has been the privatization of the financial sector.

The IP claims around 34,000 members. According to the Icelandic election studies of 1999 and 2003, the number of voters considering themselves IP members numbers around 20,000. A part of the discrepancy can probably be explained by people who have formally joined the IP in order to participate in primaries but nevertheless do not consider themselves members.

The IP has a remarkably weak class profile for a conservative party. In 1999 the party enjoyed the support of 40 percent of unskilled workers, 41 percent of skilled manual workers and middle-class professionals, while 48 percent of lower non-manual workers and 56 percent of employers and higher managerials voted for the party. The party's weakest following in any occupational group—by far—was among farmers (25 percent). In 1995 the party almost closed a gender gap, as the party's support was only 2 percent higher among men than among women, while this figure had been 9 percent and 14 percent in 1987 and 1991. The gender gap however reemerged in 1999 (5 percent) and in 2003 (7 percent).

The IP has traditionally been stronger in the urban Southwest (37.4 percent of the vote in 2003) than in the regions (27.3 percent).

After the long period (1934–70) of the strong leadership of Ólafur Thors and Bjarni Benediktsson, the IP suffered from rather weak and divided leadership for two decades. A serious leadership struggle took place in the 1970s and the early 1980s, especially between the party leader, Geir Hallgrímsson, and his deputy, Gunnar Thoroddsen. That crisis was solved in 1983, when Thorsteinn Pálsson became leader. Pálsson's leadership was generally considered weak, as exemplified by his short-lived coalition government in 1987–88. He became the first IP leader to lose his post in the leader election at the party convention.

Davíd Oddsson (born 1948), then deputy leader of the IP, successfully challenged Pálsson for the party leadership just before the Althingi election of 1991. A few weeks later he became a member of Althingi for Reykjavík, as well as prime minister in a coalition he formed with the SDP. After the 1995 election he continued as prime minister, now in a coalition with the PP. Oddsson, educated as a lawyer, had become mayor of Reykjavík in 1982, when the IP regained a majority in the city council, which it lost in 1978, having been in power since the party was founded. The party kept a comfortable majority in the municipal election of 1986, and increased that majority in 1990. Despite winning the party leadership contest in

a close vote in 1991, Oddsson quickly obtained a firm grip on the party and became generally considered a strong leader.

In a historical perspective, the period between 1971 and 1990 was a difficult one for the IP. The party spent a longer time in opposition than in government, had several bad results at the polls, and suffered from internal disputes and weak leadership. Under the strong leadership of Oddsson the party's fortunes changed for the better. Oddsson became the longest serving prime minister in Icelandic history (1991–2004), first in a coalition with the Social Democrats, but from 1995 with the PP. In the 2003 election the IP's strength was reduced form 40.7 percent in 1999 to 33.7 percent. The government coalition nevertheless continued with a reduced majority, but as a part of a new coalition deal between the IP and the PP, the PP-leader, Foreign Minister Halldór Ásgrímsson, took over the prime minister's post in September 2004, when Oddsson became foreign minister.

PROGRESSIVE PARTY, PP
(Framsóknarflokkurinn)

The Progressive Party (PP) was founded as a parliamentary group in 1916. In its first years, the party was almost exclusively a farmer's party, and it had close ties to the cooperative movement. Since 1923 the PP has on average polled around 25 percent of the vote, which made it for decades the second largest party in the country. In the last 25 years the PP has however polled under 20 percent in six out of eight elections.

Until 1987 the PP was always stronger in the Althingi than among the voters, due to the electoral system. This was especially pronounced before 1942 and contributed to the strong position of the party in the coalition system of that period: from 1917 to 1942, it spent only five years in opposition and held the premiership from 1927 to 1942.

In the 1940s the party lost its role as "the natural party of government" to the IP. Nevertheless, the PP has chaired seven coalitions in the postwar period, and, since 1971, it has been in opposition for only four years.

While the PP was clearly a cadre party at the beginning, it developed the formal characteristics of a mass party in the 1930s.

The PP is a member of the Liberal International, and it is affiliated to the association of center parties in the Nordic Council. The party's youth organization is a member of the International Federation of Liberal and Radical Youth (IFLRY) and the Nordic Youth

Center Association (NCF). While the party's women's organization is not a formal member of any international organization, it has informal cooperation with its Nordic counterparts, as well as inside the Liberal International.

The PP may be labeled a center or an agrarian party in terms of domestic policy. For decades the party's aims were clearly the defense of the interests of farmers and the more sparsely populated regions. While the PP has supported some of the liberalizing economic measures of recent years, it was critical of foreign investment and EFTA membership in the 1960s and has been the major champion of extensive government programs on rural development. In 1993, half of the party's members of Althingi voted against the ratification of the treaty on the European Economic Area, while the other half abstained. While the PP has opposed an Icelandic application for membership in the European Union, party leader Halldór Ásgrímsson has stongly emphasized that such an application might be necessary in the near future.

The PP has supported Iceland's membership in NATO, but it has been critical of the Keflavík base and, at times, supported its removal.

The PP claims 9,300 members, while the Icelandic election study of 2003 suggests that around 7,000 voters consider themselves party members.

In its early decades the party's electoral support was almost exclusively in the rural areas. While the PP has been quite successful in broadening its electoral appeal, it nevertheless remains much stronger in the three regional constituencies (26.3 percent in 2003) than in the urban Southwest (12.7 percent).

The class profile of the PP is weak, except that it still enjoys 50 to 60 percent support among farmers, a group that, however, in numbers has been reduced to electoral insignificance.

Party leader Halldór Ásgrímsson (born 1947) was a university lecturer in business studies before he entered the Althingi for the East in 1974. He was minister of fisheries in 1983–91, minister of justice in 1988–89, and became foreign minister in 1995. Ásgrímsson had been deputy leader since 1980 when he took over the leadership post from Steingrímur Hermannsson in 1994. While Hermannsson, who left politics to become one of the three directors of the Central Bank, was widely considered to be opportunistic, anti-European, and leftist, Ásgrímsson is considered more center-right and more pro-European.

Since 1971 the PP has been a member of government coalitions except for four years. Ásgrímsson became prime minister in 2004.

SOCIAL DEMOCRATIC ALLIANCE (SDA)

(Samfylkingin)

In 1999 a major restructuring of the left wing of Icelandic politics took place when the old rivals, the Social Democratic Party (SDP) and the left socialist People's Alliance (PA) joined hands with the Women's Alliance and the People's Movement and formed an electoral alliance, which a year later became a formal party, the Social Democratic Alliance (SDA). A major characteristic of Icelandic politics in the 20th century had been that the SDP was one of the weakest social democratic parties in Europe (usually obtaining around 14 percent of the votes) while the PA was one of the stongest left socialist parties (around 17 percent of the votes). Numerous attempts to unite the left into one large social democratic party along Scandinavian lines had always failed. Now the attempt succeeded in the sense that, in its first election in 1999, the new Social Democrats (SDA) obtained 26.8 percent of the vote and became the second largest party, and in 2004 the party obtained 31 percent, thus becoming the first party apart from the IP since the 1930s to break the 30 percent barrier. On the other hand, the attempt to unite the left in onc party failed, as the more orthodox left socialists formed a new party, the Left Greens, continuing the fourth main stream in Icelandic party politics.

The Social Democratic Party (SDP) had been founded in 1916 as the political arm of the labor movement. The party was organizationally tied to the Icelandic Federation of Labor (founded at the same time) until 1942.

The SDP was founded as a democratic socialist party and was clearly a working-class party. It maintained that politics were about economic distribution and the living conditions of the working class—a very radical conception in a period when politics was dominated by the struggle for independence from Denmark.

The SDP grew continuously in strength for its first two decades, and polled over 20 percent of the vote in 1934. The party lost some ground in the 1937 election, and from 1942 it was usually the smallest of the four major parties, receiving 14 to 16 percent of the vote. This history is in stark contrast to the development of the social democratic parties in Scandinavia. The socialist bloc in Iceland became smaller than in the other Nordic countries, and, until the formation of the Social Democratic Alliance in 1999, the Icelandic Social Democrats had been the smaller of the two major socialist parties within that bloc (except in the 1987 and 1991 elections). This can partly be explained by the frequent splits the SDP suffered, losing its left wing each time.

The SDP first joined a coalition government (with the PP) in 1934, having supported a PP minority government in 1927–31. The party was in government for around two-thirds of the remaining part of the 20th century, holding the premiership in one majority coalition (Stefánsson, 1947–49) and two minority cabinets (Jónsson 1958–59; Gröndal 1979–80). The SDP worked with all other major parties in coalitions. Of special interest is the extraordinarily long coalition partnership of the SDP with the IP 1959–71, an unusual political combination by European standards.

After 1971 the SDP had mixed fortunes. While the party polled only around 10 percent of the votes in 1971 and 1974, it won a major victory in 1978 with 22 percent. After a split leading to the formation of the short-lived Alliance of Social Democrats, the SDP was again down to 11.7 percent in 1983. The party recovered in the elections of 1987 and 1991, receiving over 15 percent, but after yet another split and the emergence of the People's Movement, the SDP obtained only 11.4 percent of the vote in 1995.

From 1971 the SDP remained in opposition (except for 1978–80) until 1987. Since then the party was continuously a member of various government coalitions until 1995.

The People's Alliance (PA) was descended from the Communist Party and other breakaway groups from the SDP. The Communist Party was founded in 1930 by radical SDP members as an orthodox communist party and a member of Comintern. It won its first seats in the Althingi in 1937 with 8.5 percent of the vote. In line with Comintern policy, the Communists demanded that the SDP join it in a Popular Front, but the SDP main body refused. Again, the left wing of the SDP broke off and formed the United Socialist Party with the Communists in 1938. The new party became larger than the SDP in its first election in 1942 with 16.2 percent of the vote. The United Socialist Party was not a Comintern member, but it was clearly pro-Soviet in foreign policy, and most of its major leaders had been prominent Communists. The party held cabinet posts in a coalition with the IP and the SDP in 1944–47. In 1956, after another split in the SDP, the PA was created as a loose electoral alliance between the United Socialist Party and the former SDP group. The PA immediately took a role in the government coalition of 1956–58. After a decade out of power, the PA re-created itself as a formal political party in 1968 and

the United Socialist Party was dissolved. The PA took part in the governing coalitions of 1971–74, 1978–79, 1980–83, and 1988–91. It never held the portfolios of prime minister, foreign affairs, or justice, but it was allotted the finance ministry both in 1980 and 1988.

The 1968 reorganization led to a split in the PA, led by former SDP leader Hannibal Valdimarsson and others, who formed the Union of Liberals and Leftists. This group had considerable success in 1971 (8.9 percent of the vote and five seats), largely at the expense of the SDP. The party lost seats in 1974 and disappeared from the Althingi in 1978.

The organization of the Social Democratic Alliance is similar to that of the other Icelandic parties, except that the leader is elected by all members in a postal vote. This method of selecting the leader had first been used by the People's Alliance in 1995. The old SDP had been the first formal mass party in Iceland and to some extent showed the way toward present party organization and intraparty democratic procedures.

Like the old SDP, the new SDA is a member of the Socialist International and the social democratic group in the Nordic Council. The party and its youth movement are also affiliated to various international and Nordic social democratic organizations. The People's Alliance was never affiliated with any international organizations but was a part of the left socialist group in the Nordic Council, a place that now has been taken over by the Left Greens.

The domestic policy of the Social Democratic Alliance is a fairly conventional version of European social democracy with a mix of market solutions and emphasis on the welfare system, and it is probably closer to the policy of Scandinavian social democrats than was the case with the old SDP. The domestic policy of the SDP had evolved along lines similar to other European social democratic parties: emphasis on nationalization and class struggle was dropped while adherence to the principles of the market economy, accompanied by a strong welfare state, became core issues of the party program. The fact that the SDP lost its left wing several times probably put its mark on party policy, which seemed closer to the political center than was the case with the Scandinavian social democrats. Since 1978 the SDP increasingly supported radical liberalization measures in the Icelandic economy, long marked by more state involvement and political patronage than has been common in Western Europe. Jón Baldvin Hannibalsson, SDP leader from 1984 to 1996 and minister of foreign affairs 1988 to 1995, led the Icelandic negotiations resulting in a membership of the European Economic Area in 1994. Before the 1995 election, the SDP—always the least nationalistic of the major parties—came out in favor of an Icelandic application for membership in the European Union—the only party to do so. Support for EU membership has become the European policy of the Social Democratic Alliance.

While the People's Alliance had clearly been farthest to the left on the Icelandic political spectrum, the party became more pragmatic in the last decades of the 20th century, abandoning its former socialist aims of extensive public ownership and increasingly accepting market solutions. The party—especially when in opposition—was nevertheless critical of many of the economic liberalization measures carried out in the 1980s and 1990s, and generally supported extensive public welfare services. Emphasis on environmental issues had also increased, just as was the case among left-socialist parties in Scandinavia.

The People's Alliance combined its socialist policies with a strong emphasis on nationalism. For decades, opposition to NATO membership and the U.S. military base in Keflavík formed a core of the party program, and those issues were among the most hotly debated in Icelandic politics. This was one of the major cleavages between the SDP and the left socialists, as the SDP was closest to the IP on the foreign policy dimension, supporting Icelandic membership in NATO and the base in Keflavík. From 1978, however, the People's Alliance participated in government coalitions without demanding radical changes in security policy and, in the 1990s, those issues were hardly raised by the party in the public debate. The People's Alliance was critical of foreign investments and opposed Icelandic membership in the European Union. In 1993 the PA—in opposition—voted against Icelandic membership in the European Economic Area, even though the party had been a member of the previous government that largely negotiated the treaty. Now the Left Greens have largely taken over the old left socialist foreign policy platform, including a strong emphasis on nationalism and opposition to EU membership.

The Social Democratic Alliance claims around 14,000 members, while the 2003 election survey indicates that around 8,000 voters consider themselves as members. In 1999 the party had a weak occupational profile, except that it was very weak among farmers (8 percent), as had been the case with the old SDP, and exceptionally strong among middle-class professionals, including public sector "caring" professions (36 percent)—as had been the case with the People's Alliance. The party had much stronger support among women

than among men, both in 1999 (+11 percent) and 2003 (+13 percent).

In 2005 the party faces a leadership contest, as the present deputy leader, Ingibjörg Sólrún Gísladóttir, a popular former mayor of Reykjavík and the party's prime ministerial candidate in the 2003 election, has announced that she will challenge party leader Össur Skarphéđinsson for the leadership post before the next party convention.

LEFT GREENS
(Vinstrihreyfingin—grænt frambod)

The formation of the Left Greens in 1999 was the result of the attempt to unify the left in the Social Democratic Alliance. The idea of unifying the left was born out of the theory that its fragmentation had given the right-wing Independence Party a position of influence in Icelandic politics that could be broken by a unified party of the left. The end of the cold war and increasing acceptance of the market by the left generally was felt to facilitate such a move. Attempts to put forward joint lists in local elections, moreover, indicated that such cooperation might work. Negotiations on an electoral alliance of the left-wing parties began in 1997 and included the Social Democrats, the People's Alliance, and the Women's Alliance. After a difficult process of negotiations the three parties reached an agreement (in 1998) and put forward a joint platform for the upcoming election. The platform bore all the hallmarks of a difficult compromise, being intended to satisfy a broad spectrum of opinion, from fairly moderate social democrats to radical socialists. In the end it probably satisfied no one, being too vague to satisfy either those on the right or the radicals on the left. The latter, in fact, split away from the People's Alliance rather than go through with the unification and formed the Left Greens, a new party of left-socialists and environmentalists. The split in the People's Alliance was a serious blow to the Social Democratic Alliance, which could hardly claim to speak for the unified left as it set out to do.

The Left Greens were uninhibited by the sort of large-scale compromise out of which the Social Democratic Alliance grew. Under the assertive leadership of a former People's Alliance MP, Steingrímur Sigfússon, the Left Greens provided a clear-cut alternative for voters on the far left. Combining the traditional egalitarian values of the left with environmentalism and pacifism, the party had no difficulties in forming relatively clear policies on many of the issues that were giving the Alliance greatest difficulties. In many respects, the

Left Greens could be seen as the heir to the traditions of the People's Alliance—including opposition to the U.S. military base and NATO membership—even if the People's Alliance was formally part of the Alliance.

The Left Greens established themselves as a real party in the 1999 election, obtaining 9.1 percent of the votes and six MPs. The party consolidated itself in 2003, despite minor losses at the polls (8.8 percent and five MPs). The 1999 and 2003 Icelandic Election Studies make clear that, among voters, the Left Greens are considered the successor of the People's Alliance as the alternative farthest to the left in Icelandic politics. The party claims 1,300 members, a number confirmed by the 2003 election study. In 1999 the Left Greens had a remarkably weak occupational profile, obtaining 8 to 10 percent in all groups, including employers and higher managers. There was no gender gap in the following of the party, neither in 1999 nor 2003.

Minor Political Parties

Challenges to the four-party format of Icelandic politics have become more frequent in recent years. While most minor parties contending elections in the postwar period did not win seats, several short-lived parties have had members elected to the Althingi: the National Preservation Party in 1953 (2 members), the Union of Liberals and Leftists in 1971 (5) and 1974 (2), the Social Democratic Alliance in 1983 (4), the Citizen's Party in 1987 (7), the People's Movement in 1995 (4), and the Liberal Party in 1999 (2) and 2003 (4).

Only one new party, the Women's Alliance, showed more preservance, as it had members elected in four consecutive Althingi elections after its initial success in 1983. The party focused on women's issues and its policies were left-of-center. In 1987 the party doubled its share of the vote with 10.1 percent. While the party held its own in 1991 (8.4 percent), it suffered badly in 1995 (4.9 percent). The party had lost its most prominent leader in the local elections of 1994, when Ingibjörg Sólrún Gísladóttir left her Althingi seat in order to become mayor of Reykjavík after the victory of a joint list of all parties except the Independence Party. A feud concerning candidate selection, disagreements on policy, and the fact that the new party on the left wing, the People's Movement, was led by a popular female politician may also have contributed to the party's difficulties. Besides, women have had increasing success in the old parties. In 1998, for instance, 27 percent of Althingi members were female, while the corresponding figure was 5 percent when the Women's Alliance

emerged. The Woman's Alliance joined the new Social Democratic Alliance in 1999. Some prominent members of the party, however, joined the Left Greens or quit politics.

Other Political Forces

Besides the political parties and the administration, major interest groups—increasingly independent of the political parties—play an important role in the political system. The interests of agriculture and fisheries have traditionally greatly influenced government policy. In recent decades, the Federation of Labor (ASÍ) and the Federation of Employers (VSÍ) have increased their influence on policy making, as governments have tended to offer them certain "policy packages" in return for moderate settlements and peace in the labor market. Interest groups have, for example, influenced legislation on the quota system in fisheries, agricultural policy, indexing of loans, welfare benefits, unemployment measures, mortgages, and taxation—such as the reduction of VAT on food from 24.5 percent to 14 percent.

National Prospects

After seven years of recession the economy started to improve in 1994 and has been booming since. For the first time in decades, economic stability and low inflation have been maintained for 15 years (since 1990), largely due to restraint in the labor market. Foreign investment in power-intensive industry has been increasing. Some Icelandic companies in the retail and financial sectors have been extremely successful abroad. Unemployment has been low. The economy, long characterized by excessive state involvement by Western European standards, has been greatly liberalized, and major privatization has taken place. Iceland became a founding member of the European Economic Area in 1994. The economic future looks bright and living standards can be expected to stay among the highest in the world.

In the last decades, the political parties have experienced decreasing power, increasing electoral volatility, and less internal cohesion. The scope for arbitrary decisions of individual politicians has decreased, partly due to increased professionalization of the administration, less state involvement in the economy, and the growth of critical and nonpartisan media. Despite a major restructuring of the left wing of Icelandic politics in 1999, the four party format nevertheless seems to have survived. The fact that a large social democratic party and a small left socialist party now constitute the left wing of the spectrum is, however, a major change, making the Icelandic system more similar to the Scandinavian party systems, and greatly changing the Icelandic game of government coalition formation.

Further Reading

Hardarson, Ólafur Th. "Iceland." *European Journal of Political Research* 22 (1992): 429–35; 24 (1993): 451–53; 26 (1994): 327–30; 28 (1995): 369–73; 30 (1996): 367–76; 32(1997): 391–98; 34 (1998): 423–27; 36 (1999): 419–22.

———. "The Icelandic Electoral System 1844-1999." In *The Evolution of Electoral and Party Systems in the Nordic Countries.* Ed. A. Lijphart and B. Grofman. New York: Agathon Press, 2002: 101–66.

———. *Parties and Voters in Iceland.* Reykjavik: Social Science Research Institute/University Press, 1995.

Hardarson, Ólafur Th., and Gunnar Helgi Kristinsson. "Iceland." *European Journal of Political Research* 38 (2000): 408–19; 40 (2001): 326–29; 41 (2002): 975–77; 42 (2203): 975–78; 43 (2004): 1024–29.

———. "The 1999 Parliamentary Election in Iceland." *Electoral Studies* 20 (2001): 219–34.

Indridason, Indridi H. "A Theory of Coalitions and Clientelism: Coalition Politics in Iceland 1945-2000." *European Journal of Political Research* 44, no. 3 (May 2005): 439.

Kristinsson, Gunnar Helgi. *Farmers' Parties. A Study in Electoral Adaption.* Reykjavik: Social Science Research Institute, 1991.

———. "From Home Rule to Sovereignty: The Case of Iceland." In *Lessons from the Political Economy of Small Islands: The Resourcefulness of Jurisdiction.* Ed. G. Baldacchino and D. Milne. New York: St. Martin's Press, 2000.

———. "Iceland." In *Semi-Presidentialism in Europe.* Ed. R. Elgie. Oxford: Oxford University Press, 1999: 86–103.

———. "Iceland and Norway: Peripheries in Doubt." In *Prospective Europeans.* Ed. J. Redmond. London: Harvester-Wheatsheaf, 1994.

———. "The Icelandic Parliamentary Election of 1995." *Electoral Studies* 14, no. 3 (1995): 332–36.

———. "The Icelandic Presidential Election of 1996." *Electoral Studies* 15, no. 4 (1996): 533–37.

———. "The Icelandic Progressive Party: Trawling for the Town Vote." In *From Farmyard to City Square? The Electoral Adaption of the Nordic Agrarian Parties.* Ed. David Arter. Aldershot: Ashgate, 2001: 132–61.

———. "Parties, States and Patronage." *West European Politics* 19, no. 3 (1996): 433–57.

Kristjánsson, Svanur. "From Party Rule to Pluralist Political Society." In *Party Sovereignty and Citizen Control.* Ed. H. M. Narud, M. N. Pedersen, and H. Valen. Odense: University Press of Southern Denmark, 2002: 107–66.

———. "Iceland. A Parliamentary Democracy with a Semi-Presidential Constitution." In *Delegation and Accountability in Parliamentary Democracies.* Ed. K. Strom, W. C. Muller, and T. Bergman. Oxford: Oxford University Press, 2003.

Nordal, Jóhannes, and Valdimar Kristinsson, eds. *Iceland. The Republic.* Reykjavik: Central Bank of Iceland, 1996.

Ólafsson, Stefán. "Variations within the Scandinavian Model: Iceland in a Scandinavian Comparison." In *Welfare Trends in the Scandinavian Countries.* Ed. E. Hansen et al. New York: M.E. Sharpe, 1993.

Thorhallsson, Baldur. "The Skeptical Political Elite versus the Pro-European Public: The Case of Iceland." *Scandinavian Studies* 74, no. 3 (2002): 349–78.

———, ed. *Iceland and European Integration: On the Edge.* London: Routledge, 2004.

REPUBLIC OF INDIA
(Bharatiya Ganarajya)

By Stanley A. Kochanek, Ph.D.
Revised by Srikrishna Ayyangar

With a population of more than a billion in 2005, India is one of the poorest, most diverse, and most heterogenous countries in the world. Although Hinduism is the dominant religion, India contains all of the major world religions; it is subdivided into a myriad of castes; and it has 18 major languages plus a vast array of smaller languages, dialects, and tribal tongues. In its diversity and continental size, India is more like the multistate European Union than the more integrated and unified federal system in the United States.

The System of Government

India is a federal republic with a British-style parliamentary form of government. Over the past 50 years since independence, the governmental system has evolved from a highly centralized state dominated by one party to one that has become increasingly federalized, fragmented, and controlled by unstable multiparty coalitions and alliances.

Though its roots are much deeper, the contemporary Indian political system dates from August 15, 1947, when its long and unique struggle for independence from British rule finally succeeded. Independence brought partition on religious lines between secular but predominantly Hindu India and Muslim Pakistan.

Newly independent India drafted a constitution modeled on the British and other existing constitutions. The constitution, which entered into force on January 26, 1950, provides for a democratic republic, secular, parliamentary, and federal in character. It is one of the longest and most detailed written constitutions in the world and one of the most frequently amended.

EXECUTIVE

The president of the republic is the head of state and supreme commander of the military forces but exercises the executive power only formally. The president is elected to a five-year term by an electoral college composed of the elected members of both houses of the national Parliament and of the lower houses of the state legislatures. Voting is weighted to allow for population differences between the states. The president is supposed to be a nonpartisan figure, but in practice candidates have been elected only if they were acceptable to the prime minister.

From the beginning, the president was intended to exercise his or her power only with the closest advice of the prime minister and the cabinet. His primary role was to be symbolic, much in the manner of the British monarch, although there was considerable discussion of the extent of the president's discretionary powers. Any ambiguity was removed by the Forty-Second Amendment to the constitution in 1976 and the Forty-Fourth Amendment in 1978, which explicitly required the president to act in accordance with the advice of the cabinet.

Thus, effective executive power belongs to the prime minister and the cabinet (formally the Council of Ministers.) The prime minister is appointed by the president and must be able to command majority support in the Lok Sabha, the lower house of Parliament. If there is a recognized leader of a party or coalition that commands a majority in the Lok Sabha, the president has no discretion. With the emergence of coalition government, the president's discretionary power to appoint the prime minister has increased.

The prime minister is responsible to the Lok Sabha, which may force the prime minister from office at any time by demonstrating the lack of majority support for him. Since 1979 several Indian prime ministers have been forced to resign in the face of an impending vote of no confidence or failure to maintain majority support.

The president appoints the members of the Council of Ministers on the advice of the prime minister and removes them in the same way. Within the cabinet, the prime minister has always been the strongest figure; the collective decision-making process of the British system of cabinet government is much less characteristic of India, where the prime minister and his formal and informal advisers (who may or may not be members of the cabinet) predominate. Cabinet ministers, therefore, mainly are occupied with implementation of policy decisions affecting their governmental ministries and with day-to-day administrative responsibilities.

Ministerial departments are staffed by a powerful and prestigious civil service, the modern successor to the almost legendary Indian Civil Service of British colonial days. At the apex of the modern civil service is the Indian Administrative Service, an elite cadre of highly qualified, competitively selected administrators who exercise wide-ranging power over implementation and administration of government policy subject only to the supervision of politically responsible ministers.

India has had 17 prime ministers in 50 years of independence. Jawaharlal Nehru and his daughter, Indira Gandhi, governed for 30 of those years. Mrs. Gandhi served from 1966 to 1977, when her Congress Party was defeated by a coalition of opposition parties that took the name Janata (People's) Party after 21 months of authoritarian rule under the draconian emergency provisions of the Indian constitution. The

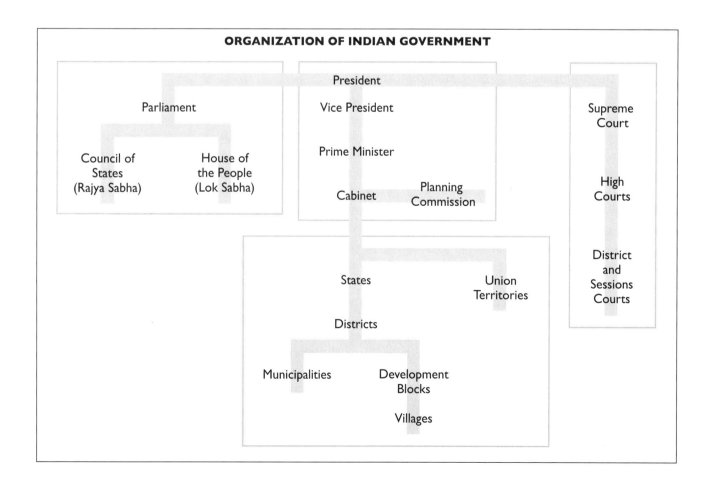

ORGANIZATION OF INDIAN GOVERNMENT

President

Parliament

Vice President

Supreme Court

Council of States (Rajya Sabha)

House of the People (Lok Sabha)

Prime Minister

High Courts

Cabinet

Planning Commission

District and Sessions Courts

States

Union Territories

Districts

Municipalities

Development Blocks

Villages

Janata Party formed a government under Prime Minister Moraji Desai, who served from 1977 to mid-1979, when the party split. Charan Singh then became the prime minister. New national elections resulted in Mrs. Gandhi's return to power in January 1980. Mrs. Gandhi was succeeded by her son Rajiv Gandhi following her assassination on October 31, 1984. Rajiv Gandhi led his Congress (I) Party to an overwhelming victory in the December 1984 general elections. Rajiv's policy failures, his centralization of power, and a series of corruption scandals involving defense contracts resulted in his defeat in the November 1989 elections.

The defeat of the Congress Party, however, led to a hung Parliament. For the first time since independence no single party was able to secure a majority and India entered an era of unstable coalition and alliance politics. Following the 1989 elections, the National Front, a loose multiparty coalition, elected V. P. Singh as prime minister. Friction within the National Front, however, led to the downfall of Singh in less than a year. Singh was replaced by Chandra Shekhar, supported by the Congress Party. This unstable alliance lasted only four months, and Indians were forced to go to the polls for the second time in less than two years in the midst of major political and economic crises.

The uncertainty that dominated the 1991 Lok Sabha elections was further compounded by the assassination of Rajiv Gandhi by a Sri Lankan Tamil during an election meeting in Tamil Nadu. Rajiv's assassination had a dramatic impact on the election results. During the first round of voting that had preceded the assassination, the Congress had suffered severe reverses. However, in the delayed second and third rounds of voting, a significant sympathy vote in favor of the Congress Party enabled the party to win 227 seats—just 29 seats short of a majority. P. V. Narasimha Rao, the newly elected Congress leader, was able to form a minority government that gradually increased its support and survived for a full term of five years.

The Congress revival, however, proved to be short-lived as the party, tainted by charges of corruption, suffered its worst defeat in history in the April–May 1996 elections. The defeat of the Congress, once again, resulted in a hung Parliament that was more fragmented then ever before. Because the Bharatiya Janata Party (BJP) had won the largest number of seats in the election, the president of India asked the party leader, Atal Behari Vajpayee, to form a government. Vajpayee, however, was forced to resign 13 days later when faced by the prospect of losing a no-confidence motion in Parliament. The president then invited the National Front–Left Front, a coalition of 13 regional and national parties, to form a government. The Front elected H. D. Deve Gowda, a former chief minister of Karnataka, to be prime minister. Gowda headed a minority government supported by the Congress Party, which refused to join the coalition cabinet. Gowda lasted less than a year and was forced to resign when the Congress Party withdrew its support. He was replaced on April 21, 1997, by Inder Kumar Gujral, a candidate more acceptable to the Congress Party. The Gujral government lasted until December, when new parliamentary elections were called. In March 1998 Vajpayee again became prime minister when the BJP cobbled together a coalition of over a dozen and a half regional parties following the 1998 Lok Sabha elections.

In the 2004 elections the Congress came back to power primarily because of the support it gained from striking pre-electoral alliances with state parties. The BJP was taken by surprise. Since their partners, the All-India Anna-Dravida Munnetra Kazhagam (AIADMK) and the Telegu Desam Party (TDP), performed poorly in their respective states, the BJP alliance failed to win the majority. At the last minute, Congress Party leader Sonia Gandhi gave up her position as prime ministerial candidate in favor of Manmohan Singh, because she felt that her prime responsibility was to promote the welfare of the Congress Party and not her personal ambition to lead the nation. Singh's candidacy was received tepidly because doubts were being cast about his political ability to push forward economic reforms, since the parties on the left are his primary alliance partners.

LEGISLATURE

The Indian Parliament is bicameral. The more important lower house is called the Lok Sabha, or "house of the people." It has 543 members directly elected from single-member district constituencies based on population and two seats filled by nomination. Elections are normally held at five-year intervals. The five-year limit has been abridged only once when, in 1976, the life of the Lok Sabha was extended by one year by Indira Gandhi under the emergency provisions of the constitution. The extension was renewed a year later. Parliamentary elections may be called at less than five-year intervals by the president acting on the advice of the prime minister.

There are 79 Lok Sabha seats reserved for members of the Scheduled Castes, or untouchables. Another 40 seats are reserved for members of Scheduled Tribes. These reserved seats are allocated among the states on

PRIME MINISTERS OF INDIA, 1947–2004

Prime Minister	Party	Dates
Jawaharlal Nehru	Congress	8/15/47–5/27/64
Lal Bahadur Shastri	Congress	6/9/64–1/11/66
Indira Gandhi	Congress	1/24/66–3/24/77
Morarji Desai	Janata	3/24/77–7/8/79
Charan Singh	Janata	7/28/79–1/14/80
Indira Gandhi	Congress	1/14/80–10/31/84
Rajiv Gandhi	Congress	10/31/84–12/1/89
V. P. Singh	National Front	12/2/89–11/10/90
Chandra Shekhar	Samajvadi Janata	11/10/90–6/21/91
P. V. Narasimha Rao	Congress	6/21/91–5/16/96
Atal Behari Vajpayee	BJP	5/16/96–6/1/96
H. D. Deve Gowda	Janata Dal	6/1/96–4/11/97
I. K. Gujral	Janata Dal	4/21/97–3/19/98
Atal Behari Vajpayee	BJP	3/19/98–5/21/2004
Manmohan Singh	Congress	5/22/2004–

the basis of the proportion of their populations that fall into the respective Scheduled category. Electorates for the reserved seats are made up of all classes of Indian citizens, but only Scheduled Caste or Scheduled Tribe members may stand for such seats. These provisions for special representation are constitutionally temporary, but they have been regularly extended. In another special category, the president of India is empowered to appoint up to two Anglo-Indians (descendants of mixed British-Indian marriages or liaisons) to the Lok Sabha.

By constitution, the Lok Sabha must meet at least twice each year with no more than six months between sessions. In practice, it usually meets three times a year.

The upper house of Parliament is the Rajya Sabha, or "council of the states." It has 250 members, 12 of whom are appointed by the president from among Indians distinguished in the arts and professions. The remaining members are elected by the state legislatures to fixed terms, with approximately one-third retiring every second year. Thus it is possible that the partisan majority in the Lok Sabha will not coincide with the majority in the Rajya Sabha, which has happened on several occasions.

The two houses of Parliament have the same power over ordinary legislation; both must pass bills in agreed form. However, money bills may be introduced only in the Lok Sabha, and the Rajya Sabha has only the power of delay. If a money bill is amended or rejected by the Rajya Sabha, it needs merely to be repassed by the Lok Sabha in the original form to be sent to the president for assent. The Rajya Sabha exercises independent jurisdiction in a limited range of issues relating to the states.

JUDICIARY

India's constitution makers took the notion of parliamentary supremacy from the British model but tried to graft onto it an independent judiciary and judicial review system based largely on the American model. At the apex of an integrated national judicial system is the Supreme Court of India. It consists of a chief justice and not more than 25 other judges appointed by the president. Judges of the Supreme Court serve until they reach the age of 65, unless removed by an elaborate and difficult parliamentary procedure. The chief justice is normally the most senior judge in terms of age, although there have been a few controversial cases of "supersession," that is, the appointment of a less senior judge as chief justice.

The Supreme Court has broad original and appellate jurisdiction that extends to civil and criminal matters and especially to matters of constitutional interpretation and relations between the center (the national government) and the states. The exercise of these powers has led to considerable conflict between governments committed to greater or lesser degrees of social reform and a court equally committed to the protection of fundamental rights outlined in the constitution. The conflict between court and government has been waged in a variety of ways over the years. Many of the 90 amendments to the Indian constitution have been designed to reverse some Supreme Court ruling striking down an act of Parliament. The most substantial attack on the Court came in 1976 when Mrs. Gandhi's government pushed through Parliament the very detailed and extensive Forty-Second Amendment Act that, among other things, placed very stringent limitations on the power of the Supreme Court to review acts of Parliament on constitutional grounds. The Supreme

Court itself struck down part of this amendment and the Janata Party government further altered it in the Forty-Fourth Amendment in 1978. The fundamental difficulty of reconciling parliamentary supremacy with judicial review remains one of the troublesome issues facing the Indian political system.

One of the most important developments in India in recent years has been the renewal of judicial activism. The Supreme Court has begun to promote public-interest litigation (PIL) based on a reinterpretation of the constitution to include equal treatment under the law and due process. In keeping with this new activism the Supreme Court has encouraged class-action suits, has treated letters written to judges as writ petitions, has acted upon newspaper reports, has appointed committees to investigate the facts of a case, has summoned experts to obtain their views, and has even made public authorities investigating charges of corruption on the part of public officials directly responsible to the Court. The result has been a massive expansion of civil, political, economic, and social rights. Supreme Court activism has also spread to the lower courts. The Court's new role, however, has brought it into conflict with both the executive and the legislature and has led to efforts by both to restrict the Court's action.

REGIONAL AND LOCAL GOVERNMENT

Although India is a federation composed of 28 states and 7 union territories, Indian federalism is weighted heavily toward the central government. The union territories are ruled by the central government under a variety of arrangements. The states are organized mainly along language lines. The central government may and occasionally has redrawn state boundaries. The structure of state government is similar to that of the central government. The executive power is vested in a governor who is appointed by the president of India on the advice of the prime minister. The governor is appointed for a five-year term and is largely a figurehead whose powers and role are analogous to those of the national president.

Real political and administrative power is exercised by a chief minister (analogous to the prime minister at the national level) and his council of ministers who are appointed by the governor and are collectively responsible to the legislative assembly. Most states have a unicameral legislature. The legislative assemblies are composed of between 60 and 500 members chosen by direct election from territorial constituencies based on population. The legislative assemblies function in a manner similar to the Lok Sabha at the national level. Six states have bicameral legislatures with a smaller legislative council functioning alongside the legislative assembly.

Members of the legislative council are elected indirectly by the assembly or appointed by the governor to fixed terms with approximately one-third retiring every second year.

The Indian constitution divides the functions of government between the states and the central government through three detailed lists. The Union List contains areas exclusively reserved to the national government, including defense and military forces, atomic energy, foreign affairs, railways, shipping, air transport, posts and telegraph, currency, international trade, banking, insurance, mining, and nonagricultural income and corporate taxation. The State List contains items reserved to the states, including public order, police, prisons, local government, public health, agriculture, land and land tenure, property tax, and tax on agricultural income. The Concurrent List contains items on which either the states or the national government may act, including criminal law, preventive detention, marriage and divorce, contracts, economic and social planning, social security, labor, education, and civil procedure. In the event of conflict between the national government and state action on matters on the Concurrent List, the national government position prevails. Moreover, a reserve clause grants the national government exclusive jurisdiction over all areas not enumerated in one of the lists. In periods of emergency or with the concurrence of two-thirds of the Rajya Sabha, the national government may act on matters on the State List.

Finally, if the president "is satisfied that a situation has arisen in which the government of the State cannot be carried on in accordance with the provisions of this Constitution," he may, on the advice of the prime minister, suspend the state government and rule directly from New Delhi. This is referred to as "president's rule" and has been used with increasing frequency since the 1960s.

The Electoral System

Although the Rajya Sabha and the legislative councils are indirectly elected, the more important Lok Sabha and the legislative assemblies are elected directly. Since 1967 all electoral constituencies have been single member. Candidates must be Indian citizens at least 25 years of age. Most successful candidates are nominated by recognized parties, although a large number of independents always stand for election. A candidate must put up a deposit of 10,000 rupees (about $218 in 2005) to run for a Lok Sabha seat and 5,000 rupees for a legislative assembly seat. A candidate must poll at least one-sixth of the votes cast in that constituency in order to have his deposit refunded. The candidate receiving a simple plurality of the valid votes cast in the constituency wins.

Vacancies caused by death, resignation, or removal from office are filled through by-elections that are watched carefully as signals of political trends.

Ballots list candidates by party symbol, in English and in the local language(s). Voting is secret and carefully supervised. Although there have been charges of corruption, intimidation, and "booth capturing," most observers agree that Indian elections are remarkably free, fair, and orderly.

All Indian citizens 18 years of age or over are eligible to vote. Registration rolls are kept by the Election Commission, an independent agency charged with responsibility to ensure fair and efficient conduct of elections, and are updated regularly at the initiative of the Commission. To insure against double voting, voters' fingers are marked with indelible ink. Voters are not counted until the final polling day is under way, and returns are not released until all polling is completed.

With approximately 605 million eligible voters, India has the largest democratic electorate in the world. Voter turnout has been relatively high. Since 1952 the average voter turnout has been 57.1 percent of the eligible voters. The highest turnout was in 1984 following the assassin of Indira Gandhi when 64.1 percent of the eligible voters turned out. The lowest turnout occurred in the first two elections of 1952 and 1957 when it was only 45.7 percent.

The Party System

ORIGINS OF THE PARTIES

Most, but not all, Indian political parties grew out of the independence struggle. The Congress Party, which has held power on the national level for most of the years since independence, is the direct descendant of the Indian National Congress, the umbrella organization that led the independence struggle from 1885 until independence in 1947. As an umbrella organization, the Congress was highly aggregative, seeking to unite disparate ideologies and personalities in the service of self-rule. With independence at

Party	Seats Won	Seats Contested	% Votes
LOK SABHA ELECTIONS, 2004 **(VOTER TURNOUT 58.07%)**			
Congress (I)	145	417	26.53
Congress (I) Allies[a]	77	122	9.29
	(222)	(539)	(35.82)
Bharatiya Janata Party (BJP)	138	364	216
BJP Allies[b]	51	223	11.75
	(189)	(587)	(32.91)
Left Front[c]	61	119	8.34
BSP	19	435	5.33
Other Parties[d]	50	1320	14.20
Other Independents	2	2385	3.79
Total	543	5435	100.39

[a]Congress (I) allies and number of seats: Rashtriya Janata Dal (21), Dravida Munnetra Kazhagam (16), National Congress Party (9), Pattali Makkal Katchi (6), Jharkhand Mukthi Morcha (5), Telengana Rashtra Samiti (5), LJNP (4), Marumalarchi DMK (4), People's Democratic Party (1), Muslim League (1), Republican Party of India (A) (1), Independents with Congress support (1)

[b]BJP allies and number of seats: Shiv Sena (12), Biju Janata Dal (11), Janata Dal (U) (8), Akali Dal (Badal) (8), Telugu Desam Party (5), West Bengal Trinamool Congress (2), Mizo National Front (1), Sikkim Democratic Front (1), Indian Federal Democratic Party (1), Nagaland People's Front (1), Independents (1)

[c]Left front and allies: Communist Party of India (M) (43), Communist Party of India (10), Revolutionary Socialist Party (3), Forward Bloc (3), Kerala Congress (1), Independents (1)

[d]Other parties: Samajwadi Party (36), Rashtriya Lok Dal (3), Janata Dal (S) (3), Asom Gono Parishad (2), Samajwadi Janata Party (R) (1), National Conference (2), National Loktantrik Party (1), Majlis e Ittehadul Musalmeen (1), Muslim League Kerala State Committee (1)

hand, ideological and personal differences led to defections from the Congress.

An early ideological split led to the establishment of the Socialist Party in 1947. Personality differences created a break between Charan Singh and the Congress in Uttar Pradesh, India's largest state, and the establishment of the Bharatiya Kranti Dal in 1967. A combination of ideology and personality led to a major "split" in the Congress in 1969 and the establishment of the Congress (O). Since 1969 the Congress has experienced repeated splits due to personality clashes and factionalism that have considerably weakened the party and filled the ranks of the opposition. Almost all of the Indian parties—except the Communist Party, Bharatiya Janata Party, and some of the regional and state parties—arose from these defections or splits in the Congress Party.

THE PARTIES IN LAW

Political parties are not given significant treatment in the constitution of India and have little special status in Indian law. Independent candidates have essentially the same legal rights and responsibilities as party candidates: nomination procedures, financial limits, and reporting requirements are the same.

Parties recognized by the Election Commission have reserved symbols. To be recognized a party must meet one of two criteria. It must either exist and participate in political activity for a period of five years or secure at least 6 percent of the votes cast in the state for the Lok Sabha or Vidhan Sabha (state assembly) elections. In the 2004 elections there were six recognized national parties and 36 recognized state parties with reserved symbols.

PARTY ORGANIZATION

Most Indian parties profess to be mass organizations based on dues-paying members; in reality, few are. Only the Congress, the Indian People's Party (BJP), and the Communist Party have sustained such a mass character over any length of time. The BJP and the Communists are numerically smaller and confined to a narrower geographical area than Congress. One of the reasons for the relative success of the Congress in the past was that it was a coalition party composed of diverse castes and communities and of disparate groups espousing different emphases in government policy. Over the years, however, the Congress has become less coalitional and more personalistic in character, a process hastened during Indira Gandhi's and her son Rajiv's tenure. While the leadership still remains personalistic under Sonia Gandhi, the party struck alliances with other parties in the 2004 elections. Now both ruling and opposition parties have entered into alliances with other smaller parties reflecting a new

trend in the party system of coalitional arrangements clustering toward a bipartisan political system.

None of the other parties has been of the coalition type, except the Janata briefly during its incumbency from 1977 to 1979. Other parties tend to be ideological, personalistic, or regional.

The main parties maintain national and state organizations. Real power usually is divided between these two sets of organizations in shifting measures. The work of running campaigns rests with the state or local units of the party. While state or local units often carry substantial political power, the national organization usually exerts major influence over the allocation of tickets (nominations). Although the details of party organization differ from party to party and from time to time, all the main national parties are structured to reflect the division of electoral and administrative structures into states and districts.

As in most parliamentary systems, there is a certain amount of tension and conflict between the parliamentary and organizational wings of the parties. Such conflict has been most pronounced in the ruling Congress Party. However, the Janata also experienced major differences when in power from 1977 to 1979, and these resulted in a split of the party in mid-1979. Such differences often have been seen at the state level.

CAMPAIGNING

Indian political campaigns have a festive air. People turn out in large numbers at political rallies and other appearances by candidates. Candidates circulate extensively in their constituencies, usually traveling from village to village by jeep, sometimes on foot or by elephant. In urban areas, parties canvass door to door. Signs, banners, and graffiti play a prominent role in campaigns. Party notables move extensively around the state or country making personal appearances in tightly contested constituencies.

Radio and television are government-controlled and have not played prominent roles in campaigning. However, beginning in 1977 in some state elections and in the 1980 national elections, all recognized parties were provided with campaign time on radio and television. But an increase in the number of channels since the broadcasting sector was liberalized in the 1990s has increased the media attention for political campaigns.

Campaign expenditures are sharply limited by law. In 1998 each candidate for the Lok Sabha was permitted to spend not more than Rs 1,500,000 ($32,830) in election expenses. Each candidate is required to maintain a daily documented account of expenditures that must be submitted to the relevant election official. Failure to comply with these regulations may result in a candidate's disqualification from serving in either house of Parliament for three years.

However, it is widely agreed that these limits are wholly unrealistic and that Indian elections are vastly more expensive. A well-known Indian news magazine (*India Today*, March 31, 1996) reported a candidate for a seat in the Lok Sabha might have to spend anywhere from Rs 500,000 to Rs 50 million ($10,943 to $1,094,331).

Political finances are the subject of much rumor and speculation and little hard data. Parties devote a good deal of effort to raising money. Some of the devices used include the collection of membership dues, the sale of advertisements in party publications, the sale of space and decorations at party functions, requests for direct donations, and, it has been charged, pressures bordering on extortion and solicitation of bribes. The large industrial families—the Birlas, the Tatas, and the like—have a tradition of financial support for political movements that goes back to well before independence. Other sources of funds include small-time traders, local industry lobbies, cooperatives, nonresident Indians, the underworld, government contracting, and various regulatory approvals. The Congress Party has been the main beneficiary of financial support from the business houses, but other parties have increased their share depending on their relative strength.

During the cold war Communist Parties were widely believed to have received support from outside India, and there have been repeated charges that other parties, including the Congress, received covert monies from the U.S. Central Intelligence Agency. However, hard evidence about sources of financial support for Indian parties is fragmentary and should be approached with caution. In any event the end of the cold war has sharply reduced incentives by outsiders to fund Indian parties.

INDEPENDENT VOTERS

Party membership figures in India are highly unreliable. Personalist parties rarely have any formal membership outside Parliament. Even in mass-based parties, frequent defections, splits, and factional conflicts make available figures highly unreliable. Voting rolls do not indicate party identification, but public opinion studies indicate that a surprisingly large proportion of the voters expresses identification with parties. Recent elections suggest that party identification may be less indicative of voting behavior than orientation to personalities and issues. Since 1971 Lok Sabha and state assembly elections have generally occurred at different times. Therefore, since voters usually cast only one ballot for one member of the Lok Sabha, ticket splitting is normally impossible.

Major Political Parties

INDIAN PEOPLE'S PARTY

(Bharatiya Janata Party; BJP)

HISTORY

The BJP was founded in 1980 after the breakup of the governing Janata Party coalition. It is the current manifestation of the former Jana Sangh (People's) Party with its long tradition of militant Hindu nationalist politics. The Jana Sangh was established in 1950 largely by a cadre of the Rashtriya Swayamsevak Sangh (RSS), or National Volunteer Organization, a paramilitary group and by some figures from the Hindu Mahasabha, a militant Hindu political party. The initiative for a new party was led by Dr. S. P. Mookerjee, a former Hindu Mahasabha leader and former member of Nehru's cabinet. Beginning with the first general election in 1952, the Jana Sangh gradually replaced the Hindu Mahasabha as the voice of Hindu cultural militancy.

Since its creation the strategy of the Jana Sangh and its successor, the BJP, has oscillated between the propagation of militant Hindu nationalism based on ethnoreligious mobilization and a more pragmatic approach based on moderation and coalition building designed to broaden the movement's electoral appeal. The basic dilemma of the leadership has been to maintain its militant core support based on the paramilitary National Volunteer Organization (RSS) and its cadre and the need to temper that ideology in an effort to develop a more centrist appeal designed to win power. Initially, in the years following its creation in the 1950s the Jana Sangh followed a militant Hindu nationalist strategy. This strategy, however, had a limited impact on the electorate, and the party was marginalized by the strong appeal of the Congress Party and the popularity of its leader, Jawaharlal Nehru.

In an effort to break out of its isolation, the Jana Sangh shifted to a more pragmatic strategy in the 1960s that saw it begin to build electoral support in the Hindi-speaking belt of North and Central India. Its electoral success enabled the party to participate in coalition governments in several states and to gain control of municipal governing bodies. This strategy continued into the 1970s as the Jana Sangh supported the opposition movement led by Jayaprakash Narayan, opposed emergency rule from 1975 to 1977, and joined the broad-based Janata coalition that defeated the Congress Party for the first time since 1947 in the 1977 parliamentary elections. Following the elections, the Jana Sangh became incorporated into the new Janata Party that brought an end to its formal existence.

Following the breakup of the Janata Party, the bulk of the former Jana Sangh members left the Janata Party to form the BJP under the leadership of Atal Bihari Vajpayee, a former Jana Sangh leader who had served as the foreign minister in the Janata government. Under Vajpayee the BJP attempted to build a new Hindu nationalist party that would be more open, centrist, and broadly based than the old Jana Sangh. The party adopted a moderate program based on Gandhian socialism, nationalism, democracy, value-based politics, and positive secularism. This new program, however, upset the party's traditional hard-core supporters in the RSS and generated considerable internal dissent. Members of the RSS became increasingly alienated from the party and began to drift toward the more militant appeals of the Congress Party under Indira Gandhi. The attraction of RSS members to the Congress increased sharply following the assassination of Indira Gandhi by her Sikh bodyguards. The assassination, Sikh separatism, anxiety over isolated incidents of Muslim conversions of low-caste Hindus, and growing insurgencies along India's northern border created a sense of insecurity and a Hindu backlash that resulted in a massive victory for Rajiv Gandhi and a stunning defeat of the BJP in the 1984 elections. Elements of the RSS contributed to this victory by actively working on behalf of Rajiv, and several prominent RSS leaders openly endorsed him.

The defeat suffered by the BJP in the 1984 elections resulted in a change of leadership, policy, and program as the party attempted to return to its roots. The more liberal Vajpayee was replaced as leader of the party by L. K. Advani who had close ties to the RSS. Under Advani the BJP adopted a more militant Hindu nationalist position and a strategy of ethnoreligious mobilization. The shift in BJP policy coincided with a sharp rise in communalism that was heightened by the agitation surrounding the long-simmering dispute over the Babri Masjid (Mosque) in Ayodhya. Hindus claimed that the Babri Masjid had been built by the Mughals on the site of a destroyed Hindu temple that had marked the birthplace of Lord Rama, a Hindu deity. They wanted the mosque demolished and replaced with a new Ramjanmabhoomi temple. The BJP used the religious symbol of the Babri Masjid/Ramjanmabhoomi during the 1989 elections in an effort to mobilize the Hindu vote. This strategy helped the BJP improve its position throughout North and West India. Its success was further enhanced by its strategy of election alliance with the newly formed National Front, a coalition composed of the Janata Dal and several regional parties.

Although the 1989 elections resulted in a hung Parliament, V. P. Singh, the leader of the Janata Dal, was elected prime minister with the support of a diverse group of opposition parties including the BJP. The BJP, however, withdrew support in November 1990 in response to Singh's decision to implement the recommendations of the Mandal Commission, which had called for the reservation of 27 percent of all central government jobs for backward castes.

The fall of the V. P. Singh government and its successor led to the dissolution of the government and new elections in 1991 that were dominated by the twin issues of Mandir (temple) and Mandal (reservations for backward castes). The BJP actively campaigned for the construction of a Hindu temple at Ayodhya and opposed the further reservations based on caste as an attempt to divide the Hindu nation. The BJP's campaign resulted in a major victory for the party across states in North and West India and significantly increased its strength in the Lok Sabha. Although the Congress Party was able to form a government thanks to a wave of sympathy that followed the assassination of Rajiv Gandhi, the BJP appeared destined to become a dominant force in Indian politics. Encouraged by its electoral success, the BJP continued its campaign to build a temple at Ayodhya. The movement peaked when Hindu militants succeeded in destroying the mosque in December 1992. The destruction of the mosque led to the outbreak of the worst communal riots in India since partition.

The seemingly unstoppable success of the BJP in the early 1990s, however, was brought to a crashing halt in the November 1993 state assembly elections in which the party was defeated in North India, its traditional stronghold. The defeat made clear that the BJP's militant strategy of ethnoreligious mobilization had reached its limits. As a result the party was forced to change its militant strategy and adopt a more moderate approach. The BJP began to play down its emphasis on ethnoreligious mobilization and, in an effort to broaden its base, focused on socioeconomic and national issues. As part of this new strategy the BJP also entered into a series of electoral alliances in preparation for the 1996 parliamentary elections. The 1996 elections, however, ended in another hung Parliament. Although voter support for the BJP increased only marginally, its electoral alliances expanded the number of BJP seats significantly and the party emerged as the largest single party in the Lok Sabha. Because of its position as the largest of the 28 parties represented in Parliament, the president of India turned to the BJP and asked it to form a government. The newly formed BJP government, however, lasted only 13 days when the largely secular opposition refused to support it.

Although the 1998 Lok Sabha elections produced a highly fractured mandate and another hung Parliament, the BJP again emerged as the largest party, with 179 seats and 25.47 percent of the vote. In addition, its 12 regional allies won 73 seats for a total of 252 seats that was just 20 seats short of an absolute majority. The BJP was able to cobble together a broad-based unstable coalition government when a combination of independents, small regional parties, and the Telugu Desam Party, a former member of the United Front, agreed to support a BJP-led government.

Despite sound economic performance on the macroeconomic front, the BJP was not able to return to power in the 2004 elections. It came back with a lesser tally of 138 seats, even though its vote share had marginally dropped to 22.16 percent. Further, its key ally, the Telugu Desam Party, had been convincingly defeated, reducing that party's share from 12 to 4 seats. Its other ally, the DMK, aligned with the Congress a few months before the elections and came back with an additional 10 seats from its earlier tally of six seats.

ORGANIZATION

The party's organizational strength depends on the RSS, a paramilitary cadre group. The RSS provides a tightly knit, well-organized, disciplined body of party workers. The connection, however, has been a mixed blessing for it also creates tension over control of party policy and strategy and has limited efforts to develop electoral alliances.

POLICY

Initially the BJP tried to be more open and liberal than the Jana Sangh. The disastrous defeat of the party at the polls in 1984, however, forced a major change in policy. The party reaffirmed its commitment to the integrity and unity of the county, democracy, value-based politics, positive secularism, Gandhian socialism, and—most important of all—building a polity in

India that conformed to Indian culture and traditions. While continuing to emphasize Hindutva (literally, Hindu-ness), a term which has become the equivalent of Hindu/nationalism, the BJP in the 1990s moved away from Gandhian socialism and became an ardent critic of state intervention in the economy and a strong supporter of the Indian private sector against the forces of globalization and competition from foreign multinationals.

In foreign policy, the Jana Sangh took a militantly anti-Pakistan position, rejecting the legitimacy of the 1947 partition and advocating reunification of the subcontinent by force, if necessary. The responsibilities of office seemed to alter Jana Sangh perspectives, especially those of A. B. Vajpayee, who took a more benevolent approach to neighboring countries, including Pakistan, a stance that created some intraparty conflict. Once out of power, some of the old militancy returned to the rhetoric of BJP leaders. The BJP supports a strong national defense, including the development of an effective nuclear capability. BJP made good on this commitment when India conducted five nuclear tests in May 1998 and declared itself to be a nuclear weapons state.

MEMBERSHIP AND CONSTITUENCY

The BJP, like the Jana Sangh before it, draws its main support from upper-caste, middle-class Hindus living in urban areas but has also extended its base to include nonelite intermediate castes. It has proved remarkably attractive to urban youth, and the Vidyarthi Parishad, the student affiliate of the RSS, is India's largest student organization. Geographically, its main strength has been in the Hindi-speaking areas of North and West India, but the party remains weak in the South and East.

FINANCING

Initially the BJP relied heavily on dues and contributions from its ideological supporters. The growing success of the party, however, has begun to attract increased support from Indian industrialists.

LEADERSHIP

The BJP leadership has begun to age. The most prominent leader is A. B. Vajpayee (born 1926), who has been responsible for the strategy of broadening the geographical base of the party. His most important colleague is the former RSS leader and Janata minister, L. K. Advani (born 1927). The next generation of leaders includes the general secretaries, Pramod Mahajan and Arun Jaitley, the urbane face of the party; the party president, Venkaiah Naidu; and Narendra Modi, the chief minister of Gujarat, who was the chief campaigner for the party in the northern states and is the voice of the culturally hard-line cadre of the party.

PROSPECTS

Many observers believe that the BJP has the best prospects to become a viable alternative to the Congress (I) among the opposition parties. Its organization, the breadth of its appeal, and strong leadership set it apart from most other Indian parties. The isolation and weakness of the BJP in the South and East, however, requires a strategy of alliance formation with regional and caste parties. It was this strategy that enabled it to come to power in March 1998. But this strategy also creates a basic dilemma that the party has faced throughout its history. A policy of pragmatism does not appeal to its RSS cadre and core supporters who are committed to the party's more militant ideology. They also oppose the use of caste appeals as contrary to the unity of Hinduism. Yet, given the weakness of its appeal in the South and East, an alliance strategy represents the only hope the party has of coming to power at the national level.

At the state and local level, BJP prospects are somewhat better. The party has become a major political force in the states of the North and the West.

COMMUNIST PARTY OF INDIA (CPI)

HISTORY

Founded in 1925, the Communist Party of India was initially a part of the Communist International and became closely connected with the Communist Party of Great Britain. In the 1930s it collaborated with the Congress in the independence movement. This relationship, however, was never an easy one and broke down completely after Nazi Germany invaded the Soviet Union. Shifting their stance, the Communists advocated collaboration with the British (and the Soviets) in the "antifascist war," while the Congress launched an anti-British noncooperation movement and demanded immediate independence. Legalization of the Communist Party in 1942 gave it the opportunity to broaden its organization while the Congress leaders were immobilized in British jails.

After the war and with the coming of independence, the Communists were divided over the appropriate approach to parliamentary democracy and to the Congress government. This has been a basic issue inhibiting the unity of the Communists throughout the postindependence period.

When the Soviets in 1953 began to woo the international nonaligned movement and its most prominent leader, Nehru, the CPI opted for competitive electoral politics within the parliamentary framework. In 1957 the CPI led a coalition government in the southern state of Kerala. Congress-led street agitation forced that government from office in 1959.

In 1964 the party split, with the more moderate group under the leadership of S. A. Dange retaining the party label and a close relationship with the Soviet Union. The more militant wing, led by E. M. S. Namboodiripad, a former chief minister of Kerala, and Jyoti Basu, later to become chief minister of West Bengal, left to form the Communist Party of India (Marxist), or CPM. The basic cause of the split was a longstanding difference over how to relate to the ruling Congress. Dange, adhering to the Soviet view, argued that the Congress represented an anti-imperialist force and should be opposed only on domestic issues. Namboodiripad and Basu argued for implacable opposition to the Congress.

The CPI never regained the strength it had possessed before the split, but it did play a prominent role in national politics again in 1969 when its support for Mrs. Gandhi's faction of the Congress provided the necessary parliamentary margin to permit her to retain the prime ministership. The party supported Mrs. Gandhi until the end of the 1975–77 state of emergency. This association with emergency hurt the CPI in the 1977 general elections, and the CPI formally shifted policy and began to take a more critical line.

The relationship to Mrs. Gandhi led to yet another split in the CPI in 1981. The general secretary of the party, C. Rajeswara Rao, argued that the party's support for Mrs. Gandhi during the emergency period had been a mistake. Dange and some of his followers disagreed and left the party to form the All-India Communist Party (AICP).

Since abandoning its cooperation with the Congress (I), the CPI has opposed Congress dominance and the communalism of the BJP and has worked closely with the CPM. Still, the CPI has never fully recovered from the 1964 split and its alliance with the Congress (I). The party's electoral support has declined from 23 seats and 5 percent of the vote in 1967 to 10 seats and 1.4 percent of the vote in 2004. Unlike the CPM, the CPI became part of the United Front government in 1996–98, and its general secretary, Indrajit Gupta, was given charge of the powerful portfolio of home minister.

Like all other left parties, it is also supporting the Congress. Its historical differences with the Congress did not allow its leaders to join the Council of Ministers. Party leader A. B. Bardhan became the speaker of the lower house in 2004.

ORGANIZATION

The CPI claims to have a highly organized structure operating on the basis of democratic centralism. In fact, the state organizations have considerable autonomy, and there is a substantial amount of fragmentation and factionalism. To the extent that power is centralized, it is lodged with the general secretary.

The party has an extensive publication program that includes journals, such as *New Age,* published directly by the party; *Link,* a news magazine that generally follows a Marxist line; and books on technical as well as political subjects. In addition, the party used to distribute subsidized publications from the Soviet Union.

It has acquired control of the All-India Trade Union Congress and operates youth, peasants', and women's organizations.

POLICY

Prior to the collapse of the Soviet Union the CPI always had a close relationship with the Soviets, and Soviet attitudes toward existing Indian governments was often a function of Soviet relations with the particular government. Soviet views, however, were only one among several factors influencing CPI policy and actions.

On domestic issues, the CPI follows classic Marxist policy positions favoring secularism, rapid industrialization, nationalization of large-scale industry, land reform, and collectivized agriculture. In foreign policy, the CPI favored a pro-Soviet position on global issues and an anti-imperialist posture on regional issues.

The collapse of communism in Eastern Europe and the Soviet Union, the breakup of the USSR, and the end of the cold war have accentuated ideological confusion within the CPI and the Communist movement in India. The movement has yet to come to grips with these momentous changes. Its policy remains anti-imperialist, anti-American, and antimarket. The party has also failed to come to grips with the rise of communalist and xenophobic forces.

MEMBERSHIP AND CONSTITUENCY

The CPI electoral strategy emphasizes a broad rural constituency and the urban working class. In Kerala and Bengal, the CPI has done well among middle peasants and is the dominant Communist influence in the fragmented urban trade union movement. The CPI lost much of the traditional Communist support in West Bengal and Kerala to the CPM.

FINANCING

The CPI uses all the customary devices to raise money. In the past, it apparently raised substantial funds through the sale of subsidized Soviet publications. There were also persistent and generally accepted rumors that the CPI received substantial direct funding from the Soviet Union.

LEADERSHIP

S. A. Dange's dominant role in the party precluded the rise of other important leaders. His age—he was born in 1899—had already led to a lessening of his grip even before he left the party. The present general secretary is A. B. Bardhan.

PROSPECTS

Dange's departure offered an opportunity for the CPI to begin to forge some sort of left unity with the CPM. Although the two parties have actively cooperated with each other, complete unity remains a distant dream. The CPI continues to remain on the fringes of Indian politics, important only in intermittent coalitions in Kerala and West Bengal and its influences in some trade union circles.

COMMUNIST PARTY OF INDIA (MARXIST) (CPM)

HISTORY

The CPM split from the CPI in 1964 over issues of militancy, ideology, and personality. It favored a more militant opposition to the Congress government. It felt the Maoist notion of peasant-based revolution was more relevant to the Indian situation than the worker-based ideas of Marx and Lenin advocated by the CPI.

The CPM gained credibility among Marxist voters when the CPI sided openly with Mrs. Gandhi after 1969. The CPM position of firm opposition to her rule, especially during the emergency period in the mid-1970s, resulted in considerable electoral success among left voters, especially in the election of 1977 when the CPM was allied loosely with the Janata coalition. The CPM has been highly successful in challenging Congress (I) candidates, especially in West Bengal. In state politics, the CPM has been even more successful. It has headed the state government in West Bengal since 1977, first with Jyoti Basu as chief minister and then since 2000 with Buddhadeo Bhattacharya; it has also extended its base into Tripura, next door. After leading the Kerala government under E. M. S. Namboodiripad from 1967 to 1969, the CPM continued to be a major factor in that state.

Although the CPM is given the status of a national party by the Indian Election Commission, the party's support is limited to West Bengal, Kerala, and Tripura. In the 1998 Lok Sabha elections the CPM won 32 seats and 5.18 percent of the vote. Unlike the CPI, the CPM refused to join the United Front government in 1996–98 but agreed to give it external support. However, in the 2004 elections the CPM played a key role in helping Congress form the government. This was the first time that CPM had won 43 seats. Along with its allies, it became a key member in the present government.

ORGANIZATION

The organizational structure of the CPM is similar to that of the CPI—strongly centralized on paper but state-based in practice. In West Bengal, Jyoti Basu managed to retain a more disciplined control over his party than is usual in India. In 2000 Jyoti Basu relinquished office of chief minister of Bengal to his protégé, Buddhadeo Bhattacharya, who has tried to open the economy to private sector investment, thereby incrementally changing the economic profile of the state.

POLICY

Over the years the CPM has distanced itself from its ideological moorings, especially in its stronghold of West Bengal. Many diehard Marxists and Maoists are dismayed at the sellout. While the CPM has opposed the Structural Adjustment Program adopted by the Rao government in 1991, the party in West Bengal has publicly embraced the principles of an open economy and foreign direct investment in the state by foreign multinationals. The party, however, continues to oppose dismantling of the public sector. In foreign policy the CPM supports a strong defense, non-alignment, resistance to American imperialism and cancellation of military cooperation with the United States, and opposes attempts to impose the Nuclear Nonproliferation Treaty and the Comprehensive Test Ban Treaty on India.

MEMBERSHIP AND CONSTITUENCY

The CPM has done better than the CPI in the traditional communist strongholds of West Bengal and Kerala, but less well in Uttar Pradesh, Andhra, and Bihar. It has targeted landless laborers in rural areas and has done well in that constituency. It has had less success with organized urban workers.

FINANCING

As a participant in the government in West Bengal and Kerala, the CPM has access to traditional sources of funds in these states. In the past there have been occasional rumors of financial support from the People's Republic of China. The CPM has no central treasurer and relies heavily upon mass collection of funds by local party units and trade unions affiliated with the party. All party MLAs and MPs are expected to contribute part of their income, and all card-carrying members must contribute, including police and bureaucrats.

LEADERSHIP

With the death of E. M. S. Namboodiripad in March 1998, Jyoti Basu (born 1914) became the last of the old guard. Both were veterans of left-wing and union politics. Basu, trained in law, came from a prominent elite Bengali family. Namboodiripad was widely regarded as the most intellectually sophisticated of contemporary politicians. Although they had dominated the party since the 1964 split from the CPI, their prominence attracted a highly competent younger group of leaders. As of 2005 the general secretary was Prakash Karat.

PROSPECTS

Since 1980 the CPM has come full circle. Founded as a revolutionary alternative to CPI reformism, the CPM itself has become increasingly reformist. The most radical wing of the party left in 1969 to form the Communist Party of India, Marxist-Leninist. The party has provided land reforms and local government reform to its rural constituency, but in the process it has become increasingly divorced from attempts to revolutionize the masses. The dilution of its ideological position and nearly 30 years of power in West Bengal have had a negative effect on the commitment of its cadre, have resulted in the stagnation of its electoral support, and have obscured the party's transformational agenda. In short, the left in India has become increasingly confused by international developments and has been unable to cope with the rising importance of cultural nationalism, the rise of communalism, and the growing appeal of the BJP.

INDIAN NATIONAL CONGRESS (I)

HISTORY

The Indian National Congress was founded in 1885 as an organization devoted to expanding opportunities for Indians in the colonial regime and incorporating Indian elite opinion in policy making.

The first two decades of the 20th century brought a deep struggle over philosophy and direction between the early great Congress leaders, B. G. Tilak (1856–1920) and G. K. Gokhale (1866–1915). Gokhale was highly educated in the Western tradition, moderate, elitist, and secular. Tilak was a prominent scholar of the Hindu scriptures, more radical, and wanted to mold the Congress in the Hindu tradition, broaden its mass appeal, and transform it into a more militant organization. Tilak's influence gave the Congress an increasingly Hindu character in spite of continuing professions of secularism.

Mohandas K. Gandhi became the dominant Congress leader in 1920 and remained so until his assassination in 1948. Gandhi was convinced that Congress had to retain its secular character in order to succeed as an umbrella organization. But he also realized that the movement depended on the mobilization of mass participation. Hindu symbolism and philosophical principles provided ready tools for mobilizing the masses. Throughout his years at the helm, Gandhi struggled to balance the commitment to secularism with the necessity of mobilizing the Hindu masses. In the end, however, the predominantly Hindu character of the Congress so frightened significant Muslim elites that independence could be won only at the price of partition.

Gandhi's leadership and philosophy left a profound mark on the postindependence party. He came to be revered as a saint by the Hindu masses. He was universally called Mahatma, "great soul." His philosophy and strategy of nonviolence (*ahimsa*) and noncooperation based on soul force (*satyagraha*) and his commitment to secularism, mass participation, village self-sufficiency, and reform of the most discriminatory features of the Hindu caste system continue to be touchstones for the modern Congress Party.

The two principal lieutenants of Gandhi, Jawaharlal Nehru and Sardar Vallabhbhai Patel, presided over the transformation of the national movement into a modern political party. As expected, the Congress formed the first independent government under Nehru. Although Congress never won a majority of the popular vote, the electoral system and the fragmentation of the opposition parties ensured that Congress usually would have a majority in the Lok Sabha. Congress used to receive between 41 percent and 49 percent of the vote in each national election, but in the 1990s and 2000s that number has slipped; in 1996 and 1998 it polled only 28.8 percent and 25.9 percent, respectively, and in 2004 it polled 26.53 percent. At the state level, Congress has been less dominant. It often lost control of state governments to regional parties or to coalitions even before it began to lose power at the center from 1989 onward. Since then, their vote share has remained the same in states like Andhra Pradesh, Madhya Pradesh, and Rajasthan, and in many other states the party does not enjoy the dominant status it used to.

Despite frequent splits and defections, leadership of the party has shown remarkable continuity. Nehru was the dominant leader from 1948 until his death in 1964. Lal Bahadur Shastri was prime minister from 1964 until his sudden death in 1966, but much real power in the party rested with a group of party bosses known as the "Syndicate." The Syndicate played a prominent role in the selection of Nehru's daughter, Mrs. Indira Gandhi (no relation to Mahatma Gandhi), as Shastri's successor and struggled with her for power until a major split occurred in 1969 between pro-Syndicate and pro-Gandhi factions. Her victory was confirmed by the electorate in 1971, and she remained the dominant figure in the party until her death in 1984. In fact, her role was so strong that the party is now officially labeled Congress (I) for Indira.

The combination of a fragmented opposition and a massive wave of sympathy votes following the assassination of Indira Gandhi on October 31, 1984, enabled the Congress Party under the leadership of Rajiv Gandhi to win a massive victory in the 1984 elections. The new prime minister's lackluster performance, his inability to reshape the Congress, and a series of corruption scandals weakened Rajiv, and the Congress went down to defeat in the 1989 general elections.

The elections, however, produced a hung Parliament as coalition and alliance politics replaced the era of Congress dominance. Like its predecessor, the Janata Party, the new Janata Dal–led National Front government proved to be weak and unstable and collapsed. As a result, India was forced to go to the polls once more in 1991 only to have tragedy strike again. In the midst of the campaign, Rajiv Gandhi, like his mother, was struck down by an assassin. As was the case in 1984, the assassination produced a last-minute wave of sympathy votes in favor of the Congress. Although the party fell just short of a majority, it was able to form a government and returned to power under the leadership of P. V. Narashimha Rao, who was able to survive a full five-year term.

The Rao government came to power in the midst of the most serious economic crisis in postindependence Indian history. Rao's success in handling the economic crisis, however, was undermined by his inept handling of the crisis in Ayodhya when Hindu militants succeeded in destroying the Babri Masjid and communal riots broke out in many parts of India. His leadership was further undermined by charges of corruption.

The Congress Party entered the 1996 elections for the first time without a member of the Nehru-Gandhi dynasty at the helm and plagued by corruption scandals, factionalism, and major defections. The result was the worst defeat of the Congress Party in its history. The party won only 140 seats in the Lok Sabha and 28.8 percent of the vote. Rao was forced to step down as leader of the Congress Party and was replaced by Sitaram Kesri, the longtime party treasurer.

In the 1998 Lok Sabha elections, Sonia Gandhi, Rajiv's Italian-born widow, finally decided to officially enter the political arena and campaigned actively on behalf of the Congress. Despite her active role in the campaign, however, the Congress was able to win only 141 seats and 25.88 percent of the vote. The main impact of the Sonia factor on the elections was to stem the tide of defections from the Congress, boost party morale, and halt the further erosion of support for the party. Following the elections, control of the party was again placed in the hands of a member of the Nehru-Gandhi dynasty when Sonia was elected president of the party to replace Sitaram Kesri.

Before the 2004 elections the Congress broke from tradition by establishing pre-electoral alliances with state-level parties. This tactical move brought the Congress back to power, but with the acceptance of a changed political scenario where its predominance in the party system has waned.

ORGANIZATION

Congress (I) is a highly structured party. Basic organizational units exist at the district, the state, and the national levels. The annual conference of the party is composed of the members of the Congress committees at the state and district levels. The conference elects the Congress president to a two-year term and chooses the All-India Congress committee (AICC). Real power, however, is in the Congress working committee (CWC), often called the Congress high command, which has 20 members, 13 of whom are appointed by the Congress president.

The Congress president is usually selected by the prime minister if the Congress is in power. Sometimes, in order to ensure control of the party organization, the prime minister may assume the Congress presidency, as Nehru did in the early 1950s and, later, Indira and Rajiv Gandhi and P. V. Narasimha Rao. At other times, the prime minister will ensure that a trusted loyalist holds the position. The two most recent

Congress presidents, Sitaram Kesri and Sonia Gandhi, have been elected by the party membership. The Congress (I) Party has an elaborate structure on paper but a weak organizational base. Despite the party's constitution, internal party elections were not held from 1972 until the early 1990s and most committees were ad hoc or nonexistent. Lacking a popular state leadership, the party in most states was forced to rely on the national party to resolve contentious policy and personnel issues. The result was that issues are often not addressed by the center until the problem has reached crisis proportions. Despite the return of some degree of internal party democracy, the Congress organization remains weak, factionalized, and semiparalyzed. The unexpected death of second-level leaders such as Madhav Rao Scindhia and Rajesh Pilot has exacerbated the situation. Horizontally, the party is divided into the old guard, such as Arjun Singh, Natwar Singh, Pranab Mukherjee, and very young and inexperienced leaders, such as the sons of the deceased leaders mentioned above. Vertically, the party is differentiated by those who are aligned with Sonia Gandhi and have little organizational popularity, such as Ambika Soni and Margaret Alva, and the truncated minority group of middle-level leaders, such as Ghulam Nabi Azad, who maintain the party's electoral base.

The daily newspaper the *National Herald* was founded by Nehru and is closely tied to the Congress (I). After the CPI gained control of the All-India Trade Union Congress, the Congress Party organized the Indian National Trade Union Congress (INTUC). Congress (I) also has women's and youth organizations.

POLICY

Until Rao's economic reforms of 1991, Congress (I) had espoused moderate socialism and a planned mixed economy aimed at rapid economic growth, self-sufficiency, and industrialization. It now supports liberalization, deregulation, privatization, and opening up of the Indian economy to foreign direct investment and trade. It also supports a secular state with egalitarian values and special programs for victims of discrimination. Land reform and national integration planks have been consistently incorporated into its party manifestos.

Under Nehru, the Congress developed a foreign policy based on nonalignment, that is, active participation in international affairs while refraining from alliance with either superpower bloc. Despite the end of the cold war nonalignment continues as the declared policy of the party. At the height of the cold war, American support for Pakistan and the development of warmer relations between the United States and China encouraged a closer relationship between India and the Soviet Union and the USSR became India's chief arms supplier. Although the Congress government signed a long-term Treaty of Friendship with the Soviet Union in 1971 (in the midst of the Bangladesh crisis), the Congress (I) still adhered to a fiercely nationalistic form of nonalignment. Congress (I) favors a strong defense posture with as much self-sufficiency as possible. The Congress favors a nuclear weapons–free world and complete disarmament and refuses to sign the Nuclear Nonproliferation Treaty or the Comprehensive Test Ban Treaty.

Congress (I) has professed a desire for friendly relations with India's neighbors in South Asia but has expected them to acknowledge and accept India's leading role in the area. The party attaches special importance to relations with Pakistan. While desiring more normal relations, Congress (I) clearly expects Pakistan to recognize India's pre-eminent role in the subcontinent and opposes international military assistance of sophisticated weapons to Pakistan.

MEMBERSHIP AND CONSTITUENCY

In the past, Congress has claimed as many as 10 million primary members and over 300,000 active members, although most observers agree such claims probably overstate the facts. Both membership categories contribute to party finances by payment of dues, although the amount for primary members is nominal. Active members may be assigned specific party duties and are eligible to hold party office.

The success of Congress had rested on the maintenance of the traditional if incongruous coalition of Muslims, Scheduled Castes, Brahmins, industrialists, landless laborers, and well-to-do landowners. The loss in 1977 was apparently the result of the defection of large numbers of Muslim and Scheduled Caste voters, especially in North India. Minority groups of all sorts, especially religious minorities, have joined the Congress coalition, reflecting the widespread perception that the opposition parties' commitment to secularism is suspect. The Congress electoral defeats of 1996 and 1998 reflected the gradual loss of support among its old constituents to various opposition parties. Some evidence indicates that the Congress is also having difficulty recruiting new support among young voters, who do not remember the Congress role in the independence movement.

Geographically, Congress traditionally has enjoyed strong support in the South except in Tamil Nadu. However, its solid base of support in the Hindi belt of North India has been sharply eroded. Congress also has had to fight more competitively in the eastern and western regions of the country.

FINANCING

As the ruling party for most of India's independent history, the Congress has had a decided advantage over other parties in raising funds. Many observers have asserted that Congress fund-raising efforts have sometimes been rather like extortion. In the early days of independent India, Congress enjoyed a near monopoly over political contributions from businesses and still receives substantial support from such sources. Party dues also provide significant funds, and the party is also in a position to command resources from abroad.

LEADERSHIP

The temporary eclipse of the Nehru-Gandhi dynasty saw the emergence of weak, colorless, elderly, old-style Congress leaders. Following the assassination of Rajiv Gandhi the Congress turned to P. V. Narasimha Rao, a loyal supporter of the dynasty. Despite diabetes and heart bypass surgery, Rao at age 69 (born 1921) was the most senior member of the party leadership and was a compromise candidate. The defeat of the Congress in the April–May 1996 elections and charges of corruption forced the resignation of Rao and the selection of Sitaram Kesri, an 80-year-old compromise candidate.

The persistence of the Nehru-Gandhi legacy is demonstrated by Sonia Gandhi. Following her husband's death, Sonia continued to play a significant behind-the-scenes role in Congress Party affairs, and in mid-1997 she officially became a member of the Congress Party. She actively campaigned for the Congress in the 1998 Lok Sabha elections, and, following the elections, the 52-year-old Sonia was elected president of the Congress.

Given its long history and extensive governmental experience at the national and state levels, the Congress Party has a large pool of talent and potential leaders. Many of the most prominent, however, have been tainted by charges of corruption. Still, given the Indian contexts, many of these leaders may be rehabilitated. Indeed, in the 2004 Union Council of Ministers, Manmohan Singh had to include senior leaders such as Pranab Mukherjee, Shivraj Patil, Arjun Singh, Natwar Singh, and Priyaranjan Dasmunshi, among others, despite the party's pre-electoral claim that it was a younger, rejuvenated party. The problem that Sonia Gandhi faces as the party leader is that she is left with very old and very young leaders. With the exception of Manmohan Singh, she has very few peers who have served in office and thereby have some professional experience to lead the country. The real problem facing Gandhi and the 120-year-old party is the need to develop a new generation of local and state leaders capable of coping with the massive challenges India faces as it enters the 21st century.

PROSPECTS

The decline of the Congress has been the most significant political development in the past 50-plus years of Indian democracy. The party has seen its old coalition of Brahmins, Scheduled Castes and Tribes, Muslims, and other minorities gradually erode as former Congress supporters have drifted away to the BJP, caste, and regional parties. The party's assumption that a return of the Nehru-Gandhi dynasty will result in its return to power may well be wishful thinking. Neither Indira nor Rajiv was able to build or maintain a sustainable party base, and the Italian-born Sonia Gandhi also lacks the charisma, experience, and skills needed. The party needs new leadership and a new program, and it must rebuild its social base for it to return to power as a majority party. In short, while the Congress will continue to play an important role in Indian politics, the days of Congress dominance have passed.

PEOPLE'S PARTY

(Janata Dal; JD)

The Janata Dal was formed in 1988 when a group of centrist parties and factions combined to form a new party led by V. P. Singh, a former minister in Rajiv's government. The Janata Dal then joined with a group of Congress dissidents and the regionally based parties to form the National Front to contest the 1989 general elections. The National Front won 144 seats in the elections, of which the Janata Dal won 141.

Although the 1989 elections produced a hung Parliament, the results were seen as a mandate for V. P. Singh to become prime minister. The experience of Singh's coalition, however, turned out to be a replay of the Janata experience of 1977 to 1979. Despite his enormous popular support, Singh's leadership of the Janata Dal was challenged by Chandra Shekhar and Devi Lal, two of his chief competitors. In August 1990, in an effort to head off the challenge and strengthen his support, Singh suddenly announced that he had decided to implement the party's electoral pledge to carry out the recommendations of the Mandal Commission and reserve 27 percent of all central government jobs for members of the backward castes,

Devi Lal's chief constituency in the Punjab. The announcement, however, transcended the issue of factional politics within the Janata Dal and touched off a firestorm of protest and criticism throughout India. The action also alienated the BJP, one of the key backers of the National Front, and the party withdrew its support. On November 9, 1990, Singh lost a vote of confidence in the Indian Parliament and was forced to resign. He was replaced by Chandra Shekhar, who split the JD and was elected prime minister with the support of the Congress Party. Chandra Shekhar's party, the Janata Dal (S), was so dependent on Congress support that it proved to be short-lived and Indians were forced to go to the polls. Chandra Shekhar's Janata Dal (S) was later converted into the Samajwadi Janata Party (SJP).

As India embarked upon the 1991 elections, a hung Parliament appeared to be inevitable. The assassination of Rajiv Gandhi, however, produced a last-minute wave of sympathy votes for the Congress and its new leader, P. V. Narasimha Rao. Rao was able to form a government that lasted the full five-year term of Parliament.

The 1996 elections ended in another hung Parliament, and the Congress Party suffered its worst defeat since 1947. Although the largest bloc of seats was won by the BJP, the party was not able to command a majority in Parliament. In an effort to isolate the BJP, a broad alliance of 13 national and regional parties hammered together a United Front minority government that commanded the support of 180 Lok Sabha members. The United Front was supported by the Congress Party, which refused to join the new government. The Janata Dal was the largest constituent in the United Front with 45 seats. The other major components of the United Front were the CPI, the CPM, and 10 regional parties. The United Front elected H. D. Deve Gowda, a Janata Dal leader and former chief minister of Karnataka, as prime minister. The new government clearly reflected the anti–upper-caste politics of the post-Mandal era. The coalition, however, proved to be extremely unstable, and Gowda was forced to resign after less than a year in office. The United Front replaced Gowda with I. K. Gujral, a weak compromise candidate whose government survived until December 1997. Riven by splits and internal factionalism, the Janata Dal suffered a devastating defeat in the 1998 elections, winning only six seats and 9 percent of the vote.

Since then, the Janata Dal has lost its popularity as a national party because it has been broken up into smaller factions led by powerful leaders. With V. P.

Singh being infirm and I. K. Gujral sequestered, the remaining leaders have, with the exception of George Fernandes, been relegated to representing regional aspirations. However, taking on a regional character has increased their influence at the national level since the prospects for power depend on the nature and size of a coalition.

The organization of the Janata Dal at the regional and local level is rudimentary and ad hoc, consisting of little more than the personal followers and clients of its regional leaders and members of Parliament.

The Janata Dal advocates the eradication of poverty, unemployment, and wide disparities in wealth, the protection of minorities, and a policy of nonalignment. As leader of the United Front, it was pledged to implement a common minimum program that called for the continuation of the policy of economic liberation begun by Rao in 1991, social justice, and a foreign policy that would stress better relations with India's neighbors.

The Janata Dal, which has been an important force in the states of Bihar, Karnataka, and Orissa, has been almost wiped out in these states. It has lost its Backward Castes (OBCs) and minority vote base to the BJP and breakaway parties that had left the Janata Dal.

The Janata Dal has no central collection system, and each factional leader depends upon his own base of financial support from business houses and industrial lobbies in their respective states. Very little is collected from its membership, and there have been no membership dues for years.

The spiritual leader of the Janata Dal is V. P. Singh, who is no longer active but is consulted during times of crisis. The most important leaders are all regionally based. In Orissa the Janata Dal has been split into two factions: one that supports Naveen Patnaik, who is the son of legendary Biju Patnaik, and another that is a loyalist; both claim to be the true inheritors of Biju's legacy. In Karnataka the Janata Dal has been riven by factions between S. R. Bommai, Deve Gowda, and supporters of late Ramakrishna Hegde. In Bihar the Dal has been divided between Laloo Yadav and his detractors in the Janata Dal (U) such as Sharad Yadav, Ram Vilas Paswan, and Nitish Kumar.

Throughout its brief history, the Janata Dal has been plagued by an unending capacity for schism. The Janata Dal (S) left in late 1990, the Samata Party split in 1994, Laloo Prasad Yadav broke away in July 1997 to form the Rashtriya Janata Dal, and Ramakrishna Hedge created the Lok Shakti Party to fight the 1998 elections. Factionalism has all but destroyed the party as a national political force.

Minor Political Parties

ASOM GANA PARISHAD (AGP)

The Asom Gana Parishad, or Assam People's Council, was born in 1985 out of the student agitations in Assam against the influx of Bangladeshi refugees in the 1980s. Following the signing by Rajiv Gandhi of the Assam Accord that attempted to settle the refugee issue, the party won a majority of the seats in the 1985 state assembly elections. The failure of the Rajiv government to implement the accord, however, led to a return of insurgency and president's rule. The AGP was defeated by the Congress in the 1991 Lok Sabha elections, and the party split. In the 1996 elections, however, a reunited AGP-led alliance defeated the Congress and was returned to power in the state. The party also won five seats in the Lok Sabha and became part of the United Front government in June 1996. The AGP was unable to win any seats in the 1998 Lok Sabha elections. In the 2004 elections it won two seats.

BHUJAN SAMAJ PARTY (BSP)

The Bhujan Samaj Party (literally, "party of society's majority") was founded in 1984 to speak on behalf of India's untouchables or Dalits (oppressed). The party began making its presence felt in the late 1980s but scored its first really big success in the 1993 state elections in Uttar Pradesh when it won 67 seats and 12 percent of the vote and formed a coalition government with the Samajwadi Party. This Dalit and Backward Caste alliance, however, disintegrated in June 1995, and the BSP formed its own government with the support of various opposition parties. The BSP government, however, lasted only a few months and the state was placed under presidential rule.

The BPS won 10 seats in the Lok Sabha elections of April–May 1996 and 67 seats in the October 1996 state assembly elections. Since the state assembly elections resulted in a hung Parliament, Uttar Pradesh was again placed under president's rule. Finally in March 1997 the BSP and the BJP agreed on a unique coalition arrangement whereby the cabinet would be based on equal representation of each party and the chief ministership would rotate between the two parties. Leadership for the first six months was to be provided by Mayawati, the 42-year-old leader of the BSP in Uttar Pradesh and close confidant of Kanshi Ram, the founder of the party. The BSP won five seats and 4.68 percent of the vote in the 1998 Lok Sabha elections. In addition to Uttar Pradesh, the BSP also has some support in the Punjab and Madhya Pradesh and sees itself as an All-India voice of the Dalits.

The strength of the BSP is in its stable vote base among the other backward castes. Typically, it has restricted itself to securing all the votes at the social margin, consistently since its inception. It limited itself to few states in the North. But in the 2004 elections it contested 435 seats, which is higher than the seats contested by even the Congress or the BJP. While it won 19 seats with 5.33 percent of the votes, it also reflects the confidence that the party has in its social base in the country. Further, it has not aligned with either the BJP or the Congress-led coalition. With 19 seats it has a significant role to play in tilting the balance in favor of any coalition, if the established alliances are in trouble.

COMMUNIST PARTY OF INDIA
(Marxist-Leninist; CPML)

In 1967 an apparently spontaneous peasant revolt broke out in the Naxalbari District of West Bengal. The West Bengal state government, dominated by Communists, adopted a policy of crushing the rebellion. Some leftists—believing the government's actions contrary to the dictates of Marx, Lenin, and Mao—joined forces with the Naxalbari peasants. Dubbed Naxalites, they vowed violent actions against authority, especially in the rural areas of Bengal and Andhra. The central and state governments made determined efforts to stamp out this movement and incarcerate its leaders.

In 1969 several factions of Naxalites came together to form the CPML. The party was banned during the emergency from 1975 to 1977, and factional disputes raged for years over the issue of violent revolutions versus an electoral strategy. The party has now turned to a parliamentary strategy but has not been especially successful at the polls. It has failed to gain any representation at the state or national levels.

DRAVIDA MUNNETRA KAZHAGAM (DMK)–DRAVIDIAN PROGRESSIVE FEDERATION & ALL-INDIA ANNA-DRAVIDA MUNNETRA KAZHAGAM (AIADMK)

The heir to the anti-Brahmin Dravidian nationalist movement in South India, the DMK was founded in 1949 by C. N. Annadurai to press the claims of Tamil cultural and linguistic autonomy. Its platform of radical populist economics and cultural nationalism

bordered on secessionism but served to gain the party control of the Tamil Nadu state government in 1967.

Rivalries that were primarily personal in nature but related to the party's relations with Mrs. Gandhi's Congress followed Annadurai's death in 1969 and led to a split in 1972. Two factions emerged. The old title of DMK was retained by the group led by M. Karunanidhi. A new group, under the leadership of film idol M. G. Ramachandran (universally known as M.G.R.), claimed to be the true followers of Anadurai and called itself the All-India Anna DMK (AIADMK). These two parties have dominated the politics of Tamil Nadu for the last 15 years, with the DMK controlling the state government until 1976 when presidential rule was imposed. The AIADMK ruled Tamil Nadu from 1977 to 1989.

Following the death of M.G.R. in 1987, the party split into two factions, one led by his wife, Janaki, and the other by his protégé costar Jayalalitha, and lost the 1989 elections to the DMK. The party united again under Jayalalitha and was swept back into power in 1991. The AIADMK began to run into trouble again when Jayalalitha was accused of corruption and using state funds to finance her foster son's wedding in September 1995. The party was defeated in the April–May 1996 elections and replaced by a DMK government led by M. Karunanidhi. At the national level the DMK joined the United Front government in June 1996 and Murasoli Maran of the DMK was allotted the industry portfolio. In the 1998 Lok Sabha elections, the AIADMK, in alliance with the BJP, made a remarkable comeback and won 18 seats. The party became a major force in the BJP government and was given four seats on the Council of Ministers. Both parties have learned to play a strategic game with the BJP and the Congress, striking alliances and withdrawing them in apparently whimsical ways, but primarily based on local electoral prospects. AIADMK withdrew support to the BJP government after 1998, then the DMK, which was earlier a Congress ally, began to support the BJP until 2003, and finally both parties reverted to their 1998 positions by switching loyalties again for the 2004 elections.

Responsibilities of office have muted whatever secessionist zeal lingered in these parties, though they both continue to champion states' rights and resist the spread of Hindi cultural and linguistic preeminence.

SAMAJWADI PARTY (SP)

The Samajwadi (Socialist) Party was formed by a group of Janata Dal dissidents led by Mulayam Singh Yadav, the leader of the Yadav community in Uttar Pradesh, in 1992. The party formed a coalition government with the Bahujan Samaj Party in Uttar Pradesh in 1993 that lasted until June 1995. In the 1996 general elections the SP won 17 seats and became a key component of the United Front government in which Mulayam Singh Yadav served as defense minister. The party won 110 seats in the assembly elections in Uttar Pradesh in October 1997. The SP represents the Backward Castes. In the 1998 Lok Sabha elections, the SP won 20 seats and 4.95 percent of the vote.

Even though the party tally jumped to 35 seats in the 2004 elections, its offer to join the government coalition in return for representation in the Union Council of Ministers was rebuffed by the Congress-led government.

SAMATA PARTY (SP)

The Samata (Equality) Party was founded in early 1994 following a split with the Janata Dal. The party is led by George Fernandes, a veteran socialist and trade unionist, and Nitish Kumar. The party is based largely in Bihar and in 1996 won eight seats in the Lok Sabha, six from Bihar and one each in Uttar Pradesh and Orissa. The party had an electoral alliance with the BJP in Bihar and is considered a BJP ally at the national level. In the 1998 Lok Sabha elections, the party won 12 seats and Fernandes became the defense minister in the BJP government.

Their most influential leader, George Fernandes, organized a merger with the Janata Dal (U) in 2003, and he is now the president of the latter. The Samata Party now consists of members who did not want to merge with Janata Dal (U). They have been allowed to retain the party name but have a different symbol.

SHIROMANI AKALI DAL (SAD)

The Shiromani Akali Dal is a Sikh communal party confined to the Punjab. Its roots go back to early Sikh nationalism. It has supported greater autonomy for Sikhs. Some even support the notion of Khalistan, an independent homeland. The extremists became increasingly assertive in early 1984, and Indira Gandhi ordered the army to occupy Amritsar's Golden Temple, the major Sikh temple that had become a center for the militant campaign. The attack, resulting in several hundred deaths, angered many Sikhs, as did the bloody anti-Sikh riots that broke out in the wake of Mrs. Gandhi's assassination by two of her Sikh bodyguards.

A moderate Sikh faction of the Akali Dal worked out an agreement with Rajiv Gandhi in July that envisaged returning the state to civil rule. Elections in September 1985 witnessed a victory for the Akali Dal Party, the first time it had won a majority on its own. The militant faction of the Sikhs renounced the agreement, and in early 1986 extremists again seized the Golden Temple and turned it into a center of the Khalistan campaign.

At the height of Sikh militancy the Akali Dal split into a half dozen factions. In the April–May 1996 Lok Sabha elections the party faction led by two-time Chief Minister Prakash Singh Badal won eight seats, and in the February 1997 assembly elections the party won 75 seats in alliance with the BJP. In both the 1998 and 2004 Lok Sabha elections the party again won eight seats. Stridently anti-Congress, the Akali Dal has become an ally of the BJP and demands a broad-based confederate structure in contrast to militant Sikhs who demand a separate Sikh nation.

SHIV SENA

Founded in the 1960s as an anti-immigrant movement centered in Bombay, the Shiv Sena fostered the building of Maratha pride and demanded that Maharashtrans be given preferences in jobs in the city. The movement expanded its influence in several urban areas outside Bombay in the 1970s and 1980s and increasingly took on a more antiminority, Hindu nationalist color. The Shiv Sena became more prominent in the 1990s as a result of its strong support of the Ayodhya issue and its alliance with the BJP at the state and federal levels. The party won 15 seats in the 1996 Lok Sabha elections and supported the short-lived BJP government. In 1998 the party won only six Lok Sabha seats, but in 2004 it won 12 seats. The Shiv Sena also governs the state of Maharashtra in alliance with the BJP. The party combines religious militancy with regionalism and is led by its founder, Bal Thackeray, a onetime cartoonist.

TAMIL MAANILA CONGRESS (TMC)

The Tamil Maanila Congress was formed by a group of Congress dissidents in Tamil Nadu who were expelled from the Congress in April 1996. The dissidents opposed P. V. Narasimha Rao's alliance with the AIADMK in the state. The party won 20 of the 39 Tamil Nadu seats in the 1996 Lok Sabha elections and 39 seats in the state assembly in alliance with the DMK. In 1998, however, the party won only three Lok Sabha seats. The party is led by G. K. Moopanar, former general secretary of the Congress, and P. Chidambaram, a former Congress minister. Chidambaram was the finance minister in the United Front government, and the party held four other seats on the Council of Ministers.

Chidambaram parted ways from Moopanar in 1998 when the latter aligned with the AIADMK for the Tamil Nadu assembly elections, forcing the former to start the TMC Democratic Front. Moopanar died in 2001, and his son took over the reins, only to eventually merge with the Congress by 2002. Eventually Chidambaram also dissolved his party and joined the Congress in 2004. He is the finance minister in Manmohan Singh's cabinet.

TELEGU DESAM PARTY (TDP)

During the early 1980s New Delhi intervened repeatedly to establish an effective government in Andhra Pradesh, a state ruled by a faction-ridden Congress (I) Party. A succession of chief ministers imposed by the central government aroused the ire of many voters in the state who were disgusted with the pervasive corruption of Congress (I) politicians and with national officials seeming lack of concern for an effective government in the state. On March 21, 1982, the leading matinee idol, N. T. Rama Rao, announced his intention to establish a new party, the Telegu Desam, to restore a clean government that would serve the interests of the common people. In January 1983 state assembly elections were held and the new Telegu Desam won 185 of 261 seats. The Desam resisted the pro–Rajiv Gandhi electoral tide in the 1984 general elections and 1985 assembly vote by winning a large majority of the seats.

N. T. Rama Rao developed a populist program including a number of social welfare schemes such as providing free lunches to all schoolchildren. On the national level, N. T. Rama Rao was a major figure in the unsuccessful move to unify the opposition prior to the general elections in the 1980s.

Andhra switched over to the Congress in 1989 and then back again to Rao in 1994. A rift developed within the family, however, when Lakshmi Parvathi, Rao's biographer, whom he married in August 1993, began playing an active role in party offices. The result was a revolt by Chandrababu Naidu, Rao's son-in-law, who toppled him in August 1995. On Rao's death in January 1996, the leadership of his faction was taken over by his wife. In the 1996 election, however, the TDP-Naidu faction won 16 Lok Sabha seats and the Parvathi faction none. Naidu became chief minister and one of the key state leaders responsible for creating the United Front government.

In the 1998 Lok Sabha elections the party won 12 seats. Following the elections, the TDP resigned from the United Front and provided the 12 critical votes that enabled the BJP to win its vote of confidence in March 1998. As a reward for its support of the BJP government, a member of the party was elected speaker of the Lok Sabha. In 2004 the party won five seats.

MUSLIM LEAGUE

The remnants of the major Muslim political organization of preindependence days, most of whose leaders went to Pakistan, the Muslim League of today is a small party devoted to the welfare of Muslims in Kerala. It occasionally has participated in coalition governments at the state level. The party won two seats in the 1998 Lok Sabha elections and one seat in the 2004 elections.

NATIONAL CONFERENCE

The National Conference is the most popular party in Jammu and Kashmir and has been a tool for giving Kashmiri Muslims a special role in their government in a state that Pakistan claims as its territory. The leading figure of the National Conference during the troubled postindependence period was Sheikh Mohammed Abdullah, who served as the state's chief executive until his arrest in 1953. After signing an agreement in 1975 accepting the state's constitutional relationship with India, Abdullah returned as chief minister and retained that post until his death in September 1982. His son, Dr. Farooq Abdullah, was his father's hand-picked successor. Prime Minister Indira Gandhi is believed to have worked to split the National Conference in mid-1984, which brought G. M. Shah, Abdullah's bitter rival, to power. However, Shah's government was unpopular and ineffectual. Following widespread communal riots in early 1986, the prime minister imposed governor's rule.

Although the National Conference was again elected to power in 1987, the government was dismissed in 1990 amid mounting unrest. Despite several efforts, no elections could be held due to an increasingly bloody insurgency by Muslim separatists. The success of the relatively peaceful parliamentary elections in May 1996 led to a decision to hold full-scale state assembly elections in September 1997. Amidst widespread allegations of voter coercion, the National Conference led by Farooq Abdullah won a massive two-thirds majority, enabling the national government to restore local government in Kashmir for the first time since 1990. In the 1998 Lok Sabha elections the party won two seats.

In the 2002 assembly elections the National Conference summarily lost to the People's Democratic Party, led by the ex–Janata Dal leader Mufti Mohammed Sayyed and his daughter Mehbooba Mufti, and formed the government with Congress's support. Thereafter, Mehbooba Mufti and Omar Abdullah, who took charge of the National Conference from his father, Farooq Abdullah, have emerged as the political leaders of the region. The National Conference retained its seats in the 2004 elections.

Other Political Forces

ORGANIZED LABOR

Due to the character of social, economic, and political change, organized labor in India has declined as a political force. Employment in the organized sector has decreased from 9.7 percent in 1971 to 9 percent in 1991. This decline has been accompanied by an increasing fragmentation of the working class and deunionization. Of the 27 million Indians employed in the organized sector in 1991, only 6 to 7 million belonged to trade unions. This small group of unionized workers, moreover, is represented by some 50,000 trade unions organized into 12 highly politicized central federations. The top five labor federations and their political affiliations are the Bharatiya Mazdur Sangh—BJP; the Indian National Trade Union Congress—Congress (I); the Centre of Indian Trade Unions—CPM; the Hind Mazdoor Sabha—originally socialist, now Janata Dal; and the All-India Trade Union Congress—CPI. While fragmentation has long plagued the Indian trade union movement, the problem has become compounded by the development of sectarianism and criminalization. The only significant effort to organize the unorganized sector in India is being made by nongovernmental organizations (NGOs).

STUDENTS

The largest student organization is the All-India Students Organization (Akhil Bharatiya Vidyarthi Parishad; ABVP), which is affiliated with the RSS and dominates many of the campuses of North India. It provided an important source of campaign workers for the Jana Sangh and the Janata Party and now provides valuable assistance to the Bharatiya Janata Party. The Congress (I), through the Youth Congress, and the Marxists also have been able to attract periodic activity on their behalf from groups of students.

BUSINESS

The Indian business community is the best-organized sector of Indian civil society, and its influence has increased significantly since the beginning of economic liberalization of the Indian economy in 1991. Due to the internal divisions of the business community based on caste, region, and the competition between foreign and indigenous capital, India has three major apex associations that represent business. The largest and most broadly based apex association representing indigenous business is the Federation of Indian Chambers of Commerce and Industry. The Associated Chambers of Commerce and Industry is the oldest, and, although it initially represented foreign capital, it now represents indigenous business groups as well. The newest, richest, and most influential apex association is the Confederation of Indian Industry. Since 1991 these associations have increasingly been consulted by government on major issues involving economic policy. The business-government relationship, however, still remains strained, and the Indian equivalent of Japan Inc. remains a distant dream.

FARMERS AND PEASANTS

Following the green revolution of the 1960s, Indian farmers began to organize movements under a variety of nonparty banners to fight for rural interests against a perceived urban, industrial bias. These new farmers' movements were organized by cultivating landowners producing commercial crops in irrigated areas located largely in northern and western India. Farmers' movements began to play a major role in pressing their demands on government in the 1980s but declined in the 1990s and 2000s as they attempted to play a more direct political role. The vast majority of the peasantry, however, especially landless labor, remains unorganized, and attempts by political parties to develop peasant movements have had limited success. Although each major party has a peasant organization, these organizations have had much less influence on policy than the more articulate and organized farmers' movements. The major farmers' movements in India are the Bharatiya Kisan Union (BKU) Punjab, Bharatiya Kisan Union (BKU) Uttar Pradesh, Bharatiya Kisan Sangh Gujarat, Shetkari Sanghatana Maharashtra, Karnataka State Farmers' Association (Karnataka Rajya Ryota Sangha or KRRS) Karnataka, and Tamil Nadu Agriculturalists' Association (Tamilaga Vyavasavavigal Sangham or TVS) Tamil Nadu.

NONGOVERNMENTAL ORGANIZATIONS

One of the most significant recent developments in India has been the rise of the NGO sector. NGOs began to mushroom in India in the late 1970s as new issues and new forces began to emerge outside the framework of formal politics and government in an attempt to develop new relations with the rural and urban poor. It is estimated that India has some 100,000 NGOs, of which 20,000 are active. Of these some 14,000 are foreign-funded. NGOs have become active in welfare, relief, charity, development, health, education, and local planning. More recently they have become champions of women's rights, civil liberties, ecology, bonded labor, child labor, and alternative development strategies. Though they are far from being characterized as India's fifth estate, they have become an important force. The 1990s, however, saw a rising tide of criticism of the NGO sector for lack of coordination, proliferation, politicization, nepotism, and lack of accountability.

CASTE

Caste is a hierarchical ordering of status groups, membership in which is based on birth. Caste groups have been the major institution organizing human relationships and interactions in India for centuries. Inevitably, a system so deeply imbedded in Indian society has influenced and been influenced by the modern political system. No single factor influences politics in India more deeply than caste, but this influence is felt most fully at the local level.

Caste groupings and more formal Caste Associations have become mediating and mobilizing institutions in Indian politics. They use and are used by political parties at the local level. They interpret political issues and positions to their members and convey caste political interests to the parties and administration. They mobilize voters, workers, and sometimes money and candidates.

SCHEDULED CASTES

Historically the most economically and socially disadvantaged groups in Indian society, the Scheduled Castes are separate castes grouped together for legal and administrative purposes. The Indian constitution outlaws the most extreme forms of discrimination against untouchability and provides special protections in parliamentary representation, civil service employment, and education. Untouchability, however, is still widely practiced in rural India, and members of the Scheduled Castes remain heavily overrepresented among the poorest, least employed, and most illiterate in Indian society.

Until recently, untouchables generally have looked to the Congress (I) Party as the source of protection for their interests. However, while there have always been significant untouchable political movements, the Dalits, as they now prefer to call themselves, are beginning to seek political power on their own. The most important untouchable movement, the Scheduled Caste Federation founded in 1942 by Dr. B. R. Ambedkar, the most prominent untouchable leader of the modern period, was largely confined to Maharashtra and central Uttar Pradesh.

Attempting to broaden its appeal to Non-Scheduled oppressed groups, the Scheduled Caste Federation took the name Republican Party of India (RPI) in 1956. It achieved considerable success at the state level in Maharashtra and at the municipal level in Agra City in the late 1950s and 1960s, but factionalism has reduced its importance in more recent times.

A more militant student-based group called the Dalit (oppressed) Panthers emerged in Maharashtra in the 1960s and developed some influence by forging links between rural and urban groups.

In the late 1970s, another organization, the All-India Backward and Minority Communities Employees Federation (BAMCEF), began to organize the Scheduled Castes and other oppressed groups on a broader geographical basis. It used the now-significant number of Scheduled Caste government employees—holders of reserved posts in the civil service—as an organizing base. Led by Kanshi Ram, the BAMCEF has been transformed into the Bahujan Samaj Party.

MUSLIMS

The most prominent minority in India is the Muslim minority. With over 138 million Muslims, India has the third largest Muslim population in the world. Yet, Muslims are only about 13 percent of the Indian population. At the time of the partition of British India, many of the Muslim elite migrated to Pakistan. The Muslim population, geographically scattered and without its traditional leadership, turned to the Congress Party for protection. That support began to erode during the 1975–77 emergency when many Muslims felt themselves the victim of overzealous bureaucrats seeking to implement the government's slum removal and sterilization programs. Since then Muslims have been more selective in their support of various political parties.

Muslim confrontations with the police and with other social groups have become more frequent as the Muslim community has become more assertive politically and socially. This assertiveness is a sign of its growing self-confidence and owes much to the openness of the democratic political system and to a growing middle class more willing to speak out on the community's behalf. Some Muslims support the Jamaat-e-Islami, a tightly organized paramilitary organization, which is roughly the counterpart of the Hindu RSS.

National Prospects

Fifty years of independence have produced a mixed picture of success and failure for India. Among the developing countries of the world, India has been generally recognized as a political success but a near economic failure. Despite a variety of problems, Indian democracy has served the country well. Its great socialist experiment, however, has produced neither growth nor equity, as the country remains plagued by poverty, illiteracy, disease, massive unemployment, and despair. As India enters its second 50 years of freedom, however, there is considerable hope that its new policy of economic liberalization and globalization will transform the country into an important economic and political force.

Perhaps India's most important success has been the resilience of its democratic order. The basic political framework based on mass franchise, parliamentary government, and an independent judiciary has withstood the test of time and has acquired increased legitimacy. These institutions have played a major role in helping to reconcile India's diverse social, economic, and cultural interest. Dormant institutions like the courts and the election commission have become revitalized and have come to play an increasingly important role.

While India's institutional system has remained intact, its party system has been transformed significantly. The party system has been marked by the gradual decline of the once-dominant Congress (I) Party, repeated failure of centrist alternatives parties to survive, the stagnation of the Communist left, the rise of the Hindu nationalism of the BJP, and the regionalization of parties. None of the national political formations is capable of governing without relying on the votes of regionally based parties that draw their support from caste and religious groups that have become electorally powerful. As a result of the transformation

of the party system, India is faced by an era of weak, unstable coalition and alliance governments. These weak governments may not be in a position to make the kind of tough choices that face the country in the coming years, especially in the economic sphere.

The Indian economy has not been an especially notable success, although in the late 1990s and early 2000s this started to change. India's most important economic achievement has been in feeding its vast population, warding off famine, and avoiding the horrors of mass starvation that occurred during the British period and in Mao's China. As of 2005 about 25 percent of the population lived below the poverty line, and 40 percent of the adult population was illiterate; both numbers were significantly better than they were in the mid-1990s. In the industrial sphere, India's vibrant private sector has been overshadowed by a massive, inefficient public sector that remains a major legacy of India's socialist past. The liberalization policies of the Rao government began the process of reducing state intervention in the economy, ending protection, and joining the global economy. Successive governments did not stray from this path, thereby ensuring an average growth rate of 6 percent and maintaining inflation at less than 15 percent. Export-oriented sectors such as information technology received the right incentives to integrate themselves very successfully with the global economy. With the largest population between 18 and 60 years of age anywhere in the world, India, along with China, is emerging in the eyes of the developed world as the biggest economic opportunity and challenge for this century.

The collapse of the Soviet Union and the end of the cold war have totally undermined the cornerstone of India's foreign policy of nonalignment. Indian leaders and foreign policy officials, however, continue to insist that nonalignment remains relevant and have failed to engage in a fundamental review of India's future role in the post–cold war world. Another legacy of the past is the continued dominance of Indo-Pakistan relations in Indian foreign policy and the problem of its relations with its neighbors. Indo-American policy also remains prickly due to differences over nuclear weapons and missile development and deployment. The May 1998 explosions of five nuclear devices further complicated India's political, economic, and foreign policy future. However, in 2005 India signed an agreement with the United States that promised to lift U.S. sanctions on Indian access to non-military nuclear technology.

These various economic, political, and foreign policy problems will continue to strain the capabilities of India's political system. India's biggest challenge will center on its ability to deal with the problems and opportunities of globalization, the development of cultural nationalism, and the need to maintain political stability and effective government in an era of coalition and alliance politics.

Further Reading

Barnett, Marguerite Ross. *The Politics of Cultural Nationalism in South India.* Princeton, N.J.: Princeton University Press, 1976.

Bava, Noorjahan, ed. *Non-Governmental Organizations in Development: Theory and Practice.* Delhi: Kanishka, 1997.

Brass, Paul R. *The Politics of India since Independence.* Cambridge: Cambridge University Press, 1994.

Brass, Tom. *New Farmers' Movements in India.* London: Frank Cass, 1995.

Butler, David, Ashok Lahiri, and Prannoy Roy. *India Decides: Elections 1952-1995.* New Delhi: Books and Things, 1995.

Drèze, Jean, and Amartya Sen. *India: Economic Development and Social Opportunity.* Delhi: Oxford University Press, 1996.

Frankel, Francine. *India's Political Economy, 1947-77.* Princeton, N.J.: Princeton University Press, 1978.

Frankel, F. R., et al. *Transforming India: Social and Political Dynamics of Democracy.* New Delhi: Oxford University Press, 2000.

Gould, Harold, and Sumit Ganguly, ed. *India Votes: Alliance Politics and Minority Governments in the Ninth and Tenth General Elections.* Boulder, Colo.: Westview Press, 1993.

Graham, Bruce. *Hindu Nationalism and Indian Politics: The Origins and Development of the Bharatiya Jana Sangh.* Cambridge: Cambridge University Press, 1990.

Hardgrave, Robert L. Jr., and Stanley A. Kochanek. *India: Government and Politics in a Developing Nation.* 6th ed. New York: Harcourt Brace Jovanovich, 2000.

Hasan, Z. *Parties and Party Politics in India.* Oxford: Oxford University Press, 2002.

Jaffrelot, Christopher. *The Hindu Nationalist Movement.* New Delhi: Penguin Books India, 1996.

Joshi, Vijay, and I. M. O. Little. *India's Economic Reforms: 1991-2001.* Delhi: Oxford University Press, 1997.

Kochanek, Stanley A. *Business and Politics in India.* Los Angeles: University of California Press, 1974.

———. *The Congress Party of India: The Dynamics of One-Party Democracy.* Princeton, N.J.: Princeton University Press, 1968.

Lewis, John P. *India's Political Economy and Reform.* Delhi: Oxford University Press, 1995.

Mallick, Ross. *Development of a Communist Government: West Bengal since 1977.* Cambridge: Cambridge University Press, 1993.

———. *Indian Communism: Opposition, Collaboration and Institutionalization.* Oxford: Oxford University Press, 1994.

Malik, Yogendra K., and V. B. Singh. *Hindu Nationalists in India: The Rise of the Bharatiya Janata Party.* Boulder, Colo.: Westview Press, 1994.

Omvedt, Gail. *Reinventing Revolution: New Social Movements and the Socialist Tradition in India.* Armonk, N.Y.: M. E. Sharpe, 1993.

Panandiker, V. A. Pai, and Ajay Mehra. *The Indian Cabinet: A Study in Governance.* Delhi: Konark, 1996.

Rajagopal, A. *Politics after Television: Religious Nationalism and the Reshaping of the Indian Public.* Cambridge: Cambridge University Press, 2001.

Ray, Rabindra. *The Naxalites and Their Ideology.* Delhi: Oxford University Press, 1988.

Sen Gupta, Bhabani. *Problems of Governance.* New Delhi: Konark, 1996.

REPUBLIC OF INDONESIA
(Republik Indonesia)

By Michael Malley, M.A.
Revised by Joel Selway

An archipelagic country of 241 million people (2005 est.), Indonesia stretches 3,000 miles along the equator from the Indian Ocean to the Pacific. Although it consists of more than 13,000 islands, only about 6,000 are inhabited. Its population is the fourth largest in the world. Nearly 60 percent of the country's people crowd onto the island of Java, which accounts for just 7 percent of the country's land area. The rest is spread mostly among Sumatra, Sulawesi, Maluku, Bali, and the Indonesian parts of Borneo and New Guinea. Nearly 90 percent of the population professes Islam, making it home to more Muslims than any other country. Christian, Hindu, and Buddhist minorities are prominent in certain regions.

The census does not record ethnic identity, but it is estimated that about 40 percent of Indonesians are ethnically Javanese, traditionally found in eastern and central Java. Other major ethnic groups include the Sundanese in western Java; the Acehnese, Minangkabau, and Batak in Sumatra; the Dayak and Banjar in Borneo; the Bugis in Sulawesi; and the Balinese in Bali. Indonesians of Chinese descent, numbering fewer than 10 million, live mostly in urban areas and control many major economic activities.

HISTORY

Prior to 2002 the constitution provided few checks and balances on executive power. More than three decades of rule by President Soeharto's authoritarian New Order regime (1966–98) institutionalized executive domination over all other branches of government. The New Order regime claimed legitimacy as the upholder of the 1945 constitution and the national ideology, *Pancasila*, which is contained in the document's preamble. The brief, hurriedly written constitution was adopted at the beginning of the revolution against Dutch colonialism (1945–49) but replaced by a provisional constitution in 1950 that instituted a system of parliamentary democracy. Amid regional rebellions and parliamentary instability, President Soekarno declared martial law in 1957. Two years later, under army pressure, he disbanded the elected Constitutional Assembly and restored the 1945 constitution. In 1966 the army forced Soekarno to cede power to its commander, General Soeharto. Soeharto became acting president in 1968 and remained president until 1998, when massive demonstrations and the defection of key military and bureaucratic supporters led him to resign. His vice president, B. J. Habibie, assumed the presidency and began to grapple with widespread pressures for political reform. He acknowledged that he was a transitional leader and promised to revise the country's electoral laws and hold elections in 1999.

Elections were held as promised in 1999. Forty-eight parties competed in what international observers declared as free and fair elections, though not void of problems. Megawati Soekarnoputri's party took firm control of the House of People's Representatives with Golkar (Soeharto's party) coming in second. Megawati was expected to win the presidential election in the same year due to mass popular support. However, Islamic conservatives and remnants of the old regime were opposed to Megawati, a woman, assuming rule over Indonesia—the world's largest Muslim country. In a shock election, the People's Consultative Assembly (MPR) elected Abdurrahman Wahid (better known as Gus Dur) as president. Gus Dur's National Awakening Party had come in third in the parliamentary elections, and his election caused mass demonstrations on the streets of Jakarta. As a token of appeasement, Wahid appointed Megawati as vice president. Nevertheless, demonstrations continued over the next two years and increased as two financial scandals broke out in the Wahid administration. Parliament dismissed Wahid in July 2001 and Vice President Megawati took over the reins of government.

In August 2002 the MPR passed significant constitutional amendments, which moved Indonesia closer to democracy. For the first time in Indonesia's history, the chief executive was to be elected by popular and direct vote. In addition, the changes stripped the MPR of its power and removed all reserved seats for the military and other special function groups. In its stead, the constitution allows for a bicameral legislature to pass laws. Moreover, the executive is now responsible only for initiating legislation rather than having the power to make statutes. Lastly, the constitutional changes created two new institutions: first, an independent electoral commission to oversee elections; second, a Constitutional Court with the power of judicial review.

The System of Government

Indonesia is a unitary state with a presidential system of government. It has a bicameral legislature.

EXECUTIVE

The amendments to the constitution passed in 2002 had the primary goal of checking and reducing the powers of the president. The 1945 constitution allowed for enormous presidential powers, which Soeharto took full advantage of. Under Soeharto, the government operated more under presidential and ministerial decrees than legislation. Futhermore, there were no term limits on the president. Thus, when Soeharto resigned in 1998, he was the world's second longest serving head of state.

According to the 2002 constitutional amendments, which became effective in 2004, the president and vice president are elected under a joint ticket by the direct voice of the people. If none of the candidates wins a majority in the first round, the top two candidates compete in a second round. The candidate with the most number of votes becomes president.

Under the new presidential powers, the president can submit laws to the Indonesian House of Representatives (the DPR), but not make statutes as in the past. The president and vice president also have a two-term limit. Moreover, the president can be impeached by the People's Consultative Assembly (the MPR) after the Constitutional Court has investigated and submitted its verdict. Lastly, the president cannot freeze or dissolve the DPR. The impact of these changes on the dynamics between the president, the DPR, and the Constitutional Court has yet to take effect. Nevertheless, the changes are large enough that the office of president is sure to be significantly reduced in importance, giving way to the more deliberative body of the DPR.

LEGISLATURE

In addition to checking the president's power, the 2002 constitutional amendments also significantly changed the legislative branch of government. Under the 1945 constitution, the People's Consultative Assembly (MPR) was the highest political body with unlimited power. The MPR was made up of about 80 percent members elected and 20 percent appointed from the military. This afforded the military significant influence in Indonesian politics. The MPR was solely responsible for electing the president and setting the broad outlines of state policy.

Under the amended constitution, the MPR has limited responsibilities and powers. It can amend or draw up a constitution, act as an electoral college, and impeach the president (although it has no exclusive powers to impeach). Moreover the MPR is now made up wholly of directly elected members. The joint bodies of the DPR and the Regional Representatives Council (DPD) now constitute its entire membership. The MPR is no longer responsible to set state policy.

The legislative branch is now bicameral, similar to the American system of House and Senate. The Indonesian House of Representatives (which is historically but inaccurately referred to as "parliament") is known as the Dewan Perwakilan Rakyat or DPR. It is the main legislative-making body in the Indonesian system. In order to make DPR candidates more accountable to their con-

stituencies, the 2002 amendments changed the closed list proportional representation system to an open list system. Theoretically, this should allow candidates further down on the party's list to win seats. However, the amendments set a district quota on the minimum number of votes these candidates have to win. This quota is very high and there are doubts that this revised system will effect greater constituency accountability.

The Indonesian "Senate" is known as the Regional Representatives Council, the Dewan Perwakilan Daerah or DPD. The DPD is not entirely like the American Senate. It does not have equal powers with the DPR, and is primarily charged with proposing, discussing, and monitoring laws relating to regional autonomy. The DPD also provides consideration to the DPR over bills on the state budget and on bills related to taxation, education, or religion. Each of the 33 provinces, regardless of its size, has four representatives in the DPD. Candidates to the DPD must not be formally affiliated to any party, even though they might be supported by parties. The electoral system is the single non-transferable vote (SNTV). Thus, the top four candidates with the most votes from each province are directly elected to the DPD.

In the elections held in May 2004, Soeharto's old party, Golkar, won the most seats in the DPR (21.6 percent). Megawati's party, Partai Demokrasi Indonesia Perjuangan, came in second with 18.5 percent of the vote. The party of Megawati's presidential challenger Susilo, Partai Demokrat, came in fifth with 7.5 percent of the vote.

JUDICIARY

The members of the Supreme Court (Mahkamah Agung) are appointed by the president. The Court has both original and appellate jurisdiction but no power of judicial review. It has never played a significant autonomous political role, and the doctrine of separation of powers is not legally recognized. The New Order regime tended to fill high-level posts in the Department of Justice as well as seats on the Supreme Court with military lawyers and judges. Indonesians widely regard the courts as subject to political influence and bribery.

Since Soeharto's dismissal in 1998, there is hope that the judiciary will take on a more autonomous role. The 2002 amendments introduce a clear separation of powers between the three branches of government, with proper checks and balances. The most significant of these changes is the introduction of the Constitutional Court (Mahkamah Konstitusi). It has the power to review laws, determine disputes over the authorities of state institutions in the Constitution, decide over the dissolution of a political party, and decide disputes over the results of general elections. It shares judicial power with the Supreme Court (Mahkamah Agung) and is comprised of nine "constitutional justices," appointed by the DPR, the Supreme Court, and the president. The Supreme Court is given a boost to its independence through the creation of the Judicial Commission. The Judicial Commission possesses the authority to propose candidates for appointment as justices of the Supreme Court. This serves as a check on the presidential power to appoint justices.

REGIONAL AND LOCAL GOVERNMENT

Indonesia is divided into 33 provinces, which are sub-divided into regencies (*kabupaten*) and municipalities (*kota*), respectively. According to the 1945 constitution, each level of government had a Regional People's House of Representatives (Dewan Perwakilan Rakyat Daerah or DPRD) whose members are elected. However, the laws governing regional autonomy (*otonomi daerah*) were antiquated and had been abused by Soeharto. Thus, revision of the 1974 and 1979 laws on regional government were a chief demand of anti-Soeharto forces. Under Soeharto, regional governments were tightly governed by the Department of Home Affairs. As at the national level, regional legislators consisted of 80 percent elected members and 20 percent appointed by the armed forces. Regional executives were approved by the national government. Moreover, the government party (Golkar) won a majority in every province after 1987 until its end in 1998. Moves to reform decentralization laws were set in motion before Soeharto resigned. In 1995 a pilot program shifted administrative responsibilities from the provincial to the district level, which the government party had less control over. In 1997 a new law on regional finance was passed. However, regional autonomy was not really achieved until the passing of Law No. 22/1999 on Regional Governance, and Law No. 25/1999 on Fiscal Balance between the Centre and the Regions. Law 22/1999 introduced the devolution of a wide range of public services to the regions, and it strengthened the elected regional councils, which received wide-ranging powers to supervise and control the regional administration. Law 25/1999 raised regional economic capabilities. In addition, it reduced regional funding gaps and created a funding system that reflected the new division of functions among levels of government.

The Electoral System

New Order officials proudly claimed that they held elections six times in 30 years. In contrast, during the country's first two decades of independence, national elections were held just once, in 1955. However, those elections were also widely regarded as the only truly fair elections in the country's history until 1999. Under the New Order, elections were used as instruments to legitimate the regime, not to change the government. To this end, electoral rules were made to appear scrupulously fair, but the political system as a whole was structured to produce a predictable outcome—victory for the ruling party.

The electoral system was given a dramatic overhaul under the 2002 constitutional amendments. Chief among these changes was the establishment of the new Election Commission. The National Election Commission (KPU) is an independent, permanent and nonpartisan body consisting of 11 members. All members enjoy equal voting rights.

Its primary role is to organize the elections, monitoring polling booths and canvassing, and ultimately counting votes. As a complimentary institution, the new Constitutional Court has the sole authority to adjudicate disputes concerning the election results. The existence of two adjudicating institutions at different stages of the elections will ultimately result in a fairer electoral system overall. The president and vice president are no longer elected by the MPR. The old system, which still proved to be undemocratic in the 1999 post-Soeharto elections, was replaced with a two-round majority system process. In order to win the election, a candidate's vote must satisfy two criteria. First, a ticket must receive 50 percent plus one of the votes. In addition, at least 20 percent of the votes must be in at least one half of the Provinces.

The DPR is now fully elected. The military no longer has reserved seats, and was not allowed to vote at the first 2004 election. Another significant change is that the DPR, DPRD-1, and DPRD-2 moved from a closed to an open list proportional system. In addition to marking their party choice, voters can add a mark for the one candidate of their choice within the party's list. The final change is the creation of a second legislative chamber at the national level, the DPD, which replaces the weak consultative body. The DPD uses the single non-transferable vote (SNTV) system of representation—the first four candidates with the most votes from each province will be directly elected to the DPD.

New election participation criteria have also been introduced. At the party level, a political party qualifies for election participation only if it meets one of two conditions: the party is operational in at least two-thirds of the provinces, or it is operational in at least two-thirds of the regencies within the province where it intends to run. At the individual level, for the DPD, only individuals who have a specified minimum number of supporters in their relevant province (number changes with province size) can participate.

New electoral districts have also been created. There are now 69 electoral districts for the DPR (previously 27—one per province), 211 DPRD-1 electoral districts, (27 in 1999), and 1,645 DPRD-2 electoral districts. Critics have argued that the redistricting results in proportionality, with the risk that many small parties may disappear. Proponents argue that in order for the Indonesian party system to mature this is exactly what the country needs.

The Party System

ORIGINS OF THE PARTIES

Legally, the New Order permitted only three parties to exist: Golkar, Development Unity, and Indonesian Democracy. In the latter years of Soeharto's reign, dissidents announced the creation of alternative parties, but since these were considered illegal they remained tiny and were not allowed to contest elections. The most prominent was the Democratic People's Party, many of whose young founders were jailed on government charges of inciting violence and disrupting the electoral process.

The army founded Golkar in 1964 as a political federation of labor unions and veterans' cooperatives that it sponsored. The army aimed to compete with Communist and radical nationalist parties and their affiliated organizations that dominated politics at that time and opposed the army. When President Soeharto decided in 1969 to hold elections to legitimate his new government, he instructed his associates to transform Golkar into the government's own electoral vehicle.

The other two parties are amalgams of parties that flourished in the country's brief period of multiparty democracy in the early 1950s. Dozens of parties existed during that era, but four dominated. In the 1955 election, the Indonesian Nationalist Party earned 22 percent, the modernist Muslim party Masyumi took 21 percent, the traditionalist Muslim party Nahdlatul Ulama won 19 percent, and the Communist Party carried 16 percent. After taking power in 1966, Soeharto banned the Communist Party for its alleged involvement in the assassination of several officers on October 1, 1965. He also permitted members of Masyumi, which Soekarno had banned in 1960 for its alleged role

in regional rebellions, to form a successor known as Muslim in Indonesia.

When elections were finally held in 1971, Golkar faced nine opponents and defeated them handily. It received 63 percent, while its nearest competitor, Nahdlatul Ulama, gained just 19 percent. Despite this massive victory, the new government was not satisfied with its ability to dominate the political system. In 1973 it forced the nine minority parties to "fuse" into just two. The four Muslim parties were incorporated into the Development Unity Party, and the five nationalist and Christian parties merged into the Indonesian Democracy Party.

In 1977 and 1982 Development Unity garnered more than a quarter of the votes, while Indonesian Democracy failed to reach even 10 percent and Golkar took 62 percent to 64 percent. In 1987 and 199, Development Unity sank to 16 to 17 percent and Indonesian Democracy peaked at 15 percent in 1992. Indonesian Democracy's rise came entirely at Golkar's expense, driving its share of the vote down from 73 percent in 1987 to 68 percent in 1992. Fearful of Indonesian Democracy's growing strength, the government undermined the party's leadership in the run-up to the 1997 elections. As a result, Golkar achieved a record 74 percent, Development Unity improved to 22 percent, and Indonesian Democracy plunged to a mere 3 percent. Following the fall of Soeharto, B. J. Habbie announced that elections would be held in 1999 and what happened to the party system in Indonesia can be described as nothing short of feverish. In the wake of the elections, a little less than 200 political parties registered to take part in the momentous event, although only 48 qualified to participate. By the 2004 elections this number had fallen to less than 50. It is clear that Indonesia's party system is immature and at times chaotic, driven more by personalities than specific agendas. Nevertheless, in both the 1999 and 2004 elections, six or seven parties took just over 80 percent of the parliamentary votes. Thus, the fledgling Indonesian party system shows signs of consolidation.

PARTY ORGANIZATION

Under Soeharto, political parties were forced to organize in a determined fashion. The result was two opposition parties that were merely loose federations of previous parties and social organizations. Membership was not required, and parties tended to be fissured along outside organization lines. In this way, Golkar effectively ensured the weakness of opposition parties. Parties also tended to be highly centralized under the

New Order regime. This was due to the forbidding of party organization at the village level. If all else failed, Golkar (via the government) would directly intervene in party leadership struggles. In 1996 the government used blatant coercion to remove the popular head of the Indonesian Democracy Party, Megawati Soekarnoputri, in preparation for the 1997 elections.

Following the reform movement of the late 1990s and beyond (known as *reformasi*), party organization has been less centralized, after the general pattern of Indonesian politics. Although most of Indonesia's leading political parties have roots back to the 1950's, they should be viewed as new parties created during *reformasi*. A leading characteristic of *reformasi* parties is that they have emerged as personality-driven rather than agenda-driven. Although Indonesian voters may have party affiliations, their voting behavior often contravenes party affiliation, favoring the most charismatic candidate. This has led to parties being associated with their leaders rather than their ideology. Thus, when a leader dies (physically or politically), the party loses much of its identity. This has a number of consequences for the Indonesian political system. Chief among these outcomes is the difficulty in forming coalitions along party lines, which hinders executive-legislative cooperation. Explicitly, if the president has a particular platform, he or she might not be able to get anything done. As the party system has matured, the top parties have begun to identify increasingly with issues. In time, they will hopefully occupy concrete positions in the political spectrum.

CAMPAIGNING

During New Order, the government attempted to exert as much control over campaigning as it did over other aspects of the electoral process. A successful campaign was one that proceeded, in the jargon of government officials and military officers, in a manner that was "safe, orderly, and smooth" (*aman, tertib, lancar*).

To ensure that the campaign proceeded this way, parties had to comply with many restrictive rules. Campaigning was permitted for only about four weeks and then had to cease during a "quiet period" (five days in 1997) immediately prior to the polls. During the campaign, the parties were required to obtain police permits to hold rallies, and the content of their speeches and other campaign materials had to be vetted by the national office of the General Election Institute before being disseminated to regional party branches. Parties were forbidden to criticize each other or government policies, and under no circumstances could they question the state ideology, *Pancasila*.

Campaigns were centrally coordinated affairs, largely because the government insisted on maintaining centralized control over the parties and the electoral process. The General Election Institute determined when and where each party could campaign, ostensibly to prevent conflict between rival parties and competition for venues. Typically, national party leaders traversed the country to appear with local officials at large public rallies. To attract the largest possible crowds, nationally known entertainers were flown from Jakarta to regional campaign sites. However, a party's ability to attract large crowds during its campaign has not been a useful indicator of electoral support, as Indonesian Democracy discovered in 1992 and Development Unity found out in 1997.

Violence was a feature of all election campaigns under the New Order, since the regime readily resorted to the use of security forces to manipulate the minority parties and secure overwhelming electoral victories. However, violence increased in the 1990s, particularly on Java. The causes of campaign violence are complex but are clearly related to two factors. One is the accumulation of minority parties' political grievances, especially the impossibility of effecting real political change through elections. The second factor is the growing number of unemployed urban youth who seek opportunities to protest the economic injustices they attribute to the government. Such people gravitated to Indonesian Democracy in 1992, and then to Development Unity in 1997.

In 1997 the government attempted to institute a "dialogical" style of campaigning in order to avert the potential for mass violence that surfaced in 1992. It forbade motorcades and parades and encouraged party spokespersons to discuss platforms on television rather than at large rallies. These restrictions failed, partly because Golkar supporters insisted on staging their own parades, which provoked a cycle of conflict, counterparades, and further violence. Campaigning during *reformasi* has been more open than at any time in Indonesia's postcolonial history. The 2004 elections saw widespread and mass political rallies, canvassing, television appearances, and parades. Such a healthy campaigning period offers signs that Indonesia is adapting well to its democratic freedom. Some incidents of violence and protest occurred but nothing in comparison to the incidents of the late 1990s. Campaigning for the 2004 presidential elections took on a personality tone, as expected. Five candidates ran promising results on some issues, but with no specific details on how to implement policy to achieve such results. More effective was the self-positioning of candidates vis-à-vis the rest of the field. For example, one of the top five candidates, Amien Rais, positioned himself as the only true reformer of the presidential contenders. Mudslinging has also been incorporated skillfully by opposition candidates. A familiar attack of the 2004 elections came against presidential hopeful General Wiranto, whose campaign suffered from human rights allegations leveled against him over his role in Indonesia's former province of East Timor.

Major Political Parties

FUNCTIONAL GROUP PARTY

(Partai Golongan Karya; Golkar)

Golkar began as an army-based party to counter the Communist Party and the ultra-nationalist parties that dominated Indonesian politics in the 1950s. Soeharto used Golkar to consolidate his power, and subsequently to guarantee the New Order government consistent majorities of the vote (ranging from 62 percent to 75 percent in the elections from 1971 to 1997). Yet despite Soeharto's hard-and-fast fall in the mid-1990s, Golkar managed to transform itself as a reformist party operating under a "new paradigm" with a new "spirit of reform." Akbar Tandjung, a minister in the Soeharto government, took over the party reins in July 1998. Despite the negative image associated with the Soeharto dictatorship, Golkar had an advantage over the new parties: a support base of existing bureaucrats, whom Golkar attempted to manipulate as they did throughout the New Order. In the 1999 elections Golkar was the only organization capable of reaching the outer reaches of the huge Indonesian archipelago. Its ability to do this was directly related to the bureaucracy's ability to influence local attitudes.

During the 1999 elections the party's platform was to present Golkar as a sensible choice for voters because of its moderation, experience, expertise, commitment to a law-based state, and pluralism. For example, Golkar campaigned on its ability to lead the country out of the economic crisis. The party's election slogan, "New Golkar, Together for Development" (*Golkar Baru, Bersatu Untuk Maju*), underlined this uneasy mix of experience with new thinking. Golkar received 22.4 percent of the national vote and 26 percent of parliamentary seats, coming in second behind Megawati's PDI-P. Thus, it was obvious that Golkar continued to

represent a significant part of the country's interest. Supporters of Golkar were concentrated most strongly outside of Java.

In the 2004 elections the party decided on General Wiranto, former head of the armed forces and defense minister, as its official candidate for the presidency, demonstrating the party's continued close links with the military. However, any suggestion that Golkar was still a militaristic party disappeared with the party's winning 21.6 percent of the vote and 128 of the 550 parliamentary seats—the most of any of the competing parties. This landslide victory signified that Golkar truly had transformed itself from its dictatorial past to a popular party in the new Indonesian party system.

INDONESIAN DEMOCRACY PARTY—STRUGGLE

(Partai Demokrasi IndonesiaPerjuangan; PDI-P)

PDI-P is a secularist, but nationalistic party that emerged in the 1950s era of parliamentary democracy. PDI-P came to the forefront of Indonesian politics under Megawati's leadership after the fall of Soeharto. Following a failed bid to win the presidency in 1999, then vice president Megawati replaced the corrupt Wahid in 2001. In 2004 she stood in the final stage of the presidential elections against Susilo Bambang Yudhoyono of the Democratic Party, barely beating third-place Wiranto for a place in the final round. Megawati's initial popularity was hindered by her performance in office, especially her failure to revive the ailing economy.

PDI-P is a heavily personalistic party. It is headed by Megawati Soekarnoputri and centers on her leadership. Some followers have even gone so far as to label her as the long-awaited *ratu adil* (just ruler) of Javanese folklore. Even less extreme followers are solidly devoted to her. Soekarnoputri is the daughter of Indonesia's first president, Soekarno, and it is perhaps the blood of leadership running through her veins that has obliterated any challenge to her leadership in the party. Her massive popularity can in part be attributed to the unpopularity of the outgoing dictator, Soeharto. In comparison to his gross abuse of power, her modest deportment earned much goodwill from the people as head of one of the only two legal opposition parties during the New Order. In 1996 the Soeharto government ousted her as leader of the Partai Demokrasi Indonesia. Thus, at its beginnings, PDI-P positioned itself as a party representing victims of past injustice.

PDI-P was seen as a strong supporter of democracy in the 1999 elections, its reformist agenda advocated gradual rather than radical change. Indeed, during the talks for constitutional reform in 2001, Megawati herself was not sure Indonesia was ready for direct presidential elections.

In 1999 PDI-P easily won the largest percentage of parliamentary (DPR) seats. Among 48 contending parties, PDI-P won 33.7 percent of the popular vote. Despite this success in the DPR, PDI-P was unable to transform its popular mandate into obtaining the presidency in the ensuing October 1999 session of the MPR. With PDI-P unable to build a large coalition, and criticized for its arrogance, Amien Rais of the National Mandate Party garnered the support of the Central Axis (an alliance of Muslim parties) and built a coalition that kept Megawati out of office. The Central Axis refused to see a secularist woman become the nation's next president. PDI-P's seemingly insignificant consolation prize, the vice presidency, turned out to be a hidden fortune, as a nation sensitive to corruption removed Wahid from office just two years later.

The party enjoys a broad base of support. Although its initial support came from the urban and rural lower classes, in the 1999 elections PDI-P garnered votes from all income and educational levels relatively evenly. The party's strongest bases are in Java and Bali, but election results suggest good support all over Indonesia.

NATIONAL AWAKENING PARTY
(Partai Kebangkitan Bangsa; PKB)

In 1998 Indonesia's largest Muslim organization, the Rise of the Islamic Scholars (Nahdlatul Ulama or NU) founded the PKB. The NU, which is estimated to have over 30 million members, made up the initial support base of the PKB. Because the NU is clearly identified with traditional Javanese forms of Islam, PKB's main area of strength is on the island of Java amongst the *pesantren* (rural religious school), small traders, and landowners. However, religious tenets do not transform into party policy in general. Its membership is open to all religions—part of PKB's emphasis on tolerance toward Indonesia's pluralistic society.

In the first post-Soeharto elections, PKB took the third largest share of the vote and the presidency. PKB's parliamentary success continued in the 2004 elections, when it again secured the third largest share of the vote. In terms of percentage of the vote, in 1999 and 2004, PKB won 12.6 percent and 11.8 percent, respectively. However, the party's popular vote does not transform into an equal proportion of seats in the DPR. For

example, in 1999, the PPP, who earned just 10.7 percent of the popular vote, took 58 seats compared to the PKB's 51. Likewise, in 2004, two parties with less share of the vote took more seats than the PKB: the PPP with 8.3 percent and 58 seats, and the PD with 7.5 percent and 57 seats. The PAN with just 6.5 percent of the vote (almost half that of PKB) took the same number of seats, 52. This seat allocation is reflective of PKB's narrower support base (mainly Java), while the PPP and other parties have more support outside Java.

PKB's significance has not lain only in its parliamentary seats. In October 1999 the PKB took the presidential reins in the figure of Abdurrahman Wahid. While it is true that Megawati's failure stemmed from PDI-P's inability to relate with other parties, it does not explain the dexterity of political bargaining the PKB displayed in bringing its candidate to the forefront. The PKB was able to market itself as a moderate choice for all parties, and the parties compromised on Wahid. The presidency did not remain long in their hands, however, as Wahid was promptly removed on charges of corruption not two years into his term. Nevertheless, Wahid's ousting had little effect on the party's popularity, mainly due to the underlying support of the NU. Although PKB took a slightly smaller percentage of the popular vote in 2004, its number of seats in Parliament remained the same.

UNITED DEVELOPMENT PARTY
(Partai Persatuan Pembanguna; PPP)

In 1973 Soeharto attempted to suppress the threat of the four leading Islamic parties by a strategy of unite and conquer. The result was the PPP. As the second of only two legal opposition parties during the New Order, the PPP has retained popular support and, in the two elections since Soeharto's fall, have taken the third most parliamentary seats. PPP has maintained this strength despite the reemergence of parties that were once component parties of the PPP. The PPP has several advantages over other parties competing for the Islamic vote. Foremost among these advantages is the party's legacy as the major opposition party prior to Soeharto's fall. In addition, the PPP has a support base that spreads all over Indonesia. PPP is based on Islam, but in both post–New Order elections it has chosen to emphasize moderation. The party does not favor implementation of Islamic sharia law, but maintains that policies should conform to Islamic principles.

PPP finished the elections with a very respectable 10.7 percent of the national vote. Due to distortions caused by the electoral system, the PPP's 10.7 percent earned the party 12.6 percent of the elected seats in Parliament, making it the third largest party. In 2004, the PPP gained just 8.3 percent of the vote, but retained 58 seats in the DPR. The PPP was also instrumental in the 1999 presidential elections. Hamzah Haz led the party to support eventual winner Wahid over the Golkar candidate, B. J. Habbie. The significance of this political maneuvering cannot be underestimated in terms of Indonesia's democratic survival. The reaction of the masses to another Golkar president may well have led to widespread and violent protests. Ironically, PPP was instrumental in ousting Wahid just two years later. In the 2004 presidential elections, PPP candidate Hamzah Haz was defeated in the first round with just 3 percent of the national vote.

NATIONAL MANDATE PARTY
(Partai Amanat Nasiona; PAN)

PAN is the least personalistic of all the leading parties in Indonesia. At its early stages, the party was led by a number of prominent reformers and introduced an ideological platform rather than centering on a single personality. The party was instrumental in the student protests of 1998 that led to Soeharto's fall. However, the party has become increasingly focused on Amien Rais. Amien Rais was a prominent Muslim intellectual and head of the Muhammadiyah, and thus has important connections to maintain a solid support base for the party. During the 1998 protests, Amien was a major supporter of the student movement. As a result, he became known as the "Father of Reform" (*Bapak Reformasi*). In November 1998 Amien Rais committed the party to a less radical agenda of reform, giving the party a different tone than its supporters had anticipated. This was the first of a number of divisive events that have weakened PAN. Indeed, since its inception, the party has been haunted by factions. Initially, PAN was unable to unify all modernist Muslims leading to the formation of a splinter party known as the Partai Bulan Bintang (PBB), which is notably more Islamic-leaning in its platform. Subsequently, PAN has been split into two factions: the modernist Muslim faction led by A. M. Fatwa and the liberal faction led by Secretary-General Faisal Basri. Amien straddled both factions trying to keep the party together, but Faisal walked out of the party in late 2000. Faisal accused the PAN of becoming increasingly personalistic.

It is this personalization that led to the party's disappointing performance in the 1999 elections. PAN was expected to be a major contender for the lead-ing number of seats in Parliament. However, Amien's identification with Islamic organizations deterred non-Muslims and tainted PAN's claims to be an "open" political party. The party ended up with just 7.1 percent of the vote. PAN gained few votes outside of the modernist Muslim stream, which also led to the party's increased commitment to Islam. Later on in 1999, Amien orchestrated shrewd coalition-building efforts to keep Megawati from becoming president. It was hoped that Amien would become the preferred candidate of this coalition, but he was unable to overcome the charismatic Wahid. In 2004 Amien gained just over 14 percent of the popular vote in the presidential elections. The party took 52 seats (9.5 percent) in the enlarged DPR despite attracting only 6.4 percent of the vote.

DEMOCRAT PARTY
(Partai Demokrat; PD)

The Democrat Party is a personalistic party centered on the figure of General Susilo Bambang Yudhoyono (SBY), who failed to be chosen vice president in 2001. SBY was responsible for important reforms in the armed forces following the collapse of the New Order. The party was established by a number of persons from the MPR and academics. Viewed as inconsequential prior to the 2004 elections, the PD enjoyed success beyond everyone's expectations. While gaining just 7.5 percent of the vote in the parliamentary elections, the party gained 57 seats (10.4 percent) in the DPR, making it the fourth largest party in the House. In addition, Susilo Bambang Yudhoyono won the presidential election.

The PD's dogma emphasizes nationalism, religion, pluralism, and humanitarianism. With a militaristic leader, it is not surprising that one of its main goals is also to protect the territorial integrity and promote the unity of Indonesia. Susilo was a military officer during the Soeharto regime and his inability to completely erase that connection from his image may ironically win him the presidency. Disillusioned by Megawati's inability to take hold of the economy and stabilize employment and prices, Indonesians have looked back somewhat nostalgically to the relative stability under Soeharto. While his military connections may have worked against him at first, as the elections evolved, SBY's popularity increased. Other domestic issues that have turned the public to a military leader include the separationist conflict in Aceh and the rising incidence of acts of terror. His administration severely challenged not long after taking office by a massive earthquake and a resulting tsunami that killed more than 220,000 people in the region around the Indian Ocean.

PROSPEROUS JUSTICE PARTY
(Partai Kedilan Sejahtera; PKS)

Despite being one of Indonesia's youngest political parties, PKS has quickly risen to a powerful standing in the political arena. The PKS is a successor to the PK (Justice Party) formed in 1998, which was part of the Central Axis that thwarted Megawati's first presidential campaign in 1999. The Justice and Prosperity Party and the Justice Party merged into one party on July 3, 2003. In the 1999 elections the Justice Party won only 1.4 percent of the vote. Consequently, it failed to meet the electoral threshold to participate in the next election without forming a new party or changing its name. The party's leader, Hidayat Nurwahid, is known for his ideological proximity to the alleged chief of Jemaah Islamiya, Abubakr Bashir. Moreover, PKS is regarded as a radical Islamic party. Specifically, the party has a goal of transforming Indonesia into an Islamic society. However, PKS is committed to allowing the population to decide to switch to an Islamic society via the democratic process.

PKS's 2004 general election campaign was not based on Islamic doctrine. Rather, the party emphasized its commitment to tackling graft, reviving the economy, and the party's record of social service and education in urban Indonesia. PKS campaigned on a motto of "clean, honest and caring" Islamic values. Thus, PKS won the support of many disaffected voters, especially in Jakarta. Despite its religion-free campaign, the party's support base remains rooted in Islamic organizations. During the campaigning period, PKS revealed that Muhammadiyah supported PKS.

In a field of 24 parties in the general elections, PKS came in sixth, with 7.3 percent of the vote and 45 seats (8.1 percent). The party's votes came from middle-class and educated voters, including young professionals who were attracted by PKS's tough stance on graft. However, the party was successful in attracting the urban poor, especially in Jakarta, where PKS finished as the largest party. Despite passing the 5 percent threshold required to put up a presidential candidate, PKS did not field a candidate. The party wanted to convince its supporters that it was concentrating its efforts solely on reforming the DPR. Initially, PKS threw its support behind PAN presidential hopeful Amien Rais. With Amien Rais suffering defeat in the first round, PKS joined the coalition of parties supporting Susilo Bambang Yudhoyono's presidential campaign. Some PKS supporters were upset with the party throwing its support behind SBY. Many had hoped the party would join with PAN to establish an opposition bloc in the DPR. Regardless of this decision, the PKS head, Nurwahid, will be an important figure in Parliament.

Minor Political Parties

Since Soeharto's fall, hundreds of political parties have been formed in Indonesia. However, there are strict rules on competing in general elections. As a result, only 48 parties competed in 1999. In 2004 this number had been cut in half. In 2004, of the 24 contending parties, 17 won seats in the DPR. The two dominant parties were Golkar and PDI-P, which won over 100 seats each. There are about five parties that won around 50 seats: PPP, PD, PAN, PKB and PKS. Three parties won around 10 seats and can be deemed as minor parties. They include the Reform Star Party (PBR), the Prosperous Peace Party (PDS), and the Crescent Star Party (PBB). Seven parties won five or less seats. They are the United Democratic Nationhood Party (PPDK), the Concern for the Nation Functional Party (PKPB), the Justice and Unity Party of Indonesia (PKPI), the Freedom Bull National Party (PNBK), the Pioneers' Party (PP), the Indonesian National Party Marhaenisme (PNIM), and the Indonesian Democratic Vanguard Party (PPDI).

Other Political Forces

Under Soekarno's principle of "Guided Democracy," the Armed Forces of the Republic of Indonesia (ABRI) played a significant role in Indonesian politics from the 1950s up until *reformasi*. This continued under the leadership of General Soeharto, and the military saw itself as the guarantor of political stability and economic development. The military was reserved a certain number of seats (about 20 percent) in Indonesia's most powerful body, the MPR. Moreover, military officers occupied various powerful positions in Soeharto's government. In addition to political positions, the military owned and operated their own commercial enterprises. As the post–World War II generation of military officers was replaced by a younger, less politically interested generation of officers, the stage was set for the political transformations witnessed in the late 1990s. In addition, in Soeharto's latter years, he became increasingly concerned with projecting a personal style of leadership and saw the military less and less as an ally.

ABRI has continued to demonstrate uncertainty in defining its new role in a more open and democratic Indonesia. In the early years of *reformasi* the military, especially Wiranto and Habbie, were tainted by Black Friday, a day when civil security forces killed 16 and injured over 400 demonstrating protestors. Following Black Friday, the military established four general principles to guide this reduction in ABRI's political role, known as "New Paradigm." First, ABRI does not need to be at the forefront of politics, as it was in the New Order. Second, the military will no longer occupy key positions, but instead will only influence the process of decision making. Third, that influence will no longer be exercised directly, but only indirectly. And fourth, the military will share roles in political decision making with nonmilitary partners.

Under the new constitution, seats are no longer reserved for military appointees. In the recent 2004 elections two of the three main contenders were ex-military leaders. These leaders, however, do not have a history of involvement in the inner circle that allowed so much violence to spread during the New Order era. The new president, Susilo Bambang Yudhoyono (SBY), has shown a strong commitment to civilian control of politics. In June 1998 SBY, then chief of the army's influential Social and Political Affairs Directorate, published a reform proposal that declared ABRI's commitment to democratic reforms and called for Indonesia's ratification of international human rights conventions. SBY also supported limits on presidential powers so that the military could not be misused by an unpopular president seeking to quell opposition. In 2000, as chief minister for security and political affairs under Wahid, he refused to declare a state of emergency. It is likely that the prevalence of ex-military officers is merely due to the fact that they are simply the only ones with political experience. As civilian institutions begin to churn out capable individuals, the military connection of politicians is sure to diminish further.

National Prospects

The future of the Indonesian political system is bright. Political reforms have been instituted that put the country on the road to democratization. The instability that occurs with every new democracy has been moderate. There have been two successful, consecutive elections, and political violence at the 2004 elections was low. A key issue in the 2004 elections was the elimination of corruption, demonstrating Indonesia's openness and progress. Though personalities are still a major part of the party system, several parties have become strong, regular contenders for power, and party platforms in the 2004 elections emphasized more issues. Political power is changing hands often, and without violence and protest. Corrupt politicians are being ousted swiftly. These are healthy signs for Indonesia's political transition.

Despite these positive movements, Indonesia faces several tough challenges if it is to survive the infancy period of democracy and develop into a regional leader. Indonesia is a vast country with huge ethnic diversity, and the government will have to prioritize national security. However, the military must handle separatist attempts carefully. Failure to do so could result in entrenched civil war in several parts of the country. In addition, there is a possible misunderstanding afoot from the onslaught of religious conservatism. International observers have expressed fear at the success of radical Islamic groups such as PKS in the recent elections. Though their electoral platforms were void of Islamic rhetoric, the goals of conservative political parties remain unchanged—to create an Islamic state. Whether this poses a threat to democracy is not yet known. There are three possible scenarios. First, the conservative parties will respect the democratic system and pursue their party goals by the people's mandate. The recent elections suggest that this is the likely way. Second, the parties attempt to overthrow the democratic system and force Islamic law on the country. This scenario is unlikely, due to the existence of moderate Islamic groups, and a clear political preference for secular parties. Moreover, there would unlikely be militaristic support for such an agenda. Indonesia is simply too vast to achieve such a goal without either military or mass support. Third, the government, either through international pressure or desire to gain a majority, seeks to stamp out Islamic parties or confuses party agendas with the terrorist dilemma. This third option cannot be ruled out.

Lastly, Indonesia must achieve economic stability. Currently, a third of the labor force, 40 million people, is unemployed. The government is unable to sustain a growth in GDP above 5 percent, the average rate in the Soeharto era, leaving millions jobless. Critics blame the government's sluggishness and inconsistency toward removing impediments to domestic and foreign investment. But it is a simple notion that 40 million unemployed will not be appeased by theoretical improvements for a sustained period of time. The next president will have to move fast to revive the economy, or risk social instability transforming into political instability.

Further Reading

Adam, Schwarz. *Indonesia: The 2004 Election and Beyond*. Singapore: Institute of Southeast Asian Studies, 2004.

Antlöv, Hans and Cederroth, Sven, eds. *Elections in Indonesia: The New Order and Beyond*. London: Routledge, 2004.

Bresnan, John. *Managing Indonesia: The Modern Political Economy*. New York: Columbia University Press, 1993.

Crouch, Harold. *The Army and Politics in Indonesia*. Rev. ed. Ithaca, N.Y.: Cornell University Press, 1988.

Liddle, R. William. "A Useful Fiction: Democratic Legitimation in New Order Indonesia." In *The Politics of Elections in Southeast Asia*. Ed. R. H. Taylor. London: Woodrow Wilson Center Press and Cambridge University Press, 1996.

———. "Indonesia: Suharto's Tightening Grip." *Journal of Democracy* 7, no. 4 (October 1996): 58–72.

———. "Indonesia's Democratic Past and Future." *Comparative Politics* (July 1992): 443–62.

Mackie, Jamie, and Andrew MacIntyre. "Politics." In *Indonesia's New Order: The Dynamics of Socio-Economic Transformation*. Ed. Hal Hill. St. Leonards, New South Wales: Allen and Unwin, 1994.

Porter, D. J. *Managing Politics and Islam in Indonesia*. London: Routledge, 2002.

Schwartz, Adam. *A Nation in Waiting: Indonesia in the 1990s*. St. Leonards, New South Wales: Allen and Unwin, 1994.

Schwartz, A., and J. Paris. *The Politics of Post-Suharto Indonesia*. New York: Council of Foreign Relations, 1999.

Simons, G. *Indonesia: The Long Oppression*. New York: St. Martin's Press, 2000.

Suryadinata, L. *Elections and Politics in Indonesia*. Singapore: Institute for Southeast Asian Studies, 2002.

Vatikiotis, Michael R.J. *Indonesian Politics under Suharto: Order, Development and Pressure for Change*. London: Routledge, 1993.

ISLAMIC REPUBLIC OF IRAN
(Jomhuri-ye Eslami-ye Iran)

By Pooya Alaedini, Siamak Namazi, and Lawrence G. Potter
Revised by Fred H. Lawson, Ph.D.

Iran, a country of 68 million people (2005 est.), serves as the nexus between the Caspian Sea and the Persian Gulf and connects the steppes of Central Asia to Anatolia and continental Europe. To the north, Iran is bounded by the Republic of Azerbaijan, the Caspian Sea, and Turkmenistan, to the east by Afghanistan and Pakistan, to the south by the Sea of Oman and the Persian Gulf, and to the west by Iraq and Turkey. Covering some 1.648 million square kilometers, Iran's topography is often likened to that of a bowl with the Alborz Mountains creating the northern rim and the Zagros Mountains the western and southern rims. The center of the country is arid and dry for the most part, while the Alborz Mountains have created a fertile crescent around the Caspian Sea. Most of Iran's major cities, including Tehran, Tabriz, Shiraz, and Mashhad, were built along the foothills of mountains where a traditional system of irrigation canals, *qanats*, delivered needed water.

While the majority of Iran's population is considered to be Persian, the country is diverse in terms of ethnicity and language. Most of the population is Twelver Shiite Muslim, while religious minorities include Sunni Muslim, Zoroastrian, Jewish, Christian, and Bahai. In addition, Iran is the largest host to refugees in the world and currently shelters close to 1.5 million displaced persons from Afghanistan and Iraq. The country is undergoing rapid urbanization, and the urban areas now claim 60 percent of the total population, compared with only 31 percent in the 1950s. Iran

possesses one of the youngest populations in the world, with 30 percent of the people 15 years old or younger.

The country's urban population was largely responsible for the overthrow of the monarch, Shah Mohammad Reza Pahlavi (reigned 1941–79, died July 27, 1980, in exile). A coalition of clerics (*ulama*), merchants (*bazaaris*), liberal reformers, Islamic radicals, Communists, and guerrilla organizations united behind Ayatollah Ruhollah Khomeini and brought the monarchy to an end on February 11, 1979. This broad coalition fell apart shortly after victory, and Islamic radicals loyal to Khomeini managed to consolidate power by pushing out the liberals and carrying out mass arrests and executions of the Communists and guerrillas between 1980 and 1982.

The System of Government

Iran is officially an Islamic Republic, following the approval by 98.2 percent of eligible voters of a referendum on March 29–30, 1979. Modeled on Khomeini's ideas of *velayat-e faqih* (rule of the Jurist), an unorthodox conception of Islamic government, the community is to be guided by the most respected religious scholar (the *faqih* or Leader), who rules in the absence of the Twelfth Imam. This Imam, a descendant of the Prophet Muhammad, went into "concealment" in the ninth century and is expected to return at the end of the era

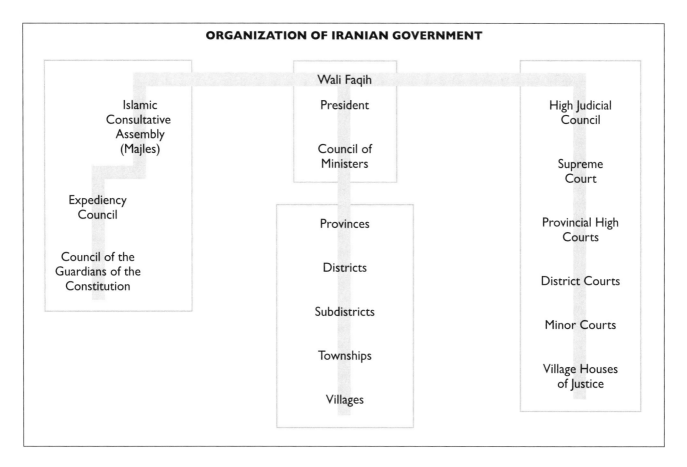

ORGANIZATION OF IRANIAN GOVERNMENT

Wali Faqih

Islamic Consultative Assembly (Majles)

President

Council of Ministers

High Judicial Council

Expediency Council

Supreme Court

Council of the Guardians of the Constitution

Provinces

Provincial High Courts

Districts

District Courts

Subdistricts

Minor Courts

Townships

Village Houses of Justice

Villages

to establish a golden age. Until that time, the Imam's will is transmitted to the people through inspired ayatollahs (*mojtahids*). Ayatollah Khomeini ruled Iran as *faqih* until his death in June 1989.

After Khomeini's death there has been no absolute source of authority in Iran. While one can readily identify the heads of different state institutions and political movements, it is often difficult to tell which actor holds the trump cards on a particular issue.

LEADERSHIP

The 1979 constitution maintained that the highest political and religious authority of Iran is the Leader (*faqih*). The Leader has extensive powers: he nominates the religious jurists on the Council of Guardians, appoints the highest judicial authorities, and is designated commander in chief of the country's armed forces. He can declare war. He must sign the order formalizing the election of the president and can dismiss the president if the Supreme Court finds him politically incompetent (a fate that befell Abolhasan Bani Sadr, the first president of the Islamic Republic, in June 1981).

The description of the Leader's powers was largely designed to fit the person of Ayatollah Khomeini, who

enjoyed unparalleled popular and religious legitimacy. He was a grand ayatollah and a source of emulation (*marja'-e taqlid*) in the Shiite religious hierarchy. Not surprisingly, the issue of succession was always on the minds of the rulers of post-revolutionary Iran. Originally, Ayatollah Hosain Ali Montazeri was designated as Khomeini's successor, but after a series of disagreements between the two over the powers of the leadership in late 1988 and early 1989, Montazeri was dismissed as the future Leader. Khomeini failed to recommend a new figure before his death.

After Khomeini's death no grand ayatollah in Iran had the ambition to take over the political reins. In fact, the *ulama* of Iran traditionally eschewed direct political involvement and saw their mandate as constructive criticism of the system. According to the constitution, "the task of appointing the Leader shall be vested with the experts elected by the people," that is, the Assembly of Experts. Should there be no decisive majority of the people in favor of one *faqih*, three to five candidates are to be appointed by the Assembly of Experts to serve on a Leadership Council.

Consequently, in June 1989, the first debate the Assembly of Experts faced was whether to opt for a single person or a group of *faqihs* to take over Khomeini's position. With the support of Ali Akbar Hashemi Rafsanjani, then Speaker of the Majles (the Parliament) and one of Khomeini's most trusted advisers, Hojjatoleslam Hosein Ali Khamenei was nominated as a compromise candidate and won majority support. The government and the media then began referring to him as ayatollah, and he was proclaimed Leader of the Islamic Republic. Later his authority was downgraded and the function as the highest religious authority was delegated to Grand Ayatollah Araki.

Khamenei, too young and lacking religious eminence, worked hard to increase his religious authority by appeasing the conservative *ulama* of Qom. However, his ambition to become the religious source of emulation was hindered following the death of Grand Ayatollah Araki in 1995, when Iran was left with no grand ayatollahs and the country's high-ranking clergy were forced to announce new sources of emulation. Khamenei's candidacy was rejected, and he was told that he lacked the needed religious credentials, though in an apparent face-saving compromise, he was included on a list of 10 ayatollahs who had the potential to become *mojtahids* in the future.

Notwithstanding, Khamenei is still the highest-ranking official of the Islamic Republic, and the Leadership as an institution maintains a great deal of power and authority. During the 1990s the Leadership came under severe criticism by Islamic reformers and liberals, who charged that Khamenei was out of touch with the needs of the country and the Iranian people. The charges prompted a concerted counterattack by defenders of the system of *velayat-e faqih,* who mobilized a variety of clerical and parastatal institutions, most notably the Revolutionary Guards Corps, to restore both the institutional prerogatives of the Leader and the personal influence of Khamenei.

EXECUTIVE

The Leadership was not the only office of government severely affected by the death of Ayatollah Khomeini. Under the original constitution of 1979, the president of the Islamic Republic was elected by a majority of popular votes cast, for a four-year term, and he could be reelected only once. He would preside over a cabinet of 26 members and would appoint the prime minister, who remained in power unless he lost the confidence of Parliament. The Leader has the power to dismiss the president.

Concurrent with the appointment of Ali Khamenei as the new leader, Rafsanjani was elected president of the republic and the post of prime minister

was eliminated. In effect, the political authority of Khomeini was now embodied in a Khamenei-Rafsanjani dyad. This arrangement attested to the political skills of Rafsanjani, who quickly proved himself adept at increasing the power of the political institution he controlled.

In many ways, the arrangement was also ideal for purposes of maintaining the new regime. One of the most complex tasks that Khomeini had mastered in his ascent to power was balancing conservative and radical Islamic forces. To retain both pillars of support, Khomeini often resorted to contradictory messages in various speeches, one day praising the concept of private ownership as one that is guaranteed and encouraged by Islam, and the next speaking to the grievances of the *mostaz'afan* (oppressed and poor masses). Similarly, in the duet comprised of Khamenei and Rafsanjani, the responsibility to appease different power centers was divided: Khamenei attempted to maintain good relations with the *ulama* and Islamic radicals, while Rafsanjani took a more moderate position and appealed to the *bazaaris*, technocrats, and intellectuals. The country's remaining secular leftists were gradually removed from the political scene.

The official powers and responsibilities of the president are rather vague in the Iranian constitution. Article 113 states: "After the office of Leadership, the president is the highest official in the country. He is the one responsible for implementing the constitution and acting as the head of the executive, except in matters directly concerned with [the office of] the Leadership." The real power of the executive branch, however, rests in its control over Iran's oil revenues, which account for nearly three-quarters of the country's foreign exchange income. The executive also has primary authority over government expenditures.

During his eight years in power, Rafsanjani filled executive posts with his supporters. Key Cabinet positions were given to moderates and technocrats close to him, with a few compromises to the radicals. He further bypassed the legislative checks and balances by often appointing candidates ousted or rejected by the Majles' special advisers and vice presidents—positions not subject to parliamentary oversight.

While such maneuvers were effective in helping Rafsanjani retain credibility among his supporters, it further complicated the political landscape of the Islamic Republic and created institutions with vague and overlapping mandates. However, the Rafsanjani legacy paved the way for the prominence of technical expertise as the basis for filling government offices, rather than strictly revolutionary and Islamic credentials. Hence, the number of moderates in key cabinet positions increased.

In May 1997 Mohammad Khatami won the presidential elections with nearly 70 percent of the total votes. Khatami represented a new generation of postrevolutionary leaders. His primary supporters included students, women, intellectuals, and artists, who hoped that the new president would loosen the existing constraints on individual expression. After a year-long honeymoon, during which he took steps to relax official controls on newspapers, called for greater access for women to senior administrative positions, and authorized the formation of political parties, Khatami ran into strong resistance from forces opposed to political and social liberalization.

President Khatami's efforts to revitalize the sagging local economy provoked opposition as well. He quickly alienated the administration of the powerful Foundation of the Oppressed, and angered former president Rafsanjani by openly criticizing earlier attempts to promote private enterprise on the grounds that they had led to a renewed concentration of wealth. More important, his unwillingness to stand up to protect university students and journalists who engaged in public protest to demand greater freedom of expression greatly diminished his prestige among those who had been his most enthusiastic early supporters.

Khatami won reelection to the presidency in May 2001 but exercised less and less power over political outcomes. At a rally on the campus of Tehran University in December, he was put on the defensive by angry students and attempted to mollify them by insisting that he had only "limited powers" to carry out a reform program. When he visited the city of Bam in December 2003 to survey the devastation inflicted by a massive earthquake, he was greeted by catcalls and local representatives refused to meet with him. His steadily falling prestige tended to weaken the institution of the presidency as well, and by early 2004 the Leader had become the more important of the two offices.

In June 2005 a new presidential election was held, and a former student radical leader and mayor of Tehran, Mahmoud Ahmadinejad, defeated a number of candidates, including Rafsanjani, to become the country's first non-cleric president in 24 years.

LEGISLATURE

The Majles-e Shura-ye Eslami (Islamic Consultative Assembly), commonly referred to as the Majles, is composed of 270 members elected for four-year terms.

There are 265 geographical seats, plus 5 seats reserved for recognized religious minorities. The Majles holds open sessions, barring exceptional conditions. These discussions are made public by radio, and the minutes are readily available in various media. The 1979 constitution empowers this body to make laws and approve international agreements, as well as to conduct investigations into all the affairs of the country.

The Majles is by no means a rubber stamp for the executive. There is often spirited debate, and the Majles has frequently asserted its independence by refusing to confirm some of the choices of the president for cabinet posts. In fact, when Mohammad Khatami was elected president, analysts immediately evaluated his political skills by how he passed his moderate cabinet through a radical legislature. In addition to veto power over the cabinet, the Iranian legislature has final approval of the five-year plans that set the tone for the country's development and investment policies. The Second Five-Year Plan, which was in effect until March 2000, was originally drafted by moderates in the executive branch to emphasize industrialization. However, radicals in the Majles chose to modify the plan and change its direction to emphasize agricultural development.

In the 1996 elections radicals and moderates competed fiercely for seats. As a result of those elections, 100 of the 270 seats in the Majles were clearly connected to radical forces led by the Speaker, Hojjatoleslam Nateq Nuri. Groups affiliated with moderate factions won about 90 seats. The remaining 80 deputies were considered independent or having only loose contacts with major political factions.

Parliamentary elections in February 2004 returned the radicals to power, after the Council of Guardians had disqualified more than 3,500 reform candidates. Only 51 percent of eligible voters turned out to cast a ballot, despite strenuous efforts by the Revolutionary Guards Corps to mobilize the inhabitants of impoverished urban neighborhoods and areas of the countryside that had previously had relatively low participation rates. The new speaker, Gholam Ali Haddad Adel, enjoyed close personal ties to Khamenei, which helped to reestablish a strong political alliance between the Majles and the Leader.

COUNCIL OF GUARDIANS

This council, known as Shura-ye Negahban, is an extremely powerful 12-member group that determines whether laws passed by Parliament conform to Islamic principles and can be ratified. It is responsible for interpreting constitutional law and supervising elections. Of its membership, six clerics are appointed by the *faqih*, the other six, whose selection must be confirmed by the Majles, are nominated by the High Judicial Council and are laymen lawyers. Members are elected for six-year terms. At times, this group has refused to concur with measures passed by the Majles, notably those on land reform. The Council of Guardians is headed by Ayatollah Ahmad Jannati. In the 2000 and 2004 parliamentary elections this body took an active part in skewing the candidate pool by rejecting prospective candidates whom it considered to exhibit a "lack of respect for Islam." During the first five years of the 21st century, the Council of Guardians vetoed approximately one-third of the bills adopted by the Majles on similar grounds.

EXPEDIENCY COUNCIL

The Council on Determining the System's Expediency (Majma'-e Tashkhis-e Maslehat-e Nezam), or the Expediency Council, has become one of the key institutions of the Islamic Republic. Created in 1986 by Khomeini's personal decree, the Expediency Council is a mediator and arbitrator between the Majles and the Council of Guardians. Originally, this role essentially amounted to mediation between the moderate and radical forces in the Islamic Republic.

The Expediency Council's influence and power were increased after Khomeini's death. This move was made to appease the members of the Council of Experts who favored a Leadership Council rather than a single Leader. As Rafsanjani neared the end of his second and last term as president under the constitution, a group of his supporters started a debate over amending the constitution to allow him a third term. Such a move was widely opposed, even by Rafsanjani himself. But the true political prowess of Rafsanjani has always been redefining the political institutions of Iran to suit his ambitions. Hence, in March 1997, just two months before the presidential elections, it came as no surprise when Khamenei declared that the Expediency Council was to assume increased responsibility. At that time, Khamenei doubled the number of the Leader's appointees to 26, declared that the Expediency Council would serve as his main advisory body, and appointed Rafsanjani as the Council's chairperson.

ASSEMBLY OF EXPERTS

The main duties of the Assembly of Experts have been to draft the constitution, to name the Leader, and to make amendments to the constitution. The first Assembly of Experts was a 75-member group (60 of whom were clerics) elected in August 1979 to draft the Islamic Republic constitution. These elections were boycotted by opposition groups when it became obvious that dissenting viewpoints would be excluded. The first Assembly was disbanded when the constitution was completed. A second, 83-member Assembly of Experts was elected in late 1982 to choose Khomeini's successor, seeking to avoid a political vacuum after his death. In November 1985 it chose Ayatollah Montazeri, who was later dismissed from the post. After Khomeini's death in 1989, the Assembly of Experts formed once again and elected the current Leader, Ali Khamenei.

JUDICIARY

In principle, the judiciary is an independent force. Its responsibilities are overseen by the five-member High Judicial Council, made up of the head of the Supreme Court, the attorney general, and three judges. They serve for five-year terms, with the possibility of extension for another five. Ayatollah Mohammad Yazdi, a radical cleric, is currently the chairman of this council and head of the judiciary. The power to appoint and dismiss the head of the judiciary lies in the hands of the Leader, and hence the judiciary stands independent of the executive and legislative powers. Consequently, there have been several occasions when the judiciary has blocked the executive branch's policies.

Trials are to be held openly and the public is allowed to attend, unless this is incompatible with public order, which it often is. Judges issue findings on cases, which must be based on Islamic principles. The court system is overloaded due to a scarcity of judges with religious qualifications. In January 1998 a few female judges were allowed to preside over the courts of the Islamic Republic for the first time.

Besides the general courts of the country, a number of "revolutionary courts" were formed in the early days of the revolution. Led by *ulama*, these courts were responsible for the execution and imprisonment of "traitors" in the Pahlavi regime, and wide disparities in sentences for the same crime were common. Although the revolutionary courts were officially merged with the country's general courts in 1984, traces of them still exist.

REGIONAL AND LOCAL GOVERNMENT

There has always been a strong tradition of local government in Iran, although power was increasingly centralized in Tehran under the monarchy. Provincial heads, as well as the mayor of Tehran, were appointed directly by the shah, and the minister of the interior was the main influence in selecting provincial officials. The only authority elected on a local level was the village headman.

Iran is currently divided into 30 provinces (*ostan*), headed by governor-generals (*ostandar*). However, as a result of rapid population growth and the urban boom, as well as political considerations, these divisions are constantly changing. Provinces are divided into districts (*shahrestan*) headed by governors (*farmandar*). Districts are divided into subdistricts (*hakhsh*) administered by lieutenant governors (*bakhshdar*). Subdistricts are divided into townships (*dehestan*) led by sheriffs (*dehdar*). Townships are divided into villages (*deh*), which are led by a headman (*kadkhoda*).

Elections for local councils were held for the first time in February 1999. Voter turnout was reported to be extremely high, although precise numbers were not released. A second round of municipal and provincial council elections in February 2003 saw considerably lower participation rates, estimated at no more than 20 percent of eligible voters in Tehran, Isfahan, Shiraz, and Mashhad.

The Electoral System

Members of the Majles are elected by direct and secret ballot. The first elections were held in two rounds, in March and May 1980; the latest elections took place in February 2004. A candidate has to have a majority to win on the first ballot; otherwise, there are more rounds of voting. This system makes it difficult to fill seats in many constituencies. Also, there have been instances of ballots for entire areas being disqualified and the election process repeated, which certainly adds to voter distrust.

Candidates who wish to run for office must be approved by the Council of Guardians, which drastically pares the list of aspirants. No standard criterion has been declared as the basis of this selection process. Thus, of over 200 candidates who registered to run in the presidential election of 1997, all but four were disqualified and no adequate explanation was provided for a person's disqualification; likewise, in 2005 over 1000 candidates were disqualified, leaving only seven to run for president.

Suffrage is universal in the Islamic Republic, an ironic fact given that Khomeini criticized the shah for extending voting rights to women. The voting age is 15, and assistance in reading the ballot is provided to illiterates. The vote of youth was a major factor in the victory of Khatami, who during his campaign had courted young people, women, and intellectuals. Around 90 percent of eligible voters participated in the 1997 presidential election. Khatami managed to win the support of 20 million people, or approximately 70 percent of the total participants.

In 2005 the turnout was only 59 percent. The victor, Mahmoud Ahmadinejad, drew considerable support from the poorer classes, reflecting his appeal as a long-time radical who spoke out against improved relations with the United States and his promise to address persistent economic problems.

The Party System

Until 1998 there were no officially recognized parties in the country, although the 1979 Iranian constitution allowed for their formation provided they did not oppose the principles of Islam or undermine national sovereignty and unity. The Islamic Republic Party, officially sanctioned in the one-party system that was established after the revolution, was disbanded in 1987. As a result of increased polarization within the government and the general public, the formation of new parties out of the existing factions has begun to occur.

POLITICAL FACTIONS WITHIN THE RULING COALITION

While Khomeini was able to defuse disagreements among the ruling coalition, factional fighting intensified after his death because of real differences among various groups within the regime. At the same time, the survival of the regime has been always at the top of each faction's agenda, and so far the existence of differences has not resulted in open hostilities. The main actors can be categorized as the radicals, the moderate pragmatists, the Islamic conservatives, and the liberal reformers.

Major Political Parties
ISLAMIC SOCIETY OF ENGINEERS
(Jame'e-ye Eslaami-e Mohandesin; ISE)

This organization is the party of President Mahmoud Ahmadinejad, who won the 2005 election. Interestingly, the ISE did not support Ahmadinejad during the election but instead backed Ali Larijani.

SOCIETY OF COMBATANT CLERGY

(Jame'eh-ye Rohaniyat-e Mobarez; JRM)

This party is one of the main bastions of power among the radicals who have dominated the Islamic Republic since its inception.

It enjoys institutional support from the Revolutionary Guards Corps, which took a more active part in defending the existing political order after a number of large-scale riots erupted in spring 1992. Its interests are also furthered by the more militant Ansar-e Hizbullah (Supporters of the Party of God), which emerged in the fall of 1997 and has played an active role in suppressing dissent on university campuses.

ASSEMBLY OF COMBATANT CLERICS

(Majma'-e Rohaniyun-e Mobarez; MRM)

This party split from the JRM in 1987. It is also known to dominate Sazman-e Mojahedin-e Enqelab-e Eslami, the Organization of the Crusades of the Islamic Revolution.

Mohammad Khatami, the former president of Iran, is the best-known figure affiliated with this organization. Other prominent figures include Mir Hosein Musavi (former prime minister), Behzad Nabavi (former minister), Musavi Ardebili (former head of the judiciary), and Mehdi Karrubi (former Majles Speaker).

The pro-Khatami faction has recently announced the formation of a new political party, called the Islamic Iran Participation Party. The newspaper *Khordad* seems to be publishing the views of this group.

EXECUTIVES OF CONSTRUCTION

(Kargozaran-e Sazandegi)

The pragmatist grouping formed around the personality and ideas of Rafsanjani. In January 1996 a group of Rafsanjani's close aides and advisers drew up a platform to compete in the Majles elections. This faction, which is composed of the technocratic elements in the regime, was formally to be known as Kargozaran-e Sazandegi (Executives of Construction). It is now an officially recognized party.

Besides Rafsanjani, other members of the Kargozaran include Gholam Hosain Karbaschi (former

mayor of Tehran), Abdollah Nuri (former minister of the interior), and Mohsen Nurbaksh (governor of the Central Bank of Iran). This faction's ideas and policies are supported by the newspapers *Hamshahri*, *Bahman*, and *Iran*.

ISLAMIC IRAN PARTICIPATION FRONT

(Jebheye Mosharekate Irane Eslaami)

This liberal reformist party is led by Mohammad Reza Khatami, the brother of former president Khatami. Its candidate in the 2005 presidential election, Mostafa Moin, was among the approximately 1,000 candidates who were disqualified prior to the election.

Minor Political Parties

There are numerous smaller parties in Iran. Those that back the regime are often dominated by larger and more powerful parties. Internal opposition to the Islamic Republic remains amorphous and sporadic. The only organizations that expressly reject the existing political order and engage in a modicum of activity inside the county are the Liberation Movement of Iran (Nahzat-i Azadi-ye Iran) and circles close to it, as well as the National Front of Iran (Jebhe-ye Melli-ye Iran) and the Iranian Nation Party (Hezb-e Mellat-e Iran). A major part of opposition activity in Iran has been carried out by intellectual circles gathered around a few relatively independent journals and magazines and by independent writers, clerics, artists, and lawyers.

LIBERATION MOVEMENT OF IRAN

(Nahzat-e Azadi-ye Iran)

The LMI, led by Ebrahim Yazdi (a minister in the postrevolutionary transitional government) has remained active since the revolution. It was founded by Mehdi Bazargan, the late Ayatollah Mahmud Taleqani, and others in 1957. They hoped the party, influenced by Shiite Islam and European socialism, would show Islam's relevance to modern politics in a way the traditional *ulama* could not. For years, this party and its publications provided public criticism of Khomeini's policies. In the 1980 elections Liberation Movement candidates won five seats; the party boycotted the 1984 elections. Bazargan sought to run for president in 1985 but was disqualified by the Council of Guardians. He did not oppose the formation of an Islamic Republic but wanted to reform it by persuasion and public protest, not violent action.

Ebrahim Yazdi became secretary-general of the party after Bazargan's death in 1995. LMI remains tolerated despite its criticism of the government, though several of its leaders have been frequently harassed or arrested. LMI and circles close to it have tried to participate in different Iranian elections with very little success. Yazdi was arrested in late 1997 but was released on bail shortly thereafter without being charged. While calling for democracy, the rule of law, and free elections, the LMI supported President Khatami against the conservative and radical factions in the ruling coalition.

NATIONAL FRONT OF IRAN (INF)

(Jebheh-ye Melli-ye Iran)

The old National Front was not a political party as such but rather a coalition of parties opposed to the shah, originally formed in 1949 by Dr. Mohammad Mosadeq. Most National Front leaders were arrested after the fall of Mosadeq's government in 1953, and the movement was reconstituted as the National Resistance Movement. This, in turn, was banned by the government in 1956.

The new National Front was established in 1977 and played a relatively important role in the early days of the revolution. Its ideology is secularist and slightly left-of-center; it was opposed to the establishment of an Islamic Republic. Support for the party has been drawn from professionals and the educated middle class. INF was led by secular supporters of Mosadeq, notably Karim Sanjabi and Shahpur Bakhtiar. There was a rift between the two in the fall of 1978. Sanjabi concluded a pact with Khomeini, then in exile in Paris, to work together for the overthrow of the shah. He went on to become foreign minister in the first postrevolutionary government, although he resigned in April 1979. Bakhtiar, who did not oppose the idea of constitutional monarchy, served as the last prime minister under the shah. The National Front expelled him from the party, and he left Iran in February 1979 after trying to prevent the return of Khomeini. He was assassinated in France in 1991.

Today, although INF is not officially recognized and is often harassed, the party continues its activities in Iran under the direction of a central council. Supporters of the party are also active in Western Europe and North America, where they publish several periodicals. While in the years following the revolution the party was squeezed out by the more radical groups, there still exists a moderate, centrist constituency for the program of the National Front. Among the prominent members of the National Front coalition who are still close to the party are Daryoush Forouhar and his Iranian Nation Party (Hezb-e Mellat-e Iran), which has boycotted the presidential and Majles elections in the past.

Other Political Forces

OPPOSITION IN EXILE

There are many Iranian groups outside the country that oppose the current government in Iran. The opposition in exile remains, however, fragmented and is characterized by constantly shifting alliances. The programs of these groups span the political spectrum: from royalists who want to restore the Pahlavi family to the throne to those who argue for a constitutional monarchy to nationalists and leftists.

The National Iranian Resistance Movement, which aimed to establish a social democratic government, was the first exile group to be formed in Paris (in 1979) and was for a while one of the largest and best-funded groups. It was led by Shahpur Bakhtiar.

Royalist groups are primarily directed by the family of the late shah (who never abdicated) or his former top officials. Some support the return to the throne of the shah's son, who declared himself Reza Shah II upon reaching the age of 20 on October 31, 1980. Reza has pledged that as a constitutional monarch, he would reign but not rule. He has kept a low profile and spends most of his time in the United States and Europe.

The significance and membership of the once-powerful leftist parties have been severely reduced as a result of both the crackdown on their activities inside Iran and the collapse of the Soviet bloc. There are nevertheless several Iranian leftist groups that have kept active through their publications in Western Europe and North America. Their platforms cover the entire leftist spectrum, from hard-line Stalinists and Maoists to those believing in socialism through parliamentary means. Many of these groups have been formed through split-offs from the Tudeh Party (the original postwar Communist party of Iran) or Fada'yan (originally Sazman-e Cherik-ha-ye Fadai-ye Khalq-e Iran), while others may be considered newer groups.

ORGANIZATION OF THE CRUSADERS OF THE IRANIAN PEOPLE

(Sazman-e Mojahedin-e Khalq-e Iran)

With the secular leftist parties and royalists in disarray, the Mojahedin has become the most cohesive Iranian opposition group in exile. The Mojahedin was formed in 1966 and initiated military operations in 1971. The group was a major force in the 1978–79 revolution. Following the revolution, however, the Mojahedin broke decisively with the clerical regime, on June 20, 1981, after authorities opened fire on a huge demonstration organized by the Mojahedin to protest the dismissal of President Bani Sadr by Khomeini.

The leader of the group, Mas'ud Rajavi, and President Bani Sadr were forced into exile in France and formed a short-lived coalition. The Mojahedin continued its activities from Paris until the French government closed down its headquarters in 1986. The Mojahedin's leadership as well as other party members then moved to Iraq where they formed an army of several thousand fighters, responsible for unsuccessful attacks on Iranian soil. Women are reported to constitute a major component of this army, which is under an all-female leadership council with Rajavi's wife, Maryam Azdanlu Rajavi, as commander. The Mojahedin has organized an extensive structure in Europe and North America to lobby against the regime in Iran.

The Mojahedin was a respected organization in Iran because of its long guerrilla struggle against the shah. Its ideology, emphasizing Shiite Islam, socialism, and Iranian nationalism, proved to have strong appeal to the lower classes, who carried out the revolution. However, this appeal has been seriously compromised because of disillusionment with the group's leaders who have built personality cults around themselves, its violent tactics that kill civilians, its ties with Iraq, and the apparent lack of a viable platform.

SHIITE CLERICS

The clerical group has been estimated to include 300,000 persons, a large number of whom are lower-ranking *ulama* active on a local level, preaching in mosques throughout the country and providing religious leadership and education. Middle- and higher-ranking clerics are called *mojtahids*. The title *hojjatoleslam* ("proof of Islam") is below the rank of ayatollah ("sign of God"), of which there are thought to be about 100 at present. The highest-ranking ayatollahs are called grand ayatollahs, of which there are only a handful.

The ranks of the Shiite clergy, and the number of mosques, swelled after the revolution. Formerly, low-ranking *ulamas* were not held in high esteem, but now they have achieved new power and prestige. Before the revolution there were about 10,000 theological students in Iran; today their numbers have increased considerably, two-thirds of them in Qom.

The image of the Iranian *ulama* generally conveyed by the foreign media is that of a fanatically intolerant, monolithic establishment. This image, however, is misleading, for it does not take into account the serious personal and ideological disagreements that characterize intracleric politics.

Khamenei is not a grand ayatollah and therefore cannot be a *marja'* (source of emulation) for Shiite Muslims. To justify his position as Leader, the constitution was changed in 1989 to separate the office of *faqih* from that of the *marja'*. This change, however, goes against the spirit of Khomeini's conception of *velayat-e faqih* (the rule of the Jurist). At the same time Khamenei was appointed by the Council of Experts to the position of Leader Grand Ayatollah Araki was chosen as *marja'* (the highest religious authority).

With the death of Araki and a few other grand ayatollahs in the early 1990s, the problem of *marjaeiyyat* (the position of the source of emulation) has been brought to the forefront once again. Of the clerics with credentials to be *marja'*, almost none seems to be on good terms with the low- and middle-ranking clerics who control Iran.

In 1997 Ayatollah Montazeri challenged the establishment by questioning the credentials of Khamenei as Leader. Montazeri's office was attacked in response, and demonstrations against him were staged in front of his residence in Qom. Several high-ranking clerics and leading political figures support Montazeri. The outcome of this struggle and the inherent contradiction in the present ruling arrangement have important implications for the fate of the regime.

MILITARY

The two shahs of the Pahlavi dynasty were both authoritarian figures closely identified with the military. They pampered it and used it as their primary instrument for modernizing the nation and asserting central control from Tehran. Before the revolution the shah's armed forces (413,000 men in uniform, plus 300,000 reserves) were equipped with the best military hardware available. This formidable force was, however, impotent during the revolution. Afterward, the officer corps was discredited for having supported the shah, and many high-ranking officers were executed, imprisoned, or fled the country, and Iran's military was severely weakened.

The postrevolutionary rulers continued to mistrust the army, which they considered foreign-oriented. In order to protect itself from a potential coup d'état, the new regime created the Revolutionary Guards Corps as a counterweight to the army. After Iraq's invasion of Iran in 1980 and the ensuing eight-year war, the Revolutionary Guards grew enormously. The Leader is the commander in chief and supervises both forces.

Today the Corps is structured much like the army with its own ground, air, and naval forces. It has a draft, just like the regular army. All males are required to register for military service at the age of 18 for two years, unless they enter university, in which case they serve after obtaining their degree. At present, the regular armed forces consist of 400,000 men, while the Revolutionary Guards are composed of 120,000 men. Due to demographic changes, Iran's armed forces will be inflated in the future since more men are drafted each year than discharged.

The Revolutionary Guards also control the *basij* (mobilization) forces, which is a large volunteer force (formed in November 1979) used primarily as unpaid militia. The regime is increasingly trying to transform this group from that of a revolutionary force to a civilian one.

The Revolutionary Guards are known to interfere in politics, usually on the side of the radicals, despite a clear legal ban on doing so.

FOUNDATIONS

One of the most powerful forces of postrevolutionary Iran are the quasi-governmental public foundations (*bonyads*). These parastatal organizations have grown into major political and economic nodes of power in the Islamic Republic. With immense financial means at their disposal, some foundations are known to have created and implemented their own policy agenda, including aiding radical groups outside the country. Two foundations deserve particular attention.

The Foundations of the Oppressed and of War Veterans (Bonyad-e Mostaz'afan and Bonyad-e Janbazan) were created atop a number of prerevolutionary foundations. These organizations not only inherited the riches of the Pahlavi Foundation, they also took charge of the properties and businesses confiscated by revolutionary courts. The Foundation of the Oppressed is currently Iran's richest financial institution and controls a lion's share of the country's economic activity. Said to be the richest foundation in the world, it is headed by Mohsen Rafiqdust, the former head of the Revolutionary Guards. Numerous charges of corruption have been leveled against this organization, and while no one has yet dared to accuse Rafigdust himself, his brother was tried and convicted for the embezzlement of hundreds of millions of dollars.

The 15th of Khordad Foundation (Bonyad-e Panzdah-e Khordad) is best known for having placed a bounty on the head of Salman Rushdie, the British author of Indian descent against whom Khomeini issued a *fatwa* that condemned him for writing *The Satanic Verses*. This organization is well known for its militant ideology and is led by Hasan Sanei, one of the most radical figures in Iran today. In 1998 Sanei was included in the expanded Expediency Council. Some analysts see this move as an attempt to integrate Sanei and the 15th of Khordad Foundation within the system and make the organization more accountable.

BAZAARIS

Historically, a significant political force in Iran has been the merchants of the *bazaar*, or *bazaaris*. The *bazaar* refers to a nationwide network of merchants and shops that has long played a key role in financing the clerical establishment, including Islamic schools and social welfare activities.

Bazaaris played a crucial role in ogranizing antiregime demonstrations in 1978-79. Following the success of the revolution, many *bazaaris* were able to grab high positions in the newly formed government. They quickly turned the state agencies into huge profiteering centers that have been in direct competition with the traditional *bazaar*, so that the *bazaar* has lost much of its former social and economic importance. The establishment of trading houses within ministries has accelerated this trend.

Bazaari interests have since the early 1960s been represented by the Society of the Islamic Alliance (Jamiyat-e Mo'talefeh-ye Islami), which organized support among urban tradespeople for Khomeini and other critics of the monarchy. After the revolution, members of this organization managed to seize control of a variety of lucrative enterprises, which gave them a stake in the existing order. The society thus opposed fundamental change to the postrevolutionary political economy, despite harboring a principled interest in the spread of private enterprise and market relations.

INTELLIGENTSIA

Under the monarchy, a rather large group of modern intelligentsia arose. Such people did not hold the clerics in esteem, although some were religious (e.g., Mehdi Bazargan). They included those who supported the regime and its modernizing efforts as well as those who opposed it, including liberals and leftists. While the intelligentsia was instrumental in the revolution, it hoped that the new government would be a liberal, if not secular, regime. As a result, the intelligentsia became a favorite target for removal by the postrevolutionary regime after the failure of the transitional government of Bazargan. Many fled abroad (one estimate places the number at 1 million).

With the imposition of general restrictions on political activity, the intelligentsia has directed its activities toward cultural and social issues. While secular intellectuals have been confined to literary or nonpolitical cultural activities, the liberal-religious intelligentsia has entered into important debates on the role of religion in the government and on the new, liberal interpretations of Islam.

Intellectuals of all stripes played a major role in the 1997 presidential election. Khatami's plaform, which advocated the rule of law, the expansion of civil society, and greater freedom of expression, appealed directly to this particular group. As it became clear that the new president was going to be unable to carry out his ambitious campaign promises, however, disillusion and frustration steadily spread among the educated elite.

ORGANIZED LABOR

Trade unions as such do not now exist in Iran. Between 1945 and 1953 several trade unions were formed, particularly in Tehran and the oilfields, and there were many strikes. However, from 1953 until 1979 any attempt to organize a labor movement was strongly suppressed. After 1959 the government permitted the formation of "official" trade unions, which were not allowed to strike or engage in political activity (unless it was to support the regime). There were about 1,000 such unions by 1978.

After the fall of the monarchy, many factory owners fled the country and workers took over the factories, which they ran through workers' councils. The postrevolutionary regime has generally taken an ambivalent position toward the workers' councils. With the worsening economic situation, many labor strikes have been recorded in the country and have been crushed by the government to prevent further escalation of labor activity. Today, two government-sanctioned, national labor organizations exist in Iran, the House of Workers and the Islamic Society of Workers, with the latter established to counterbalance the former.

YOUTH

With the rise of the fertility rate in the years following the revolution, Iran has experienced a drastic demographic change. As a result, over half of the country's population either was born after the revolution or has no recollection of the prerevolutionary period and the revolutionary struggle. While the regime has tried its best to educate youth to its own liking, this group constitutes a disaffected and potentially antagonistic force. With Iran's high unemployment rate and unpopular social restrictions, the government will not be able to satisfy the demands of this segment of the society. Their aspirations were apparent during the 1997 presidential election, in which those young people who could vote became a major force behind Khatami's victory.

UNIVERSITY STUDENTS

While students played a prominent role in the ouster of the shah, the extent of their support for the postrevolutionary regime is unclear. After the 1978–79 revolution, university campuses remained a major scene of political activity. As a result, all colleges and universities were closed in the spring of 1980 in the wake of rioting. They reopened in 1983 after developing a new "Islamic curriculum." Preference is given for entrance to those with a "correct" political and religious background and to war veterans.

Students presently constitute a large and disaffected group. There is severe competition to matriculate, and, upon acceptance, there are many limits on behavior and political activity. The government has responded to the problem of space availability by establishing the semiprivate, low-quality Islamic Open University, which has branches in many large and small towns. Since the only possible line of political activity on Iran's university campuses has been through the Islamic student associations, secular students have been severely restricted.

Islamic student associations have recently become platforms for protest. Many such organizations have invited liberal-religious intellectuals to deliver speeches. As a result, there have been a number of confrontations between such groups and radical students who, with the help of the mob, have tried to prevent such gatherings. As part of this trend, Heshmat Tabarzadi, the secretary-general of the Union of Students' Islamic

Association and the editor of the weekly *Payam-e Daneshju* (Students' Message) was fined and banned from working at any publication for five years. He had called for a curtailment of the powers of the Leader, in line with a democratic society. This provoked a physical attack on him by a pro-regime mob.

WOMEN

Although Iranian women were a major force in the revolution of 1978–79, they became a main target of restriction once the Islamic regime was established. They were forced to cover their hair and dress modestly in public and were encouraged to limit their role in the society to that of housewives. Some university majors and government positions were rendered off-limits to women. Several laws, which previously protected the rights of women in the family, were revoked or modified.

These major setbacks have not remained unchallenged. The major challenge has come from both the women who essentially believe in the regime and those who have adopted an Islamic discourse to fight for women's rights. Women's magazines such as *Zanan* and *Zan-e Ruz* used religious texts to call for a change or a new interpretation of laws. As a result of these and other efforts by women's organizations, female Majles deputies and other women close to the ruling elite, and independent women's rights advocates, some restrictions have been lifted. All academic subjects are now accessible to women, and a law to protect the rights of women in marriage was passed in 1992. More recently, a female vice president was appointed by President Khatami, and the previous ban on women becoming judges was lifted. Women were a major force behind the election of Khatami.

MINORITY RELIGIOUS GROUPS

About 90 percent of the people of Iran adhere to the Twelver Shiite branch of Islam. Minority religious groups include Sunni Muslims, Bahais, Christians (of different churches), Jews, Zoroastrians, and a few other sects within Shiism. Under the monarchy, there existed a general atmosphere of religious tolerance. As a result, the members of most minority religious were apprehensive at the prospect of a militant Shiite regime coming to power following the 1978–79 revolution.

According to the 1979 constitution, Zoroastrians, Jews, and Christians are the only recognized non-Muslim minorities and are to be left free to follow their religious precepts. These minority religious have traditionally been protected in Muslim societies, which regard their members as "People of the Book." They are represented in the parliament as follows: Zoroastrians and Jews each have one representative; the Assyrian and Chaldean Christians, together, have one representative; and the Armenian Christians of northern and southern Iran each have one representative. There is a provision for a small increase in representation, should their numbers increase.

Bahais, probably the largest non-Muslim minority (over 300,000), are generally reviled by the regime for being apostates from Islam and are not recognized as a legitimate religious group. They are not mentioned in the constitution and have no seat in Parliament.

ETHNIC GROUPS

What constitutes a distinct ethnic group in Iran is difficult to answer. A combination of language, religion, and cross-border proximity to similar groups seems to determine a group's self-identification as a distinct ethnicity in Iran. Most Iranians speak Persian or one of its major dialects (Luri, Bakhtiari, Caspian coast or Baluchi). Persian is a subgroup of the Indo-European family of languages, and is the official language of Iran. It is spoken as a first language by approximately 60 percent of Iranians. The rest speak either a Turkic tongue (Azerbaijani, Turkoman), a Semitic language (Arabic, neo-Syriac), Kurdish or Armenian (a non-Persian Indo-European language).

Kurdish and Baluchi Iranians have long desired autonomy within Iran, although in most cases not actual independence. They have their own political organizations, as well as armed factions that have actively opposed the regime. Government warfare against Kurdish rebels was carried out at the same time as the war against Iraq.

The main political association supported by the Kurds has been the Iranian branch of the Kurdistan Democratic Party, which was led by Abdorrahman Qasemlu until his assassination. The party slogan is "Democracy for Iran, Autonomy for the Kurds." The other Kurdish group, the Kumala, has been important in urban areas, especially Sanandaj.

Azerbaijani speakers are the largest linguistic group in Iran after Persian speakers. Although Azerbaijani is a Turkic language, similar to the official language of the neighboring republic of Azerbaijan, this minority community is well-integrated in Iranian society, and its members make up a considerable proportion of the country's economic and social elite.

A significant percentage of ethnic groups still profess some degree of affiliation to an *il*, which can be defined as an organized pastoralist group based on kinship relations, formerly under the leadership of an *Ilkhan*. There are, however, no accurate figures on such populations, and calculation is difficult because many people who may ethnically belong to an *il* now live in urban areas.

Most *ils* have not played a significant role in national politics since the early part of the 20th century, and this fact does not seem likely to change. They had a long history of hostility toward the Pahlavi regime, which attempted, with some success, to integrate them into a modern state by disarming and settling them and forcing them into the state educational and military systems. The present regime, like the monarchy, represents an urban, centralized government and seeks in similar ways to extend central control to *ili* areas. While the general climate of the first postrevolutionary decade was conducive to the political involvement of the *ils*, with the subsequent consolidation of the regime, most activities of this kind have subsided.

National Prospects

After more than a quarter century of instability due to revolutionary turmoil and war, the Islamic Republic of Iran continues to survive. Early predictions that this unprecedented experiment in modern Islamic governance would collapse as a result of external attack, international isolation, or internal mismanagement proved incorrect. Not even the death of the undisputed Leader, Ayatollah Khomeini, led to the undoing of the new order. Yet a major crisis seems to be escalating in the domestic arena, as the hopes that were kindled by the election of Muhammad Khatami as president in 1997 have largely expired. After a brief political, social, and cultural opening, when it appeared likely that autonomous civic associations, political parties, and independent newspapers and journals might take root and flourish, forces threatened by the turn toward liberalization reasserted control.

In the wake of Khatami's landslide victory, three competing nodes of power emerged inside the regime. One advocated opening up the political system, institutionalizing the rule of law, reducing restrictions on social and cultural life, building bridges to the outside world, and improving the country's technical and intellectual infrastructure. A second favored restoring a vanguard political organization, protecting the principles associated with Khomeini's peculiar interpretation

of social justice, reinvigorating a form of command economy, and standing firm against the Siren song of global imperialism. The third, and mediating, position reflected the fundamental pragmatism of the Rafsanjani years, when institutional balance and a mixed economy provided opportunities for the enrichment of a privileged few.

Each current had an identifiable leader: Khatami the reformer, Khamenei the radical-conservative, and Rafsanjani the pragmatist. Khatami's aura faded dramatically during his second term as president, generating more despondency and apathy than rage among his various constituencies. The one area in which his administration met with a degree of success was in reestablishing ties to the international arena, as the governments of Europe, East Asia, and Russia pursued mutually beneficial economic and cultural relations. Only the United States persisted in labeling the Islamic Republic an outlaw regime, whose actions could destabilize a vital region of the world. Repeated fulminations from Washington poisoned Khatami's efforts to promote basic changes in Iranian society that might have been interpreted as creeping Americanization. More important, they augmented the influence of radical activists, who took advantage of U.S. military intervention in the Gulf and Central Asia to rally popular support behind a return to the policies that characterized an earlier phase of the postrevolutionary era. In this project they were joined by a small but growing contingent of neoconservatives, who opposed the liberalization measures introduced by Khatami and demanded stricter adherence to presumed Islamic values. This faction appeared to be victorious with the election of Mahmoud Ahmadinejad in the 2005 presidential election.

These struggles play out in the context of a rapidly growing population, stagnant oil prices, and intense competition for Iranian products on global markets. Consequently, the government continues to have great difficulty meeting the day-to-day needs of the general public. Persistent unemployment and inflation remain critical problems that provoke occasional outbursts of popular violence, and they were important in the election of Ahmadinejad, who promised to focus on addressing these economic problems. To this point, the authorities have permitted the Revolutionary Guards Corps and Ansar-e Hizbullah to take the lead in suppressing discontent. But relying on brute force to maintain order is likely to prove successful only in the short run. Moreover, the religious establishment in Qom, whose senior figures have monopolized the interpretation of Shiite juisprudence for more than three decades, faces the prospect that a rival center of authority will shortly take shape in the historic seminary and pilgrimage cities of southern Iraq. Each component of Iran's ruling coalition appears to face an uncertain future.

Further Reading

Ansari, Ali M. *Iran, Islam and Democracy*. London: Royal Institute of International Affairs, 2000.

Azimi, Fakredin. "On Shaky Ground: Concerning the Absence or Weakness of Political Parties in Iran." *Iranian Studies* 30, nos. 1–2 (winter/spring 1997).

Bayat, Asef. *Street Politics: Poor People's Movements in Iran*. New York: Columbia University Press, 1997.

Hooglund, Eric. *Twenty Years of Islamic Revolution*. Syracuse, N.Y.: Syracuse University Press, 2002.

Isfandiyari, Halah. *Reconstructed Lives: Women and Iran's Islamic Revolution*. Baltimore: The Johns Hopkins University Press, 1997.

Kamrava, Mehran and Houchang Hassan-Yari, "Suspended Equilibrium in Iran's Political System," *Muslim World* 94 (October 2004)

Moslem, Mehdi. *Factional Politics in Post-Khomeini Iran*. Syracuse, N.Y.: Syracuse University Press, 2002.

Rahnema, Saeed, and Sohrab Behdad, eds. *Iran after the Revolution: Crisis of an Islamic State*. London: I. B. Tauris, 1995.

Schirazi, Asghar. *The Constitution of Iran: Politics and the State in the Islamic Republic*. Translated by John O'Keene. London: I. B. Tauris, 1997.

REPUBLIC OF IRAQ
(Al-Jumhuriyya al-'Iraqiyya)

By Soeren Kern

Formerly part of the Ottoman Empire, Iraq was occupied by the United Kingdom during World War I. It was declared a League of Nations mandate under British administration in 1920. Iraq became independent on October 3, 1932.

Following the overthrow of the pro-Western monarchy of King Faisal II in 1958 and a coup in 1968, Iraq became a center of Arab nationalism under the control of the ruling Ba'th (Renaissance) party. In 1972 the Ba'thists nationalized the Iraq Petroleum Company; the resulting oil revenues made Iraq rich. When Saddam Hussein became president in 1979, petroleum made up 95 percent of the country's foreign exchange earnings.

However, the 1980–88 Iran-Iraq war, the 1991 Gulf War following Iraq's invasion of Kuwait in August 1990, and the subsequent imposition of international sanctions had a devastating effect on its economy and society and reduced Iraq to a pre-industrial state.

Saddam Hussein's regime collapsed in April 2003, three weeks into a major U.S.-led military campaign. Iraq was governed for a year by the "Coalition Provisional Authority (CPA)" led by the United States and the United Kingdom. On March 8, 2004, the U.S.-appointed Governing Council signed an interim constitution. The transfer of sovereignty to the interim government took place on June 28, 2004. A newly elected democratic government was in place by April 2005, and voters approved a new constitution in October 2005.

Iraq now faces a period of uncertainty and transition. Although free from the tyranny of Saddam Hussein, the most pressing problems facing Iraq include the restoration of civil order, the creation of a new political system, and reconstruction.

The System of Government

Iraq is now a federal republic with a parliamentary style of government. A permanent constitution was written after the January 30, 2005, national elections for a transitional National Assembly; the document was approved by voters in a referendum in October 2005. New parliamentary elections were scheduled for December 2005.

EXECUTIVE

According to the 2005 constitution, the prime minister is responsible for the day-to-day running of the government through the ministries; he is also commander in chief of the armed forces and is responsible for choosing the members of the cabinet. The president acts as the head of state and oversees the work of the prime minister.

LEGISLATIVE

The constitution calls for two legislative bodies: the Council of Representatives and the Federation Council. The former is the most important body. It consists of one representative per 100,000 Iraqi citizens. The

ORGANIZATION OF IRAQI GOVERNMENT

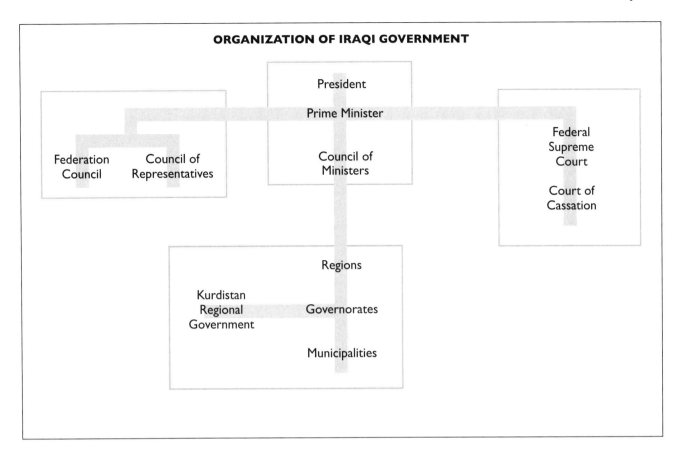

members are directly elected to four-year terms. Its functions include passing federal laws, electing the president, and ratifying international treaties. The Federation Council includes representatives from various regions and is apparently designed to address regional needs; this body is overseen by the Council of Representatives.

JUDICIARY

The Federal Supreme Court is the highest court in Iraq. It hears judicial appeals, settles disputes between the federal government and the regional authorities, and arbitrates other federal legal issues. The Supreme Court will consist of members based on a method to be determined by the Council of Representatives. The constitution also calls for a Court of Cassation.

REGIONAL AND LOCAL GOVERNMENT

The constitution calls for regions, governates, and local municipalities. Each region will be allowed to draft its own regional constitution that defines the structure of the regional government; the capital city of Baghdad is given special consideration to form its own local governing council. The region of Kurdistan is allowed additional powers of self-governance and autonomy.

The Electoral System

The January 2005 elections for the transitional national assembly marked the country's first direct multiparty parliamentary elections since 1953. Each voter was able to select one entry on the ballot, whether a party slate or independent candidate. All Iraqis 18 years of age or older on January 1, 2005, were eligible to vote. The vote was a single national ballot, with no constituencies or regional representation. For the most part, voters cast a single vote for a list of candidates from a party or coalition of parties. Seats in the transitional assembly were allocated by proportional representation (if a party received 20 percent of the vote, it would receive 20 percent of the seats in the assembly). The party's seats were filled from its candidates list, starting from the top and counting down until the seats are filled.

Following the adoption of the new constitution in October 2005, new parliamentary elections were scheduled for December. The constitution allows for direct election of members of parliament by secret ballot.

The Party System

More than 120 parties were approved to run candidates for the transitional National Assembly in January 2005. A total of 83 slates of candidates were registered for the January elections. Many of the parties banded together to form broad alliances for the election. It was unclear how many of the newly formed parties, not to mention the broad alliances, would establish themselves as permanent players in Iraq's political scene.

Major Political Parties

UNITED IRAQI ALLIANCE

This 240-member alliance was backed by Ayatollah Ali al-Sistani, Iraq's leading Shiite religious authority. It contained representatives of the country's main Shiite religious parties. Its members won nearly half of the votes for the transitional National Assembly and ended up gaining 140 out of the 275 seats. The alliance included the Supreme Council for the Islamic Revolution (Sciri), headed by Abdulaziz al-Hakim, and Da'awa, headed by Ibrahim Jaafari, who became the country's prime minister in April 2005. The alliance also included Ahmed Chalabi, leader of the Iraqi National Congress, as well as Hussein al-Shahristani, an independent Shiite politician and nuclear scientist, who is a close adviser to Sistani. Many of the Shiite politicians featured on the alliance developed close ties with Iran when they were forced into exile during the regime of Saddam Hussein. The alliance also included a number of other Shiite and Turkmen parties and some independent Sunnis and tribal leaders. Followers of the radical Shiite cleric Moqtada al-Sadr considered joining the alliance but decided against it because of theological differences with Sistani.

KURDISTAN ALLIANCE

This alliance included Massoud Barzani's Kurdistan Democratic Party and Jalal Talabani's Patriotic Union of Kurdistan, the two leading Kurdish parties that have shared power in the semi-autonomous Kurdish regions of northern Iraq. The list also included six smaller Kurdish parties. The alliance won 75 seats in the January 2005 elections, second only to the United Iraqi List.

IRAQI LIST

This alliance included the Iraq National Accord, a secular-leaning party headed by Iyad Allawi, Iraq's interim prime minister, along with several other secular parties. The list campaigned on security and law and order and favored a secular and nonsectarian Iraq. It won 40 seats in the January 2005 elections.

IRAQIS' PARTY LIST

This secular party was led by Iraq's Sunni interim president, Ghazi al-Yawar. The list contained 80 candidates from different sections of Iraqi society and included ministers, governors, tribal leaders, and clerics. It won five seats in the January 2005 elections.

IRAQI ISLAMIC PARTY

This party, led by Mohsen Abdel Hameed, was the biggest Sunni party and was dominated by members of the formerly outlawed Muslim Brotherhood. It initially presented a list of 275 candidates but withdrew from the elections in late December because of security concerns. Without the Iraqi Islamic Party, however, no other party or candidate had enough support to attract the popular Sunni vote.

Minor Political Parties

PEOPLE'S UNION

This 275-candidate list included the Iraqi Communist Party led by Hamid Majid Moussa. It won two seats in the January 2005 elections.

INDEPENDENT NATIONALIST ELITES AND CADRES

This 180-candidate alliance represented the Shiites of Sadr City, the impoverished Baghdad suburb dominated by followers of the rebel cleric Moqtada al-Sadr. It won three seats in the January 2005 elections.

IRAQI INDEPENDENT DEMOCRATS

This 76-candidate list represented a secular party headed by Adnan Pachachi, a prominent Sunni politician and former foreign minister.

IRAQI DEMOCRATIC GATHERING

This party was led by Mishaan Jibouri and was linked to the Jibouri tribe, one of the largest and most powerful Sunni Muslim tribes in Iraq. The party pushed for the return of former members of Saddam Hussein's Ba'th Party to government.

CONSTITUTIONAL MONARCHY

This was a moderate Sunni-dominated group that sought to restore a constitutional monarchy. Its 275-candidate list was headed by Sharif Ali Bin Hussein, a cousin of Iraq's last king.

CHRISTIAN LISTS

Due to a dispute over the order of candidates appearing on the list, the Christians split it in two. However, the manifesto of the National Rafidayn List and the Two Rivers Coalition was essentially the same, with a focus on safeguarding the rights of minorities, including the Chaldeans and Assyrians. Their campaign also underlined the importance of teaching the Assyrian language, which is spoken by about 1 million Iraqi Christians living in Baghdad, Kirkuk, and Mosul.

Other Political Forces

LOCAL GOVERNORATES

The 2005 constitution promotes federalism, a system of government that gives local areas substantial control over their own affairs, strengthens the unity of the entire country, and prevents any region or group from dominating the others. Yet, in many areas of the country, the central government is seen as lacking in legitimacy and control.

FOREIGN FIGHTERS

Much of the violence and chaos in Iraq following the ouster of Sadaam Hussein has been tied to foreign insurgents pouring into the country to battle the U.S.-led coalition forces and all Iraqi forces and institutions that sought to forge a new democratic system.

National Prospects

Iraq's economy is dominated by the oil sector, which has traditionally provided about 95 percent of foreign exchange earnings. With the exception of its southern neighbor, Saudi Arabia, Iraq has more oil buried underneath it than any country in the world: Iraq is estimated to hold 115 billion barrels of proven oil reserves and possibly much more undiscovered oil in unexplored areas of the country. Iraq also is estimated to contain at least 110 trillion cubic feet of natural gas.

Ultimately, the U.S.-led invasion of Iraq in March–April 2003 resulted in the shutdown of much of the country's oil production facilities. A joint UN and World Bank report released in the fall of 2003 estimated that Iraq's key reconstruction needs through 2007 would cost $55 billion. In October 2003 international donors pledged assistance worth more than $33 billion toward this rebuilding effort.

In July 2004 a U.S. National Intelligence Estimate painted a pessimistic picture for the future of Iraq, including the possibility of civil war. The 50-page report raised serious questions about Iraq's ability to achieve political solutions in subsequent years, noting the country's limited experience with representative government and its history of violence.

Further Reading

Birdsall, Nancy, and Arvind Subramanian, "Saving Iraq from Its Oil." *Foreign Affairs* (July–August 2004).

Byman, Daniel L., and Kenneth M. Pollack. "Democracy in Iraq." *Washington Quarterly* (summer 2003): 119–36.

Cordesman, Anthony H. *Playing the Course: A Strategy for Reshaping U.S. Policy in Iraq and the Middle East.* Washington, D.C.: Center for Strategic and International Studies, 2004.

Crocker, Bathsheba. "Reconstructing Iraq's Economy." *Washington Quarterly* (autumn 2004): 73–93.

Diamond, Larry. "What Went Wrong in Iraq." *Foreign Affairs* (September–October 2004).

Hashim, Ahmed S. "Iraq: From Insurgency to Civil War?" *Current History*, January 2005, 10–18.

IRELAND
(Éire)

By Alan J. Ward, Ph.D.

Ireland is located in five-sixths of the island of Ireland, on the western edge of Europe. It has an area of nearly 70,000 square kilometers (27,000 square miles) and a population of just over 4 million (2005 est.), approximately 93 percent of whom identify as Roman Catholics. Of the remainder, 3 percent are members of the Anglican Church of Ireland.

Irish is the first official language of Ireland and English the second. The English text of the constitution uses Irish terms for certain offices and institutions: Oireachtas (Parliament), Dáil Éireann (House of Representatives), Seanad Éireann (Senate), taoiseach (prime minister), and tánaiste (deputy prime minister). This use of Irish will be followed in this account, as will the customary use of Irish names for three political parties, Fianna Fáil, Fine Gael, and Sinn Féin.

When the island of Ireland was partitioned by the United Kingdom in 1921, the six counties in the northeast, which contained the majority of the island's Protestants, became a self-governing region of the United Kingdom, known as Northern Ireland. The remaining 26 counties became independent in 1922 as the Irish Free State (Saorstát Éireann), with the constitutional status of a British Dominion under the Crown, like Canada. In 1936 all references to the British Crown were deleted from the Free State constitution (Bunreacht na hÉireann), and in 1937 Eamon de Valera's government introduced a new constitution, which was approved by a plebiscite. The state was renamed Ireland (Éire). The constitution was wholly republican in form, but Ireland retained the External Relations Act of 1936, which authorized the king of England, as head of the British Commonwealth, to act formally for Ireland in external relations. In this way, the country retained a relationship with Britain until 1949, when the Republic of Ireland Act was implemented and Ireland withdrew from the Commonwealth. The state continues to be called Ireland in the constitution, but the names Irish Republic and Republic of Ireland are also widely used.

The System of Government

Ireland is a unitary republic with a parliamentary form of government. Amendments to the constitution require the approval of the Oireachtas and a public referendum.

EXECUTIVE

The Irish head of state is the president (Uachtarán na hÉireann). The constitution specifies that most of the president's powers are exercised at the direction of others: the taoiseach, the Government, or Dáil Éireann. These include the power to appoint ministers, summon and dissolve the Oireachtas, and assent to bills.

The president has seven discretionary powers, but the advice of the Council of State must be sought on five of these, including the most important, the decision

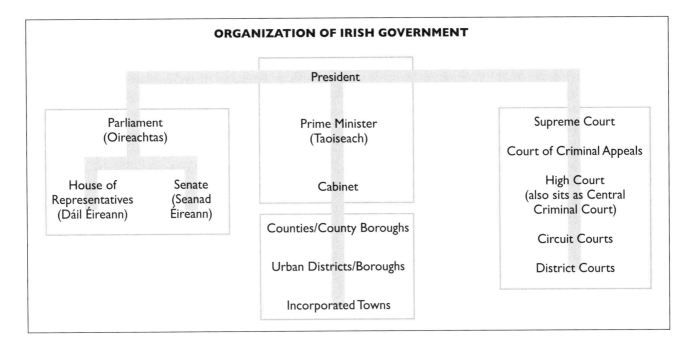

ORGANIZATION OF IRISH GOVERNMENT

President

Parliament (Oireachtas)

House of Representatives (Dáil Éireann)

Senate (Seanad Éireann)

Prime Minister (Taoiseach)

Cabinet

Counties/County Boroughs

Urban Districts/Boroughs

Incorporated Towns

Supreme Court

Court of Criminal Appeals

High Court (also sits as Central Criminal Court)

Circuit Courts

District Courts

to submit a bill to the Supreme Court for a test of its constitutionality. The statutory members of the Council are the taoiseach, tánaiste, chief justice, president of the High Court, attorney general, presiding officers of the two houses of the Oireachtas, and people who have held office as taoiseach or chief justice in the past. The president is not required to seek the Council's advice when appointing up to seven additional members of the Council and deciding to dissolve, or not dissolve, Dáil Éireann on the advice of a taoiseach who has lost the support of a majority in the Dáil.

The president must be at least 35 years of age, serves a seven-year term, and may be reelected only once. Elections are partisan, and most presidents have been members of the largest party, Fianna Fáil. Until 1990 presidents conducted the office in a low-key manner, but the Independent Labour president Mary Robinson (1990–97) may have set new expectations for the office by speaking out on public issues and representing Ireland on frequent overseas visits. President Robinson resigned on September 12, 1997, some months before the completion of her term, to take up a position as UN High Commissioner for Human Rights. A new president had to be elected within 60 days of her resignation. A Presidential Commission, composed of the chief justice of the Supreme Court and the two presiding officers of the Oireachtas, performed the essential functions of the office until November, when the Fianna Fáil candidate, Mary McAleese, a native of Northern Ireland, was elected president.

As in all parliamentary countries, the effective executive in Ireland is not the president but a cabinet, known in Ireland as the Government, which is selected from the majority in the lower house of the Oireachtas, Dáil Éireann. The Government must resign if it loses the support of the majority, by losing a general election, a vote of no confidence in the Dáil, or a vote on the budget. Ireland adopted this model before independence, when the first Dáil Éireann was formed during the War of Independence in 1919. The model was retained when the Irish Free State constitution was adopted in 1992 and was confirmed in the constitution of 1937.

The Irish Government is composed of ministers selected from the Oireachtas to head government departments. The constitution limits the number to 15, and no more than two may sit in the Seanad. The taoiseach, tánaiste, and minister for finance must sit in the Dáil. Seventeen ministers of state, or junior ministers, have been established by ordinary law to support ministers, and these must also sit in the Oireachtas.

The constitution recognizes the special role of the taoiseach, or prime minister, in various ways. Appointed by the president on the nomination of the Dáil, the taoiseach alone nominates ministers and ministers of state to the president for appointment, as well as the attorney general, who need not sit in the Oireachtas. The taoiseach alone may request the president to dismiss members of the Government. It is the taoiseach's responsibility to request the president to dissolve the Dáil and call for a general election. The request must be granted if the taoiseach has the support of a majority in the Dáil, but it may be denied if that support has been lost. In practice, no president has ever denied a request for a dissolution. If the taoiseach resigns or dies in office, the whole Government is deemed to have resigned. In a coalition, some of the taoiseach's powers may be circumscribed because coalition partners will want a say in the disposition of certain offices.

The taoiseach is clearly preeminent in the government, but the constitution requires the Government to meet and act as a collective body in many matters, including the presentation of appropriations bills to the Dáil, the conduct of foreign relations, and most instructions to the president. In 1992 the Government decided that all its decisions would be announced as if taken unanimously, and in 1924 it decided that the appearance of unanimity required all Government proceedings to be confidential. It therefore resisted court subpoenas. A constitutional amendment in 1997 confirms secrecy of proceedings but permits court access to documents in some circumstances.

Ministers represent their own departments in Parliament. The Ministers and Secretaries Act of 1924 recognizes each minister as a "corporation sole," which is to say, as personifying the department in law, and it always acts in the minister's name.

The members of the Government control the executive departments, of course, but party discipline enables them to dominate the legislature as well. Standing Orders, which are the rules of each house, have been written to favor the Government in significant ways. The members of the Government also supervise the large, semistate sector of "state-sponsored bodies." These account for roughly 10 percent of Ireland's GDP, and they engage in a variety of commercial, marketing, research, and regulatory activities. Their governing boards are appointed by ministers, and the Oireachtas has very limited influence over them.

The Supreme Court has the constitutional power to reject legislation as unconstitutional, but other formal checks on the Irish Government are weak. Backbench deputies on the Government's side can influence its policies in the privacy of party meetings, but they are socialized to accept its dominance in the Oireachtas itself. Members of opposition parties have very little influence in the Oireachtas.

Government dominance is most evident when a single party forms a majority Government, but Irish governments have been formed with four kinds of support, each of which tends toward a different degree of dominance. First, a party may be able to form a single-party, majority Government, and it gives the Government the greatest degree of control. Second, the Government may be formed by a majority coalition composed of two or more parties. The composition and programs of the Government will be, of necessity, compromises between coalition partners. Third, if no party controls a majority of seats in the Dáil, a single party may be able to form a minority Government without a coalition if it has the support of other parties or independents on votes of confidence and budget votes. This places the government in a precarious position. Finally, and least common in Ireland, a coalition may form a minority government under the same conditions.

LEGISLATURE

The Oireachtas is defined by the constitution as a tricameral institution, comprising the president, Dáil Éireann, and Seanad Éireann, but in practice, the Oireachtas is always taken to mean an assembly of two chambers, Dáil Éireann and Seanad Éireann.

Dáil Éireann has 166 members and is the primary house of the Oireachtas. Elections are by popular vote using single transferable votes (STV) in multimember constituencies. The Dáil may sit for a maximum of five years but can be dissolved in a shorter period at the request of the taoiseach. The Dáil elects a chairman (Cathaoirleach) and deputy chairman (Leas-Cathaoirleach) after each general election, usually from a Government party. The seat of a sitting chairman is not contested at a general election unless he or she is retiring. The Dáil has exclusive responsibility for nominating the taoiseach and approving his nominees for the Government. The taoiseach, tánaiste, and minister for finance must sit in the Dáil, and money bills, which deal with taxes, appropriations, and public loans, must be introduced there by the Government. Once approved, a money bill is forwarded to the Seanad, which has 21 days to make comments, but it may not offer amendments. The Dáil may accept the Seanad's recommendations, or it may vote to send the original bill to the president for signature. Nonmoney bills may be initiated in either house, but in practice very few are introduced in the Seanad. That house has 90 days to consider a nonmoney bill sent to it from the Dáil, and if it does not return the bill in this period or amends it in ways that are unacceptable to the Dáil, the Dáil may vote to send the original bill to the president for signature. The 90-day delay may be abridged for reasons of public peace, security, or emergency, as determined by the taoiseach with the president's concurrence. In practice, the Seanad has rejected only a handful of Government bills, and it almost never amends them in ways that are unacceptable to the Government.

The great majority of bills that become law in Ireland are introduced by the Government in Dáil Éireann. A small amount of time is available for private members' bills, but it is dominated by opposition parties rather than individual members. Party members are expected, and in some parties are required, to vote as directed by the party on all bills except votes of conscience.

The Dáil sits for fewer than 100 days a year. It appoints standing committees to handle the third, or committee, stage of some noncontroversial bills, but most bills pass through all of their stages in the full house, sitting as itself or as a "committee of the whole." Select committees are established annually to consider specialized topics. Some are reappointed year by year, such as the Public Accounts Committee, the Procedure and Privileges Committee, the Joint Committee of Dáil and Seanad on Commercial State-Sponsored Bodies, and the Joint Committee on Secondary Legislation of the European Union, but they do not consider legislation and there are no committees to review financial estimates.

The Seanad has 60 members and is very much a secondary chamber. In addition to the constitutional restrictions on its powers discussed above, the Senate is subjected to party discipline and is invariably dominated by the Government. Indeed, the taoiseach nominates 11 senators, enough to ensure the government's control. The Seenad sits for fewer days than the Dáil.

JUDICIARY

The Irish judicial system was inherited from Britain. Irish law is derived from British common law, British statutes that applied to Ireland at the time of independence and have not been amended by Irish statutes, the Irish constitution, and Irish statutes passed subsequent to independence.

The lowest court is the district court, which is divided into 23 districts to hear minor civil and criminal cases. More serious cases go to the circuit court, which is divided into 8 circuits. Next in authority is the High Court, a panel of 17 judges who handle the most serious cases and hear appeals from lower courts in civil cases. When hearing criminal cases the High Court sits as the Central Criminal Court. Criminal appeals are heard by the Court of Criminal Appeal, which includes both High Court and Supreme Court judges. The High Court is permitted by the constitution to consider the constitutionality of laws in its decisions. The Supreme Court is the court of final appeal from decisions of the High Court and the Court of Criminal Appeal, and it is required to consider the constitutionality of bills referred to it by the president before signing them into law. Irish judges are appointed by the president on the recommendation of the Government.

Early Irish Supreme Court justices were trained in the British tradition and practiced typically British judicial restraint, but since the 1960s they have been interpreting the constitution quite broadly to nullify acts of the Oireachtas. The Irish constitution includes specific rights of citizens, several based upon Catholic teachings, that courts must apply, and a 1983 referendum added the prohibition of abortion to this list. In addition, since Ireland joined the European Economic Community (now the European Union) in 1972, Irish courts have been bound by European law and European Court decisions.

REGIONAL AND LOCAL GOVERNMENT

Ireland is a unitary state. All local governments operate under powers granted by the Oireachtas and may only perform tasks permitted by law. Councils were occasionally suspended by the Government, and local elections were postponed several times, most recently in 1990. Since 1999, however, the constitution has recognized local government, and elections must be held at least every five years.

The major local government functions are public housing, roads and traffic, water supply, sewage, environmental protection, planning and development, and recreation. Expenditures are funded, in order of importance, by central government grants, local government charges for goods and services, and taxes on business and industrial property. The central government exerts considerable influence by making laws with respect to local government, making grants for roads, housing, and other purposes, and coordinating certain activities, such as planning. Local governments spend about 5.5 percent of Ireland's GNP, approximately 65 percent for current expenditures and 35 percent for capital expenditures.

In order of descending levels of responsibility, there are 29 county councils and 5 county borough councils, 49 urban district councils and 6 boroughs, and 30 boards of town commissioners. Elections to five-year terms are by proportional representation and are contested by parties. Each jurisdiction has a manager, a public servant who is appointed by the authority on the recommendation of the Local Appointments Board, a central government agency. Elected members set general policy, the annual tax rate, and public borrowing. The also enact by-laws to regulate local matters, such as traffic and parking. Managers administer according to these policies, but they are typically experienced sources of advice to local councils. About 25,000 people are employed in local government.

Eight regional authorities were established by law in 1994 composed of representatives from local governments. They coordinate regional public services and advise on the implementation of certain European Union programs. In addition, there are regional tourism organizations, vocational education committees, county enterprise boards, fisheries boards, and harbor authorities.

The Electoral System

The minimum voting age for all elections in Ireland is 18, and balloting is secret. The electoral register is prepared by an annual house-to-house survey. Elections for president are by all registered voters in Ireland using the single transferable vote. Candidates must be nominated by 20 members of the *Oireachtas* or 4 county councils. Voters indicate their preferences among the candidates, and if no candidate wins a majority on the first count, the second preferences of the candidate with fewest votes are redistributed to the remaining candidates, as happened, for example, in 1990.

Dáil elections are by proportional representation and secret ballot using the STV system in multimember constituencies. There are 41 constituencies, and the number of seats varies between 3 and 5. Constituencies are revised at least every 12 years, and the boundary commissioners are required by the constitution to maintain a ratio of electors to deputies of between 1:20,000 and 1:30,000. Commissioners are also required to consider county boundaries, geographic features, and continuity in relation to constituencies, which is why permissible variations in constituency size are helpful.

The Dáil electoral system operates as follows. On their ballots, voters number candidates in their order of preference up to the number of seats to be filled. The minimum number of votes required to elect a member is the "quota," which is determined by the formula: the number of valid ballots votes cast/(number of seats + 1) plus one. By this measure, the quota is 25 percent plus one in a three-seat constituency, 20 percent plus one in a four-seat constituency, and 16.66 percent plus one in a five-seat constituency. When the ballots are counted, the first preferences for each candidate are sorted. Should a candidate reach the quota at this point, the second preferences of votes that are surplus to the quota are redistributed to other candidates. Should no other candidate reach a quota, the second preferences of the candidate receiving the least number of first preferences are redistributed. This process proceeds at length, redistributing the surplus votes of winners and then the second preferences of the bottom candidates, until all the seats are filled. Parties influence the outcome by directing how their supporters should cast their preferences. From 1997 candidates for the Dáil have been subject to spending limits for campaigns, but they may receive verifiable expenses from the state if they can secure at least 25 percent of the quota for their districts.

The Dáil electoral system produces a house whose membership approximates quite closely the proportion of votes cast for each party. About 80 percent of voters usually see their first- or second-preference candidates elected. In Britain, by contrast, a majority of seats are won by candidates who poll less than a majority of votes and only a minority of voters can claim a role in electing a member of Parliament. However, because the quotas in Ireland are very high, by proportional representation standards, the STV system somewhat underrepresents small parties, the Green Party and Sinn Féin, for example. STV also has the effect of making deputies compete against members of their own parties for high preferences, and a deputy may lose a seat to a member of the same party who cultivates the constituency more assiduously. Deputies spend a great deal of time performing constituency service to protect their seats.

Labour and the smaller parties do not offer candidates in all constituencies, which limits the proportion of the nationwide vote they can receive. In recent years approximately 13 percent to 14 percent of Dáil members have been women. Though far from satisfactory, this is a substantial increase over the 8 percent of November 1982 and 7 percent of 1989.

Proportional representation makes it difficult in Ireland for a party to form a government alone with a majority of seats in the Dáil. This happened nine times after 1922 but not once since Fianna Fáil lost office in 1981. Elections are more likely to lead to coalition or minority governments.

The Senate has 60 members, selected in three ways. Two groups are selected by elections, which must be held within 90 days of the dissolution of the Dáil, using STV and postal ballots. Forty-three members are elected from five panels representing broad vocational constituencies: agriculture, industry and commerce, labor, culture and education, and administration. The distribution of seats per panel is set by law. Candidates to the panels are nominated by recognized nominating bodies or by members of the Oireachtas. The electorate for this group of senators is members of the local councils and deputies from the new Dáil, about 1,100 voters. Next, three senators each are elected by graduates of the National University of Ireland and the University of Dublin (Trinity College). The third form of selection is by nomination. Eleven senators are appointed on the nomination of the incoming taoiseach.

When designing the constitution in 1937, de Valera did not view the Senate as a chamber in which vocational interests would be represented per se. Rather, he thought that elections in vocational panels would produce senators of distinction who would represent the interests of Ireland as a whole. In the event, however, the Seanad has been a disappointment by any standard. Other than the university members, who are usually Independents, the nominations process has always been dominated by political parties, and the taoiseach's nominees ensure that the chamber is always friendly to the Government.

The Party System

Parliamentary systems depend on political parties. Without them, governments would have to construct new majorities issue by issue and would be exposed to defeat, and hence resignation, day by day. Disciplined parties bring stability and have been a feature of the Irish political system since independence. They contest elections at every political level. Parties that are registered by the clerk to Dáil Éireann and have no fewer than seven members elected at the previous general election receive subsidies from state funds in proportion to the votes they received. Each candidate's party, if any, is identified on the ballot, and parties are allocated free TV and radio broadcasts during general elections. They are prohibited by law from television and radio advertising during campaigns.

The present Irish party system reflects the events that accompanied the end of the Irish War of Independence. The war was concluded with the Anglo-Irish Treaty of December 1921, which caused a devastating split in Sinn Féin, the party that had led Ireland in the war. The treaty was accepted as the best they could

secure from Britain by the Irish negotiators, led by Michael Collins and Arthur Griffith, but it recognized the Irish Free State as a British Dominion, under the Crown, and left Ireland partitioned. When both the Dáil Éireann Executive (cabinet) and the Dáil itself approved the treaty by very narrow margins, the more radical Irish nationalists, led by Eamon de Valera, left the Government and the Dáil.

This schism led to the Irish Civil War of 1922–23 and laid the foundations for the Irish party system. The present-day Fine Gael and Fianna Fáil parties, the largest parties in the state, are the descendants of the pro- and antitreaty factions of Sinn Féin in 1922. Because the two major Irish parties were primarily defined by their attitudes to the Anglo-Irish Treaty, rather than by social class or economics, and because the people of the Irish Republic are religiously and culturally homogeneous, Irish party politics has not reflected the class and religious cleavages that are characteristic of continental European parties.

Between 1922 and 1932, treaty supporters, now known as the Cumann nGaedheal Party, constituted the Government of the Irish Free State, but in 1932, the Fianna Fáil Party, formed by opponents of the treaty, took power for the first time. Between 1932 and 1989, Irish party politics revolved around the question of whether Fianna Fáil or an anti–Fianna Fáil coalition led by the successor to Cumann nGaedheal, Fine Gael, would form the Government. Fianna Fáil formed 14 governments and anti–Fianna Fáil coalitions 7 in this period. Since 1989, however, Fianna Fáil itself has led coalition governments. Coalition building is often a tortuous exercise, but it is possible in Ireland because of the nonideological character of the major Irish parties.

Fianna Fáil and Fine Gael move about on the political spectrum from time to time, and at present both can be identified in the center-right part of the European political spectrum. Ireland has one of the lowest levels of support for left-wing parties of any country in Europe for three major reasons: the treaty split stifled the development of class-based parties; Ireland has a small, industrial working class; and the Roman Catholic Church has been extremely hostile to socialism.

In the 1970s Fine Gael appeared to move toward European social democracy, and it formed coalition governments with the Labour Party in 1973, 1981, and 1982. In the late 1980s, however, it became quite conservative in its economic policies, and in 1993 Labour formed a coalition with Fianna Fáil, which had taken a centrist position on economic policy. When this government broke up in 1994, Fine Gael formed another coalition with Labour and a small party to Labour's left, the Democratic Left. It appeared to move again in a social democratic direction. After the general elections of 1997 and 2002, Fianna Fáil formed coalitions with the Progressive Democratic Party, which is conservative on economic policy but liberal on social issues. Labour has often been the kingmaker because the traditional political enemies, Fianna Fáil and Fine Gael, have been unable to form coalitions together. But ancient enmities are dying, and there is nothing in the ideologies or policies of these two that would forever preclude such a union. Because of proportional representation, minor parties and independents have always been able to meet the election quotas in some seats, and they have often held the balance of power in the Dáil.

With the exception of the small Green Party, Irish political parties are hierarchically organized. A small central office staff in Dublin coordinates the activities of the party and reports to the national executive, a body of representatives from local branches and members of the Oireachtas that manages the party between annual conferences. There are usually several local branches (or *cumann* in Fianna Fáil) in each constituency, but candidate selection is handled by constituency-level bodies. The national executive may influence selections, but most authority lies at the local level. The centerpiece of the party is an annual or biennial conference (or Árd Fhéis) attended by delegates from local branches, members of the Oireachtas, and members of the national executive. This meeting features an address by the party leader and is increasingly staged for the benefit of broadcast media. The party leader is typically elected by members of the Dáil, but Fine Gael adds senators and members of the European Parliament to the electorate.

Party policy is officially set by the national conference, but when in office, a Government effectively sets party policy. Even in opposition, the leaders of a party in the Dáil have a great influence on policy. The Green Party has made an effort to deviate from this model, with a "coordinator" rather than a leader, and it develops policies by consensus.

Since 1997 Irish parties have been required to publish their accounts. They draw their funds in part from members' contributions or donations, and from private gifts from individuals, corporations, and trades unions, but by far the largest source of funds is annual grants from the state.

Major Political Parties

FIANNA FÁIL
(Soldiers of Destiny)

Fianna Fáil has been the largest party in the state since 1932. It was formed by Eamon de Valera in 1926 when he and a majority of treaty opponents abandoned their opposition to the Irish Free State. They entered the Dáil for the first time in 1927 and took office in 1932 as a minority government with Labour Party support. Since then Fianna Fáil has been the only party to form a single-party government.

Fianna Fáil was led by de Valera until he became president in 1959. The party was more inclined to press for the reunion of Ireland than Fine Gael, more protectionist in trade, less inclined to welcome secular influences from abroad, and more protective of traditional Irish values, including the Irish language. The Catholic hierarchy supported this policy of cultural isolation. The fact of Ireland's partition enabled Fianna Fáil to make electoral capital out of republican nationalism. The party has always been conservative on economic, cultural, and moral issues but has also espoused a brand of social populism that expresses support for the poor and underprivileged. In World War II, de Valera's Finna Fáil government adopted a policy of neutrality that evolved into abstention from military alliances in the postwar years.

De Valera's successor as party leader and taoiseach, Séan Lemass, began the process of modernizing the Irish economy in the 1960s and opened Ireland to foreign trade and investment. His government negotiated Irish entry into the European Economic Community in 1972. Lemass also began to change Fianna Fáil's position on Northern Ireland and twice met the prime minister of Northern Ireland, Terence O'Neill, for talks in Belfast and Dublin. Fianna Fáil now accepts that Irish unification must come about by the decision of the people of Northern Ireland themselves and by reconciling the two communities there. In December 1993, the taoiseach, Albert Reynolds, signed a joint declaration on peace with the British government that confirmed these policies, and in 1998, his successor, Bertie Ahern, also Fianna Fáil, signed the Belfast Agreement that cemented them into law.

Fianna Fáil sits in Europe with the European Democratic Alliance, which includes the French Gaullists. The European Democratic Alliance is customarily placed to the left of the larger European People's Party, the Christian Democrat group in Europe.

FINE GAEL
(Tribe of Irish People)

In 1923 the protreaty Sinn Féin republicans took as their name Cumann nGaedheal. The party became Fine Gael in 1933 in an amalgamation with the smaller Center Party. Fine Gael is today the second largest party in Ireland. As Cumann nGaedheal it formed the government of the Irish Free State until 1932, under the leadership of William Cosgrave, but since then it has only been in government as the largest party in a number of coalitions.

Fine Gael has been less confrontational to Britain than Fianna Fáil, less committed to republican nationalism, less protectionist on economic issues, less populist, and more committed to a pluralist Ireland, but it was a Fine Gael–led coalition that clarified Ireland's republican status in 1949 and withdrew Ireland from the British Commonwealth. In its early years the party was identified with large farmers and professional classes and had a weak party organization. In the mid-1960s, however, it changed its image and became a socially progressive party. The redefinition was led by Senator Garret FitzGerald, who became leader of the party and subsequently taoiseach in Fine Gael-Labour coalitions from June 1981 to February 1982 and November 1982 to 1987. FitzGerald also signed the Anglo-Irish Agreement of 1985 with British prime minister Margaret Thatcher, which committed both countries to pursue a peace in Northern Ireland based on respect for both the Unionist and Nationalist traditions and the consent of the majority in the province. The agreement was an important step toward the Belfast Agreement of 1998.

In a very testing period for the Irish economy, Fine Gael became too conservative in economic matters for its Labour coalition partner and the FitzGerald coalition collapsed in 1987. The party returned to power in 1994 in a Fine Gael–Labour–Democratic Left coalition under Taoiseach John Bruton. The party went into opposition in 1997.

Fine Gael has been the leading Irish supporter of the European Union. It sits with the second largest group in the European Parliament, the European People's Party, a Christian Democrat coalition.

IRISH LABOUR PARTY

The Irish Labour Party was founded in 1912 by the trades union leaders James Connolly, James Larkin, and William O'Brien. The party did not contest the 1918 United Kingdom general election or the 1921 Irish elections for fear of splitting the anti-British vote, and when it did contest the Irish general election in 1922 it found that its class-based politics could not compete with the highly charged politics of the Anglo-Irish Treaty. In addition, Ireland had only a relatively small industrial working class of the kind that supported successful left-wing parties elsewhere in Europe. Because of the abstention of antitreaty deputies from the first Irish Free State Dáil, Labour became the official Dáil opposition and is credited with playing an important part in the development of Irish parliamentary government. It has consistently taken third place among Irish parties since Fianna Fáil entered constitutional politics in 1927 but has participated in many coalition governments. In 1999 the Labour Party merged with the smaller Democratic Left, formerly the Workers' Party, which was itself an offshoot of Sinn Fein.

In 1990 the Labour Party nominated the Independent Labour senator Mary Robinson for president of Ireland. She had resigned from the party in 1985 to protest the Anglo-Irish Agreement, which she thought unfair to Unionists in Northern Ireland. She won the election and served from 1991 to 1997.

Labour is a social democratic party committed to social and economic equality. It has its greatest strength in Dublin, where a majority of its branches are located, and is weakest in western Ireland. It currently has 12 affiliated trades unions, representing about half of Ireland's trade unionists. In the European Parliament, it sits with the Party of European Socialists, the largest group, and it is also a member of the Socialist International.

Minor Political Parties

A large number of minor parties have come and gone in Ireland since 1922, but the following have figured in recent elections.

PROGRESSIVE DEMOCRAT PARTY

The Progressive Democrat Party was founded in 1985 by Desmond O'Malley, a former Fianna Fáil government minister who was expelled from the party in 1984. Though relatively libertarian, by Irish standards, on social and moral issues, it is neoliberal on economic issues and believes in minimizing government intervention in the economy. Mary Harney, who was elected to succeed O'Malley in 1993, was the first woman to lead an Irish political party. The party has formed coalition governments with Fianna Fáil, including following elections in 1997 and 2002.

GREEN PARTY

The Green Party, formerly the Green Alliance and the Ecology Party of Ireland, dates to 1982 as an environmental protection party but now takes positions on a wide range of issues. It is committed to a participatory political system in which decisions are taken at the lowest effective level. It recognizes world peace as a necessary precondition for environmental protection and supports the redistribution of the world's resources from rich nations to poor. The party operates nonhierarchically, rotating leadership positions annually, and seeks to make policy by consensus.

SINN FÉIN

(We Ourselves)

Sinn Féin is the lineal descendant of those members of the antitreaty Sinn Féin who did not follow Eamon de Valera into constitutional politics in 1926 and have survived a number of schisms. It operates in both the Irish Republic and Northern Ireland, where it is the largest nationalist party.

Sinn Féin is committed to Britain's withdrawal from Ireland and the reunification of the island under a socialist government. It believes that the Unionist majority in the North will come to accept its place as a minority in Ireland as a whole. Its organization is based on local branches, and it has a very strong international support network, particularly in the United States.

SOCIALIST PARTY

Militant Tendency, a Trotskyite group, became the Irish Socialist Party in 1996. Organized in both the Irish Republic and Northern Ireland, it stands for public ownership and democratic socialist planning.

Other Political Forces

Ireland has a great variety of organized groups lobbying for interests and causes: business, agriculture, labor, humanitarian, and charitable. Their influence is felt primarily in public opinion and the executive, because members of the Oireachtas have so little independent power that lobbying them is largely ineffective. Many groups have become client groups for particular govern-

ment departments and are routinely included in processes of government consultation. In 1973 the National Economic and Social Council (NESC) was launched from the Department of the Taoiseach with representatives from the government and "social partners." Its membership includes representatives from government, trades unions, business and employer organizations, farmers' associations, and, since 1996, community and voluntary organizations. There is a government appointed chairperson. The NESC produces plans for national economic and social policy, industrial policy, housing, social service priorities, agriculture, rural development, and emigration. The Department of Finance and other key government departments have public-private partnership units to coordinate the partnership process. Through their roles in the process, interest groups can have more influence on public policy than members of the Oireachtas, where partisanship inhibits cooperation.

The Catholic Church in Ireland continues to be an influential body, less through directions it gives governments than through its leadership of Irish Catholics. However, its influence is declining because of the growing secularization of Ireland. Against the wishes of the church, for example, Irish voters legalized divorce in a 1996 referendum.

About 70 trade unions are affiliated with the Irish Congress of Trades Unions, which operates in the Irish Republic and Northern Ireland. Most unions are quite small, but the ICTU itself is powerful in the public-private partnership process. Twelve trade unions are affiliated with the Labour Party.

National Prospects

The Irish Republic is a stable democracy and is likely to remain so. It has one of the healthiest economies in Europe and is firmly committed to membership in the European Union. There are no bitter cleavages in the country, economic, ethnic, or political, and whereas developments in Northern Ireland divided Irish political parties in the past, all the major parties now agree that the reunification of Ireland must depend on reconciliation between the Nationalist and Unionist communities and the consent of the majority in the North. With the issue of the North neutralized, the politics of the Irish Republic will revolve around social and economic issues. Proportional representation will continue to inhibit the formation of single-party, majority governments, but the pragmatic nature of the major parties will make coalition politics possible.

There are likely to be few changes in Ireland's constitution. The Constitutional Review Group appointed by the Government reported in 1996 in favor of only minor changes, and governments seem uninterested in even these. The Commission did recommend, however, that there should be an independent review of the role and composition of the Seanad, and this may come about.

Further Reading

Coakley, J., and M. Gallagher, eds. *Politics in the Republic of Ireland*. 3d ed. London: Routledge, 1999.

Chubb, B. *The Government and Politics of Ireland*. 3d ed. New York: Longman, 1992.

Dooney, S., and J. O'Toole. *Irish Government Today*. 2d ed. Dublin: Gill and Macmillan, 1998.

Gallagher, M. *Political Parties in the Republic of Ireland*. Manchester: Manchester University Press, 1985.

Keogh, D. *Twentieth-Century Ireland: Nation and State*. New York: St. Martin's Press, 1995.

Lee, J. J. *Ireland, 1912-1985: Politics and Society*. Cambridge: Cambridge University Press, 1989.

Morgan, D. G. *Constitutional Law of Ireland*. 2d ed. Dublin: Round Hall, 1990.

Ward, A. J. *The Irish Constitutional Tradition: Responsible Government and Ireland*. Washington, D.C.: Catholic University of America Press, 1994.

STATE OF ISRAEL
(Medinat Yisrael)

By Bernard Reich, Ph.D., and Gershon R. Kieval, Ph.D.
Revised by Tamar Gablinger

Israel is a small country in size and population, located in the Middle East on the eastern shore of the Mediterranean Sea and bordered by Jordan, Syria, Lebanon, and Egypt. It is a multiparty parliamentary republic of some 6.2 million people (2005 est.), of whom 76.8 percent are Jewish; 15.7 percent Muslims (mostly Sunni); 2.1 percent Christians; 1.6 percent Druze, and 3.7 percent others—mostly non-Jewish immigrants from the former-USSR who would not like to be included as "Christians." Israel also controls territories occupied in the 1967 war ("Six-Day War"): the Golan Heights (occupied from Syria); the West Bank—Judea, Samaria and East Jerusalem (occupied from Jordan)—and the Gaza Strip (occupied from Egypt, though never claimed by that country). The Sinai Peninsula, also occupied during the war, has been returned to Egypt under the terms of the 1977 Peace Accord between the two countries. Egypt, however, renounced its interest in the Gaza Strip (as had Jordan regarding the West Bank, in 1988), and Israel withdrew its settlers and military forces from the territory in 2005. The occupied population does not enjoy civil rights and does not have Israeli citizenship, unlike the above-mentioned Palestinian citizens of Israel. In addition, approximately 200 settlements of Israeli citizens in the occupied territories are recognized by the Israeli government (dozens more are not recognized)—the majority of them in the West Bank. Most of the settler population lives in East Jerusalem. Different attempts to settle the dispute between Israel and its neighbors, including the Palestinians, have been made.

Since 1990 the Israeli political system demonstrated instability, marked by the assassination of Prime Minister Rabin (1995), and by frequent amendments to the electoral laws and Government Law as well as changes in the party system and coalition formations. The 1993 "Oslo Accord," which was intended to gradually settle the dispute between Israel and the Palestinians, was not upheld by either side (including clashes in 1996 during which more than 100 were killed within two weeks; and never-ending and terror attack retaliations). In September 2000 a second Palestinian intifada (uprising) broke out in the occupied territories, bringing further instability into the political and social system.

HISTORY

Although Israel achieved its independence in May 1948, the origins of the political system predate the founding of the state. During the period of the British Mandate (1922–48), the Jewish community in Palestine (the *Yishuv,* or settlement) established institutions for self-government, including the Assembly of the Elected (Asefat HaNivcharim), a representative body chosen by secret ballot. The party system appeared with the first election to the Assembly in 1920, and a system of proportional representation was used to distribute the Assembly's seats.

The Assembly met annually and elected the National Council (Vaad Leumi) to exercise administrative responsibility for Jewish communal affairs between

Assembly sessions. The National Council functioned alongside the Jewish Agency for Palestine, which was created on the authority of the League of Nations Mandate and which included Jewish organizations sympathetic to the idea of a Jewish national home. The Jewish Agency acted as the international diplomatic representative of the *Yishuv*, conducting negotiations with Great Britain, the mandatory government, and the League of Nations, in addition to fund-raising and establishing a network of communications with foreign governments. After the United Nations adopted a plan for the partition of Palestine in 1947, a National Council of State was chosen from the National Council and the Jewish Agency executive. This provisional government consisted of a state council (which served as a legislature), a cabinet elected from among the state council's members, and a president elected by the state council. The executive of the National Council became the cabinet. The provisional government functioned from May 14, 1948 (Israel's independence day) until February 14, 1949, at which time the state council's authority was transferred to the first Knesset (Assembly), a popularly elected, unicameral parliament.

Although Israel has no formal written constitution, a number of Basic Laws have been passed that are intended in time to form portions of a consolidated constitutional document. Laws include those on the Knesset (1958); the Lands of Israel (1960); the President (1964); the Government (1968, amended in 1992 and amended again in 2001); the State Economy (1975); the Army (1976); Jerusalem, the Capital of Israel (1980); the Judiciary (1984); the State Comptroller (1988); Human Dignity and Liberty (1992); and Freedom of Occupation (1994).

The System of Government

Israel is a parliamentary democracy with a unicameral legislature.

EXECUTIVE

The president is the head of state and is elected by the Knesset for a seven-year term. He may not be reelected. His powers and functions are primarily formal and ceremonial. The president has the task of selecting a member of the Knesset to form a government. The political composition of the Knesset in practice determined this selection in most cases. However, the presi-

dent played a crucial role in determining which person was to form the next cabinet in 1984 and 1990 in situations in which different combinations of parties could have gained the support of the Knesset. As of 2005 the president was Moshe Katsav, who was the first Likud Party member and the first immigrant from a Muslim country to hold this position.

The prime minister as head of government is the chief executive officer and wields considerable power. He or she determines the agenda of cabinet meetings and has the final word in policy decisions, although such decisions are often arrived at by hard bargaining and compromise among the coalition of parties participating in the government.

After establishing a coalition, the government is to be approved by the majority of the Knesset members and all coalition agreements should be presented to parliament. During the period between 1996 and 2001 the Government Law was amended to include direct election of the prime minister by the public. However, in 2001 the current form was reestablished, and the prime minister is elected indirectly, by the Knesset.

The legislators hoped that by amending the Government Law and enacting direct election of the prime minister, they would reduce his or her dependency on smaller coalition partners. However, the result was the erosion of power base for the larger parties in favor of smaller ones, mostly those who represent the interest of the ultra-orthodox Jews, which were able to extract political concessions for their support of governmental decisions. The two ballot system enabled the voters to vote separately for a candidate, who would have been more likely to succeed, and for a smaller party, which represents a more radical ideology. Not fulfilling its purported goal, the law was amended again.

From the outset, Israel's governments have been coalitions of several political parties. This is the result of the intensity with which political views are held, the proportional representation voting system, and the multiplicity of parties. These factors have made it all but impossible for a party to win an absolute majority of seats in the Knesset. Despite the constant need for coalition governments, they have proved to be quite stable; only once, in 1990, has a government been forced from office by a vote of no confidence. A new government is constitutionally established when it receives a vote of confidence from the Knesset. The maximum term of a government and the Knesset is four years.

The stability of Israel's cabinets and political life has several bases. Until recently, political life in Israel has been dominated by a small and relatively cohesive elite that has held positions in government and other major institutions since the period preceding independence. The periods of elite domination in the Israeli system could be divided into periods of complete domination of MAPAI (1932–65), including the delegitimization and exclusion of other parties (the right-wing Herut—later Likud—and the Communist MAKI); a period of bipolar power base with the right-wing Likud Party (1965–84); a period of power-sharing with the Likud, within Unity Governments (1984–90) and a period of instability, since 1990, in which each side attempts to achieve a landslide victory and to exclude the other (Labor Party bloc in 1992 and 1999; Likud Party bloc in 1996, 2001, 2003). The two power blocs include not only the Likud Party or the Labor Party, but smaller right- and left-wing parties, respectively, who are natural coalition parties for the larger ones. Rigorous party discipline in the Knesset has helped to curb irresponsible action by individual Knesset members.

The coalition system has resulted in the acceptance of bargaining as a procedure for the allocation of government portfolios and the distribution of power, as well as being a factor in determining government policy. This has permitted the religious parties, particularly the National Religious Party and SHAS (Sephardi Torah Guardians), to play strong roles in government decision making because they are essential components of any parliamentary majority.

LEGISLATURE

The Knesset, a unicameral body of 120 members, is the supreme authority in the state. The Knesset's main functions are similar to those of other modern parliaments and include votes of confidence or no confidence in the government, legislation, participation in the formulation of national policy, approval of budgets and taxation, election of the president, and general supervision of the activities of the administration. Legislation is usually presented by the cabinet, although a member of the Knesset (MK) can initiate private bills. Bills are drafted by ministerial committees in consultation with the Ministry of Justice, approved by the cabinet, and sent to the Speaker of the Knesset, who sends the bill to the appropriate committee for consideration. The legislation is read and voted on three times and is passed by a simple majority of MKs present at the time of the vote. An absolute majority is required for the election of the president and state comptroller for successful motions of no confidence, and for changes in the system of proportional representation and the Basic Laws.

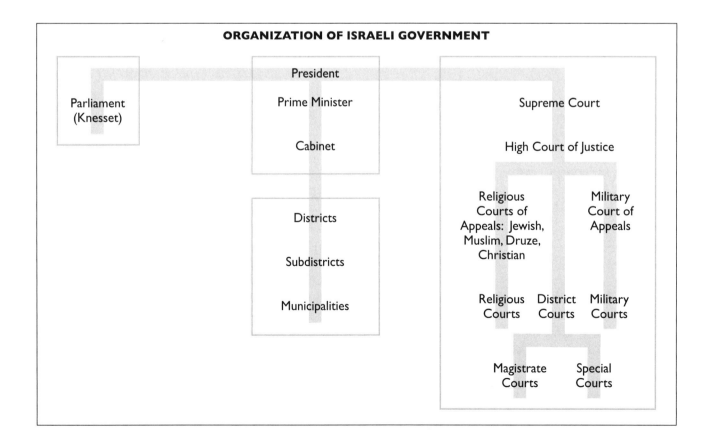

The state comptroller's office, which functions as an arm of the Knesset, oversees the accounts and operations of government ministries and other state bodies. Critical reports from the comptroller usually bring reforms.

JUDICIARY

The judiciary consists of two court systems, secular and religious. Judges for both types of courts are appointed by the president upon recommendation by the nominations committee chaired by the justice minister. This committee consists of the president of the Supreme Court and two other Supreme Court justices, two MKs, one other cabinet member, and two members of the Chamber of Advocates (Israel's bar association). The Supreme Court is the highest court in the land. It hears appeals from lower instances in civil and criminal cases, (and quasi-judicial issues) and sits at a "further hearing" on its own judgment. It also rules as a first instance as the "High Court of Justice" (BAGATZ—"Bet Din Gavoa Le'tzedek"), regarding the legality of the actions of state authorities: issuing writs of habeas corpus, protecting the rights of Israeli citizens (as well as the Palestinian population in the occupied territories) and protecting the individual from arbitrary actions by public officials. The Supreme Court does not have the power of judicial review, but it may invalidate administrative actions and ordinances it regards as contrary to Knesset legislation. There are five district courts and numerous municipal and magistrate courts on the local level. The military courts are under the purview of the Military Court of Appeals, which is responsible to the Supreme Court.

Religious courts have jurisdiction over personal matters including marriage and divorce, alimony, inheritance, and so on. The High Rabbinical Court of Appeal is the highest Jewish religious court and is overseen by the Ashkenazic and a Sephardic chief rabbi. Its decisions are final. Christian and Muslim courts function in the same capacity.

All judges are tenured, holding office until death, resignation, mandatory retirement at age 70, or removal for cause.

REGIONAL AND LOCAL GOVERNMENT

Israel is divided into six administrative districts under the jurisdiction of district commissioners and 15 subdistricts overseen by district officers. These officials are appointed by and responsible to the interior minister. A district official drafts legislation pertaining to local government, approves and controls local tax rates and budgets, reviews and approves by-laws and ordinances passed by locally elected councils, approves local public works projects, and decides matters of grants and loans to local governments.

Local and regional councils are elected by universal, secret, direct, proportional balloting. Mayors are chosen from among these councilmen with the same sort of coalition bargaining as occurs in the Knesset. Kibbutzim (collectives), Moshavim (cooperatives), and other types of settlements are also governed by elected councils. Local governments are responsible for providing education, health and sanitation services, water, road maintenance, park and recreation facilities, firehouses, and setting and collecting local taxes and fees.

The Electoral System

Elections for the Knesset are national, general, equal, secret, direct, and proportional. Every citizen 18 years of age or older has the right to vote but must be 21 years old in order to be a candidate for a Knesset seat. The same rules apply to local elections. In 2001 the Knesset restored a single-ballot system, after a short period (1992–2001) in which there had been separate ballots for the prime minister and for the Knesset, and the prime minister had been elected directly and independently of the Knesset.

In the elections to the Knesset, the individual voter casts a ballot for a party list, not for an individual candidate. The list is prepared by each party, which ranks from 1 to 120 candidates on the list. Parties determine their lists by different methods, some by means of primary elections among registered party members and others by means of selection by a party committee or other body. The list stands for the entire country as a single constituency; there are no by-elections. If a seat in the Knesset becomes vacant, the next person on that party's list takes the seat. Elections are held by law at least every four years but can occur more frequently if the Knesset dissolves itself. Between 1992 and 2001 it was possible for the prime minister to resign, therefore calling for early elections. Participation is very high, averaging about 80 percent of eligible voters.

Elections are supervised by the Central Election Committee, composed of representatives of each political party in the outgoing Knesset and chaired by a justice of the Supreme Court.

The proportional representation system is based on the d'Hondt system. Parties receiving at least 2 percent of the valid votes cast are entitled to a seat in the Knesset. The distribution is determined by dividing the total number of valid votes for all the lists that obtained at least 2 percent of the valid vote by the number of Knesset seats, the result being the quota required to obtain one seat. Each list receives the largest number of seats that can be determined by this process. The remaining seats are then distributed to those parties with the largest number of surplus votes. Any leftover seats go to the parties that have already won the greatest number of seats.

The Party System

ORIGINS OF THE PARTIES

Most of Israel's political parties trace their origins to various Zionists and non-Zionist forces that have existed in the country before 1948. The main forces before 1948 included—in the Jewish political arena—four main groups: the Zionist "left," the Zionist "right," the non-Zionist and Zionist religious movements, and the non-Zionist communists. In addition to these groupings, the pre-1948 Arab-Palestinian political arena included its own varieties of nationalist and socialist movements, similar to their contemporaries in other Arab societies in the area. However, after 1948, most Arab political leaders have not been active in Israel and the political activity among the Israeli Arabs has been marginalized. Besides the parties that existed before 1948, a few new parties (most of them small or of temporary success) have entered the political arena, owing to Israel's latest political experiences. They include parties representing specific ethnic groups (especially the recent immigrants from the Soviet Union as well as ultra-Orthodox Sephardim) and parties representing a liberal political ideology, such as Shinui.

THE PARTIES IN LAW

The only restriction on the formation of a new party is that its list may be disqualified if its candidates espouse the aim of destroying the state or the state's democratic character or if its program is determined to be racist. New parties must collect signatures of supporters and post a bond before being allowed to campaign. These requirements, which are easily met, have permitted the creation of a large number of parties. The bond is forfeited if the party does not win at least one seat. Access to radio and television is provided by the government in proportion to the parties' strength in the outgoing Knesset, with a minimum set aside for each party and each new list. The state also provides some financial assistance to the parties according to the number of seats held in the previous Knesset. New parties elected to the Knesset receive funding retroactively based on the number of seats won in the election. Campaign expenditures are limited by law. All election expense accounts are audited by the state comptroller but are made public only in aggregate. Campaign donations also are restricted by law.

PARTY ORGANIZATION

Political activity in Israel is highly ideological, often personalistic, and often based upon alliances of two or more parties. Charismatic individuals (e.g., David Ben-Gurion, Menachem Begin) often contribute to a party's success, and the formation of electoral alliances (GAHAL, Labor–MAPAM Alignment, Likud–Tzomet-Gesher) help the individual parties maximize their strength and influence on policy without losing their ideological identities. Smaller parties may consist of no more than one or two Knesset members and their loyal supporters, who are generally highly organized.

Israeli parties are marked by centralized leadership. In most parties, the central committee and party oligarchs are chosen by party elections but control the party machinery and in some cases determine the rankings on the party's national election list and thus the candidates' chances of winning a seat in the Knesset. This central control extends to the local government level. Party branches are often permitted more flexibility in choosing candidates for local office, but party necessities may also require that such candidates be chosen by the party nominating committee or be imposed by the requirements of an alliance or government coalition agreement. The parties are highly disciplined. All viewpoints may be aired in annual conventions, and intense bargaining can occur between factions. But once a policy is decided upon, members are expected to support it, keep silent, or quit the party.

In addition to campaigning and party business in the Knesset, the major parties engage in a great variety of other activities: publishing; housing projects; recreational facilities; various types of cooperatives; banking; and in the case of the religious parties, large educational systems. All the major parties maintain a variety of auxiliary organizations for youth, women, and other special groups.

Israeli party membership as a percentage of eligible voters is unusually high. Membership is not required, but many voters join a party as a matter of civic duty and "fraternal" responsibility and to participate in intraparty elections. There are also some practical advantages to party membership and activity since the parties have considerable patronage to distribute. Consequently, party membership serves also as a mobilization mechanism for some. Their economic activities can provide both employment and security for party members.

Within the major groupings of left, center-right, and religious parties, the life of parties and alignments is fluid. Parties form, merge, split, dissolve, change names, and reform. Many small parties are formed primarily to advocate a special point of view on a narrow subject and have little hope of winning a Knesset seat. Others are the personal followings of major political figures who can lead their supporters into and out of alliances and mergers as necessary to further their effect on policy or advance their personal ambitions. Some of these small parties do not clearly fit into the three major groupings (left, right, religious) but from time to time may become aligned with one of them. Many parties form in preparation for national elections and dissolve or merge soon after. In 2003, 28 parties contested the election, while 13 secured the minimum percentage of the valid votes to obtain a seat in parliament. The Likud and the right-wing parties won this election in a landslide: The Likud secured 925,279 votes (38 seats), while Labor-Meimad secured 455,183 votes (19 seats). This campaign saw the rise of a new "centrist," neoliberal political party, Shinui, which secured 386,535 votes (15 seats).

CAMPAIGNING

Political campaigning takes place both within the parties and between the parties on the national scene. Within the parties, the goal is to achieve leadership positions and high positions on the election list; nationally, it is to secure as many votes as possible for the party. Campaigning focuses more on parties than on individuals, although at times individuals have been made the focus of opposition efforts. The campaigns involve television and radio appeals, substantial use of newspaper and magazine space, and rallies. Given the small size of the country and its population, extensive appearances of the parties' leading candidates throughout the state are an important aspect of the campaign. Generally, the parties seek to rally their traditional supporters and to sway the small number of uncommitted voters. Foreign and security policy issues have assumed greater saliency over domestic issues in recent elec-

tions, and security-related developments have often affected the outcome, such as in 1981 and 1996.

Currently, the larger parties are the Israeli Labor Party, Likud, SHAS, and Shinui. The instability of the system, however, could change the power relations. Smaller parties include the Democratic Front for

POLITICAL PARTIES AND KNESSET ELECTION RESULTS, 1996–2003

Party	1996 % (seats)	1999 % (Seats)	2003 % (Seats)
Labor[1]	26.8 (34)	20.2 (26)	14.5 (19)
Likud	25.1 (32)	14.1 (19)	29.4 (38)
Shinui	—	5 (6)	12.3 (15)
Shas	8.5 (10)	13 (17)	8.2 (11)
Am Ehad[2]	—	1.9 (2)	2.8 (3)
DFPE	4.2 (5)	2.6 (3)	3.0 (3)
Hamerkaz	—	5 (6)	0.06 (0)
National Union	—	3 (4)	5.5 (7)
NDA	—	1.9 (2)	2.3 (3)
NRP	7.8 (9)	4.2 (5)	4.2 (6)
The Third Way	3.1 (4)	—	—
UAL	2.9 (4)	3.4 (5)	2.1 (2)
UTJ	3.2 (4)	3.7 (5)	4.3 (5)
Yachad[3]	7.4 (9)	7.6 (10)	5.2 (6)
Yisrael Baa'liya[4]	5.7 (7)	5.1 (6)	2.2 (2)
Yisrael Beytenu[5]	—	2.6 (4)	—

[1] In 1999 the Labor Pary ran under the name One Israel (Yisrael Achat).

[2] After the 2003 elections re-integrated into the Labor.

[3] Yachad is the current name of the party participating in 1999 as Meretz.

[4] Yisra'el Ba'aliya dissolved after the 2003 elections into the Likud.

[5] In 2003 ran together with Haichud Haleumi in one list.

Peace and Equality, the National Religious Party, the National Union, United Torah Judaism, Yachad, and the Arab parties.

RESULTS OF THE DIRECT ELECTIONS FOR PRIME MINISTER: 1996–2001

Candidate	Party	Percentage
May 29th, 1996		
Benjamin Netanyahu	Likud	50.3%
Shimon Peres	Labor	49.6
May 17th, 1999		
Ehud Barak	Labor	56.08
Benjamin Netanyahu	Likud	43.92
February 6th, 2001		
Ariel Sharon	Likud	62.39
Ehud Barak	Labor	37.61

Major Parties

ISRAEL LABOR PARTY

(Mifleget HaAvodah HaYisraelit)

HISTORY

The Israel Labor Party came into being in 1968 as a result of the merger of three labor parties: MAPAI (Mifleget Poalei Yisrael; Israel Workers Party), Achdut HaAvodah (Unity of Labor), and Rafi (Reshimat Poalei Israel; Israel Labor List). MAPAI originated with the union of two smaller parties in 1930, but the roots of the movement can be traced back to the turn of the 20th century in Europe, especially Russia. MAPAI soon became the dominant party in Israel. The two parties that formed it had established the trade union federation Histadrut in 1920, and under their leadership Histadrut became the embodiment of Jewish Palestine. MAPAI controlled it as well as the National Assembly and the Jewish Agency. Many of the noted figures in the creation of Israel came out of MAPAI—Ben-Gurion, Moshe Sharett (Shertok), Golda Meir (Myerson), Moshe Dayan, and others.

After Israel became independent, MAPAI consistently won the largest number of votes in Knesset elections, usually about one-third of the total. It was the leading member of all government coalitions and ordinarily held the key portfolios of defense, foreign affairs, and finance, as well as the prime ministership. The party permeated the government, the bureaucracy, the economy, and most of the other institutions of Israel.

Achdut HaAvodah, originally the party of Ben-Gurion in the 1920s, exhibited a militant class consciousness in its early years. It was merged with MAPAI from 1930 to 1944, when it left in disagreement with MAPAI's gradualist policies, the prohibition of party factions, and the general exclusion of more radical elements from MAPAI leadership. It rejoined MAPAI in 1965.

Rafi appeared in 1965, when Ben Gurion and his protégés Moshe Dayan and Shimon Peres left MAPAI, partly out of dissatisfaction with the leadership of Levi Eshkol. Rafi advocated more technocratic efficiency in government, the transfer of some of the Histadrut's functions to the state, and reform of the electoral system in favor of single-member districts with simple plurality elections. Rafi stood alone for only one election (1965) and gained a respectable 10 seats in the Knesset. However, it strength derived from its leaders. These 10 seats also had significance, as for the first time the hegemony of MAPAI had been broken, and Rafi could then, theoretically, form a coalition with GAHAL.

In 1969 Labor formed an election Alignment (*Maarach*) with MAPAM, a socialist Zionist party that championed the cause of Israel's Arab population and promoted a solution to the Arab-Israeli conflict. The two parties retained their own organizations and memberships. The Alignment continued MAPAI's dominant position until 1977. A combination of elements contributed to the loss of the *Maarach* power, for the first time in Israeli history: lackluster leadership, corruption scandals, the loss of trust in the party after the 1973 Yom Kippur War, and the founding of the Democratic Movement for Change made way for the Likud victory.

In 1984 the Alignment emerged as the largest party in the Knesset, and its leader, Shimon Peres, was given the mandate to form the new government. He formed a Government of National Unity with himself as prime minister for the first two years of the government's tenure and with Likud leader Yitzhak Shamir as prime minister for the last two years. The Alignment was the leading force in Parliament and the government. Peres's decision to form a coalition with the rival Likud bloc prompted MAPAM to leave the Alignment. To compensate in part for the loss of MAPAM's six Knesset seats, the Alignment co-opted Ezer Weizman and his Yahad faction (three Knesset seats) upon entering the 1984 unity coalition. Weizman and Yahad formally joined the Labor Party in 1988. The Labor Party won one less seat than Likud in the 1988 election, and the two parties joined in a new Government of National Unity, albeit dominated by Likud. That government lasted until the spring of 1990 when Labor withdrew over Likud's unwillingness to participate in a U. S. peace initiative. Labor subsequently engineered a successful vote of no confidence (the first ever in Israel's history) bringing about the government's downfall. Although given the first chance to form a new coalition, Peres was unable to do so, and a new Likud government was eventually fashioned.

Yitzhak Rabin, former chief of staff and hero of the 1967 Six-Day War, led the Labor Party to a decisive victory in the 1992 election, although Labor fell short of a parliamentary majority of its own, and he quickly formed a coalition government. The election victory marked a dramatic personal political comeback for Rabin, who returned to the prime ministership 15 years after having been forced to resign the leadership of Labor and relinquish the position of prime minister because of a financial scandal. But the victory did not represent a return to Labor's political dominance in Israel. Rather, it represented a classic case of voters punishing the incumbents, Likud, for years of "bad government" and other failures. Prime Minister Rabin was assassinated by an Israeli right-wing extremist in November 1995. Shimon Peres was returned to the prime ministership and became his party's candidate to run in Israel's first direct election for prime minister in May 1996. Peres narrowly lost that election, although Labor won two more seats in the Knesset than Likud. In 1997 Ehud Barak, former chief of staff and Rabin's hand-picked successor, was elected to replace Peres as Labor Party chairman.

Barak made some fundamental changes in the party, renaming it "One Israel," thus alienating some of its hard-core supporters. Two parties have joined Barak's "One Israel"—Gesher, David Levy's party (that later returned to the Likud); and MEIMAD (Medina Yehudit, Medina Demokratit; JSDS, Jewish State, Democratic State), a party representing moderate religious Zionists, headed by two rabbis, Yehuda Amital and Michael Malkior. Barak managed—as he had promised during his election campaign—to pull Israeli troops out of southern Lebanon. However, his inability and ineffectiveness in dealing with the second Palestinian uprising in September 2000 brought about his downfall. He had to resign as prime minister in 2001, and, in the 2003 elections the Labor Party (returning to its former name) was beaten by a landslide. Peres regained his position as party leader, reportedly "temporarily" (but as a matter of fact until a challenger to the leadership would manage to topple him). In 2003 another party joined Labor—"One People" (Am Echad), headed by Amir Peretz, the head of the Histadrut (the major labor union). Peretz formerly had left the Labor Party to form this unionists' party, claiming that Labor had lost its social way.

ORGANIZATION
The Labor Party is organized regionally and nationally, but with "branches" and a center. The party executives are democratically elected. The party has women, youth, and regional organizations. Its close connections with the Histadrut, however, have weakened, and the Histadrut is now closely aligned, politically, with its head, Amir Peretz, who heads the small faction "One People" ("Am Echad").

POLICY
Labor was a nationalist (Zionist) and socialist party. However, after 1965 there was erosion in the socialist policies and the party adandoned most of its socialist ideology. Nevertheless, some of the activists in the party still support unionist or socialistic ideals, and the party uses in general more "socialist rhetoric" than its counterpart, the Likud. Its platform, for example, still supports a social welfare state, a state-planned and publicly regulated economy with some room for the participation of private capital, full employment, minimum wages, and the right to strike. Similarly, the Labor platform supports the separation of religion and state, while in fact the party has made concessions to its religious coalition partners. It nominally supports equality for minorities, but also supports the free immigration of Jews to Israel, which is not expanded to include free immigration in general. It accepts the possibility of returning some—or all—of the occupied territories in exchange for peace.

MEMBERSHIP AND CONSTITUENCY
Some 70,000 people are registered members of the Labor Party. The number tends to significantly increase before party primaries, general elections, and other important decisions. As a mass party, support of the party could be found in all sectors of Israeli society. Some ethnic and class predispositions still exist—more Ashkenazi or Israeli-born; as well as better educated; and most of the residents of Kibbutzim and Moshavim (collectives and cooperatives) citizens tend to support the Labor Party.

FINANCING

Data on the party's financing are unavailable. Most income is derived from membership dues and contributions.

LEADERSHIP

As of 2005 Shimon Peres was the leader of the party. The party, however, suffered a major leadership crisis in the late 1990s and early 2000s. This crisis deepened after Ehud Barak lost the premiership in the 2001 elections due to the changes he had tried to implement in the party. Peres has been part of the party's leadership since the 1960s, and he was one of Ben-Gurion's protégés and was appointed two times to the prime ministership: in 1984–86 (in a coalition government with the Likud party) and in 1995–96 (after Rabin was assassinated).

Peres's leadership is challenged by several in the party. Ehud Barak, who was the party leader between 1997 and 2001 (and prime minister from 1999 to 2001), resumed his claim to the party premiership in 2004, after his resignation from political life in 2001. Other challengers to the leadership include Amir Peretz (the head of the Histadrut workers' union and of the "One People" faction) and Matan Vilnai, a former army general. A recent addition to the leadership candidates is Ami Ayalon, a former commander of the navy and of the secret services (SHABAK) who joined the party in 2004 and who leads an independent peace movement.

PROSPECTS

The popularity of the Likud and the leadership crisis in the Labor Party both lessen the chances of Labor regaining power. The party's different factions—unionists, socialist and free-market supporters, political "hawks" and "doves"—do not contribute to a healthy diversity, but rather to constant conflict and an inability to determine a unified line, agreed by most of the members of the party. The party is not able to win the hearts of those who support Likud or Likud coalition governments, including hawkish voters and nationalists, the Ultra-Orthodox community (about 15 percent of the population), and immigrants from the former USSR (another 15 percent of the population), who prefer to vote for the Likud or parties that would align with it in a possible coalition.

LIKUD

HISTORY

Likud is an alliance of parties, the central element of which is the historical "Herut" party that existed (as part of the Revisionist Movement) before 1948. The name "Likud" has been in use since 1973, and the alliance crystallized at the time of the 1977 elections. It consisted of the GAHAL alliance (Herut and Liberals); the La'am alliance (the State List and the Free Center); Achdut (a one-man faction in the Knesset); and Shlomzion, Ariel Sharon's former party. Since then, other parties have joined Likud, most notably, Tzomet, Gesher, Yisrael Ba'aliya, and Tami as well as other one-man factions in the Knesset. Likud came to power in Israel in 1977, ousting the Labor government for the first time since Israel became independent. Although it retained its government position after the 1981 elections, its majority in the Knesset seldom exceeded two or three votes. In 1984 it lost its plurality and joined with the Labor Alignment to form a Government of National Unity in which it shared power and ministerial positions.

Likud emerged with one more seat than Labor in the 1988 election, and a new Government of National Unity was formed but with somewhat less power sharing. That government fell in 1990 in an unprecedented vote of no confidence, but Likud was able to fashion a new coalition government without Labor's participation. Likud suffered a stunning setback in the 1992 elections and found itself in opposition for the first time since 1977. In 1996 the new Likud leader, Benjamin Netanyahu, won Israel's first-ever direct election for prime minister, slightly edging Labor candidate Shimon Peres by ninetenths of 1 percent. Likud, running in an electoral alliance with the Tzomet and Gesher Parties, won 32 Knesset seats compared with Labor's 34, but Netanyahu was able to put together a Likud-dominated coalition commanding 66 seats in Parliament with the religious parties and two new centrist parties. In 1999 Netanyahu lost the elections in favour of Ehud Barak, the Labor (then "One Israel") candidate. In 2001, after Barak's resignation, Ariel Sharon won the prime ministerial direct elections (since then the law has been changed, and direct elections are no longer held), and attempted to form a coalition with the same results. In 2003 the Likud won by a landslide (mostly because of Labor's weakness and loss of votes in favor of Shinui), absorbing the Russian immigrants party Yisrael Ba'aliya and putting together a coalition with the National Union, the National Religious Party, and Shinui. Likud is a center-right, strongly nationalist party, and one strongly assertive in foreign policy.

As mentioned before, Likud is an alliance of several historical right-wing parties, but its main component is Herut. Herut is descended from the Revisionist movement of Vladimir Zeev Jabotinsky (1880-1940), who settled in Palestine after World War I and is regarded by many as the leading Zionist figure after Theodor Herzl, Zionism's founder. The Revisionists advocated militant ultranationalistic action as the means to achieve Jewish statehood. Revisionism called for the creation of a Jewish state in "Greater Israel" (all of Palestine and Jordan), and, until recently, among Likud's symbols—those of Herut—one could find a map of "Greater Israel" with a shotgun replacing the Jordan River. It also supported rapid mass immigration of Jews into Palestine, formation of a free-enterprise economy, rapid industrialization—as opposed to agricultural settlements—to increase employment opportunities, a ban on strikes, and a strong army. In order to effect these policies and because they were outnumbered by leftist and moderate elements in the Zionist Organization, the Revisionists formed the New Zionist Organization in 1935. Their rejection of the socialist and liberal Zionist leadership and its conciliatory policy toward the mandatory power led Revisionists to form two paramilitary groups: Irgun Zvai Leumi (ETZEL), founded in 1937, and the even more radical Lohame Herut Y'srael (LEHI, alter. "Stern Gang"), founded in 1939–40. ETZEL was commanded by Menachem Begin after 1943. Betar, the Revisionist youth movement, was founded by Vladimir Jabotinsky in 1920 and continues as the Herut youth wing today. Begin founded Herut in June 1948 to advocate the Revisionist program within the new political context of the State of Israel.

Another smaller Likud faction is "Gesher." Founded by Likud's prominent politician at the time, David Levy, in 1995, Gesher was mostly based on Levy's charisma and strong following. With Gesher, Levy joined the Likud at the time of the 1996 elections, but in 1998 he left the alliance, contributing greatly to the fall of the Netanyahu government in 1999. Gesher then joined the Labor Party, participating with Labor and Meimad as "One Israel." In 2001 Levy left the Labor government again and returned to the Likud. Despite these frequent political turning points, Levy still maintains a stronghold of supporters in the Likud.

ORGANIZATION

The Likud is a mass membership party, with a large body of regionally elected members—the Likud "Center" ("Merkaz")—responsible for decision making for the party. The Likud Party center attracts different factions identifying with this party, from neoliberal businessmen to nationalist-religious settlers. The Likud Center assembles, at least, every six months and elects—among its other functions—the Likud list for the Knesset and the party's Secretariat (main executive body, nominating the party's executives). The party also operates several movements organizing youth ("Beitar"), students, women, and Jews from the Diaspora ("World Likud"). The Likud's younger members (aged less than 35) are also organized in the "Young Likud."

POLICY

Likud, as an alliance of several factions and as a mass party, includes numerous main streams. The party's platform supports a free-market economy with a minimum of controls, and advocates the "inalienable" right of Jews to settle anywhere in Israel, including the occupied territories.

MEMBERSHIP AND CONSTITUENCY

According to the latest internal elections information, some 200,000 Israelis (2004) are Likud members, making it the largest party (in membership) in Israel, with more than 4 percent of the registered voters as its members. Likud membership, in fact, has become a means to influence national politics or to empower specific sectors and patronage systems.

Likud's constituency, as appropriate for such a mass party, consists of several sectors in Israeli society. In general, its voters tend to be more traditional, with many of them from the lower classes, drawn to its nationalistic ideology as well as to a certain populist and antiestablishment image that it possesses since the days that Herut served as the main opposition party to the MAPAI government (Labor's precursor). The Likud also enjoys support from more Oriental Jews (Jews of Middle Eastern origin) than does the Labor Party. However, the party also attracts those in the middle classes interested in fewer government controls on the market; and ultranationalists interested in influencing the government's policies "from the inside."

FINANCING

Most of the Likud income derives from membership dues and from donations. In addition, the annual income of the Likud's faction in the Knesset (including that from state funding to political parties), stands at $7 million.

LEADERSHIP

Since the early days of the Revisionists and Herut, the movement has been characterized by strong, charismatic leadership. Menachem Begin was Herut leader between 1948 and 1983. He was regarded by many as a heroic figure because of his role as a leader of the underground in the Israeli struggle for independence. He was also a skillful politician and a charismatic figure. Upon Begin's retirement, Yitzhak Shamir became prime minister and party leader, although he was challenged within Herut by Ariel (Arik) Sharon and David Levy. In 1993 Benjamin Netanyahu was elected Likud leader, and in 1996 he was elected prime minister. However, Netanyahu, partly because of his fierce neoliberal political economy, and partly because of his personality, lost the 1999 elections to Ehud Barak. After he lost the elections, Netanyahu temporarily resigned from political activity, but resumed his activity after a year. Netanyahu is still one of the main challengers for the Likud's leadership, and he was appointed foreign minister (and, in Sharon's second government, finance minister).

After Netanyahu's resignation, Ariel Sharon assumed leadership of the Likud, and in 2001 he was elected prime minister. Sharon, who was the minister of defense during the 1982 invasion to Lebanon, was considered to be a hard-liner. Other prominent figures in the Likud's leadership include Ehud Olmert, former chief of general staff Shaul Mofaz, Foreign Minister Silvan Shalom, and Limor Livnat.

PROSPECTS

The Likud is as of 2005 Israel's strongest party, and despite some leadership struggles, it enjoys stability and mass popularity. Likud is expected to remain Israel's prominent party. Its main challenge is to maintain the balance between the party's nationalistic base and the party's own ideology while pursuing the compromise required by a peace process with the Palestinians and perhaps also with Syria. Netanyahu's economic policies have also drawn much criticism.

SHAS

(Sephardi Torah Guardians)

SHAS split from the ultra-Orthodox Agudat Yisrael and contested the 1984 election. While ideologically close to Agudat Yisrael, the former Sephardi chief rabbi, Ovadia Yosef, and other Sephardi rabbis decided to leave the Ashkenazi-dominated Aguda and set up SHAS after Aguda leaders refused to place enough Sephardi candidates on the party's list for the 1984 election. The founders of SHAS wished to secure the funds, political jobs, and other forms of support that they felt had been denied them. Eliezer Schach, an Ashkenazi rabbi and leader of non-Hasidic elements within Aguda, helped in the creation of SHAS. (Hasidism comprises several ultra-Orthodox, somewhat mystical, sects, whose leadership tends to be hereditary.) Schach was troubled by the influence of Aguda's Hasidic trends over its non-Hasidic members and thought the formation of

a separate Sephardi ultra-Orthodox party would force Aguda's Hasidic leadership to pay more attention to the non-Hasidic segment of the party. SHAS won four Knesset seats in 1984.

SHAS's strength increased to six Knesset seats in the 1988 election. The party's success was largely the result of its participation in the previous Government of National Unity. SHAS controlled the Interior Ministry—traditionally the bastion of the NRP—which enabled it to channel funds through local governments to provide services to its constituency of *haredi* (pious) Sephardi Jews. SHAS also exploited the Sephardi-Ashkenazi split among Israelis, stressing in its platform the restoration of Oriental culture to a position of prominence in Israeli society.

Although SHAS gained some votes in the 1992 election, it did not manage to increase its Knesset representation beyond the six seats it already held. During the election campaign, the party's advertisements and statements by its leaders strongly suggested that SHAS intended to throw its lot only with a Likud-led government. When it became clear, however, that Labor had won the election and would be in a position to block a Likud-led coalition, SHAS leaders reconsidered their options and eventually decided to join the new government headed by Yitzhak Rabin.

SHAS made significant gains in the 1996 election, increasing its seats in parliament to 10 and confounding the preelection predictions of pollsters. The party continued to stress to its constituents a combination of ethnic pride and traditional values to compensate for the sense of cultural alienation felt by many of them. SHAS also exploited the strong mystical tendencies among potential SHAS voters, distributing 150,000 amulets blessed by the elderly mystic Rabbi Yitzhak Kadourie. In addition, it benefited from having as its spiritual mentor the former Sephardi chief rabbi, Ovadia Yosef, who was popular even among non-Orthodox Orientals. In the prime minister's race, the party's leaders refused to back either Likud leader Netanyahu or Labor leader Peres and allowed their followers to vote for either candidate. In this way, Yosef left all options open for joining either a Likud- or a Labor-led coalition afterward. In 1999 SHAS fared even better, reaching a peak of 17 seats in the Knesset, becoming the third largest political party. The party joined Ehud Barak's Labor coalition government, and, after it fell in 2001, joined the coalition headed by Ariel Sharon and the Likud. In the 2003 elections, however, the strength of SHAS weakened and it won only 11 seats, making it the fourth largest party (after the newcomer Shinui, which used anti-SHAS rhetoric for most of its campaign). For the first time in its history, due to Shinui demands, SHAS has not been called to join the coalition. One of the reasons for the loss of votes is the indictment of former party leader Arie Deri and his removal from the movement.

ORGANIZATION

SHAS formed a council of sages known as Moetzet Hachmei Ha-Tora to guide major policy decisions and its leadership is closely linked to the former Sephardic chief rabbi, Ovadia Yosef. SHAS has built an extensive social service network, including low-fee day care centers and afternoon schools, in the poor neighborhoods of Jerusalem, Tel Aviv, and underdeveloped towns throughout the country.

POLICY

SHAS was founded to promote the interests of Sephardi ultra-Orthodox and traditional Sephardim. It argued that the Torah was its platform and regarded itself as a movement of spiritual awakening. It seeks to ensure government support for the party's network of educational and social organizations. Throughout the years, the party leadership demonstrated relative pragmatism on the question of the occupied territories and supported the government's position on the subject, in concession for social benefits to its institutions. Rabbi Ovadiah Yosef has famously ruled that Israel is allowed to return territories in exchange for "true" peace. On the other hand, the constituency of SHAS consists mostly of poor and alienated Israelis, who are easily persuaded to support ethno-nationalist and fundamentalist rhetoric. Therefore, the party's rank and file is more hawkish.

MEMBERSHIP AND CONSTITUENCY

No reliable data on SHAS membership are available. SHAS attracts a mostly poor, alienated constituency—outside the scope of the original constituency of Sephardic ultra-Orthodox—which feels excluded from mainstream politics and tends to support enthnoreligious political movements. It is especially popular in poor neighborhoods of the big cities, and in the poor periphery.

FINANCING

No reliable information on SHAS financing is available.

LEADERSHIP

The former Sephardi chief rabbi of Israel, Ovadia Yosef, is the spiritual mentor of SHAS. The party is led by Eli Yishai, who replaced Arie Deri, the former, and still charismatic, party leader, who has been indicted for corruption. There is an apparent tension between supporters of the two leaders.

PROSPECTS

SHAS plays an important role in the center of the religious camp and is a potential partner in any Likud- or Labor-led coalition. The party's supporters, however, likely will continue to support Likud candidates as long as Labor is identified with the secular forces that religious voters see as threatening the Jewishness of the state. However, given the support of nationalist and religious ideology in the right wing, and the fact that those ideas are popular among its voters, SHAS is more likely to support right-wing coalitions.

SHINUI—THE CENTER PARTY
(Shinui—Mifleget Hamerkaz)

HISTORY

Shinui (lit. "Change") was originally founded as a small protest group by Professor Amnon Rubinstein of Tel Aviv University in the wake of the 1973 Yom Kippur War. It sought to effect changes in the Israeli political system and in the political culture. It developed a party organization, but did not have a charismatic candidate. In 1976 it joined with others to form the Democratic Movement for Change (DMC, Hatnua Hademokratit Leshinui, DASH), which secured 15 seats in the 1977 elections and in fact was one of the major elements in the "turnover," the Mahapach, and the loss of Labor power for the first time in the country's history.

The DMC was constituted under the leadership of a former IDF chief of staff, the archeology professor Yigael Yadin, who served as a deputy prime minister under Begin after the 1977 elections. In 1979, just two days before the final signing of the peace agreement with Egypt, the party split and Shinui joined the opposition. The party dissolved just prior to the 1981 elections and the Shinui faction emerged as an independent party, gaining two to three seats in the 1981, 1984, and 1988 elections. Approaching the 1992 elections, Shinui amalgamated with RATZ and MAPAM, to form a new party—MERETZ. MERETZ participated successfully in the 1992 elections, winning 12 seats, with two Shinui representatives. In 1996 its power declined to nine seats (still, with two Shinui seats).

In 1997 MERETZ leaders decided to unite the different factions into one party. Elements within Shinui's ranks expressed their objection. They claimed that the new party represented a socialist line, opposed to Shinui's liberal tradition, and that the smaller faction's voice was unheard. Thus, a decision to run again as an independent party emerged.

Shinui's parliamentary leader, Avraham Poraz, decided to grant the leadership to Yosef ("Tomi") Lapid, a popular journalist and famous TV talk show star. The party presented a solid liberal platform. Its main campaign topic, however, was the alleged preference of the ultra-Orthodox community in the Israeli political system. It openly called for drafting Yeshiva students and canceling many of the benefits enjoyed by the ultra-Orthodox community as well as other "status quo" agreements made by the Likud and the Labor as concessions to their religious partners. This issue was the main cause of the party's success, first as it gained six seats in 1999, and then as it won 15 seats in 2003. After its major success in 2003, Shinui joined the Sharon coalition on the condition that the ultra-Orthodox parties would be left out of the coalition. In December 2004 Shinui ministers were dismissed from their posts after voting against the budget (which included 290 million shekels of "special" allotment for the ultra-Orthodox parties) and left the coalition.

ORGANIZATION

Two major institutions set the policy of the party. The first one is the Shinui Council, which consists of 168 members. This is the highest authority of the party and it decides the party's platform and elects its candidates for the Knesset. The members of the Shinui Council are elected by the party members; 60 of them in national elections and 90 are sent from the local branches (each branch sends representatives according to his relative strength). The remaining 18 places are secured places. The secretariat is the executive body, which is responsible for implementing decisions of the Shinui Council. It is also responsible for carrying out the daily activities of the party. This body numbers 45 members, who are elected from within the Shinui Council. Shinui is part of the World Federation of Liberal political parties, and it has a youth organization.

POLICY

Shinui's platform is a mixture of purist neoliberal economic policies and a liberal approach in all that is related to individual choice, especially the separation of religion and state. Its economic policies support the privatization of public holdings, sharp reduction in social benefits and subsidies, and a free-market economy without any government intervention. On the other hand, it is aligned with the Israeli left in supporting an agreement to make some territorial compromises in exchange for peace.

MEMBERSHIP AND CONSTITUENCY

Shinui presents itself as the "bourgeoisie" party. Its voters are usually well educated, relatively affluent (middle class), and secular.

LEADERSHIP

Shinui's charismatic leader is Yosef (Tomi) Lapid. Lapid, who survived the Holocaust as a child, was a leading journalist and author before he made nationwide fame with his appearances in a political TV talk show. Lapid's spontaneous and populist reactions contributed to his popularity. The party's former leader, Avraham Poraz, decided to withdraw his claim for leadership in order to ensure the party's success at the polls. He is still considered the party's main ideologue.

PROSPECTS

Shinui is currently the third largest party in the Israeli Parliament, enjoying popularity despite its inability to fulfill its election promises when in government. It could, however, end up like many meteors in the Israeli political arena. Tzomet, the Center Party, the Third Way, and the DMC before it all attempted to establish an alternative to the largest parties and to present a different agenda. Like those parties, it might disappear after disappointing its voters. On the other hand, given the weakness of the Labor Party, and given the fact that Shinui has a solid constituency, it might continue existing, though it may lose some of its power.

Minor Parties

YACHAD—TOGETHER/ SOCIAL DEMOCRATIC ISRAEL

YACHAD (Yisra'el Chevratit Demokratit)

YACHAD was formed in 2003 from several left parties and factions: MERETZ, an alliance between several formerly independent parties; SHAHAR, a faction that seceded from the Labor Party, led by Yossi Beilin; and the Democratic Choice (HaBchira HaDemokratit), a one-man Knesset faction, led by Roman Bronfman.

YACHAD was supposed to unite voters of the left into one social democratic party, after the downfall that MERETZ suffered in the 2003 elections. MERETZ was formed prior to the 1992 elections from the merger of three smaller left-wing parties: Shinui, RATZ (HaTenua

Lezchuyot HaEzrach Uleshalom; The Movement for Civil Rights and Peace) and MAPAM (Mifleget Poalim Meuhedet; United Workers' Party). In 1997 Avraham Poraz and most of the other members of Shinui left the party and formed a separate party.

The Movement for Civil Rights and Peace was founded in 1973 by Shulamit Aloni (born 1928), a former Labor Party member and civil rights activist. RATZ did well following the 1973 war when there was substantial discontent with the Israel Labor Party. It won three seats in the 1973 elections and joined the government coalition for a brief period in 1974. Its position declined in the 1977 and 1981 elections, and, following the latter, Aloni pledged her party's support to Labor in an effort to block Likud's efforts to form the new government. The party changed character in the 1980s. It became a party whose membership was drawn from a variety of older groups: the historical MCR, including various liberals and secularists, the academics of the "Group of 100" (including former Peace Now and Labor Party doves), and other disaffected left-wing voters. Its constituency was primarily the "middle-class" Ashkenazi population, and its platform featured full civil rights for all Israelis. Yossi Sarid (born 1940), another former Labor Party activist, assumed a significant role in shaping the party's dovish foreign policy. The MCR's greatest success at the polls came in 1988 when it won five Knesset seats.

MAPAM was organized in 1948 when HaShomer HaTzair merged with radical elements from Achdut HaAvodah. From its beginnings the party was more Marxist than MAPAI. The former Achdut HaAvodah members left in 1954 because of MAPAM's pro-Soviet orientation and acceptance of Arabs as party members. Although the party's domestic policy was essentially indistinguishable from MAPAI's, MAPAM's share of the vote in national elections declined steadily before it joined the Alignment for the 1969 elections. MAPAM ended its alliance with Labor in September 1984 over the issue of the formation of the Government of National Unity with Likud. MAPAM ran as an independent party list in the 1988 election, winning three seats in the Knesset.

The Democratic Choice was formed in 1999 by two members of the immigrants party "Yisrael BeAliya" who objected to the government's social policy. The faction split once more, when Roman Bronfman aligned with MERETZ. Yossi Beilin and Ya'el Dayan, both Labor members of the Knesset, formed SHAHAR in 2002, after failing to win a "realistic" place on the party list. In 2003 Beilin and Dayan, with few of their supporters, aligned with MERETZ.

In the 1992 election MERETZ, with Shulamit Aloni at the head of the party list, ran on a platform stressing the need for territorial compromise in order to resolve the Arab-Israeli conflict and a freeze on the expansion of existing settlements and building of new settlements in the occupied territories. It advocated the reform of Israel's electoral system in order to broaden political participation and make parties and Knesset representatives more accountable to the public. The party also called for greater pluralism and tolerance in the country's educational system, a strict separation between religion and state, and the conscription of Yeshiva students into the army. The new party won 12 seats in the election, two more than the movement's component groups held in the outgoing Knesset. MERETZ joined Labor in the government formed by Yitzhak Rabin, with Aloni appointed as education minister. In 1993 Aloni was removed from that post because of her frequent attacks against the Orthodox Jewish community and sidelined in the relatively minor post of minister of communications, science, and culture. At the same time, Yossi Sarid was brought into the cabinet as environment minister. Sarid replaced Aloni as party head prior to the 1996 election, in which MERETZ won nine seats.

After the outbreak of the second intifada in 2000, MERETZ, still a firm supporter of the Oslo Agreements, lost many of its voters. In the 2003 elections to the 16th Knesset, YACHAD won six seats, less than what MERETZ alone had held in the 15th Knesset. The party's leader is Dr. Yossi Beilin, the leader of SHAHAR.

DEMOCRATIC FRONT FOR PEACE AND EQUALITY (DFPE)

(Hachazit Hademokratit leshalom uleshivyon; HADASH)

A Communist party was active in Palestine before the establishment of the State of Israel. Unlike its counterparts, this party did not exclude Arab membership. The Israeli Communist Party (MAKI—Miflaga Komunistit Yisrealit) was founded in 1948. Communist representatives have been continuously represented in the Knesset since the first Knesset, though they have been excluded by MAPAI from any potential power. The Communist Party, in its different forms, generally secures a large proportion of their support from Israel's Arab population. On average, the Communists have secured three to five seats in the Knesset. MAKI split in 1965, with a group critical of the USSR remaining with the old name and the New Communist List

(RAKAH—Reshima Komunistit Hadasha), the party recognized by Moscow, secured its dominance as "the" Communist Party. In 1977 RAKAH allied with the Black Panthers, a left-wing protest movement founded by immigrants from North Africa and other Islamic countries, naming itself the "Democratic Front for Peace and Equality" (DFPE, or in Hebrew, HADASH—Hachazit Hademokratit leshalom uleshivyon).

As with Communist parties worldwide, the collapse of the Soviet Union led to an internal crisis. The support of the party declined and this was followed by contemplations on the continued adherence to communist ideology. It aligned with political forces in the Arab sphere, which are more (Arab) nationalist than Communist. In 1996 it aligned with the National Democratic Assembly (BALAD—Brit Leumit Demokratit—Altajamuu' Alwatany Aldimokraty) and secured five seats. In the following elections, in 1999, it participated independently of BALAD and won three seats. In 2003 it won three seats after it aligned again, this time with the Arab National Movement (TAAL—Tenuaa' Aravit Leumit), a move that brought about considerable internal criticism, especially from the Jewish members of the party.

Its platform calls for the total withdrawal of Israel from the occupied territories, including from southern Lebanon; the establishment of a sovereign, independent Palestinian state alongside Israel in the territories occupied by Israel in 1967, with eastern Jerusalem as its capital; and the cancellation of all "strategic" agreements between Israel and the United States.

NATIONAL RELIGIOUS PARTY (NRP)

(Miflaga Datit-leumit; MAFDAL)

HISTORY

Founded in 1956, the NRP was a full merger of Mizrachi (short for "spiritual center"), formally established as a party in Palestine in 1918, and HaPoel HaMizrachi (Mizrachi Worker), founded in 1922. HaPoel retained a degree of independence as the trade union section of the party responsible for immigration and absorption, labor and vocational affairs, housing, settlement, culture, pension funds and economic affairs, and so on. The central NRP organization was responsible for policy, party organization, religion and rabbinical relations, and publications. From its beginning, this party of Orthodox religious Zionists began to have an impact on the movement, electing 19 percent of the delegates to the 12th Zionist congress in 1921. The NRP has

participated within the mainstream of Jewish life and the activities of the State of Israel since independence, has been a significant partner in almost all of Israel's governments, and consequently has wielded substantial political power.

Since the early 1980s the NRP has suffered from internal differences over issues and leadership that have led to the creation of factions—each with its own leadership and agendas—and breakaway parties. Prior to the 1981 election, Aharon Abuhatzeira, the scion of an important Moroccan rabbinical family, bolted from the NRP and formed TAMI (Tenuah LeMassoret Israel; Movement for Jewish Tradition) as a North African-oriented religious party. Abuhatzeira broke away from the NRP in part over the issue of ethnic representation, but he was also upset by the perceived lack of support he received from the NRP leadership during his trial for corruption. His new party list won three seats in the 1981 election, drawing support from the Oriental community, and appeared to have a major electoral impact on the NRP, which saw its Knesset strength cut in half from 12 to six seats. TAMI's political fortunes, however, declined steadily thereafter. In the 1984 election it won only one seat, and in 1988 Abuhatzeira was coopted into Likud and guaranteed a safe slot on its list of Knesset candidates.

The NRP further splintered in 1984 when its right-wing faction broke away and joined with several other right-wing politicians to form the Morasha (Heritage) party. Morasha won two seats in the 1984 election, and the NRP again lost ground, falling to four seats in Parliament. Morasha collapsed in 1988 when its former NRP component left to rejoin the NRP. The reintegration of the right-wing faction strengthened the nationalist tendencies within the NRP. Changes within the party leadership also contributed to the party's rightward swing. Yosef Burg, the party's moderate elder statesman, was no longer influential in party affairs and his successor as party leader, Zvulun Hammer, was himself replaced by Avner Shaki. Shaki, a Sephardi, was an ardent supporter of the Gush Emunim (Bloc of the Faithful) settlement movement in the West Bank and was committed to retention of all the occupied territories. Shaki also took a less conciliatory position on domestic religious issues, particularly the question of changing the Law of Return to recognize only those conversions to Judaism performed according to Orthodox religious law. Though the NRP suffered a small additional percentage loss in popular vote in the 1988 election, it managed to secure five Knesset seats.

In response to the NRP's rightward trend, party doves left in 1988 and formed the Meimad (acronym for "Jewish State–Democratic State") Party. The new parry list fell about 7,000 votes short of the threshold (then 1 percent) for attaining a seat in the 1988 election and later joined the Labor Party.

The NRP won six Knesset seats in the 1992 election. It reinstated Hammer as head of its list, dropping Shaki to the second slot, and used the double entendre "NRP Right at Your Side" as its campaign slogan. The party's campaign identification with the political right wing, and implicitly with Likud, virtually ruled out any chance that NRP leaders would be able to maneuver after the election to join the new Labor coalition under Prime Minister Rabin.

The NRP fared much better in the 1996 election, winning nine seats. The party's platform called for applying Israeli sovereignty over greater Jerusalem, including the Gush Etzion settlement bloc and the settlements of Ma'ale Adumim and Givat Ze'ev; strengthening Jewish settlement throughout the West Bank, including Hebron (due to be handed over to Palestinian administrative control under terms of the Oslo accords); and retaining all of the Golan Heights. Since the 1992 elections, there has been only one diversion from its usual achievements of five to six seats in the Knesset. In the 1996 elections, using an ultra-nationalist campaign, it managed to win nine seats. However, in the 1999 elections it retained only five seats, and, in the 2003 elections it won six seats, under the leadership of its new leader—since the death of Hammer in 1998—Efraim ("Effi") Eitam.

ORGANIZATION

Officially, important decisions are passed through the NRP "center," a body of some 750 representatives of the party's local branches. In fact, however, there have not been new elections to the "center" since 1989, and its power is highly limited. Leadership is elected by the "center" but is usually, in actual fact, nominated. The party also has a women and a youth organization.

The NRP is related to an array of bodies and mobilized groups that have been founded by Mizrahi or are ideologically connected to it, including a youth movement (Bnei-Akiva), sports organization (Elitzur), a housing company (Mishav), and many more.

POLICY

The NRP was founded to emphasize the need for legislation based on Judaic religious law (*Halacha*) and protective of a "Torah-true" tradition. It actively supports Jewish immigration, the development of the private sector, and government support of all religiously necessary religious activities, including a religious school system and rabbinical councils in every city and town. These aims have been constant since the founding of NRP's predecessors, and they have been realized to a large degree. With only some minor intraparty disagreement, the NRP view was that it was organized for religious purposes and had no particular role to play in political, economic, or foreign affairs. It was able to cooperate effectively with MAPAI and Labor primarily because of its willingness to defer to the left on foreign and defense questions in return for support on religious matters.

With the Israeli capture of the West Bank and the Sinai Peninsula in 1967, however, NRP attitudes began to change. The capture of ancient Israeli cities—Hebron, Shechem (Nablus), and Old Jerusalem—was seen as a miraculous achievement in fulfillment of the covenant between God and the Jewish people. The NRP believed that the return of any of the territory of historic Israel to Arab control would be a repudiation of that covenant. On that basis, NRP "hawks" sought to focus the party's efforts on the rapid settlement of the new territory with the aim of securing it for Israel in perpetuity.

Although "hawks" are to be found in all of the NRP factions, they appear to be concentrated in the youth faction, which originally sought to reform the party organization, in part to increase the opportunities for newer and younger members in the party and government. They also wanted to increase NRP's independence in the coalition with the Labor Party. After 1967 the youth faction sought to appeal to non-traditional voters with the slogan "no return of any part of Eretz [historic land of] Israel." Largely because both groups are composed of the same people, the youth faction has strong but informal ties with Gush Emunim, the leading movement of West Bank settlers. In some respects, the youth faction considers itself the political representation of the Gush Emunim. Youth faction leaders have come to increasing prominence in both the NRP and the government.

MEMBERSHIP AND CONSTITUENCY

There are several thousand members in the NRP, but because of the ineffectiveness of the party mechanism, it is difficult to know how accurate this information is. Voting support comes primarily from the ranks of the Orthodox religious Zionists, while less-affluent Orthodox (or non-Zionists) voters tend to vote for SHAS or other parties in the past several years. One of the more important power bases of the NRP consists of voters in the "ideological" settlements in the occupied territories, namely, those who came to settle the area for nationalistic, messianic, and religious motives.

FINANCING

No reliable information on NRP financing is available. Membership dues and donations provide the bulk of the party's income.

LEADERSHIP

The factionalism of the NRP reflects both personal conflicts and differing policy perspectives. Yosef Burg was the party leader from its founding until the late 1970s and served in most Israeli cabinets up until 1977. A man of great political skills, he worked successfully to maintain and expand the religious foundation of the state. His seniority and role as head of the largest faction (Lamifneh) secured his dominant position in the party, but he did not dictate its positions or policies. His influence was, in part, the result of his shrewd use of patronage in allocating jobs in the party and the party-controlled institutions. As a government minister, he was also able to distribute many public jobs in the religious and educational establishments and a variety of posts controlled by the Ministry of the Interior. Zvulun Hammer, who for many years was also head of the youth faction, served as party leader until his death in January 1998. Hammer was appointed education minister in the 1996 government of Prime Minister Netanyahu.

The current leader of the NRP is Efraim ("Effi") Eitam. Eitam, who is a decorated brigadier-general, leads a nationalistic and hawkish line. In 2004 he resigned from his post in Sharon's government because of his refusal to support Sharon's plans to resettle some of those in the Palestinian territories.

PROSPECTS

The NRP is firmly entrenched in the right-wing nationalist camp allied with Likud. It will continue to play a key role as a coalition partner for Likud, and press it—from the right—not to make any concessions on settlements with the Palestinians.

NATIONAL UNION

(Ha'ihud Ha'Leum)

The National Union was founded in 1999, uniting three parties—Herut (a group that seceded from the Likud, using its historical name to symbolize its commitment to the original Herut ideology); Moledet ("Motherland"); and Tkuma ("Resurrection"). A year later, Herut left the party, and Yisrael Beitenu ("Israel—

Our Home"), a nationalist party founded by and for immigrants from the former USSR, joined in. The three factions still operate somewhat independently but run as one party.

The founder of the party was Rehavam ("Ghandi") Zeevi, a former army general who advocated a policy of "voluntary transfer" (de facto, expulsion) of the Palestinian population. Zeevi was the minister of tourism in Sharon's coalition when he was assassinated by a Palestinian in 2001. After Zeevi's death, Avigdor Liebermann, the leader of Yisrael Beitenu, became the new leader of the party, and the National Union withdrew from the coalition. Liebermann and Benny Elon, Moledet's new leader, joined the government again after the 2003 elections, but they were dismissed by Sharon because of their refusal to support his plan to disengage gradually from Palestinian territories. The party continues to support a hard-line nationalist policy, rejecting any compromise with the Palestinians.

UNITED TORAH JUDAISM (UTJ)

(Yahadut HaTorah Hameuchedet)

United Torah Judaism (UTJ) was formed prior to the 1992 election as a result of the merger of two ultra-Orthodox parties, Agudat Yisrael (Association of Israel) and its offshoot, Degel HaTorah (Flag of the Torah), which constitute the united party's two main factions.

Agudat Yisrael, the world organization of Orthodox Jews founded in 1912 by various rabbis and other religious leaders in Europe, was at first opposed to Zionism, believing that Israel should wait for divine redemption and the coming of the Messiah and that the establishment of a political state in Palestine was heretical. Although it boycotted the institutions of the Jewish community in Palestine, it eventually gave partial backing to the Zionist endeavor when it supported the establishment of Israel (but without ascribing any religious significance to it) and, upon becoming a political party in 1948, participated in the institutions of the state. As an independent party until 1992, it was represented in Parliament and supported most of the coalition governments, but after 1952 it refused to accept a cabinet portfolio. Its voting strength lies in Jerusalem and Bnei Brak and consists mostly of Ashkenazim.

In 1984 SHAS broke away from the Ashkenazi-dominated Aguda to contest that year's Knesset elections. The defection of the Sephardi wing of the party appeared to cost Aguda some of its support in the election; its Knesset representation was cut in half from four to two seats.

Agudat Yisrael was again split in 1988. This time, Rabbi Eliezer Schach, who had helped to engineer the creation of SHAS four years earlier, left Aguda with his followers over what he saw as the growing influence within the party of the Lubavitch Hasidic sect and its leader, Brooklyn-based Rabbi Menachem M. Schneerson. So, on the eve of the 1988 election, Schach formed the rival ultra-Orthodox party Degel HaTorah. This development led Schneerson to mobilize his followers to vote for Agudat Yisrael, and his efforts were largely responsible for Aguda's success at the polls. It secured nearly three times the number of votes it had in 1984 and increased its Knesset seats from two to five. Degel Ha-Torah won two seats.

Degel HaTorah was all but negotiated out of existence prior to the June 1992 election when Rabbi Schach agreed that the party join Agudat Yisrael in a unified list called United Torah Judaism. Also joining the bloc was a small breakaway party from SHAS, the Moriah party. Schach accepted the fifth and seventh spots on the joint list for his Degel HaTorah representatives, but the new electoral alliance won only four seats in the election, as compared with the seven seats that the three constituent groups had held in the outgoing Knesset. The Moriah Party representative, who had the number two slot on the party list, was forced by a preelection promise to resign his seat in order to allow Degel HaTorah to take up the party's fourth and final seat in the new Knesset.

United Torah Judaism retained its four Knesset seats in the 1996 election but was the only religious party that failed to increase its representation. The party fell solidly behind Likud leader Benjamin Netanyahu in his bid to become prime minister; heeding the injunction of Agudat Yisrael's Council of Torah Sages to vote for the candidate who would be more likely "to work in the spirit of religion and Jewish tradition." In the 1999 and 2003 elections it gained five seats.

All crucial UTJ decisions on policy are made not by the party's Knesset members or its membership but by Agudat Yisrael's 12-member Council of Torah Sages, composed of revered rabbis, heads of yeshivas (religious schools), and members of Hasidic dynasties. Besides the council, the party's central institutions are the great assembly, composed of representatives of the local branches, the central world council, and the world executive committee. It has its own school network in which religious instruction is a major part of the curriculum. The government supplies most of the funds for the school system.

UTJ is primarily concerned with enhancing the role of religion in the state and is opposed to all forms of secularism. Its support for the Netanyahu coalition was secured on the basis of a lengthy coalition agreement containing numerous concessions to the group's religious perspectives, for example, strict Sabbath laws and revision of legislation to accommodate orthodox Jewish principles. The parliamentary leader is Meir Porush, son of a longtime Agudat Yisrael member of the Knesset, Rabbi Menachem Porush.

ARAB PARTIES

During Israel's War of Independence (1948) most of the political leadership of the Palestinians, along with most of the elite, left the territory of Palestine-Israel. The population that was left in the territory received citizenship and the Israeli Declaration of Independence called on them "to preserve peace and participate in the upbuilding of the State on the basis of full and equal citizenship and due representation in all its provisional and permanent institutions." In practice, however, a military government was imposed on most Arab-Israeli villages between 1948 and 1966, and the political activity of the Arab population was closely monitored and manipulated by MAPAI. The political activity was mostly limited to "daughter" parties sponsored by MAPAI (and sometimes also other Zionist parties), with MAKI (the precursor of the DFPE) as the only exception. The only political leader of that time who is worth mentioning is Toufiq Toubi, one of the leaders of the DFPE and the only pre-1948 leader who remained in the territory.

In the mid-1970s independent Arab parties began to consolidate and, with it, the support of the DFPE, which posed itself as the only established alternative, soared. The Arab-Israeli constituency is divided between those who vote for nationalistic (Palestinian) parties; those who choose to support the Islamic Movement and its representatives in the political arena; and those who choose to support the Communist and other parties, which do not define themselves as "Arab" parties. It is noteworthy that more than half of the Arab Israelis vote for various "Jewish" parties—Yachad, Labor, Likud, or others—and that there are as many Arab MKs from the Likud, Labor, and Yachad as there are from "Arab" parties. It is also worth mentioning that voting rates in the Arab population are much lower compared to the Jewish participation, due to unwillingness to recognize the state.

The two parties claiming to be "Arab" are the United Arab List (UAL, Reshima Aravit Meuchedet, RA'AM) and the National Democratic Assembly (NDA, Brit Le'umit Demokratit, BALAD). The UAL was formed in 1996 as a union between three forces: the Arab Democratic Party (ADP), parts of the Islamic Movement, and the National Unity Front. The ADP was founded by Abd el-Wahab Darawshe in 1988, after Darawshe seceded from the Labor, because of its policies regarding the first Palestinian Intifadha. (Darawshe won one seat.) The Islamic Movement began its activity in Israel in the 1970s, as the Israeli version of the political forces ran by Islamists elsewhere in the Middle East and based on the model of the Muslim Brotherhood. It gained momentum after the rise of the Ayatollah Khomeini in Iran in 1979. In 1983 it participated for the first time in local elections, and won the control over two councils. The united party won four seats in 1996, five seats in 1999, but only two seats in 2003, presumably because of the refusal of some elements in the Islamic Movement to participate in the elections. The head of the UAL is Abd al-Malek Dahamshe, a lawyer who became more religious while serving a sentence in an Israeli prison for recruiting members to the PLO's Fatah faction.

A second "Arab" party is the National Democratic Assembly (Brit Leumit Demokratit. BALAD, or in Arabic—Altajamuu' Alwatany Aldimokraty), which tends to be more national-secular than its counterpart. The NDA was founded by Azmi Bishara, a philosophy professor who heads the party, and began its course by aligning with the DFPE in the 1996 elections. In the 1999 elections Bishara's extreme Arab nationalism brought him two seats, and in 2003 the party increased its power to three seats.

Other Political Forces

Outside of Israel's turbulent parliamentary sphere, social and political movements attempt to affect the government's policies or to press the politicians. Two of the most important movements—Shalom Achshav on the left and Gush Emunim on the right—can be traced to the disappointment of young voters from the political establishment after the 1973 "Yom Kippur" War.

Gush Emunim ("Bloc of the Faithful") is a loose movement of those supporting (and inhabiting) the settlements in the occupied territories (in Judea, Samaria, East Jerusalem, and the Gaza Strip, and only to a lesser extent also in the Golan). Gush Emunim was founded after the 1973 war by Orthodox youth—mostly by those inspired by the theology of Rabbi Zvi Yehuda Kook—and operates as an independent, nonpartisan political movement, but it is in fact closely connected to the NRP. Gush Emunim still exists, but

currently other names are more often in use, describing different groups within the settler community (the institutionalized YESHA Council, the anti-establishment "Hills' Youth," etc.).

An array of peace movements is also active in Israel. Shalom Achshav ("Peace Now") was founded in 1978 by IDF reservists, supporting a peace initiative with Egypt. It has been the primary force behind the protests against the Israeli involvement in Lebanon and supported governmental peace negotiations. The inability of Peace Now to react to the new realities after the second intifada broke brought other peace movements to prominence, including the non-Zionist Gush Shalom ("Peace Bloc"), headed by Uri Avneri; the Siruvniks movement that supports those who refuse to serve in the IDF because of the occupation; and the "National Accord" (Ha-Amana Ha-Leumit), led by Ami Ayalon and the Palestinian leader Sari Nuseybe, which tries to aim at the political center.

The main trade union, the Histadrut, is not as strong as it was in the 1950s and 1960s, when it was one of MAPAI's tools to control Israeli politics. It is, however, still a stronghold for the large and powerful unions, such as those of the Electricity Company or the Aviation industries (it has also been criticized for not protecting workers who are less powerful and are employed by personnel companies). Its head, Amir Peretz, still maintains power and is the most prominent figure representing Socialist and unionist ideology in Israel.

National Prospects

The continued drift to the right in Israeli public opinion in the early 2000s was partially caused by an unrelenting wave of Palestinian terrorist attacks and its disappointment of any possibility of sustainable peace in the region after the collapse of the Oslo Accords in 2000. The free market economic policies of the Likud government and the processes of international globalization have reshaped the political identities of the Israeli voters: those who are alienated and excluded from the political and economic processes find themselves identifying with nationalistic ethnoreligious rhetoric, the sort propagated by SHAS, the National Union, the Arab nationalist and religious parties, the NRP (to a lesser extent), and, ironically, also the Likud.

Those who feel threatened by the political ethnoreligiosity as manifested by SHAS tend to support the party that seeks to represent the Israeli bourgeoisie, Shinui. However, Shinui, which campaigned in the

2003 elections almost solely against the ethnoreligious policies, might find itself in dire straits if its disappointed voters cast their votes for other parties. Those who support free-market policies might find themselves within the Likud or the Labor, while those who voted for Shinui only because of its anti-religious rhetoric might support Yachad. The fate of Shinui, despite its tremendous success in the 2003 elections, might be similar to that of other attempts to establish a "liberal" or "third way" party in Israel.

Nevertheless, the Arab-Israeli conflict remains Israel's most important challenge. Failed peace initiatives and the need for personal security are other reasons for the success of the Likud in the 2003 elections. The emergence of the Likud as the dominant party in the 2003 elections was helped by the fact that the Likud center gained strength of its own accord. Some groups joined the center in order to change Likud's policies, a move that these groups perceived as the most effective means to affect the state's policies. The political system continues to reflect diversity, but it also manifests instability, which adds to the uncertainty expressed in public opinion.

The Israeli withdrawal from the Gaza Strip in 2005 provided a small opening for new peace prospects, but the Israeli-Palestinian divide was likely to remain one of the world's most enduring political conflicts in the years to come.

Further Reading

Arian, Asher. *The Choosing People: Voting Behavior in Israel.* Cleveland: Case Western Reserve University Press, 1973.

——, ed. *The Elections in Israel—1969.* Jerusalem: Jerusalem Academic Press, 1972.

——, ed. *The Elections in Israel—1981.* Israel: Ramot, 1983.

Arian, Asher, and Michal Shamir, eds. *The Elections in Israel: 1984.* New Brunswick, N.J.: Transaction, 1986.

——, eds. *The Elections in Israel, 1988.* Boulder, Colo.: Westview Press, 1990.

——, eds. *The Elections in Israel, 1992.* Albany: State University of New York Press, 1995.

——, eds. *The Elections in Israel—1996.* Albany: State University of New York Press, 2001.

——, eds. *The Elections in Israel—2001.* Jerusalem: The Israeli Democracy Institute.

——, eds. *The Elections in Israel—2003.* Jerusalem: The Israeli Democracy Institute.

Aronoff, Myron J. *Power and Ritual in the Israel Labor Party.* Rev. ed. Armonk, N.Y.: M.E. Sharpe, 1993.

Elazar, Daniel J., and Howard R. Periniman, eds. *Israel at the Polls 1981.* Bloomington: Indiana University Press, 1986.

Elazar, Daniel J., and Shmuel Sandler, eds. *Israel's Odd Couple: The Nineteen Eighty-Four Knesset Elections and the National Unity Government.* Detroit: Wayne State University Press, 1990.

——, eds. *Who's the Boss in Israel: Israel at the Polls, 1988–89.* Detroit: Wayne State University Press, 1992.

——, eds. *Israel at the Polls, 1992.* Lanham, Md.: Rowman and Littlefield, 1995.

Reich, Bernard. *A Brief History of Israel.* New York: Facts On File, 2005.

——. *Historical Dictionary of Israel.* Metuchen, N.J.: Scarecrow Press, 1992.

Reich, Bernard, and Gershon R. Kievab. *Israel: Land of Tradition and Conflict.* 2d ed. Boulder, Colo.: Westview Press, 1993.

——, eds. *Israel Faces the Future.* New York: Praeger, 1986.

——, eds. *Israeli Politics in the 1990s: Key Domestic and Foreign Policy Factors.* Westview, Conn.: Greenwood Press, 1991.

Sager, Samuel. *The Parliamentary System of Israel.* Syracuse, N.Y.: Syracuse University Press, 1985.

Shapiro, Yonathan. *The Road to Power: Herut Party in Israel.* Albany: State University of New York Press, 1991.

Shindler, Cohn. *Israel, Likud and the Zionist Dream: Power, Politics, and Ideology from Begin to Netanyahu.* New York: St. Martin's Press, 1995.

REPUBLIC OF ITALY
(Repubblica Italiana)

By Jeffrey K. Hass, Ph.D.

Italy is a recent newcomer to the Western European community of nation-states. Originally a peninsula of smaller kingdoms, Italy only became a nation-state, with a constitutional monarchy, in 1861. The impetus to unification was driven by an elite from the Piedmont region. Initially Italy was not a democracy, as only 2 percent of the population enjoyed suffrage rights until 1919, when all males were given the right to vote. This introduction of universal male suffrage caused a split between the mass electorate and the elite. With growing discontent and economic downturn after World War I, Italian society split along class lines, as the working class turned more and more to emerging socialist and communist parties and movements and the middle class followed the lead of the elites and exchanged power for security with Benito Mussolini's emerging reactionary Fascist Party. Fascism contributed to certain future developments in Italian politics. First, Italy's centralization and unification were completed under Mussolini. Second, through the Lateran Pacts of 1929, the Catholic Church received a privileged position (Catholicism was legally admitted as the national religion), which brought Catholic organizations into politics and eventually gave birth to the powerful Christian Democratic Party. Additionally, fascism gave political legitimacy and moral authority to the Socialists and the Communists, who helped lead the Resistance movement and thus emerged from World War II as a contending power with the Christian Democrats. Third, by siding with the Fascists, the bourgeois elite and middle class traded future political legitimacy for security. After World War II and the horrors of fascism, right-wing elite and middle-class bourgeois parties were dead in the water; a mass electorate remembered how bourgeois interests had sold out the nation, and so until 1994 there was no bourgeois party with serious political support.

THE 1970S AND 1980S

The 1970s and 1980s were not kind to the Italian republic. The 1970s saw the continuation of civil strife from the late 1960s, except that radical right-wing and left-wing groups joined in the fray. One infamous radical left-wing organization was the Red Brigade, which used violence to splinter the political system. The Red Brigade's most daring and successful adventure was the kidnapping and murder of a former prime minister, Aldo Moro, in March–May 1978. This was replaced in the 1980s by organized crime (the Mafia). Historically the descendants of the private armies feudal landowners used in the 15th and 16th centuries, the Mafia, through penetration into the economy and politics, had become the new threat to stability. Particularly in the South, the Mafia could harass and threaten even state officials; judges and prosecutors tracking Mafia activities for legal action were targets of Mafia violence and helped trigger an anticorruption and anticrime wave that began to sweep Italy in the late 1980s.

Through the 1970s and 1980s Italian development followed two paths: greater local industrial development aided by effective, responsive local government in the North; and less effective, more corrupt and contentious local politics and business in the South. As more money concentrated in the North and stories of corruption and violence disseminated from the South, a reaction began. Some talk of secession by northern regions emerged, especially in the rhetoric of the radical party Northern League (Lega Nord). As well, political parties and elites in the North began to organize regional parties focusing more closely on local interests and in opposition to the power of the central government. This fault line between North and the South was not necessarily new. The two halves had different institutional histories, with regional association dominating the North and clan politics dominating the South, and the economies were primarily industrial (north) and agricultural (south). This gave Italy the semblance of an artificial nation that, united by culture, language, and religion, was less unified and integrated than from afar might appear to be the case. However, this fault line became more apparent by the 1990s, when right-wing parties started drawing on the reaction of northern voters against southern corruption and central government.

One important event was increasing openness about corruption and the rising passion to do something about it. Corruption investigations and scandals led to the fall of leading parties and, in the end, helped with the fall of the First Republic. A 1992 sting operation in Milan uncovered large kickback schemes; resulting plea bargaining led to more investigations and uncovered a trail of scandal and kickbacks leading to high government officials (including the former Socialist prime minister, Bettino Craxi) and members of the Christian Democrats. Additional disclosure revealed that a kickback system dubbed *Tangentopoli* permeated Italian politics and society. High-ranking government officials were forced to resign; public sentiment became so strong against the ruling politicians that not only did the electorate turn against them for alternative parties but also mobs at times threatened Parliament. The only two important parties that were not much harmed by corruption scandals and investigations were the Party of the Democratic Left (PDS), the former Communist Party, and the Italian Social Movement–National Right (MSI), the neofascists. As a result of the impact of the corruption probes, both these parties scored well in local elections, to the detriment of the formerly powerful Christian Democrats, which was relegated to electoral impotence. Ironically,

this once-dominant party was quickly felled and has not recovered since.

THE 1990S TO THE PRESENT

Political shifts occurred in the 1990s with the collapse of the First Republic, owing to party splits, changes in electoral rules, and the rise of regional and right-wing parties. Left-wing parties, tainted by corruption, also had problems dealing with national problems, such as a sluggish economy and a $1 trillion national debt (one-tenth of which was being channeled to political parties illegally). When the left-wing parties could not handle corruption charges or political problems and when electoral laws and intraparty fighting led to political realignments, the time was ripe for a major change in the political landscape and, as a result, the rise of the right. Briefly in 1993 Central Bank head Carlo Ciampi was asked to become prime minister and form a government; but his government was short-lived. Another short-lived government led President Scalfaro to dissolve Parliament early in 1994 and call for new elections (under new electoral rules).

These elections changed the face of Italian politics. Arguably the most important and controversial actor in this whole scenario was the media millionaire Silvio Berlusconi, whose party owed its existence to its boss's drive and to an existing business network. Berlusconi united his right-wing Forza Italia with right-wing Alleanza Nationale, the regionalist anticenter, pro-market Lega Nord, and other smaller parties to bring a right-wing government to power in 1994, riding the wave of anticorruption feeling, the disorganization of former major parties, and the threat of a Communist resurgence (as the PDS had taken several mayoral races in 1993). This alliance, called the Freedom Pole (Polo della Libertà), obtained a majority of seats in Parliament. Berlusconi became prime minister. However, this alliance proved short-lived, as the Lega Nord, under the guidance of its fiery leader Umberto Bossi, soon withdrew its support from the alliance. By the latter half of the year Berlusconi was investigated for conflict of interests (for keeping his businesses in a blind trust that he could still control while prime minister), and Berlusconi's brother Paolo was investigated for kickbacks. Silvio Berlusconi tried to hamper judicial and investigatory power into his brother's affairs (through use of an emergency decree), but this was blocked by the threat of resignation by the anticorruption leader Antonio Di Pietro. Finally, amid the scandals and squabbling within the Freedom Pole alliance, the Northern League withdrew, and Berlusconi resigned. Lamberto Dini, an economist, became the new prime minister in 1995 and attempted neo-orthodox economic reforms in the face of the Freedom Pole's opposition. Social benefits were cut and legislation was introduced to regulate the media (following allegations that Berlusconi had used his media empire unfairly in his election campaign). In 1995 Berlusconi was indicted for kickbacks to tax inspectors, although he did avoid one possible problem when a referendum supported Berlusconi's right to own three major television networks (which the government claimed amounted to near-monopoly power).

Berlusconi's first term as prime minister atop the right-wing coalition was marked by domestic and international concerns, not only with the tone of his and his coalition's rhetoric but also with his domination of the Italian media. Western governments distanced themselves from the governing coalition, with its sometimes neofascist language. Berlusconi also faced the prospect of formal legal investigations over charges that he bribed judges in the 1980s. To add to governance problems, the Northern League, the most radical of the right-wing coalition, opted out of the alliance. Under these domestic and international pressures, Berlusconi temporarily lost his grip on power. The final blow came when President Oscar Scalfaro's nominated prime minister, Antonio Maccanico, could not create a coalition government. This forced Scalfaro to dissolve the parliament and call for a new election in 1996. In a close race, Olive Tree, a center-left coalition led by PDS, emerged victorious by a narrow margin over the Alliance for Freedom (essentially the Freedom Pole without participation of the Northern League). Center-left control of the government was tenuous, however, because the ruling coalition depended on the good will of an alliance with the Communist Refoundation Party (unreformed Communists who disagreed with the main party's renunciation of communism after 1989). Other allies were found, but the two successive center-left coalition governments were unstable and did not last long.

By 2000 the right-wing parties were rebuilding their alliance. The Northern League had faired badly in regional elections after its uncooperative behavior in the 1990s and radical rhetoric. The new right-wing coalition, Freedom House, was once again led by Berlusconi's Forza Italia. The alliance parties made significant gains in local elections in 2000, setting the way for electoral victory in 2001. Partly this reflected the strength of the right, and partly it reflected the inability of the Communists and leftist Social Democrats to come to a working agreement for shared electoral and governing strategies. Berlusconi's fortunes on the

world stage also improved as well. In his first term as prime minister he was not a favorite of the Western community because of fears that his right-wing tactics and image, coupled with his accumulation of immense economic and media power, bordered on neofascism. While this reality did not change, Berlusconi focused on improving his image abroad. He was able to make some inroads in parts of the international community when he joined American president George W. Bush and British prime minister Tony Blair in the "war on terror," including providing both moral support and troops for the U.S.-led incursion into Iraq. While this endeared him to the American and British political elite, it did not improve relations with antiwar leaders and publics on the European continent, who continued to view him with suspicion.

Despite the improvement of his fortunes in 2001, Berlusconi did not reign supreme, and in 2004 he was beginning to show signs of vulnerability. The popularity of his Forza Italia party was slipping in the polls, and his attempts to reform and improve the economy were bearing little fruit. Berlusconi came to power with ambitious plans to change Italy's economy and bring it out of the doldrums. His attempt to liberalize Italy's thicket of paternalist labor laws was partially successful, although it did cause outrage among some sections of the Italian public and in Europe more generally. (That his finance minister left office did not help the government's image or Berlusconi's efforts.) Accusations of corruption continued to hound him, in particular a trial over accusations of bribing judges. Further, while the Northern League fared badly in Chamber of Deputies elections (the lower house of Parliament), it contributed important seats to the Freedom House alliance in the Senate.

The Freedom House coalition collapsed in early 2005, leading to Berlusconi's resignation. However, not long after he was able to form a new coalition government that included his Forza Italia party, the Northern League, the National Alliance, and the Union of Christian Democrats.

The System of Government

Italy is a republican unitary state, with a functional constitution dating to 1948. The fundamental political system is parliamentary. As a unified country Italy is, in spite of its long history, a relative newcomer, with unification finalized only in the 20th century.

After the dark period of fascism, the Italian polity was restructured along democratic lines. However, due to the particularities of political institutions, Italian politics remains less than stable and for the outsider rather confusing. Recent radical changes both in electoral procedure and the organization of political parties, intended to bring greater stability, has made the Italian political landscape as confusing as it had been previously.

The Italian governmental system provides the sources of political instability—Italy has had more than 50 governments in the postwar era—and yet still remains able to provide a basic framework to keep politics from sliding into chaos. The executive has the duty of formulating and implementing policies and for maintaining order within the country. However, because of institutional restrictions and because of the structure of Italy's party landscape—in particular, the plethora of parties—it is difficult for a government to remain in power long. Thus, Parliament is the ultimate seat of power and sovereignty in Italy.

The Italian system is grounded in a constitution, which provides general rules of political conduct. The constitution provides the rules for selection for powers and for structures of the various branches and levels of government. Further, the constitution guarantees certain political and social rights: the existence of a minimum wage, state-sponsored vocational training, gender equality in the workplace, a welfare safety net (for the unemployed, the disabled, and the unfortunate), the right to form trade unions and to strike, the inviolability of private enterprise and private property (except in cases of "general interest").

However, constitutional rules are broad enough that much of the important political reality is governed by political structure and institutions, in particular, the structure of parties and the electoral system that shapes that structure. Electoral rules and party structures shape the resulting political landscape, which in turn accounts for policies and for the political instability that has hampered Italian politics since World War II.

EXECUTIVE

The executive in Italy, as in much of Europe, has two parts: a president and a prime minister. The president is mostly an international figurehead representing Italy on the world stage and in international negotiations; however, the president also has some powers that occasionally are of political importance. The first power is symbolic: the president can act as a national figure for uniting and rallying the country. Such symbolic power and the use of the presidential "bully pulpit" help the president mobilize political forces and common voters. Second, the president does have some official institutional powers. The president can suspend legislation—sending it back to Parliament for

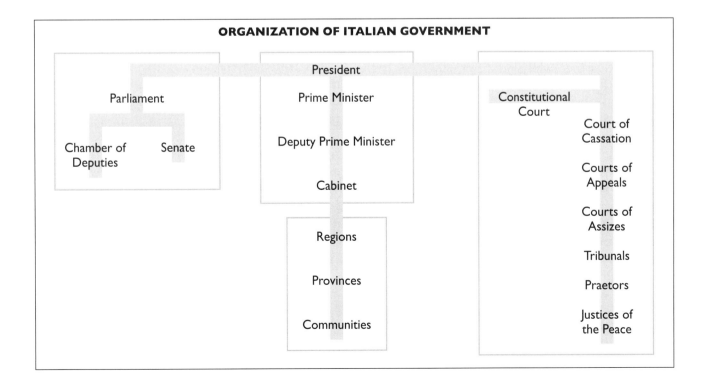

reconsideration, although if the two chambers pass the bill once again with a majority of votes, then the president's weak veto is overturned. Presidential acts are considered valid only if they are countersigned by the prime minister, giving some degree of control over the president. Also, the president nominates the prime minister, which can constitute real power if Parliament is at loggerheads over just whom to nominate. Finally, after consultation with heads of both parliamentary chambers, the president can dissolve Parliament and call for early elections. In the case when a president cannot serve out his term, he is replaced by the speaker of the Senate; new elections are to be held within 15 days except in extreme circumstances.

The real executive power in Italy belongs to the prime minister and the Council of Ministers (Consiglio dei Ministri). Ministers are proposed by the president; the government then formulates its political program within 10 days and submits itself and the program to each chamber of Parliament. Both chambers must pass a majority vote of confidence if this new government is to be confirmed (although if only one chamber does not pass a vote of no confidence, after changes a new vote must be undertaken).

The government may issue decrees and provisional measures in exceptional cases or other cases of necessity; however, these decrees are good for only 60 days and must be submitted within five days to Parliament, which then debates whether these government decrees should become law. Other powers of the ministers are proposing and implementing policy and overseeing the activities of the state bureaucracy. Reform policies—for example, neo-orthodox policies of austerity and privatization, to lower Italy's budget deficit—are the responsibility of the cabinet, which must not only formulate these policies but also then make sure they will not face opposition in Parliament and that the state bureaucracy will implement them. One result of the power of ministries and government positions and the link between government and parties is that parties have used control of the government to place their own members into bureaucratic positions, turning the government into a tool of party patronage; this practice came back to haunt the Christian Democrats in the 1980s.

The prime minister and other ministers are assembled by the president, who then presents them to Parliament within 10 days for a vote of confidence; this requires knitting together a parliamentary coalition. The work of crafting a coalition embodies the weakness of the prime minister and cabinet—and of the executive and the Italian system in general. Prime ministers do have a great deal of direct power;

however, given the parliamentary watchdog vote of no confidence, the prime minister and his cabinet can find themselves in tenuous positions if a supporting coalition in Parliament breaks down. This means that the parties and party bosses have greater power in influencing the executive than in many other parliamentary democracies in Europe, for a government's support depends on brokering between larger and smaller parties in the politics of coalition building. For example, prime ministers have fallen because of splits within their own party. This has led to one major problem with the Italian executive, the rapid turnover of governments and ministers in the postwar period, because of lack of firm support or a firm coalition within Parliament. Until 1986 the longest term for any one government was four years (that of Socialist Bettino Craxi, from August 1983 to 1987). From 1945 to 1995 Italy had 55 different governments and ruling coalitions; this was due mostly to instability fostered by two factors. The first was the electoral system, which allowed for a large number of parties to enter Parliament and which, as a result, did not encourage the thinning of the ranks to a few powerful parties that could win majorities outright or lead stable coalitions. A second reason was internal instability of the parties themselves; for example, the Christian Democrats often suffered splits within their own ranks, leading members of the ruling Christian Democratic coalition to levy a vote of no confidence against a prime minister and government headed by other members of their own party.

LEGISLATURE

Italy's national legislature is the Parliament (Parlamento), which is composed of two houses, the Chamber of Deputies (Camera dei Deputati) and the Senate (Senato della Repubblica). The Chamber of Deputies is composed of 630 representatives; the Senate is composed of 315 members chosen through direct elections plus former presidents and their appointees known as senators-for-life. The length of a legislative term is five years, although this term can be ended ahead of time if the speakers of the two chambers agree to do so and the president, after consulting with them, dissolves Parliament and calls for new elections.

The two chambers open their two annual sessions in February and October, although it is not uncommon for a session to continue into the next session, meaning a continuous convocation. There is no stipulation in the constitution or other laws making one house "upper" and the other "lower"; in principle, both have equal legislative powers, and both have the same legal chance to send a member to a ministerial post. Each chamber has special committees (11 to 14 in each), which are where legislation is initially debated before being brought to the floor for a vote. Each committee has a president who has the power to control the committee's agenda, giving this individual certain legislative and procedural powers. Legislation is more often than not introduced by the executive (especially the ministers) into both chambers, although members of Parliament, members of parliamentary committees, and regional representatives and councils may introduce bills, and citizens' groups may introduce petitions (if 50,000 signatures are collected in support); while the executive submits many important bills, nonexecutive groups (especially parliamentary members) can be at times active in submitting legislation on their own. After being debated in committees, the bill might (if passed by committee) be sent to the chamber for a floor vote. For a bill to become law it must be passed by majority vote in both houses. There are two cases when this path is not used for legislation. First, a popular referendum (which needs at least 500,000 signatures of registered voters or the formal support of five regional councils to be legitimate) can be called by the public; however, referenda cannot alter or address budgetary laws, amnesties, or international agreements. The second alternative method is for a bill to be passed straight out of the committees without a floor vote; this, however, is rare.

These are the formal powers of the legislature. Just as important are the structure of parties within the legislature and the effect this has had on Italian politics. Previous electoral law allowed for any party to hold a seat in Parliament if it obtained votes; this led to a Parliament made up of numerous parties and deprived larger parties such as the Christian Democrats and Communists of the ability either to rule through majority or to have a commanding enough plurality that creating a coalition would require inviting only a few ideologically close parties. The result has been constantly changing coalitions, as no single group has the power to dominate Parliament. Further, political shifts within parties have led to intraparty fighting, which also threatens potentially stable coalitions. Such a precarious nature of Italian parties can be seen in the breakup of the larger parties (the Communists and Christian Democrats) in 1993 and 1994 into several smaller groups.

Actual coalitions have changed over time. Until 1963 the coalitions making up the government were centrist and center-right; after 1963, centrist and cen-

ter-left coalitions began to dominate. The years 1992–93 witnessed instability within the coalition system, as no "stable" coalition (defined broadly in the Italian context) could be created. Recent coalitions (from 1993 on) have turned back to a neo-orthodox center-right type of coalition. This began with economic problems and corruption scandals within the government and the major parties. At the same time, media magnate Silvio Berlusconi, using his media empire to promote his political party Forza Italia and its allies the Northern League (Lega Nord) and the neofascist National Alliance (Alleanza Nazionale), came to prominence on a regionalist platform and a conservative reaction against scandals and instability of the 1992–93 crisis years. Bertusconi's coalition lasted from May to December 1994, when it was replaced (following a scandal involving Berlusconi) with a technocratic government of Lamberto Dini, backed by the Northern League, the Partito Popolare (formerly of the Christian Democrats), and the Democratic Party of the Left. This government lasted until February 1996, when it was replaced in April 1996 (following the parliamentary elections, called early) with a return to the center-left and a government led by a coalition of center-left parties (former Socialists and Christian Democrats) called "Olive Tree."

The center-left Olive Tree failed to maintain its electoral popularity. Partly this was due to the right's consistent use of Berlusconi's media power and the rise of right-wing (especially ethnic or nationalist) sentiments in the electorate. A major cause of the center-left's failure to hold on to power was the split between Olive Tree and the Communist Refoundation, which, after 1998, decided to contest elections against, rather than in conjunction with, Olive Tree parties. This split part of the center-left vote, allowing Berlusconi's Freedom House to return to power in 2001; following the collapse of this coalition in 2005, Berlusconi was quickly able to form a new government with most of his party's partners on the right.

JUDICIARY

While the Constitutional Court—the highest court in the land—was established in the 1948 constitution, it did not become functional until 1956. This Court is composed of 15 members; the number rises to 31 in cases of impeachment; Parliament appoints the additional 16. Originally, five judges are appointed by the president, five by a joint session of Parliament, and five by the judiciary itself; the constitution now states that 10 are chosen by various levels of judges within the legal system and five are chosen by Parliament, all selections made from a pool of legal academics and lawyers with at least 15 years' experience. Except in extreme cases, "special" judges are forbidden by the constitution (most likely a rejection of fascist policies). The formal powers of the Court include decisions on the constitutionality of policies and laws; mediating disputes between the federal and regional governments; and running impeachment proceedings.

The judicial branch is formally independent from other branches and answerable only to the law; this has given judges some independence and helped them sweep aside fascist policy legacies and, at times, push the battle against organized crime. The overall judicial system in Italy is grounded in civil law; judicial review of laws is reserved for the Constitutional Court, so that the Italian system resembles the Continental rather than the Anglo-American system (where precedent, common law, and judicial interpretation of laws are important political procedures). Judges below the Constitutional Court may become judges only after a rigorous examination, making the judiciary resemble the bureaucratic civil service.

REGIONAL AND LOCAL GOVERNMENT

The constitution provides for regional autonomy, with a focus on decentralizing some powers to the local level. The hierarchy of local government runs from the regions (20) to the provinces to the communities. Italy's 20 regions are defined in the constitution as the following: Piedmont; Valle d'Aosta; Lombardy; Trentino–Alto Adige; Venetia; Friuli-Venetia Julia; Liguria; Emilia-Romagna; Tuscany; Umbria; Marches; Latium; Abruzzo; Molise; Campania; Apulia; Basilicata; Calabria; Sicily; Sardinia. Regions have a certain degree of autonomy from the federal government, and some regions enjoy additional political autonomy: Sicily, Sardinia, Trentino–Alto Adige (actually more functionally a province but having autonomy like a region), Friuli-Venetia Julia, and the Valle d'Aosta. Regional powers and responsibilities include organizing local planning, transportation, tourism, hospitals and charities, local police, artisanship, agricultural and forestry issues, vocational training, local fairs and markets, and other local duties. Regions are responsible for collecting their own taxes and providing for part of their own finances (although taxation on exchange between regions, or any other regulation of interregional exchange, is forbidden by the constitution). Local branches of the federal administration are overseen by a federal representative.

The local legislative body is the regional council; its powers include legislation at the local level and the proposal of bills to the national Parliament. Any legislation adopted by the regional councils must be sent to the local federal government representative, with has 30 days to approve the legislation or, in cases of unconstitutionality or incongruity with federal laws, to reject it. The executive branch is the Junta, headed by a president. The duties of the Junta and the president include implementation of local level laws and representing the region to other regions, to the national administration, and to foreign bodies as well. The regional council is elected by the local population, and deputies of the regional council in turn elect the members of the Junta and select the president of the Junta. The regional council may be dissolved ahead of electoral schedule if the federal government finds it in violation of federal laws or the constitution.

Decentralization has been an important political consideration in Italy in the postwar era, partially in reaction to fascist centralization. Historically, Communists and Social Democrats came into conflict over regional reform and autonomy in the postwar world. Communists favored regional decentralization because, given their power bases in the regions rather than at the national level, such reforms favored the increase of Communist power. The Social Democrats, being more of a national party, opposed regionalization for just this reason.

Provincial and community levels have less power and autonomy than the regional level. However, local elections at the community level do have some importance, as these set the government for the various towns. Communists did well in local elections in the 1970s and early 1980s, but they have witnessed a decline from the late 1980s on.

The Electoral System

Italy's electoral system has certain unique characteristics that mark it off from other Western democracies. Most differences are in parliamentary elections, where major changes occurred in 1993 and 1994. Suffrage is extended to Italian citizens who are 18 years old or older, except in elections to the Senate, in which suffrage extends to those 25 and older.

The election of the president for a term of seven years is fairly straightforward. The president, who must be at least 50 years old to stand for the office, is selected by Parliament during a joint session of the two chambers, in which there are an additional three delegates from each region (except Val d'Aosta, which sends only one additional delegate). To win office a candidate must receive two-thirds of delegates' votes. Should no one gain this majority, a second round occurs, where victory also requires a two-thirds majority. If this does not produce a winning candidate (and it usually does not), a third round is undertaken, where a candidate needs only an absolute majority.

The previous system that ran from 1948 to 1992 contributed to the survival of smaller parties and maintained perpetual instability of governments. The changes to electoral procedure were supposed to encourage the winnowing of parties to a few powerful groups. However, parties now form electoral coalitions that keep alive Italy's tradition of multiple parties within the legislature. (The emergence of some parties to dominance has as much to do with recent political events such as the corruption scandals and new right-wing power base as the electoral procedures.) In the old system, the Senate was elected by a combination of direct elections and proportional representation conducted at the regional level. To win a single-member constituency, a candidate had to receive at least 65 percent of votes cast; in the case of any candidate failing to obtain such a number of votes, that seat was transferred to the general proportional representation pool for that region. The Chamber of Deputies was elected by a double proportional representation system. Regions received a number of seats to the Chamber, and parties received seats according to the proportion of votes they received in the general count, as manipulated by a complex formula. Some seats would be left unfilled this way, and those shifted to the national proportional representation pool and distributed among parties receiving more than 300,000 votes. This system was criticized for its complexity and contribution to instability, and it was also tarnished (as was much of the political system generally) by the scandals of the 1980s.

The new system has retained some of the complexities of the older system, but it has been streamlined somewhat. To be a Chamber candidate an individual must be 25 years old and have suffrage rights. For Chamber elections Italy is divided into 26 constituencies (plus the Valle d'Aosta region, which has only one seat); the number of seats per constituency is equal to that constituency's percentage of the overall Italian population. Constituencies are further divided into single-seat districts; the number of districts is equal to 75 percent of that constituency's seats. Thus three-fourths of all seats are from single-member districts, while one-fourth is left for proportional representation

on the basis of the entire constituency rather than on districts. Voters receive two ballots, one for the single-seat race and one for the proportional list. This allows voters to split their votes between one for a particular person and one for a particular party. For the Chamber of Deputies, 475 members are now elected through a first-past-the-post system from the single-seat constituencies; this is the equivalent of American elections to the House of Representatives- where the candidate with the plurality of votes in his or her constituency wins a seat. The remaining 155 members are selected by a complex proportional system that favors "good losers." Once votes are tabulated nationwide, the proportional seats are distributed. Only parties overcoming a national 4 percent barrier can receive proportionally allocated seats. Further, the number of seats a party may receive is affected by the *scorporo*, a "price" paid for single-seat victories. In essence, the number of votes a party receives for purposes of proportional counting is diminished by the number of seats the second-place candidate gets in the constituency where a party's candidate has won the single-seat race. Thus, parties that lose in the single-seat races gain some ground in the proportional race, because parties that win in the single-seat races then lose votes they would have received on the second (proportional) ballot. This "good loser" system is unique to Italy.

Senators are elected by a combination of plurality and proportional representation systems. In the plurality system—also known as "first past the post"—the candidate with the most votes at the end of the day is declared the winner (rather than requiring 65 percent of the vote). The Senate also splits its members by single-seat mandate and proportional representation. To stand as a candidate an individual must be at least 40 years old. A constituency receives a number of Senate seats equal to its proportion of the overall population, although there are two stipulations to this constitutional rule: no constituency will have fewer than 10 senators, and the Molise constituency has only 2 and Valle d'Aosta has only 1. According to the recent electoral law, 232 members win their positions through first-past-the-post systems in their home constituencies; 83 members are selected through a proportional system. Constituencies are divided into 20 single-member districts for the 232 single-member seats, which follow a first-past-the-post system. The remaining 83 are distributed to parties based on the general number of votes they received from the party affiliation of individual candidates; these seats are distributed at the constituency level rather than at the national level (as is the case for the Chamber of Deputies). There is also no minimum percentage barrier, as there is for the Chamber of Deputies. Further, the *scorporo* works somewhat differently for Senate races: a party with a losing candidate receives votes for the proportional seats based on the number of votes its losing candidates received. This complicated and confusing system allows smaller parties a fairer chance at representation (and would seem to promote the continuance of representation of smaller parties, and thus the fragmentation of Parliament).

PARLIAMENTARY ELECTIONS, MAY 13, 2001

Party/Coalition	Chamber of Deputies	Senate
Casa delle Libertà (Freedom House)	368	177
– Forza Italia	{196}	
– Alleanza Nazionale	{99}	
– Lega Nord	{30}	
– Biancofiore	{40}	
– Nuovo Partito Socialista Italiano	{3}	
Ulivo (Olive Tree)	252	125
– Democratici di Sinistra	{172}	
– La Margherita	{85}	
– Il Girasole	{16}	
– Partito dei Comunisti Italiani	{10}	
Rifondazione Comunista	11	3
Lista di Pietro Italia dei Valori	—	1
Democrazia Europea	—	2
Lista Pannella Bonino	—	—
Ulivo-SVP	—	3
Südtiroler Volkspartei	3	2
Movimento Sociale Fiamma Tricolore	—	—
Union Valdôtaine (Valdostian Union, regionalist)	1	1
Aleanza Lombardia Autonoma	—	1

In spite of the confusion and constant governmental changes, the general orientation of Italian politics has been fairly stable.

These trends reflect a common wisdom about Italian postwar politics up until the crises of the late 1980s: the fascist legacy hurt the initial formation of right-wing movements, helping the left and center-left parties establish a stranglehold on politics. Two factors hindered right-wing formation: first, this legacy left political domination with the Christian Democrats, Communists, and Socialists and made advancement of center-right parties difficult; second, because of Italy's social structure (a state presence in the economy, bifurcation between the industrial North and the agricultural South, a small individualist bourgeoisie), organizing and mobilizing of potential right-wing support were difficult. In short, no right-wing party could gain ground without some system shock.

This system shock came in the late 1980s and early 1990s, with economic problems, the collapse of leftism at the end of the cold war, and political scandals. This drove many voters away from the left to regionalist or right-wing parties untainted by corruption. Further, entrepreneurship and the growth of a bourgeoisie provided the soil for right-wing groups, so that when Berlusconi entered the political scene, serendipity had provided the opportunity for a major political shift. This occurred in 1994.

Berlusconi's right-wing alliance, Freedom House, has remained a dominant force ever since. Italian politics, in the wake of a global move to neo-orthodox politics and away from socialism and state-centered policies, has noticeably shifted to the right and, barring a serious economic downturn due to neo-orthodox market reforms or political scandals, should remain viable after almost 50 years of marginality.

The Party System

HISTORY

Italy's party system did not begin to take shape until the 20th century. While the Socialist Party was founded in 1892, it remained marginalized, as its support base, the working class, did not have the right to vote. Catholic groups initially remained outside politics, a protest against the Catholic Church's loss of power in the face of secular unification and centralization. However, as the Socialist Party began to gain strength, Catholic organizations came together to form in 1919 the Catholic Popular Party. The Socialist and Catholic Parties remained apart from each other, and this helped the rise to power of Mussolini's Fascist Party, which in 1926 outlawed all other political parties. As suggested earlier, the fascist period shaped the following political period: the Lateran Pacts brought Catholicism back into social domination, and helped give Catholic groups a firmer organizational base; and the struggle with fascism gave political legitimacy and capital to the Socialist and Communist organizations (which managed to hurt each other through splits and feuds borne of Stalin's antisocialist policies). Opposition to fascism made a temporary alliance between Socialist and Catholic groups possible, but this alliance fell apart in the postwar era. In the postwar world the Communists were kept out of power but still managed to gain a following among the working classes and certain industrialized northern regions; the Socialists and Christian Democrats became the leading parties but could not gain sufficient dominance to create durable coalitions. Additionally, party splits and an electoral system favorable to small parties led to a plethora of political parties and a consistently fragmented Parliament.

This was the general landscape for most of the postwar era. However, the situation changed in the 1990s. First, investigations into corruption led to shocks within the parties. Second, the changes in the electoral system encouraged and sped up centrifugal tendencies within the parties. The final factor was the weakening of the left, and especially of the Communist Party, in the late 1980s, and the rise of regional and conservative forces, led by the mercurial Silvio Berlusconi. The result was splits and realignments and a major reconfiguration of the party landscape.

In postwar Italy political parties have popped up like mushrooms after a storm, although some of these mushrooms have been far larger than others. This is due to two primary factors. The first is Italy's fractured nature: a liberal industrialized North and a conservative agrarian South, with less of a sense of national unity than other European countries. The second is the Italian electoral system, which allowed many small parties into Parliament and did not weed out these minor parties but instead encouraged their marginal existence. Yet in spite of the plethora of parties, a few parties managed to dominate, in particular the Christian Democrats and the Communists.

ORGANIZATION

Before the recent party breakups, political parties in Italy had two important features: they were mass par-

ties, and they centered themselves and their actions on ideologies and ideological identity. Joining most parties required sponsorship by someone inside the party, in order to test for ideological "purity," and joining a political party was an ideological statement of sorts. And yet in spite of the stress on ideology, Italian parties were notorious for being factionalized. These factions are less based on splinters within the ideological framework than they are centered on personal networks and personalized groups or clans within parties. In this way, ideology served as the glue holding mass parties together, and yet the parties were rent through and through with networks of personal cliques and loyalties that weakened them.

Parties are linked with many other organizations in society. Parties have cells and formal ties with unions, with movements, with associations, and other political or nonpolitical organizations. These links are partly personal but also partly ideological, bringing political ideology into everyday life to a degree not seen in many other Western democracies. And the personal or clan side makes its way into the party-society structure as well. While many ties are ideological in nature—such as ties between parties and local cultural festivals—other links are patronage. For example, parties with influence in an area will get their people placed in local government, or a party drawing support from a region will use its parliamentary power either to get people from that region jobs in the state bureaucracy or to provide benefits, such as housing, government contracts, and the like.

Internal organization of most parties does not differ from mass parties elsewhere. On the one hand, there are institutions of democracy that promote mass participation. Local cells elect members of sections and section heads, who then select the provincial committees, which select the regional committees, and so on to the top. This provides some local grassroots influence and power. For most parties, national congresses that set the party programs are held every two years. However, this democracy is dulled by the need for everyday organization, which means the rise of a party elite and a party bureaucracy. This system gives party elites patronage power within the party (similar to patronage through the state) and the ability to reproduce their own power.

RIGHT-WING PARTIES

The Italian right saw renewed strength in the 1994 elections, owing to Berlusconi's resources and increased right-wing party organization, along with the discrediting of the left-wing and centrist parties through news of scandals and corruption and through economic problems left-wing policies could not solve. Further, the return of the right was enhanced by the rise of Silvio Berlusconi and his Forza Italia party.

LEFT-WING PARTIES

The two basic left-wing camps are the Socialists and the Communists, broken through a Comintern-dictated split in 1921. In the postwar era both camps played on their partisan activities for legitimacy and popularity; the Socialists were able to become a legitimate governing party (although they had only one Socialist prime minister, Craxi) and the Communists remained in opposition.

The Italian Communist Party, formerly the largest Communist Party west of the Iron Curtain, was founded in 1921 following a Comintern-inspired split between Socialists and more radical Communists. During fascism the PCI was illegal and its leaders threatened or jailed; some, such as Palmiro Togliatti, escaped Italy, while others, such as Antonio Gramsçi, went to prison. The persecution under fascism did not, in the end, hurt the party; if anything, the PCI's resistance to fascism provided a certain moral power that helped the PCI survive the period and prosper afterward. Further, the PCI had always maintained some distance from Stalin and the Comintern; therefore, when Stalin's excesses were revealed in the 1956 "secret speech," the Italian Communists did not lose face or legitimacy as other Western European Communist Parties did.

After World War II the Communists temporarily took part in government in a three-way alliance with the Socialist Party and the Christian Democrats; however, PCI participation in government came to an end with the onset of the cold war. Initially the Socialists supported the Communists, but by the 1960s the Socialists moved closer (tactically) to the Christian Democrats in order to participate in the executive branch. This did not necessarily hurt the PCI; with the Socialists in some way involved in running the country, the PCI could remain an opposition force loyal to its party base (the working class); and indeed the PCI remained until recently not only Italy's second largest party but also the guardian of the left wing. By the 1970s, with the threats of neofascist parties' growing (although still small) success and the example of right-wing reaction against a left-wing government in Chile, the PCI turned to "strategic alliances" with other pro-democracy parties; this helped raise the PCI's

support to over 30 percent of the electorate. However, this alliance also hurt the PCI, which was now more involved with the government and would lose some of the support among the left-wing dissatisfied elements in society (such as the working class). By the 1980s, with the loss of popular leader Enrico Berlinguer and with the problems of moving closer to the ruling parties, the PCI's support slipped, so that by 1987 PCI was only the third largest party. Of little comfort was the loss of support among party strongholds—the working class, especially in the industrialized North.

By 1989 some factions within the PCI came to the decision that a change was needed. The PCI had been slowly moving away from more radical policy and opposition tactics to become more of a social-democratic party; further, the fall of the Communist East bloc in 1989 sealed the fate of Communist Parties everywhere. In February 1991 the different tensions within the party over its future came to a head, and PCI split into two parties: the Democratic Party of the Left (Partito Democratico della Sinistra; PDS) and more traditional Communists, who broke off to form Communist Refoundation (Rifondazione Comunista; RC). The PDS suffered in the early 1990s from its split and from the taints of corruption that all major parties endured. However, in the 1994 elections the PDS regained some lost ground; as a response, Massimo D'Alema, the new head of PDS, organized for the 1996 elections the l'Ulivo (Olive Tree) coalition, consisting of the PDS, smaller liberal parties, and small parties from the Christian Democrats.

In 2004 the Olive Tree coalition became the Federation of All United in the Olive Tree (Unite Nell l'Ulivo). In 2005 this coalition aligned with a broader center-left coalition called the Union (L'Unione) in the hopes of capturing the 2006 elections.

CENTRIST PARTIES

After the corruption scandals that hit politics in the 1980s, the change in electoral rules, and the rise of the Italian right and right-wing parties to prominence, the political center in Italy has become difficult ground to hold. Once, the center-right Christian Democrats (Democrazia Cristiana; DC) were the most dominant Italian political party. Their collapse in the 1990s left Italy without a strong centrist party able to stand between left and right. Further, Italy's political atmosphere has become more charged, as former Communists and center-left parties have formed coalitions against the energized right-wing parties such as Forza Italia and Lega Nord.

Major Political Parties

FORWARD ITALY

(Forza Italia; FI)

The most important right-wing party since the 1990s is Silvio Berlusconi's Forward Italy (Forza Italia; FI). The party and its leader, who served a brief stint as prime minister in 1994 and then again from 2001 onward, are inextricably linked; the party owes its fortunes to the leader, and the leader owes his ability to enter politics to the party network that brought electoral support. Berlusconi owed his rise to prominence to his media empire (three television networks that attained approximately 45 percent of the audience market), built through competition with inefficient state-run media outlets and through his control of the popular Milan football (soccer) team. Berlusconi himself also enjoyed personal acclaim as an entrepreneur who had built his own entertainment empire through his own hard work and had provided Italians with entertainment outside of that provided inefficiently by the state.

In January 1994 Berlusconi created Forza Italia on the basis of his media connections and of the Milan football team's various clubs, which became the equivalent of party cells. Berlusconi and Forza Italia rode a wave of antipolitician sentiment in 1994, but this was not the only political force to bring Berlusconi and his party to power. Berlusconi noticed that in spite of the window of opportunity open in the early 1990s, left-wing parties were numerous and could form their own alliances to return to power; hence, the emerging right wing had to form political alliances as well to pool their voters and resources. In 1994 Berlusconi was able to forge the Freedom alliance among his party, the right-wing Alleanza Nationale (which was popular in the South), and the new party Lega Nord, whose more regionalist agenda remained anti-insider and could deliver northern voters.

FI's and Berlusconi's ideological appeal came from two sources: no stain from political scandals (or from a political past) and adherence to neoliberal policies. The first benefited enormously, as Berlusconi could position himself and his party and alliance against the entrenched interests using the state to maintain their own power. The second built on the first, as Berlusconi could emphasize entrepreneurship, individualism, and a neoliberal economic platform that would lower corruption and bring economic growth (as his own personal history testified). He stressed anticommunism as well, although in the 1990s this tactic does not have

the power it did in the cold war. Finally, Berlusconi was seen as a strong individual who could set right Italian politics and sweep away the old corruption.

Berlusconi's coalition collapsed in 1996 after the Northern League pulled out. However, the coalition reformed in 2000, allowing it to form a new government and for Berlusconi to regain the prime ministership. The coalition collapsed again in 2005, but Berlusconi was quickly able to form a new government and remain prime minister.

NATIONAL ALLIANCE

(Alleanza Nationale; AN)

Bringing up a more radical right wing was the Italian Social Movement (MSI), which in 1994 changed its name to MSI–Alleanza Nazionale and in 1995 simply to Alleanza Nationale (AN). Established in 1946, the MSI reflected much of the ideology and worldviews of the discredited (and in 1952 illegal) Fascist Party. In 1972 MSI merged with the Monarchist Party and became known as Movimento Sociale Italiano–Destra Nazionale (Italian Social Movement–National Right), but problems after the 1976 elections led moderate members to break off and form their own party, Democrazia Nazionale (National Democracy).

AN's policy is anti-Communist and right-wing. This has come to hurt AN, which saw its fortunes start to drop until the 1994 elections, when in a party cartel it reversed the decline. The MSI had a strong organizational framework that the AN appeared mostly to have inherited—branches throughout Italy attached to youth and student movements, to women, to war veterans, and to some trade unions. Originally having roots in the north (where fascism had been at its strongest), the MSI slowly "migrated" south, a process helped when MSI "swallowed" the Monarchist Party. MSI tries to appeal in part to disillusioned youth; its rules permit one to join at the age of 14. While MSI had more of a pseudofascist appeal, AN has tried to moderate this image somewhat while remaining a right-leaning party.

AN ideology is problematic, mostly because party platforms and grassroots support do not necessarily meet, and the party's right-wing image is vague enough to attract many right-wing voters who have no other real party to turn to. AN, as MSI before it, took a strong positive view toward some Western ideals, toward corporatism, anticommunism, lower-middle-class populism (which made it difficult, until the 1990s, to espouse right-wing radical free-market reforms), and more conservative social views (such as stances against abortion and divorce). Certain aspects of MSI ideology, such as more open admiration for fascism and hints of anti-Semitism and racism, have been dropped or pushed into the background (along with party leaders espousing these views). Most important in the ideology is a sense of "anti-insider" politics: criticisms of the centrist and left-wing parties that had led Italy for so long.

When one turns to the rank-and-file support, however, the ideological picture of AN gets muddled. While a sizable number of supporters still hold to an AN that is oppositionist and outside the system, more supporters now believe that AN should ally itself with other parties and enter the government. Further, against the traditional views of the party, a majority of supporters favor sexual equality; and a majority are not hostile to Catholicism, which contradicts historical anti-Catholic views of MSI and AN. One surprise on the ideological front—both for official AN views and views of supporters—is the lack of anti-immigrant sentiment. Given the influx of immigrant workers and the rise of anti-immigration right-wing politics throughout Europe (especially in France), one would expect a right-wing protofascist party like MSI/IAN to play this card; however, both AN and its supporters have refrained from making anti-immigration policies a centerpiece of party platforms. This does *not* mean that AN will *not* play this card in the future, however.

MSI's biggest problem, which appears to have been overcome in the 1990s with the formation of AN, was the creation of a veil of legitimacy. The MSI had two political stains that it had to wash out: first, its ideological and imagined links with fascism and, second, 1970s right-wing terrorism. In spite of MSI's freedom from corruption scandals, these stains were problematic. Several events helped bring the MSI (and then the AN) into legitimacy and respectability. The first was the collapse of the Christian Democrats and the Communists in 1992; this allowed an opening for new parties to grab up electoral votes. Second was party leader Giafranco Fini's ability to put together a network of political contacts that allowed AN to engage in political alliances in elections—and thus to overcome one of MSI's major problems, political isolation due to lack of political alliances. Third was the political air of 1993–94, when MSI changed its name to AN and when AN linked up with Berlusconi and Forza Italia, whose coattails added to AN's increasing popularity. Berlusconi's open support for AN in 1993—when Berlusconi himself was still popular—helped AN in local elections and propelled the party forward in 1994 national elec-

tions. The AN has remained part of Berlusconi's coalition since that time.

NORTHERN LEAGUE
(Lega Nord; LN)

Occasionally, small regionalist parties arise and compete in Italian politics, such as the Union Valdôtaine (drawing from the small Val d'Aosta) or Sardinia's Sardo d'Azione. However, until the 1990s they could not compete with the larger national parties. Only in the 1990s, with the change in electoral rules and the creation and realignment of parties, did one regionalist party arise to play more than a marginal role in politics: the Northern League (Lega Nord; LN). The Northern League began as an association of smaller northern regionalist parties, the most important of which was the Lega Veneta, stemming from Venice. The Venetian League surprised observers in the 1980s and refused to die; when it began to lose popularity, Leagues in other northern cities were already established political forces. In the late 1980s these small regional movements and parties unified into the umbrella Northern League, which in 1990 regional elections scored well, garnering nearly 19 percent of the vote.

The League's growing popularity was greatly helped by the breaking scandals, especially in 1992. These scandals ended the stranglehold the Christian Democrats and Socialists had held in northern towns and brought the Northern League, as the remaining important regional party, into prominence in 1993 local elections and then in 1994 national elections.

The basic ideology of the Northern League is regionalist. The League, rather than taking strong abstract positions, focuses on more concrete issues. One set of issues concerns misuse of public funds by the major parties. The League has supported fiscal reform and lower taxes; relatedly, the League has voiced the outrage of northern voters that their tax money is drained away to Rome and southern Italy, where it is used in corrupt patronage and never finds its way back to honest development in the North. Another set of issues the League supports is pro-market reforms. This stems from the individualist "Protestant Ethic" views of many northern elites and voters: that, as Berlusconi might suggest, development and growth come from hard work by individuals and not through state-led programs or the welfare state. Yet another set of issues is regionalist identity. Although the League is not secessionist, it does exude an antisouthern sentiment, regarding northern Italy as developed and European while seeing southern Italy as underdeveloped, flooded with immigrants and thieves, controlled by the Mafia, and in general rather immoral. The League is more pro-European than some other parties. One caveat should be mentioned at the end, however. While these are the general sentiments voiced by League leaders and supporters, the Lega Nord, unlike many of the pre-1990s parties, does not really have a formal, worked-out party ideology; this purposive vagueness acts, in a sense, as a "big tent" for general discouragement and disillusionment with southern Italy, the welfare state, and the failures of postwar policies. So instead of formal programs, the League champions general issues such as devolution of political power and anticenter sentiment.

In terms of party organization, the League is not a preeminent example of the modern party, as Forza Italia or the pre-1990s Communists are. The party has a very loose structure, making it more of an umbrella social movement than a true organized party. It does not have the party machine—cells, a party press—that, for example, Forza Italia has. Further, Lega Nord has been wary of electoral alliances; while it did ally itself with Berlusconi in 1994, the League proved to be a less-than-charming partner, and its quick break with Berlusconi brought down the Berlusconi government in 1994, not long after it had formed. In 1996, rather than join an electoral alliance with Forza Italia and Alleanza Nationale, the Northern League decided to go it alone—and its vote count actually increased by a small margin.

The general portrait of the Lega Nord supporter is a male, with less-than-average education, either from the working class or from small individual businesses, who lives in a rural locale. However, given the League's loose structure, determining actual party membership and other party procedures is difficult at present.

Despite the hopes of the outspoken Bossi, electoral support for Lega Nord beyond its northern confines has been slipping, and even in the North Lega Nord does not have the same appeal as in the past. Likely this is because of radical claims that northern regions should secede from Italy, as well as its leader's xenophobic rhetoric. Poor showing in regional and European elections before 2000 were a warning that Lega Nord might be losing steam, and Bossi brought his party back into Berlusconi's alliance before 2001 to save his party a share of political power. In the 2001 elections Lega Nord received less than 4 percent of the overall vote, suggesting that its political base was becoming confined to specific groups. (The party did not gain a single seat in the Chamber of Deputies through proportional representation.) While Lega Nord no longer has the same political clout as several

years before, the Freedom House coalition still needs Lega Nord seats in the Senate to maintain its majority there. This means that Bossi remains an important player, and he has continued to threaten to leave the right-wing coalition if his partners do not give in to his demands. While Berlusconi and partners continue to tolerate Bossi, it is uncertain how long they will do so, especially if Lega Nord drops further in the polls in the next parliamentary election.

DEMOCRATICS OF THE LEFT
(Democratici di Sinistra; DS)

This party was formerly the Democratic Party of the Left (PDS). Before the 2001 elections PDS set out to increase its strength by merging with several smaller, minor left-wing parties. The newly expanded center-left party was renamed Democratici di Sinistra (Democrats of the Left, DS). This did not particularly change the party's ideology and policy stance, and it made DS the leading member of the Olive Tree coalition. However, continued lack of agreement over electoral and governance strategies persists between the DS and its chief rival on the left flank, the Communist Refoundation Party (PRC). Until 2005 both parties competed against each other in local races, rather than joining forces against right-wing parties, dividing their electoral strength and keeping them from truly challenging Forza Italia and Freedom House. However, the DS-led Olive Tree coalition united with the PRC and related parties in 2005 to form the Union. This will increase its chances of capturing the 2006 elections.

COMMUNIST REFOUNDATION PARTY
(Partito della Rifondazione Comunista; PRC)

When the former Communist Party renamed itself PDS and softened its platform to the center-left in 1991, the radical left minority decided to maintain a Communist party and ideology. Led by Fausto Bertinotti, a former trade union activist, this group formed the PRC, Communist Refoundation Party, to preserve a more leftist version of Marxism in Italian politics. While the PRC has managed to maintain support among a small portion of the Italian leftist electorate, its electoral strength has been in slow decline, partly because of its more old-fashioned Marxism in a post-Soviet political world, and partly because in comparison to PDS and Olive Tree, PRC alone has been too weak to be the left's challenger to Berlusconi's coalition. PRC originally formed a pact with PDS and Olive Tree to avoid competition between center-left parties, in order to present a unified front against Berlusconi. However, PRC broke with the Prodi government over the state budget. In 2001 PRC received only 5 percent of the general vote in parliamentary elections; it had received 8.6 percent in 1996. The party elite's desire to maintain organizational and ideological autonomy and to hold to a more unadulterated communism ultimately cost political influence—ironically, after the one moment when an Italian Communist party was finally part of a ruling coalition.

In 1996 PRC and PDS came to agreements about electoral strategies, with one withdrawing in deference to the other in local races so as not to split the left-wing vote against Forza Italia and Berlusconi. The strategy worked, and PRC joined the PDS-led Olive Tree coalition into power—a first for an Italian Communist party. However, the agreement between PDS and PRC lasted only two years, and by 1999 the PRC was out of the government and the governing coalition and had set out on its own. In the wake of this split, some PRC members formed their own separate Communist party, Partito dei Comunisti Italiano (Party of Italian Communists), and returned to Olive Tree and in 2001 added 10 seats to that coalition's count in the Chamber of Deputies (although they received only 1.7 percent of the overall vote)—not enough to give Olive Tree a majority, however. While PRC challenged PDS seats in Senate races, it did not challenge Olive Tree in Chamber of Deputies races, where an unofficial agreement over electoral strategy persisted.

In 2005 the PRC joined a new center-left coalition with the DS in the hopes of winning the 2006 elections.

ITALIAN DEMOCRATIC SOCIALISTS

(Socialisti Democratici Italiani; SDI)

The SDI is the successor to the Italian Socialist Party (PSI), which emerged from World War II with an antifascist image (although not nearly as strong as the Communists' image and legitimacy). In spite of weaker organization than the Communists, the Socialists quickly became the second largest party in Italy. Still the Socialists remained a party with a core of cadres and without a more organized mass base. Throughout the postwar era the Socialists remained a moderate left-wing party: forming governments with the Christian Democrats, trying to act as mediator between sides in the tense atmosphere of 1968. The Socialists provided a degree of stability to Christian Democratic governments, supplying the necessary vote

count in Parliament to get new governments off the ground (although not being able to sustain them for long periods of time). The Socialists also took a more moderate ideological and policy line than their Communist brethren: the PSI remained pro-NATO and pro–law and order.

One major problem that the Socialists faced was constructing their own "ground" amid a two-front battle with Christian Democrats and the Communists, in essence to build its own identity separate from both the Communists and Christian Democrats and provide a left-wing "alternative." This "alternative" never materialized, and demoralization in the party continued in the 1970s. Bettino Craxi, party leader and briefly prime minister in the 1980s attempted to change the style of the Socialists; Craxi personalized both the Socialist Party and Italian politics, in this way acting as a legitimate forerunner of Berlusconi's brand of personalized politics. Craxi also tried to make the Socialists into a liberal party supporting modernity and reforms but tailored this image to the regions of the country. In the North the Socialists appealed to entrepreneurs with a stress on fiscal discipline and support of a privatization program, while in the South they advocated using the public sector and relying on clientelism and a degree of patronage (which brought on charges of corruption in the 1990s). When in the 1990s Craxi was under suspicion for corruption, the Socialist Party fell into disgrace along with its leader.

As of 2005 the party was led by Enrico Boselli. It was part of the Olive Tree coalition as well as the larger Union alliance.

FEDERATION OF THE GREENS

(Federazione dei Verdi)

This pro-environmental group entered Parliament following the 1987 elections. While the Greens appear condemned to marginality—averaging around 2.5 percent of the national vote—they were essential to the early success of the center-left Olive Tree coalition, where their small number of votes were crucial for a balance against the right wing. Like Green parties in other European countries, the Verdi focus more on environmental issues than on other political themes; this makes an alliance with center-left parties, which do not support free capitalism, more palatable than an alliance with right-wing parties, which wish to reduce state intervention (thus possibly leading to further unintended market-created environmental problems). The Greens joined the Union coalition in 2005.

DASIY–DEMOCRACY IS FREEDOM

(La Margherita–Democrazia è Libertà)

This party was formed by the merger in 2000 of the Italian People's Party (the DC's major founder) and three smaller centrist parties. In the 2001 elections the PPI-led Margherita managed to gain the second-most votes of all parties in the center-left Olive Tree coalition, reinvigorating the former Christian Democrats and the hopes of centrist parties. In 2005 this party decided against joining the new Olive Tree coalition, although it did agree to join the Union alliance.

Minor Political Parties

Below the major parties and their coalitions are numerous scattered minor parties that appear and disappear or that hang on for decades at a time but gain little representation. The Italian Republican Party was founded in 1894 and managed to survive through the 20th century, seeing some of its better showings in the 1970s and 1980s when its electoral score jumped from 2 percent to 4 percent of the general vote. This party split in the 1990s; both factions (each center-left in political orientation) joined Olive Tree at various times. The Italian Liberal Party, dominant in the 19th century, suffered in competition with the Christian Democrats and Socialists, and by the 1990s had split, with its center-right faction joining Berlusconi's various coalitions. Other local parties manage to gain the occasional parliamentary seat: for example, the Südtiroler Volkspartei, based in Bolzano (a northern province also known in German as Südtirol), gained a handful of parliamentary seats in 2001. Many of these minor parties emerged from splits of other minor parties or formerly important parties on the decline. Because the electoral system supports coalitions, the number of independent parties has not thinned as hoped, and so smaller parties persist, hoping either to gain seats through their own effort or to join larger coalitions with the demand that they gain a token seat in return for not campaigning locally against the major players.

Other Political Forces

Since World War II the military has not been an active player in Italian politics. However, other nonmilitary, nonstate forces have been important: trade unions, organized crime, and for a time terrorist groups. Italy has been noteworthy for waves of strikes, usually increasing with improvements in the economy. Trade unions historically have been more closely allied with leftist political forces, and could be more radical than left-wing parties in Parliament when they called their members out onto the streets. Since the 1980s strikes have been on the decline. This is partly due to economic stagnation in the 1990s and to some deindustrialization making unions irrelevant. (Unions are more prominent in industry and weaker in the service sector, where much of the growth in the European economies has been.) However, Berlusconi's attempts to reign in public spending as per European Union and euro-zone rules have led to increased agitation among unions, and it is possible that another wave of strikes may emerge before too long, should Berlusconi continue to push for austerity policies and decrease state spending on public works and the economy.

Organized crime has been indirectly important to politics for reasons of corruption, especially in southern Italy. Clans and factions have been informal but real structures of power. Through them, patronage and funds for politicians, judges, and other political elites—from bribes to support for a candidate or his/her opponent—made the Mafia a force to be reckoned with. The usual impact of organized crime on politics was in the realm of public policy and funding—state money going to political favorites and kickback schemes. In the 1980s and 1990s the police and judiciary launched attacks on the Mafia and political corruption, with some success. However, the Mafia and corruption are far from defeated, merely under better control than earlier.

Finally, terrorist groups occasionally played important roles in politics when they had the strength and organization to resist efforts by the state to control them. The most infamous group in the 1970s was the Red Brigade, responsible for the kidnapping and murder of Aldo Moro. Since the 1970s state efforts to control terrorist groups have been relatively successful.

National Prospects

Italy has not had one of Europe's more stable political systems—witness the constant changes in governments, the constant dissolutions of Parliament before the end of its five-year term, and the fracturing of parties since the 1990s—but also has not fallen into the same kind of chaos that has threatened other countries. Italy's instability is more a threat to policy efficacy than to the social fabric of the nation. Such instability did make policy implementation difficult; however, changing coalitions always remained in one part of the political spectrum, so that ruptures were not great and policies could be implemented.

For Italy to continue its march into prosperity, several issues must be addressed. First, there is the issue of corruption and crime. The political system in the 1980s and 1990s was crippled by scandals of political corruption, in particular by widespread and deep structures of party patronage. While patronage had its positive side—breaking class stratification and helping development of various regions, especially those in the South—it also led to recriminations of political favoritism and to the formation of right-wing reactionary groups, especially in the North. Such corruption, in spite of its ability to funnel resources to often needy patrons, also can lead to abuses of power and distraction of policies.

Corruption is not the only part of the dark underside plaguing Italy's politics: there is also the Mafia, especially prominent in southern Italy and Sicily, where Mafia families dominate and in fact are the real power, literally ousting more ineffectual state structures. These Mafia families are involved in a lucrative drug trade, spurring tensions and conflict between organized crime and the state and leading at times to bloodshed. Mafia control makes further centralization and organization of state power and authority problematic. The Mafia also contributes heavily to the problem of official corruption.

Another issue that haunts Italy is xenophobia of right-wing parties and movements, especially in the North. While this phenomenon is not unique to Italy—right-wing xenophobia and racism have emerged as minority movements and parties in Europe, from the Greater Romanian Party to the more threatening Le Pen in France—in Italy this rhetoric has made it into the ruling coalition. The Northern League and its leader, fiery Umberto Bossi, have harangued foreigners, Muslims, Jews, gays, and others, and part of the support for Freedom House and Berlusconi come from disaffected segments of Italian society who fear that foreigners might dilute Italian society and culture.

Italian politics has been more stable in the early 2000s than in the preceding two decades, if by "stability" we mean how long a government remains in power. This has not brought general contentment to Italian politics, however. Berlusconi continues to call out emotional reactions (for and against) from both sides of the political spectrum. His attempts to improve the Italian government's finances through reduction of welfare support and state spending (especially in the economy) led to a wave of strikes in November 2004. Even if his standing among some countries has improved given his talk on terrorism and world politics, he has not been entirely accepted by world leaders and publics. As in past decades, Italy's politics are right-of-center—less because of an overall conservative population and more out of the machinations of the political elite. Revisions to the electoral process have not brought consolidations of parties, and it is uncertain whether Berlusconi's right-wing coalition can long govern as well. As is the situation elsewhere in Europe and the world, the weakening of the left after 1989 has given the right an advantage, and Berlusconi and company rely on this and the leader's media empire as much as on a feeling of national unity. Italian politics retains the undercurrent of fragmentation that has haunted political life since unification in the 19th century. That has not yet led to catastrophe, but it remains a problematic issue for Italian politics.

Further Reading

Alvarez-Rivera, Manuel. "Elections to the Italian Parliament." *Election Resources on the Net.* Available online. URL: http://www.electionresources.org/it. Updated May 12, 2004.

Bartolini, Stefano, and Roberto D'Alimonte. "Plurality Competition and Party Realignment in Italy: The 1994 Parliamentary Elections." *EUI Working Paper SPS No. 95/7,* Italy, 1995.

Putnam, Robert. *Making Democracy Work.* Princeton, N.J.: Princeton University Press, 1993.

Sassoon, Donald. *Contemporary Italy: Economy, Society, and Politics.* 2d ed. London: Addison-Wesley, 1997.

Smith, Denis Mack. *Modern Italy. A Political History.* Ann Arbor: University of Michigan Press, 1997.

REPUBLIC OF IVORY COAST
(République de la Côte d'Ivoire)

By Elizabeth L. Normandy, Ph.D.
Revised by Vasilis Margaras

Slightly larger than the state of New Mexico, Ivory Coast is located in West Africa between Ghana and Liberia. Its coastline borders the North Atlantic Ocean.

There is no single dominant ethnic group in Ivory Coast. Of the approximately 60 ethnic groups, four groups make up over 67 percent of the 17 million population. They are distributed as follows: Baoule, 23 percent; Bete, 18 percent; Senoufou, 15 percent; Malinke, 11 percent. About 3 million non-Ivorian Africans reside in the Ivory Coast, including 300,000 Liberians who have taken refuge in the country as a result of the Liberian civil war. There are also sizable French and Lebanese populations. The country's major religious groups are Muslim, 35 to 40 percent; Christian, 20 to 30 percent; and indigenous religions, 25 to 40 percent.

For more than three decades, Ivorian politics was dominated by President Félix Houphouët-Boigny, who led the country to independence, wrote the constitution, and governed the country until his death in 1993. In the country's first multiparty elections in 1990, Houphouët-Boigny defeated Laurent Gbagbo, a candidate of the "democratic left" coalition. Houphouët received 81.68 percent of the vote, and Gbagbo received 18.32 percent. Alassane Ouattara was named to the newly created post of prime minister by Houphouët-Boigny. Nonetheless, real power remained in the hands of the president, who guided Outtara's decisions from behind the scenes.

On the death of Houphouët-Boigny in 1993, Henri Konan Bédié, Speaker of the National Assembly, assumed the presidency as decreed by law. In the 1995 elections Henri Bédié retained the presidency, winning 96 percent of the vote. Outtara, the most serious challenger to Bédié, was forced to withdraw from the race because of a recently enacted restrictive electoral code.

In 1999 Bédié was overthrown in a military coup led by General Robert Guei. In October 2000 Guei proclaimed himself president after announcing he had won presidential elections, but he was forced to flee in the wake of a popular uprising against his perceived rigging of the polls. In the wake of his ousting, Gbagbo named himself president, setting off a fresh round of violence between his supporters and those of Outtara. An attempted coup failed to oust Gbagbo in 2001. In March 2002 Gbagbo and Ouattara met for the first time since the start of the post-election violence and agreed to work toward reconciliation. In January 2003 Gbagbo accepted a peace deal at talks in Paris. The deal, known as the Marcoussis Peace Accord, proposed a power-sharing government made up of the competing factions, which were generally split along regional lines, with Gbagbo's support drawn mainly from the Christian-dominated South and the opposition mainly in the Muslim-dominated North. The accord also stipulated that the legal age at which someone could run for president would be reduced to 35 years.

As a result of the peace accord, the "consensus" prime minister, Seydou Diarra, was charged with forming a cabinet. Nonetheless, the country remained unstable. In August 2003 French authorities detained a group of suspected mercenaries who were planning to assassinate Gbagbo. Elections scheduled for October 2005 were postponed by Gbagbo, who invoked a law that he said allowed him to sidetrack the five-year term limit and remain as president. The African Union recommended that Gbagbo should retain his position for one additional year but urged him to appoint a different prime minister, one that would be acceptable to his foes in the northern part of the country.

The System of Government

Ivory Coast has a presidential form of government built on a separation of powers. The system is based on a new constitution adopted in 2000 following the coup by Guei.

EXECUTIVE

Most political power lies with the presidency, as stipulated by the constitution. The president has the power to submit a bill to a national referendum or initiate legislation in the National Assembly, where approval is almost automatic. He or she may appoint, dismiss, and outline the functions of the cabinet members and may appoint most other high-ranking civil, judicial, and military leaders. The president is also commander in chief of the military and may negotiate and ratify certain treaties.

The president is chosen by a direct national election for a five-year term of office. The constitution stipulates that the president be at least 40 years old, an eligible voter, and not the holder of one of several high political offices; the 2003 peace accord lowered the minimum age to 35 years. The president is elected if he receives a majority of votes cast on the first ballot or, if no candidate receives a majority, through a runoff election between the two top candidates.

LEGISLATURE

Ivory Coast's legislature is the National Assembly, consisting of 225 members. Since 1990 deputies have been selected in multiparty elections, replacing the multicandidate elections established in 1980. Deputies are elected by direct universal suffrage for five-year terms that run concurrently with the term of the president.

According to the constitution, the National Assembly meets in two regular sessions, each lasting about three months. The first session opens in April and the second in October. The primary powers of the National Assembly are the voting of laws and the authorization of taxes. The constitution stipulates that any power not expressly given to the National Assembly is outside its domain. This serves to augment the power of the president, who has fewer constitutional limits on his

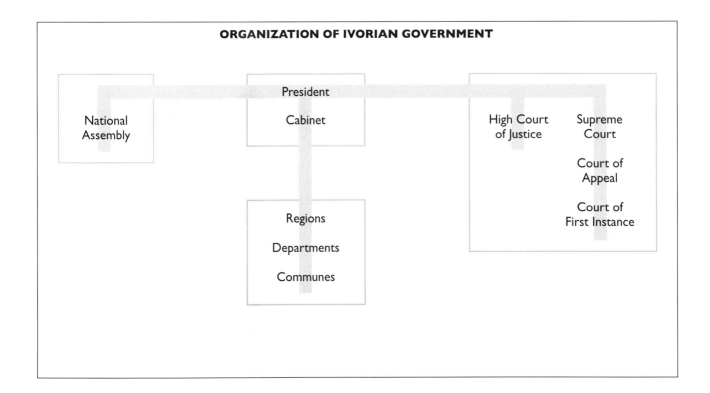

ORGANIZATION OF IVORIAN GOVERNMENT

President
Cabinet

National Assembly

High Court of Justice   Supreme Court

Court of Appeal

Court of First Instance

Regions

Departments

Communes

power. In practice, the National Assembly has little independence from the president. It does not check the president's powers, nor does he consult it. Rather, its role is to ratify executive decisions in order to give them legitimacy.

In the 2000–01 elections, the Ivorian Popular Front (FPI) won 96 seats, while the Democratic Party of Ivory Coast (PDCI) won 94 votes.

JUDICIARY

The legal system of Ivory Coast is a mixture of customary and French law. The Supreme Court's constitutional section may rule on the constitutionality of bills that have been proposed or passed by the National Assembly but not promulgated. The Court's administrative section is the court of final appeal for cases dealing with government administration and the bureaucracy, and the audit and control section oversees state expenditures and audits state accounts. The High Court of Justice, composed of deputies to the National Assembly, rules on crimes committed by government officials within the line of duty and on charges of treason against high officials, including the president. The judicial system includes a court of appeals and lower courts. Although nominally independent, the judiciary does not ensure due process and is subject to pressure from the executive in political cases.

REGIONAL AND LOCAL GOVERNMENT

Local government in Ivory Coast is modeled after the French system. The country is divided into 19 regions, which are futher divided into 58 departments, each governed by a prefect appointed by the president. There are 135 communes, each headed by a competitively elected mayor. The 37 largest towns and cities are governed by municipal councils that are also elected.

The Electoral System

Elections in Ivory Coast are direct; suffrage is universal for those 18 years of age or older. Elections are held every five years. Under a multiparty system adopted in 1990, parties are legally free to organize and run candidates for office. However, election law stipulates that candidates must meet stringent parentage, residency, and citizenship requirements. Changes to the law in 1995 require candidates to prove that both parents were born in Ivory Coast.

The Party System

Prior to 1990 Ivory Coast was in practice a one-party state dominated by the PDCI. The PDCI prevented the rise of a formal opposition by giving prominent persons who might conceivably lead such an opposition high and demanding positions in the government. The total domination of the government by the PDCI helped to make it an unofficial fourth branch of the government. Most important decisions affecting government policy actually were made by the elite of the PDCI.

In 1990 several weeks of strikes and protests of unprecedented scale and intensity revealed intense dissatisfaction with PDCI-controlled government. With the party's popularity at an all-time low and opposition parties covering the entire political spectrum forming underground, the government announced that opposition parties would be recognized officially. In the elections that followed later that year, 26 opposition parties contested the elections.

This domination ended with the 1999 coup by Guei. Following his ouster and Gbagbo's installation as president in 2000, Gbagbo's FIP has been the leading party in the National Assembly, holding 96 of the 225 seats. The PDCI remains powerful, holding 94 seats in the Assembly. Like the country itself, the parties are divided along geographic and religious lines.

Major Political Parties
DEMOCRATIC PARTY OF IVORY COAST
(Parti démocratique de la Côte d'Ivoire; PDCI)

The PDCI was formed in the late 1940s as the Ivorian branch of the African Democratic Rally (Rassemblement Démocratique Africain; RDA). The RDA was an organization formed to encourage independence for French West Africa. Although the French opposed the efforts of the RDA prior to 1951, after that date the French withdrew their support of other African groups and then allowed the RDA—and its branch, the PDCI—to dominate politics in the region. Both the RDA and the PDCI were founded by Houphouët-Boigny. The PDCI was the sole legal party between 1963 and 1990.

Prior to 1990 Houphouët-Boigny maintained his control of the party and the government through strict repression of violence and co-opting of the opposition. During the 1990 election campaign the PDCI used its control over political resources, such as the news media and government facilities, to ensure that it won the election. In 1992 the PDCI-controlled government used heavy-handed tactics to suppress the opposition. Prior to the 1995 elections the government used lethal force to control antigovernment demonstrations that had been banned by decree.

As of 2005 the party held 94 seats in the National Assembly, second only to the FPI's 96 seats.

IVORIAN POPULAR FRONT

(Front Populaire Ivorienne; FPI)

The FPI became an important party during the 1990s, and it gained even more power when Laurent Gbagbo proclaimed himself president in late 2000. In 2001 the FPI emerged as the biggest single party in parliamentary elections, gaining 96 seats out of 225.

RALLY FOR REPUBLICANS

(Rassemblement des Républicains; RDR)

The Rally for Republicans (RdR) is a party led by Alassane Ouattara, who is regularly reported to be the inspiration behind the former rebel movement. The party's main support comes from the country's northern region. Ouattara was banned from the presidential election in 2000 because of his foreign origin. As a result, RdR boycotted the presidential and parliamentary elections of 2000–01. Outtara was awarded a certificate of Ivorian nationality in 2002. In August 2002 the party was given four ministerial posts in the new government as part of an effort to help stabilize the country.

Minor Political Parties

There are numerous smaller parties in Ivory Coast. Among those that won seats in the 2000–01 elections are the Ivorian Workers Party (Parti Ivorian des Travailleurs; PIT); the Union of Democrats of Côte d'Ivoire (Union des Démocrates de Côte d'Ivoire); and the Movement of Future Forces (Mouvement des Forces de l'Avenir).

Other Political Forces

THE REBELS

The initial rebel group was the Ivory Coast Patriotic Movement, known by its acronym MPCI. When the MPCI stopped fighting the government in late 2002, two new groups attacked from the west. Both the Movement for Justice and Peace (MJP) and the Ivorian Popular Movement of the Great West (MPIGO) were included in the January 2003 round-table talks at Marcoussis in France that brought the war to a close. But it is alleged by many that both MJP and MPIGO have such close links to MPCI that they are effectively satellite movements under MPCI control. After the Marcoussis peace agreement, all three rebel movements fused into a group known as the New Forces. Guillaume Soro, the organization's political leader, announced that he would not present himself as a presidential candidate in 2005. When President Gbagbo delayed those elections, the African Union recommended that he appoint a prime minister with executive power who would be acceptable to all parties; Soro's supporters called for Soro to take that position. As of November 2005, however, Gbabgo had declined to make this appointment.

National Prospects

Once a country of stability and economic growth, Ivory Coast is today in crisis. Thousands of people died in the civil war that began after the elections in 2000, and the local and national economy has been devastated. The war is now officially over, and rebel leaders have been given seats in the government. However, the rebels still control the country's North, and plans to demobilize and disarm them have so far produced modest results. Elections were due in 2005 but were postponed by Gbabgo. In the meantime, 4,000 French peacekeepers are monitoring the cease-fire line across the middle of the country while a further 6,000 UN troops have also been deployed in the country.

Further Reading

Cohen, Michael A. *Urban Policy and Political Conflict in Africa: A Study of the Ivory Coast*. Chicago: University of Chicago Press, 1974.

Foster, Philip, and Aristide R. Zolberg. *Ghana and the Ivory Coast*. Chicago: University of Chicago Press, 1971.

Kohler, Jessica. *From Miraculous to Disastrous: The Crisis in Côte d'Ivoire*. Geneva: Center for Applied Studies in International Negotiations, 2003.

Mundt, Robert J. *Historical Dictionary of Côte d'Ivoire*. 2d ed. Lanham, Md.: Scarecrow Press, 1995.

Widner, Jennifer A. "The 1990 Elections in Côte d'Ivoire." *Issue: A Journal of Opinion* 20, no. 1 (winter 1991): 31–40.

JAMAICA

By Thomas D. Anderson, Ph.D.
Revised by Soeren Kern

Jamaica is one of the Greater Antilles with an area of about 4,200 square miles lying south of Cuba and west of Haiti in the Caribbean Sea. It is a parliamentary democracy that was granted independence from the British Empire on August 6, 1962. The capital city is Kingston. Its population is roughly 2.6 million and largely speaks English. Slightly more than three-fourths of the population is black, and another one-fifth is of mixed ancestry. Whites, Chinese, and others make up the remainder. Although about half of the population is Christian (largely Protestant), most of the rest identify with various spiritual faiths, the most important of which in Rasta Farianism, which originated in Jamaica. Agriculture is a major feature of the landscape, with about a quarter of the surface devoted to field and tree crops. However, bauxite mining, light manufacturing, and tourism are the most significant sectors of the economy.

The System of Government

Jamaica is a constitutional parliamentary democracy modeled after the British system. It has a bicameral legislature.

EXECUTIVE

The chief of state is the British monarch, represented by a governor-general appointed by the monarch on the advice of the Jamaican prime minister. The governor-general is advised by the six-member Privy Council. Effective executive power is held by the prime minister, who is leader of the majority party in the House of Representatives, to which the prime minister and cabinet are responsible. In 2003 the government of Prime Minister Percival Patterson announced a desire to create a republican form of government by 2007.

LEGISLATURE

The bicameral Parliament consists of the House of Representatives and the Senate. The House has 60 members elected by direct suffrage to five-year terms. The 21-member Senate is appointed by the governor-general: 13 members on the advice of the prime minister and 8 on the advice of the leader of the opposition. Cabinet members may be appointed from either the House or the Senate. Although Parliament is the preeminent legal authority, it is effectively under the control of the prime minister.

Bills may be introduced by either body, except for money bills, which must originate in the House. Although the Senate may delay passage of a bill by voting it down, the House may override the action by passing the bill a second time. Senate approval is required for constitutional amendments. Parliamentary standing committees handle legislative business under direction of the prime minister and his cabinet. On advice from the prime minister, the governor-general may dissolve the legislature and call for now elections at any time. Otherwise elections are held at five-year intervals.

JUDICIARY

The judicial system is based on English common law and practices. The high courts are the Supreme Court and the Court of Appeals. The Supreme Court consists of the chief justice and other judges. The chief justice is appointed by the governor-general on the advice of the prime minister and in consultation with the leader of the opposition. The other judges also are appointed by the governor-general on the advice of the Judicial Service Commission, which is chaired by the chief justice. Appeals from the Supreme Court go to the Court of Appeals, which is the highest court in Jamaica. Further appeals may be sent to the Privy Council in London, which is the ultimate court of appeals.

REGIONAL AND LOCAL GOVERNMENT

For administrative purposes, Jamaica is divided into 14 parishes; for local government purposes, Kingston and St. Andrew are grouped in the Kingston and St. Andrew Corporation, which includes the principal metropolitan area. Each parish has an elected council that administers local affairs.

The Electoral System

National elections have occurred in Jamaica since 1944. Suffrage is universal for citizens age 18 or older. Elections to the House of Representatives are held at least every five years, and seats are won by simple plurality in single-member constituencies. A nominal cash deposit is required for those who stand for office and is forfeited should the candidate receive less than 12.5 percent of the constituency vote. The boundaries of the constituencies are reviewed periodically by a standing committee in Parliament. In general, elections have been fair, although allegations of fraud were widespread after the election of 1976.

The Party System

The first open demand for greater self-government in the British West Indian possession came in 1936, when Jamaican expatriates in New York City founded the Jamaican Progressive League. This period was one of growing labor strife in the British West Indies. It began when an attempt to organize sugar workers on St. Kitts was suppressed. Two years later a general strike began in Trinidad, and related strikes and demonstrations spread to other British territories. London's reaction was to legalize unions and widen the franchise. What

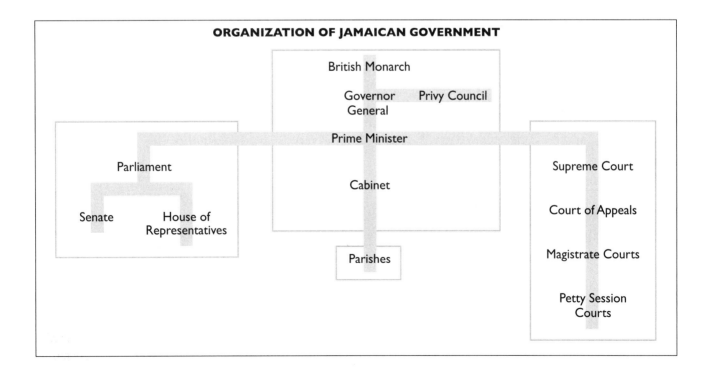

ORGANIZATION OF JAMAICAN GOVERNMENT

British Monarch

Governor General   Privy Council

Prime Minister

Parliament

Cabinet

Senate   House of Representatives

Supreme Court

Court of Appeals

Magistrate Courts

Parishes

Petty Session Courts

next evolved was a hybrid political structure peculiar to the British Caribbean.

Although conditions differed, those that developed in Jamaica were somewhat archetypal: a two-party, two-union system with labor and political elements intertwined but still distinguishable. The pairings were the Jamaica Labour Party (JLP) and the Bustamante Industrial Trades Union, arrayed against the Peoples National Party (PNP) and the National Workers Union. The unions were very similar in composition. The leaders of each normally serve in Parliament, and both unions were blanket types in that a wide cross section of worker categories was represented. A significant event in 1952 was the expulsion from the PNP of the "Four H's"—Ken Hill, Frank Hill, Arthur Henry, and Richard Hart—for espousing Marxist doctrines in violation of party rules. The policies of the PNP have varied little since the time. External influences have helped to shape the distinctive non-Marxist union/party forms, such as U.S. and Western European governments and labor unions. Especially important was the Scandinavian example of worker participation in control of an industry's operation rather than its ownership. Two towering figures had major roles in these events. Alexander Bustamante first gained national stature when he was arrested and imprisoned following labor unrest in 1938. His defense lawyer was Norman Manley, considered a national hero in Jamaica and a founder of the PNP.

The party system is open and well developed. There are no barriers to the entry of new parties or independent candidates, but none of the former and few of the latter have fared well in competition with the disciplined organizations of the two major parties. Both the PNP and the JLP are organized by constituency. Since the early years, the party structures have been more influential than those of the unions. Both parties maintain youth organizations that provide the core of their forces during campaigns as well as training for the leadership of the future. Campaign expenditures are limited by law, but few details are public knowledge. It is generally assumed that both parties receive major contributions from business and industrial enterprises.

Election campaigns are well organized and fiercely contested—unfortunately in recent years this has included serious violence. In the 1980 campaign an estimated 500 people died in campaign-related incidents. Much of the violence is attributed to youth wings of the parties, which attempt to control sections of Kingston and exclude campaigning by their opponents in these sectors.

Most violence occurs in the poorest neighborhoods where each party competes strongly for a sector of the vote that had been a deciding factor in a recent election. The 1972 and 1976 successes of the PNP were attributed to the left-wing appeals to the urban poor by Michael Manley (son of Norman Manley), whereas his failure to improve their lot and a 30 percent unemployment rate was decisive in the rout of the PNP in 1980.

In 1983 the ruling JLP called a snap election that the PNP decided not to contest. Prime Minister Edward Seaga sought to capitalize on a wave of popular support for his role in backing the invasion of Grenada in order to reaffirm his leadership. The opposition boycotted on the grounds that the voter lists had not been updated to include 100,000 new voters. As a result, the JLP won all 60 seats in Parliament, leaving Jamaica without an official opposition for the first time. It was feared that such one-party rule would harm the political system, but the PNP remained active and because the JLP permitted public participation in the House of Assembly, a lively exchange of views continued.

Major Political Parties

JAMAICA LABOUR PARTY (JLP)

The JLP was founded by Alexander Bustamante in 1943, after he took his Bustamante Industrial Trade Union (BITU) out of association with the PNP in a dispute over that party's advocacy of Jamaican independence. Most of the JLP's support came from the workers, whereas the leadership was primarily from businesses and professionals. Initially opposed to independence, the JLP first came to power in 1944 when Jamaica was granted self-government. It lost power from 1955 to 1962 but presided over the transfer of sovereignty in 1962. From 1972 to 1980 it again served as an opposition party. The JLP held power again until defeat by the PNP in February 1993. The scale of the loss (the JLP won only eight seats) was such that the JLP contended that the election was the most fraudulent in Jamaican history and that they would refuse to contest any by-elections until electoral reforms were implemented. They did, however, drop 14 of 16 court challenges in specific constituencies.

In its early years, the party was dominated by Bustamante, but, following his retirement in the mid-1960s, the strength of the constituency organizations increased as greater democracy was introduced. The party's political stance has always been right-of-center, with emphasis on free enterprise, foreign investment, and economic expansion as the best strategies to improve conditions for the island's poor. Along with a strong rural base, the JLP also draws strength from the social elite. The 1993 election defeat caused Seaga in 1995 to poll the party delegates regarding his standing. His version of the result (critics had their doubts) was a 78 percent approval rating, and he remained in the leadership post.

In national election of 1992 the party won only 10 seats in the legislature, but in 2002 it captured 47 percent of the vote and 26 seats, and it served as the main opposition party.

PEOPLES NATIONAL PARTY (PNP)

The PNP was founded in 1939 by Norman Manley. Its early policy thrust was Jamaican independence and an end to the dominance of British capital on the island. In its early years, it relied heavily on Bustamante's union for support, but, after Bustamante split with the party in 1943, it eventually developed an organization that won support both within the middle class and among labor when Manley organized the National Workers' Union in the 1950s.

Despite its early strength among the business and professional community under the leadership of Norman Manley, the party moved sharply to the left after the founder's death in 1969, when his son Michael took over. The younger Manley had been an NWU organizer and leader, and he increased the appeal of the party to the urban poor and younger voters. As prime minister from 1972 to 1980, Manley pursued a socialist policy that included nationalization of foreign holdings and social programs such as a literacy campaign, agricultural collectivization, and government-funded education through the university level. Manley identified Jamaica with the Third World and nonaligned movements and expressed solidarity with the Caribbean Marxist governments in Cuba and Grenada.

During Manley's eight years as prime minister Jamaica experienced a 17 percent drop in its economy, an increase in unemployment from 20 percent to 30 percent, and an accumulation of foreign debt that reached to over a billion U.S. dollars. The reaction of the voters was a resounding defeat of his party, although Manley retained his own seat in the House. An additional factor in this rejection was the attempt by Fidel Castro to provide money and political advice in support of the Manley campaign. Newspaper reports of these activities both swayed some voters and induced a wider turnout by others.

Despite this down period, the PNP retained is traditional solid base of support and took advantage of errors and a stagnant economy during the subsequent terms of Edward Seaga to return to power in the election of February 1988. Ill health induced Manley to give way to Percival Patterson in March 1992, and he led the PNP to victory in 1993, 1997, and 2002. The 2002 victory marked the first time any Jamaican political party has won four consecutive general elections since the introduction of universal suffrage to Jamaica in 1944.

Minor Political Parties

In the context of Jamaica's dominant two-party structure, the political alternatives could usually be more accurately termed factions. However, in October 1995 the former JLP chairman and heir apparent to Edward Seaga as party leader, Bruce Golding, formed the National Democratic Movement made up of dissidents from the major parties. However, it did not win any seats in the last two elections.

The New Beginnings Movement (NBM), with several hundred adherents, is a minor political party with only a slight political impact. The Rasta Farians ("Rastas") of the country, despite their relative informal organizational status, could be a potent political force should they decide collectively to take positions on specific issues. The movement has spread widely throughout the Caribbean as well as into Anglo-America and Britain but remains most influential in its land of origin and especially in the interior highlands (the "Cockpit" country).

Other Political Forces

Jamaicans for Justice (JFJ) is a nonpartisan human rights group that lobbies for change in the judicial system. JFJ has pushed the government to implement public policies that improve police accountability and ensure that Jamaicans have equal access to fair, correct and impartial treatment. The JFJ was especially active in the lead-up to the referendum on ratification of Jamaica's participation in the Caribbean Court of Justice (CCJ). In December 2003 three bills aimed at establishing the CCJ were tabled in the Senate, and in January 2004 JFJ filed a suit challenging, among other things, the constitutionality of the proposed method of establishment of the Court as the final court of appeals, as did four other organizations. As a result, the Senate debate on the bills was postponed to allow for the hearing of the cases in court.

National Prospects

Jamaica's political system is stable. However, the country's serious economic problems have exacerbated social problems and have become the subject of political debate. While elections have often been marred by violence, their results have always been accepted and, on the whole, political institutions have managed to retain their legitimacy. With the downturn of the bauxite market and the increasing competition for tourist dollars (especially from Cuba), the prospects for economic growth appear best in the expansion of the manufacturing sector. Expansion of the North American Free Trade Agreement (NAFTA) to Mexico, along with the continued exclusion of the rest of the Caribbean, has raised serious concerns about the likelihood of such expansion. For example, in 1997 the apparel industry suffered its first downturn in 20 years, and Mexico's membership in NAFTA was considered a chief explanation.

Jamaica is struggling to overcome lawlessness that has given it one of the world's highest murder rates and threatens to jeopardize its tourism industry, the main foreign exchange earner. The government has at times deployed army units to suppress violent unrest.

Further Reading

Alexander, Robert J. *Political Parties of the Americas: Canada, Latin America and the Caribbean.* 2 vols. Westport, Conn.: Greenwood Press, 1982.

Anderson, Thomas D. "Marxists and Non-Marxists in the Caribbean." In *A Critique of Marxist and Non-Marxist Thought.* Ed. Ajit Jain and Alexander J. Matejko. New York: Praeger, 1986.

Harriott, Anthony. *Understanding Crime in Jamaica: New Challenges for Public Policy.* Kingston, Jamaica: University of West Indies Press, 2004.

JAPAN
(Nihon/Nippon)

By Richard Leitch, Ph.D.
Revised by Soeren Kern

Japan is an island nation-state located in northeastern Asia between the North Pacific Ocean and the Sea of Japan, approximately 450 miles east of China. The Japanese archipelago consists of roughly 3,300 islands, but the four largest islands—Honshu, Kyushu, Hokkaido, and Shikoku—account for 97 percent of Japan's land area and are home to 98 percent of Japan's approximately 127 million people.

The System of Government

Japan is a constitutional monarchy with a parliamentary democracy. The monarch, known in Japan as the emperor, is chief of state but has very little authority. The prime minister as head of the government is the most important executive in the government.

EXECUTIVE

Executive authority is vested in a cabinet, numbering some 20 members, all of whom must be civilians. The cabinet consists of the prime minister, and chief cabinet secretary, ministers of state with portfolio, and several directors general of agencies, all without portfolio. The constitution stipulates that the prime minister selects and may dismiss other members of the cabinet and also states that the prime minister, as well as a majority of the cabinet ministers, must be members of the Diet. Since ministerial appointments are usually made as a reward for political loyalty to the prime minister and/or factions within the ruling party or parties, tradition has held that only under extraordinary circumstances would a member of the cabinet not also be a member of the Diet. Most often, therefore, cabinet appointments by the prime minister are considerations of political exigency rather than selections of experts on the policy facing the various ministries and agencies.

The power of the cabinet is limited by its relationship to the Diet, especially to the Lower House. Cabinet members are required to attend the sessions of both houses of the Diet and the meetings of the committees relevant to their appointment, and to reply to questions raised in these forums. In policy, the power of the prime minister is checked in legislative matters primarily by party members of the Diet—particularly its leaders—and to a lesser extent by the leaders of the opposition parties in the Diet. Cabinet power is also limited by the role of bureaucrats in the drafting and implementation of legislation: the first because of their relatively greater knowledge of the specifics of a policy issue and the second because of their ability to enforce the law. At the height of bureaucratic involvement in the process of policy formulation, it was estimated that more than four-fifths of all legislation that reached the floor of the Diet was initiated by civil servants and presented through the cabinet.

The most significant check that the legislative branch holds over the cabinet is the power constitutionally delegated to the Lower House to present no-confidence resolutions against the cabinet. The Upper House of the legislature is not empowered to present no-confidence motions, and the cabinet does not have the authority to dissolve the Upper House. If the Lower House passes a no-confidence motion (or rejects a confidence motion), the cabinet must resign en masse.

As is the case with all parliamentary democracies, Japan's prime minister is chosen from the ranks of the legislative branch. From its creation in 1955 until the general election of October 1993, the Liberal Democratic Party either held a majority of seats in the formerly 511-member Lower House of the legislature (therefore, at least 256 seats) or was able to win the support of minor parties or party independents in the unusual event that it did not win a majority of seats (only between 1976 and 1980 was this the case). Technically, these unusual situations would have made such an arrangement a coalition government, but because of the preponderance of LDP power in the relationship or the subsequent decision of the non-LDP representatives to change their party affiliation to the more powerful and better organized LDP, the instability inherent in a coalition government was virtually eliminated. Therefore, because of this LDP dominance, from 1955 to 1993 all prime ministers of Japan were members of the Liberal Democratic Party.

Conflict between the executive and legislative branches over legislation has traditionally been less frequent than is often the case in those nation-states that have a presidential form of government. Conflict between the legislative and executive branches was also lessened during the LDP reign because of the ritualized opposition role played by other political parties. The tactics of opposition parties were often determined well in advance of the presentation of an issue before the Diet, and, as their position was shared with members of the ruling LDP, everyone knew what was expected of the respective parties when the issue was ultimately presented. Conflict between the executive and legislative branches in Japan has also been mitigated because most prime ministers have been weak leaders in terms of innovative or bold policy agendas and have instead arrived at the position as a result of their seniority within the party, their ability to raise funds for the party, or sheer happenstance.

LEGISLATURE

Legislative authority is vested in a bicameral legislature called the Kokkai (Diet), consisting of the roughly 250-member Upper House, the Sangiin (House of Councillors), and the relatively more powerful 480-member Lower House, the Shugiin (House of Representatives). Of these, 180 are elected from 11 multimember constituencies by proportional representation, and 300 are elected from single-member constituencies. Members of the House of Representatives are elected for four-year terms, but as Japan has a parliamentary system, the House may be dissolved at any time during this four-year term and new elections held. Often, early elections are called by the prime minister when public opinion polls are favorable, making it likely that the will be reelected by an approving electorate. During the period between 1955 and 1993, during the Lib-

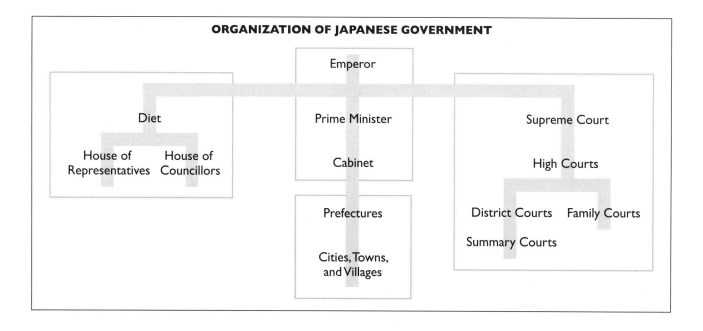

ORGANIZATION OF JAPANESE GOVERNMENT

Emperor

Diet

House of Representatives   House of Councillors

Prime Minister

Cabinet

Prefectures

Cities, Towns, and Villages

Supreme Court

High Courts

District Courts   Family Courts

Summary Courts

eral Democratic Party unchallenged dominance, dissolution of the Lower House for this reason was not uncommon. Indeed, the only time during this period that Lower House members served the duration of their four-year terms was between 1972 and 76); the average term lasted approximately 2½ years.

While "snap elections" called by the prime minister are the most frequent reason for early termination of a representative's term in office, elections are also required following a successful vote of no confidence (or rejection of a confidence resolution) against the cabinet by the Lower House, or in the event of a vacancy in the post of the prime minister, or if the cabinet resigns en masse.

In all three events described above, the composition of the House of Councillors is not affected. Members serve fixed, six-year terms, with half of the body up for election every three years. Although constitutionally weaker than the Lower House, the Upper House does have some power to influence the specifics of legislation or to delay the legislative process.

As a result of U.S. influence in drafting Japan's postwar constitution, operations in the Japanese Diet are similar to that of the U.S. Congress. Most debate on proposed legislation takes place at the committee level. Both houses of the Diet have standing and special committees, with the Lower House committees approximating the jurisdictions of the various government ministries and agencies and those of the Upper House relevant to national policy rather than to administrative matters. There are 16 standing committees in both houses, each with its counterpart in the other, and two additional standing committees (science and technology, and the environment) in only the Lower House. All are granted the right to conduct investigations of the actions of the government offices relevant to their charges, and the standing committees have their own investigative branches staffed by researchers and policy specialists. Representation on standing committees is apportioned according to the relative strength of each party's representation in the appropriate house, with chairmanships traditionally assigned to members of the ruling party or, in the case of a coalition government, ruling parties. Special committees are formed if the issue in question falls outside the scope of the standing committees and are disbanded after their findings have been reported to the Diet.

There are three distinct research offices that assist two distinct parts of policy making. Both the Lower House Legislative Bureau and the National Diet Library Research and Legislation Office assist Diet members in drafting bills. Cabinet bills are rarely the initiative of

TERMS IN OFFICE OF POSTWAR PRIME MINISTERS

Prime Minister	Term in Office
Higashikuni Naruhiko	August 1945–October 1945
Shidehara Kijuro	October 1945–May 1946
Yoshida Shigeru	May 1946–May 1947
Katayama Tetsu	May 1947–March 1948
Ashida Hitoshi	March 1948–October 1948
Yoshida Shigeru	October 1948–December 1954
Hatoyama Ichiro	December 1954–December 1956
Ishibashi Tanzan	December 1956–February 1957
Kishi Nobusuke	February 1957–July 1960
Ikeda Hayato	July 1960–November 1964
Sato Eisaku	November 1964–July 1972
Tanaka Kakuei	July 1972–December 1974
Miki Takeo	December 1974–December 1976
Fukuda Takeo	December 1976–December 1978
Ohira Masayoshi	December 1978–July 1980
Suzuki Zenko	July 1980–November 1982
Nakasone Yasuhiro	November 1982–November 1987
Takeshita Noboru	November 1987–June 1989
Uno Sosuke	June 1989–August 1989
Kaifu Toshiki	August 1989–August 1991
Miyazawa Kiichi	August 1991–August 1993
Hosokawa Morihiro	August 1993–April 1994
Hata Tsutomu	April 1994–June 1994
Murayama Tomiichi	June 1994–January 1996
Hashimoto Ryutaro	January 1996–July 1998
Obuchi Keizo	July 1998–April 2000
Mori Yoshiro	April 2000–April 2001
Koizumi Junichiro	April 2001–

the cabinet members themselves but, as the result of bureaucratic initiative and research, are often referred to as "government bills."

Zoku refer to those policy and issue-related realms in which Diet members have specialist knowledge or experience, and they act to protect the interests of affected groups by intervening in administrative and legislative matters on their behalf. For example, among others, there is an agriculture and forestry group (*norin-zoku*), a construction group (*kensetsu-zoku*), and a commerce and industry group (*shoko-zoku*). Under the multimember districts of the pre-1996 electoral system, on average, three to five representatives would hail from each district, with there rarely being two *zoku* representatives from the same district. Unless under exceptional circumstances, each representative would establish one *zoku* affiliation, which was coordinated by the LDP.

The *zoku* phenomenon was once seen as reflecting the close ties between members of the LDP, their counterparts in government ministries and agencies, and the special interest groups that they represented. This collaborative relationship became known as an "iron triangle" or, when it applied to the big-business realm of policy making, "Japan, Inc." Such a generalized, simplistic view obfuscates the conflict that was often inherent among the three groups, and it seems especially inapplicable in the post-1993, post–economic boom era.

Under Japan's revised, single-seat electoral system, representatives are now expected by the party (or compelled if they want to win a subsequent term) to develop multiple *zoku* affiliations. In contrast to the earlier era when *zoku* representatives could be considered experts on policy relating to that *zoku,* the result under the new system may be that less-than-knowledgeable Diet representatives come to rely on bureaucratic knowledge and assistance on those issues that fall outside of their primary *zoku* expertise even more than they had before. On the other hand, the likelihood of collusion among special interest groups, politicians, and bureaucrats—formerly accepted by the electorate as part of politics, but now openly criticized—may likely be mitigated.

It is normally the case that bills and other matters requiring Diet approval are first referred to the appropriate committee or committees for deliberation and then presented to the plenary session for a vote. Exception to this practice is given to those matters deemed so urgently in need of immediate legislative action that they must sidestep the committee channeling process. Following full-house deliberation, these issues are voted upon in the plenary session.

Far more frequent than immediate-action cases but again exceptional relative to the number of bills first brought before committees are those significant items over which the ruling party (or parties) and the opposition will clearly be at odds. In these instances, which are termed important or "confrontational" bills, the item is introduced before the plenary session together with an explanation as to why the item is important enough to merit exception from the normal legislative channels. It is sure then to evoke debate during the plenary session. Although such a bill is not acted upon when introduced but is instead referred to the appropriate committee or committees, with an important bill's introduction before the full house, the stage has been set for backroom brokering and negotiations between the parties. Failing an inter-party agreement before the bill once again reaches the plenary session for a vote, well-orchestrated, vitriolic harangues and displays of vote-stalling tactics by the party or parties that realize the vote may be against their cause are not uncommon.

The Diet is convened for any of three distinct sessions: regular, extraordinary, and special. By law, regular sessions must be held at least once a year. They are opened in December and last for 150 days. Extraordinary sessions are most often convened when the cabinet determines the need for such a session or when one-fourth of the membership of either house requests such a session. Special sessions are held in accordance with Article 54 of the constitution, which stipulates that upon dissolution of the House of Representatives, "there must be a general election of members of the House of Representatives within forty days from the date of dissolution, and the Diet must be convoked within thirty days from the date of the election."

The term of an extraordinary or special session is somewhat flexible, as it is decided by agreement of both houses, with the Lower House decision binding if no agreement can be reached. Yet expedience and efficiency are essential during any of these sessions, for a bill that is not approved by both houses during the same session cannot be carried over to the next session unless both houses agree to continue deliberations at the committee level. A Diet session can also be extended, in accordance with the procedure for determining the initial term of an extraordinary or special session, although the number of extensions permitted is limited to one for a regular session and two for extraordinary or special sessions. For the LDP, which from 1955 to 1989 either held an absolute majority in both houses or had the support of smaller parties when it did not, extending sessions or pro-

HOUSE OF REPRESENTATIVES ELECTION RESULTS

	2000	2003	2005
Liberal Democrats	233	237	296
Komeito	31	34	31
United Social Democratic	—	19	67
Democratic Party of Japan	127	178	113
Japan Communist Party	20	9	9
Liberal Party	22	—	—
Liberal League	—	1	—
Conservative	7	4	—
Independent/Other	17	11	24
Total	480	480	480

longing the life of a bill was a matter of intraparty, not interparty, concern. But once it lost its majority in the Upper House following the July 1989 election, the LDP was forced to consider more seriously the influence of the opposition.

The constitution establishes the primacy of Lower House decisions over those of the Upper House in four areas: enactment of laws, passage of the budget, approval of treaties, and designation of the prime minister. If the two houses vote differently on a bill, a joint committee is convened to create a compromise bill that is returned to both houses for action. In such instances, if the Upper House still votes differently from the Lower House or if agreement cannot be reached through the deliberations of a compromise committee, the decision of the Lower House prevails. Of significance, if the budget is not passed by the Upper House, then the administration continues to operate on a budget equivalent to that of the preceding fiscal year.

Before the LDP's loss of its majority in the House of Councillors following the election of 1989, the convocation of a joint committee was for 33 years a rarity. But since 1989—and especially since 1993—the joint committee has become more frequent. The constitution stipulates that if the two houses cannot agree on a compromise version, the measure becomes law if approved by two-thirds or more of Lower House members present

(Article 59). Yet since no party has ever held two-thirds of the seats in the Lower House, this scenario is possible only as a result of party alliances. In fact, the only period when these two-thirds alliances were struck was in the early years of LDP rule, and the most recent successful Lower House override of a measure other than those mentioned above (budget, treaties, and designation of the prime minister) was in 1957.

The 1996 election was the first conducted under a new electoral system that eliminated multimember districting in an effort to reduce corruption, decrease party factionalism, and create more cohesive parties in the Diet.

JUDICIARY

Article 81 of the constitution specifies that the Supreme Court is "the court of last resort with power to determine the constitutionality of any law, order, regulation, or official act." While the Supreme Court has the power of judicial review, with minor exceptions it has rarely been invoked, as the Court has taken a decidedly apolitical stance on issues involving constitutionality. On those infrequent rulings, the Court has generally maintained a status quo, pro-government, pro-public stance, in contrast to a confrontational, progressive, or individual rights position.

The Supreme Court consists of 15 members, 14 of whom are selected by the Diet from a list provided by the Court itself, while the chief justice of the Court is appointed by the emperor on the recommendation of the cabinet. Therefore, in theory, the executive, legislative, and judicial branches are responsible for determining who will serve in these 15 posts, but the actual power of appointment rests with the cabinet (Article 79). The name of justices are brought before the electorate at the first general election of members of the Lower House following the justices' appointment and are reviewed again at the first Lower House election following a lapse of 10 years and every 10 years thereafter in the same manner. A simple majority of those votes cast is needed for both continuity and termination of one's term of office. Yet because the office itself rarely questions the workings and decisions of either the executive or the legislative branch through judicial review, the members of the Supreme Court are nearly anonymous to the general electorate, and never has one who has sought a continuation of service not been returned.

In addition to the Supreme Court, which is at the pinnacle of a hierarchic judicial structure that allows for appeal of decisions, adjudication of criminal and civil matters occurs in Japan's 8 high courts, 50 district courts, 50 family courts, and some 450 summary courts. At lower levels of adjudication, however, for reasons of bringing embarrassment to those involved and a lack of willingness to air personal matters in public forums, Japanese have traditionally preferred to settle disagreements through the payment of compensation deemed appropriate by both parties in a dispute or, failing that, through mediation that does not involve the court system. The number of attorneys is therefore low relative to other democracies, especially the United States.

There is a further explanation for the low number of civil proceedings handled by the Japanese court system, and that is the inaccessibility of the system to ordinary citizens. Japan's Civil Proceedings Law, under which civil matters are adjudicated, has not been revised in more than 70 years. The procedures are archaic, as is the language, written in classical, literary Japanese, used to explicate those proceedings.

Adjudication is the purview of the judges themselves, and with the exception of the Supreme Court, in which most hearings involve only five of its 15 members, cases at all levels of the judicial system are heard before either three judges or one judge and two subordinates who are considered to be experts in legal matters. There is no jury system in Japan.

REGIONAL AND LOCAL GOVERNMENT

In keeping with the occupation authorities' belief that decentralized, local government would strengthen the foundations of democracy in Japan, the constitution provides for local government autonomy and grants these various lower levels of government the right "to manage their property, affairs, and administration and to enact their own regulations within the law (Article 94)." In practice, however, as with all unitary forms of government, Japan's 47 prefectures and other lower levels of municipal government are autonomous of the central government only to the extent that the central government, located in Tokyo, grants them that autonomy. It is a unitary form of government with generally mutual respect of the roles of each successively lower level of government, although each level is dependent to a large degree on the central government for the revenue necessary for it to carry out its functions. The primacy of the central government and its laws are recognized (and rarely have been challenged) by municipalities, either prefectural, city, or village. Nor, with rare exception, has the central government had to overtly use its power to enforce its position and make these lower levels of government conform to the policy of the center.

The Electoral System

Under the revised national-level electoral system, which applies only to elections for the House of Representatives and not to those of the House of Councillors, voters cast two votes, one for a candidate in a single-member district system and the other for a political party; the party votes are distributed on a proportional basis. Voting is by secret ballot, and for the Lower House races voters receive two ballots. For the single-seat races voters select from a list of candidates, while on the proportional representation ballot, voters must write in the name of the party. The October 1996 Lower House election was the first national election in Japan conducted under this reformulated electoral districting system that attempts to shift emphasis from individual candidates to political parties. Of the now 480-member Lower House, 300 members are elected with a plurality in single-member districts and another 180 members are selected from ranked lists of candidates on the basis of their party's proportional share of the vote in 11 electoral regions. As a concession to incumbents whose tenure might have been jeopardized under the new system, a candidate may appear on both the district and the regional ballots.

The objective of allowing dual candidacy was to make parties more significant than individual politicians, but critics complained that the system also allows those who could not win election in the single-seat constituencies to have a chance at winning in the broader-based proportional representation districts. In the 1996 election, for example, 566 candidates ran in both races, while 260 of them, which represented approximately 90 percent of all the party's Lower House candidates, were from the LDP. Of those LDP candidates who lost their single-seat races, 32 won seats in the proportional contest.

In eliminating multimember districts, the new electoral system may have addressed the structural explanation for political corruption in Japan, but it will not cease the demands of constituents on their representatives. Additionally, parties must now maintain a presence in 300 electoral districts compared with the previous 130, increasing the demand for funds.

The new electoral system also decreased the relative number of seats allocated to rural districts, recognizing that overrepresented citizens in these regions had benefited from the LDP's occasional, minor electoral reforms that failed to accurately reflect rural-to-urban population shifts. Yet even the relatively significant reapportionment brought on by the new electoral system has not eliminated the disparity between the value of an urban dweller's vote and that of most rural counterparts. For example, the smallest rural single-seat constituency has about two-fifths of the eligible voters that the largest district in Tokyo contains

To run as a party candidate in a single-seat constituency, a candidate's party must be represented in the Diet by at least five party members or have obtained 2 percent of the votes cast in the previous national election. Of course, it is also possible to run as a party independent, but the prospects for election appear slim.

Voting rights were realized in three distinct periods in Japan: a period of limited male suffrage, from 1890 to 1925, in which voting was restricted to taxpaying male citizens, with qualifications gradually liberalized to increase the size of the eligible electorate; a period of universal male suffrage, from 1925 to 1945, in which male citizens aged 25 or over, with one year prior residence in the municipality and no tax qualification, were eligible to vote; and the present period of universal suffrage, which was established in 1945 and which also reduced the voting age from 25 to 20. The Election Law provides that anyone at least 25 years of age can stand for election to the Lower House. Only those judged legally incompetent or who are serving prison sentences or have violated the election law are prohibited from voting or seeking public office.

Although the intent of the Election Law is to provide a nearly universal opportunity for political hopefuls to seek office, the selection of political candidates is fairly limited, as it is in other nation-states. Three routes are more certain than most in winning election to a national-level post: inheriting the position, having experience in the national-level bureaucracy, and having served as an elected official in lower levels of government (such as local assemblies and municipal offices).

In the hereditary-post scenario, those veteran politicians who retire because of age or illness nominate their successors, with the support of the district's constituents. Oftentimes the successor may be a relative (son, daughter, or even adopted son-in-law), but familial relations are not essential. Through the successor, the retiree can still influence politics to some degree, and the constituents can benefit from the political machine that the retiree developed over the course of several terms. The practice of hereditary

officeholding is most common in the LDP, where generally more than one-third of LDP Diet members inherited their posts.

The Party System
ORIGINS OF THE PARTIES

The first political parties in Japan were founded in 1874, when several oligarchs split with the other members of Japan's government over the issue of whether or not Korea should be invaded for, among other reasons, its refusal to recognize the legitimacy of the Meiji government. Those who advocated an invasion viewed this as an opportunity to restore pride to the samurai class, which had seen its status in society progressively decline. As their more numerous opponents were concerned that such an endeavor would prove costly to Japan's limited treasury resources, the proinvasion faction of the government lost what has been referred to as the "Great Debate of 1873" and walked away from their government posts. Their subsequent attempts to return to power focused on the betterment of former elite samurai, and the organizations they founded advanced a narrow interpretation of popular rights. It is from these early organizations that Japan's political party system was created.

PARTY ORGANIZATION

Japan has a multiparty system in which one political party, the LDP, has dominated national politics since the mid-1950s. This dominance has been tempered by the existence of several opposition parties, usually one that can be considered the primary opposition party in terms of its representation at the national level and several smaller parties that can see their relative strength temporally increase if their support is needed on legislative or parliamentary matters. For most of the post-1955 period, this main opposition party was the Japan Socialist Party (Nihon Shakaito), but the role of the opposition has been played by different parties since the 1990s, when the Japanese political system experienced major changes. A moderate range of liberal and conservative ideologies are represented through this multiparty system, which, with the exception of the Japan Communist Party, lacks the extremist parties found in some nation-states. The result is similar to what is found in most nation-states with an established two-party system characterized by leadership turnover—an appeal by the parties to the priorities and preferences of the mass of moderate voters—although the change in leadership never materialized in Japan until 1993.

Seizing their opportunity to organize at the height of anti-LDP sentiment, these new party leaders established parties that were far too dissimilar in name, platform, and justification to bode well for the long-term survivability of most. Predictably, their party names included words that expressed a sense of newness, freshness, or reform; their platforms espoused the creation of a "true" democracy, increased accountability, and progress; and their justification was based on the anti-LDP, antigovernment cynicism of the electorate.

CAMPAIGNING

In principle, contemporary Japanese elections have operated on the basis of a distinction between political activity, or activities that seek to make the public understand the party's policies and programs, on the one hand, and election campaigning, or activity that is intended to secure votes for a particular candidate in a particular election, on the other. *Koenkai*, grassroots support networks for individual politicians, serve a role in achieving both objectives and can be considered the "modern" form of party organization in Japan. A politician forms a *koenkai* or to expand and to some extent institutionalize his support among the electorate. These mass-membership support groups are created and financed by the politician, but the myth is maintained that they are organized by the Diet candidate's supporters. In addition to including ordinary citizens, who make up the majority of the *koenkai*, local officials are given official titles and positions for their support. What makes *koenkai* "modern" is the use of mass membership for supporting candidates, not the appointment of local officials to head them. *Koenkai* also usually have various groups they organize, such as youth groups and women's groups.

Under the revised electoral system, all candidates receive a certain amount of free advertising space in newspapers. While there are strict limits on how frequently individual candidates may publicize their campaign via the mass media and limits as to how much they may spend in doing so, political parties are not faced with the same degree of regulation. No candidate or party may officially advertise a campaign via the mass media until 12 days before the date of election, which is also reduced from a 14-day period under the former system. Yet within those 12 days, political parties spend billions of yen.

Recent revisions to the Public Office Election Law maintained the prohibition of house-to-house canvassing by candidates and strengthened publicity limits by not allowing posting of campaign materials from six months before the expiration of one's term of membership or before the day following dissolution of the Lower House. Penalties for campaign violators and those convicted of bribery were also increased, as each can result in a five-year deprivation of the right to seek public office and the right to vote. Under the former system, no such penalty existed. Bribery within the party, for example, by those attempting to become the party nominee in a single-seat district or attempting to improve their relative place on the party list in proportional districts, would result in a prison term of up to three years for the influence wielder and a sentence of up to three years and a fine of up to ¥1 million (approximately $9,000) for the candidate. Recent amendments to the 1948 Political Funds Control Law will, in policy at least, ban all political contributions from corporations and other organizations beginning in the year 2000. Additionally, political parties must report contributions—and their contributors and recipients—of more than ¥50,000 (approximately $450), a change from the earlier level of ¥1 million. Failure to report such contributions would result in a five-year imprisonment and a fine of ¥1 million for the party accountant.

A more significant electoral reform was the establishment of the Political Party Subsidies Law. Any political party is eligible to receive public funding, provided that it has a representation of at least five of its members in the Diet or at least some representation if less than five, in which case it must have also obtained at least 2 percent of the total number of votes cast in the latest Lower House election or in the previous Upper House election or any national election before that. It is clear from such relatively minor requirements that the intent of the reformers was to make public financing the basis for party funds.

The pool of funds is allocated in the government budget and is based on the most recent census figures multiplied by ¥250 per citizen. Half the amount is distributed to parties in proportion to the number of Diet seats it holds, with the remaining half distributed on the basis of the share of votes each party obtained in the most recent national election.

But recent trends favor a two-party system. Indeed, Japan's once fractious political system has coalesced around the LDP and its main opponent, the Democratic Party of Japan (DPJ). New Komeito is the only other major party of note.

Major Political Parties

LIBERAL DEMOCRATIC PARTY (LDP)

(Jiyuminshuto)

HISTORY

The Liberal Democratic Party was formed by the merger of the Liberal Party and the Democratic Party in 1955, at the initiative of business leaders and in response to the unification of leftist political organizations two weeks before its establishment. Despite its electoral defeat of 1993, which many commentators believed would usher in a system in which political leadership would alternate between two major political parties, a significant rival to the LDP's degree of organization, connections, and representation has yet to emerge.

ORGANIZATION

The LDP continues to be a group of groups, or factions. Leaders of the then five extant factions (named after their leaders or former leaders, which included the Obuchi, Komoto, Miyazawa, Mitsuzuka, and Watanabe factions) complied with a 1994 order of party bosses that they disband and cease their formal operations in the wake of legislation that created the new electoral system of single-member districts. In theory, this new system would have made the existence of factions superfluous. Indeed, following implementation of the revised law, there was an initial diminution in the role played by the former factions, which have since adopted some variant of the name "policy research groups."

MEMBERSHIP AND CONSTITUENCY

Despite its 1993 electoral defeat, and other relatively minor setbacks that preceded it, in terms of representation in both houses of the Diet the LDP has been the dominant political party in Japan since 1955 and remains so today.

As the LDP was in part formed by the initiative of business leaders worried about a united socialist front, business interests have been a traditional support base for the LDP. Four major economic organizations deserve mention. The Japan Federation of Economic Organizations (Keidanren), Japan Federation of Employers Associations (Nikkeiren), Japan Chamber of Commerce and Industry (Nissho), and the Japan Association for Corporate Executives (Keizai Doyukai) have been, to varying degrees, supporters of the LDP. The largest and most influential of the four, Keidanren, is a

corporation consisting of approximately 120 industrial organizations and 1,000 member companies. When it served as the principal conduit for member firms' contributions to the LDP, Keidanren was also a political force. But in 1993 the organization decided to stop collecting political donations from member businesses, limiting their purpose to the LDP. The four groups' influence as a factor to be considered in policy making and their role as mediators between the government (or, more specifically, the LDP) and the business world have declined with the downturn of the Japanese economy, which began in the early 1990s.

In November 2003 the New Conservative Party (Hoshu Shinto) was absorbed into the LDP, a move based largely because of the New Conservative Party's poor showing in the 2003 general election. The Conservatives won only four seats, and the party's leader failed to win reelection in his home constituency. In 2005 the LDP secured an excellent result. Prime Minister Koizumi Junichiro, facing internal dissension because of his plans to privatize the postal system (the Upper House rejected the plan), called an early election and was rewarded by voters, who gave the LDP an absolute majority in the Lower House.

POLICY

Historically, the LDP has ardently supported policies that benefit its major support bases, big business and agricultural interests, and, generally, it continues to do so. However, LDP-backed 1994 legislation that provides for a gradual liberalization of Japan's rice market (which had been closed to foreign competition) and other similar agricultural deregulation legislation made some agricultural supporters of the LDP reconsider their party loyalties, and subsequently their support has moved to the NFP. Similarly, as should be expected, both corporate and small business interests are divided about the repercussions of proposed deregulation measures, which the LDP generally supports, particularly those that target the energy, telecommunications, and finance sectors, as well as Japan's distribution system. Thus, one can no longer say that the party's policy interest, or even the prioritization of those interests, is as narrow as it once was.

LEADERSHIP

A new procedure for electing the party president was initiated in 1995. A candidate is elected LDP party president if he or she receives a majority of votes, with one given to each LDP Diet member and one representing every 10,000 party members who vote via mail (at present, there are some 1.5 million dues-paying

LDP party members). If no candidate garners a majority of votes, LDP Diet members determine the party president in a runoff election between the top two vote earners.

PROSPECTS

Prospects for the LDP remain strong, if only because they are the party with the most incumbents. And it is still the most popular party in Japan. Additionally, the LDP remains the only party that can truly qualify as a national party in terms of representation from a variety of districts throughout Japan. But the LDP is held together more by patronage than by ideology. For example, although Koizumi supports privatization of most industries, a large faction within the LDP opposes his neoliberal economic policies.

DEMOCRATIC PARTY OF JAPAN
(Minshu To)

HISTORY

The Democratic Party of Japan (DPJ) was established in 1996 by two former high-ranking members of Shinto Sakigake (New Party Harbinger), Hatoyama Yukio and Kan Naoto, a former minister of health and welfare. While serving in the ministerial post, Kan had acquired a sudden national reputation as an advocate of the people for his investigation into a Ministry of Health and Welfare policy of the mid- to late 1980s not to inform the public that some blood products used in Japan may have been tainted by the HIV virus.

ORGANIZATION

The DPJ grew dramatically between 1996 and 2003, when it was strengthened by a merger with the Liberal Party, led by Ichiro Ozawa. In 2003 it won 178 seats in the House of Representatives, but in 2005 it was reduced to 113 seats in the LDP landslide.

MEMBERSHIP AND CONSTITUENCY

The DPJ is a party dominated by young professionals, including bureaucrats, lawyers, doctors, aid workers, bankers, and journalists, who are able to draw on a wide variety of experience in formulating policy proposals. As a result, DPJ politicians have introduced a large number of independent bills. The party places a strong emphasis on the speedy implementation of across-the-board reform and the creation of a fairer and more inclusive social environment in Japan. The DPJ was instrumental in introducing the manifesto (party platform) to Japanese politics, marking the initiation of genuine policy debate. Specific policy proposals include increasing the consumption tax to fund the overburdened pension system; bolstering regional autonomy by moving from a system of tied subsidies to one of providing independent budgets to the regions; and making most of the highway network toll-free.

POLICY

In economic policy, the DPJ favors decentralization of the central government and the revitalization of regional economies. It also promotes regulatory reform, the transfer of powers from central to local governments, and free trade agreements with other countries. In domestic policy, the DPJ favors pension reform by integrating pension plans into a single scheme that would link the amount of benefits to the total payments of contributions made. In foreign policy, the DPJ places a priority on the Japan-U.S. alliance as an essential requirement for stability and development in the Asia-Pacific region. It also calls for an improvement in bilateral ties with China.

PROSPECTS

The DPJ has emerged as the main opposition party. It defeated the LDP by a single seat in the July 2004 upper house elections, but the LDP managed to keep the majority due to its alliance with New Komeito. Despite some speculation in 2003 that it might overtake the LDP by 2005, its status was undermined by the 2005 results. Nevertheless, many Japanese hope that DPJ strength might usher in a two-party system that puts Japanese politics on a sounder footing. A majority of Japanese favor a working two-party system, something Japan has not experienced since the end of World War II. But questions remain whether the DPJ can replace the ruling coalition. Indeed, many analysts believe the DPJ as a whole remains long on rhetoric and short on substance.

NEW CLEAN GOVERNMENT PARTY
(Komei To)

HISTORY

Often translated as "New Komeito Party," the New Clean Government Party is an offshoot of Soka Gakkai, Japan's largest lay Buddhist organization. The present party was formed as a result of a merger between the Clean Government Party (more to the left and very radical) and the New Peace Party in November 1998. New Komeito is now the third largest force in the Diet, after the LDP and the DPJ.

ORGANIZATION

Soka Kyoiku Gakkai was formed in 1930 to promote education based on Buddhism, the organization faced oppression until the end of World War II under the religious controls of the former military government.

In 1954 Soka Gakkai set up a culture department as part of its move into politics. The department's political activities were taken over in 1961 by the Komeito Political League, which went on to become Komeito and later, New Komeito. The party was officially founded in 1964 as the political wing of Soka Gakkai. Although Soka Gakkai makes no campaign donations to New Komeito, it concedes that it is New Komeito's "main supporting organization." The head of Soka Gakkai is considered the de facto head of New Komeito. The party in effect is a moderate conservative party, while at the same time it is a theocratic Soka Gakkai Buddhist party.

MEMBERSHIP AND CONSTITUENCY

The party shares its support base with the LDP, made up of white-collar bureaucrats and rural populations. It also gains support from religious leaders. But married women account for half of Soka Gakkai's core membership, and they wield immense power in the organization. Because of its religious ties, New Komeito is a great vote-gathering machine, as Soka Gakkai boasts a membership of 10 million households. Indeed, its female supporters are key vote-gatherers. As a result, the party delivers key votes in every major constituency.

At a time when the LDP's traditional support bases, including agricultural cooperatives and construction firms, are losing their influence over rank-and-file members in election campaigns, the party has become increasingly dependent on Soka Gakkai for its election victories. In the Lower House election in November 2003, the LDP sought support from Soka Gakkai in single-seat constituencies. In return, the party called on their own supporters to vote for New Komeito in the proportional representation segment. Some four-fifths percent of LDP candidates who received New Komeito endorsement were elected in the November 2003 polls. New Komeito captured 15 percent of the vote and 34 seats in 2003, though in the landslide by the LDP, its coalition partner, in 2005, New Komeito was reduced to 31 seats.

POLICY

New Komeito is, in effect, a political-religious group. Soka Gakkai's fundamental principles include promoting peace, welfare, and democracy to protect human rights, freedom of religion, and freedom of speech. Its critics say the party is determined to make Soka Buddhism the state religion of Japan.

New Komeito says its mission is to act as an "accelerator" on structural reforms and a "brake" to prevent the coalition government from leaning too far to the right. The party's proposals include reduction of the central government and bureaucracy, increased transparency in public affairs, and increased local autonomy with the private sector playing an increased role.

In foreign policy, New Komeito has been torn between its ideals and reality. The party wants to eliminate nuclear weapons and armed conflict in general. But despite its pacifist ideology, it supported the LDP's deployment of Japanese troops to Iraq.

PROSPECTS

Though in the 2003 elections New Komeito was the only party other than the DPJ to pick up more seats, increasing its bloc from 31 to 34, it fell back to 31 in 2005. Nevertheless, it is considered the new kingmaker in Japanese politics. But New Komeito has many critics, and anti–New Komeito sentiments could grow among LDP members to the extent of jeopardizing the ruling coalition. The issue of whether current relations between the LDP and New Komeito change is the key to the future of Japan's political landscape.

Minor Political Parties

SOCIAL DEMOCRATIC PARTY (SDP)
(Shakai Minshu To)

HISTORY

The original incarnation of the SDP (the JSP, or the Japan Socialist Party, and subsequently the Social Democratic Party of Japan, although for both English language renderings it was known as Shakaito) was established in 1955 with a merger of formerly disparate left-wing and right-wing socialist forces. Until its support of the LDP-dominated coalition government in 1993, the SDP had been the LDP's primary opposition for nearly 40 years.

The 1993 Lower House election proved to be a disaster for the Social Democrats who, with anti-LDP sentiment among voters at a zenith, lost what was clearly their best chance at national leadership. Then party leader Doi Takako, the first female leader of a major political party, took responsibility for the party's relatively poor showing at the ballot box, and her successor, 74-year-old Murayama Tomiichi, was selected by his coalition partners—dominated by the overwhelming plurality of LDP representation in the Lower House—as the first Socialist prime minister in Japan since 1947.

However, the minority status of the Socialists in this coalition arrangement and the perception that Murayama was unable to lead the country toward reform became apparent, and, in January 1996, the LDP replaced Murayama with one of its own, Hashimoto Ryutaro. By the early 21st century the SDP was on the verge of extinction.

JAPAN COMMUNIST PARTY

(Nihon Kyosanto)

HISTORY
Officially founded in 1922 during Japan's period of post–World War I liberalism, the Japan Communist Party (JCP) is the oldest political party in Japan. But as an organized group that has advocated radical policies, including an end to the imperial institution, the JCP was banned when liberalism took a back seat to Japan's militarist policies of World War II. Postwar occupation authorities released the jailed members of the former JCP and granted the party legal recognition. It is the only major political party that has not been included in any of the four mostly short-lived coalition governments that followed the 1993 defeat of the LDP. Its support increased in the mid-1990s, when it won 26 seats, but its support has dropped in more recent elections.

ORGANIZATION
Along with the LDP, the JCP has established itself as a well-organized political party, although, in contrast to the LDP, its grassroots appeal is generally limited to the urban electorate. A 168-member central committee elects the 38-member presidium, and the 14-member presidium standing committee. The standing committee alone determines policy, and once a policy decision is made, the party's belief in the concept of democratic centralism dictates that the decision must be followed by all party members.

MEMBERSHIP AND CONSTITUENCY
Support for the JCP is concentrated in major urban areas, and Communists have served as mayors of some of Japan's largest cities. The JCP has traditionally competed with the SDP for a share of the progressive votes, with (until recently) the SDP attracting relatively more voters. Following the LDP-SDP-Sakigake coali-

tion government, the JCP has since referred to itself as "the only opposition party," a move to attract those leftists in the SDP, moderates in the DPJ, and even some support from alienated former LDP backers. The JCP has about 400,000 members belonging to 25,000 branches.

POLICY
The JCP is the only one of Japan's major political parties that, at least ideologically and rhetorically, could be considered extremist. Among other policies, the JCP advocates a democratic revolution of the Japanese people against the rule of U.S. imperialism and a nationalization of the mass media. It also opposed nuclear weapons. In action, neither the party nor its members have displayed any radicalism or initiated any violence toward the existing social and political system. It is for this reason more than all others that the JCP is able to appeal to some members of the electorate whose primary party identification (if any) is for moderate or even conservative political parties. Some of the party's most distinctive positions, such as its call for abrogation of the United States–Japan Security Treaty, appear anachronistic and are clearly against the prevailing public sentiment.

PROSPECTS
After the collapse of the Soviet Union, the JCP—unlike other Communist parties, such as those in Europe—failed to enact any major changes in direction. This was largely because the Japan Socialist Party already had claims to the social democratic space that the JCP would have entered. This has left the JCP politically vulnerable.

Indeed, the JCP was decimated in the July 2004 Upper House elections, largely by the opposition DPJ. The Communists collapsed from 15 to 4 seats and lost all 7 of their district seats, mostly in urban prefectures. In the proportional ballot, the JCP lost 4 of 8 contested list seats.

Other Political Forces

GAIATSU

Gaiatsu literally means "pressure from outside" or, in other words, foreign governments applying political pressure on the Japanese government to change its policies. For example, most analysts recognize that *gaiatsu* had some degree of influence on Japan's rice issue, in which Japan was pressured to open its rice market to imported competition (particularly from the United States). These analysts disagree, however, on the extent to which *gaiatsu* contributed to the politicization of the rice issue and to the ultimate decision.

The influence of *gaiatsu* can be measured against the influence of the Japanese government. As far as the rice issue is concerned, some analysts argue that *gaiatsu* was weak and the Japanese government held its position not to open the rice market, and then did so only marginally. One reason that the Japanese government may have acceded is that the issue of food security is no longer so important to a generation that does not remember a Japan on the brink of starvation after World War II and in whose diet rice does not figure so prominently. On the whole, these commentators believe, the Japanese government seems to be stronger in many cases than is *gaiatsu* and cannot be bulldozed into action.

Other political observers argue that unless the Japanese government was confronted by periodic doses of *gaiatsu*, nothing would have changed in a status quo–seeking Japan. This camp therefore believes that a high degree of landmark legislation is attributable to the *gaiatsu* factor. Included among these significant policy shifts, they argue, were the decisions to liberalize Japan's rice market and to implement administrative and financial market reform (an initiative that, they claim, was the result of repeated foreign criticism of the difficulties of "doing business in Japan")—and even a movement toward understanding and admitting Japan's role in World War II.

BUREAUCRACY

For most of Japan's postwar history, civil servants—particularly those of the national government—were nearly revered for their abilities, generally beyond reproach for their steadfastness as public servants, and universally respected for the immense power that they commanded. Recently, however, the focus of reporting official corruption has shifted from politicians to civil servants. Together with a prolonged stagnation of Japan's economy, for which the bureaucracy was often attributed credit during economic prosperity, the bureaucracy has lost the public trust and is the target of administrative reform measures proposed at the national level.

The effects of the collapse of Japan's bubble economy of the late 1980s and early 1990s are still being felt. In 1996 the Diet passed legislation authorizing taxpayer funds to underwrite the bailout of seven *jusen* (housing-loan companies) saddled by billions of dol-lars worth of nonperforming loans. In the course of deliberations, it was revealed that more than a dozen former officials of the Ministry of Finance held leadership posts in these firms. In addition to the "*jusen* scandal, " other recent bureaucratic scandals involve the HIV-tainted blood dilemma, numerous cases involving officials at the Ministry of Finance, *amakudari* benefits awaiting civil servants shortly after retirement, and the perception of their less-than-transparent way of going about their duties or of describing their jobs.

Amakudari, literally "descent from heaven," refers to the practice of former civil servants, particularly those senior members of Japan's central government bureaucracy, receiving prestigious nongovernment posts in exchange for their contacts developed during their government careers. Recent legislation ruled that upon retirement, civil servants are prohibited from accepting employment in companies connected with their former ministries or agencies for two years, although this restriction can be waived if approval is granted by the National Personnel Authority.

Administrative reform is the contemporary buzzword in Japan, and all political parties have advocated it to a certain degree. Yet it is difficult to gauge how much of the drive is based, on the one hand, on a desire to decrease redundancy and inefficiency while increasing accountability and, on the other, on targeting a specific group of people who have found recent disfavor with the public.

National Prospects

Japan has the world's second largest economy, and its role on the world stage is considerable. It is a major international aid donor and a main source of global capital and credit. Moreover, in 2003, Prime Minister Koizumi deployed Japanese troops in Iraq following the U.S.-led invasion in 2003. The deployment divided public opinion, which many critics said violated the country's pacifist constitution.

But the move, seen as part of Koizumi's efforts to reshape Japan's foreign policy, could have consequences for many years to come. The government, and some elements of the public, recognize that Japan needs to continue to commit troops for the sake of its U.S.-Japan alliance, which affords the country protection against threats from neighboring China and North Korea.

Japan's relations with its neighbors are still heavily influenced by the legacy of Japanese actions before and during World War II. This is especially true of

Sino-Japanese ties, which are very chilly. Japanese and Chinese leaders have not reciprocated official visits, and they hold only occasional summits on the sidelines of international conferences in other countries. Ironically, Japan and China depend on each other for their prosperity. In fact, Japan's trade with China has surpassed that with the United States.

Japan's economy has been battered by repeated recession, deflation, and a long hangover from the collapse of its asset bubble in the early 1990s. The number of people gainfully employed has fallen, and unemployment exceeded 5 percent—a figure that would be considered excellent in many countries but was considered a disaster in Japan. Economic problems make people cautious about spending and hamper the performance of domestic companies.

Further Reading

Allinson, Gary D. *Japan's Postwar History*. Ithaca, N.Y.: Cornell University Press, 1997.

Beason, Dick, and Dennis Patterson. *The Japan That Never Was: Explaining the Rise and Decline of a Misunderstood Country*. Albany: State University of New York Press, 2004.

Gordon, Andrew. *The Modern History of Japan: From Tokugawa Times to the Present*. New York: Oxford University Press, 2003.

Hrebnar, Ronald J. *The Japanese Party System*. 2d ed. Boulder, Colo.: Westview Press, 1992.

Jain, Purnendra Jain, and Takashi Inoguchi, eds. *Japanese Politics Today: Beyond Karaoke Democracy?* New York: St. Martin's Press, 1997.

Johnson, Chalmers. *Japan: Who Governs? The Rise of the Developmental State*. New York: W. W. Norton, 1995.

Katz, Richard. "Helping Japanese Economic Reform." *Washington Quarterly* (autumn 2000): 135–53.

Kawashima, Yutaka. *Japanese Foreign Policy at the Crossroads: Challenges and Options for the Twenty-first Century*. Washington, D.C.: Brookings Institution Press, 2003.

Kohno, Masaru. *Japan's Postwar Party Politics*. Princeton, N.J.: Princeton University Press, 1997.

Lincoln, Edward J. "Japan: Using Power Narrowly." *Washington Quarterly* (winter 2003–2004): 111–27.

Masumi, Junnosuke. *Contemporary Politics in Japan*. Trans. Lonny E. Carlile. Berkeley: University of California Press, 1995.

McVeigh, Brian J. *Nationalisms of Japan: Managing and Mystifying Identity*. Lanham, Md.: Rowman and Littlefield, 2004.

Muramatsu, Michio. *Local Power in the Japanese State*. Berkeley: University of California Press, 1997.

Nathan, John. *Japan Unbound: A Volatile Nation's Quest for Pride and Purpose*. Boston: Houghton Mifflin, 2004.

Ozawa, Ichiro. *Blueprint for a New Japan*. Tokyo: Kodansha International, 1994.

Richardson, Bradley. *Japanese Democracy: Power, Coordination and Performance*. New Haven, Conn.: Yale University Press, 1997.

Sakakibara, Eisuke. *Structural Reform in Japan: Breaking the Iron Triangle*. Washington, D.C.: Brookings Institution Press, 2003.

Schwartz, Frank J., and Susan J. Pharr, eds. *The State of Civil Society in Japan*. New York: Cambridge University Press, 2003.

Tabb, William K. *The Postwar Japanese System*. New York: Oxford University Press, 1995.

Watanabe, Akio. "A Continuum of Change." *Washington Quarterly* (autumn 2004): 137–46.

HASHEMITE KINGDOM OF JORDAN

(al-Mamlaka al-Urduniyya al-Hashimiyya)

By Curtis R. Ryan, Ph.D.

Like many other postcolonial states in the Middle East, the Hashemite Kingdom of Jordan has largely artificial boundaries, drawn by European imperial powers, as the previous empire, that of the Ottoman Turks, collapsed in the wake of World War I. But since these inauspicious beginnings, what began as the British Mandate of Transjordan in 1921 evolved into the Emirate of Transjordan at the time of independence from Britain in 1946, and finally into its current form as the Hashemite Kingdom of Jordan since 1949. Jordan has, in short, evolved into a modern state that has long defied predictions of its imminent demise. The British installed two brothers of the House of Hashim, Abdullah and Faisal, respectively, in their mandates of Jordan and Iraq as a reward for Hashemite support in the Arab Revolt against the Ottoman Empire during World War I. The Hashemites originally hailed from the Hijaz area in what is today western Saudi Arabia but had been forcibly expelled by their Saudi rivals.

This kingdom of some 5.8 million people (2005 est.) is situated in southwest Asia and is bounded to the north by Syria, to the east by Iraq, to the south by Saudi Arabia, and to the west by Israel and the Palestinian territories. Given this location, Jordan was from the outset deeply involved in the various dimensions of the Palestinian-Israeli and broader Arab-Israeli conflicts. By the time of Jordanian independence in 1946, tensions were peaking in neighboring Palestine between Jews and Arabs over the issue of Zionist versus Palestinian aspirations to full statehood. The United Nations voted to partition Palestine between the two peoples in 1947,

and Israel declared its independence and statehood the following year. Within 24 hours several Arab armies had invaded the new state, joining fighting that had already begun between the two communities. One of these armies was Jordan's Arab Legion.

Following the Israeli victory and the tense peace that followed, Jordan continued to occupy the territory of the West Bank of the Jordan River (including East Jerusalem), formally annexing it in 1950. In July 1951 King Abdullah was assassinated by a Palestinian nationalist as he entered the Al Aqsa Mosque in Jerusalem. Abdullah was succeeded briefly by his son Talal, who was ultimately judged mentally unfit to rule and was in turn succeeded by his own son, Hussein, in 1953.

King Hussein's long reign (1953–99) was marked by a seemingly relentless succession of regional and domestic crises. In regional politics, further Arab-Israeli wars were fought in 1956, 1967, 1973, and 1982. Of these, the devastating Arab defeat in the 1967 Six-Day War was by far the most important for Jordan. For the Jordanians lost not only the war but also the entire territory of the West Bank—including East Jerusalem. In addition, tens of thousands of Palestinian refugees streamed into Jordan, joining those already there from the 1948 war. The large numbers of Palestinians in the kingdom led to recurrent domestic tensions between the Jordanian regular army and Palestinian guerrilla forces linked to the PLO. This spilled over into a bloody civil war in September 1970. King Hussein's bedouin-dominated army ultimately defeated and expelled the PLO forces and also pushed back an invasion force from Syria. But the legacy of tension remained decades later—between radical Arab nationalists and the conservative Hashemite regime and also between the Palestinian and "East Banker" Jordanian communities within the kingdom.

The Hashemite regime had for years maintained its claim to the West Bank and East Jerusalem, but in 1988 it renounced these claims and turned instead toward consolidating its rule east of the Jordan River. The kingdom remained under martial law from the time of the 1967 war until 1992, when it was lifted following the promulgation of a new National Charter in 1991 that aimed at creating more pluralism and political liberalization in Jordan while also ensuring that the country remains a Hashemite monarchy.

The System of Government

Jordan is a constitutional monarchy. The current constitution was established in 1952 during the brief reign of King Talal. The constitution gave increased authority to parliament, with executive power vested in the king, but ultimate authority over all branches of government is retained by the monarch. According to the Jordanian constitution, succession to the throne is guaranteed through the eldest male in direct line from King Abdullah I. Should there be no direct male heir, the eldest brother becomes king. On occasion, the king has altered this formula by decree. King Hussein, for example, maintained the line of succession from himself to his brother, Crown Prince Hasan, for more than 30 years, only changing it back to his eldest son weeks before the 1999 succession to Abdullah II.

EXECUTIVE

In accordance with the 1952 constitution, the king is head of state and government, with complete authority over the armed forces and power to appoint both the prime minister and cabinet. The king also has the authority to put laws into effect and to dissolve the legislature and call new elections. The prime minister is at least nominal head of government, appointed by the king, and in practice Jordanian prime ministers have selected their own cabinets subject to royal approval.

LEGISLATURE

Jordan has a bicameral legislature, divided between the 110-member House of Representatives (Majlis al-Nu'ab) and the 55-member House of Notables or Senate (Majlis al-Ayyan). Members of the lower house are elected by universal suffrage for four-year terms, while members of the Senate—the de facto upper house—are appointed directly by the king. The membership of the

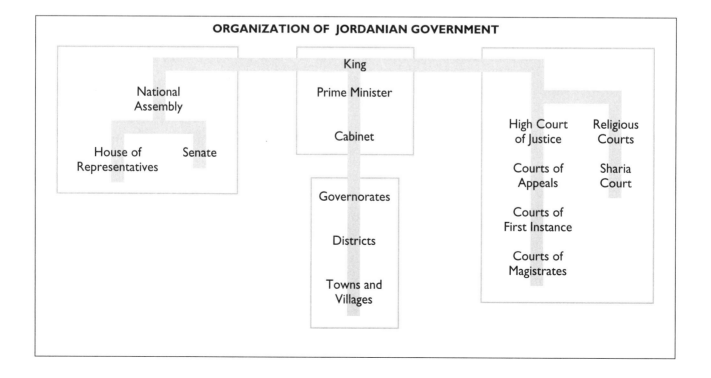

ORGANIZATION OF JORDANIAN GOVERNMENT

King

Prime Minister

Cabinet

National Assembly

House of Representatives   Senate

Governorates

Districts

Towns and Villages

High Court of Justice   Religious Courts

Courts of Appeals   Sharia Court

Courts of First Instance

Courts of Magistrates

House of Notables amounts to a veritable who's who (or who was who) of Jordanian politics.

Although the combined houses of the legislature can legally override the king's veto of any legislation, the fact that the entire Senate is made up of royal appointees effectively nullifies this as a threat to royal privilege.

JUDICIARY

The highest court in the kingdom is the High Court of Justice, centered in the capital, Amman. The court system includes a series of lower courts, including courts of appeals, courts of first instance, and courts of magistrates. In addition, and particularly in social and family matters, there are separate religious courts for the Muslim and Christian religious communities. Finally, in the rural areas of the kingdom, there are additional tribal courts for local bedouin affairs.

REGIONAL AND LOCAL GOVERNMENT

Jordan is divided into 12 provinces or governorates, each of which is headed by a governor and is further subdivided down to the level of the municipality. At that most local level, most municipalities are governed by two councils or—in the case of rural areas—by local Mukhtars, traditional village or tribal leaders.

The Electoral System

Full national parliamentary elections in Jordan only reemerged in 1989, following a more than two-decade hiatus in the wake of the 1967 war. The trigger event was the imposition of an IMF-sponsored economic austerity plan in April 1989 that led to the outbreak of rioting across the country. The riots, against both economic hardship and political corruption, prompted a shaken regime to respond with promises of elections and political reforms to begin that same year. The first of these elections took place in November 1989 and yielded a lower house of parliament in which both Islamist and secular leftist candidates were well represented.

By the time of the next round of elections, in November 1993, the regime had lifted martial law and its longstanding ban on political parties. More than a dozen newly legalized parties contested the 1993 elections, with the Islamists faring more poorly on their second attempt at national parliamentary power. This was due, in part, to a public backlash against unpopular Islamist legislation in the previous parliament but also to adjustments in the electoral law that limited each voter to one vote.

The previous electoral law had allowed voters to vote up to the number of representatives allotted for their district. Thus voters in Irbid in 1989 could vote for up to nine representatives from their city to the national parliament. In that election the Muslim Brotherhood, as the only organized group at the time, had run lists of candidates up to the exact number of seats for a district. In this way, they were able to exploit the plurality-based electoral system to gain representation well above their proportion of the overall vote. But in the 1993 elections almost the reverse happened, with the government closing that loophole and replacing it with the one-person one-vote law and also with adjusted new districts that disproportionately favored traditionally pro-Hashemite areas (such as rural rather than urban districts).

Voting rights in Jordan are universal for adults aged 18 or older. The franchise was extended to include women in 1973, but, since no new elections were held until 1989, women were unable to exercise their right to vote or run for office until that time. Within parliament, the regime reserved a number of seats for specific minority constituencies, all of which have traditionally been strong supporters of the Hashemite monarchy. These include nine seats for the rural bedouin, nine seats for the Christian community, and finally three seats for the Circassian and Chechen communities collectively. In 1993 one of the Circassian seats went to Tujan al-Faysal, the first woman in the House of Delegates. But even before that election, a number of grassroots organizations had formed that aimed to field more women candidates in the future and to mobilize blocs of women voters.

In 1997 the regime maintained its one-person one-vote formula for the electoral system, despite a threat by the opposition to boycott the election. Eleven opposition parties, led by the Islamic Action Front, chose to boycott the polls, while the regime chose to hold the elections anyway. The result, predictably, was a parliament filled with pro-regime legislators and very few opposition voices. After the death of King Hussein in 1999, the opposition hoped that the new king, Abdullah II, would be less conservative in his approach to political liberalization. But the next elections, due to be held in 2001, were repeatedly delayed by the new king, largely due to regional instability. Finally, after more than two years of delays, Jordan in June 2003 held national parliamentary elections in an effort to reengage its stalled political liberalization process. The 2003 elections were deemed especially important by both government and opposition. They were the first since 1997, the first since the dissolution of parliament in 2001, and the first under King Abdullah II.

In June 2003 the elections were finally held under still another electoral law. The new law, announced in July 2001, lowered the age of voting eligibility for men and women from 19 to 18, and increased the number of parliamentary seats from 80 to 104, with new (but still uneven) electoral districts. In February 2003 King Abdullah supplemented changes with a new decree adding six more parliamentary seats in a specific quota to ensure minimal representation for women. In the previous three elections (1989, 1993, and 1997) only one woman was elected to parliament: Tujan al-Faysal. The Islamic Action Front had originally registered its strong opposition to the women's quota, but then included for the first time a woman, Hayat al-Musayni, among its slate of 30 candidates. No Jordanian woman won a seat outright in 2003, but Musayni turned out to be the top vote-getter among women candidates overall. Ironically, therefore, the first woman seated in the new 2003–07 parliament was a conservative Islamist activist.

The Islamic Action Front succeeded in getting 17 of its party members elected (including Musayni). Aside from the IAF, five independent Islamists were also elected, including such high profile Islamists as Abd al-Munim Abu Zant, whom the IAF had expelled from membership just before the election. Most of the parliamentary seats, however, went to traditional tribal leaders or former government officials. At least 62 seats out of 110, in short, went to loyalist pro-regime figures.

The Party System

Jordan's monarchs had in the past experimented in limited ways with party systems, including a brief but fairly vibrant period in the 1950s, but each experiment ended in the state's curbing party activity. In 1957, for example, the state charged that military and party leaders were colluding in an attempt to overthrow King Hussein. This resulted in a ban on political parties that lasted for decades, aside for some brief state-directed experiments with forming loyalist parties. With the beginning of the political liberalization process in 1989, however, a new era emerged that would lead to the restoration of political parties and parliamentary life in Jordan.

With the legalization of political parties in 1992, dozens of new and old parties applied to the Ministry of the Interior for approval. Many of these were approved and went on to contest the 1993 elections. But in many ways the Jordanian party system remains fluid, with parties rising and falling, merging or splitting in two, as a result of electoral campaign fortunes or internal struggles over platform issues and party leadership.

Jordan's political parties can be discussed in two broad groupings: 1) leftist and pan-Arab nationalist parties (Jordanian Arab Progressive Ba'th Party, Jordanian Arab Socialist Ba'th Party, Jordanian Communist Party, Jordanian Democratic Popular Unity Party, Jordanian People's Democratic Party, and Jordanian United Democratic Party); and 2) centrist, conservative, and Islamist parties (Future Party, Islamic Action Front, National Constitutional Party).

Major Political Parties

JORDANIAN ARAB PROGRESSIVE BA'TH PARTY (JAPBP)

(Hizb al-Ba'th al-'Arabi al-Taqadumi al-Urduni)

One of two wings of the pan-Arab ad socialist Ba'th Party in Jordan, this wing is thought to be linked to Syria. The JAPBP has not been as successful in electoral politics as its pro-Iraqi counterpart, the Jordanian Arab Socialist Ba'th Party, but still draws support not just from Ba'thist sympathizers but sometimes also from Jordanians who favor stronger ties with Syria in general.

JORDANIAN ARAB SOCIALIST BA'TH PARTY (JASBP)

(Hizb al-Ba'th al-'Arabi al'Ishtiraki al-Urduni)

This second wing of the Ba'th Party in Jordan is said to be linked to Iraq and was blamed by the government for "inciting" the 1996 bread riots following the imposition of the IMF austerity program. Despite being singled out for such criticism, which had resulted in temporary arrests of numerous party officials, the JASBP did manage to win a seat in the 1997 elections to parliament. The JASBP was, therefore, one of few leftist opposition parties to actually contest the elections, disregarding the opposition boycott.

JORDANIAN COMMUNIST PARTY (JCP)

(Hizb al Shuyu'i al-Urduni)

The Jordanian Communist Party (JCP), recognized by the state in 1993 after an initial rejection, later lost many of its members to the other secular leftist parties such as the Jordanian United Democratic Party. Still, the JCP is one of the oldest parties in the kingdom and dates its roots to the late 1940s. The Communist Party maintains a radical stance toward most socioeconomic and political issues, has ties to its counterpart in Israel, and has openly supported a two-state solution to the Israeli-Palestinian conflict.

JORDANIAN DEMOCRATIC POPULAR UNITY PARTY (JDPUP)

(Hizb al-Wahda al-Sha'biyya al-Dimuqrati al-Urduni)

A Jordanian secular, leftist, and Arab nationalist party with ties to George Habash's Popular Front for the Liberation of Palestine (PFLP). The JDPUP became a legal party only in the 1990s, in accordance with the 1992 National Charter legalizing political parties, but it had operated as an underground party since the 1960s. Its policy stances closely correspond to those of the PFLP, including its opposition to the Palestinian and Jordanian peace negotiations with Israel.

JORDANIAN PEOPLE'S DEMOCRATIC PARTY

(Hizb al-Sha'b al-Dimuqrati al-Urduni)

Better known as "Hashd," this secular neo-Marxist party is affiliated with Nayef Hawatmeh's Democratic Front for the Liberation of Palestine (DFLP). Jut as the JDPUP corresponds closely to the PFLP, Hashd's policies strongly reflect those of its Palestinian counterpart, the DFLP. Before its legalization as a Jordanian political party in 1993, Hashd had been viewed by the government as virtually inseparable from the DFLP faction within the PLO. While opposed to what it views as the unfavorable terms of the Jordanian-Israeli Peace Treaty and the Israeli-PLO Accords, Hashd has stressed its support for a peace process in general. The party sees the current process, however, as slanted and unfair.

JORDANIAN UNITED DEMOCRATIC PARTY (JUDP)

(Hizb al-Dimuqrati al-Wahdawi al-Urduni)

In 1995 the JUDP emerged following the merger of several secular leftist and pan-Arab nationalist parties, with strong Palestinian roots. The JUDP is made up largely of pan-Arab nationalists and moderate former members of the Jordanian Communist Party (JCP). The party presents itself as a secular-left opposition force but is considerably more moderate than most other Jordanian leftist parties and has, for example, taken a moderate stance toward the Arab-Israeli peace process.

FUTURE PARTY

(Hizb al-Mustaqbal)

The Future Party is a pan-Arab nationalist and conservative party, usually well represented in parliament and even in cabinet posts. The party's leader, Sulayman Arar, was elected speaker of Jordan's lower house of parliament following the 1989 elections. In the 1997 electoral campaign, however, the Future Party surprised many on the Jordanian political scene by joining the opposition boycott of the elections.

ISLAMIC ACTION FRONT (IAF)

(Jabha al-'Amal al-Islami)

The main Islamist party in Jordan, the Islamic Action Front is the political wing of the Muslim Brotherhood. Before creating the IAF as a legal political party in 1992, the Muslim Brotherhood had been by far the kingdom's best-organized and most successful political grouping. In the 1989 elections, Islamists affiliated with the Brotherhood won 22 seats in parliament. They were so successful, in fact, that they prompted the regime to change the electoral law to the current one-person one-vote system. Despite their protests against this change, the newly formed IAF decided to compete in the 1993 elections, this time winning 16 seats. But in 1997 the IAF was one of the main parties leading the electoral boycott and thereby had no official representation in the 1997–2001 parliament (although several independent Islamists did win seats). The IAF is, in general, critical of the peace process and of Jordan's ties with the United States, but it has maintained a pro-monarchy stance as a "loyal opposition" party.

NATIONAL CONSTITUTIONAL PARTY

(Hizb al-Dusturi al-Urduni)

The NCP emerged only in 1997 following the merger of several other parties such as the Awakening Party (Hizb al-Yaqazah). The core of the National Constitutional Party, however, remained that of its main predecessor, the Pledge Party (Hizb al-'Ahd). The NCP presents itself as conservative and avowedly "pro-Jordanian" and draws support from Jordan's "tribal" communities as well as from numerous former ministers and army officers. The party advocates a Jordanian nationalism distinct from Jordan's Palestinian community. The NCP, in both its membership and party platform, is loyalist, and it is very much an establishment party. In the 1997 elections the NCP attempted to take advantage of the opposition electoral boycott to garner a core of parliamentary seats as the self-declared party of the regime. Its electoral performance, however, was less impressive, garnering only two of the 10 seats it officially contested.

Minor Political Parties

FREEDOM PARTY

(Hizb al-Huriyya)

Secular and leftist, the party advocates social democracy and a kind of reformed neo-Marxism. The Freedom Party is one of several small parties in Jordan that emerged in 1993 as offshoots of the Jordanian Communist Party.

JORDANIAN ARAB DEMOCRATIC PARTY (JADP)

(Hizb al-'Arabi al-Dimuqrati al-Urduni)

A secular leftist party supportive of Palestinian rights, it is critical of the peace treaty with Israel. The JADP experienced some electoral success in 1993, winning two seats in parliament, but since then has divided over the peace process. Some of this pro-Palestinian party's members supported the PLO's positions, including its accords with Israel, while others opposed the peace process in general.

JORDANIAN NATIONAL ALLIANCE PARTY

(Hizb al-Tajammu al-Watani al-Urduni)

This party is a conservative, pro-government, and pro-Hashemite party with strong roots in Jordan's bedouin communities.

NATIONAL PARTY

(Hizb al-Watan)

A conservative and usually proregime party, al-Watan leaders have been represented in Jordanian cabinet positions as well as parliament, although the party did oppose the regime's peace treaty with Israel.

PROGRESS AND JUSTICE PARTY

(Hizb al-Taqaddumi wa al-'Adl)

Progress and Justice is essentially a pro-government, centrist-to-conservative party that originally billed itself as economically liberal but socially conservative.

Other Political Forces

PROFESSIONAL ASSOCIATIONS

Given the 1997 electoral boycott by most opposition parties and the relative weakness in Jordan's still reemerging party system, political opposition shifted after 1997 to an institutional base in the kingdom's professional associations. These associations, particularly the Islamist-dominated engineers association, led the national campaign against normalization of relations with Israel. Other associations also organize along professional lines, with associations for pharmacists, journalists, medical doctors, and so on—and with similar levels of activism on domestic and foreign policy. While the state did try to reign in these organizations, the professional associations nonetheless provided a meaningful institutional vehicle for civil society in Jordan, especially during the absence from parliament (1997–2001) of most opposition parties.

MUSLIM BROTHERHOOD

The Muslim Brotherhood has long been the most organized political opposition group in Jordan. Even during the years when parties were banned, the Muslim Brotherhood was tolerated by the regime. As a result, when parliamentary elections resumed in 1989, the Muslim Brotherhood was the only really organized political force and used this to its advantage in the national elections that year. When the ban on political parties was lifted in 1992, the Islamic Action Front emerged as the political wing of the Muslim Brotherhood and as one of Jordan's most successful political parties. Unlike the mutual hostility that characterizes the relationship between Islamists and the state in neighboring Syria, the Muslim Brotherhood and

Hashemite monarchy have had a decades-long relationship of "peaceful coexistence."

MILITARY

As early as the foiled coup attempt of 1957, King Hussein relied on the loyalty of his armed forces to thwart serious challenges to his rule. The military was then composed almost entirely of bedouin and other "East Bank" Jordanians loyal to the Hashemite regime. Today, the army is still a bedrock constituency for the monarchy but represents a broader range of the population ever since the institution of the draft in the early 1970s.

PALESTINIANS

Estimates of the size of the Palestinian population in Jordan vary widely, anywhere from 50 percent to 60 percent of the overall population. Some still live in refugee camps, while others have more fully integrated into Jordanian economic and political life. The rift between Palestinian and Jordanian communities within Jordan tends to be exaggerated, overlooking the many overlaps between families and the number of Jordanians of Palestinian origin who are key parts of the political elite. But some level of difference does remain a source of tension, leading to charges of Jordanian domination of the public sector or of Palestinian domination of the private sector.

FOREIGN NATIONS

Throughout its existence as an independent state, the Hashemite Kingdom of Jordan has remained deeply dependent on economic assistance from external patrons. Originally, the kingdom's main ally in this regard was the United Kingdom. But since the 1960s the role of the United States and of Arab Gulf monarchies became increasingly important to the economic survival of the kingdom. In addition to these critical external aid linkages, the kingdom remains vulnerable to pressures on its domestic politics from its many powerful neighbors—in particular Syria, Iraq, and Israel.

National Prospects

The decade of the 1990s was traumatic for Jordan, beginning with the Gulf crisis over Iraq's invasion of Kuwait. Even before that, however, the kingdom had been rocked by riots over price increases and political corruption in April 1989. With the onset of the Gulf crisis and the war that followed, Jordan attempted to maintain its political and economic alignment with Iraq, while opposing the annexation of Kuwait and trying to mediate the crisis. As the crisis steadily tumbled toward war, Jordan's fence straddling was viewed as betrayal by Kuwait, Saudi Arabia, and the Western-led coalition—in particular, Jordan's key ally, the United States. The price for Jordan's Gulf crisis stand was the abrupt cutoff in economic aid from the Gulf monarchies and the United States and the expulsion from Saudi Arabia and Kuwait (after the war) of more than 300,000 Palestinians and Jordanians. These Gulf "returnees" put tremendous strain on Jordan's social services and housing sector, but ultimately the kingdom managed to weather the crisis and eventually even restored its diplomatic links (and hence its foreign aid connections) to the United States and the Gulf states. This diplomatic success was due in part to Jordan's participation in the U.S.-sponsored Middle East peace negotiations that began in Madrid in 1991. Following the surprise announcement of an Israeli-PLO accord in 1993, Jordan quickly concluded a full peace treaty with Israel in 1994. The regime appeared to rush well ahead of its populace in doing so, possibly banking on an expected financial windfall based on full economic relations with Israel and also on financial rewards from Western states. The windfall, however, never took place, and domestic discontent over the peace treaty mounted steadily, especially following the election of hard-line prime minister Benjamin Netanyahu in Israel in 1996.

Domestic anger spilled over into unrest in August 1996, when the regime implemented its second IMF-sponsored austerity program. As in 1989, riots broke out in Karak, Ma'am, and elsewhere. The 1996 riots, however, were not quite as widespread or violent as those of seven years earlier. They did, nonetheless, demonstrate clearly the level of public dissatisfaction over key issues of state policy—from economic reform to the pace of political liberalization to foreign policy issues such as Jordan's relations with Israel.

In response to mounting criticism, the regime backpedaled in the process of political liberalization by issuing a new set of restrictive guidelines for the press. Jordan's print and television media had opened up considerably since the reform process began in 1989, yielding one of the most open societies in the Arab world. For that reason, however, the regime's media restrictions were regarded by many in the kingdom as draconian. As the Oslo peace process began to collapse, domestic disaffection increased within Jordan and 11 opposition parties, led by the Islamic Action Front, organized a boycott of the November 1997 parliamentary elections. The opposition demanded that the electoral law be changed, that press freedoms be restored, and that normalization with Israel cease. None of these demands were met by election day, and so the elected Jordanian parliament included few members of either the Islamist or leftist opposition. Instead, with most of Jordan's parties sitting out the electoral process, the new parliament was tilted heavily toward conservative pro-regime figures. Thus, although the regime could expect to deal with a far more pliant parliament, it did so at the cost of setting back the minimal gains that had been made in Jordan's program of political liberalization.

The political liberalization process, along with the economic adjustment program and the peace treaty with Israel, were all meant to erase questions about the political future of Jordan and its monarchy. But as the kingdom entered the 21st century, profound questions remained about each of these areas of concern. In addition, the kingdom also faced the question of what would happen after King Hussein passed from the scene. At least in legal and constitutional terms, there had been no real "question" of succession since the king's brother, Hasan, had been crown prince for more than 30 years and was therefore the designated successor to Hussein. But in January 1999 the king surprised many observers by changing the succession and appointing his first-born son, Abdullah, to be his successor rather than Hasan. Thus what had seemed a relatively clear question of succession had instead become far more controversial. But with the death of King Hussein in February 1999, Abdullah ascended to the throne of Jordan, and in his first official act, appointed his half-brother Hamza crown prince. Yet even with this transition, the dominant questions in Jordanian politics continued to be about economic restructuring, political liberalization, and peace with Israel.

Almost immediately after the succession, the new king continued the electoral process through countrywide municipal elections in 1999. These elections even saw the return of many in the opposition who had boycotted the 1997 national parliamentary elections, suggesting that both regime and opposition were again pursuing the course of political reform. But the more important elections—the parliamentary elections scheduled for 2001—were repeatedly postponed. The myriad reasons included violence and unrest in Palestine to the west, and in Iraq to the east, as well as difficulties completing a newer system of electronic voting cards. But in 2003 the long delayed elections did finally take place, including full participation by the large Islamist movement as well as leftist and nationalist parties.

Prior to the polls, King Abdullah's government established a new electoral law, changing parliament from 80 to 110 seats, and later new legislation guaranteed women at least six seats in parliament. The regime returned to political liberalization, but only slowly and cautiously. In the atmosphere of the intifada and the Iraq war, for example, constraints on civil society—and specifically on the rights to organize public demonstrations or to question Jordan's foreign policy positions—have been severely circumscribed. To be clear, the regime program, symbolized accurately by its own slogan "Jordan First" (*al-Urdun Awalan*), has prioritized realignment in foreign policy as well as economic development in domestic policy. Domestic political reform has taken a back seat to both priorities, and has frequently suffered as a result. By 2004 the Palestinian uprising against Israeli occupation had entered its fourth year, while Iraq resistance to U.S. occupation also increased in intensity and violence. With continuing conflict between Israel and the Palestinians and sustained resistance to U.S. occupation in Iraq, Jordan was pressed between these unstable situations, as King Abdullah II attempted to respond to demands for more political reform at home while also steering the kingdom through a particularly difficult time in regional politics.

Further Reading

Brand, Laurie A. *Jordan's Inter-Arab Relations: The Political Economy of Alliance* Making. New York: Columbia University Press, 1994.

Brynen, Rex. "Economic Crisis and Post-Rentier Democratization in the Arab World: The Case of Jordan." *Canadian Journal of Political Science* 25, no. 1 (1992).

Day, Arthur R. *East Bank/West Bank: Jordan and the Prospects for Peace.* New York: Council on Foreign Relations, 1986.

Lynch, Marc. *State Interests and Public Spheres: The International Politics of Jordan's Identity.* New York: Columbia University Press, 1999.

Massad, Joseph. *Colonial Effects: The Making of National Identity in Jordan.* New York: Columbia University Press, 2001.

Nevo, Joseph, and Ilan Pappe. *Jordan in the Middle East 1948-1988: The Making of a Pivotal State.* Portland, Ore.: Frank Cass, 1994.

Robinson, Glenn E. "Defensive Democratization in Jordan." *International Journal of Middle East Studies* 30, no. 3 (August 1998): 387–410.

Ryan, Curtis R. "Elections and Parliamentary Democratization in Jordan." *Democratization* 5, no. 4 (winter 1998): 194–214.

———. "Jordan in the Middle East Peace Process: From War to Peace with Israel." In *The Middle East Peace Process.* Ed. Ilan Peleg. New York: State University of New York Press, 1997.

———. *Jordan in Transition: From Hussein to Abdullah.* Boulder, Colo.: Lynne Rienner, 2002.

———. "Peace, Bread, and Riots: Jordan and the I.M.F." *Middle East Policy* 6, no. 2 (fall 1998): 54–66.

Wiktorowicz, Quintan. *The Management of Islamic Activism: Salafis, the Muslim Brotherhood, and State Power in Jordan.* Albany: State University of New York Press, 2000.

Wilson, Mary C. *King Abdullah, Britain and the Making of Jordan.* Cambridge: Cambridge University Press, 1987.

REPUBLIC OF KAZAKHSTAN

(Kazakhstan Respublikasy)

By Roger D. Kangas, Ph.D.

Kazakhstan is located in the heart of Central Asia, just south of Russia and west of China. It is 2,717,300 square kilometers in size and has a population of 15 million (2005 est.). Given the high numbers of Russians, Germans, and Ukrainians who have left the country since independence in 1991, the population is actually smaller now than it was a decade ago.

The System of Government

Kazakhstan is a republic with a strong president, as outlined in the 1995 revised constitution. The country has a bicameral legislature.

EXECUTIVE

Like the other Central Asian states, Kazakhstan possesses a very strong president. Nursultan Nazarbayev has been president since independence, making a seamless transition from Communist Party of Kazakhstan's first secretary (appointed in 1989) to independent president. Nazarbayev was elected president of independent Kazakhstan on December 1, 1991, running unopposed. A referendum held on April 30, 1995, extended his mandate until the year 2000, preempting a 1996 scheduled election. The reported support for the referendum was 95 percent of eligible voters—a figure disputed by international observers. In October

1998 President Nazarbayev revised the constitution, eliminating the age and term limits on presidents and making terms of office seven years. He called for an early election to be held on January 10, 1999, which he promptly won with almost 80 percent of the vote.

As with the other Central Asian leaders, Nazarbayev has been able to successfully consolidate his authority. According to the most recent constitution (August 1995), the president has the authority to appoint and dismiss judges, cabinet ministers, senators, regional officials, and other bureaucrats in the government. In addition, he can call referenda at any time, can issue presidential decrees, and is responsible for all treaties and foreign negotiations. In sum, like the other Central Asian states, Kazakhstan has a strong, centralized presidential system.

The other executive is the prime minister, who has, in the past, played an important role in carrying out Nazarbayev's policies. This was especially true when the legislature was not in session, as during the 1995 dissolution of that body. At that time the prime minister, Akezhan Kazhegeldin, was in charge of implementing the president's domestic policies. It became apparent in 1997 that Nazarbayev was dissatisfied with his prime minister; he replaced him on October 10, 1997, with the former oil and gas minister Nurlan Balgimbayev. This is representative of the problems facing the "second executive" in Kazakhstan: Kazhegeldin was actually trying to wield his own authority and was also gaining a power base independent of the president. It seems that internal politics, more so than the stated "health reasons," prompted his resignation. Since that time a loyal subordinate to the president has generally held the office of prime minister. Over time, the prime minister position has evolved into more of a managerial position within the government, acting as a "chief of staff" for the executive cabinet. As of 2005 the prime ministership was held by Daniyal Akhmetov.

LEGISLATURE

Kazakhstan has a bicameral legislature consisting of the 39-member Senat (Senate) and 77-member Majlis (Assembly). The country has had three different legislatures in its short existence as an independent state. In 1991 the Soviet-era Supreme Soviet took on the role of legislature in the country, although it was dissolved in 1994 to accommodate the new constitutional arrangement. In that year elections were held for a 177-seat legislature. These elections were considered multiparty but, because of voting irregularities, were not considered free and fair by international observers. In spite of efforts by Nazarbayev to control the elections, his parties failed to gain a majority of the seats, and the 1994 legislature quickly began to assert its authority vis-à-vis Nazarbayev.

Because of an instance of "voter irregularity" in one district, the Kazakhstani Constitutional Court declared the entire 1994 election invalid on March 6, 1995. As a result, Nazarbayev dissolved the legislature five days later. A caretaker government under then prime minister Kazhegeldin took over for most of 1995, until a new constitution could be implemented and new elections called. It was at this time that Nazarbayev called for his own term extension and, on August 30, held another referendum on his new constitution, which outlined the current bicameral legislature structure. This referendum received slightly less support than the term extension, garnering only 89 percent of all eligible voters.

The powers of the current legislature are weak; it is nothing more than a rubber-stamp organization. While the members can challenge presidential legislation, they cannot address his decrees, effectively allowing the president and his cabinet to circumvent legislative oversight. In principle, the upper house represents the regions and regional governments, with the lower house representing the people. Surveys conducted by the U.S.-based group IFES (International Foundation for Election Systems) reveal that most Kazakhstani citizens cannot even name their legislator or senator and base their knowledge of politics on Nazarbayev's speeches and policies.

The Majlis held its first elections on December 9, 1995, with runoff elections in January and February 1996. It is important to note that a number of parties did not participate in the elections, protesting the 1995 annulment of the legislature. Elections were held again for the lower house on September 19, 2004 (with runoff elections on October 3, 2004). As these are for five-year terms, the next elections are not scheduled until 2009. In the Majlis, the pro-presidential parties have an overwhelming majority: the Fatherland Party (Otan) currently holds 42 seats, the Agrarian Party–Civic Party coalition (AIST) has 11, All Together (Asar) has 4, and Bright Path (Ak Zhol) and the Democratic Party each have one seat. Independent candidates, many with ties to Otan, occupy the remaining 18 seats.

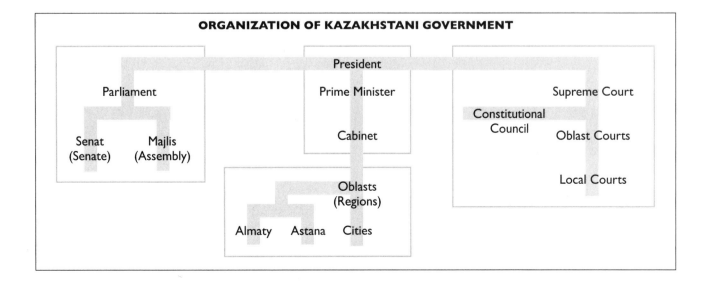

ORGANIZATION OF KAZAKHSTANI GOVERNMENT

President

Parliament

Prime Minister

Supreme Court

Constitutional Council

Senat (Senate) Majlis (Assembly)

Cabinet

Oblast Courts

Oblasts (Regions)

Local Courts

Almaty Astana Cities

JUDICIARY

The Supreme Court with 44 members oversees the constitutionality of laws and is the highest court of appeal in the country. The Court has not been active enough to give a fair assessment of its independence and position on issues. However, the fact that all justices are appointed by the president for fixed terms means that, most likely, the judiciary is subservient to the president. The 1995 constitutional crisis strongly supported this belief. There is also a Constitutional Council, consisting of seven members.

REGIONAL AND LOCAL GOVERNMENT

Up until 1997 Kazakhstan comprised 19 regions (*oblasts*) and the city of Almaty. A number of the *oblasts* have been merged into larger entities, bringing the total number down to 14; the municipal districts of Almaty and Astana each have their own councils. Various reasons have been given for reduction in the number of *oblasts*, including the need to control regional clan groups. Most likely, this streamlining is a way to more effectively control regional governments in general, particularly the *oblasts* in Russian-dominated northern Kazakhstan, where the mergers have taken place. Each province has its own legislature (Maslihat) and executive (Akim). Then former are chosen through regional election, and the latter are appointed by the president. Each Akim is also allowed to appoint a consultative body, much like the president's cabinet. Because the planning system is centralized, regional governments are largely dependent upon the central government for financial assistance. Terms are fixed for each of these officeholders at four years, although it is not uncommon for an Akim to be replaced by the president more frequently.

Kazakhstan also has a system of *mahallas,* or communal governments, that resemble rural township and urban district politics in the former Soviet system. Like the oblast governments, however, the *mahallas* have little power in the way of budgetary oversight.

The Electoral System

Kazakhstan uses three types of electoral systems in the executive and legislative branches. The presidency is determined through a nationwide election with the winner needing 50 percent plus one of the votes to win. Failing that, the top two vote getters participate in a run-off election shortly after the first vote. Nazarbayev ran unopposed in the December 1991 election. In the January 1999 race he did allow three challengers: the Communist Party chief, Serkbolsyn Abdildin, who won 13.5 percent of the vote, and two minor figures who received 4.3 percent and less than 1 percent, respectively. Nazarbayev himself received 78.3 percent of the vote. As the presidency now has a seven-year term, Nazarbayev does not have to face the voters again until 2006.

The Majlis is based on single-member districts (77) with the same 50-percent-plus-one requirement noted above. In addition, for an election to be considered valid, at least 50 percent of the electorate must participate. The Senat races are determined in two ways: 32 seats are selected via indirect elections with the legislatures of the 14 *oblasts* and the cities of Almaty and Astana each selecting 2 senators; the president is able to appoint 7 on his own.

The Party System

ORIGINS OF THE PARTIES

As with the other post-Soviet states, Kazakhstan's party system is a result of two phenomena: the Communist Party and the social organizations that emerged in the late 1980s to counter Communist Party activity. The current Kazakhstani constitution allows for opposition parties, as long as they are registered with the state.

THE PARTIES IN LAW

The current law on political parties requires that any political party that wants to register must have at least 50,000 registered members and a minimum of 70 in each province of the country. This was a change from the previous (1995) law that only required 3,000 signatories for a party registration form. Article 51 of the constitution further outlines requirements on eligibility of legislators, including residency status, language abilities, and age.

PARTY ORGANIZATION

Political parties in Kazakhstan resemble, in most ways, the structure of the former Communist Party of Kazakhstan (KPK), which differentiated between the *nomenklatura* and the masses. The former were/are the political elite within the party that held top offices, while the latter were in shop-floor groups, rural associations, and other local-level structures, called primary party organizations (PPOs). Above this level, the KPK was based on councils (*sovety*) and executive branch associations (*buro*) that operated at the district (*raion*), regional (*oblast*) and republic levels. This top level was seen in the KPK party congress, political bureau, and secretariat, which was headed by the first secretary. The current political parties in Kazakhstan bear a striking resemblance to this structure, particularly Otan and the Communists, which are in many ways the heirs to the defunct KPK.

CAMPAIGNING

Campaigning in Kazakhstan has been lackluster at best. The presidential contest of 1991 was a one-candidate affair, so any campaign advertisements and rallies were for Nazarbayev only. The legislative campaign of 1994 did see a brief flurry of activity among the opposition parties. However, the annulment of that legislature and the creation of a new body in 1995 severely weakened any trend in fostering open elections. The combination of a short electoral season in December 1995 and the fact that a number of opposition parties opted not to participate (or could not, because they were not registered) meant that, once again, voters saw little in the way of campaigning.

In the early 2000s opposition parties have tried to pressure the media into granting more equal coverage of the campaigns. In the 2004 Majlis elections there was a modest amount of campaign literature distributed and efforts to make the voting population aware of different views. Ultimately, international organizations criticized the election on both the unfair amount of "pro-government" coverage and the inability of true opposition parties to be able to register (and thus participate in the election).

INDEPENDENT VOTERS

Since party identification is still weak in Kazakhstan, it is difficult to assess the role of independent voters in the country. With most votes going to Otan party members, or "independents" supportive of that party, it can be assumed that the Soviet-era trend of supporting the major political party remains.

Major Political Parties

FATHERLAND PARTY

(Otan)

HISTORY

Founded in March 1999, Otan is really the result of a gradual evolution of the pro-Nazarbayev elite in Kazakhstan that can be traced back to the *nomenklatura* of the

Communist Party of Kazakhstan. As the Soviet Union was breaking up, Nazarbayev remained loyal to the Communist Party of Kazakhstan, although in August 1991 he had the party renamed the "Socialist Party of Kazakhstan." In October 1991 he attempted to merge the various social organizations present in the country into a "People's Congress," which was headed by the writers Olzhas Suleymanov and Mukhtar Shakhanov. However, these individuals often openly expressed their opposition to the president, and eventually this organization ran afoul of Nazarbayev. His third attempt at establishing a pro-presidential party was the Party of People's Unity of Kazakhstan (Partiya Narodnoye Edinstvo Kazakhstana; PNEK) in 1993.

The PNEK carried Nazarbayev's banner from 1993 to 1999. At that time, and perhaps in an effort to break from some potential political rivals, Nazarbayev switched his loyalty to the organization Otan. It has had several chairmen since its founding, all of whom profess loyalty to President Nazarbayev. With over 300,000 members, it is clearly the largest and most significant political party in Kazakhstan.

ORGANIZATION

Otan, as noted above, parallels the traditional party structure of the former Communist Party of Kazakhstan. There is a central administration based in the capital of Astana and *oblast* headquarters in each region.

MEMBERSHIP

Membership is based on a probationary-status system with required sponsorship of a current member. As of 2005 there were an estimated 300,000 registered members. Perhaps reflecting the post-Soviet reality in the country, party membership is not necessarily viewed as essential to upward mobility. That and the fact that Nazarbayev himself is at least publicly distanced from the party system may be seen as an explanation as to why membership figures are not higher.

POLICY

Otan is openly supportive of Nazarbayev's reform agenda and is viewed as the most pro-government party in the political spectrum. On paper, it supports a market economy, state control of the energy export industries, and the maintenance of the social welfare system. In the area of foreign policy, it supports ties with Russia while at the same time exploring relations with other regional states. This is the result of the fact that Kazakhstan shares a lengthy border with Russia and must be on good terms with this neighbor to the north.

FINANCING

Technically, "Otan" gets no funding from the government. Instead, it raises its money through membership dues.

LEADERSHIP

The chairman as of 2005 is Gani Yesimov, although most experts consider Nazarbayev himself to be the unofficial leader of the party. Technically, since Article 5 of the constitution prohibits government officials from being party leaders, Nazarbayev is forced to play this shadow role.

PROSPECTS

As long as Nazarbayev remains in power, Otan will most likely remain one of the strongest parties in Kazakhstan. Public opinion polls suggest a strong recognition of the party, as compared with others. In addition, its infrastructural support will ensure continued existence. The only problem it may face is if Nazarbayev further distances himself from the party in an effort to present himself as completely above party politics. This seems unlikely at present, given the valuable support Otan gives the president.

Minor Political Parties

The rest of the party spectrum in Kazakhstan can be considered a collection of minor parties. While there are a number of parties registered, technically making Kazakhstan a multiparty system, these tend to be limited in membership, leadership, and scope. Indeed, some are really nothing more than organizations supporting a particular political leader's opposition to Nazarbayev. Political parties in Kazakhstan are still in a state of flux and often revolve around a single individual leader. Over the past decade countless parties have emerged and then disappeared from the stage.

ALL TOGETHER

(Asar)

This party was founded by Dariga Nazarbayev, the daughter of the president, in late 2003 (officially registered on December 19, 2003). Asar's political platform emphasizes the development of a free market economy in the country and the "proper use" of energy profits, that is, for social development and pensions. More importantly, this party is seen as a potential vehicle through which Dariga Nazarbayev could launch a successful career on the way to being president. Thus, observers note that this party could develop into a serious force in the coming years. The party focuses on the younger generation of voters, with over half of the members between 25 and 35 years old. It is reported to have a membership of 177,000.

CIVIC PARTY OF KAZAKHSTAN

(Qazaqstan Azamattlyk Partiyasi)

Under the leadership of Azat Peruashev, the Civic Party is also deemed a "loyal opposition" organization to the president. With over 160,000 members this party is actually the third largest in the country.

AGRARIAN PARTY OF KAZAKHSTAN

(Qazaqstan Agrarlyk Partiyasi)

This party parallels the Aul Social Democratic Party, as most of the 100,000 registered members are from rural regions. Romin Madinov founded it in January 1999 (and registered it in March of that year). For the 2004 Majlis elections, the Agrarian Party and the Civic Party formed a bloc named AIST (Agrarian Party–Civic Party Bloc) and ran a combined ticket. This bloc is currently the second most important entity in the legislature, after Otan.

BRIGHT PATH

(Ak Zhol)

This party was founded by individuals who had expressed real opposition to the president while members of the Democratic Choice of Kazakhstan (DCK). It registered in 2002 and has since provided some criticism of the president. It purports to represent the interests of business and commerce in the country, and many of its nearly 150,000 members are supposedly from the business class.

PATRIOTS PARTY OF KAZAKHSTAN

Under the leadership of Gani Kasymov, this party was registered in mid-2000 and remains active in Kazakhstani politics. It has a membership of 132,000, about a third of whom are war veterans.

VILLAGE SOCIAL DEMOCRATIC PARTY

(Auyl Sotsial-Demokratiyalyk Partiyasi; Auyl)

Under the leadership of Gani Kaliev, Auyl was registered in the spring of 2000. A key component of this party's membership consists of farmers and rural residents.

COMMUNIST PARTY OF KAZAKHSTAN

(Kommunisticheskaya Partiya Kazakhstana; KPK)

This party was formed in September 1991 by members who opposed the reformist position of the other successor party to the Soviet-era KPK, the Socialist Party of Kazakhstan (SPK). Legally registered in March 1994, the KPK has had some difficulty in remaining a political force in Kazakhstan. For instance, the Ministry of Justice attempted to have the party banned because it favored reunification of the Soviet Union. Faced with this challenge, the KPK revised its platform to be more supportive of Kazakhstani independence. Nevertheless, it is still seen as a party that favors close ties with the other members of the Commonwealth of Independent States (CIS). In addition, the KPK's platform includes maintaining state control of most of the economy as well as the continuation of the Soviet-era welfare state.

The party faced serious problems in early 2004 when the leadership split over charges of financial mismanagement. As for membership, the Communist Party is holding at 70,000 members. An offshoot party—the Communist People's Party of Kazakhstan—also claims to have 70,000 members, although it is less visible in the country.

PEOPLE'S CONGRESS OF KAZAKHSTAN

(Narodnyi Kongress Kazakhstana; NKK)

This was seen as one of the first real opposition parties to the SPK or KPK when it was founded in the fall of 1991. Headed by the popular writer Olzhas Suleymanov, the NKK at least initially had the backing of President Nazarbayev. However, the party's periodic criticisms of the president, as well as its growing popularity, prompted the president to part ways with Suleymanov. In August 1995 Suleymanov was appointed ambassador to Italy, effectively removing him from Kazakhstani domestic politics. The party won nine seats in the 1994 election, but it did not participate in the 1995 elections. The People's Congress lost its registration in the early 2000s. Efforts to regain legitimacy have been thwarted, generally on administrative and technical grounds.

DEMOCRATIC CHOICE OF KAZAKHSTAN

(Qazaqstannyn Demokratiyalyk Tandau)

This party remains associated with Galymzhan Zhakianov, the former Akim of Pavlodar who fell out of favor with the government in the early 2000s and was imprisoned for economic crimes; he was released from prison in 2004 and sent into internal exile. This party was founded in February 2004 and purported to have nearly 90,000 members. However, in early 2005 the Supreme Court ordered it to dissolve because of the party's actions in protesting the fairness of the 2004 elections.

Other Political Forces

ETHNIC MINORITIES

Without question, the strong Russian and non-Kazakh minority in the country will remain a significant force in the near future. Even if ethnic Kazakhs reach 60 percent of the total population, as is predicted (they totaled 53 percent as of 1999, the most recent census), the fact that there is a significant minority in the country suggests that the government will always have to be mindful of this force. The most significant minority population in Kazakhstan are Russian, at 30 percent of the Kazakhstani population. Living primarily along the Russo-Kazakhstani border, the Russians have expressed great concern about being "second-class citizens" in Kazakhstan. In particular, there have been vociferous debates over the language laws, which state that Kazakh is the official language of the republic, as well as the language taught in primary and secondary schools.

Nearly 20 percent Kazakhstan is made up of nearly 100 other listed minority groups, most of them too small to be of political importance. The exceptions are the Uighurs, Uzbeks, and Germans. The Uighurs are a Turkic minority that straddles the Sino-Kazakhstani border and is more heavily represented in the People's Republic of China. The Uighurs have been a source of protests and concern in China over the past decade, and as these demonstrations increase in intensity, the PRC has become most concerned over what happens in Kazakhstan. This issue has become so sensitive that President Nazarbayev has banned several Uighur-language newspapers and does not allow political movements advocating Uighur rights to register, although several are reported to exist in Kazakhstan.

Finally, the German population represents a continuing trend for the ethnic minorities in Kazakhstan. The unification of Germany in 1990, combined with the opening of the former Soviet borders the following year, has resulted in a significant outmigration of ethnic Germans to Germany. German immigration to the Kazakh territories actually began during the czarist period, with the most significant inflow taking place in 1944 with the deportation of Volga Germans to Kazakhstan. In 1989 the German population in Kazakhstan was over 1 million. As a result of the outmigration, the population decreased by almost 50 percent, and it is now estimated that there are fewer than 600,000 ethnic Germans in Kazakhstan. Their importance, as well as that of ethnic Poles and Koreans, is that they are seen as links to these foreign countries and foundations for economic trade in the region. On the other hand, the emigration of these peoples also underscores the problems of Kazakh nationalism and the attempt to build a multiethnic Kazakhstani state.

Unlike the neighbors to the south, such as Uzbekistan and Tajikistan, Kazakhstan does not have a reputation for possessing a large, Islamic extremist threat. Indeed, the secular nature of Kazakhstani society and the multifaith environment in the country suggests that Islamic extremism will not be a concern for the country overall. Some Islamic groups may be active in southern Kazakhstan in the Shymkent region, but they are isolated.

National Prospects

The political future of Kazakhstan is open to some variation, although if Nazarbayev can maintain his hold on power, there should be no change at the top. However, unlike the situation in most other Central Asian states, there are legitimate challengers to his authority and potential coalition partners who would like nothing better than to defeat Nazarbayev in an open and fair election. One challenger, former prime minister Akezhan Kazhegeldin, was accused of illegal activities and thus prohibited from participating in the January 1999 presidential election. As a result, Nazarbayev was assured of an easy victory. In the early 2000s other potential challengers were also eliminated. For instance, Galymzhan Zhakianov of Democratic Choice was imprisoned in 2002; he was released in 2004 but placed in internal exile. In November 2005 another vocal critic of Nazarbayev, Zamanbek Nurkadilov, was found shot to death in his home.

A good deal of Nazarbayev's authority—and ability to stay in power—will increasingly be linked to his ability to turn the economy around and realize profits from energy exports. While he can pin the blame on others (as with former prime minister Kazhegeldin), such reasoning will eventually fall on deaf ears. Combining the ongoing tensions in the international energy market and the fact that the energy fields in Kazakhstan are beginning to realize their promise means that Kazakhstan should begin to profit from this natural resource. International companies are increasingly engaged in the new fields of Kashagan, for example, and pipeline routes continue to dominate the geopolitical discussions of the country. The question remains, though, whether the population as a whole will experience these benefits and thus acquiesce to the limited political opportunities in the country.

Further Reading

"Kazakhstan." *Nations in Transit 2004*. Available online. URL: http://www.freedomhouse.org/research/nattransit.htm (accessed November 17, 2005).

Kazakhstan Report on Human Rights 2004. Washington, D.C.: U.S. Department of State, 2005.

Olcott, Marthat Brill. "Democratization and the Growth of Political Participation in Kazakhstan." In *Conflict, Cleavage, and Change in Central Asia and the Caucasus*. Ed. Karen Dawisha and Bruce Parrott. Cambridge: Cambridge University Press, 1997.

———. *Kazakhstan: Unfulfilled Promise*. Washington, D.C.: Carnegie, 2002.

REPUBLIC OF KENYA
(Djumhuri ya Kenya)

By Andrei I. Maximenko
Revised by Thomas P. Wolf, Ph.D.

The Republic of Kenya, a nation of about 34 million people (2005 est.), lies astride the equator on the east coast of Africa. As in much of the continent, the population figure represents nearly a threefold increase since independence some 40 years ago.

While Kenya was generally characterized as an economic success during its first two decades of independence, subsequent stagnation combined with relentless population growth (notwithstanding the more recent HIV/AIDS plague) has kept an increasing proportion of its population in dire poverty. The plague itself makes a substantial contribution to this poverty, having produced over 800,000 AIDS orphans by 2005.

Approximately 56 percent of the population lives in conditions that reflect income below the official poverty line. By 2002 just 10 percent of the population was earning 52 percent of total national income. Such a distribution of wealth/poverty contributes not only to a considerably high level of misery—and crime—but also to the patronage linkages that underwrite much of the actual practice of everyday politics. An integral part of such linkages is corruption.

Socioculturally, Kenya is comprised of some 40 ethnic groups, although the five largest (Kikuyu, Luhya, Luo, Kalenjin, and Kamba, in that order) constitute over two-thirds of the country's total population. Also of note is the fact that while over two-thirds of Kenya's surface area is home to various pastoralist communities, these constitute only about 10 percent of Kenya's population, due to the arid or semiarid nature of the regions they inhabit. In part a reflection of such vastness, coupled with the longstanding instability across most of its northern borders (e.g., northern Uganda, southern Sudan and Ethiopia, and Somalia), much of this area remains only partly within the "law-and-order" grasp of the state.

HISTORY

Following several decades as a protectorate (marked by a number of violent military campaigns of conquest and subjugation), Kenya was elevated to colonial status in 1905, receiving several waves of British settlers over the next few decades. The first significant African nationalist organization was the Kenya African Union (KAU, a successor to the Kikuyu Central Association, banned with the onset of World War II), founded in 1944. In 1947 Jomo Kenyatta (a Kikuyu like most KAU members) became its president. Upon eruption of the Mau-Mau (also known as the Land Freedom Army) revolt in 1952, Kenyatta (among others) was arrested and remained in detention in remote parts of the colony for nine years. Although this rebellion was crushed prior to his release, it left a pair of legacies that would impact heavily on the country's subsequent political and economic development: first, that implanted colonial privilege would be preserved, whoever came to occupy the new country's most important offices, and second, that the defeated Mau-Mau and those allied to them would possess a dangerously destabilizing potential these postcolonial rulers would have to confront. In more personal terms, it also meant that the British government, to say nothing of that slice of the local settler community that was determined to stay, had to engage in a major "reinvention" of Kenyatta, as it became increasingly clear that no other leader was acceptable to the majority of the population.

Internal self-government arrived on June 1, 1963, following general elections the previous month, and full independence on December 12, 1963. Kenyatta, as leader of the Kenya African National Union (KANU), was initially prime minister, becoming president a year later when the constitution was changed to make Kenya a republic. At that time prominent members of the main opposition party, the Kenya African Democratic Union (KADU), were incorporated into the cabinet, whereupon this single opposition party dissolved itself. Significant in this regard was KADU's principal policy stance: "regionalism" (Swahili, *Majimbo*) with considerable powers shared between the center and the provinces (via elected legislators and governors and an upper house or Senate in Nairobi). These arrangements, too (most of which had never been fully implemented), disappeared with KADU's absorption, laying the foundation for an all-powerful executive and a political monopoly that lasted to 1992.

In the meantime, Kenyatta's waning health in the mid-1970s led to increasing tensions within the regime's inner circle itself. In 1976 an effort was launched to prevent the automatic succession of Vice President Daniel arap Moi to the presidency, should that office become vacant. Fortunately for Moi (and perhaps for the country's stability), this latter struggle was resolved in Moi's favor just a year before Kenyatta's death, leaving his path to the presidency largely unobstructed.

Moi, proclaimed president in October 1978 (having been serving in an acting capacity), was subsequently unchallenged as KANU's candidate for the party's presidential nomination prior to national elections held in November 1979. In the absence of any opposition party, or any national ballot for the presidency, Moi, like Kenyatta before him, needed only to retain his parliamentary seat (of Baringo Central, where he also enjoyed "unopposed" status, thus automatically capturing the seat, as he would continue to do until 1992).

In June 1982, responding to the perceived threat of the proposed launch of a new, Socialist-leaning party, the National Assembly officially declared Kenya a one-party state. Such a narrowing of political space, rather than achieving its purpose, only encouraged dissent. By the mid-1980s Mwakenya, an unofficial left-wing opposition group, emerged, taking credit for a number of "subversive pamphlets," though denying responsibility for several small-scale explosions in Nairobi's city center. This combination of growing corruption, repression, and popular discord was reflected in the 1988 elections, easily the least democratic in Kenya's history.

Within a month of those elections, President Moi shocked his own party faithful at a Special Delegates' Conference by calling for the reintroduction of a multiparty political system; a month later the National Assembly dutifully removed Section 2 (a) of the constitution that had been inserted 10 years earlier. Kenya was therefore once again a multiparty state.

Following two five-year terms (1992–97, 1997–2002), both pundits and politicians continued to wonder whether Moi would, after all, agree to exit public life. Three broad options were available should he decide not to do so: (1) to push through a constitutional amendment removing presidential term limits; (2) to legitimize an additional term by dissolving the Assembly and calling (and winning) a snap election before completing his second term, coupled with judicial sanction to block application of the "two five-year terms" constitutional provision; or (3) to violate the constitution and simply remain in office, including possible use of the military to do so.

While recurrent rumors and occasional reports by investigative journalists, along with periodic public statements by key supporters, gave some credence to each of the three options, by mid-2002 it was fairly certain that the president would, after all, retire. This was the general conclusion following Moi's surprise announcement in July that Uhuru Kenyatta, son of the country's first president, was his choice to be the ruling party's presidential candidate.

At the same time, the mainstream opposition, at work for several years trying to reach agreement on a collective election strategy, finally succeeded in doing so. Several factors contributed to this. First was the consensus that Mwai Kibaki (then serving as leader of the official opposition) should be the "compromise" presidential candidate. Coming from the largest ethnic community (the Kikuyu) and having the most senior political status given his long-serving cabinet and vice presidential experience (and the most extensive access to campaign funding), Kibaki was perhaps an obvious choice. But given widespread ambivalence about this ethnic community, such consensus depended upon two other informal conditions: that (especially considering his 70 years) he would serve for only one term, and that a new constitution would be enacted "within one hundred days" that would downsize the presidency considerably by ceding authority to a prime minister and several deputies. As such, leaders of Kenya's other main opposition-leaning ethnic groups—the Luhya, the Luo, and the Kamba—could seek support from their followers on the basis of a more widely shared distribution of executive power.

In the 2002 elections the National Alliance Rainbow Coalition (NARC) and their candidate Kibaki easily defeated Kenyatta with 62 percent of the vote (though total turnout, surprisingly, was actually slightly lower than in the previous two elections, at 57 percent). Nearly the same margin obtained for parliamentary contests, with NARC netting 125 out 210 seats. KANU, with 68 seats, now became the official opposition. Despite a few problems, the election earned strong national and diplomatic endorsements.

Well into the government's second year, severe strains were showing over the stalled constitutional review process that had produced and then ratified a draft document that the government rejected (especially those provisions relating to the executive and devolution). Further, not only had few concrete steps been taken to address the wrongs committed by the previous regime, but several blatant cases of corruption involving prominent members of Kibaki's team had been revealed as well.

Taking all such developments into account, it remained unclear as to just which, if any, of the proposed changes to the current constitution would in fact ever be implemented and, if so, when. What did seem clear, however, was that the attempt to implement a sweeping reform agenda in the context of the current constitutional structure in which so much power remained largely unaccountable had little hope of success. In the meantime, with so much rancor continuing within NARC, and with Kibaki's health still in doubt even as his closest colleagues began to insist that he would, after all, seek a second term, it remained unclear what his government would actually be able to achieve, and how another winning electoral coalition could be put together in 2007.

The System of Government

Kenya's government functions as a unitary, formally multiparty (from 1992), quasi-democratic state, with a highly centralized set of political institutions situated around an executive presidency.

EXECUTIVE

The most striking feature of executive power in Kenya is the general absence of institutional checks and balances and, hence, of accountability. In large part, this stems from the country's hybrid constitutional structure, incorporating elements of both its original, parliamentary system and particular attributes of presidentialism that were added later. For example, while elections must be held at least every five years, the president (like a British prime minister) has the prerogative to dissolve the National Assembly at any time, triggering elections, which also follow a successful no-confidence vote. At the same time, the president must himself be an elected member of the National Assembly (though very rarely, aside from attending its State Opening, have presidents made personal appearances there). Although unlikely, the possibility thus exists that a successful presidential candidate could lose his parliamentary contest, thus triggering a constitutional crisis. All presidential candidates must also be at least 35 years of age and nominated by a registered political party; as with parliamentary races, independent candidates are not allowed.

As chief executive, the president is the head of state, head of government, and commander in chief of the armed forces. Both the vice president and cabinet ministers are appointed by the president from among members of the National Assembly, with the former alone required to be an elected rather than a nominated member. The president must command a majority in the National Assembly; losing a no-confidence vote triggers his resignation and new elections. If a president dies, or a vacancy otherwise occurs during a term, the vice president becomes interim president for up to 90 days while a successor is popularly elected. However, if for any reason the vice president is either unable or unwilling to assume this interim position, the cabinet meets and selects one of its own to fill it during this same 90-day period. One glaring omission is the absence of provisions for the actual handing over of power by an outgoing incumbent (a situation that bordered on chaos following the 2002 election). Most critically, however, is the dual personality of this branch of government, a central focus of the ongoing, if still highly uncertain, review process.

LEGISLATURE

The legislative branch consists of the unicameral National Assembly. The body consists of 224 members: 210 elected by popular vote for five-year terms; 12

nominated by the president based upon the numerical party strength of elected MPs; and the attorney general and speaker, who are ex-officio members. The attorney general may not vote. Its calendar (dates of sittings, as well as dissolution, within the five-year period) is determined by the president.

From the onset of independence, the executive has dominated the legislature. After the return to multipartyism in 1992, however, and given KANU's slim majority in both the seventh and eighth parliaments, it was necessary to make increasing use of various informal mechanisms, especially cash handouts and other forms of patronage, but also physical threats in some cases, to keep a sufficient number of MPs of various parties in check. Yet in the 1997 election the mounting din for constitutional and electoral reforms, coupled with the threat of an election boycott accompanied by public rallies that often attracted state violence, eventually forced a compromise set of reforms that offered two lessons to MPs and the wider public: 1) given sufficient pressure, the executive could be forced into making at least some concessions; 2) however great the country's political divisions, most MPs are prepared to bargain with each other (whatever the truth of allegations that money from various sources constitutes a critical element in such bargaining).

This same sort of inclination to compromise was evidenced subsequently in the agreement that incorporated major civil society elements into the Assembly's hitherto monopoly control over the constitutional review process in 2001. The Assembly's new-found muscle was perhaps most concretely expressed in the establishment of the Parliamentary Service Commission in that year, giving the Assembly for the first time power to determine its own budgetary and staff needs; a subsequent effort in 2002 to alter Sections 58 and 59 of the constitution so as to deprive the president of the power of dissolution and thus accord parliament with both fixed dates for its sittings and its overall duration, failed, however. In this case, the government used the argument that as the process of complete constitutional review was underway, it would be inappropriate to make any piecemeal changes in the meantime; whether a recent renewed attempt to alter these constitutional provisions will succeed, given the difficulties in the review process, remains to be seen. Other key pending elements in the ongoing effort of legislative strengthening include the power to vet key presidential appointments and financial estimates prior to the official presentation of the annual budget, and

access to and similar vetting power over proposed expenditures in the heretofore undisclosed areas of the military and security services.

Finally, whatever additional measures are instituted to strengthen this branch of government, it can be agreed that following two massive increases in pay and benefits (that legislators awarded to themselves, one before and one immediately after the 2002 elections), Kenya's legislators are (in relative terms) among the best paid on the continent, if not the world.

JUDICIARY

Kenyan jurisprudence is based on English common law, African customary law, Islamic law, acts of the British Parliament before independence and of the National Assembly after 1963, and judicial precedent.

A chief justice and 11 puisne (associate) judges make up Kenya's High Court, which sits continuously in Nairobi, Mombasa, Nakuru, Kisumu, and Nyeri. The High Court supervises a system of subordinate courts, including provincial and district magistrates' courts and Muslim district courts, the latter ruling on questions of Islamic law relating to family and domestic affairs. The Court of Appeals issues the final verdict in contested civil and criminal cases. The president has the authority to appoint High Court and Court of Appeals judges, upon advice from the Judicial Service Commission, a body that was largely dormant during Moi's rule.

The courts are empowered to review government acts and legislation and to declare laws and acts null and void. However, the Kenyan judiciary's independence was seriously eroded through the passage in 1988 of constitutional amendments affecting the security of tenure of judges and the employment of expatriate judges who worked under contracts with the Kenyan government. During the political liberalization of the early 1990s, however, such security of tenure was restored.

Given its severely tarnished reputation under Moi, upon assuming office the current NARC government sought to implement its promise of a thorough overhaul of the judiciary. Doing so led to the departure of nearly half of this branch's most senior judges (23 High Court and Court of Appeals justices) and a substantial number of lower-tier magistrates (82 out of 300). However, several senior judges successfully appealed their suspensions, and it remained unclear as to how thorough and fair such a cleansing process would be, especially pending a final resolution of the constitutional review process.

REGIONAL AND LOCAL GOVERNMENT

Kenya is divided administratively into provinces, districts, divisions, locations, and sublocations. Provincial commissioners oversee the country's eight provinces (Central, Coast, Eastern, North Eastern, Nyanza, Rift Valley, Western, and Nairobi). The commissioners oversee the implementation of government policies through the provincial, district, and divisional officers who work under them, representing all principal ministries and departments. Likewise, they chair provincial and district security committees. Districts and divisions within districts are headed, respectively, by district commissioners and district officers. As of 2004 there were 74 districts and some 215 divisions. Notwithstanding their geographic spread, however, these civil servants are directly responsible to the president and thus should be seen as extensions of executive authority, rather than providing a genuinely two-way avenue for the expression of local needs and opinions. It should be noted that the draft constitution that emerged from the review process early in 2004 called for the scrapping of the entire provincial administration system that had become closely associated with unaccountable and oppressive executive power and having its functions assigned to popularly elected local authorities organized in a three-tier (and, critics said, financially unsustainable) structure.

Local authorities are comprised of elected members (councilors) and administrative staff. They may be any of the following five types: municipal councils, town councils, county councils, urban councils, and area councils. Local councils, though largely dependent upon Treasury support (the Local Authority Transfer Fund, or LATF) for financial viability, raise modest revenues by levying taxes and other fees with which to build and maintain roads and public housing and provide health, welfare, and education, and various other social services. Since the late 1960s, and culminating in the passage of the Local Government Act of 1974, central government, particularly through the Ministry of Local Government, has exercised real power over all local authorities. This is so even if the onset of multiparty politics allowed for considerable de facto autonomy, especially with regard to corrupt practices that fed regime-based or aligned patronage networks.

Rural people especially have participated in local governmental processes by attending general meetings (*baraza*, in Swahili) convened most often by chiefs, assistant chiefs, or district officers. While these are often orchestrated so that only approved government

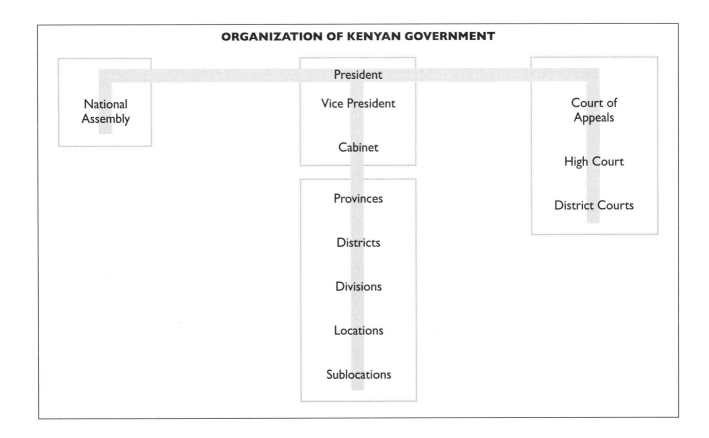

ORGANIZATION OF KENYAN GOVERNMENT

President

Vice President

Cabinet

National Assembly

Court of Appeals

High Court

District Courts

Provinces

Districts

Divisions

Locations

Sublocations

messages are communicated, they have become more spontaneous in recent years and do provide an increasingly important means of two-way communication between rulers and ruled.

The Electoral System

Under Kenya's constitution, regular presidential and legislative elections are held simultaneously every five years (or sooner, if parliament passes a motion of no-confidence or the president chooses to dissolve parliament). All citizens 18 years or older may vote. The president and members of the National Assembly are elected through direct popular vote by secret ballot. To be elected president, a candidate must receive a plurality of votes cast and at least 25 percent or more of the vote in at least five of eight provinces; failing this, a runoff contest must be held between the top two candidates within 30 days. Candidates to the National Assembly are elected in single-member districts.

As of 2005 there are 210 elected and 12 nominated members (plus the attorney general and speaker), a limit stipulated in the current constitution. With or without a new constitution, however, pressures are mounting to increase this number. As part of the pre-1997 reform package, nominated members are allocated to political parties according to the percentage of total parliamentary votes cast and received by the various parties. Previously, the allocation of these seats was a presidential prerogative. Gender should also be taken into account in these nominations and, to a large degree, has been.

Some two-thirds of those registered actually voted in the 1992 and 1997 elections, though claims of fraud in the registration and voting process in both contests cast some doubt on the accuracy of these figures. However, it is unclear just what percentage of eligible voters was actually registered.

From early 2003 the Electoral Commission put into practice a system of continuous voter registration, though access to national identity cards required for this has continued to be difficult in certain areas. Nevertheless, it is expected that whatever the national mood at the time of the next election, a significantly higher number of eligible Kenyans should find themselves on the voter rolls; whether they will return to the polls in numbers that reflect such enhanced ease of registration is another matter. Whatever the case, at least on the basis of the country's unbroken string of 11 national elections that culminated in the unprec-

edented change of regime in 2002, it seems reasonable to assume that this particular institution is firmly anchored in Kenya's political culture.

The Party System

Although it is more than a decade since the return to multiparty politics, the current state and certainly future content of the country's evolving party system remains unclear. This applies both to particular parties and to the way all of them function in relation to the country's key political institutions.

Kenya's 50-plus registered parties can be assigned to several categories. In the first are those that seek national power either individually or through preelection pacts or agreements with other parties. The second category includes those that seek parliamentary representation only, usually in terms of ethnic or, in some cases, regional identity. These may or may not field a presidential candidate (and their decision as to whether to do so may change from one election to another).

In the next category are those parties centered on a particular individual who merely seeks wider publicity that may or may not include actually contesting a parliamentary seat. Such individuals, too, may contest the presidency as well, again to attract publicity and to increase their chances in their constituency contests.

Fourth are those largely opportunistic or "parachute" parties. While initially registered mainly for personal or financial reasons, several of these have taken on a much more significant guise, when, following either a split in a major party or when one or more leading individuals within them fell out with those in control, the need for an alternative electoral vehicle arose.

A final category includes those parties that similarly have no realistic chance of winning any elective seats (even at the local government level) but are conceived in order to raise the public profile of an individual or group of individuals or a cause.

At the same time, in terms of holding and attracting support, during campaigns, and more generally, they all combine some mixture of patronage (especially when able to access state power) and populist appeals. In recent years these have been couched in terms of alleviating poverty and promoting development in general, as well as "bringing to book" those reputed to have been involved in economic and human rights crimes and abuses.

Major Political Parties

NATIONAL ALLIANCE RAINBOW COALITION (NARC)

The current ruling party, NARC, is the result of what has now been revealed as a rather fleeting inter-elite agreement for purposes of dislodging KANU. Several political parties united in a simple desire for power rather than in any vision of the purposes for which the power should be used. Two months before the 2002 election the National Alliance Party of Kenya (NAK), a working composite of over one dozen major and minor opposition parties, forged an alliance with the Liberal Democratic Party comprised of that faction of KANU that rejected Moi's imposition of Uhuru Kenyatta as his party's presidential candidate.

In this connection, suffering from increasing wrangling within his NARC party (especially from the "Rainbow" group), President Kibaki subsequently sought to shore up his parliamentary majority in June 2004 by bringing into his cabinet seven MPs from KANU and FORD–People. This move, one negotiated and agreed to by the individuals involved rather than by their parties, triggered a constitutional challenge on the grounds that it violated Kenya's identity as a "multiparty" state, even though the constitution allows the president to "appoint cabinet ministers from among Members of the National Assembly." (The High Court's judgment was pending at the time of writing.)

Indeed, in the wake of this development, one KANU Assembly member suggested publicly that should Kibaki stand again in the 2007 election, KANU would support him, and should he not, his own party leader, Uhuru Kenyatta, would be NARC's next presidential candidate.

KENYA AFRICAN NATIONAL UNION (KANU)

KANU, founded in 1960, held the reins of government from independence in 1963 to 2002. While President Kenyatta's government relegated the party as a distinct institution to the sidelines in favor of the Provincial Administration, Moi made much more active use of it, at both the national and the local levels.

Notwithstanding its long history, it is difficult to determine the true number of actual KANU members. Whatever its records may show, a national survey conducted seven months after its defeat in 2002 found only 4 percent of respondents willing to "identify

with" the former ruling party (whereas 52 percent did so with NARC).

The future of KANU's leadership remains unclear since the 2002 election. The party constitution, ratified at its March 2002 conference, provided for Moi to continue as chairman after his exit from office. In the wake of its electoral disaster, however, Moi resigned early in 2003, following which Uhuru Kenyatta was confirmed as "acting chairman." In January 2005 Kenyatta won the election for the chairmanship, easily defeating Nicholas Biwott. Kenyatta has declared his opposition to the proposed new constitution.

Minor Political Parties

FORUM FOR THE RESTORATION OF DEMOCRACY–KENYA (FORD–KENYA)

Although it has the honor of being the first opposition party to be founded after the restoration of the multiparty competition system at the end of 1991 and for a brief period embodied the hopes of nearly all those determined to bring KANU rule to an end, FORD–Kenya today represents a much narrower slice of national politics. After the 1997 election the party nearly disappeared; as of 2005 it had only a single seat in the Assembly. Other offshoots of the original party include FORD–People and FORD–Asili.

Although the party lost its standing as the official opposition after the 1997 elections when its parliamentary numbers were overtaken by DP, it continued to have some attraction to that section of the population that was anti-KANU but disinclined to support either a Luo or a Kikuyu-led party. Some party stalwarts remain optimistic that it can recover much of the broader, national appeal that FORD had at the start of the modern multiparty era.

DEMOCRATIC PARTY (DP)

The Democratic Party, like FORD, was formed in 1991. Its founders were the former minister of health and vice president Mwai Kibaki and a group of disgruntled former civil servants and older politicians. Given the strong support role Kibaki played in the KANU government during its most repressive years, such a turnabout provoked some cynicism.

Given FORD's mass following at the time and its populist appeal, the conservative (and mainly Kikuyu, but also non-African) propertied business class was clearly worried at the prospect of this "radical" party taking power. By the time of the 1992 elections, however, following FORD's split and KANU's partial resurgence, Kibaki's Nyeri District was the clear center of DP's strength, winning only a few seats elsewhere, especially in the Kamba-inhabited region of Eastern Province.

While Kibaki finished third in that presidential race, he climbed to second position in the 1997 contest, its parliamentary representation earning DP recognition as the official opposition. This reflected both the numerical clout of the Mt. Kenya communities (Kikuyu, Embu, and Meru) as well as the further fractioning of the opposition that occurred after the 1992 election. Based on his party's strength and personal seniority, he was thus its most commanding figure as the opposition strategized for the 2002 transition election, eventually gaining NARC's collective ("compromise") nomination. Like NARC's other composite members, DP's future is unclear, given the absence of a clear successor to Kibaki within the party itself.

OTHER MINOR PARTIES

Given the ethnic, elite-driven nature of Kenya's parties, a relatively minor or even unknown party today can become a most important one tomorrow. For example, the relatively obscure Social Democratic Party (SDP) for a time appeared to have the potential as a nonethnic, more policy-based (pro-reform) party. It made room for C. Ngilu when she fell out with Kibaki's DP before the 1997 election; she then ran as its presidential candidate. This enlarged profile helped boost SDP's overall parliamentary representation, while Ngilu retained her own seat. Subsequently, leadership wrangles emerged between Ngilu and the party's officials, forcing her eventual departure to a previously unknown entity, the National Party of Kenya, that later was transformed into NARC. SDP, in the meantime, has nearly vanished.

Another small party, Safina, had its registration attempts blocked by the government prior to the 1997 elections. It appears that the international stature of one of its central figures, Dr. Richard Leakey, and especially his perceived fund-raising potential, was the main reason for the regime's trepidation in this case. By the time the party was allowed to register, little time remained to organize, and it fielded no presidential candidate. Its candidates, several of whom were successful, found the party useful for two reasons: it had a more precise reform agenda than mainstream (ethnoregional) opposition parties, and it freed them from association with any ethnic identity via a party leader or presidential candidate. Although winning just a single seat in the 2002 election, it is likely that in a country such as Kenya where ethnic affiliation so dominates the political terrain, Safina, among other such marginal parties, will continue to provide useful alternative avenues of political mobility.

Other Political Forces

INTERNATIONAL DONORS

The (mainly Western) international community played an important role in promoting political changes in Kenya in the early 1990s, mainly through the withholding of development assistance and budgetary support. This led to an on-again, off-again relationship, particularly with the International Monetary Fund (IMF) and World Bank, throughout the decade and into the early 2000s. Such failure to adhere to agreed conditions also added fuel to domestic calls for reform.

Reflecting such a souring of relations, especially from the mid-1990s, international donors gave substantial support to NGOs and other civil society groups active in the areas of human rights monitoring, civic education, constitutional reform, and election preparation and observation activities. Despite expectations to the contrary, donor relations with the new Kibaki government, while certainly improved, have yet to be completely restored. Well into 2004 the World Bank had restarted a number of projects previously halted, in addition to initiating new ones, but the IMF expressed less than complete confidence in the government's commitment to implementing all agreed reform measures.

Whatever the course of such relations, the fact remains that as long as the country's current account deficit (-$459 million as of 2004) remains so large and its development needs and popular expectations so high, no Kenya government can survive for long without external support.

THE MILITARY

The military's threat to constitutional (and possible civil) order can arise through a number of scenarios. Internally, the military may itself engineer a coup in which it formally takes power, or identify civilian actors through whom it may wield influence. Externally, civilian politicians may seek to use the military for their own purposes. In either case, such situations become particularly explosive when sections of the military disagree and fighting between two or more of them ensues.

In Kenya's case, however, the longer term political importance of Kenya's military lies in its general disinclination to exert influence over politics, and similarly, to allow itself to be used by civilian power-holders. Several reasons have been cited for this. One is the high level of professionalism, encouraged by close ties with Western military forces, especially those of Britain. While U.S. military assistance and other ties have been made more subject to the vagaries of the host country's governance performance, especially with regard to corruption in arms and related purchases, the 1998 al-Qaeda destruction of the U.S. embassy in Kenya provided a strong incentive for closer cooperation along these lines.

Perhaps most important of all, the political leadership has kept a close eye on the barracks. This has taken the form of appointing and promoting senior officers in whom it has a high level of trust. It has also entailed ensuring that even in times of severe budgetary constraints the needs of the troops are well catered for.

It was, perhaps, for its past political neutrality, as well as for the rumored refusal of the military to lend any assistance to possible efforts to block the transfer of power that accompanied the transition election of 2002, that 58 percent of Kenyans expressed high trust in this institution. One may conclude, therefore, that even if future conditions may not be as supportive in maintaining a clear divide between the military and political life as has been the case to date, the country's first 40 years of success do inspire considerable confidence in this regard.

UNDERGROUND GROUPS AND MILITIAS

Beginning especially with the Mau-Mau, Kenyan political society has been periodically populated by a variety of underground or shadow-state groups. The former have arisen in periods of intense political and economic frustration, the latter when those in power, nationally or locally, feel threatened and are able to exploit mainly jobless youth to pursue political objectives of which they may have only sketchy awareness, often for immediate (if minimal) material gain.

Minimal violence associated with such gangs occurred in the context of the 2002 elections, at least after the various (and often violent) party nominations were over. Some observers concluded that this stemmed primarily from two facts: that both leading presidential contenders (Kibaki and Kenyatta) were from the same (Kikuyu) ethnic group, thus defusing tensions on this basis, and that leading figures in

KANU feared engaging in such blatantly illegal behavior, just in case their party lost.

Whatever the actual mix of reasons then, the next (2007) election will be a major test for the NARC government with regard to such militias, when once again, the stakes will be exceedingly high.

THE RELIGIOUS SECTOR

To speak of a religious "sector" in Kenya is somewhat misleading, since the positions taken by leaders of various denominations and institutions on public issues often vary as much as do those of competing politicians and parties. Yet the increased involvement of Christian and Muslim organizations and leaders is undeniable over recent years.

Direct church involvement in support of civil liberties began in 1986 with the National Council of Churches of Kenya (NCCK) speaking out publicly against the government's proposal to replace the secret ballot with a queuing system of voting (employed during the subsequent elections of 1988). These criticisms later broadened to encompass Moi's use of detention without trial and torture and the one-party system generally.

The Muslims, by contrast, were much slower to become so engaged. All Islamic organizations in Kenya are affiliated to the Supreme Council of Kenya Muslims (SUPKEM) that until the constitutional reform movement got underway in 1999 had been seen largely as KANU-leaning. Energized in part by local objections to certain security measures introduced in the aftermath of the 1998 U.S. embassy bombing and other threats, particular Muslim leaders and organizations became more vocal in a wide variety of national, secular debates.

UNIVERSITY STUDENTS AND FACULTY

At numerous times in Kenya's postcolonial history the universities, and particularly the University of Nairobi, have been flashpoints of political protest. On even more occasions, however, students have engaged in violent acts to express dissatisfaction with mundane issues closer to home, such as fee increases, poor dormitory food, and campus power failures. The underlying cause of many of the more recent outbursts was the massive and rapid expansion of the student body over the last 20 years, a process that had strong political overtones in terms of both the communities and the families that benefited most from it.

With the return to multiparty politics, certain political operators frequently sought student involvement in their campaigns and related activities, helping to imprint upon students the same kinds of divisions present in the Kenyan body politic at large.

THE URBAN POOR

Since independence Kenya's urban centers, especially Nairobi and Mombasa, have experienced very rapid growth. The country's urban population that stood at about 10 percent at independence is now nearly 30 percent. This increase reflects both steady natural growth within the urban population and steady rural-urban migration, in large part a consequence of the lack of income-earning opportunities in most rural areas. The bulk of these urban dwellers inhabit very low income areas and dwellings, many without basic necessities; Nairobi's Kibera slum alone has close to half a million residents. The wanton, often unannounced, destruction of shantytowns and expulsion of their dwellers for the benefit of politically connected developers have caused further suffering. Such oppressive conditions have made many among the urban poor extremely dissatisfied with the status quo and vulnerable to demagogic manipulation by elites, especially in exchange for material inducements, however modest. Sociocultural factors aside, however, the sober realities affecting the vast majority of residents in Nairobi and other urban centers constitute yet another extremely daunting challenge for the government.

ORGANIZED LABOR AND EMPLOYERS

Approximately half of Kenya's employees are members of the country's two dozen labor unions. With the exception of the Kenya National Union of Teachers (KNUT), all are affiliated to the Central Organization of Trade Unions (COTU). Throughout the KANU era, the government, through its Ministry of Labour, controlled union registration and also, to a large extent, internal union politics.

In the wake of NARC's electoral triumph, there was a small explosion of labor unrest, as many workers attempted to see how far they could go in improving their pay packages and working conditions, which in many cases were sorely wanting, even by local standards. By and large, the results were disappointing, with the government generally supporting employers who made only minimal concessions.

Once in office, the new NARC government, through especially the Ministry for Planning and National Development, established several advisory panels and other bodies to encourage private sector input into policy formulation and implementation. However, given its relatively small size and racial diversity, the "business community" is not likely to have much direct influence on formal political institutions, especially through the electoral process.

THE MEDIA

As in other less developed countries, most Kenyans have limited access to media, aside from medium-wave radio broadcasts. The 2003 Kenya Afrobarometer Survey revealed that while a full 77 percent of respondents listen to radio news on a daily basis, only 15 percent have access to newspapers.

Keeping this reality in mind, it should be stressed that even the more modest outreach of the press and television may have a significant impact, given that actual influence over public affairs is concentrated in the hands of relatively few people.

For their part, in both number and content, Kenya's nonstate media have reflected the prevailing political atmosphere in the country. This stems in large part from the fact that publishing or broadcasting requires a state license. The press, on the other hand, has always been in private hands. Even so, until the reopening of political competition in the early 1990s, it, too, had to stay within unofficial but clearly recognized limits, with regard to both the kind of stories covered and the editorial views expressed; several publications that demonstrated too much independence were silenced.

With regard to the electronic media, the government's Kenya Broadcasting Corporation (successor to the Voice of Kenya) continues as the only radio station with a truly national reach. It will perhaps not be until completion of the next electoral cycle before a firm judgment can be made as to how secure is this expanded freedom of expression.

National Prospects

Not since the immediate post–Mau Mau period has there been so much uncertainty in Kenyan public life. This relates to questions in three main areas: (1) whether the current set of economic policies can significantly improve the well-being of the vast majority of citizens; (2) what will be the shorter and longer term "menu" of political party choices, with what mix of individual and ethnic identity, as the next election approaches; and (3) to what extent the country's public institutions will be restructured, whether through a more thorough constitutional review or through piecemeal reform by means of ordinary legislation and executive fiat.

The increasing attention to political advantage may undermine whatever possibilities for significant economic restructuring and growth the Kibaki government brought with it. In this connection, some fear that without marked growth, further polarization based on the country's yawning class distinctions will grow, straining relations not just between rich and poor but also between Africans as a whole and the small but critical non-African slice of the population. Economic hardship may also encourage calls for those associated with past economic and human rights abuses to be held accountable, further weakening national cohesion, whatever the merits of such an application of justice.

Finally, although expectations have dropped significantly in this regard, given the vast sums invested in the review process, popular demand for a new or substantially revised constitution remains high. The promised date for such a document is now long since past, although the Assembly did finally approve a draft in 2005. Meanwhile, a fierce debate continues as to (1) its final content regarding especially the executive, devolution, the Islamic kadhis' courts, and overall state financing, and (2) the most legitimate and efficient way out of the current procedural quagmire. Here the critical choices have to do with parliament's possible role in working out a compromise concerning the content of these outstanding issues, the method of adoption of whatever document may emerge, and the timing both of implementation and of the order of sequence of its various provisions. In view of the entrenched interests that have become increasingly evident since the election, some observers have concluded that the only actual issue remaining is who will be saddled with the blame for failure. The impact such an outcome would have is difficult to surmise. Although Kenya has long been noted for its political stability, the country is currently undergoing a process of fundamental, albeit slow, change to greater political freedom.

Further Reading

Anderson, David M. "Briefing: Kenya's Elections 2002—The Dawning of a New Era?" *African Affairs* 102 (2003): 331–42.

Atieno-Odhaimbo, E. S., and John Lonsdale, eds. *Mau Mau and Nationhood: Arms, Authority, and Narration.* Oxford: James Currey, 2003.

Barkan, Joel D. "Kenya after Moi." *Foreign Affairs* 83, no. 1 (2004): 87–101.

———, ed. *Beyond Capitalism vs. Socialism in Kenya and Tanzania.* Nairobi: East African Educational Publishers, 1994.

Brown, Stephen. "Authoritarian Leaders and Multiparty Elections in Africa: How Donors Help to Keep Kenya's Daniel arap Moi in Power." *Third World Quarterly* 22, no. 5 (2001): 725–39.

Dealing with the Past: Economic Crimes and the Transition. Nairobi: Transparency International–Kenya/Law Society of Kenya, 2002.

"The Draft Constitution." In *The People's Choice: Report of the Constitution of Kenya Review Commission.* Nairobi: Constitution of Kenya Review Commission, September 2002.

Holmquist, Frank. "Kenya's Postelection Euphoria—and Reality." *Current History* 102, no. 664 (May 2003): 200–05.

Kagwanja, Peter M. *Killing the Vote: State-Sponsored Violence and Flawed Elections in Kenya.* Nairobi: Kenya Human Rights Commission, 1998.

Mbugua, Ng'ang'a. "Confusion Reigns: Political Parties Have Lost Their Identities." *Daily Nation,* August 5, 2004, 9.

Miller, Norman N., and Rodger Yeager. *Kenya: The Quest for Prosperity.* 2d ed. Boulder, Colo.: Westview Press, 1994.

Muigai, Githu. "Ethnicity and the Renewal of Competitive Politics in Kenya." In *Ethnic Conflict and Democratization in Africa.* Ed. Harvey Glickman. Atlanta: African Studies Association, 1995, 161–96.

Mutunga, Willy. *Constitution-Making from the Middle: Civil Society and Transition Politics in Kenya, 1992-1997.* Nairobi: Sareat, 1999.

Ndegwa, Stephen N. "Citizenship and Ethnicity: An Examination of Two Transition Moments in Kenyan Politics." *American Political Science Review* 91, no. 3 (September 1997): 1–18.

———. "Kenya: Third Time Lucky?" *Journal of Democracy* 14, no. 3 (2003): 145–58.

Rutten, Marcel, Alamin Mazrui, and François Grignon, eds. *Out for the Count: The 1997 General Elections and Prospects for Democracy in Kenya.* Kampala: Fountain, 2001.

Throup, David W., and Charles Hornsby. *Multi-Party Politics in Kenya: The Kenyatta and Moi States and the Triumph of the System in the 1992 Election.* Oxford: James Currey, 1998, 453–532.

Vandenberg, Paul. "Ethnic-Sectoral Cleavages and Economic Development: Reflections of the Second Kenya Debate." *Journal of Modern African Studies* 41, no. 3 (2003): 437–55.

Wolf, Thomas P. "Contemporary Politics." In *Kenya Coast Handbook: Culture, Resources and Development in the East African Littoral.* Dick Foeken, Jan Hoorweg, and R. A. Obudho. Münster, Germany: Lit Verlag, 2000, 129–55.

Wolf, Thomas P., Carolyn Logan, and Jeremiah Owiti. "A New Dawn? Kenya after the Transition." *Afrobarometer Working Paper No. 33.* Available online. URL: http://www.afrobarometer.org (accessed November 17, 2005).

REPUBLIC OF KIRIBATI

By Eugene Ogan, Ph.D.

The democratic republic of Kiribati was known as the Gilbert Islands until it achieved independence from Great Britain in 1979. Great Britain had administered the Gilbert Islands as part of a protectorate that included the Ellice Islands. In a referendum held in 1974, inhabitants of the latter voted to form a separate nation, now Tuvalu. Kiribati remains within the British Commonwealth.

Kiribati is made up of 33 islands, all of them coral atolls except Banaba, which had been a major producer of phosphate until operations ceased in the year of independence. Total land area is 823 square kilometers, including 103 square kilometers of uninhabited isles. In 2005 there were 103,000 residents, most of whom lived on the single island of South Tarawa.

Population pressures have been recognized for decades, and migration to the Solomon Islands was encouraged by the former British administration. When phosphate on Banaba was exhausted and the island was no longer habitable, Banabans were relocated to Rabi, in the Fiji group.

The System of Government

A mixture of parliamentary and presidential systems, the Kiribati government is headed by a president, or Beretitenti. Kiribati has a unicameral legislature.

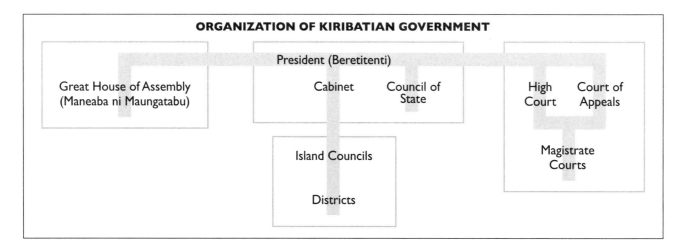

ORGANIZATION OF KIRIBATIAN GOVERNMENT

President (Beretitenti)

Great House of Assembly (Maneaba ni Maungatabu)

Cabinet   Council of State

High Court   Court of Appeals

Island Councils

Districts

Magistrate Courts

EXECUTIVE

The president is both head of state and head of government. The Great House of Assembly, or Maneaba ni Maungatabu, nominates up to four candidates from its membership, and one is chosen in a national election.

Presidents are elected to a normal term of four years and may be reelected twice. They can be removed by a no-confidence vote in the House of Assembly, in which case a Council of State serves until a new election can be held. The president selects a vice president, as many as eight ministers, and an attorney general who must be a lawyer and may or may not be elected a member of the Maneaba. These constitute the cabinet and, with the president, the executive authority.

In the 2003 election Anote Tong defeated his older brother, Harry, to win the presidency.

LEGISLATURE

Elections for the Maneaba are held every four years. It is a single-chamber legislative body, consisting of 42 total members: 40 members elected from 23 single-member or multimember constituencies; a representative of the Banaban community nominated by the Rabi Council in Fiji; and the attorney general, who serves ex officio. Each member must be elected by an overall majority of votes cast, and runoff elections are often necessary. A distinctive feature of the Maneaba is that the speaker is chosen from among persons who are not members. Except for cabinet ministers, members may be recalled by a petition of a majority of voters in their electorates.

JUDICIARY

Judicial authority is vested in a High Court, a Court of Appeals, and a system of magistrates' courts. The chief justice of the High Court is appointed by the president with the advice of the cabinet. There are 24 magistrates' courts serving every inhabited island; each has three magistrates. A primary function of magistrates' courts is dealing with land matters.

REGIONAL AND LOCAL GOVERNMENT

There are 6 districts and 21 local government councils, including town or urban councils. Council members are elected for three-year terms, but Maneaba members also serve ex officio on councils located in their electorates.

The Electoral System

The voting age is 18, but candidates for the Maneaba and presidency must be at least 21.

The Party System

There is no tradition of formally organized political parties in Kiribati. Those parties that exist are loosely organized groups that lack formal party platforms and structures. There are two major parties, the Maneaban Te Mauri Party or MTM and the Boutokaan Te Koaua Party or BTK.

Major Political Parties

PROTECT THE MANEABA

(Maneaban Te Mauri Party; MTM)

This party holds a majority in parliament with 24 out of 42 seats after the 2003 legislative elections. Its presidential candidate, Harry Tong, lost the presidential election to his brother, Anote, of the BTK.

PILLARS OF TRUTH

(Boutokaan Te Koaua Party; BTK)

This party came in second in the 2003 legislative elections, winning 16 seats. However, its presidential candidate, Anote Tong, won the presidential election.

Minor Political Parties

Minor parties in Kiribati include the National Progressive Party and the Maurin Kiribati Party.

Other Political Forces

Kiribati has no armed forces to interfere in the political system. The media is small but generally independent and able to comment on political affairs without threat of harassment.

National Prospects

Kiribati's government is notable for its political stability as well as its financial prudence, especially when compared with other Pacific Island nations. However, the country's economic situation remains gloomy. Since the exhaustion of the major phosphate deposits, fishing remains the resource with greatest potential. In 2001 Kiribati received over U.S. $15 million in aid, most of it from the United Kingdom and Japan.

Even more threatening are predictions of global warming and a consequent rise in sea level. There is much debate about the accuracy of these forecasts, but they represent a real danger for the low-lying atolls of Kiribati. If the worst-case scenario should occur, this Pacific Island nation might simply disappear.

Further Reading

Van Trease, Howard, ed. *Atoll Politics: The Republic of Kiribati.* Canterbury, New Zealand and Fiji: Universities of Canterbury and the South Pacific (Fiji), 1993.

DEMOCRATIC PEOPLE'S REPUBLIC OF KOREA
(Chosun Minjujueui Inmin Konghwaguk)

By Hun Joo Park, Ph.D.
Revised by Florina Laura Neculai, M.A.

The Democratic People's Republic of Korea, or North Korea, is a Stalinist single-party state that controls the northern half of the Korean Peninsula. Korea was divided between rival governments in the aftermath of the 35 years of Japan's colonial rule and World War II. North Korea, with a land mass of 122,370 square kilometers, about 55 percent of the total land area of the peninsula, shares a 1,025-kilometer border with the People's Republic of China along the Yalu and Tumen Rivers and a 16-kilometer border with Russia at the mouth of the Tumen River. Since the end of the Korean War in July 1953, the demilitarized zone (DMZ), a 4,000-meter-wide "no-man's-land" along the 38th parallel, has divided the Democratic People's Republic of Korea from the Republic of Korea (South Korea). As of 2005 North Korea's population stood at 22.9 million, which is about half the population of South Korea.

An examination of the history, both ancient and modern, of the Korean Peninsula sheds much light on the character and the preoccupations of the North Korean regime. Korea is an ancient country that has been a marching ground for the armies of its more powerful neighbors (China, the Mongols, Japan, the Manchus, and, to a lesser extent, Russia) and yet has managed, with great tenacity, to preserve its national identity. A tragic history has given the Korean people great determination and strength of character and has also made them highly suspicious of outsiders and, at times, rigidly conservative. The Yi dynasty, which despite foreign invasion and bitter internal rivalry between political factions lasted from 1392 to 1910, sought protection by becoming a tributary state of China, assiduously copying its political institutions and social practices. By closing itself off from all other foreign influences, it became what Westerners in the 19th century called the "hermit kingdom."

In 1876, however, Japan forcibly opened the country, in much the same manner as Japan itself was opened by the United States in 1853. The next three decades saw intense rivalry among Japan, China, and, to a far lesser extent, Russia for dominant influence in Korea, but Japan's control of Korea was set after its victories in the Sino-Japanese War of 1894–95. Although the Russo-Japanese War (1904–05) broke out primarily over their rivalry for Manchuria, Japan's victory over Russia sealed Korea's tragic fate. Japan's colonial rule, which officially began in 1910, combined policies of economic exploitation and systematic destruction of the Korean national identity. Koreans bitterly resented the Japanese, and their national resistance continued in various forms throughout the rule. The March 1, 1919, mass uprising was a culmination of such resistance.

The dream of Korean independence after the defeat of Japan in World War II gave way to the tragedy of dismemberment with the occupation of the peninsula by Soviet and American armed forces. Although the United Nations planned for Korea's reunification after nationwide elections, it never materialized. On August 15, 1945, with the early advance of Soviet troops into the peninsula, the United States proposed dividing Korea at the 38th parallel so the Japanese troops in

Korea could surrender. Stalin accepted the proposal, but that temporary division ironically hardened into two separate states. The Soviet-backed Democratic People's Republic of Korea, with its own constitution, was established on September 8, 1948, claiming control over the entire peninsula and accusing the rival Republic of Korea, established in August 1948, of being a "puppet" regime.

North Korea initiated the Korean War (June 1950 to July 1953) by invading South Korea. The war, which resulted in the death and dislocation of millions of people and the desolation of the entire peninsula, not only intensified and militarized the cold war but also locked the governments of the North and South into a stance of rigid hostility. For over four decades the peninsula has been one of the most militarized in the world.

Kim Il Sung, born near P'yongyang on April 15, 1912, fought with guerrilla units against the Japanese on the Soviet-Manchuria border between 1932 and 1945. He led the Korean Workers' Party (KWP), the ruling Communist party, after its founding in 1946, was premier after 1948, and, following the adoption of the 1972 constitution, president of the DPRK. By the early 1960s Kim had established unchallenged control of the Korean Workers' Party and thereby full state power. Kim could consolidate his position because his Kapsan guerrilla faction successfully purged every rival political faction in the North Korean government one by one. Kim first purged Pak Hon-yong's domestic faction, many of whom were Socialist intellectuals from the South who had fled to the North shortly before the Korean War. He blamed them for the failure of "liberating" the South and executed Pak. Exploiting the party membership registration issue, Kim then purged the Russian faction that Ho Ka-i led, a group neither well organized nor cohesive. Finally, Kim purged the Yenan faction, which had begun to criticize Kim's personality cult in light of the onset of de-Stalinization that took place in the Soviet Union in 1956.

Kim Il Sung built a monumental personality cult around himself, dwarfing that of Stalin or Mao. Kim then groomed his son Kim Jong Il (born February 16, 1942) as his own successor, and, beginning in 1975, he began referring to the younger Kim as the "Party Center." Kim Il Sung died of heart failure at the age of 82 on July 8, 1994, and Kim Jong Il succeeded his father as the leader of the country, thus establishing a Communist hereditary monarchy, a historically unprecedented phenomenon. The younger Kim continued his father's policies by building his own personality cult and ruthlessly controlling every aspect of North Korean society.

The System of Government

North Korea is a one-party dictatorship led by Kim Jong Il.

EXECUTIVE

As in other Communist countries, the state organization of the Democratic People's Republic of Korea is defined as subordinate to the ruling Korean Workers' Party. The state implements policy formulated by the party, which owes its dominant position to its role as representative and "vanguard" of the revolutionary working class. However, in practice, the constitutional changes in 1972 shifted the center of power from the party and its political committee to the presidency and the Central People's Committee (CPC), a kind of supra-cabinet that directs the large and unwieldy Cabinet of the State Administration Council (SAC). (The SAC has 32 ministries and 13 commissions, or supraministries.)

The head of state is the president. From 1972 when the office was established until his death in 1994, North Korea knew no other president than Kim Il Sung. The creation of this office marked the unrivaled supremacy of Kim, who was at the same time secretary-general of the Korean Workers' Party. Although the president is supposed to be elected for renewable four-year terms by the national legislature, the Supreme People's Assembly (SPA), he is in practice accountable to no one. The president is the commander of the armed forces, chief executive with control over the State Administration Council, and supreme legislator through his power to issue edicts with the force of law and the requirement that all other legislation be approved by him. The president is also responsible for approving treaties and agreements with foreign countries.

Kim Jong Il assumed the presidency in July 1994, upon his election as president of the National Defense Commission (NDC) and the Supreme People's Assembly. He was reelected to those posts in 1998. In 2003 the SPA reelected him as president of the NDC while making Pak Pong Ju premier. Despite Pak's position, virtually all power remains in the hands of Kim.

LEGISLATURE

Delegates to the unicameral Supreme People's Assembly are chosen for four-year terms in direct elections based on universal suffrage for those 17 and older. Each delegate represents a constituency of about

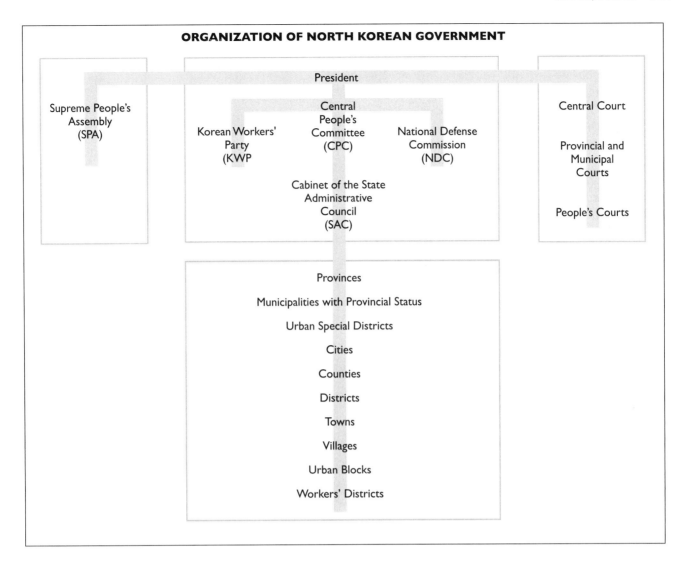

ORGANIZATION OF NORTH KOREAN GOVERNMENT

30,000 persons. The nominal powers of the SPA include the election of the president, the passing of laws, amendment of the constitution, and approval of the national budget and economic plans. Sessions are supposed to be held twice a year, in spring and late fall. When the SPA is not in session, its standing committee, elected by the deputies, acts in its name. Although the 1972 constitution defines the SPA as the "highest organ of state power," it is, in fact, a rubber-stamp organization.

The Central People's Committee, elected by the SPA for a four-year term, functions essentially as the link between party and state, the great majority of its members being members of the central political bureau (politburo) of the KWP. Its powers and responsibilities are broad, including the definition of domestic and foreign policy lines and control over the State Administration Council and Central People's Commissions dealing with national defense, foreign policy, state control, internal matters, and justice and security.

JUDICIARY

Central Court judges are elected by the SPA for three-year terms. They thus fall under the control of the state and party and have no independence. Furthermore, the procurator general, appointed by the SPA, exercises supervisory control over the court system down to the provincial and local people's courts.

REGIONAL AND LOCAL GOVERNMENT

The country is divided into nine provinces and four "special cities" (the capital, P'yongyang, Kaesong, Namp'o, and Ch'ongjin). Subnational units are divided into urban districts (the special cities and other large cities), regular cities, and some 152 counties. Each of these units has its own local people's assembly, local administration committee, and local people's committee, corresponding to the SPA, the State Administration Council, and the Central People's Committee on the national level. On the village level, there are no formal government organizations. Instead, administrative matters are the responsibility of the chairman of the local agricultural collective.

The Electoral System

Elections are managed by the party's umbrella organization, the Democratic Front for the Reunification of the Fatherland. A single slate of candidates approved by the party is presented to the electorate, and their election is automatic. Voter turnout routinely is reported at 100 percent. Most candidates are KWP members; other political groupings generally receive a few seats.

The Party System

The Democratic People's Republic of Korea is one of the most tightly regulated countries on earth, far closer in fact to the model of a totalitarian state than was the Soviet Union or the People's Republic of China. North Korea's small size facilitates efficient surveillance. Its continuing confrontation with South Korea creates a pervasive atmosphere of military discipline and mobilization. The Korean Workers' Party, which monopolizes political and state powers at both the national and the local levels, remains in total control of this isolated society.

Major Political Parties

THE KOREAN WORKERS' PARTY (KWP)

(Chosun Nodongdang)

HISTORY

The Korean Workers' Party was established in August 1946 as a coalition of diverse elements, including Korean Communists who had been based in the Soviet Union before and during World War II, particularly in the Maritime Province bordering Manchuria and Korea. Others had been in China and were closely associated with the Chinese Communist movement. A third group consisted of underground resistance fighters who had operated within Japanese-occupied Korea. The party structure and principles were modeled after those of the USSR's Communist Party; a number of its most prominent members had been members of the Soviet party. The party's development after 1946, however, was unambiguously in the direction of one-man rule under its secretary-general, Kim Il Sung. In the early years, Kim, who owed his position as KWP leader to Soviet support, had to recognize and deal with the somewhat divergent viewpoints of other party leaders even if no one seriously challenged his supremacy. As briefly discussed earlier, however, a series of purges eliminated other factions, so that by 1956 all sources of potential opposition to the Kapsan faction's dominance were eliminated. Kim reorganized the KWP and subjected it to intense and unremitting doses of ideological remolding. In the 1960s a campaign to idolize Kim and his revolutionary achievements was initiated and has remained the dominant theme of North Korean political life.

ORGANIZATION

The highest organ of the Korean Workers' Party is its party congress, whose delegates are elected by members of provincial and special city party congresses. Although it is supposed to be convened every four years, the congress has in fact met much less frequently. As is the case in other one-party systems, the congress, meeting so infrequently and with a membership of over 3,000, is not the effective locus of decision making but only a platform for the promulgation of decisions made by a much smaller group of leaders.

Power is concentrated in even smaller concentric circles. The central committee convenes the congress and acts in its name when it is not in session. Technocrats formed the largest single group in the central committee following the sixth party congress in 1980. The political bureau is elected by the central committee. The standing committee of the political bureau is composed of North Korea's most powerful leaders.

The secretariat is a national-level party organ that has nine secretaries heading different party departments, including the inspection committee (responsible for party discipline), an audit committee (responsible for finances), a military committee, and a liaison bureau (in charge of relations with underground "revolutionary" elements in South Korea). Other central committee departments deal with a variety of matters such as agriculture, fisheries, science and education, and propaganda and agitation. The party publishes *Nodong Sinmum* (The Workers' News), a daily newspaper, and *Kulloja* (The Laborer), a theoretical journal.

There are party congresses, committees, and secretariats on all subnational levels as well as smaller party units in rural villages. The basic unit of the party on the local level is the cell, to which all party members must belong.

Important mass organizations include the Socialist Working Youth League, which schools future party members, and the Young Pioneer Corps for children. The Democratic Front for the Reunification of the Fatherland also comprises a number of groups coordinated by the party. Among them are the general association of Korean residents in Japan, which organizes support for the P'yongyang regime among Japan's more than 600,000 Korean nationals.

POLICY

Kim Il Sung is revered not only as the revolutionary leader who liberated Korea from the Japanese (the role of the Soviets being glossed over) but as the creator of the *Juch'e* (self-reliance or independence) ideology, originally conceived of as an adaptation of Marxist-Leninist ideology to the Korean context. *Juch'e* ideology is more consistent with traditional Korean Confucian thoughts or Korean nationalism than with proletarian internationalism. *Juch'e* somewhat repudiates Soviet and Chinese models of socialist construction, but it has also over time shown a tendency to depart from the theoretical foundation of the revolution, Marxism-Leninism. While the Chinese Communists have always modestly described "Mao Zedong Thought" as only an application of universal Marxist-Leninist truths, in the DPRK the thought of Kim is known as "Kim Il Sung *Jueui*," a full-class "ism" equal and perhaps superior to Marxism-Leninism.

To understand the *Juch'e* ideology fully, one must look at the origins of the idea, which was the changing international political context of the 1960s. First, the Sino-Soviet rift became increasingly clear in the early 1960s. Second, once Soviet Communist Party leader Khrushchev's de-Stalinization campaign began in earnest, Kim's autocracy and personality cult began to be criticized. Third, during the Chinese Cultural Revolution in the late 1960s, the Red Guards openly criticized Kim as a bureaucratic revisionist who was indulging in

a luxurious, decadent bourgeois lifestyle. It was in this context that Kim advocated *Juch'e* in order to maintain distance from the big Communist brothers. It also came at a time when economic aid from the Soviet Union and China was declining. It goes without saying that the idea of *Juch'e* has been stretched too far to justify the Kim family dictatorship and North Korea's extremely isolationist policies.

Kim pursued a policy of self-reliance in the military sphere as well. As a result, the military share of North Korea's government budgets increased, imposing a serious burden on the country's economy. The militarization of society has increased the importance of the military in North Korean politics, especially since Kim Il Sung's death. The appointment of Choe Gwang, the most prominent veteran military man, as defense minister in October 1995 also suggested that the military was increasingly the real locus of power in North Korea.

The great preoccupation of the P'yongyang government since the end of the Korean War has been its hostile and competitive relationship with the Republic of Korea. Technically, the peninsula is still in a state of war. The North Korean leaders, former guerrilla fighters, have turned their country into a tightly disciplined armed camp. No fewer than 1.2 million men are in military uniform in a total population of 23 million, and most of them are deployed offensively close to the demilitarized zone. DPRK actions against the South have included border provocations, armed infiltration of the Republic of Korea, and, most dramatically, terrorist acts such as the attempt to assassinate South Korean president Chun Doo Hwan on October 9, 1983. While on a state visit to Rangoon, Burma, Chun narrowly escaped death when a bomb set off by North Korean agents killed 17 South Koreans, including four cabinet ministers.

These hostile acts have alternated in a very unpredictable fashion with gestures of conciliation, such as the North Korean offers of rice, clothes, and medical supplies to South Korean victims of floods in September 1984. In 1985 people from both the North and the South were allowed to visit family members on the other side of the DMZ for the first time since the Korean War. Throughout the latter 1990s and early 2000s relations with South Korea improved somewhat. Kim Dae-jung, who was elected president of South Korea in 1997, established a "sunshine policy" of increasing engagement with North Korea. During these years South Korea supplied significant humanitarian aid to North Korea, which was experiencing a major famine.

In the 1990s North Korea played its nuclear card by withdrawing from the Nuclear Nonproliferation Treaty in March 1993. It apparently paid off, since in October 1994 South Korea, Japan, and the United States agreed to give North Korea $5 billion worth of nuclear power stations of the sort that cannot easily be used to make nuclear bombs and 500,000 tons of free fuel per year until the completion of the new reactors. North Korea agreed to engage in preliminary talks to hold four-party (North and South Korea, the United States, and China) peace talks, as South Korea and the United States jointly proposed in April 1996. North Korea's interests in agreeing to come to the negotiating table seemed to lie in its desire to normalize diplomatic relations with the United States as well as to secure more economic aid. North Korea's insistence on U.S. troop withdrawal from South Korea as a precondition to the four-party talks was a major stumbling block to further progress. In the early 2000s North Korea further antagonized its neighbors and the international community in general by expelling UN weapons inspectors and withdrawing from the Non-Proliferation Treaty.

MEMBERSHIP AND CONSTITUENCY

It is estimated that the number of KWP members could have been as high as 3.2 million at the time of the sixth party congress (1980), a sharp rise from the 2 million announced by the KWP in 1976. This could have been due to the induction of a large number of the "Three Revolution Workteams," a mass political mobilization movement. Overall, about 15 percent of the total population are party members. Recruits must be recommended by members in good standing and must serve a one-year probationary period.

Criteria for party membership include personal commitment to its ideology, loyalty to Kim Il Sung and now to Kim Jong Il, and proper class background. Former revolutionary fighters, workers, and poor peasants have generally been perceived as the most revolutionary classes and thus most eligible for party membership. In recent years, however, technical and administrative expertise has been seen as important as class background, and such skills play an increasingly central role in the selection of party cadres and management personnel. Schools for the training of KWP cadres include the college of people's economic management, the Kim Il Sung higher party school, and the Kumsong political college.

FINANCING

Information on party financing is unavailable. It can be assumed that as in other Communist states, party members pay a portion of their income in dues and that direct government support is considerable.

Minor Political Parties

Parties other than the KWP do exist, but they are completely subordinate to the KWP and must acknowledge its leadership. Two such parties are the Korean Social Democratic Party and the Young Friends Party (Ch'ondogyo Chongu). Ch'ondogyo is a religious movement founded in the 19th century.

Other Political Forces

There are no other political forces in North Korea.

National Prospects

North Korea is an ethnically homogenous population. Its dominant religions are Buddhism and Confucianism. It had a GDP of $40 billion in 2004. North Korea finds itself totally ill prepared to adapt to drastic changes that are taking place in the post–cold war era. North Korea's economy is in shambles, in part because the Soviet Union, its biggest aid donor and trade partner, collapsed, and in part because its Stalinist economic management has utterly failed. Both the Soviet Union in 1990 and China in 1992 normalized their diplomatic relations with South Korea, while the North still has no equivalent ties with the United States or Japan. It joined the United Nations together with South Korea in 1991, only because it became clear that it was no longer able to block the UN from accepting South Korea as a member. In the mid-1990s there was increasing evidence that North Korea was developing atomic weapons, but this crisis was overshadowed by the starvation crisis of the North Korean people. However, the international community's focus on the North Korean atomic weapons program remained, and in 2002 U.S. president George W. Bush said that North Korea was a part of the "axis of evil" (along with Iran and Iraq). In December 2002 North Korea expelled the UN weapons inspectors, and in January 2003 it withdrew from the Non-Proliferation Treaty. In 2004 the International Atomic Energy Agency announced that it had strong evidence that North Korea had provided Libya with uranium. Because of North Korea's insularity and Kim Jong Il's habit of employing highly antagonistic rhetoric toward the United States and any other country that dared criticize it, the international community remained alarmed about North Korea's nuclear ambitions. As of 2005, however, neither the United States nor North Korea's neighbors had reached any consensus on how to deal with the nuclear threat from North Korea.

With regard to North Korea's future and the reunification of the two Koreas, various scenarios are conceivable. Any of these variants could materialize: the "big bang" scenario, as in the case of German unification or Romania's collapse; a military confrontation, although it would be suicidal for the North Korean regime; a stalemate; or a smooth transition to reunification. Only time will tell what will actually transpire. But given the fact that the North Korean regime has trouble even feeding its own people, the question of what kind of reunified Korea will be built on the peninsula is critically dependent upon how South Korea responds to this historic challenge.

Further Reading

Cha, V., and D. Kang. *Nuclear North Korea: A Debate on Engagement Strategies.* New York: Columbia University Press, 2003.

The Economist Intelligence Unit Limited. *North Korea: EIU Country Profile, 1996-97.*

Lee, Chong-Sik. *Korean Workers' Party: A Short History.* Stanford, Calif.: Hoover Institution Press, 1978.

Lee, Hong Yung. "The Korean Question in Post–Cold War East Asia." Unpublished typescript, May 1997.

Satterwhite, David H. "North Korea in 1996." *Asian Survey* 37, no. 1 (January 1996).

Scalapino, Robert A., and Chong-Sik Lee. *Communism in Korea.* 2 vols. Berkeley: University of California Press, 1972.

Sigal, L. V. *Disarming Strangers: Nuclear Diplomacy with North Korea.* Princeton, N.J.: Princeton University Press, 1998.

"A Subversive Weapon." *The Economist.* August 23, 1997.

REPUBLIC OF KOREA
(Daehan Minguk)

By Hun Joo Park, Ph.D.
Revised by Mary Hendrickson, Ph.D.

The Republic of Korea (ROK), or South Korea, is a budding and prosperous democracy. Democratization has advanced considerably since 1987, when the shift to democracy occurred. The government consists of a system of power that is shared by a president and unicameral legislature. While the president has traditionally held the greater balance of power, recent assertions of power by the legislative branch may foreshadow a shifting equilibrium between the branches. The Republic of Korea is one of the most successful developing countries in the postwar era. Through some 30 years of condensed industrialization and modernization, it has evolved to rank among the largest 15 economies in the world. Its per capita GNP grew from one of the lowest to $11,000 by 2004. Korea maintains a favorable balance of trade with exports of $193.8 billion in 2003; its economy also performs well over time on other economic indicators. South Korea controls the southern half of the Korean Peninsula, with a land area of 98,477 square kilometers, or about 45 percent of the total area of the peninsula. Its population in 2005 was 48.4 million (about twice that of North Korea), with Seoul, the capital, one of the largest cities in the world, with 11 million inhabitants.

HISTORY

The ancient country of Korea, unified since 668 A.D. and with at least 2,000 years of continuous and distinct sociocultural history, has trodden a tough, if tragic, modernization path. Confronted with colonialism at the end of the 19th century, the 500-year-old Yi dynasty found itself unable to modernize the country and preserve independence. It fell under Japan's exploitative totalitarian rule in 1910, but, in reality, Japan's ruthless rule over Korea had already begun after the Sino-Japanese War of 1894–95. At the end of World War II Japan's surrender prompted the United States to propose to the Soviet Union the use of the 38th parallel as a temporary dividing line for governing the nation as part of an international trusteeship. That division hardened into two separate states: the Republic of Korea in the southern part of the peninsula and the Stalinist Democratic People's Republic of Korea, or North Korea, in the northern part.

The Korean War, which began in June 1950 with the invasion of the South by the armed forces of the North intent on "liberating" the entire Korean Peninsula, had a formative influence on the development of the political system of the Republic of Korea. Millions of people were dislocated, including an influx of refugees from North Korea and workers repatriated from Japan, which was a cause of great social and political instability in the postwar years. The threat of further aggression from the North led political leaders to establish a highly centralized, authoritarian order, under which dissent and opposition were linked with Communist subversion, often without justification. American military support of the Seoul government made South Korea the keystone of the U.S. defense perimeter in East Asia. Even today, after the fall of the

Soviet Union, the cold war continues on the Korean Peninsula.

During the period from 1948 to 1960, known as the First Republic, Syngman Rhee, a political science Ph.D. from Princeton University, was president of the Republic of Korea. Rhee was one of the most prominent leaders of the struggle for national independence. Having been the first president of the Korean government-in-exile in Shanghai in 1919, he enjoyed quite a bit of prestige. That he was descended from Yi Song-gye, founder of the Yi dynasty, gave him an added aura of legitimacy, particularly among the country's tradition-oriented peasants who made up the majority of the population. His anti-Communist credentials also gave him an edge in getting U.S. backing for his bid to become the country's first president. His administration, however, was marked by pervasive corruption and favoritism, and Rhee himself had no tolerance for critics or political opponents. Rhee was already 73 years old in the first year of his presidency. He refused to support the establishment of a parliamentary system of government in which the legislature would have supreme power, insisting instead on a centralized presidential system that would give him broad powers as chief executive. Rhee's first four-year term was to end in August 1952, and the National Assembly had defeated a constitutional amendment sponsored by him that would allow for a popularly elected president, rather than one chosen by the Assembly. Rhee declared martial law in May 1952 and forced the Assembly to pass the amendment. In 1955 a second constitutional amendment was passed, also through the use of dubious methods, to allow Rhee to succeed himself indefinitely. However, student and popular outrage over his autocratic and often brutal methods forced him to retire in 1960, after some 142 students were killed by the police during demonstrations early that year.

THE SECOND REPUBLIC AND MILITARY COUP

South Korea experienced a brief period of democratic rule during the Second Republic, which lasted from April 1960 to May 1961. The constitution was revised once again, this time to provide for a parliamentary form of government. Chang Myon, a leader of the opposition Democratic Party, was chosen as prime minister. Bitter struggles between Democratic Party factions and continued instability in the nation as a whole gave a small group of military officers under Major General Park Chung Hee the opportunity to seize power on May 16, 1961.

Park dissolved the National Assembly and established a junta, called the Supreme Council for National Reconstruction. Military officers took over high-level administrative positions in the government. Under martial law, all political activities were suspended, and many politicians of the Rhee era were "blacklisted." In June 1961 the Korean Central Intelligence Agency (KCIA) was established to carry out surveillance of civilian and military opponents of the new regime. Its founder and first director was Colonel Kim Jong Pil, a member of the junta and nephew of Major General Park through marriage. Kim also played a central role in organizing the government-sponsored Democratic Republican Party. Under the new constitution of the Third Republic, which allowed for popular election of the president, Park retired from the military and ran for election as the Democratic Republican Party candidate, winning narrowly in October 1963 against Yun Po-sun of the opposition New Democratic Party.

Spectacular economic growth during Park's 16-year rule as president transformed South Korea from a predominantly rural, agricultural country into an urbanized, industrial one exporting manufactured products to world markets. The South Korean "miracle" insured support for Park's regime, as individual incomes steadily rose. Close links with Japan were seen as essential for economic development, and thus a South Korea–Japan treaty normalizing relations between the two countries was ratified in June 1965. There had, however, been substantial opposition, particularly among students, given the history of Japanese colonialism, and violent demonstrations led to the imposition of martial law. Park won the presidential elections in 1967 and 1971 with rather narrow margins of votes against New Democratic Party candidates Yun Po-sun and Kim Dae Jung. Like Rhee in his time, Park had the constitution amended in 1969 to allow himself a third term in 1971.

The decade of the 1970s saw Park establish dictatorial authoritarian rule. In October 1972 he proclaimed martial law and dissolved the National Assembly. A month later, he held a national referendum on the *yushin,* or "revitalization," constitution that established the Fourth Republic. The new constitution gave absolute power to the president over the executive, legislative, and judiciary branches. The president was to be elected by an electoral college of the National Conference for Unification, a body consisting of some popularly elected 2,359 members, and there were no limits to the number of terms that one person could serve as president. In effect, the *yushin* constitution practically guaranteed Park's lifelong presidency.

Continued popular opposition caused Park to enact Emergency Measure Number Nine (May 1975), which made it a crime to criticize the *yushin* system or advocate its revision. The KCIA became increasingly powerful and feared as it used harsh methods to silence opposition, even among Koreans overseas. The most spectacular example was the KCIA kidnapping of the New Democratic Party leader, Kim Dae Jung, from a Tokyo hotel in August 1973, an event that caused a serious rupture in South Korean–Japanese relations and underlined the regime's increasingly poor human rights record. Thousands of South Koreans were jailed or put under house arrest, including the Second Republic president, Yun Posun, and the dissident poet Kim Chi Ha; many were subjected to brutal treatment.

The domestic and international crises of the late 1970s hastened the downfall of Park's rule. By then, there were clear signs of failure of the heavy and chemical industrialization drive, on which President Park staked so much political capital. Inflation was rampant, unemployment soared, and the ruling party for the first time failed to win more popular votes than the opposition in the 1978 National Assembly election, despite the less than perfectly free and fair electoral environment. In 1979 Korean exports experienced a negative growth in real terms, the second oil shock hit, and, in 1980, Korea's economy contracted by 4.8 percent.

As antigovernment demonstrations erupted across the country, Park's lieutenants split into hard-liners and moderates. The head of the hard-liner camp was Cha Ji Chul, chief of the presidential security forces, who argued for harsher repression to crack down on any form of antiregime opposition. Kim Jae Gyu, director of the KCIA, took a more pragmatic stance and advocated dialogue rather than outright confrontation with the opposition and demonstrators. Park generally leaned toward Cha Ji Chul's side. During a party on October 26, 1979, Kim Jae Gyu shot both Park and Cha in a desperate plot to change course. The assassination of Park led to the collapse of the *yushin* (reform) system and the brief restoration of civilian rule under an acting president, Choi Kyu Ha. In December 1979 Choi abolished Emergency Measure Number Nine and released a large number of political prisoners who had been jailed under its provisions. These included Kim Dae Jung, who had been under house arrest following his kidnapping from Tokyo to Seoul. The political scene was enlivened as both the Democratic Republican Party under Kim Jong Pil and the New Democratic Party under Kim Young Sam and Kim Dae Jung began jostling in anticipation of presidential and National Assembly elections, which were to follow the promised establishment of a more liberal constitutional order.

Factional struggles within the parties, strikes by workers demanding higher wages and better working conditions, and a wave of student unrest, however, provided the military with yet another opportunity to establish its dominance over the political system. Major General Chun Doo Hwan, head of the Defense Security Command, established his control over the military by leading younger generals in a successful move to oust the chief of staff, General Chung Seung Hwa, and other Park-era senior military officers, on December 12, 1979. On May 17, 1980, Chun reacted to increased student militancy, aimed at removing the military from politics, by proclaiming martial law. His decree banned all forms of political activity, closed the headquarters of political parties, outlawed strikes, and muzzled journalists. The universities were closed, and the National Assembly suspended. Opposition leaders were arrested on charges of corruption and sedition. In Kwangju, the capital of South Cholla Province, Kim Dae Jung's home region and long a center of opposition sentiment, the brutal treatment of student demonstrators by the police and army paratroopers sparked a revolt by the general populace that lasted nine days and reportedly resulted in the death of up to 2,000 people. The official death toll was 189.

The junta established the Special Committee for National Security Measures with power in the hands of four men: Generals Chun Doo Hwan, Cha Kyu Hun, Roh Tae Woo, and Chung Ho Yung. A campaign of "social purification" was initiated. Some 9,000 people—members of the National Assembly, government officials, managers of state-run corporations, and educators—were fired from their posts. Nearly 200 magazines and newspapers were closed, and several hundred journalists were sacked for promoting "corrupt influences." Kim Dae Jung and a number of his supporters were tried by a military court; Kim was sentenced to death on charges of subversion in September 1980.

THE FIFTH REPUBLIC

President Choi Kyu Ha resigned on August 16, and Chun, now a five-star general, retired from the military to run for the presidency. With the support of the military, Chun was approved as interim president by the National Conference for Unification, which acted as an electoral college. Chun's new constitution (the Fifth Republic), ratified in a referendum on October

22, 1980, constituted only a slight modification of the *yushin* constitution. The Chun constitution abolished the National Conference for Unification, limited the presidency to a single, nonrenewable seven-year term, and made it more difficult for the president to proclaim martial law and dissolve the National Assembly. Both the Chun and *yushin* constitutions, however, provided for indirect, rather than direct, election of the chief executive.

After three years of harsh repression of all political activities unauthorized by the state, South Korean politics entered a period of softening by 1984. No authoritarian regime can rule by coercion alone. As Korea's economy had recovered its confidence and the GNP growth rates started to pick up again, Chun took a much more conciliatory attitude. By combining carrots and sticks, Chun tried to prolong his own grip on state powers. Despite the pent-up societal demand for democracy and the direct presidential election system, Chun attempted to maintain the existing rules of the game at least until after the election of his hand-picked successor. In April 1987 Chun issued an order to prohibit any discussion of constitutional changes. But 1987 was not 1980.

In the mass demonstrations that followed Chun's order, office workers as well as students and factory workers in Seoul took to the streets to demand democracy. Against such a backdrop came the famous June 29, 1987, declaration by Roh Tae Woo, then the official presidential candidate of Chun's Democratic Justice Party (DJP). The eight points that the declaration contained included the restoration of Kim Dae Jung's political rights and constitutional revision for a directly elected presidential system. Given the ruling party's incumbency premium of about 35 percent and the popularity of the two Kims (Kim Dae Jung and Kim Young Sam), the DJP's strategy must have been to divide the opposition and rule. No matter what the political calculation behind the June 29th declaration, it laid the groundwork for Korea's transition to democracy.

The outcome of the first presidential election under the Sixth Republic in 1987 turned out to be disastrous not only to the two Kims but to those who wished to see the end of the military domination of the country's politics. Roh, who helped Chun to seize power by illegally bringing his front-line division to Seoul, was elected to the presidency with 36 percent of the popular vote. Kim Dae Jung and Kim Young Sam split the opposition vote by getting 27 percent and 28 percent, respectively. Nonetheless, the process of democratization was now set in motion.

TRANSITION TO DEMOCRACY

In the National Assembly elections of 1988, the governing party, for the first time in the nation's history, failed to obtain a simple majority. In order to resolve the ruling party's minority dilemma in the legislature, Roh merged the Democratic Justice Party with Kim Young Sam's party to form the Liberal Democratic Party, a grand conservative coalition. Subsequently, Kim Young Sam managed to win the presidential nomination of the ruling party through an open competition and thereby the presidential election in 1992.

In December 1997 the former political prisoner Kim Dae Jung of the National Congress for New Politics Party was elected the eighth president, serving a single term. His presidency marked the first instance of a peaceful transition from an opposition party. Kim had a reputation as a courageous political dissident who championed democratic causes. Kim's enemies made numerous assassination attempts; he completed two jail sentences, and he was exiled for a time to the United States. The agenda of his presidency was economic recovery and reform. Notably, though, his historic efforts to reengage with North Korea earned him a Nobel Peace Prize in 2000. A summit between North Korea's leader Kim Jong Il and President Kim resulted in the North-South Declaration of Cooperation aimed at joint humanitarian and economic endeavors.

Roh Moo-hyun was narrowly elected president in December 2002 and assumed the presidency in February 2003. Roh is a former human rights activist and labor lawyer. His initial period in office proved challenging and controversial. Public confidence in his leadership sank during his first year in office amid a faltering economy and a labor strike that Roh failed to manage decisively. On March 12, 2004, parliament voted to impeach Roh, coinciding with a dip below 40 percent in his public approval ratings. Prime Minister Goh Kun temporarily assumed the presidency while the impeachment case was heard. Grounds for impeachment were weak, resulting in a public outcry against an act the people considered to be blatantly political. In parliamentary elections in April 2004, the Uri Party, associated with Roh, benefited from the anti-impeachment sentiments, winning a majority of parliamentary seats. The Millennium Party, which sponsored the impeachment measure, was reduced to only nine seats, and the Grand National Party (GNP) lost its majority. In May 2004 the Constitutional Court overturned the impeachment and returned Roh to office.

The System of Government

South Korea is a democratic republic with a strong president and a unicameral legislature.

EXECUTIVE

The constitution provides that the president is head of state, commander in chief of the military, and chief executive. Since 1987 the president is directly elected to a single, nonrenewable, five-year term. The president appoints the State Council (cabinet), which, in addition to the president, includes the cabinet ministers, the prime minister, and deputy prime ministers. The prime minister is appointed by the president with approval of the National Assembly.

Korea is a presidential system of government, with a system of separation of powers incorporated into the constitution, based upon the American model. While power was traditionally concentrated in the executive branch and the presidency, legislative powers expanded under the Sixth Republic's 1987 constitution. Executive dominance is historically rooted in Confucian state-centric tradition, which found strong reinforcement in the Japanese "colonial totalitarianism" and the subsequent military authoritarianism. The *yushin* constitution, for example, afforded the president the power to dissolve the National Assembly and to appoint one-third of its members, which assured a majority for the ruling party. In addition, the president appointed Supreme Court justices and could issue emergency decrees without approval of the National Assembly.

The 1987 constitution stripped the president of the powers to dissolve and appoint members to the National Assembly, to appoint judges, and to issue emergency degrees without legislative approval. The national assembly retains the right of consent to matters that lie mainly within the executive realm, such as ratification of treaties and declaration of war. Aside from the stronger powers of the National Assembly under the 1987 constitution, there is evidence that the strong powers of the presidency may be giving way to a greater balance of powers, as evidenced by parliament's assertion of power in the attempted impeachment of President Roh in 2004.

The State Council, chaired by the president with the prime minister as vice chair, deliberates on policies within the purview of the executive branch. Members include the executive (cabinet) ministers and the ministers without portfolio. Matters referred to the State Council, according to the constitution, include declarations of war, foreign policy issues, proposals to hold national referenda, proposed treaties, budget proposals, emergency orders, and certain appointments.

The National Security Council advises the president on the formulation of foreign policy and national security, and a National Economic Advisory Council assists in formulation of economic policies. In accordance with the constitution, an Advisory Council of Elder Statesmen may be established, chaired by the immediate former president or another individual appointed by the president.

LEGISLATURE

The National Assembly is a unicameral body consisting of a minimum of 200 members, elected by popular vote to four-year terms. Most members are elected from single-member districts, with the remainder appointed by political parties through a proportional representation system based on the number of seats won by each party. Bills may be introduced by either the National Assembly or the executive branch. The constitution provides that bills passed by parliament be promulgated by the president within 15 days unless he vetoes the bill. In that case, the bill is returned to the National Assembly with an appended explanation of objections. The president may request that the National Assembly reconsider the bill. The legislature may override the president's objections by two-thirds votes. Bills automatically become law if the president fails to promulgate them within five days.

The National Assembly's powers grew following the Fifth Republic. As previously stated, the president's power to dissolve the Assembly was eliminated in 1987. In addition, sessions of the Assembly were increased in length and may be easily convened by a smaller number of members. The Assembly's powers have been enlarged, including its ability to investigate administrative affairs and approve emergency measures put into effect by the president.

JUDICIARY

The Constitutional Court, the supreme organ of judicial review, was established in the 1988 constitution. The nine justices serve six-year renewable terms. The president of the Court is appointed by the president with consent of the National Assembly. The constitution prohibits justices from joining any political party or participating in politics. Jurisdiction of the Court extends to judicial review of legislation and governmental acts, impeachment, and decisions relating to dissolution of political parties. In passing judgment

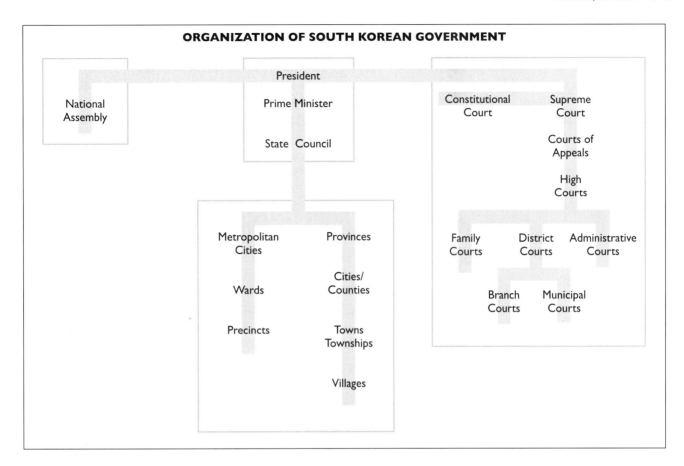

ORGANIZATION OF SOUTH KOREAN GOVERNMENT

on these matters, six justices must be in agreement. Despite its relative infancy, the Court had by July 2002 declared 228 laws or decrees unconstitutional and revoked approximately 160 government acts.

The court system in South Korea also consists of a Supreme Court, intermediate appellate courts, and courts of original jurisdiction. The Supreme Court is the highest court, hearing appeals from the High Courts and appellate divisions of the district courts and the Family Court. The High Courts are intermediate appellate courts. The District Courts are courts of original and general jurisdiction. The Family Court and Administrative Court are specialized courts of original jurisdiction. The District Courts and High Courts are divided into geographic districts to hear cases. District Courts have appellate divisions that hear cases from Branch Courts, Municipal Courts, or single-judge District Courts.

REGIONAL AND LOCAL GOVERNMENT

South Korea is a unitary system of government in which the central government possesses authority to determine the geographical boundaries and powers of subnational units. Under a revised Law on Local Autonomy passed in 1986, local governments were granted more autonomy from the national government. The local elections of June 1995, under President Kim Young-Sam, marked the beginning of a new era for local autonomy in South Korea. Funds for local governments have increased, although most of the budgets for these governments come from the national level, creating a dependent relationship.

The Republic of Korea is divided into nine provinces, the special city of Seoul, and five other special cities: Pusan, Taegu, Inch'on, Kwangju, and Taejon. Each has a legislative council that is elected by popular vote. The special cities and other large cities are divided into wards and precincts, while the provinces are divided into cities and counties. Provincial governors and mayors of province-level cities are also elected by popular vote. Counties are divided into towns, townships, and villages.

The Electoral System

The Central Election Management Commission was established in 1963 to oversee the management of elections and referenda campaigns, the voting process, and vote counts. Prior to 1987, along with democratization, the commission's independence was compromised by interference from government officials. The Commission is created by the 1987 Constitution and consists of nine members appointed for six-year terms by the president (3), National Assembly (3), and chief justice of the Supreme Court (3). The chairperson, the chief justice by custom, is elected from among the members. Members of the Commission are prohibited from joining political parties or participating in politics. The Commission oversees and appoints district commissions that, in turn, manage local elections involving heads of local government and council members. The Commission has the right to investigate allegations of election improprieties or irregularities, including corruption, bribery, publication of false information, misuse of election funds, and breach of election campaign regulations.

The constitution provides for direct election by secret ballot of the president and National Assembly by voters who are at least 20 years old. Prior to 1987 presidential elections were direct only in the periods of 1952–60 and 1963–71. Indirect systems of election were previously used. The one-term presidency and four-year term without limits for the National Assembly were established in 1987 as well. Presidential candidates must be at least 40 years of age and have lived for at least five years in the country. The system of elections to the National Assembly is changeable by legislative act, but, in recent years, three-quarters of the members are selected by plurality in single-member districts, with the remainder elected through proportional representation. Candidates in single-member districts may be either nominated by political parties or run as independents.

The Party System

ORIGINS OF THE PARTIES

Political parties first appeared in South Korea at the end of World War II. The decade of the 1950s was marked by the struggle between the Liberal Party, which Syngman Rhee established in 1951, and the Democratic Party, which originally supported Rhee but opposed his altering of the constitution to establish a strong presidency. The short-lived Second Republic saw the Democratic Party in power, but much weakened by factional infighting. Between 1963 and 1972, the first decade of Park Chung Hee's presidency, the dominant group was the government-sponsored Democratic Republican Party (DRP). During this period, relatively fair and open competition existed between the DRP and the opposition New Democratic Party (NDP). The establishment of the *yushin* system in 1972, however, undercut party politics. The president was now selected by the National Conference for Unification, whose members could not be affiliated with political parties, and the powers of the National Assembly were curtailed. The DRP itself became, in a sense, superfluous, and a battery of emergency regulations put a tight lid on the activities of opposition groups.

The unsettled period between the assassination of Park in October 1979 and Chun Doo Hwan's complete control of state powers in May 1980 saw increased activities by political parties, particularly the NDP, although at this time it was split into rival factions led by Kim Young Sam and Kim Dae Jung. On May 17, 1980, however, Chun Doo Hwan's military extended martial law to the entire nation, dissolved the National Assembly, prohibited all political activities and assembly, imposed tight censorship on press and media, closed universities, made labor strikes illegal, and banned rumors, slanders, or defamation of the government. Chun's harsh political repression continued unabated until 1984.

THE PARTIES IN LAW

Under the Political Party Act as amended on December 27, 1993, a group of 20 or more initiators who are not teachers, public officials, or other persons with the status of public officials can legally start the process of founding a political party. But any political party must have district parties that number one-tenth or more of the total regional election districts for the National Assembly members, which means 26 or more branch chapters. Moreover, any party's registration can be revoked if it does not obtain seats in the general election for the National Assembly members and does not get more than two-hundredths of the total effective votes.

To register as candidates for the election of the National Assembly members, party nominees need nomination letters and a deposit of 10 million won. In addition to the deposit money, independent candidates are required to submit recommendations from 300 to 500 voters.

The Political Funds Act on March 16, 1994, was revised in 1999 to increase regulation of campaign contributions. Among other things, virtually all major campaign funds continue to flow to candidates by way of political parties. It is so in part because the law prohibits individuals' direct contributions or "independent" expenditures to affect electoral outcomes, while it does not regulate political parties' expenditures "on behalf of" candidates.

The Election for Public Office and Election Malpractice Prevention Act of March 16, 1994, meticulously and strictly regulates the manner in which the elections take place through the Central Election Management Committee. For instance, the law stipulates that the period of the presidential, National Assembly, and local elections be 23 days, 17 days, and 14 days, respectively.

CAMPAIGNS AND ELECTIONS

Regionalism continues to be a major factor in voter preference. For example, in the 1996 election to the National Assembly, the New Korea Party of President Kim Young Sam won all 21 seats contested in Pusan, which is near Kim's hometown; the ruling New Korea Party (NKP) Party also picked up 17 out of 23 seats in the president's native province of South Kyongsang. In contrast, the National Council for New Politics, Cholla Province–based Kim Dae Jung's party, captured 36 out of 37 seats in Kwangju and the two Cholla Provinces. Further, Kim Jong Pil's United Liberal Democrats won 17 out of 21 sets in his native region, the two Ch'ungch'ong Provinces.

The election of President Roh Moo-hyun in 2002 represented the first left-leaning government in South Korea's history, drawing upon support of young voters in an election campaign that featured approval for continuing relations with North Korea, governmental programs to address social problems, as well as anti-American sentiments. Roh was selected as the Millennium Party's nominee in the first national primary held in South Korea. He went on to be narrowly elected and subsequently changed political parties to join the new Uri Party. Roh, a relative unknown prior to the election, successfully campaigned to young voters using electronic democracy, including a "fan club" for Roh on the Internet, illustrating the growing importance of the Internet and cell phones as a new vehicle for reaching voters in a country with an exceptionally high concentration of homes connected to the Internet. Increased use of televised candidate debates in 2002 also provided Roh with the opportunity to present his issues directly to the voters. The Central Election Management Commission also used its Web site to publicize extensive candidate information, including voting records and campaign sources, and created a special section of the Web site that appealed to young voters.

Major Political Parties

Political parties in South Korea tend to be centralized, revolving around a dominant politician who draws support on a regionalist basis. Candidate selection for parliament tends to be the prerogative of a small group of party leaders. Members do not pay dues or participate in the formation of the party platform. While the Uri Party has a slightly more leftist orientation, major Korean parties generally adhere to centrist positions that are not easily differentiated by the voter.

URI PARTY

(Uri Dang; UP)

The Uri Party was established in November 2003 as a splinter group from the Millennium Democratic Party in support of then-president Roh Moo-hyun. The party stunned the Korean establishment by winning 152 parliamentary seats in the 2004 elections, the largest number of seats in parliament; UP became the first left-leaning party to hold a parliamentary majority in South Korea. The party is a reform-oriented, liberal/social democratic party that has gained its support from young people, students, city dwellers, and voters in the Jeolla region. While the party won seats based upon a slight anti–United States bent, Roh has agreed to work with the United States in negotiations concerning North Korean nuclear weapons, and the president sent soldiers to Iraq as part of a peacekeeping mission led by the United States.

The UP's power decreased in 2005, as it failed to capture a single seat in by-elections held in six electoral districts.

GRAND NATIONAL PARTY

(Hannara Dang; HD)

Grand National Party is a coalition of the old New Korea Party and the Democratic Party. On January 23, 1990, in order to break from the problem of a "ruling minority and opposition majority" (yoso yadae), President Roh Tae Woo merged his ruling Democratic Justice Party with two opposition parties, Kim Young Sam's Reunification and Democracy Party (RDP) and Kim Jong Pil's New Democratic Republican Party (NDRP), into a grand conservative alliance to create the Democratic Liberal Party. The creation of DLP in the image of Japan's Liberal Democratic Party was not well received by the public. However, by taking the chance to merge his party with the ruling DJP, Kim Young Sam, who had perpetually been in the opposition, subsequently won the governing DLP's nomination for the presidency in 1992. After suffering a big loss in the local elections in 1995, President Kim renamed the party the New Korea Party.

During the 1997 presidential campaign, the contender Lee Hoi Chang changed the New Korea Party's name to Grand National Party. This was seen as Lee Hoi Chang's attempt to remake the party in his own image, since he was in the middle of an unsuccessful campaign and then-president Kim had been only lukewarm about supporting his candidacy.

Although figures on party membership are not readily available, both the 1992 presidential election and the 1996 National Assembly election showed that popular support for the party was generally more balanced throughout the nation than for the opposition parties. Because of the government's pro–Kyongsang province development policies that have been in effect since Park Chung Hee seized power in 1961, political support for the ruling party in the two Kyongsang provinces remains pronounced.

The party supports a close ROK alliance with the United States, and it expressed concern over U.S. withdrawal of some of its troops from South Korea in 2004. The GNP describes itself as a "conservative-progressive" party. Major policy concerns include maintaining close relations with the United States, strengthening a free-market economy, and moving cautiously toward greater cooperation with North Korea. In 2004 the GNP captured 121 of 299 seats in the National Assembly, becoming the main opposition party to a new majority party, URI. It gained back six seats in by-elections held in October 2005.

Minor Political Parties

MILLENNIUM DEMOCRATIC PARTY (MDP)

(Saechonnyon Minju Dang)

Founded by Kim Dae Jung as the National Congress for New Politics, the party became the Millennium Democratic Party in 2000. Kim was elected president in 1997, pursuing improved relations with North Korea, for which he received the Nobel Peace Prize. President Roh Moo-hyun also pursued the presidency as an MDP candidate, succeeding Kim in February 2003. However, supporters of Roh left the party in 2003 to form the Uri Party. The Millennium Party is a liberal party that

has lost support over the issue of impeachment of Roh, which it supported.

UNITED LIBERAL PARTY

(Jayu Minju Yonmaeng)

The United Liberal Party is a right-wing conservative party that is supported by a rural constituency and favors stronger government at the regional and local levels. The party was founded in 1995 by farmers and fishermen. It held four seats in parliament in 2004.

DEMOCRATIC LABOR PARTY (DLP)

(Minkook Dang)

The Democratic Labor Party is a left-wing social democratic party that attracts support from farmers, factory workers, and the urban poor. The party was organized by the Korean Federation of Trade Unions in 1997 and had 10 seats in the National Assembly in 2004.

Other Political Forces

MILITARY

The dominant role of the military in the political system has been a feature that the Republic of Korea shares with many developing countries; yet, in light of Korea's long history, it is something of an aberration. Traditionally, it has been civilian scholar-officials versed in the Confucian classics, rather than military officers, who have held political power. Popular disapproval of the military, particularly among students and intellectuals, grew out of the conviction that military rule per se was illegitimate, no matter what its accomplishments. Yet the ruling military circle saw itself as the only group in society with the training, discipline, and organization needed to run the state in an efficient manner. It has taken credit, with much justification, for the spectacular modernization of South Korea in the post-1961 period.

The army was established in November 1948. All male youths are required to undertake some form of military service.

In contrast to the situation in the early 1960s when South Korea lacked trained administrators and professionals and officers took over a broad range of functions, there is now a large, highly educated class of civil servants, technocrats, and managers with whom the military must cooperate in the national interest. The election of Kim Young Sam, the first civilian president since 1961, and his successful purge of politicized military officers, who centered around the Chun Doo Hwan–controlled secret military society *Hanahoe* (literally, One Society) signaled the end of the prolonged military dominance of South Korean politics.

UNITED STATES

The Republic of Korea's most important foreign relations have been with the United States. The United States has supported South Korea militarily and economically since before the outbreak of the Korean War, and a continued U.S. commitment to the peninsula has been seen both in Washington and in Seoul as essential to the country's security. During the administration of President Jimmy Carter, there was talk of a phased withdrawal of ground troops, the most visible sign of American commitment. But when intelligence reports in 1978 and 1979 revealed that North Korea had greater military strength than was previously estimated, this idea was dropped. Although the Reagan administration's support of Korea's new military regime under the leadership of Chun Doo Hwan aroused significant anti-American feelings, especially among intellectuals and militant students during the 1980s, the continued presence of American troops undoubtedly has played an important role in keeping peace and stability intact. In the post–cold war era, the United States has reaffirmed its security commitments to South Korea by deciding to maintain troops, albeit at a somewhat reduced level.

JAPAN

The specter of 35 years of Japan's colonial rule over Korea still haunts the relations between Japan and South Korea. The years since 1965 have seen close cooperation between the two neighboring countries, particularly in the economic sphere. The two countries co-hosted the World Cup in 2002. However, the rise of Japan's military capability and the gradual increase of its willingness to use its forces overseas in the post–cold war era cause concern to South Korea as well as to China. It is all the more the case given Japan's lack of reflection on its past militarism. There is no doubt that Japan remains one of South Korea's most important allies and partners. But Japan's position on Korean unification seems to remain ambiguous, as it does not wish to see a unified, strong Korea.

CHINA

While maintaining its traditional relations of comradeship with North Korea, China has been rapidly deepening its economic relations with South Korea, particularly since the establishment of diplomatic ties in 1992. The trade volume between the two countries reached about $60 billion by 2000, and is estimated to reach $100 billion by 2008. China seems to seek closer links with prosperous South Korea because both nations fear the possibility of the rise of a Japan-centered order in East Asia. Concerning the Korean unification issue, China clearly does not want to see the collapse of the North Korean regime and the consequent instability and trouble on its border, but it may not want to see Korea united soon either.

National Prospects

The Republic of Korea has come a long way in modernizing the country in terms of both economic and political development. Ever since its initial, if belated, efforts at modernization were hijacked by Japan, the nation has suffered many traumatic experiences, including Japan's colonial rule, which systematically tried to degrade and destroy the Korean identity; the Korean War, which caused excruciating societal pain, dislocation, and turmoil; and the wrenching process of condensed, if desperate, economic development. To South Korea, which has found its own path to modernization and present-day prosperity and thereby regained some of its national confidence, the two issues that seem to be most critical and challenging are Korean identity and national reunification.

In the midst of growing globalization pressures that appear to drive the convergence of diverse political economies, Korea finds itself undergoing a crucial historical moment when it can and must make strategic choices on how to continue to modernize the country. Yet, the popularity of liberal parties, such as Uri, suggests the possibility of a mixed economy that incorporates some welfare state measures. The American model of high productivity and competitiveness by deregulation and freer market competition appears tough to resist. But the questions remain: Which social path do South Koreans want to pursue? What do they as a people value most?

The reunification problem is tied, in part, to national security issues. Negotiations over North Korea's nuclear weapons program have involved the United States, Japan, China, as well as Russia and North and South Korea. In the end, reunification may well be a matter of time, given the nation's long history as a unified country and the people's strong desire for reunification. But what kind of country will unified Korea be? Unification would have unanticipated consequences, despite careful planning, politically, culturally, and economically.

Further Reading

Amsden, Alice H. *Asia's Next Giant: South Korea and Late Industrialization.* Oxford: Oxford University Press, 1989.

Clifford, Mark L. *Troubled Tiger: Businessmen, Bureaucrats, and Generals in South Korea.* Armonk, N.Y.: M. E. Sharpe, 1994.

Eckert, Carter J., et al. *Korea Old and New: A History.* Seoul: Ilchokak, 1990.

Federal Research Division, Library of Congress. "A Country Study: South Korea." October 1, 2004.

Henderson, Gregory. *Korea: The Politics of Vortex.* Cambridge, Mass.: Harvard University Press, 1968.

Koh, B. C. "South Korea in 1995." *Asian Survey* 36, no. 1 (January 1996).

———. "South Korea in 1996." *Asian Survey* 37, no. 1 (January 1997).

Lee, Hong Yung. "South Korea in 1992." *Asian Survey* 33, no. 1 (January 1993).

"Survey: South Korea." *The Economist,* December 7, 2004.

KUWAIT

(Dawlat Al-Kuwayt)

By Jill Crystal, M.A.
Revised by Ghassan Salame, Ph.D.
Further revision by Curtis R. Ryan, Ph.D.

Kuwait is a nation of more than 2.3 million people (2005 est.) at the northwest end of the Persian Gulf. It is governed by an emir from the Sabah family. Kuwait first emerged as a semiautonomous political unit in the early 18th century when it was settled by the Bani Utub branch of the Arabian Anazah confederation. The ascendancy of the Sabah family dates from about 1756, when the leading families appointed a Sabah sheikh to represent them in dealings with the Ottoman Empire. In the 19th century Kuwaiti rulers, caught on the fringes of empires and fearing Ottoman, Persian, and Wahhabi incursions, acquiesced to the growing British influence in the Gulf region. In 1899 Sheikh Mubarak (founder of the current ruling line) negotiated a treaty with Great Britain that secured Kuwait's independence from the Ottomans in exchange for British control over its foreign relations. The association with Great Britain, which continued until independence in 1961, consolidated the Sabah family's control over domestic politics.

The Kuwaiti constitution was promulgated on November 11, 1962. In international politics, Kuwait's existence as an independent state remained tenuous. Its current borders were established at the 1922 Uqair Conference attended by Britain, Iraq, and Saudi Arabia. Kuwait remains threatened by its neighbors, however, particularly by Iraq, which laid claim to the sheikhdom's territory in a 1961 proclamation. That claim has been revived on many occasions and resulted, ultimately, in the August 2, 1990, Iraqi invasion and conquest of Kuwait. Following months of regional and international tension, the emirate was liberated by a U.S.-led coalition in the 1991 Gulf War.

Kuwait, originally a pearling and trading economy, became increasingly dependent on oil after World War II. In 1936 Sheikh Ahmad had granted a concession to the Kuwait Oil Company (jointly owned by British Petroleum and Gulf Oil). In 1973 Kuwait acquired a 25 percent share in the company and took over full ownership in 1976. Production rose to 1.076 billion barrels a year by 1972 but fell to 607 million barrels in 1980 in line with the state's conservationist policy following the 1973 price increases. Kuwait's current reserves are among the highest in the world and, at current production levels, will last for over a century. The consequences of a transformation to an oil-based economy were to give Kuwait one of the highest per capita incomes in the world (almost $20,000) and to increase its dependence on foreign trade and foreign laborers (who now constitute more than half the population). The large revenues, paid directly to the rulers, freed the Sabahs from much of their historical dependence on merchant allies and financed a large bureaucracy to administer new welfare and development projects and to redistribute wealth through state employment.

The System of Government

Kuwait is a semiconstitutional monarchy governed by an emir from the Sabah family who rules in conjunction with senior family members through an appointed Council of Ministers.

EXECUTIVE

In accordance with the 1962 constitution, Kuwait's chief executive, the emir, is chosen from male descendants of Sheikh Mubarak. Since 1915 all of Kuwait's emirs but one have been chosen alternately from the Salim and Jabir branches of the Sabah family. The actual selection is made privately by senior family members. In this manner, Kuwait's present emir, Sheikh Jabir al-Ahmad al-Sabah (born 1928 in the Jabir line), was named heir apparent and crown prince in 1966. He acceded to power peacefully in December 1977 on the death of the emir Sheikh Sabah al-Salim al-Sabah (of the Salim line). The present crown prince (a Salim), appointed February 1978, is Sheikh Jabir's second cousin, Sa'ad Abdullah al-Salim al-Sabah. The crown prince held the title of prime minister until 2003, when the emir named Sheikh Sabah al-Ahmad al-Sabah as prime minister.

The emir has very broad powers but governs within the informal constraints set by family consensus. Intrafamily disagreements are managed and family control assured by the direct recruitment of family members into the highest and most sensitive administrative posts.

LEGISLATURE

Kuwait's National Assembly (Majlis al-Umma) was first elected in 1963. Subsequent elections were held in 1967, 1971, and 1975. In August 1976 the Assembly was dissolved and several articles of the constitution was suspended by decree of the emir. The Assembly's functions were assumed by six appointed legislative committees under the Council of Ministers.

Several factors led to the suspension of the National Assembly in 1976. The Assembly had grown popular as a forum for public opinion and criticism of government policies. Debates over oil company agreements and production levels and over social policy (especially housing) sometimes included verbal attacks on members of the Sabah family. The government had become concerned about internal security problems precipitated by terrorist activity and the rise of a leftist opposition. The Assembly had also become an effective forum for Middle Eastern issues, of particular importance to the country's non-Kuwaiti majority, who at the time included 300,000 resident Palestinians. Just prior to its dissolution, the Assembly adopted pro-Palestinian resolutions condemning Syrian involvement in the Lebanese civil war, in opposition to the government's officially neutral position. The dissolution of the Assembly was accompanied by press curbs, the introduction of new censorship rules, the arrest of several leftists, and the dissolution or suspension of several newspapers, social clubs, and professional and trade unions.

In February 1981 new elections were held and the Assembly reconvened with new guidelines. The Assembly consists of 50 seats, two in each of 25 constituencies. Election is by simple plurality for four-year terms. The majority of seats were filled, as in previous elections, by conservative government loyalists and members of traditionally allied families. Within this group, some observers saw a shift in predominance from the established commercial elite toward tribal bedouin leaders (who took 23 of the 50 seats), toward

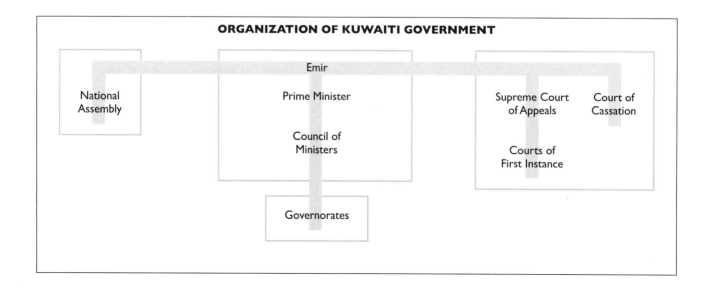

ORGANIZATION OF KUWAITI GOVERNMENT

National Assembly

Emir
Prime Minister
Council of Ministers

Supreme Court of Appeals   Court of Cassation

Courts of First Instance

Governorates

younger technocrats (who took 13 seats), and toward Sunni Muslim "fundamentalists" (5 seats). The election was viewed as a defeat for more radical Arab nationalists who, under the leadership of Dr. Ahmad al-Khatib of the Arab Nationalist Movement, had held a third of the seats in the 1976 Assembly but won no seats in the 1981 election. It was also a defeat for the Shiite Muslims, who ran several candidates but won only four seats.

This realignment was partly attributable to a redistricting that affected many previously radical and Shiite areas. New elections were held on February 20, 1985. The results showed a reemergence of the secular Arab nationalist movement led by Dr. Ahmad al-Khatib (5 seats) and some erosion of the Islamic fundamentalist group, two of whose leaders were defeated.

Following the liberation of the emirate from Iraqi occupation, new Assembly elections were held in 1992 in which most of the new representatives were opponents—or at least critics—of the regime. This Assembly, and its successors, included a strong Islamist influence that has been demonstrated in a number of pieces of legislation. In 1994, 39 of the 50 delegates backed a request from the Assembly to the government to make the sharia the only legal system in the emirate. This was promptly rejected by the government. But in 1996 an Islamist-sponsored proposal to introduce gender segregation in colleges and universities was passed in the National Assembly.

The issue of women's suffrage came before parliament twice again in 1999 but ultimately was defeated. After the first bill was defeated by a mere two votes, the emir shocked many even in the feminist movement by granting women full political rights by royal decree. Yet this too remained subject to a parliamentary vote for its confirmation as law, and once again the legislature defeated the proposal, this time by a much larger margin. The anti-suffrage vote was based largely on an alliance within parliament of Islamists and traditional tribal MPs. Liberal activists and many Shiite MPs supported the measure but with insufficient numbers to win a legislative majority. The surprise support of the monarchy, however, led many observers to conclude that women's political rights would now be inevitable, even if subject to further delays. In 2005 the parliament finally approved constitutional amendments that granted full political rights to women. The first female cabinet minister was appointed in June 2005.

JUDICIARY

Kuwait's judicial system, as reorganized in 1980, has three levels. The highest court is the Supreme Court of Appeals, although the emir can act as a de facto final appeals court. There is the national Court of First Instance and summary courts in each administrative district. The legal code is drawn primarily from the Egyptian and Ottoman codes, with the constitutional stipulation that legislation not conflict with the shariah (Islamic law). "Acts of Government" are outside the jurisdiction of the courts.

REGIONAL AND LOCAL GOVERNMENT

Kuwait's administration is highly centralized. However, Kuwait City, Ahmadi, Jahra, and Hawalli are, administratively, provincial governorates, with governors and municipal councils appointed by the emir. Smaller administrative divisions are the same as electoral constituencies.

The Electoral System

Suffrage is restricted to adult (age 21), literate, male Kuwaiti citizens; beginning in 2007 women age 21 and over will likewise have the right to vote. Citizens are defined as persons whose families lived in Kuwait before 1921. Members of the police and armed forces cannot vote, nor can foreigners, some 60 percent of the population. Kuwait's National Assembly includes 50 parliamentary seats, with two seats for each of the emirate's 25 electoral districts. The 15 members of the Kuwaiti cabinet serve also as ex officio members of parliament and are permitted to vote in the chamber's deliberations. For the elected full members of parliament, however, districts range greatly in population size. For this reason the topic of redistricting to a more demographically even format is a perennial issue of debate within Kuwaiti politics. Islamists in particular argue that the system of uneven districts weighs against more rural and conservative voters, and hence against much of their political base. In the 2003 elections, however, Islamist candidates continued to do well, winning 21 seats compared to 14 seats to progovernment candidates, 12 for independents, and most surprisingly a mere 3 seats for liberal MPs.

The Party System

Candidates run on individual platforms since political parties are illegal in Kuwait.

Major Political Parties

There are no political parties in Kuwait.

Minor Political Parties

There are no political parties in Kuwait.

Other Political Forces

POLITICAL BLOCS

In the 1990s, despite the continuing ban on political parties, a number of political "tendencies" did emerge. These political tendencies, if not political parties, include two predominantly Sunni Muslim groupings: the Islamic Constitutional Movement and the Islamic Popular Group. The former is the more moderate of the two and may have ties to the Muslim Brotherhood in various Arab countries. Both the Islamic Constitutional Movement and the Islamic Popular Group had some success in the 1992 and 1996 elections, and both have been represented in the Kuwaiti Council of Ministers. Other political tendencies include the Kuwaiti Democratic Forum, a secular liberal grouping pressing for an end to corruption and royal nepotism in political life, and the Islamic National Alliance, which is the main group organizing Kuwait's Shiite Muslims. Since 1997 the liberal Kuwaiti Democratic Forum has been increasingly superceded by the National Democratic Forum (NDF). The NDF is a secular bloc that supports women's suffrage and other liberal reforms.

RULING-FAMILY, TRIBAL, AND MERCHANT LEADERS

Kuwait has had more success than neighboring Gulf sheikhdoms in settling intrafamily disputes peaceably. Since the time of Mubarak, succession has been confined, relatively smoothly, to the Jabir and Salim lines. Personal ambitions within the family, loosely associated with either traditionalist or more modern points of view, are the primary sources of dispute.

Tribal and merchant families, whose input into the decision-making process has declined since the development of an oil economy, have not presented an overt challenge to the regime. Nonetheless, these somewhat overlapping groups may offer the greatest potential threat to regime stability. They have been mollified economically by the business opportunities associated with increased oil revenues. Politically, they have been partially co-opted into the state through the Assembly and ministerial posts. Still, their autonomous corporate existence, their own media—notably *Al-Qabas*, a daily newspaper—and historical claim to political participation could provide the basis for a loyal or disloyal opposition. This became especially clear following the withdrawal of Iraqi forces from Kuwait in 1991. Kuwait's mercantile and technocratic elites in particular pushed for democratization in the emirate, many contesting the elections of the reconstituted National Assembly in 1992. In that first post–Gulf War election, critics of the regime took a majority of the new Assembly's seats.

WOMEN

Kuwait women played a major role in the resistance to Iraqi occupation in 1990–91 by conveying messages, harboring dissidents, and smuggling supplies. Since then the regime has frequently cited their heroism, yet their demands for political rights were thwarted just as often. This remained all the more glaring given the widespread social rights that Kuwaiti women enjoy, including universal education and fairly extensive job opportunities. Women comprise a clear majority of university students in the country and also hold jobs as professionals in the government and private sector. In the continuing quest for full political rights, Kuwaiti women organized a pro-suffrage movement through networks such as the Women's Cultural and Social Society, a longstanding feminist organization. They also organized through more recent political creations such as the Women's Issues Committee and through support of the National Democratic Forum. Their efforts paid off in 2005, when the Assembly passed constitutional amendments giving women full political rights by 2007.

MILITARY

The military is subject to firm, and personal, Sabah control. Disturbances have been reported in recent years within the police force and at the infantry school. There is some potential for a disenchanted prince within the military establishment to use his position in alliance with other groups to create opposition for the regime.

SHIITE MUSLIMS

Estimates of the number of Shiite in Kuwait vary. Some 10 percent of the total population may be Shiite, while the number of Kuwaiti nationals who are Shiite may be as high as 20 percent. Most of these latter are probably Persian in origin. While a small portion of the Shiite community is influentially placed in commerce, the community's impact on policy has been slight. Still, Kuwaiti Shiites are increasingly organized in backing candidates from the Islamic National Alliance in elections to the National Assembly.

NON-NATIONALS

The citizens of Kuwait remain a minority in the emirate, constituting at the most 45 percent of the population. Palestinians and Indians have historically formed the two largest groups of non-nationals. Crucial to the economy, these non-nationals, some now of several generations' standing, have few political rights and little chance of acquiring them through citizenship. They cannot organize independent trade unions; they cannot own property, stock in Kuwaiti businesses, or companies without a Kuwaiti partner. They enjoy only limited access to the benefits of the welfare state.

Non-nationals, however, have so far provided only sporadic opposition to the regime. Their capacity to organize is minimized by internal cleavages (language, culture, and occupation), fear of deportation, and self-interest in keeping lucrative if insecure jobs. Their long-term threat to the regime lies, first, in their potential nuisance value in alliance with other disaffected groups, and, second, in their contacts abroad. The Kuwaiti border with Iraq is difficult to close effectively against the movement of people, money, weapons, and ideas. Activities of the Palestine Liberation Organization, while financially supported by Kuwait outside its borders, have long worried the Kuwaiti regime, given the large Palestinian population in the emirate up until the 1991 Gulf War.

Kuwait's rulers are well aware of the trade-offs involved in having such a large non-national population. In the months surrounding the constitutional crisis of 1976, the government deported thousands of foreign (primarily Arab) workers. New deportations (mainly Iranian this time) took place in 1985. At the same time, the government made some social services available to foreigners and opened a few loopholes for acquiring Kuwaiti citizenship.

The 1991 Gulf War, however, changed the situation for Palestinians in particular. Following Iraq's defeat and withdrawal, groups of Kuwaiti vigilante groups executed an unknown number of people accused of collaborating with Iraq, and many of those accused and executed were Palestinians. Upon reassuming power in Kuwait, the restored Sabah regime took vengeance on the Arab regimes and organizations it viewed as supportive of Iraq, such as Jordan, Yemen, and the PLO. Kuwait promptly expelled tens of thousands of Jordanian, Palestinian, and Yemeni guest workers (whose positions were largely filled by workers from other Arab states and from South Asia).

National Prospects

Thus far Kuwait has maintained a high degree of political stability through a combination of cautious leadership, a cohesive ruling coalition, government largesse, and alliances with powerful external states—such as Great Britain and the United States. Domestically, merchant and tribal allies of the regime have profited from business ventures, while the bulk of the Kuwaiti population has benefited from the massive distribution of oil wealth in the form of direct transfer payments, guaranteed state employment (the state is Kuwait's largest employer), and free or subsidized housing, health care, and education. As extensive social services have become the norm, however, they may be seen less as examples of the rulers' largesse and more as rights that the individual, as a citizen, can claim from the state.

Kuwait's leaders also face possible trouble from the internalization of external threats. Iraqi claims to Kuwait and its oil had been a recurrent problem even before the 1990 invasion and could easily be revived by any regime in Baghdad. The Arab-Israeli conflict, which insinuated itself into local politics, most notably in the 1976 Assembly suspension, continues to be monitored closely by Palestinians and other Arabs. After the Iranian revolution and subsequent Iran-Iraq War (1980–88), Kuwait also had to contend with growing Shiite unrest (manifested in demonstrations and bombing incidents) and with security problems associated directly with the war itself. Iran bombed Kuwaiti refineries and tankers several times during the war, as a warning against aid to Iraq.

This sensitivity to the regional political environment, coupled with potential internal threats, became much more evident after 1983. On December 12, 1983, a truck bomb exploded in the vicinity of the American embassy and other bombs exploded at five other sites. Attempts against the life of the editors of two Kuwaiti newspapers (*Al-Anba* and *As-Siyassa*) followed, as did the assassination of an Iraqi diplomat. On May 25, 1985, the emir escaped an attack on his motorcade in which at least four people were killed.

Six weeks later bombs were planted in two popular cafés, killing 10 people and injuring 56. Kuwaiti courts and government officials accused pro-Iranian Shiite militants of having perpetrated these acts. Iran systematically denied any involvement, but Kuwait deported thousands of Iranians and Lebanese and Iraqi Shiites from the emirate.

These internal security concerns of the 1970s and 1980s, however, paled in comparison with the external security threat demonstrated in Iraq's invasion of Kuwait in 1990. But even after the U.S.-led coalition defeated and expelled Iraq from Kuwait, both domestic and regional security tensions remained very real for the Sabah regime. The Sabahs attempted to rectify any resurgent external threats by completing a string of alliances with major world powers, including military defense commitments from the United States, United Kingdom, France, and Russia and an agreement on military cooperation with the Peoples' Republic of China. In short, Kuwait had established military linkages to all five permanent members of the UN Security Council. In addition, since 1981 Kuwait has been a member of the Gulf Cooperation Council along with Bahrain, Oman, Qatar, Saudi Arabia, and the United Arab Emirates.

In 2003 Kuwait was among the very few Arab states to support the U.S. invasion of Iraq. While the emirate refused to send troops to participate in the U.S. occupation, the regime did strongly support the overthrow of Saddam Hussein. After the war, however, Kuwait's security situation actually declined, as terrorism increased in Iraq and throughout the region, due in large part to local hostility to the U.S. occupation. That hostility also extended to regimes (such as the Kuwaiti monarchy) that are perceived to be too close to the United States.

On the domestic front, the key recent issues have been conservative pressures from Islamist members of the National Assembly, on the one hand, and liberalizing pressures from groups supporting women's suffrage and political rights, on the other. A third key issue continues to be the conflict between reformers seeking to clean up public life and resisting members of the "old guard" of Kuwaiti politics. A June 1997 assassination attempt on Abdullah al-Naybari, a leading reformer in the National Assembly, served to underscore this line of tension. Naybari had led the first post–Gulf War investigations into charges of corruption and embezzlement within the government. Several Kuwaitis and Iranians were arrested for the attack, but many Kuwaiti democracy advocates took the attack to mean that the continuing investigations were coming too close to powerful government figures.

Kuwait's small size, vulnerable strategic location, and dependence on foreign labor all render it particularly susceptible to domestic unrest and especially to external disputes in the Persian Gulf region. The granting of suffrage to women beginning in 2007 should ease one pressure on the regime, but the tension with Islamic militants remains significant, as evidenced by the January 2005 skirmishes between militants and police.

Further Reading

Al-Ebraheem, Hassan Ali. *Kuwait and the Gulf: Small States and the International System.* London: Croom Helm, 1984.

Crystal, Jill. *Oil and Politics in the Gulf: Rulers and Merchants in Kuwait and Qatar.* 2d edition. New York: Cambridge University Press, 1995.

Hoyt, P.D., "Legitimacy, Identity, and Political Development in the Arab World." *International Studies Review* 42, no. 1 (May 1998): 173–76.

Kostiner, J. *Middle East Monarchies: The Challenge of Modernity.* Boulder, Colo.: Lynne Rienner, 2000.

Lesch, Ann M. "Palestinians in Kuwait." *Journal of Palestine Studies* 20, no. 4 (summer 1991).

Tetreault, Mary Ann. "Autonomy, Necessity, and the Small State: Ruling Kuwait in the Twentieth Century." *International Organization* 45, no. 4 (autumn 1991).

———. "Civil Society in Kuwait: Protected Spaces and Women's Rights." *Middle East Journal* 47, no. 2 (spring 1993).

KYRGYZ REPUBLIC

(Kyrgyz Respublikasy)

By Eugene Huskey, Ph.D.

Kyrgyzstan is a small, mountainous country in Central Asia. Bordered by China on the east, Uzbekistan on the west, Kazakstan on the north, and Tajikistan on the south, Kyrgyzstan has a population of 5.1 million (2005 est.) living in a territory roughly the size of England.

The country takes its name from the indigenous ethnic group, the Kyrgyz, who account for almost 65 percent of the population. Historically a nomadic people, the Kyrgyz belong ethnically and linguistically to the Turkic world, whose members populate territories stretching from Manchuria and Siberia in the east to Bulgaria and Turkey in the west. Islam is the dominant religion among the Kyrgyz, though its influence is far more evident in the south than in the north of the country. Among the other ethnic groups in Kyrgyzstan are several indigenous Central Asian peoples, such as the Uzbeks (18 percent), as well as numerous European settlers, including Russians (12 percent), Ukrainians (1 percent), and Germans (1 percent). The European groups migrated to the region during the past century while the country was under Russian and later Soviet rule. Whatever their ethnic background, citizens of the country are known as Kyrgyzstanis.

One of the 15 former republics of the USSR, Kyrgyzstan claimed state sovereignty in August 1991, though complete independence arrived only with the final collapse of the Soviet Union in December 1991. Unlike several other Soviet republics, Kyrgyzstan had never experienced statehood before. Indeed, it acquired the status of a territory in the Soviet Union only in 1936. Although the Kyrgyz trace their roots as a people to the 1,000-year-old legendary figure of Manas, Kyrgyzstan's statehood is an unintended by-product of the Soviet colonial era.

In the transition from Communist rule, the political leadership of Kyrgyzstan has sought to establish a new identity for the country by abandoning the Soviet political inheritance and lessening Russian cultural influence. The indigenization of cultural policy, for example, led to the replacement of Russian place names with Kyrgyz counterparts. The country's name changed from Kirgizia (sometimes spelled Khirgizia) to Kyrgyzstan. The main street in the capital of Bishkek (formerly Frunze), which previously bore the name of the Soviet secret police chief, Dzerzhinsky, became Erkindik (Freedom) Prospect. To revive the Kyrgyz language, which had gone into decline in the Soviet era, the parliament of Kyrgyzstan passed a language law that favored Kyrgyz at the expense of Russian. These and other measures prompted such a large exodus of highly trained Russians and other Europeans that the president of Kyrgyzstan scaled back the indigenization campaign in 1994 to stem the tide. Recent concessions to the dwindling Russian population include the passage of legislation designating Russian as an official language. Kyrgyz remains the country's state language.

The System of Government

Like France and Russia, Kyrgyzstan has adopted semi-presidential institutional arrangements, which divide executive authority between a directly elected president and an appointed prime minister who requires the confidence of parliament. Thus, where the president is the head of state, the prime minister is the head of the government.

EXECUTIVE

The Kyrgyzstan constitution of 1993, the first in the independence era, grants the president broad powers over the shaping and execution of domestic and foreign policy. He has the authority to appoint—with the consent of parliament—the leading figures in the government and the judiciary, he may declare war or introduce a state of emergency, he has the right to submit issues to popular referendum, and he enjoys wide decree-making powers. After a referendum expressing a lack of popular confidence in parliament, the president may dissolve the legislature and call new elections.

The president maintains a staff of approximately 100 officials to assist him in overseeing the work of the prime minister and his government (Council of Ministers) and the regional authorities beneath them. In 2004 the government was composed of 25 members besides the prime minister, including three vice premiers, twelve ministers, and numerous heads of state committees and agencies. Approximately 17,000 civil servants work in the country's ministries and local administrations.

Like French president Charles de Gaulle at the beginning of the Fifth Republic, the first president of Kyrgyzstan, Askar Akaev, helped to define the office of the presidency. A Kyrgyz physicist and computer specialist who spent his early adult life in Leningrad (now St. Petersburg), Akaev made the presidency the institutional engine of economic and political reform in Kyrgyzstan. At the same time, he championed the politics of inclusion, serving as a mediator among various political, ethnic, and regional interests. As a result, in terms of its political power, the presidency towered above the government, the legislature, and the judiciary during his tenure in office. However, in 2005, widespread dissatisfaction with his government, including suspicions that he had interfered with the legislative elections of early 2005, led to massive street protests (known as the "Tulip Revolution") that forced him into exile in March; Kurmanbek Bakiev was named interim president in advance of presidential elections in July. Bakiev won those elections and became the country's second post-independence president. However, the imme-

diate post-election period was filled with political unrest and street violence, leaving his authority in question.

LEGISLATURE

Through referendums engineered by the country's president, Kyrgyzstan has periodically altered the structure, size, and powers of its national legislature. Following the introduction of the constitution of 1993 and the passage of a referendum in October 1994, Kyrgyzstan replaced a 350-person legislature inherited from the Soviet era with a smaller bicameral parliament, known as the Jogorku Kenesh, or Supreme Soviet. A successful referendum in February 2003 led to yet another revision of the legislative framework of the country. With the February and March 2005 elections the Jogorku Kenesh became a unicameral legislature with only 75 deputies. The elections were widely denounced as unfair, and the resulting protests forced President Akaev into exile. The new parliament named Kurmanbek Bakiev as interim president and prime minister, and Bakiev and the new parliament agreed to a deal in which he would retain the interim executive posts until a July presidential election, and in return the old parliament would dissolve in favor of the new 75-member body.

JUDICIARY

Kyrgyzstan inherited from the Soviet era a variant of the Continental civil law system. Although president and parliament have remade the country's legislation in recent years through the issuance of new laws and decrees, they have left virtually intact the structure of legal institutions. Criminal proceedings as well as civil disputes between individuals are heard in courts of general jurisdiction, which operate at every administrative level, from the district and city courts at the bottom of the judicial hierarchy to the Supreme Court at the top. The only significant structural change to the Soviet judicial inheritance was the recent elimination of a separate hierarchy of courts to hear commercial cases. Commercial disputes, which had previously been decided in special arbitrazh courts, are now heard in the courts of general jurisdiction.

Conflicts between branches or levels of government are matters for the new nine-person Constitutional Court in Bishkek, which has thus far been reluctant to challenge powerful political interests. There are also courts of elders (aksakal), designed to revive traditional Kyrgyz justice in less serious cases.

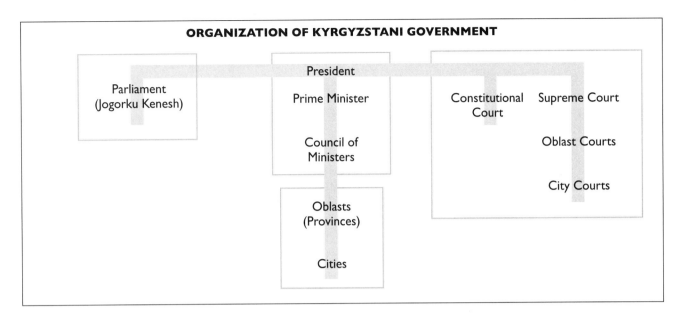

ORGANIZATION OF KYRGYZSTANI GOVERNMENT

President
Prime Minister

Parliament
(Jogorku Kenesh)

Council of
Ministers

Constitutional   Supreme Court
Court

Oblast Courts

City Courts

Oblasts
(Provinces)

Cities

All judges are nominated by the president and confirmed by parliament, though the justices on the country's highest courts are said to be "elected" by the legislature. Constitutional Court justices serve 15-year terms, while members of the Supreme Court have 10-year terms of office. All other judges serve 7-year terms after an initial probationary term of three years. Higher court judges may be removed from office for high treason and other crimes by a two-thirds vote of parliament, based on a finding of wrongdoing by the Constitutional Court. Lower court judges enjoy no such security in office. They may be removed administratively for disreputable conduct or failing a performance evaluation or judicially on the basis of a conviction in a higher court.

REGIONAL AND LOCAL GOVERNMENT

Kyrgyzstan is a unitary government divided into seven regions—Batken, Chu, Issyk-Kul (or Ysyk-Kol), Jalal-Abad, Naryn, Osh, and Talas—and the capital city of Bishkek. The regions are in turn divided into a total of 51 major cities and rural districts. Formerly part of the Osh region, Batken was created in 2000 in the wake of recent incursions by armed Islamists into this southwestern region of the country.

Each region has its own governor, known as an *akim,* and a legislative assembly, or *kenesh.* Within the regions, there is an *akim* and *kenesh* in each rural district and major city as well as a kenesh in each village and settlement. Whereas the *kenesh* are popularly elected, an *akim* serves at the pleasure of the executive official at the next administrative level. Thus, President Akaev appoints the regional governors, and they in turn select the *akimy* in the cities and districts beneath them. Only in the case of Bishkek is the *akim* directly elected by the population, a novelty in all of Central Asia. In this executive-dominated system, the *akimy* wield almost unlimited power in their locales; the role of the *kenesh* is consultative at best.

Despite President Akaev's ability to appoint and dismiss the regional governors, he was able to impose a tight rein on local bureaucracies, an indication of the weakness of the state in Kyrgyzstan. With their own bases of local support as well as political allies among deputies and executive officials in Bishkek, the regional akimy became power brokers in Kyrgyzstani politics. Thus, the most effective check on presidential power comes not from the legislature or the courts but from the regional elites.

The Electoral System

Members of the 75-seat parliament are elected every five years in single-member districts. The districts are of roughly equal size, ranging from 31,000 to more than 36,000 voters. Contests for parliamentary seats are decided by a two-round system similar to that governing presidential elections.

The president of Kyrgyzstan is elected for a five-year term and may not hold the office for more than two terms in succession. However, in 1998 the Constitutional Court ruled—contrary to its Russian counterpart—that for electoral purposes President Akaev's first term would not count because it commenced before the adoption of the constitution; he was thus able to extend his tenure until being forced from office in 2005. Eligibility for the presidency is limited to Kyrgyz-speaking persons between the ages of 35 and 65 at the time of election. In addition, they must have lived in the country for not less than 15 years prior to nomination. To stand for the presidency, candidates must receive no fewer than 50,000 signatures from the electorate. If a candidate obtains an outright majority in the first round of the presidential election, he or she is declared the winner. If no candidate receives a majority, the top two vote getters proceed to the second round, where the candidate with the most votes wins. In both instances, elections are only valid if no less than half of the electorate has voted.

Direct presidential elections have taken place in Kyrgyzstan in October 1991, December 1995, October 2000, and July 2005. In the first election, Askar Akaev ran unopposed; in the second, he won with minimal opposition, garnering almost 72 percent of the vote. Prior to the 1995 contest the president's desire to avoid the risks and unpleasantness of an election campaign led him to seek a second term a year early by popular referendum, which would have asked the electorate to vote "Yes" or "No" on extending his tenure for another five years. Facing parliamentary opposition to this unconstitutional move, Akaev accepted a compromise: he would stand in a contested election a year before the expiration of his first term. With his popularity buoyant in the fall of 1995, in part because of the national celebrations of the Manas millennium, Akaev did not wish to lose the political advantages of the moment, especially given the economic downturn that was expected the following year.

In the October 2000 election, Akaev was re-elected to a third term after receiving almost 75 percent of the vote in an election in which over 77 percent of the eligible voters cast ballots. Even more than in the previous election, the President and his supporters employed the power of the state to prevent a free and fair electoral contest. The president's most potent challengers were denied access to the ballot and the remaining contenders were unable to reach the electorate because of steps taken by the president's camp to limit their exposure through the mass media.

Frustration with Akaev's actions and with the country's economic malaise, combined with suspicions that the president interfered in legislative elections in February and March 2005, led to street protests that forced him into exile. Kurmanbek Bakiev was named

interim president and prime minister. In the presidential elections held in July, Bakiev won a landslide victory. Felix Kulov became prime minister.

The Party System

Party development, which is still in its infancy in Kyrgyzstan, has been hampered by the remoteness of many regions of the country, by an electoral system that encourages regional rather than party loyalties, and by Akiev, who found it easier to dominate a country that has a multitude of weak, fractious parties. Of the more than 40 parties registered with the Ministry of Justice in 2004, most were groups of notables with little support outside the capital. Although official documents indicate that several parties have more than 10,000 members, the accuracy of those figures is in question. In the 1990s the Communists maintained the only party that had a sizable membership (25,000 in 1997) as well as constituency organizations throughout the country, but the Communist Party was never able to transform its organizational advantages into parliamentary seats. In 1995 only three of the 105 members of the Jogorku Kenesh were elected on the Communist ticket.

Throughout the latter half of the 1990s, the most successful parliamentary faction was the Social Democratic Party. Founded in December 1994, just in time to contest the 1995 parliamentary elections, the Social Democrats represented the interests of Kyrgyzstan's regional political elites and officialdom. They won 14 seats in the new parliament, far more than any of their rivals. Trailing the Social Democrats, with four seats each, were the Unity of Kyrgyzstan Party and the Party of National Renewal "Asaba" (Flag). The former, registered in June 1994, is a Westernizing party committed to "a decisive continuation of economic reform." Its leader is Amangel'dy Muraliev, appointed governor of the Osh region in 1996. Asaba, on the other hand, has championed the defense of ethnic Kyrgyz interests. Registered in the last days of the Soviet era, Asaba has pressed for the revival of Kyrgyz language and culture.

In the campaigns preceding the local elections of 2004 and the parliamentary elections of 2005, the most active parties were Adilet (Justice), Moia strana (My Country), the Communist Party of Kyrgystan, and Alga, Kyrgyzstan! (Forward, Kyrgyzstan!). Although most parliamentary seats were contested by several national parties, elections for the regional, district, and village assemblies were far more likely to be nonpartisan. National parties are only just beginning to recruit candidates for subnational elections.

Major Political Parties

ADILET

(Justice)

Claiming a membership of 35,000 persons, Adilet was allied to Akaev's administration and was working with Moia Strana and Alga, Kyrgyztan! to assure the election of persons associated with President Akaev in 2005. The honorary chairman of the party is Chingiz Aitmatov, the famous Kyrgyz novelist who has been residing for some years in Europe.

ALGA, KYRGYZSTAN!

(Forward, Kyrgyzstan)

Formed in September 2003 to present candidates in the 2004–05 election cycle, Alga, Kyrgyzstan! is the latest incarnation of a pro-presidential party in Kyrgyzstan. It brings together several former parties and electoral blocs into what is called in Russia a "party of power," that is, a party whose primary social base is the existing political and administrative elite. Like parties of power elsewhere in the post-Communist world, such as United Russia, it lacks a clear ideology and is oriented instead toward the maintenance in power of the current ruling group. Whereas the party claims to have 40,000 members, independent observers put the figure at approximately 7,500.

AR-NAMYS

(Dignity)

Headed by President Akaev's most formidable adversary, Felix Kulov, Ar-Namys enjoyed very limited electoral success up until 2005, in large part because Kulov remained in prison, a victim of the prosecutorial politics of the Akaev administration. His release from prison following the ouster of Akaev was followed by his appointment as prime minister in September 2005. Registered in August 1999, Ar-Namys reportedly has 11,000 members, several of whom live in exile in the West.

MOIA STRANA

(My Country)

A pro-Akaev party founded in 1998, Moia Strana is headed by the deputy prime minister in charge of trade and development, Dzhoomart Otorbaev. The party reports a membership of 3,000 persons.

NARODNOE DVIZHENIE KYRGYZSTANA

(Popular Movement of Kyrgyzstan)

Founded in 2004, this movement brought together nine opposition parties that rallied behind Kurmanbek Bakiev as their common candidate for the 2005 presidential election. This political bloc was remarkable for the diversity of the parties involved, which ranged from those on the right, such as the Republican Party, to those on the left, such as both of the Communist Parties of Kyrgyzstan. It was a measure of the frustration, and perhaps desperation, of the opposition to Akaev's rule that it was willing to put aside its philosophical and personal differences to support a common candidate. Bakiev was named interim president following Akaev's ouster, and in the July 2005 presidential election Bakiev coasted to victory with 88 percent of the vote.

COMMUNIST PARTY OF KYRGYZSTAN/PARTY OF COMMUNISTS OF KYRGYZSTAN

The Communists in Kyrgystan divided at the end of the 1990s into two parties: the Party of Communists of Kyrgyzstan and the Communist Party of Kyrgyzstan. Where the former reportedly has 25,000 members, the latter has only 10,000. Until his death in August 2004, the former head of the Kyrgyz Communist Party in the Soviet era, Absamat Masaliev, was the leader of the Party of Communists of Kyrgyzstan.

Minor Political Parties

Unlike many mature Western democracies, in which vibrant minor parties exist alongside two or three major political parties, Kyrgyzstan's smaller parties play a minor role in the country's political life. They are often little more than a circle of political associates based in the capital who have the ambition, but little means, to participate in electoral and parliamentary politics. Among such parties are the Party of Urbanites of Bishkek and the Republican Popular Party of Kyrgyzstan. Given the new electoral rules and smaller parliament, minor parties are likely to fare even less well in the future.

Other Political Forces

Although Kyrgyzstan's civil society is more developed and active than that of neighboring Central Asian countries, it lacks the diversity and financial and political autonomy that one finds in the West. There is a rich assortment of nongovernmental organizations (NGOs) in Kyrgyzstan, whose concerns range from women's issues to the environment, but they are heavily funded by sources outside of Kyrgyzstan, which raises questions about the NGOs' long-term viability. Among the more visible social groups are those that represent the interests of the country's many ethnic communities. Akaev's government was intent, however, on co-opting these and other social groups into a coalition of institutions supportive of the president. One vehicle for this co-optation was the Assembly of Peoples of Kyrgyzstan, which brought together representatives from all of the country's ethnic communities. Such "pocket groups" may not be considered, however, as independent political forces. As a result of the limited vitality of society itself, most politics takes place within the state, especially at its epicenter, in the presidential administration.

National Prospects

During its first years of independence, Kyrgyzstan earned a reputation as an oasis of democracy in the authoritarian desert of inner Asia. The new state promoted a free press, private political associations, and a market economy and in so doing attracted the sympathy and financial assistance of the West. Yet the very openness and competitiveness of the new politics in Kyrgyzstan made the country difficult to govern at a time of declining economic production and increasing social stratification and ethnic tension.

In the mid-1990s President Akaev began to resort to authoritarian measures as a means of imposing discipline on an ever-more-fractured state and society. During the summer and fall of 1994, he closed two opposition newspapers and—in violation of the constitution—revised institutional arrangements by plebiscite and engineered the early dissolution of parliament. Although the new, and more corrupt, parliament elected in February 1995 did not contain a presidential majority, it was so divided that it presented only a weak challenge to presidential rule.

Akaev's dominance of Kyrgystani politics and society was further entrenched by his reelection in 1995 and 2000 and by the passage of numerous referendums that increased the powers of the presidency. His dramatic ouster in the Tulip Revolution of March 2005 reflected the growing tumult of the political scene in the country, a fact that was further in evidence in the months following the revolution, when several members of parliament were assassinated.

In the fall of 2005 it was unclear whether President Bakiev could retain his authority amid the continuing political violence in the country. If he does, he will face formidable challenges in reviving a moribund economy. An infusion of money and expertise from the IMF and other Western institutions has enabled Kyrgyzstan to introduce its own currency, tame inflation, and put in place part of the infrastructure of a market economy. But as elsewhere in the former Soviet territories, large-scale corruption has accompanied the privatization of the economy, as business and bureaucratic interests conspire to protect their own ventures against competition. Moreover, without a renegotiation of the external loans received in the early and mid-1990s, servicing the national debt may force Kyrgyzstan to make deeper, and politically dangerous, cuts in state spending on essential services such as health, education, and welfare. The question for the future is whether political democratization in Kyrgyzstan can survive and advance amid a painful economic and political transition.

Further Reading

Abazov, Rafis. "The Parliamentary Elections in Kyrgyzstan, February 2000." *Electoral Studies*, no. 3 (2003): 545–53.

Edgeworth, Linda, William Fierman, and Chitra Tiwari. *Kyrgyzstan: Pre-election Assessment*. Washington, D.C.: IFES, 1994.

Huskey, Eugene. "An Economy of Authoritarianism? Askar Akaev and Presidential Leadership in Kyrgyzstan." In *Power and Change in Central Asia*. Ed. Sally N. Cummings. London: Routledge, 2002.

———. "Kyrgyzstan: The Fate of Political Liberalization." In *Conflict, Cleavage, and Change in Central Asia and the Caucasus*. Ed. Karen Dawisha and Bruce Parrott. Cambridge: Cambridge University Press, 1997.

———. "Kyrgyzstan: The Politics of Demographic and Economic Frustration." In *New States, New Politics: Building the Post-Soviet Nations*. Ed. Ian Bremmer and Raymond Taras. Cambridge: Cambridge University Press, 1996.

———. "National Identity from Scratch: Defining Kyrgyzstan's Role in World Affairs." *Journal of Communist Studies and Transition Politics*, no. 3 (2003): 111–38.

———. "The Rise of Contested Politics in Central Asia: Elections in Kyrgyzstan, 1989–1990." *Europe-Asia Studies*, no. 5 (1995).

Imart, Guy. "Kirgizia-Kazakhstan: A Hinge or a Fault Line." *Problems of Communism*, no. 5 (1990).

Olcott, Martha. "Central Asia's Catapult to Independence." *Foreign Affairs*, no. 3 (1992): 108–30.

———. "The War on Terrorism in Central Asia and the Cause of Democratic Reform." *Demokratizatsiya*, no. 1 (2003): 86–95.

Pryde, Ian. "Kyrgyzstan's Slow Progress to Reform." *World Today*, June 1995.

———. "Kyrgyzstan: The Trials of Independence." *Journal of Democracy*, no. 1 (1994).

LAO PEOPLE'S DEMOCRATIC REPUBLIC

(Sāthālanalat Paxāthipatai Paxāxon Lao)

By Martin Stuart-Fox, Ph.D.

Laos, a nation of 6.2 million people (2005 est.) on the Southeast Asian mainland, is a member state of the Association of Southeast Asian Nations (ASEAN). More than 60 percent of the population are lowland ethnic Lao; the rest comprise more than 40 different mountain tribes (including upland Tai and Hmong). The present regime seized power on December 2, 1975, when the forced abdication of King Savāngvatthanā brought the six-century-old Lao monarchy to an end.

The System of Government

Laos is a single-party Communist state. Government is the monopoly of the Lao People's Revolutionary Party (LPRP), which directed the Lao Communist movement in its revolutionary struggle against both French colonial domination and the former Royal Lao regime. In this it was strongly supported by neighboring Communist North Vietnam.

EXECUTIVE

The party controls all three arms of government, but under the Lao constitution, enacted in 1991, the state president wields more than just symbolic power. Elected by a two-thirds vote of the National Assembly, he or she issues decrees, appoints the prime minister, and decides on promotions in the judiciary and the military (as head of the armed forces). This position was first held by the powerful secretary-general (subsequently president) of the LPRP, Kaisôn Phomvihān. After Kaisôn's death in 1992, power was shared between the state president and the president of the party, but after 1998 the two positions were again combined.

The state president appoints the prime minister, who in turn nominates a cabinet of 13 ministers and a president of the Committee for Planning and Cooperation. All appointments must be endorsed by the National Assembly.

LEGISLATURE

The National Assembly (Saphāthaeng Xāt) is the supreme legislative body. Elections to the 109-member Assembly take place every five years, the most recent being in February 2002. Members of government are not, however, drawn from the National Assembly; they are appointed by the prime minister. All have been members of the LPRP; with the single exception of one long serving "neutralist minister." The government is defined as "the administrative organization of the state" and is responsible for drafting laws, strategic development plans, and national budgets (in accordance with the policies of the party) for ratification by the National Assembly. Though some debate does take place, the National Assembly essentially provides a rubber stamp for party and government decisions. Six committees of the National Assembly oversee its work: law; economic planning and finance; social and cultural affairs;

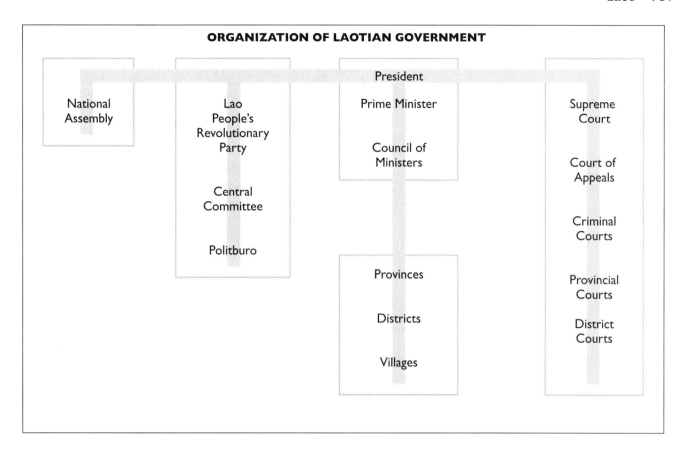

ORGANIZATION OF LAOTIAN GOVERNMENT

President

National Assembly

Lao People's Revolutionary Party

Central Committee

Politburo

Prime Minister

Council of Ministers

Provinces

Districts

Villages

Supreme Court

Court of Appeals

Criminal Courts

Provincial Courts

District Courts

ethnic affairs; national defense and securities; and foreign affairs. A Standing Committee, consisting of the president, three vice presidents, and two other members, meets when the Assembly is not in session.

JUDICIARY

The president of the People's Supreme Court and the Public Prosecutor General are appointed (and can be dismissed) by the National Assembly. Not until 1989, however, was a recognizable judicial system formally adopted and the courts separated from the State Prosecutor's Office. Criminal and civil codes followed, and since 1993 all laws have been published in the trilingual judicial gazette (in Lao, English, and French). Thus a legal framework is painstakingly coming into being to replace the arbitrary use of state power in people's courts. Provincial and district courts function at those levels of administration, though there the new legal framework is less likely to be observed.

REGIONAL AND LOCAL GOVERNMENT

From 1975 until 1991 people's councils in all 16 provinces and the municipality of Viang Chan (Vientiane)

and at the district level were popularly elected, all candidates being "vetted" by the party. The new constitution, however, eliminated elected bodies at both these levels of administration. The reason for this appears to have been twofold: to strengthen central government control in the face of continuing regionalism and to strengthen the "leading role" of the party. Province governors and district and village chiefs are appointed by the party, though not without some popular consultation. They have responsibility for implementing decisions taken at each higher level.

The Electoral System

Elections are straightforward in the LPDR. They take place at the national level only in single-member constituencies. The winners are those who poll the largest number of votes. Not all candidates must be members of the LPRP, but party endorsement is required through the Lao Front for National Construction. This ensures that only a limited number of candidates contest any seat.

The Party System

Laos is a Communist state with a single legal political party, the Lao People's Revolutionary Party (Phak Paxāxon Pativat Lao).

Major Political Parties

LAO PEOPLE'S REVOLUTIONARY PARTY

(Phak Paxāxon Pativat Lao)

HISTORY

The party traces its history back to the Indochina Communist Party (the ICP), founded in 1930 by the veteran Vietnamese Communist Ho Chi Minh. With the breakup of the ICP in 1951, Lao members began organizing their own party, with Vietnamese assistance. In 1955 they formed the Lao People's Party, forerunner of the LPRP (the name adopted at the party's second congress in 1972). The party concealed its existence, however, behind the facade of the Lao Patriotic Front (Naeo Lao Sang Xāt), led by the charismatic Prince Suphanuvong. Real power meanwhile lay in the hands of the party secretary-general, Kaisôn Phomvihān, son of a Vietnamese father and a Lao mother.

Under the provisions of the 1954 Geneva Agreements that brought the First Indochina War (against French colonialism) to an end, two provinces were set aside for regroupment of Communist (Pathēt Lao) guerrillas. Not until 1959 was the country reunited through formation of a coalition government that included two Communist ministers. Such a coalition, in the context of the cold war, was not acceptable to the United States, which engineered its overthrow. Three years later, as the country descended into civil war, the incoming Kennedy administration agreed to the neutralization of Laos at another conference at Geneva that endorsed formation of a second coalition government in 1962.

Very soon, however, Laos became caught up in the Second Indochina (Vietnam) War. For a decade, until the cease-fire of 1973, the Pathēt Lao, directed by the LPRP and with the support of its North Vietnamese allies, fought the U.S.-supported Royal Lao regime. In 1974 a third coalition government was formed, this one with half the ministerial positions going to the LPRP (to reflect the fact that the Pathēt Lao by then controlled fully two-thirds of the country, though less than half the population). Following Communist victories in Cambodia and Vietnam in April 1975, the LPRP moved to seize full power. Royal Lao bureaucrats and military officers were interned in reeducation camps, and in a bloodless coup on December 2, 1975, the LPRP declared the formation of the Lao People's Democratic Republic.

ORGANIZATION AND MEMBERSHIP

From some 300 to 400 members in 1955, the LPRP grew to a membership of 25,000 by the time it seized power in 1975, and to 100,000 when it held its seventh congress in 2001 (still accounting for less than 2 percent of the population). It is organized, as are other Communist parties, on a Leninist basis with cells at all administrative levels and throughout the bureaucracy, the military, and mass organizations. Party committees function at the local, district, and provincial levels, each electing members to the next higher committee. At the apex stands the central committee of 53 members elected at the seventh party congress in March 2001, who in turn elected the 11-member political bureau (politburo), where actual power within the party resides.

At the seventh party congress, the dominance of the army within the party was confirmed. Of the 11 politburo members, no fewer than seven were generals or former generals and one was a former colonel. Just as significant, three of the 11 members were from ethnic minorities, while regions outside the capital were well represented in both the politburo and the central committee. Educational standards of members also improved, with a majority claiming postsecondary qualifications of one kind or another.

LEADERSHIP

At the seventh party congress, General Khamtai Siphandôn (concurrently state president) was elected president of the LPRP with General Samān Vinyakēt, president of the National Assembly, and General Chummali Xainyasôn, state vice president, at numbers two and three. Former state president Nuhak Phūmsavan retired from the politburo, which was increased in size from nine to 11 members.

POLICY

The LPRP claims to exercise power on behalf of the worker-peasant alliance (the Lao proletariat is minute) through the system of democratic centralism in the name of Marxism-Leninism. What this means in practice is that all decisions are made by the politburo and central committee and communicated down the party hierarchy to be implemented, not to ensure the victory of Marxist-Leninist ideology (which has been largely forgotten) but to ensure that the party retains its monopoly of political power.

To this end the party keeps as tight control over all the media as it can. There is no press freedom. The party publishes its own newspaper, *Paxāxon* (The People), as do some mass organizations and the army. An English-language paper, *The Vientiane Times,* appears three times a week, and there is a French publication. The most popular magazine (*Vannasin*) features short stories and articles on Lao culture. The medium the party cannot control is television beamed into Laos from Thailand. Lao and Thai are closely similar languages; all Lao understand Thai, and most Lao prefer Thai TV to their own rather dowdy single government channel.

Minor Political Parties

There are no other political parties in Laos.

Other Political Forces

MASS ORGANIZATIONS

The principal mass organization is the Lao Front for National Construction (Naeo Lao Sang Xāt), which has branches all over the country and representatives from all ethnic and religious groups. Its purpose, along with that of other mass organizations, according to the constitution, is to "unite and mobilize" the people to build a new and modern Lao society as directed by the LPRP. This it does by developing political consciousness among all the multiethnic Lao people and among all social classes.

The other sanctioned mass organizations are the Federation of Trade Unions for the benefit of the Lao working class, the Lao Women's Union grouping women's organizations, and the Lao People's Revolutionary Youth Union for young people.

OPPOSITION

With the ending of the cold war and inclusion of both Laos and Vietnam in ASEAN, Thailand no longer supports armed opposition to the Lao regime. Lao and Hmong refugee camps in Thailand have been closed down. Hmong were blamed for two attacks on buses in 2002 that left two dozen dead. But only a dwindling handful of diehard Hmong continue to oppose the government from their mountain hideouts south of the Plain of Jars.

Internal opposition surfaced briefly in the late 1980s when a group of intellectuals called for introduction of multiparty social democracy. Three ringleaders were arrested, charged with plotting against the government, and sentenced to 14 years' imprisonment. All calls for their release have been ignored, and one of the three has subsequently died.

In 2004 an organization calling itself the Free Democratic People's Government of Laos claimed responsibility for a series of small bombs in Viang Chan and southern Laos that killed one person and injured several more. This movement claims to represent internal opposition to the Lao regime but is probably based in Thailand.

Buddhism now flourishes in the LPDR, and it is not unusual to see members of the politburo on their knees as a mark of respect to Buddhist monks. Many temples have been repaired and refurbished, not least to encourage rapidly developing tourism. The modus vivendi that thus exists between Buddhism and the LPRP makes it most unlikely, therefore, that the Buddhist Sangha (monastic order) will become a vehicle for political opposition to the regime. The party is much more suspicious of Christianity, and the freedom of worship of Lao Christians has been curtailed.

Many Lao refugees abroad who previously opposed the regime have since 1990 returned to visit their homeland. Some have invested money, and some have returned to live in Laos. The regime has generally welcomed returnees, providing they do not involve themselves in politics. What prevents more Lao returning is the "nationality law," which prohibits dual nationality: Lao who live abroad are most reluctant to relinquish their acquired nationalities. While many Lao abroad still detest the regime, more now seek to compromise with it rather than plot its violent overthrow.

National Prospects

Since 1989, when the last Vietnamese troops were finally withdrawn, Laos has resumed its traditional position as a neutral "buffer" state enjoying friendly relations with all its neighbors. While relations with Vietnam remain close, as fellow Communist states and wartime allies, relations with both Thailand and China have also become warm and friendly. Laos has also actively developed its relations with both Burma (Myanmar) and Cambodia.

As a member of ASEAN, Laos will inevitably develop ever-closer ties with its neighbors. In April 1994 the first bridge was opened across the Mekong River between Thailand and Laos; two more followed and more are planned. Road and bridge building are priorities for the Lao government, and for foreign aid donors, as these will link Vietnam with Thailand and Thailand with southern China (Yunnan). A feasibility study has been carried out for a rail line from Thailand to Yunnan to pass through Laos.

This growing transport network will assist in integrating the states of mainland Southeast Asia into a single expanding market, linked to both the rest of ASEAN and to southern China. The strategic position of Laos makes it central to such a project, which holds out opportunities for future growth and development.

At present, however, Laos remains one of the UN's "Least Developed Nations," with an annual per capita income of only about U.S. $1,900. The value of imports is double that of exports, and the country is heavily dependent on foreign aid and soft loans from the World Bank and the Asian Development Bank. Some light industry is in production (especially textiles), but the principal exports are hydropower and timber, with gold and copper set to increase. In late 2004 the country gained the status of Normal Trade Relations with the United States, which will lower tariffs on exports.

Laos has great potential as an exporter of electricity and has an ambitious program to build a series of huge dams on fast-flowing tributaries of the Mekong. In 2005 the World Bank approved a loan for one such dam. Timber, minerals, and agriculture provide other opportunities for investment and development that promise to turn around the Lao trade deficit in the longer term.

In conclusion, therefore, the prospects are for steady if not spectacular economic growth and for continued political stability under the watchful eye of a party that is now Communist only in name—provided further economic reforms are implemented and corruption contained.

Further Reading

Bourdet, Yves. *The Economics of Transition in Laos.* Cheltenham, England: Edward Elgar, 2000.

Evans, Grant. *The Politics of Ritual and Remembrance: Laos since 1975.* Chiang Mai, Thailand: Silkworm Books, 1998.

——. *A Short History of Laos: The Hand in Between.* Crows West, Australia: Allen and Darwin, 2002.

Ngaosyvathn, Mayoury, and Pheuiphanh Ngaosyvathn. *Kith and Kin Politics: The Relationship between Laos and Thailand.* Manila: Contemporary Asia Press, 1994.

Savada, A. M., ed. *Laos: A Country Study.* 3d edition. Washington, D.C.: Library of Congress, 1995.

Stuart-Fox, Martin. *Buddhist Kingdom, Marxist State: The Making of Modern Laos.* 2d edition. Bangkok: White Lotus, 2002.

——. *Historical Dictionary of Laos.* 2d edition. Metuchen, N.J.: Scarecrow Press, 2001.

——. *A History of Laos.* Cambridge: Cambridge University Press, 1997.

——. "Laos 1995: Towards Regional Integration." *Southeast Asian Affairs* ISEAS (1995): 177–95.

——. *Laos: Politics, Economics and Society.* Boulder, Colo.: Lynne Rienner, 1986.

Zasloff, J. J., and L. Unger, eds. *Laos: Beyond the Revolution.* London: Macmillan, 1991.

REPUBLIC OF LATVIA
(Latvijas Republika)

By Jeffrey K. Hass, Ph.D.

On August 21, 1991, following the failed Soviet putsch, the Latvian Supreme Soviet declared Latvia independent of the Soviet Union, beginning the process of building democracy. Like its two Baltic neighbors, Lithuania and Estonia, Latvia has enjoyed a happier transition to democracy and capitalism than other former Eastern bloc or Soviet republics. While disputes over policy, territorial boundaries, economic policy, and definition of citizenship have been problematic and while Latvia's economy bottomed out in 1992 and 1993, the country has enjoyed relative political calm and recent economic growth.

While it may perhaps be early to talk about a stable, never-changing political system, Latvia's polity has come closer to institutionalization than other post-Soviet states except Estonia.

Culturally Latvia is far from homogeneous—a potential political problem in the past, present, and future. According to official data, "Latvians" (ethnically defined) make up 57.7 percent of the population; Russians are 29.6 percent (a result of migration from other Soviet republics before 1991). The official language is Lettish ("Latvian"); Lithuanian and Russian are prevalent as well.

The System of Government

Latvia is a parliamentary republic with a strong, unicameral legislature and a weak president.

EXECUTIVE

The executive branch is headed by two figures, the president and the prime minister. The president, who sits for a three-year term (and who cannot sit for more than two consecutive terms), is the nominal head of state but is not a powerful figure in Latvian politics; the constitution holds the president as a figurehead who represents Latvia in the international arena and has other circumscribed powers. For example, no bill can come into force with a presidential signature alone; the prime minister must countersign bills. The constitution gives the president unilateral political power only in two cases: inviting a figure to become prime minister and form a government and suggesting that the parliament he dissolved. In the first case, the president can invite a prime minister to form a government only after the previous prime minister has resigned or failed to survive a parliamentary no-confidence vote. In the second case, the president may suggest that the Saeima (parliament) be dissolved; however, such a decision must go to a nationwide referendum. If the referendum receives a majority of votes cast, the Saeima is dissolved and new elections will be forthcoming. If, however, the referendum does not receive majority support and fails, then the president is dismissed from office and the Saeima elects a new president to serve out the remainder of the three-year term. Unlike some countries, such as Russia, where the president has the power to dissolve the legislature, the Latvian constitution makes such an action a double-edged sword, forcing the president not to take such action lightly.

In spite of such institutional obstacles to a strong presidency, the first president, Guntis Ulmanis, tried to move beyond his legal means—not confining himself to the presidential bully pulpit or his duties in the realm of diplomacy and foreign policy (including talks with Russia about removing troops and bringing Latvia closer to NATO and the European Union). In 1995 the Saeima was divided into two roughly equal groups to the right and to the left, making support for a prime minister and government difficult; Ulmanis attempted to play power broker to put in his favorite for prime minister but finally had to turn to a compromise candidate (Andris Skele) on the third try. The law gives only so much room for presidential maneuver.

The prime minister is the head of the government and as such answers to the Saeima concerning the status and outcomes of policies and for problems within the government and Council of Ministers. In essence this makes the prime minister, rather than the president, the real executive authority. First, legislation becomes law only with the prime minister's cosignature. Second, by heading the ministries that form the apex of the government, the prime minister and the Council of Ministers have direct control over policy implementation and day-to-day operations (albeit at some bureaucratic distance). Third, in cases of urgent need occurring between sessions of parliament, the Council of Ministers has the right to issue temporary decrees with the force of law. However, the Council cannot issue such decrees on just any subject. For example, Council decrees cannot, among other matters, amend elections, judicial procedures, the state budget, or laws passed by a sitting parliament.

The president and the prime minister are not only beholden to parliament to account for their actions; they owe their positions to parliamentary election. The prime minister must be approved and can lose office to a vote of no confidence. In Latvia, the president is not elected by direct popular vote but by parliament. Presidential "elections" were held in 1993 and 1996. In July 1993, at the convocation of the first pure post-Soviet parliament, three individuals came forward as presidential candidates: Guntis Ulmanis won on the third ballot; the second post-Soviet presidential election saw parties in the Saeima challenge Ulmanis. Ulmanis maintained a moderate policy program, and this helped him win 53 of 97 ballots in the first round of voting, returning him to the presidency for a second term. In 1999 Vaira Vike-Freiberga, a women of Canadian and Latvian extraction and an academic, succeeded Ulmanis to the presidency.

LEGISLATURE

The Saeima, or parliament, is the locus of political power in Latvia. The Saeima is a unicameral body composed of 100 seats and is elected for a term of four years. When a newly elected parliament meets for the first time, the deputies elect a board that acts as the organizing head of the Saeima. This board consists of a chairman, two deputy chairmen, and two secretaries; the chairman acts in the role of speaker of parliament. The Saeima also has 10 committees that make up 100 positions; thus, in theory every Saeima member can become a member of a parliamentary committee. These committees are one path for submitting legislation; if five or more members of a committee so act, they can present a bill for a vote in parliament. (A bill can also

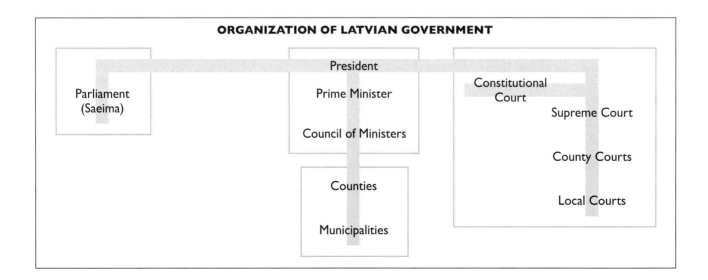

ORGANIZATION OF LATVIAN GOVERNMENT

Parliament (Saeima)

President
Prime Minister
Council of Ministers

Counties
Municipalities

Constitutional Court
Supreme Court
County Courts
Local Courts

be brought up by the president, Cabinet of Ministers, or one-tenth of eligible voters.)

Parliament wields not only legislative power but ultimate political sovereignty. The president is selected by the Saeima, and the prime minister must answer to parliament. If the president dies, the next in line is not the prime minister, as in some countries (such as Russia); instead, power goes to the chairman of the Saeima. While the executive branch proposes and implements administrative policy, these policies are embedded in the legal framework formed by Saeima decisions. Parliamentary deputies enjoy not only immunity from criminal prosecution but also from recall: according to the constitution, deputies cannot be recalled from their office and can be disciplined only by the Saeima itself. (Only in the case of defamation or revealing information about another's private life can deputies become liable to prosecution.) Even in cases of criminal activity, a Saeima member cannot be prosecuted until the Saeima decides to sanction such prosecution.

Legislation is the primary duty of the Saeima. Laws pass if they receive a majority vote (51 votes). While the president can send legislation back to the Saeima for reconsideration, the Saeima can override the veto with a simply majority (51) a second time in support of the proposed bill. The president then cannot raise his initial objections a second time, that is, the president cannot veto a bill with the same objections twice. One-third of the Saeima can motion to suspend implementation of a law for two months or can request the president to suspend implementation. The law in question is then submitted to a nationwide referendum if one-tenth of the voters request it; otherwise, the law goes into force at the end of the two-month waiting period. If in the referendum a majority does not support the draft law, then it will not go into force.

Only laws and measures on the budget, on taxes and customs duties, on military service, on declaration of war or peace, on a state of emergence, and on foreign treaties cannot be subject to a nationwide referendum. Further, two-thirds of the Saeima may vote that a law is "urgent," which means that the president may not demand a second review of the law and a referendum cannot be called to judge it. Finally, the Saeima can amend the constitution if new articles are passed by a two-thirds majority after three readings; two-thirds of Saeima deputies must be present for such constitutional changes to be valid.

JUDICIARY

The judiciary is in the process of being reorganized. For the first half of the 1990s, Latvia used the system it inherited from its Soviet past, namely, district, regional, and administrative courts, along with a newly created Supreme Court. Each level handles both criminal cases and civil cases (disputes), and appeals move up the chain to the Supreme Court, which is the final arbiter of legal conflict. The Constitutional Court has the right to determine the constitutionality or unconstitutionality of laws.

REGIONAL AND LOCAL GOVERNMENT

Latvia is divided into 26 counties (*rajons*) and seven municipalities. At the local level, the highest political body is the local council, ranging from 15 to 120 members (depending on the region) and sitting for a five-year term. The council is run by a chairman and board elected by the council deputies. In local politics, members of the Latvian National Independence Movement have faired well and dominate, whereas candidates linked to the Communist Party have fared poorly.

The Electoral System

The Latvian Constitution holds that election to the Saeima is through proportional means—that is, voters receive a list with parties and then vote for a party. Those parties receiving more than 5 percent of votes cast receive a number of seats equal to the percentage of votes they received out of the total votes cast for parties that overcame the 5 percent barrier; votes for parties that do not cross the 5 percent barrier are, therefore, wasted votes.

Latvia has not been blessed with stable governments, reflecting fragmentation in parliament—not unusual when many different parties are represented (a problem in Italy suffered for decades)—and unstable power bases. Anatolijs Gorbunovs was the first post-Soviet parliamentary chairman, backed by a majority coalition led by Latvia's Way. This coalition soon splintered, and Latvia's Way tried several times to build a successful, stable coalition. The 1994 elections led to another round of negotiations to form a new government, and, after several rounds of voting, businessman Andris Skele became prime minister. After the 1998 elections Latvia's Way was again heading the ruling coalition in alliance with nationalist parties For Fatherland and LNNK (FF/LNNK) and the center-left New Party. Villis Kristopans was named prime minister, but he survived only nine months due to constant political crises. Skele returned, leading a coalition of FF/LNNK and the new People's Party. This government succumbed to internal rivalries and disputes over privatization and collapsed in 2000. The 1998 coalition returned with a new leader and prime minister, Riga's mayor, Andris Berzins—which survived until the 2002 elections. In 2002 Latvia's Way, the leading party in the 1990s, failed to overcome the 5 percent barrier. The New Era Party won the largest number of seats (26), followed by the coalition For Human Rights in a United Latvia. Einars Repše of the New Era Party became prime minister at the head of a center-right coalition. In February 2004 Repše's coalition collapsed, and Repše resigned his post. A coalition led by the Greens and Farmers Union formed a new government, with Indulis Emsis becoming the first European prime minister from a Green party. However, Emsis's government lasted only nine months before collapsing after the parliament rejected his government's budget. Aigars Kalvitis of the People's Party became the new prime minister, heading a four-party coalition.

The Party System

As in other former Communist countries, talking about coherent "parties" is difficult. While there are formal party groupings, parties in Latvia may disappear and new parties sometimes are created, making the party landscape somewhat in flux. Further, the last few years have seen shifting coalitions of parties, who ally or merge in order to increase their potential electoral support and voting power in the Saeima. Finally, party organization and discipline do not always seem very strong, since candidates may run on their party's list in one district and on a list for a coalition in a district where that party is weaker. Hence, there may be a low correlation between the "rank and file" (which may be rather low), programmatic stance, positions of deputies in parliamentary debates, and leadership within one party.

In the 1990s the two dominant parties were Latvia's Way (Latvijas celsh) and Saimnieks, but both suffered reversals of fortune: Saimnieks lost all its parliamentary seats in the 1998 election, and in 2002 Latvia's Way lost all its seats as well (it had 21 in 1998). Latvia's Way was founded in 1993 on the basis of political organizations that had championed Latvian independence from the USSR. Aiming for support from

entrepreneurs and the middle class, Latvian's Way promoted radical economic reform, but this created backlash. Saimnieks, which drew support from the *nomenklatura* (Soviet-era economic elite), was founded for the 1995 parliamentary elections and merged with the Democratic Party. It joined a coalition government after the 1995 election but left the coalition in 1998. It strongly supported a change in Latvia's citizenship laws and successfully obtained such a change. This was its last success, as it lost all its seats in the 1998 election and has not reappeared since.

On the left a coalition emerged to maximize electoral success: For Human Rights in a United Latvia (Par Cilveka Tiesibam Vienota Latvija). The electoral alliance received the second largest number of votes (18.9 percent) and seats (25) in the 2002 elections. It was made up of three parties, the People's Harmony Party (Tautas Saskanas Partija), the Latvian Socialist Party, and the minor partner Lidztiesiba Savieniba. For Human Rights gained much of its support from the Russian-speaking population. By itself the People's Harmony Party achieved electoral representation (5.6 percent of the vote and 6 seats in 1995), but the coalition had better success. In 2002 another left-wing party, the Latvian Social Democratic Workers' Party, lost all 14 seats it won in the 1998 elections.

In the center is the New Era (Jaunais laiks) Party, and toward the center-right are the People's Party, the Latvian Farmers' Union, and the Green Party of Latvia. Further along the right-wing nationalist spectrum are two formerly important parties who merged to form For Fatherland and Freedom/Latvian Independence Movement.

Major Political Parties

NEW ERA PARTY

(Jaunais laiks)

This party was founded in 2000 by Einars Repše and in 2002 won the most seats in the legislative elections. Repše formed a coalition government and served as prime minister until 2004, when the coalition collapsed and he resigned. Linked to domestic and foreign (especially Scandinavian) businessmen, New Era enjoys healthy financial support, and its recruitment of cultural figures to its ranks has helped its popular image as well. The party's platform addresses issues primarily of corruption but also market development.

PEOPLE'S PARTY

(Tautas Partija)

This center-right party was founded in 1998 by Andris Skele and populated by deserters of Latvia's Way, the Christian Democratic Union, and LNNK. Like the right-wing parties from which it originated, People's Party focuses on right-wing populist issues such as supporting society's moral fiber, protecting the traditional family, and defending the nation. People's Party nationalism is not total, however: it has ties with Russian business. The party won 20 seats in the 2002 legislative elections, and in 2004 it formed a new coalition government, with Aigars Kalvitis as the new prime minister.

LATVIAN FARMERS' UNION

(Latvijas Zemnieku savien ba)

The Farmers' Union is conservative and protectionist, and while it has taken on board former Communists from other defunct parties, the party remains center-right. This party joined a coalition with the Greens in 2002, and in 2004 the alliance formed a brief government with Green Party leader Emsis Lemulis as prime minister.

GREEN PARTY OF LATVIA

(Latvijas Zaļā partija)

Founded in 1990, this party formed an alliance with the Latvian Farmers' Union in 2002 that captured 12 seats in parliament. In 2004 the Green Party's Emsis Lemulis became the first Green Party prime minister in European history when he formed a brief minority government. The government collapsed after only nine months, and a new center-right coalition came to power.

FOR FATHERLAND AND FREEDOM/LATVIAN NATIONAL INDEPENDENCE MOVEMENT

(Apvieniba Tevzemei un Brivibaik/LNNK)

In 1995 For Fatherland and the Latvian National Independence Movement received 12 percent and 6.3 percent of the vote, respectively; in 2002 they merged to form For Fatherland and Freedom/Latvian National Independence Movement (Apvieniba Tevzemei un Brivibaik/LNNK) and promptly received only 5.4 percent of the vote. Both promoted nationalist issues, including nationalist citizenship laws, and rejected diplomatic compromises with Russia.

PEOPLE'S HARMONY PARTY

(Tautas Saskanas Partija)

This party was formed in 1994 by Jānis Jurkāns, who has remained its leader since then. It has long been popular with ethnic Russians. In 1998 it joined the For Human Rights in a United Latvia coalition, which won 25 seats in the 2002 parliamentary elections. However, People's Harmony pulled out of the coalition in 2003.

LATVIAN SOCIALIST PARTY

(Latvijas Sociālistiskā partija)

This party was founded in 1994 and has long drawn its strength from the Russian-speaking population. In 1998 it joined with two other Russian-oriented parties, People's Harmony and Equal Rights, to form the For Human Rights in a United Latvia coalition. The coalition enjoyed significant success in the 2002 elections but gradually fell apart, with People's Harmony pulling out in 2003 and the Latvian Socialist Party following not long after.

EQUAL RIGHTS

(Lidztiesiba Savieniba)

Like its former coalition partners in For Human Rights, this party gets its support from the Russian-speaking population.

Minor Political Parties

There are numerous smaller parties in Latvia, most of which have no representation in the Saeima. These include the Peoples Movement for Latvia on the far right, the Democratic Party on the center-left, and the Latvian Unity Party on the left.

Other Political Forces

The tensions between ethnic Latvians and Russians have been a factor in the country's political system since independence, and will likely remain one into the future.

National Prospects

Latvia has two major political problems, those having to do with ethnic issues and those having to do with political gridlock. On the ethnic front, the problems are mainly between ethnic Latvians and Russians, who make up one-third of the Latvian population. While citizenship had been a thorny issue, it appears to have been solved for the present. While some groups claim political abuse, the actual abuse is not particularly abominable.

The second potential problem is political gridlock. With most parties hovering around a center ground, political disputes are more like those in the United States—conflicts between rival political ambitions rather than over different ideological views and policies. With the Saeima split in half, forging political coalitions and bold political policies has proven to be difficult. However, if viewed in the context of politics in other former Soviet nations, perhaps such political gridlock of the American variety is a sign that Latvia is in good shape.

Perhaps Latvia's crowning achievement after independence has been its invitations into two important Western families: NATO and the European Union. NATO membership has caused some tension with Russia, but it also offers a modicum of security Latvians had long desired. EU membership promises access to markets and provides opportunities for labor mobility that likely will help Latvia's post-Socialist economic development.

Further Reading

Arter, David. *Parties and Democracy in the Post-Soviet Republics.* Aldershot, England: Dartmouth, 1996.

Galbreath, David. "The Politics of European Integration and Minority Rights in Estonia and Latvia." *Perspectives on European Politics and Society* 4, no. 1 (May 1, 2003): 35–53.

REPUBLIC OF LEBANON
(Al-Jumhuriyyah Al-Lubnaniyyah)

By As'ad Abukhalil, Ph.D.
Revised by Rima Habasch, Ph.D.

This small but strategically located country has long served as a link between one region and another: in modern times it has linked the Arab world and the Mediterranean world. It consists of some 130 miles of coastline on the Mediterranean sea and comprises with its mountains some 4,000 square miles. It has been an integral part of the Arab East, or the Levant, for much of its recent history. Its location has shaped its history and society: Lebanon's relatively isolated mountainous environment has allowed various sectarian groups from throughout the region to seek haven on its territory to avoid fear and persecution. This history of welcoming various peoples is probably responsible for the richly diverse composition of its population.

The last official census was conducted by the French in 1932, and successive governments have considered the sectarian distribution of the population a state secret that could potentially destabilize the country. In reality, the Christian establishment avoided conducting a new census because it did not want to confirm the fact that Muslims now form the overwhelming majority of the Lebanese population, contrary to the French figures in 1932. Population figures are important because the political posts in government are still distributed along sectarian lines, with the Christians enjoying significant privileges, including the post of president of the republic.

Lebanon is a modern creation; it was fashioned from the legacy of the Ottoman Empire in part as a response to European demands for a Christian entity tied to the West. The League of Nations granted France mandate authority over Greater Syria, an area that included Lebanon. The French designed the political system of Lebanon and shaped the constitution, which was enacted in 1926. Lebanon was established as a republic, and the Christians were given supreme political positions. In 1932 the French announced the result of a comprehensive census that found the Christians to be the majority of the population. In response, political posts were divided according to an arithmetic formula of sectarian weights, to the advantage of the Maronites and of the Christians in general. Lebanon won its independence in 1943, and the Sunni and Maronite elites reached an understanding that become known as the National Pact. This unwritten agreement was essential for the operation of the political system from 1943 until the civil war in 1975.

According to the terms of the National Pact, the Christians were to promise not to seek foreign, that is, Western Christian, protection and to accept Lebanon's Arab "face," a partial recognition of Lebanon's ties to its Arab surroundings and its gratitude to its Arab/Islamic heritage. In return, the Muslims were to agree to recognize Lebanon's independence and the legitimacy of the state with its 1920 boundaries and to renounce aspirations of a union with Syria or with any other Arab country. The pact also reinforced the sectarian division of political powers: it specified that the Maronites will have the presidency, the Shiites the ceremonial speakership of parliament, and the Sunnis the prime ministership. Other top security positions were also reserved for Maronites. Until the outbreak of the civil war in 1975, representation in the parliament was based on a 6:5 ratio of Christians to Muslims. The Ta'if Accord changed this ratio to 1 to 1.

In 1975 a civil war broke out that was to last for at least 16 years. While the Lebanese government officially declared the end of the war, one can still disagree with the notion that all sources of conflict have been amicably resolved in that country. The war began as the product of acute socioeconomic injustices and as a result of the distribution of political power according to an outmoded formula of sectarian (im)balance. Shiites, among other groups, became increasing unhappy over their small share of power given their large demographic share of the population. Leftists battled rightists, and some Muslims battled some Christians, while outsiders (primarily Israel and Syria) intervened heavily on this side or that. The PLO in Lebanon also fought alongside the leftist/Muslim coalition of forces. Syrian troops intervened heavily in Lebanon in 1976 to crush the power of the PLO and its Lebanese leftist allies, while Israel intervened at several times and invaded the country in 1982 to install its ally Bashir Gemayyel as president and to expel PLO forces from Lebanon. The civil war caused significant damage to the national economy and the Lebanese currency and was marked by assassination, kidnappings, massacres, and mutilation of bodies.

In September 1989 the Lebanese Parliament met in special sessions in the city of Ta'if in Saudi Arabia to discuss formulas and plans for constitutional and political reforms. These sessions were attended by 31 Christian and 31 Muslim deputies out of the 73 surviving members of the 1972 parliament. They met again in October 1889 in an effort to put an end to the civil war and to respond to popular demands for serious constitutional reforms.

The resulting agreement, known as the Ta'if Accord, shifted some powers from the president to the Council of Ministers and called for equal sectarian representation of Christian and Muslims in parliament. The agreement also promised to end "political sectarianism," although no firm timetable was specified. The agreement also included a comprehensive settlement of the Lebanese civil war, which entailed the dissolution of all militias in Lebanon. The identity of Lebanon was declared to be Arab and Lebanon's relations with Syria were officially and juridically characterized as "distinctive." The agreement included a promise of Syrian evacuation of troops from Lebanon. Thereafter, the administration of Ilyas Hrawi adopted the agreement and parliament amended the constitution to incorporate those reforms. Observers still disagree whether the

Ta'if agreement was actually implemented and whether those reforms are sufficient to end national discord in Lebanon.

While important provisions of the Ta'if Accord were implemented, others have not been addressed. For example, decentralization of government has yet to be fully implemented. Furthermore, the Council for Economic and Social Development, which is foreseen in the Ta'if Accord, has not been created as of the early 2000s.

Other provisions of the Ta'if Accord have been changed or not fully implemented. For example, the increase in the number of parliamentary seats from 108 to 128 as stipulated by the Ta'if Accord is viewed by some as a violation of the accord. The Ta'if Accord foresaw the establishment of a Constitutional Council, whose role is to verify the constitutionality of new laws upon request of 10 members of parliament.

In 2005 Syria's influence and presence in Lebanon generated international headlines. In February, former Lebanese prime minister Rafik Hariri was killed in a car bomb attack in Beirut. Many observers, both domestic and foreign, suspected that Syrian elements were behind the attack. Huge anti-Syria protests combined with international outrage at the assassination finally forced Syria to withdraw its troops from Lebanon, a process that was completed in April. However, violence along the pro- and anti-Syrian divide in Lebanon continued in subsequent months.

The System of Government

Lebanon is a parliamentary republic with a strong president and a unicameral legislature.

EXECUTIVE

The original constitution gives great powers to the president. He or she is commander in chief of the army and security forces; can appoint and dismiss the prime minister and cabinet; promulgates laws passed by parliament and may also propose laws, enact urgent legislation by decree, and veto bills; and can dissolve parliament under certain circumstances. The president also has powers over the government bureaucracy.

The sectarian system, however, puts some constraints on the powers of the president because national concord requires mutual agreement among the various sects. The Ta'if agreement has transferred some of the

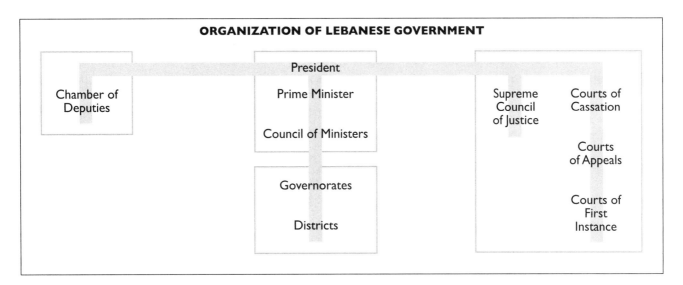

ORGANIZATION OF LEBANESE GOVERNMENT

President

Chamber of Deputies

Prime Minister

Council of Ministers

Governorates

Districts

Supreme Council of Justice

Courts of Cassation

Courts of Appeals

Courts of First Instance

powers of the president to the collective Council of Ministers, over which he or she presides. Furthermore, the Maronite president has to try to obtain the support of the Sunni Muslim prime minister.

The president is elected by parliament, and not by a direct vote of the citizenry. This has facilitated corrupt practices such as bribery of members of parliament. The president serves for a six-year term and may not succeed himself, although the constitution may be amended toward that end, as was the case with Bisharah Al-Khuri and recently with Emile Lahoud, whose term was to end in 2004 but was extended by parliament for an additional three years. A quorum of two-thirds of the deputies is required to hold a special session for the election of the president, and a two-thirds majority of deputies attending is required for the president to be elected on the first ballot. In the second round, a simple majority suffices.

The Ta'if agreement strengthened the powers of the Council of Ministers, which includes the president, the prime minister, and the ministers. The president consults with the deputies before naming a prime minister. The designated prime minister then conducts his own consultation before designating the ministers. Sectarian sensibilities and the terms of the National Pact are often more important criteria than specialization and merit. The prime minister is the highest Muslim official in the country and can bring great authority to the position, as did billionaire Rafik Hariri during his two terms (1992–98 and 2000–04). The prime minister presides over the Council of Ministers and is responsible for running the day-to-day affairs of the government. The powers of the prime minister, however, vary by personality. Some presidents have selected

weak individuals with no power bases as subservient political tools. The Ta'if Accord extended the term of the speaker of parliament from one to four years.

The country is theoretically administered through the Council of Ministers, although the president, the prime minister, and the speaker of parliament often reach decisions in informal meetings without consulting with the cabinet members. Ministers do not necessarily mind as long as they receive support for their pet projects and as long as they are able to serve their own personal and political objectives.

LEGISLATURE

Legislative power is vested in a unicameral Chamber of Deputies, which has seldom exercised its legislative authority because the president, with or without the Council of Ministers, often legislates by special decree. The constitution gives parliament powers for dealing with budgetary oversight and amendment of the constitution, but the president can easily manipulate the deputies through an exploitation of the sectarian system and through direct dealing with the sectarian political bosses, known as *zu'ama'*.

Deputies are elected every four years by popular vote, but according to a strict sectarian formula that designates the sectarian affiliation of every candidate for every seat. The citizens are then forced to select according to sectarian/political considerations.

The civil war disrupted parliamentary life in Lebanon, and no election was held from 1972 until 1992. The credibility of the 1992 election was questioned by many because many Christians boycotted it in protest of Syrian influence in Lebanon. The 1996 elections, however, were more representative, although they too were marred by fraud and irregularities. Party politics have played a small part in electoral politics because sectarian leaders dominate the list making and campaigning. The electoral system also discourages nonsectarian parties.

To be eligible for election, an individual has to be at least 25 years of age. The number of seats in parliament accorded with a 6-to-5 formula, to the advantage of Christians, but the formula is now 50-50, that is, 50 percent Muslim and 50 percent Christian.

The most recent parliamentary elections were held in 2005. The anti-Syrian Rafik Hariri Martyr List won 72 out of the 128 seats. The Amal-Hezbollah alliance won 35 seats.

JUDICIARY

The judicial system is supposed to mirror that of France; the Ministry of Justice has official authority over the judicial system. But the Supreme Council of Justice, an independent body appointed by the Council of Ministers, exercises actual jurisdiction over the various courts. There are 56 courts of first instance, with 17 in Beirut alone. Cases from these courts can be appealed to one of 11 courts of appeals, each of which has a three-judge panel. Above these are four courts of cassation, on which sit three judges each. Three of these courts adjudicate civil cases, and one hears criminal complaints.

Several other courts exist outside of this framework. There are, for example, an appeals court for administrative matters and the Judicial Council, which includes the most senior judge of the courts of cassation and four other judges appointed by the government and which rules on cases of public security. Other specialized courts exist to deal with matters relating to the military, the press, and business affairs.

While the French legal system inspired the organization of the judiciary, personal status laws remain the domain of the sectarian religious leadership within each community. In issues dealing with marriage, divorce, burial, and inheritance, the state has given total control to the clerical establishment. Secularists and feminists regard this monopoly over personal status laws as harmful to the cause of equality and liberty; it also impedes the process of national construction of one identity. The clerical establishments encourage the perpetuation of sectarian identities, and they insist on commanding the loyalty of the various sectarian groups.

In a country known for sectarian loyalties, patronage, and elite rivalries, political interference in judicial affairs is quite common. Judicial appointments, even in the era of the so-called second republic (in reference to post–civil war Lebanon), are the product of sectarian considerations. Informal meetings between the president, the prime minister, and the Speaker decide very crucial appointments, with each of them thinking about the interests of the sect. Thus, the judge in question is loyal to the individual leader who was responsible for his or her appointment. This minimizes the independence of the judiciary and makes it susceptible to political and sectarian pressures.

REGIONAL AND LOCAL GOVERNMENT

The operation of the government in Lebanon has been highly centralized; citizens from outside the capital often complain that simple governmental transactions require a visit to the capital. The state has not tried to ease the burden by decentralizing its structure. The civil war heightened fears of partition of the country and demands by right-wing groups of decentralization intended to split the country into Christian and Muslim sectors. After the political defeat of the Maronite-oriented groups, the state has insisted on a unified Lebanon, which only weakens the operation of local governments.

The country is divided into six provinces, or governorates (*muhafadhah*): Beirut, Al-Biqa', Mount Lebanon, the South, the North, and Jabal'Amil. The last one was created in the 1980s to satisfy Shiite demands. All governorates, except Beirut, are divided into districts (*qada'*). The Ministry of Interior has oversight and fiscal responsibility over the local administrations. The governor, who is appointed by the Council of Ministers, is the highest-ranking official in each province. He or she must come from a region different from that of the region he or she is assigned to administer. The governor heads the Council of the Governorate, which includes a representative of the Ministry of Finance and the deputy governors (*qa'immaqam*), who are also appointed by the Council of Ministers.

The Ta'if Accord emphasized the strengthening of local government and the decentralization at the governorate level. There has been, however, little parliamentary consensus or support on this issue. A law that increased fiscal autonomy of municipalities was passed in 1997. However, the more than 30 sources of funding, on which municipalities have been relying, make local planning and budgeting difficult. The system of government structure remains centralized, and most municipalities suffer from a lack of resources. Many local development projects continue to be undertaken by the central government.

The first municipal elections after the Ta'if Accord—the first after more than 25 years—were held in 1998 after numerous postponements. The elections saw a high voter turnout of an average of 60 percent. The single most important outcome of the elections was the increased strength of Hezbollah and the weakening of Christian parties. In 2001 municipal elections were held for the first time since 1963 in the newly liberated areas in South Lebanon.

The most recent mayoral and municipal elections were held in May 2004. Voter turnout was low, especially in Beirut. In Mount Lebanon and South Lebanon voter turnout was higher. Considered as a test of the existing powers, the elections saw the defeat of the list supported by Hariri in his home town Saida.

The Electoral System

The Ta'if Accord stipulated the electoral district be based on the *muhafaza* (governorate), rather than on the smaller *qada* (district). In the election of 1996 electoral districts were based on both the *muhafaza* (governorate) and the *qada*, as for example was the case of Beirut. Taking the *muhafaza* as the basis would have reduced the number of electoral districts from 26 to 6. More importantly, as the *muhafaza* constitutes a multisectarian district, candidates would need the support of all sects rather than relying solely on one or two sects, as would be the case for the smaller *qada*.

Suffrage is extended to all males age 21 and over, with voting being compulsory, and to all females age 21 and over with an elementary school education.

The Party System

The study of Lebanese political parties is made difficult due to the fragmentation of the political culture into narrow, sectarian subcultures. Most Lebanese political parties and organizations, not to mention political leaders, mobilize members of a particular sectarian group. The explosion of the civil war in 1975 only reinforced sectarian political identities and marginalized those parties that championed secular reforms of the political system. This excessive fragmentation, which goes beyond the Muslim-Christian distinction to include denominations within each of the two religions, requires a typology of parties based on the type of sectarian identity promoted by the party and on the sectarian composition of party members.

Origins of Lebanese political parties predate the founding of independent Lebanon in 1943: some existing political parties in Lebanon trace their roots to the 1920s and 1930s. This era witnessed the formation of small political identities following centuries of grand identities based on either Islam or pan-Arabism. To be sure, identities based on sectarian loyalties have been a feature of Lebanese society for centuries, but those identities were only channeled in modern political formations in this century. The formation of political parties reflected an attempt by sectarian leaders to adjust to the consequences of the creation of the Lebanese republic. They wanted to mask their sectarian agendas behind an ostensible national outlook encompassing the whole of Lebanon and its people. Also, the Lebanese electoral system sometimes required the election of a leader by a multisectarian constituency, although the narrow sectarian districts often served the interests of sectarian agitation and representation.

Major Political Parties

CURRENT FOR THE FUTURE

(Tayyar Al Mustaqbal)

This party formed the main faction of the Rafik Hariri Martyr List for the 2005 parliamentary elections. In the aftermath of Hariri's assassination and the withdrawal of Syria's military troops from Lebanon, the party won 36 seats, the most of any party, and led the larger coalition to a resounding victory. The party is led by Rafik Hariri's son Saad, who appears poised to take his father's place on the country's political scene.

LEBANESE PHALANGIST PARTY

(Hizb Al-Kata'ib Al-Lubnaniyyah)

One of the oldest parties in Lebanon, this party was founded in 1936 by Pierre Gemayyel in imitation of Nazi youth organizations, which he observed in Germany. The party was formed to reject calls for uniting Lebanon with its neighbors and insisted on a special Christian identity for Lebanon. The party became a sophisticated political machine benefiting from its blatant sectarian agenda, which was useful during the 1958 sectarian civil war. The party's motto emphasized allegiance to "God, homeland, and family," and it has promoted a conservative political agenda that blamed Lebanon's problems on outsiders (Syrians, Egyptians, Iranians, Palestinians, and others). It has been recently revealed that the party had benefited from secret ties to Israel, which helped fund the party's electoral campaigns. It professed its dedication to democracy, private property, and the free-enterprise system, and it consistently expressed its detestation of communism and Arab nationalism. Members of the party have been predominantly Christians, and Maronites have led the party over the years.

It founded one of the early militias in Lebanon and succeeded in attracting members by provoking clashes with the PLO forces in the country. It was one of the main fighting forces on the right during the civil war, and the Lebanese army helped it in training and the supply of matériel. Pierre's son, Bashir, emerged as the main right-wing leader in Lebanon in the wake of the 1975–76 phase of the civil war. The 1982 Israeli invasion of Lebanon boosted the fortunes of the party, and the Israeli occupation army ensured the election of Bashir as president, although he was assassinated days after his election. He was succeeded by his brother Amin, who led Lebanon in one of the worst periods of its contemporary history. Many Lebanese still blame him for intensifying the conflict and for worsening Lebanon's economic problems. Pierre died in 1984, and the party never recovered. It was later headed by the former deputy George Sa'adah, who failed to reunite the party. Many former leaders and members formed their own organizations and refused to acknowledge the leadership of Sa'adah, who failed in the 1996 elections. He died in 1998. The leader of the Phalangist Party, Amin Gemayyel, returned from his long stay in France in 2000.

In 2005 the party joined the anti-Syrian Rafik Hariri Martyr List, which won the elections.

LEBANESE FORCES

(Al-Quwwat Al-Lubnaniyyah)

This coalition of right-wing militias was officially established in the summer of 1976 in the wake of the death of William Hawi, the head of the military apparatus of the Lebanese Phalanges Party. Bashir Gemayyel wanted to unify "the Christian rifle" to end the competition and wars between the various Christian militias in East Beirut. He also wanted to ensure utmost loyalty and obedience by Christian fighters. The role of the Forces gradually grew from that of a joint command of militias to that of a political-military apparatus with a large budget. It soon dominated the political leadership in East Beirut and marginalized the roles of other parties, organizations, and personalities. Bashir eliminated by force the presence of rival militias and arranged for the killing of rivals.

The Lebanese Forces was supported and financed by Israel and paved the way for the 1982 Israeli invasion of Lebanon. The election of Bashir to the presidency brought more prestige to the Forces, although his death brought about a decline in its effectiveness; previously dormant parties were revived and the leadership of the Christian camps was no longer monopolized by one man. The Lebanese Forces was tied to the massacres of Sabra and Shatila in 1982, which resulted in the death of innocent Palestinians residing in refugee camps. The Forces was briefly aligned with the Syrian regime under the leadership of Elie Hubayqah, but he was ousted and replaced by Samir Ja'ja' in 1986. Ja'ja' led the Forces through the difficult wars with General Michel Aoun, but he was arrested in 1994 for plotting the assassination of a rival and the bombing of a church. Like other militias, the Forces was disbanded but was then registered as a new political party. Ja'ja' was pardoned in 2005 and moved to France. In the 2005 parliamentary elections the party won six seats and was part of the Rafik Hariri Martyr List.

PROGRESSIVE SOCIALIST PARTY

(Al-Hizb At-Taqaddumi Al-Ishtiraki; PSP)

This party was founded by the famed Druze leader Kamal Jumblat in 1949. He invited a group of multi-sectarian intellectuals to form the leadership, but the party quickly became a sectarian Druze party despite its secular agenda. It served as a political vehicle for this influential Druze za'im. Jumblat was a key parliamentary leader and played a crucial role in the 1958 civil war. By 1975 Jumblat had emerged as one of the most important opposition leaders in the country, and he founded and headed the Lebanese National Movement, which supported political reforms and the PLO in Lebanon. Jumblat wanted to defeat the Phalangist-led forces in Lebanon but was thwarted in his efforts by the Syrian regime. He was assassinated in 1977 and was immediately succeeded by his son Walid.

Walid quickly ended the feud with the Syrian regime and reorganized the PSP's militia in preparation for a major showdown with the Lebanese Forces. In the 1983–84 War of the Mountain, Jumblat consolidated his leadership within the Druze community and the party emerged as one of the most effective militias in the country. The party won seats in the 1992, 1996, 2000, and 2005 elections; in the latter it joined the Rafik Hariri Martyr List. The party does not serve as more than a tool for Walid Jumblat.

AMAL MOVEMENT

(Harakat Amal)

The original name of this organization is Harakat Al-Mahrumin (Movement of the Disinherited), but its name after 1978 became known by the acronym of its military arm Afwaj Al-Muqawamah A1-Lubnaniyyah (Detachments of the Lebanese Resistance), or AMAL. The word also means "hope" in Arabic.

The history of this movement is closely associated with the role of its founder Imam Musa As-Sadr, who came to Lebanon from Iran in 1959 and organized the political movement of the Shiite community. Israeli bombardment of South Lebanon in the 1960s, when the Palestine Liberation Organization (PLO) was emerging as a political and military force in Lebanon, radicalized the community, which was—and is—the poorest community in the country. As-Sadr called on the Lebanese state to defend the villages of South Lebanon and to bring about economic improvement in the lives of Shiites. The role of As-Sadr was boosted in 1969 when he was elected chairman of the Higher Islamic Shiite Council. He founded the council to separate the demands of the Shiites from the political demands of other Muslim sects in the country; he wanted to assert an independent Shiite voice after decades of Sunni leadership of all Muslim sects in Lebanon. While As-Sadr did not call for a revolution, he supported "armed struggle" to fight back against Israeli forces in Lebanon.

The civil war did not help the cause of the movement: its role was marginalized as many Shiites flocked to Lebanese and Palestinian radical organizations that offered them arms and ideologies. In 1976 the movement was ejected from areas under the control of the PLO and its Lebanese allies because it supported Syrian military intervention in the country. The movement was dormant until 1978 when pro-Syrian As-Sadr "disappeared" while on an official visit to Libya. His supporters blamed the Libyan regime, while the regime denied responsibility. This coincided with two other important developments that affected the Shiite political culture: the PLO rule in South Lebanon was growing increasingly unpopular due to various acts of misconduct and thuggery (committed by both Lebanese and Palestinian gunmen), and the Islamic revolution in Iran was popularizing a form of religious-inspired mobilization. This propelled the movement again into prominence, and the Shiite sectarian identity became the cornerstone of the movement's ideology.

The movement's strong pro-Syrian orientations were confirmed and consolidated in 1980 when Nabih Birri assumed the leadership of the movement, which has been under his command ever since. The Israeli invasion of 1982 produced a split in the movement, but Birri succeeded in steering the organization away from Iranian hegemony. The movement launched a war against the Palestinian refugee camps in 1987, which dragged on for three years. Birri became a minister in 1984 and was elected to the Speakership of parliament (the highest Shiite post in the government) in 1992. Birri was elected speaker of parliament for a third term in 2000. The movement was disarmed along with other militias during the first administration of Ilyas Hrawi (1989–95). The movement won four parliamentary seats in the 1992 elections, and its list won overwhelmingly in the South in the 1996 parliamentary election, in which Amal and Hezbollah unified their list. In the parliamentary elections of 2000 the Amal-Hezbollah list achieved a landslide victory, but in 2005, in the wake of Syria's withdrawal of its troops from Lebanon, the list was soundly defeated by the Rafik Hariri Martyr List.

PARTY OF GOD

(Hezbollah)

This party was officially established in the wake of the Israeli invasion of 1982, but its formation can be traced back to the 1960s, when militant Shiites expressed unhappiness with the moderate agenda of Imam Musa As-Sadr. The party was formed in opposition to the Amal movement, and the Islamic republic in Iran played a key role in its formation. The existence of the party was announced in 1984. Shaykh Muhammad Husayn Fadlallah, who has been considered the spiritual guide of the party, has played a major role in the party's history and in widening its appeal among Lebanon's Shiites. While the party stressed the need for an Islamic republic in Lebanon, it has been mostly known through press reports linking it to anti-American acts of violence in Lebanon, including the kidnapping of American hostages in Lebanon in the 1980s. The party has refused to disarm and continues to launch acts of national resistance against the Israeli occupation of South Lebanon.

In the parliamentary elections of 2000 the Amal-Hezbollah list achieved a landslide victory and won all 23 seats allocated for South Lebanon. It is believed that without a joint list with Amal, Hezbollah, which took 12 of the 23 seats, would have gained more seats. In 2005 the alliance again won all 23 seats in South Lebanon, but nationally it was soundly defeated by the anti-Syrian Rafik Hariri Martyr List.

Minor Political Parties

SYRIAN SOCIAL NATIONAL PARTY

(Al-Hizb As-Suri Al-Qawmi Al-Ijtima'i)

This is one of the oldest parties in the country. It was founded by Antun Sa'adah in 1932 and quickly became one of the most influential parties in the entire Arab East, attracting scores of intellectuals and workers. The party advocated the unity of Greater Syria, which includes the Fertile Crescent and Cyprus. Sa'adah coined the slogan "Syria is for the Syrians and the Syrians form one nation" to summarize his vision. He opposed sectarianism and called for Christian-Muslim brotherhood within the context of Syrian nationalism. He strongly denounced the clerical establishment in Lebanon.

The party clearly reflected fascist organizations of the time: this can be seen in its ideology and organizational structure, which focuses on blind allegiance to the personality of the leader (Sa'adah). The party's ideology is virulently anti-Semitic, and Sa'adah understood nationalism in racial terms. Sa'adah declared an armed revolt against the Lebanese state, and he was executed without trial in 1949. The party recovered from the death of its founder and continued to expand in the region. It was originally right-wing and supported Kamil Sham'un in the 1958 revolt. The most serious crisis in the party's history was the coup attempt—the only one of its kind in Lebanon—launched by the party in 1961. The coup failed and the Shihabi regime led a brutal campaign against party members, which resulted in its temporary exclusion from Lebanese political life. While in jail, many party leaders decided to move the party in a more leftist direction and to express solidarity with Arab nationalist parties in Lebanon. Party leaders were released from jail in 1969, and they worked to revive party activity.

The party suffered from many splits in its history and from conflicting claims of allegiance to the personality of Sa'adah, and all party members are required to salute his picture before party meetings. The party participated in the Lebanese civil war as a member of the Lebanese National Movement and received aid from the PLO. A pro-Syrian branch of the party opposed the Lebanese National Movement, especially when the latter fought against the Syrian army in 1976. The two factions were temporarily reunited in 1978, but other splits continued to tear the party apart. There are now at least two parties that use the name of the party and both claim to be the authentic heirs of Sa'adah. The major party won two seats in the 2005 parliamentary elections.

FREE PATRIOTIC MOVEMENT

(Tayyar Al-Watani Al-Horr)

This party was founded in 2005 by General Michel Aoun, who served as prime minister between 1988 and 1990 and who was exiled to France for many years before returning to Lebanon in May 2005. The party draws support from both Muslim and Christians and claims to be the only major party in Lebanon not based on a religion. In the 2005 elections the party won 14 seats, and it also formed a larger alliance (the Aoun Alliance) that captured a total of 21 seats.

Other Political Forces

Opposition against government policy increased in the early 2000s over issues related to socioeconomic policies, absence of the rule of law, and the growing corruption in the Lebanese government. The most vocal opposition to government policies, the General Confederation of Lebanese Workers, was muted by government intervention and manipulation of its presidential elections.

Syria has long played a central role in Lebanon's political scene. This role dimmed somewhat in 2005 following the assassination of former prime minister Rafik Hariri, which many blamed on Syrian military police. Domestic and international outrage pressured Syria into withdrawing all of its troops from the country, but there is little doubt that Syria still retains a significant presence in the country. That presence is supported by a large number of Lebanese, as evidenced by the massive demonstrations in favor of the Syrian presence in the aftermath of Hariri's assassination.

National Prospects

As Lebanon continues on the path of reconstruction and national conciliation, some people remain skeptical about its ability to end once and for all the national discord and sectarian hatred. The government of President Emile Lahoud was largely overshadowed by the prominent personality of his prime minister, Rafik Hariri. Hariri had emerged as the single most important architect of postwar Lebanon, and his international reputation had secured him a stable political status that few prime ministers have had in modern Lebanon history. His reconstruction plans, however, earned him the hostility of advocates of the poor in Lebanon. It is widely believed that his plans for postwar Lebanon were based on the old economic formula for prewar Lebanon, which stressed the service sector of the economy at the expense of agriculture and industry, where most of the poor are employed. In addition, his plans did not address the problem of acute centralization that has characterized modern Lebanon. Poor Lebanese residing in remote areas of the country still depend on the services and government agencies centered in Beirut. His assassination in 2005 opened a new round of political upheaval in Lebanon and led both to the withdrawal of Syrian troops from Lebanon and a huge victory for pro-Hariri parties in the 2005 legislative elections.

The formula of political reform known as the Ta'if Accord also created resentment on the part of large segments of the Christian population, which felt that Syrian political dominance in Lebanon caused a reduction of their political power. They especially criticized the marginalization of important opposition figures, such as General Michel Aoun, who was in exile in France until May 2005. Many Christian leaders cheered the withdrawal of Syrian troops from Lebanon in 2005, a move they had long called for.

The single most important achievement of the Ta'if Accord was the reestablishment of internal security. With the exception of Hezbollah, the major militias were integrated into the army.

The current challenges faced by the government include increasing levels of poverty. The funding of the ambitious postwar reconstruction program through borrowing has made Lebanon one of the most indebted states in the world. Economic decline and the government's failure to address the growing gap between rich and poor and corruption at the governmental level have added to the socioeconomic distress. Whether the new government of Prime Minister Fouad Siniora, which was organized following the 2005 legislative elections, can address these issues remains to be seen.

Further Reading

AbuKhalil, As'ad. *Historical Dictionary of Lebanon.* Lanham, Md.: Scarecrow Press, 1998.

Ajami, Fouad. *The Vanished Imam.* Ithaca, N.Y.: Cornell University Press, 1986.

Azar, Fabiola, and Etienne Mullet. "Muslims and Christians in Lebanon: Common Views on Political Issues." *Journal of Peace Research* 39, no. 6 (November 2002): 735–46.

Beydoun, Ahmed. *Identité confessionelle et temps social chez les historiens libanais contemporains.* Beirut: Lebanese University, 1984.

Collings, Deirdre, ed. *Peace for Lebanon?* Boulder, Colo.: Lynne Rienner, 1994.

Dagher, Carole H. *Bring Down the Walls: Lebanon's Postwar Challenge.* New York: St. Martin's Press, 2000.

El Khazen, Farid. *The Breakdown of the State in Lebanon, 1967–1976.* Cambridge, Mass.: Harvard University Press, 2000.

———. "Political Parties in Post-war Lebanon: Parties in Search of Partisans." *Middle East Journal* 57, no. 4 (autumn 2003): 605–24.

Gilmour, David. *Lebanon: The Fractured Country.* New York: St. Martin's Press, 1983.

Gordon, David. *Lebanon: The Fragmented Nation.* London: Croom Helm, 1980.

Goria, Wade. *Sovereignty and Leadership in Lebanon.* London: Ithaca Press, 1985.

Hanf, Theodor. *Coexistence in Wartime Lebanon.* Translated by John Richardson. London: I.B. Tauris, 1993.

Hudson, Michael. *The Precarious Republic: Political Modernization in Lebanon.* New York: Random House, 1968.

Khalaf, Samir. *Lebanon's Predicament.* New York: Columbia University Press, 1987.

Khalidi, Walid. *Conflict and Violence in Lebanon.* Cambridge, Mass.: Harvard University Press, 1979.

Norton, Augustus Richard. *Amal and the Shi'a.* Austin: University of Texas Press, 1987.

Owen, Roger. *Essays on the Crisis in Lebanon.* London: Ithaca Press, 1976.

Petran, Tabitha. *The Struggle over Lebanon.* New York: Monthly Review Press, 1987.

KINGDOM OF LESOTHO
(Mmuso wa Lesotho)

By B. David Meyers, Ph.D.

Lesotho, a nation of slightly fewer than 2 million people, is completely surrounded by South Africa. Most of the nation's GNP is provided by citizens working in South Africa. The country's tumultuous political history has seen a series of clashes involving the king, partisan leaders, the military, and the forces of neighboring states.

Formerly the British territory of Basutoland, Lesotho received its independence in October 1966. Moshoeshoe II, the paramount chief of the Basotho, was recognized as king of a constitutional monarchy. In the last elections before independence, the Basotho National Party (BNP), helped by funds from South Africa, narrowly defeated the Basotho Congress Party (BCP), and the BNP's leader, Chief Leabua Jonathan, became the nation's prime minister.

Relations between Jonathan and King Moshoeshoe were often turbulent, and, by 1970 the king had once been placed under house arrest and, another time, sent overseas in the first of three periods of exile. When he returned from exile, the king agreed to respect the constitutional nature of the monarchy and to refrain from any political activities. Jonathan, meanwhile, further consolidated his own power. In January 1970, when the opposition BCP had seemingly won a majority of seats in elections to the National Assembly, Jonathan suspended the constitution, jailed his opponents, and established rule by decree.

In 1986 South Africa, angered that Lesotho had given sanctuary to antiapartheid African National Congress guerrillas, imposed a blockade on its tiny neighbor. The blockade sparked a military coup, led by General Metsing Lekhanya, who seized power from Jonathan and agreed to expel the guerrillas. In March 1990, following a power struggle between the king and the general, the military government again exiled Moshoeshoe. After seven months the king returned, but rather than refrain from politics, he insisted that military rule be ended and elections held. Lekhanya again deposed him, and the nation's senior chiefs put his son, Letsie III, who promised to keep out of politics, on the throne.

In 1991 another coup, led by Colonel Phisoane Ramaema, ousted Lekhanya and announced that the army would return to barracks following free elections. After a number of postponements, these elections were held in March 1993, and a new government took power.

This elected government, headed by Prime Minister Ntsu Mokhehle, quickly ran into problems with the military as armed units fought one another, killed the deputy prime minister, and killed or abducted other cabinet members. Intervention by neighboring Botswana, South Africa, and Zimbabwe was needed to diffuse these crises. In August 1994, after a series of such violent disturbances, King Letsie dissolved parliament, dismissed the Mokhehle government, and replaced it with one that included the leader of the opposition BNP. Intervention by leaders of the same neighboring states restored the elected government, forced Letsie to abdicate, and reinstated his father, Moshoeshoe.

On January 15, 1996, King Moshoeshoe was killed in an automobile accident and was, again, succeeded by Letsie. In February there was another unsuccessful coup attempt.

Violence again racked Lesotho in 1998. In that year's elections the Lesotho Congress for Democracy (LCD) won 60 percent of the popular vote, which resulted in the capture of 79 of the 80 seats in the National Assembly. Opposition parties claimed the polling was rigged, and thousands of angry people took to the streets. Reports of another attempted military coup followed by the arrest of a number of officers increased the widespread disorder. In September, South African and Botswanan soldiers, who had entered Lesotho to quell the unrest, fought pitched battles with members of the Lesotho Defense Force.

Although neutral observers denied the opposition's claims of electoral fraud, it was widely agreed that there was an explosive asymmetry between the opposition's 40 percent of the popular vote and the resultant single Assembly seat. In an effort to reduce this discrepancy, before the 2002 elections 40 additional seats (known as Proportional Representation seats) were added to the Assembly. These were divided among the minority parties in proportion with their polling strength.

The System of Government

Lesotho is a constitutional monarchy in which the king plays mainly a ceremonial role. The legislature is bicameral.

EXECUTIVE

The Lesotho king is intended to reign as a ceremonial head of state with no executive power. In theory such a constitutional monarch provides continuity and stability to a political system. Only in the last decade has this been the case in Lesotho as both Letsie and his father, despite promises to the contrary, were politically active. Since his return to the throne in 1996, Letsie has refrained from interfering in the political process.

Executive authority is vested in the Council of Ministers, which is headed by a prime minister who is the leader of the majority party in the National Assembly. Ntsu Mokhehle, leader of the Basotho

Congress Party and later its virtual successor, the Lesotho Congress for Democracy (LCD), served as prime minister from 1993 to 1998. When he stepped down in May 1998, he was replaced by Pakalitha Mosisili, who won a second term in 2002.

LEGISLATURE

Lesotho has a bicameral legislature consisting of a Senate and National Assembly. The Senate includes the country's 22 principal chiefs and 11 members appointed by the government. In efforts to increase popular support, the composition of the more important National Assembly has twice been altered. In 1993 the Lesotho Congress for Democracy (LCD) won all 65 seats, completely excluding the opposition. In 1998 the Assembly was expanded to 80 single-member constituencies, but LCD's 60 percent of the popular vote was sufficient to capture all but one of them. As part of the effort to avoid the violence that followed that election, the composition of the Assembly was again altered by adding 40 seats that are proportionately distributed among the minority parties. In the 2002 elections the LCD again won 79 of the contested seats and thus maintained control of the Assembly and government. The Basotho National Party (BNP), which had received 22.4 percent of the popular vote, was awarded 21 of the Proportional

LESOTHO NATIONAL ASSEMBLY: PERCENT OF POPULAR VOTE AND SEATS BY PARTY, 2002

Party	% Vote	Seats
Lesotho Congress for Democracy	54.9	79
Basotho National Party	22. 4	21
Lesotho Peoples' Congress	5.8	5
National Independent Party	5.5	5
Basutoland African Congress	2.9	3
Basutoland Congress Party	2.6	3
Lesotho Workers Party	1.4	1
Marematlou Freedom Party	1.2	1
Khoeetsa ea Sechaba/ Popular Front for Democracy	1.1	1
National Progressive Party	0.7	1

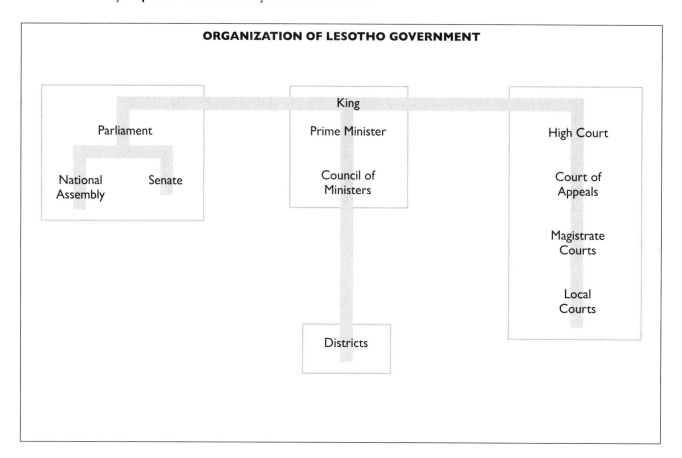

ORGANIZATION OF LESOTHO GOVERNMENT

Representation seats, while eight other parties divided the remaining 19.

JUDICIARY

At the top of the judicial system is a High Court that has the power of judicial review of legislative acts. Below it is a Court of Appeals and a number of subordinate magistrate's courts. Members of the two high courts are chosen by the government and appointed by the king.

The legal system is based on English common law and Roman-Dutch law. There is a movement to change the Roman-Dutch legal system as it is thought to discriminate against women. At the local level courts administer customary tribal law.

REGIONAL AND LOCAL GOVERNMENT

The nation is divided into 10 administrative districts. Outside of the urban areas, the country is divided into numerous chiefdoms, whose traditional leaders fulfill many of the functions of local government. Local elections were held in 2005 for the first time since independence.

The Electoral System

Since the election law changes of 2002, there is popular polling for the 80 single-member, first-past-the-post seats and then the distribution of 40 additional seats among the minority parties. This system encouraged 19 parties to participate in that year's National Assembly contests. Postelection recriminations were considerably less frequent than previously, and most observers believed that the elections were fair. Voters must be 18 years of age.

The Party System
ORIGINS OF THE PARTIES

Political parties in Lesotho began with the formation of the BCP in 1952, more than a decade before independence. Lesotho's conservatives saw the BCP programs as radical and formed their own party, the BNP, to protect their positions and beliefs as the country moved toward independence. With the exception of the period of military rule when political activity was suspended, one or the other of these two parties controlled the government from independence until the rise to dominance of the Lesotho Congress for Democracy (LCD).

CAMPAIGNING

In the most recent elections, most party platforms were highly similar as ideological and other differences were subordinated to a focus on the national problems of the deteriorating economy, AIDS, and growing famine. In their campaigns, politicians discussed both national and local concerns but seldom offered clear-cut alternative policies. Posters focused on the party leaders, and a part of LCD's success was often linked to the personal popularity of former prime minister Ntsu Mokhehle.

Major Political Parties

LESOTHO CONGRESS FOR DEMOCRACY (LCD)

The LCD was organized in June 1997 by Ntsu Mokhehle, who was at the time the nation's prime minister and the leader of the Basotho Congress Party (BCP). Mokhehle quit the BCP, which he had founded, in reply to a challenge launched by young, self-proclaimed "progressives," who wished to remove him from the party leadership. Almost half of the BCP's members of parliament followed Mokhehle into the new party. Pakalitha Mosisili, who had been Mokhehle's deputy as both party leader and prime minister, was among those who made the switch. When age and ill health forced Mokhehle's retirement, Mosisili assumed both the government and the party offices.

The LCD supports the development of a Socialist economy and favors the limitation or abolition of the governmental role of chiefs. In recent elections it campaigned, as did the other major parties, on the promise of more jobs and a continued fight against poverty.

BASOTHO CONGRESS PARTY (BCP)

The BCP was formed in 1952 under the leadership of Ntsu Mokhehle. From the time of its founding, the party encouraged Lesotho's national independence and opposed the advancement of ties to neighboring South Africa. Party policies have also included the development of a socialist economy and have supported efforts to limit or abolish the governmental roles of the traditional chiefs.

The BCP won the 1960 elections but lost to the BNP in 1965, the last elections before independence. It was apparently winning in 1970 when Jonathan annulled the election results and arrested Mokhehle and other BCP leaders. During the years of Jonathan's rule, the BCP temporarily split between those who chose to accept participation in his government of national unity and those who followed Mokhehle into exile.

The 1997 split left the once-powerful party with a minority of its former members. In the 1998 elections the BCP came in third in the popular vote and captured no seats in the Assembly. In 2002 it received 2.6 percent of the vote and was awarded three of the Proportional Representation seats. The BCP is headed by Tseliso Makhakhe.

BASOTHO NATIONAL PARTY (BNP)

The BNP was formed in 1958 under the leadership of Leabua Jonathan, a minor chief. Originally much more conservative than its BCP rival, it supported the traditional chiefs, opposed communism, and sought good relations with South Africa. With the support of the chiefs and their followers and the Catholic Church, and with financial support from South Africa, BNP won the 1965 elections and led the country at independence. During the 1970s and early 1980s the BNP dominated Lesotho politics. During this period Jonathan became an opponent of South African apartheid, and there were clashes between the two countries. The growing problems with South Africa and the rise in power of the BNP's radical Youth League were the major reasons for the 1986 military coup that removed the party and its leader from power. Jonathan died about a year later.

In the 1993 elections the BNP, under the leadership of Evaristus Sekhonyana, received only 16 percent of the popular vote and won no seats. Its prospects were further damaged when Sekhonyana supported King Letsie's brief dismissal of the elected government in August 1994. It is widely believed that the BNP's leaders have been involved with numerous military efforts to overthrow the government.

The BNP remains the most conservative of Lesotho's major parties. In 1998 it received 24 percent of the popular vote but captured only one Assembly seat. In 2002 it again came in a distant second place, winning 22.4 percent of the popular vote and being awarded 21 of the Proportional Representation seats. The party is led by Major General Justine Metsing.

Minor Political Parties

In addition to the three major parties, 16 minor parties contested the 2002 elections. Seven of them gained at least one of the Proportional Representation seats in the Assembly, while some of the others disappeared almost immediately after the polling was completed. Of the minor parties, only one, the Marematlou Freedom Party (MFP), has ever held a directly elected Assembly seat. The MFP, a royalist party, has the support of some of the chiefs but has been unable to move Lesotho's more traditional/conservative voters from their support of the BNP. In 1992 the MFP received only 1.2 percent of the popular vote and was awarded one PR seat. The party is led by Vincent Malebo.

Other Political Forces

Within Lesotho, the 2,000-strong army has been, and seemingly remains, a powerful political actor. The army's long distaste for the governing party comes originally from its years of bloody struggle against the BCP's armed wing. In recent years the regular forces have mutinied over demands for a pay raise. The army has continually resisted the government's efforts to exert control and has killed some political leaders and held others captive. Only threats of South African intervention have prevented, pacified, or ended various army threats to, and actions against, the elected government.

During the 1960s the Roman Catholic Church was politically powerful and was supportive of the BNP. More recently, church leaders have issued calls for internal peace and for holding a national conference on peace, democracy, and stability, but, in general, they appear peripheral to the political system. Lesotho's labor unions have often compounded the nation's problems with their own strikes and economic demands.

More than anything else, Lesotho's political fate has often been largely in the hands of neighboring South Africa. The decision by South Africa to use fewer foreign miners has hurt Lesotho's already-poor economy, while South African diplomatic and military power has diffused or decided its series of political crises.

National Prospects

After years of lurching from crisis to crisis, Lesotho has recently enjoyed a measure of political stability. Unfortunately, the LCD government has been unable to alleviate the continued problems of a deteriorating economy, widespread shortages of food, and an AIDS pandemic.

Further Reading

Southall, Roger, and Fox, Roddy. "Lesotho's General Election of 1998: Rigged or de Rigueur." *Journal of Modern African Studies* 37, no. 4 (1999): 669–97.

REPUBLIC OF LIBERIA

By Elizabeth L. Normandy, Ph.D.
Revised by Dora Ioveva

Liberia is located in West Africa. It lies between Sierra Leone and Ivory Coast (Côte d'Ivoire) and borders the North Atlantic Ocean. It has a land area of 38,250 square miles, slightly larger than the state of Tennessee.

Liberia's population is estimated at 3.4 million people (2005 est.), excluding the approximately 1.4 million refugees residing in the surrounding countries of Côte d'Ivoire, Guinea, Ghana, Sierra Leone, and Nigeria. Approximately 160,000 Liberians died between 1990 and 1997 as a result of the civil war. In addition, at least 7,000 refugees from Sierra Leone fled into Liberia as the result of a May 1997 coup in Sierra Leone.

Indigenous African ethnic groups make up 95 percent of Liberia's population. These groups include the Kpelle, Bassa, Gio, Kru, Grebo, Mano, Krahn, Gola, Gbandi, Loma, Kissi, Vai, and Bella. Americo-Liberians, descendants of the African Americans who settled the territory in the 19th century, make up 5 percent of the population. Those who practice traditional African religions are 70 percent of the population, while 20 percent of the remainder are Muslim and 10 percent are Christian.

Liberia has a republican form of government established in 1847 and patterned after the United States. From 1877 to 1980 Liberia was ruled by the True Whig Party (TWP), which was dominated by the Americo-Liberian elite. Americo-Liberian domination of Liberian politics ended in April 1980, when a coup brought a military regime, led by Samuel K. Doe, to power. Doe was elected to the post of president in 1985, returning Liberia to a civilian republican form of government. An armed insurrection in 1989 resulted in the death of Doe and brought to power a series of interim governments that held office between 1990 and 1997, as an expanding array of rebel factions carried out a bloody struggle for control of the country. In July 1997 Charles Taylor, leader of the rebel faction that began the insurrection, was elected to the presidency in the first multiparty elections since 1985. However, the civil war continued until 2003, when the United Nations finally brokered an end to the conflict. As part of the agreement, Taylor under heavy international criticism for meddling in Sierra Leone's civil war was exiled to Nigeria, and an interim government known as the National Transitional Government of Liberia was installed. Gyude Bryant was named interim president. New presidential and legislative elections were scheduled for 2005.

The System of Government

Liberia is a unitary republic. The constitution of 1984 calls for a strong presidential system with a bicameral legislature.

EXECUTIVE

Under Liberia's constitution, approved by a national referendum in 1984, executive power is vested in a president who is head of state, head of government, and commander in chief of the armed forces. The president is elected through universal suffrage for a six-year term. The president appoints a 16-member cabinet.

Following the death of Samuel Doe in 1990, Amos Sawyer was inaugurated as interim president. The Interim Government of National Unity (IGNU) was backed by ECOWAS, a regional organization of West African states that had put an 8,000-member peace-keeping force known as ECOMOG into the country. The Sawyer government entered into a cease-fire with the rebel forces, a truce that lasted for two years until October 1992. A July 1993 peace accord created a five-member transitional authority, the Liberian National Transitional Government (LNTG), to rule until elections were held. The council contained representatives of the three major factions in the war and two independent members agreeable to the principal factions. Presidential aspirants were barred from membership on the interim council, and transitional officeholders were prohibited from running for president.

Amid bickering over the composition and leadership of the transitional government, David Kpormikor was named chairman of the council. An amendment to the 1993 peace accord in December 1994 provided for the replacement of the transitional government, and in September 1995 Wilton Sankawulo became the head of the five-member council until elections could be held in August 1996. The council included representatives of at least three rebel factions in the civil war, and the leaders of the major factions influenced the selection of the cabinet. Continued fighting prevented elections from being held, and, in August 1996 Ruth Perry was selected to serve as interim leader until elections in 1997. In July 1997 Charles Taylor defeated Ellen Johnson-Sirleaf and 11 other candidates to become president. Taylor's cabinet included some of his former adversaries. As part of the U.N.-brokered peace agreement in 2003, Taylor resigned the presidency and went into exile. Gyude Bryant was named interim president. Bryant appointed the cabinet, with members drawn from among the groups participating in the peace agreement. New presidential elections held in 2005 indicated that Johnson-Sirleaf won the voting. She was thus poised to become the first female president of an African country.

LEGISLATURE

Liberia's 1984 constitution provides for a bicameral legislature. The 30 members of the upper house, the Senate, are elected for a nine-year term. Members of the 64-seat House of Representatives are elected for six-year terms. There is no limit on the number of terms a legislator may serve.

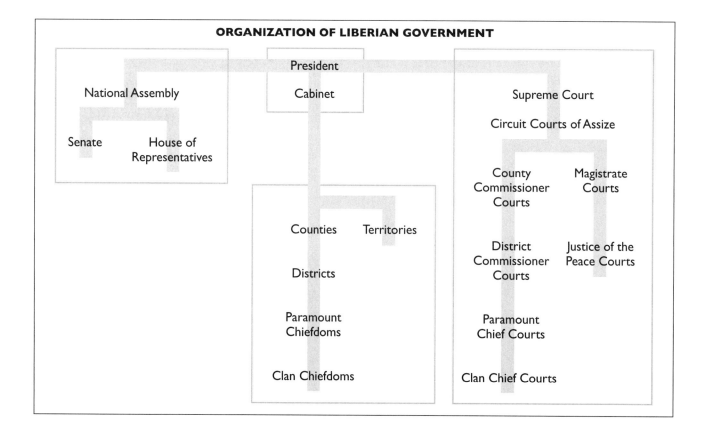

ORGANIZATION OF LIBERIAN GOVERNMENT

There are two seats for each of Liberia's 15 counties in the Senate and one representative for every 20,000 people in the House of Representatives. The passage of laws requires the approval of both houses and the president. The president has veto power, but a presidential veto can be overridden by a two-thirds majority of both houses.

Liberia does not have a strong tradition of legislative independence. Until the election of Samuel Doe, the True Whig Party dominated the executive and the legislative branches.

In March 1994 a unicameral Transitional Legislative Assembly was established. Members of the 35-seat body were appointed by the leaders of the major factions in the civil war. In July 1997 Charles Taylor's National Patriotic Party (NPP) captured a majority of the 90 seats in the bicameral legislature. When the U.N.-brokered peace agreement was reached in 2003, the legislature was suspended, and an interim Legislative Assembly was installed. It contained 76 members drawn from among the various factions that signed the peace agreement. The interim legislature was dissolved in 2005, following legislative elections for both houses to reinstate the permanent legislature. The Congress for a Democratic Change (CDC) won 15 seats in the House of Representatives, the Liberty Party won nine, and the Unity Party and the Coalition for the Transformation of Liberia each won eight.

JUDICIARY

The constitution of Liberia provides for an independent judiciary with power vested in the People's Supreme Court and several lower courts. Magistrates' courts and circuit courts exist at the local level. The Supreme Court comprises a chief justice and four associate justices. They and the judges of the lower courts are appointed by the president and approved by the Senate. Traditionally, Liberia has maintained a dual legal system: statutory law based on Anglo-American common law for the modern sector, and customary law based on unwritten tribal practices for the indigenous sector. Efforts to unify the legal system have not been successful.

REGIONAL AND LOCAL GOVERNMENT

Liberia is divided into 15 counties administered by superintendents who are the direct representatives of the president. They are appointed by the president and approved by the Senate. Each county also has a county council. The capital city of each county is governed by a mayor and a city council. The counties are divided into districts administered by district commissioners. The districts are further divided into smaller units administered by paramount, clan, and town chiefs who are locally elected. Monrovia, the capital city, is administered by a city corporation that levies and collects taxes on real property within the city limits. Historically, local governments have had very little fiscal or administrative autonomy from the central government.

The Electoral System

Liberia's constitution calls for a multiparty system and an Elections Commission to conduct and supervise all elections for public office. Election is by universal suffrage exercised by citizens 18 years of age or older. Citizenship is available only to people of black ancestry and is conferred by birth or naturalization.

During the 2005 elections, which marked the end of the transitional government, voter turnout was estimated at nearly 75 percent for the first round of presidential voting and 61 percent in the second round. Losing presidential candidate George Weah claimed that the election was marred by voter fraud, but international observers including the United Nations, European Union, and Carter Center declared that the elections were for the most part free and fair.

The Party System

For more than a century, Liberia was effectively a one-party state dominated by the True Whig Party. In the years preceding the 1980 coup, the most significant opposition came from the Progressive Alliance of Liberia (PAL) and the Movement for Justice in Africa (MOJA). Headed by Gabriel Baccus Mathews, PAL was founded by Liberian students in the United States and began functioning in Liberia in 1978. In early 1980 PAL registered as a political party under the name Progressive People's Party (PPP). Formed in Liberia in 1973 as a campus-based intellectual movement, MOJA was a pressure group led by Drs. Togba Nah Tipoteh and Amos Sawyer from the faculty of the University of Liberia. It focused on labor grievances and endorsed industrial action.

The 1980 military coup resulted in the destruction of the True Whig Party. When the ban on political parties was lifted in 1984, the Americo-Liberians combined with indigenous Liberians to form the Liberian Action Party (LAP). In the 1985 elections four parties, Doe's NDPL, the LAP, the Unity Party (UP), and the Liberia Unification Party (LUP), won seats. Two other parties and their leaders were banned. These were the Liberia People's Party (LPP) headed by Amos Sawyer and the United People's Party (UPP) headed by Gabriel Baccus Mathews.

By 1996 the political party system consisted of many of the same parties that had existed in 1985 plus the newly created party of Charles Taylor, the National Patriotic Party (NPP). These parties were the National Democratic Party of Liberia (NDPL), led by Augustus Caine and formerly the party of Samuel Doe; the Liberian Action Party (LAP), led by Emmanuel Kromah and formerly supported by Americo-Liberian elements; the Unity Party (UP), led by Joseph Kofa and preparing to run Johnson-Sirleaf for president in 1997; the United Peoples Party (UPP), led by Gabriel Baccus Mathews and banned in the 1985 election; and the Liberia People's Party (LPP), led by Dusty Wolokollie and formerly headed by Amos Sawyer, interim president of Liberia from 1990 to 1993.

By 2005 all of these same parties were still in existence. They were joined by the Congress for Democratic Change (CDC), which won the most seats (15) in the 2005 House elections, and the Liberty Party, which won nine House seats.

Major Political Parties

CONGRESS FOR DEMOCRATIC CHANGE (CDC)

The CDC was led by George Weah, a former football (soccer) player who contested the 2005 presidential election. In the first round of voting he came in first, but in the second round he received fewer votes than the UP's Ellen Johnson-Sirleaf. The party won 15 seats in the 2005 House election and three seats in the Senate election.

LIBERTY PARTY (LP)

The LP's candidate in the 2005 presidential election, Charles Brumskine, came in third in the first round of voting and was thus eliminated from the second round. The party won nine House seats and three Senate seats in the 2005 legislative elections.

UNITY PARTY (UP)

The UP's Ellen Johnson-Sirleaf ran unsuccessfully for president in 1997, but in 2005 she scored a landmark victory, apparently becoming the first democratically elected women to head an African country. Educated at Harvard, Johnson-Sirleaf later became an economist for the World Bank. Her educational an professional credentials appeared to play a large role in her 2005 victory, as her opponent, the football star George Weah, lacked any such credentials. The UP won eight House seats and three Senate seats in the 2005 legislative elections.

LIBERIAN ACTION PARTY (LAP)

The LAP joined the four-party Coalition for the Transformation of Liberia (COTOL) ahead of the 2005 elections. The coalition won eight House seats and seven Senate seats in the elections.

LIBERIAN UNIFICATION PARTY (LUP)

The LUP likewise joined the COTOL alliance for the 2005 elections. The coalition won eight House seats and seven Senate seats in the elections.

UNITED PEOPLE'S PARTY (UPP)

For the 2005 legislative elections the UPP joined the LPP in the Alliance for Peace and Democracy. The coalition won five House seats and three Senate seats.

LIBERIA PEOPLE'S PARTY (LPP)

The LPP was the second member of the two-party Alliance for Peace and Democracy in the 2005 legislative elections. The coalition won five House seats and three Senate seats.

Minor Political Parties

Other parties with representation in the legislature following the 2005 elections include the NPP (four House and four Senate seats), the NDPL (one House and two Senate seats), the New Deal Movement (three House seats), and the All Liberia Coalition Party (two House seats and one Senate seat).

Other Political Forces

The United Nations, through a unit known as the United Nations Mission in Liberia (UNMIL), played a key role in helping to end the 14-year civil war in 2003. UNMIL retained a strong presence in the country even after working with the warring factions to disarm, a process that was completed in late 2004.

National Prospects

The new government of Liberia, presumably to be led by Ellen Johnson-Sirleaf, faces a number of formidable challenges. It must rebuild the economic infrastructure destroyed by the civil war. It must repatriate refugees and restore water, electricity, and social services. And it must maintain peace and stability. The international community was heavily involved in the rebuilding efforts and in providing basic humanitarian assistance. In February 2004 the United States pledged $200 million in relief aid and rebuilding efforts to the country, with other nations pledging an additional $320 million.

Further Reading

Adebajo, A. *Building Peace in West Africa: Liberia, Sierra Leone, and Guinea-Bissau*. Boulder, Colo.: Lynne Rienner, 2002.

Clapham, Christopher. *Liberia and Sierra Leone: An Essay in Comparative Politics*. London: Cambridge University Press, 1976.

Dolo, Emmanuel. *Democracy versus Dictatorship: The Quest for Freedom and Justice in Africa's Oldest Republic—Liberia*. Washington, D.C.: University Press of America, 1996.

Dunn, D. Elwood, and Svend E. Holsoe. *Historical Dictionary of Liberia*. Lanham, Md.: Scarecrow Press, 1985.

Hlophe, Stephen S. *Class, Ethnicity and Politics in Liberia: A Class Analysis of Power Struggles in the Tubman and Tolbert Administrations from 1944–1975*. Washington, D.C.: University Press of America, 1979.

Jackson, Robert H., and Carl G. Rosberg. *Personal Rule in Black Africa: Prince, Autocrat, Prophet, Tyrant*. Berkeley: University of California Press, 1982.

Kieh, George K., Jr. *Dependency and the Foreign Policy of a Small Power: The Liberian Case*. Lewiston, N.Y.: Edward E. Mellen Press, 1992.

Liebnow, J. Gus. *The Evolution of Privilege*. Ithaca, N.Y.: Cornell University Press, 1969.

———. *The Quest for Democracy*. Bloomington: Indiana University Press, 1987.

Lyons, T. *Voting for Peace: Postconflict Elections in Liberia*. Washington, D.C.: Brookings Institution Press, 1999.

Pham, J. P. *Liberia: Portrait of a Failed State*. New York: Reed Press, 2004.

Weller, Marc., ed. *Regional Peacekeeping and International Enforcement: The Liberian Crisis*. New York: Cambridge University Press, 1994.

SOCIALIST PEOPLE'S LIBYAN ARAB JAMAHIRIYA

(Al-Jamahiriya al-Arabiya al-Libiya al-Sha'abiya al-Ishtirakiya)

By Ronald Bruce St. John, Ph.D.
Revised by Curtis R. Ryan, Ph.D.

The Socialist People's Libyan Arab Jamahiriya, a nation of 5.7 million people (2005 est.), is a unitary state governed by a unique organization of congresses and committees. This system of government evolved slowly after the Libyan Free Unionist Officers Movement, led by a Central Committee of 12 officers, executed a well-planned coup d'état on September 1, 1969, and overthrew the monarchy that had ruled the United Kingdom of Libya since independence in 1951.

The Central Committee soon renamed itself the Revolutionary Command Council (RCC), and, on December 11, 1969, it replaced the 1951 constitution with a Constitutional Proclamation, which described the Libyan Arab Republic as a free Arab democratic republic constituting part of the Arab nation, with Islam as the religion of the state and Arab unity as its overall objective.

The System of Government

Libya is essentially a military dictatorship under the control of Colonel Muammar al-Qaddafi. The RCC is designated the highest authority in the country and exercises both executive and legislative functions. As such, it is empowered to take whatever measures it deems necessary to protect the regime or the revolution. Such measures may take the form of proclamations, laws, orders, or resolutions. The Constitutional

Proclamation specifically gives the RCC power to declare war, conclude and ratify treaties, appoint diplomatic envoys and receive diplomatic missions, proclaim martial law, and control the armed forces.

The RCC is further empowered to appoint a Council of Ministers consisting of a prime minister and ministers; the Council's function is to implement the state's general policy as defined by the RCC. The RCC may also dismiss the prime minister and ministers; the prime minister's resignation automatically results in the resignation of the entire Council of Ministers.

The 1969 Constitutional Proclamation was to remain in force until the completion of the so-called nationalist democratic revolution, when it would be superseded by a permanent constitution. This has never occurred, and since Libya's political system has experienced continuous change since the overthrow of the monarchy, the system functioning today bears little resemblance to the one detailed in the proclamation. Moreover, there is some doubt as to whether the Constitutional Proclamation will ever be replaced by a constitution. The Green Book, the economic and political manifesto of Qaddafi, describes human-made law, including constitutions, as illogical and invalid, concluding that the genuine law of any society is either tradition (custom) or religion.

EXECUTIVE

Qaddafi, initially chairman of the RCC, is the head of state. The general secretary of the General People's

Congress (GPC) is the chief executive, and the General Secretariat of the GPC is the chief executive's staff and advisory body. The General People's Committee (or General Popular Committee), comprised of a general secretary and 19 secretaries, serves as a cabinet, replacing the former Council of Ministers, which was abolished in 1977.

Qaddafi was the general secretary of the GPC from 1977 until early 1979, when he relinquished the post to concentrate on what he described as "revolutionary activities with the masses." He has retained his position as de facto commander in chief of the armed forces and adopted the new title of leader of the revolution. During Qaddafi's tenure as general secretary of the GPC, the remaining members of the RCC initially formed its General Secretariat. They also resigned their posts in 1979 to focus on revolutionary activities. Regardless of position or title, Qaddafi and the former members of the RCC control and direct the Libyan government. Members of the General Secretariat of the General People's Congress are selected by them and serve at their convenience. Members of the General Secretariat, in turn, appoint members of the General People's Committee who serve three-year terms.

The objectives of the revolution have remained constant since the overthrow of the monarchy and can best be summarized within the major goal statements of freedom, socialism, and unity. The emphasis on freedom is the result of Libya's long history of foreign domination and exploitation. In practical terms, it means complete political and economic independence from any foreign direction or control. Through socialism, more often referred to as social justice, the revolution seeks to insure equal access to law and justice, to achieve a more equitable distribution of wealth, and to eliminate class differences. With the issuance of part two of Qaddafi's Green Book in 1977, the socioeconomic revolution in Libya became increasingly radical and pervasive. Unity is sought both domestically and internationally. On the national level, the objective is to unite society in purpose and effort by a centralized political authority. Internationally, the goal is overall Arab unity, and, in pursuit of it, the government repeatedly has proposed mergers with neighboring Arab states.

LEGISLATURE

The national-level representative body is called the General People's Congress (GPC), which was created in 1976. Delegates to the GPC are usually the chairpersons of the basic people's congresses and the branch or municipal people's committees, as well as representatives from the university student unions and the national federation of unions and professional associations. The number of delegates varies from session to session but generally approximates 1,000.

Scheduled to meet annually, normally for two weeks in January or February, the GPC is the major arena in which the plans, programs, and policies of the government are discussed and ratified. Formal ratification carries with it the responsibility of implementation by

ORGANIZATION OF LIBYAN GOVERNMENT

the people's committees, people's congresses, and trade unions and associations. At its first session in 1976, the General Secretariat of the GPC began submitting major government policies and plans to the GPC for review and authorization. Both the general administrative budget and the 1976–80 development budget were submitted, for example, as well as several major domestic and foreign policy items. This practice was continued thereafter. At the fifth session of the GPC (January 1–6, 1980), for example, a progress report on the 1976–80 five-year plan and a draft of the 1981–2000 national socioeconomic plan were discussed, as were a wide range of other domestic policy and foreign policy questions ranging from an amendment to the social security law to the bilateral pacts that Libya had concluded with other states in 1979. Nevertheless, there are limits to the subjects the head of state will allow on the GPC agenda. Libya's intervention in Chad, for example, was not discussed at the sixth session of the GPC (January 3–7, 1981).

With the abolition of the RCC and the Council of Ministers in 1977, both executive and legislative power was theoretically vested in the GPC. In reality, the GPC has delegated much of its major responsibility to the General Secretariat and the General People's Committee. In December 1978, for example, the GPC authorized the General People's Committee to appoint ambassadors and the secretary of foreign affairs to receive the credentials of foreign diplomats.

The fourth session of the GPC (December 1978) illustrated some of the limits of its power and authority. In the first two days of the Congress, several representatives called for an increase in salaries, although the recently published second part of the Green Book had called for their abolition. Other representatives demanded an end to the military draft after the General Secretariat had announced universal conscription for all young people. As a result of these and similar actions, the meeting was adjourned on the third day, officially out of respect for the death of the president of Algeria. Unofficially, delegate independence convinced the general secretary and the General Secretariat that they had to reassert their control over the revolution. After the adjournment, several people's committees were told to select new members before the GPC reconvened, and mobile election teams representing the government were dispatched to monitor those reelections. Similarly, when the ninth session of the GPC (February 1984) opposed three key proposals put forward by Qaddafi, he criticized the reactionary nature of the body and later revised the delegate makeup to ensure that such opposition was not repeated.

While the General Secretariat closely supervises the activities of the General People's Congress, the GPC does serve as a clearinghouse and sounding board for the views of the Libyan people as transmitted by their representatives on the congresses, committees, and functional organizations. Moreover, for the first time in the nation's history, subnational government requires popular participation in the selection of local leadership and allows popular involvement in the local policymaking process. At the same time, it provides an effective organization for the national leadership to communicate its ideas and objectives to the people. In this regard, while Qaddafi and the former members of the RCC remain the primary decision makers, the current political system has produced a level of representation and participation hitherto unknown in Libya.

JUDICIARY

From the beginning, the RCC indicated that it intended to place the nation's entire juridical system in an Islamic context. On October 28, 1971, the RCC established a Legislative Review and Amendment Committee, composed of the leading legal experts in Libya, to make existing laws conform with the basic tenets of the Islamic code of law, the sharia. Two years later, the RCC promulgated a law that merged the existing civil and sharia courts into a single juridical system.

The revised court system consists of four levels: Summary Courts, Courts of First Instance, Courts of Appeals, and the Supreme Court. The Summary Courts, existing in most villages and towns, are the primary level of the system. The Courts of First Instance serve as a court of appeal for the Summary Courts. In addition, they are the court of original jurisdiction for all matters involving more than 100 Libyan dinars. A Court of Appeals sits in each of three cities: Tripoli, Benghazi, and Sabhah. As its name suggests, it hears cases referred from a Court of First Instance. The Court of Appeals has no original jurisdiction except for cases involving felonies or high crimes. The Supreme Court sits in Tripoli and is composed of five chambers specializing in civil and commercial, criminal, administrative, constitutional, and personal matters. Each chamber consists of a five-judge panel with the majority establishing a decision. Before its formal abolition, the RCC appointed all judges; now, they are appointed by the GPC with the General Secretariat and the secretary of justice probably making the actual decision. With the exception of political cases, both judicial independence and due process of law generally appear to have been respected since 1969.

In addition to the regular court system, certain other bodies are involved in the administration or enforcement of justice. The Supreme Court for Judicial Authorities plays an administrative role, supervising and coordinating the various courts. The prime responsibility of the Council of State is to deliver advisory legal opinions for government bodies on draft legislation or other actions or regulations they are contemplating. A People's Court has been convened periodically to try crimes against the state. Plots and conspiracies against the state have also been referred to special ad hoc military courts convened for that purpose.

REGIONAL AND LOCAL GOVERNMENT

There are three levels of subnational government in Libya: the zone, the municipality or branch municipality, and the national. At the lowest level, zone residents elect a zone people's committee (or popular committee) to administer the affairs of the zone. The zone does not include a congress or legislative body.

The next echelon of government is the municipality. In the case of Libya's larger urban areas, municipalities are divided into branch municipalities; Tripoli, for instance, is divided into five branches. There are approximately 190 municipalities or branch municipalities, although the total number fluctuates. All zones are components of either a municipality or a branch municipality. Each municipality or branch municipality elects a legislative assembly known as the basic people's congress (BPC). Meeting quarterly, the BPC makes recommendations or decisions on administrative matters within its jurisdiction, such as roads, sewage, water, and public clinics. The BPC also debates the agenda of the GPC in advance of its annual meeting. The BPC selects its own chairman as well as a five-member people's committee, which has day-to-day administrative responsibility. All voting in the BPC is public; it is either a show of hands or a division into yes-or-no camps.

In those instances where a municipality is divided into two or more branches, a municipal People's Leadership Committee is established to coordinate the activities of the branch people's committees. The municipal people's leadership committee is made up of the chairperson and deputy chair of the branch people's committees. They select one of their number to be chair, who is, effectively, the mayor of the municipality. In those municipalities not large enough to be divided into branches, the chair of the municipal people's committee

serves as mayor of the municipality. In 1978 the General People's Committee at the national level was decentralized to include a similar structure at the municipal level. Municipal general people's committees are elected by the BPC for a term of three years. They are responsible for the coordination of activities between the General People's Committee and the BPC.

In addition to the zone and municipal committees and congresses, Libyan workers are organized into unions or professional associations. Each union or professional association elects its own people's committee (also known as popular committee) to administer its affairs. In turn, these People's Committees participate in the federation of unions at the national level. The national federation of unions and professional associations sends representatives to the GPC to address issues of special relevance to the unions, but these representatives are not allowed to vote on major policy issues. While the unions and professional associations bring necessary expertise to selected issues, Qaddafi has insisted that their views as citizens be represented through the people's committees and the BPCs.

Libyan universities are managed to a large degree by student unions. Under this system, each college or faculty in Libya's three universities (Tripoli, Benghazi, and Beida) elects a chairperson and a committee (also known as cabinet) to administer the college. Representatives of these committees form the university student union, which, along with the president of the university, is responsible for running the university. The president of the university serves at the pleasure of the members of the student union. Like unions and professional associations, university student unions attend the GPC in a nonvoting capacity.

A completely new echelon of subnational government, the revolutionary committee, was also established in 1979. Revolutionary committees now exist in virtually all government departments and agencies as well as within the BPCs, the people's committees of the union and professional associations, the university student unions, and the armed forces.

The revolutionary-committee system was established to raise the political consciousness of the people, especially in those areas that seemed to be influenced by traditional or petit bourgeois ideas or individuals. It was also expected to counter the growing tendency of BPCs to advocate parochial interests and concerns instead of taking a broader view of the nation's needs. Examples of this latter tendency were the excessive budgetary demands made by BPCs at the Fourth General People's Congress and the reluctance of people's committees west of Tripoli to support the reallocation of coastal farming land.

Revolutionary committees report directly to Qaddafi. He convenes the revolutionary committees both individually and en masse. Since all members are self-proclaimed zealots, the revolutionary committees have become the true cadres of the revolution. In the words of Qaddafi, "the People's Committees exercise administrative responsibilities while the Revolutionary Committees exercise revolutionary control."

The Electoral System

The Declaration of the Establishment of the People's Authority declares that direct popular authority is the basis for the political system in the Socialist People's Libyan Arab Jamahiriya. The people exercise their authority through the people's committees, people's congresses, unions and professional associations, and the General People's Congress. Elections are direct, and all voting consists of a show of hands or a division into yes-or-no camps. Suffrage and committee/congress membership are open to all Libyan citizens 18 years of age or older in good legal and political standing.

In theory, the residents of each zone elect their own people's committee. Similarly, the residents of each branch municipality or municipality elect their own basic people's congress. The members of a BPC then elect a chairman and a five-member branch or municipal people's committee. The General People's Congress is made up of the chairmen of the BPC, the branch and municipal people's committees, and representatives of the people's committees for unions, professional associations, and student unions.

In reality, the revolutionary committees severely limit the democratic process by closely supervising committee and congress elections at the branch and municipal levels of government. Revolutionary committees scrutinize the professional and revolutionary credentials of all candidates for the basic people's congresses, professional people's committees, and the municipal General People's Committees; only approved candidates actually stand for election.

The Party System

The RCC has continued the monarchy's ban on the organization and operation of political parties. The only exception to this was the 1971 formation of the Arab Socialist Union (ASU) modeled after the Egyptian ASU under Nasser. But even by the mid-1970s, the ASU

disappeared from the Libyan political scene. In effect, the December 1969 Decision on the Protection of the Revolution, the penal code, and law number 71 of 1972 render political party activity of any sort a crime and constitute a strict legal injunction against unauthorized political activity.

Like many Islamic thinkers, Qaddafi rejects the political party system. This is not because it is fundamentally incompatible with the Koran or the sharia but rather because he is unfavorably impressed with party organization and competition. In the Green Book, he describes the political party as the modern dictatorial instrument of governing and the party system as an overt form of dictatorship.

Qaddafi's condemnation of the political party system is multifaceted. He argues that political parties, because they are generally made up of people of similar beliefs, represent and promote the interests of only a segment of society. Such segments form parties to attain their ends and impose their doctrines on society as a whole. Moreover, in such a system, competition between parties frequently escalates, often resulting in the dominant party or parties ignoring the rights and interests of minority-party members. In a final criticism, Qaddafi argues that political parties, in their struggle to gain power, often destroy the accomplishments of their predecessors, even if those accomplishments were for the general good. His solution to these dilemmas is the system of congresses and committees that he has established.

GENERAL PEOPLE'S CONGRESS SYSTEM

The development of Libya's current political system has been an evolutionary process that very likely is still incomplete. To understand this system and how it functions, it is necessary to trace its progress from the traditional, tribal-based monarchy, which the RCC overthrew in 1969, to the formal Declaration of the Establishment of the People's Authority in 1977.

The members of the Revolutionary Command Council shared similar backgrounds, motivations, and worldviews. Most were from lower-middle-class families and minor tribes and attended the Libyan military academy at a time when a military career offered opportunities for higher education and upward socioeconomic mobility. The language of the RCC was the language of Arab nationalism guided by the precepts of the Koran and sharia, strengthened by a conviction that only the revolutionary government understood and spoke for the masses.

The September 1, 1969, coup d'état was completed without the participation of any organized civilian groups, and initially the RCC maintained the military character of the revolution. In the early days, it exercised both executive and legislative functions, enshrining its right to do so in the December 1969 Constitutional Proclamation. Later, the RCC appointed civilians to the Council of Ministers to help operate the government, but even then it reserved supreme authority in all fields for itself. It sat at the top of the pyramid, issuing proclamations, laws, and resolutions; insuring support of the armed forces; overseeing the activities of the government; and creating new institutions to promote the objectives of the revolution.

The RCC's chairman, Qaddafi, quickly became the dominant figure in the revolutionary government. While never given formal authority over his RCC colleagues, Qaddafi was able to impose his will through a combination of personality and argument. In theory, the RCC functioned as a collegial body with the members discussing issues and policies until enough of a consensus evolved to establish a unified position. In practice, as the revolution unfolded, Qaddafi increasingly exercised the final choice in major decisions and Libyans increasingly looked to his public statements to guide their own behavior. In late 1975 he issued part one of the Green Book, titled "The Solution to the Problem of Democracy." Part two followed in the fall of 1977 and part three in early 1979.

The executive-legislative system comprised of the RCC and the Council of Ministers operated into 1977; however, on September 1, 1976, the seventh anniversary of the revolution, Qaddafi introduced a plan to reorganize the government. The key feature of his proposal was the creation of a new, national-level representative body called the General People's Congress (GPC) to replace the RCC as the supreme instrument of government. The details of the plan were included in the Declaration of the Establishment of the People's Authority issued on March 2, 1977, which fundamentally revised the governmental organization described in the 1969 Constitutional Proclamation. The March 1977 declaration also changed the name of the country to the Socialist People's Libyan Arab Jamahiriya. *Jamahiriya* was a newly coined Arabic word with no official definition but unofficially has been translated as "people's power" or "state of the masses."

Qaddafi was designated general secretary of the GPC, and the remaining members of the now-defunct RCC made up the General Secretariat. A General People's Committee was also named to replace the Council of Ministers, whose 26 members were termed secretaries instead of ministers.

On June 11, 1971, Colonel Qaddafi announced the formation of the Arab Socialist Union (ASU), an official mass-mobilization organization patterned after the Egyptian counterpart of the same name. The ASU system was envisioned as an organization from local to national level that would provide the masses with an opportunity to participate in the establishment and execution of local policies; it also could function as a pervasive network of organizations throughout Libyan society, capable both of monitoring citizens at all levels and of becoming a source of support for revolutionary policies.

The ASU was organized at the national, governorate, and basic (local) levels. Both the basic and *muhafaza* units consisted of two main organizations: a congress (or conference) representing the general membership and a committee for leadership. Membership was based both on geography (places of residence) and function (occupation or workplace). Application for membership was made either where the individual lived (a *mudiriya* or *mahalat*) or at the workplace; however, the individual could not join the ASU at both levels. The basic committee consisted of 10 people elected by and from the basic congress to serve as its executive body. The governorate congress consisted of two or more representatives elected from each basic unit, with the actual number elected depending on the size of the basic unit's membership. The governorate committee consisted of 20 people elected by and from the congress members.

Membership in the ASU was open to any Libyan citizen of the working people who was 18 or more years of age, in good legal standing and sound mental health, and not a member of the royal family or associated with the previous monarchical government or specifically barred by the RCC. The charter of the ASU specified that 50 percent of all ASU members must be workers and farmers.

The ASU structure at the national level was the National General Congress (or Conference), a forerunner of the General People's Congress. The Congress was made up of 10, 14, or 20 representatives from each governorate, as well as members of the RCC, the Council of Ministers, and delegates from the army, police, youth and women's organizations, professional associations, and trade unions. The term of the National General Congress, scheduled to meet every two years, was six years. The ASU was firmly controlled by the RCC with Qaddafi serving as president and the other members of the RCC designated the Supreme Leading Authority of the Arab Socialist Union.

By 1972 the ASU was dismantled, since the RCC's rigid direction and control stifled local initiative and suffocated local leadership. The former district and subdistrict divisions were abolished, thus reducing subnational administration to the governorate and municipality. The principal organ of local government at both levels became the council, which had both executive and legislative powers. At the governorate level, executive power was exercised by the governor; at the municipal level, by the mayor. Both governors and mayors were appointed by the RCC.

On April 15, 1973, Qaddafi proclaimed a popular revolution and called for the Libyan people to elect people's committees. Like the ASU, the people's committee structure was given both a geographical and a functional basis. Geographically, committees were formed at the zone, municipal, and governorate levels. At the zone level, direct popular elections were used to fill the seats on the people's committee. Later in 1973 the RCC promulgated Law No. 78 to clarify the administrative responsibilities of the people's committees. The law transferred the functions and authority of the governorate and municipal councils established in 1972 to the people's committees at the same levels. The chairs of the governorate people's committees, in effect, became the governors and the chairs of the municipal people's committees became the mayors. The RCC also authorized the election of people's committees in public corporations, institutions, companies, and universities as well as in other sectors, such as hospitals, convalescent homes, and government printing plants.

The creation of the people's committee system was a significant stage in Libya's political evolution. For the first time in Libya's history, the subnational political system actively encouraged popular participation in the selection of local leadership and allowed substantial local involvement in the local policymaking process. With its formation, the RCC increased the political involvement and experience of the Libyan people and focused their attention on the issues of most importance to the local community.

Still not satisfied with the level of popular involvement and participation, Qaddafi at the 1974 National Congress called for a further refinement of the subnational administrative machinery. The Congress responded by stressing the primacy of the people's committees in administrative affairs and by recommending the elimination of the governorates. In February 1975 the RCC issued a law abolishing the governorates and reestablishing a Ministry of Municipalities. Within five years, another RCC law formally established the municipality as the single geographical and administrative subdivision in Libya.

Major Political Parties

There are no political parties in Libya.

Minor Political Parties

There are no political parties in Libya.

Other Political Forces

THE MILITARY

The September 1969 coup d'état was totally military in conception, planning, and execution. It was accomplished without the participation or even knowledge of organized civilian groups. In the early years the RCC insisted on maintaining the military direction of the revolution. Under attack from all facets of the former elite structure, the RCC worked to create a reliable coercive arm capable of sustaining the revolution.

To a certain degree, the military has become the most representative institution in the country; it now draws its membership from all strata of society. Recognizing this fact, Qaddafi has integrated the armed forces and sought to instill in them a spirit of unity, discipline, and professionalism. Within a year of the coup, the military establishment tripled in size, largely due to the merger of regional and specialized security forces; it continued to grow in quantity and quality throughout the 1970s. In May 1978 the government issued a conscription law making military service compulsory; in January 1979 it was announced that women would be conscripted along with men. Expenditures for equipment also increased dramatically throughout the decade, and Libya's armed forces entered the 1980s with the highest ratio of military equipment to manpower in the developing world. As of 1999, the latest figures available, Libya spent nearly 4 percent of its gross domestic product on military-related items.

Military opposition has grown as Qaddafi has increasingly advocated a people's militia to offset the power of a professional military organization. His insistence on compulsory military service for women, a measure opposed by the GPC in 1984, was especially unpopular in the military. Most observers agree that any significant challenge to the revolution will probably originate within the armed forces, particularly the army, as the military is the only group in the country with the required power and organization.

Qaddafi's strongest bases of support are the military and also the revolutionary youth committees designed to socialize youth into the Green Book principles and to guard these "revolutionary" principles zealously. But one of the paradoxes of Libyan politics is that just as the armed forces remain the strongest source of regime support, they are also the most likely source of any successful opposition. There have, indeed, been numerous coup attempts since the original 1969 coup d'état itself. In 1975 groups of army officers rebelled against Qaddafi but were repressed. In 1984 army units linked to opposition Libyan exiles attacked Qaddafi's own military stronghold but were beaten back in a bloody fight. And in 1993 units revolted in several locations throughout the country, but they too were ultimately defeated by loyalist military forces.

PETIT BOURGEOISIE

After 1977 the regime followed an increasingly radical socioeconomic policy that included housing redistribution and currency exchange, leading to the state takeover of all import, export, and distribution functions by the end of 1981. The resultant widespread redistribution of wealth and power directly affected the economic well-being of different sectors of the population, activating dormant political opposition. Particularly affected were the members of the petit bourgeoisie, which had prospered after 1969 as the revolutionary government's emphasis on the service and housing sectors created lucrative opportunities in trade, real estate, and small consumer manufacture.

Opposition is not limited to a single socioeconomic group; it also includes farmers, the educated elite, and even middle-level and senior-level government officials. Outside the country, opposition exists among student groups and self-imposed exiles, with a number of organized opposition groups operating in Western Europe and the Middle East. The largest and most active of these groups is the National Front for the Salvation of Libya (NFSL), founded in Khartoum in 1981 and since then operating out of Egypt and the United States. The attempted military coup of 1984 was instigated by military officers sympathetic to the NFSL.

However, the opposition is badly fragmented and must deal with a considerable amount of support for the regime, especially among the younger, less well-to-do elements of society. This support has been generated by Qaddafi's charismatic leadership and the regime's distributive economic policies. Qaddafi has taken extraordinary and often violent measures to stifle opposition at home and abroad and to limit any collaboration between domestic and foreign opponents. The regime has in particular taken aim at Libya's growing Islamist movement. The regime began to reemphasize the role of the sharia in Libyan political life in the 1990s while also cracking down on those suspected of having Islamist sympathies. In this regard, the Qaddafi regime may have been deeply influenced by the unrest and violence between government and Islamists in neighboring Algeria.

National Prospects

After more than 30 years in power, Qaddafi is the longest-serving ruler in the Middle East. While Libya's political system has seen little change under Qaddafi's rule, the same cannot be said for foreign relations. After decades of overt and mutual hostility, Qaddafi's regime abruptly changed directions in its foreign policy beginning in the late 1990s. The shift in Libyan policy became clear in 1999 when the Qaddafi regime agreed to extradite to the United Kingdom two former Libyan intelligence agents. The agents then stood trial for the 1988 bombing of Pan Am Flight 103 over Lockerbie, Scotland, which killed 270 people. Following the extradition of the agents, which had been a longstanding demand of the British government, Britain then restored diplomatic relations with Libya.

The Qaddafi regime had been subjected to severe economic sanctions by the United States, the European Union, and the United Nations, which together served to cripple Libya's economic development and in particular its oil industry. Due in large part to these external constraints, and the internal domestic political pressures that they generated, the regime chose to dramatically shift its foreign policy in hopes of ending the sanctions and ensuring its own survival. Qaddafi had long used the wealth generated by the national oil industry to tacitly and sometimes quite explicitly buy off key sectors in Libyan society. The longer the sanctions cut into Libyan economic development, and, more importantly, into government revenue, the more problematic this domestic cooptation process became. Ultimately, the regime was forced to change its external strategies in order to end its pariah status.

In 2003 this process continued as the Libyan government agreed to a deal with the United States under which Libya would accept responsibility for the 1988 bombing over Lockerbie, thereby removing the last obstacle to a financial compensation plan for the families of the victims. The U.S. government then removed most of its economic sanctions on Libya in exchange for Libya's cooperation in disclosing and destroying its programs for weapons of mass destruction (WMD). The European Union then quickly followed suit, as the EU also lifted its 18-year embargo against Libya.

Yet just as Libya's international standing appeared to be improving dramatically, some suggested that Qaddafi's regime may have been involved in a foiled attempt to assassinate Crown Prince Abdullah of Saudi Arabia. Still, in the absence of conclusive evidence regarding either Libyan guilt or innocence, the normalization process continued between Libya, the United States, and the European Union. The question remained, however, whether this amounted to the beginning of the end for the Qaddafi regime, or whether it had indeed secured a new lease on life, by shifting its external relations in order to avoid domestic political reform.

Further Reading

Alexander, Nathan (Ronald Bruce St. John). "The Foreign Policy of Libya: Inflexibility amid Change." *Orbis* 24, no. 4 (winter 1981).

———. "Libya: The Continuous Revolution." *Middle Eastern Studies* 17, no. 2 (April 1981).

Allan, J. A. *Libya: The Experience of Oil.* London: Croom Helm, 1981.

Anderson, Lisa. *The State and Social Transformation in Tunisia and Libya, 1830–1980.* Princeton, N.J.: Princeton University Press, 1986.

Davis, John. *Libyan Politics: Tribe and Revolution.* Berkeley: University of California Press, 1987.

Deeb, Marius, and Mary Jane Deeb. *Libya since the Revolution: Aspects of Social and Political Development.* New York: Praeger, 1982.

el-Fathaly, Omar I., and Monte Palmer. *Political Development and Social Change in Libya.* Lexington, Mass.: Lexington, 1980.

el-Kikhia, Mansour. *Libya's Qaddafi: The Politics of Contradiction.* Gainesville: University Press of Florida, 1998.

Haley, P. Edward. *Qaddafi and the United States since 1969.* New York: Praeger, 1984.

al-Qaddafi, Muammar. *The Green Book, Part I: The Solution to the Problem of Democracy.* London: Martin Brian and O'Keefe, 1976.

St. John, Ronald Bruce. "The Ideology of Mu'ammar al-Qaddafi: Theory and Practice." *International Journal of Middle East Studies* 15, no. 4 (November 1983).

———. "Libya's Foreign and Domestic Policies." *Current History* 80, no. 470 (December 1981).

Vandewalle, Dirk. *Libya since Independence: Oil and State-Building.* Ithaca, N.Y.: Cornell University Press, 1998.

Wright, John. *Libya: A Modern History.* Baltimore: The Johns Hopkins University Press, 1982.

PRINCIPALITY OF LIECHTENSTEIN
(Fürstentum Liechtenstein)

By Valerie O'Regan
Revised by Florina Laura Neculai

The Principality of Liechtenstein, located between Switzerland and Austria, is a 160-square-kilometer sovereign state with a population of 33,717 (2005 est.). The Principality of Liechtenstein is the result of the unification in 1719 of the earldom of Vaduz and the domain of Schellenberg by Prince Johann Adam Andreas von Liechtenstein. However, the territory is historically known to have been inhabited since the 3rd millennium BCE. In the period from 1815 to 1866 the principality was part of the German Confederation. In 1852 Liechtenstein concluded a customs union with Austro-Hungary that lasted until 1919, when the dualist empire collapsed. In 1924 the Principality of Liechtenstein joined a customs union with Switzerland and adopted the Swiss currency, a union that continues to the present day. Over the years, Liechtenstein has become a member of the Council of Europe (1978), United Nations (1990), European Free Trade Association (1991), European Economic Area (1995), and the World Trade Organization (1995).

The System of Government

Liechtenstein is a hereditary constitutional monarchy ruled by the princes of the House of Liechtenstein, which is one of Europe's oldest noble families (the first mention dates from 1136) and has over 100 members, some of whom still live in Liechtenstein. The prince, Hans-Adam II, born in 1945, assumed executive authority in 1984 and succeeded his father, Prince Franz Josef, to the throne upon his death in November 1989. On August 15, 2004, Prince Hans-Adam II delegated day-to-day running of the country to his eldest son, Prince Alois.

EXECUTIVE

The powers of the prince are stated in the Constitution of 1921 that was finally modified in 2003 after discussions about reform that had been taking place since 1992. According to the Constitution of 2003, the prince is the head of the state and the representative of the state abroad, but both the prince and the people govern the state. The prince has the power to convene and dismiss parliament or to prorogue or discontinue it for three months and to make government appointments upon parliamentary recommendation. Under the new constitution, the government loses its mandate if it loses the confidence of those to whom it is responsible, that is, the sovereign and parliament. The same rule applies for any member of the government if s/he loses the confidence of the prince and parliament. In this case, a joint decision of dismissal of both the prince and parliament is required.

These new constitutional provisions raised concern about the increasing power of the prince over the government. However, the prince, who also has the right of veto over legislation, usually works with the government, particularly with the head of government, until they reach an agreement. The reigning prince also has the power to nominate the magistrates, to pass emergency decrees, and to release prisoners. The Constitution of 2003 maintains the immunity of the prince's person but makes the prince subject to a vote of no confidence from the people who, from now on, also have the right to vote for abolition of the monarchy.

LEGISLATURE

The sovereign executes legislative power in conjunction with the unicameral legislature, the Landtag. The Constitution of 1921 provided for a 15-member parliament, but following a 1988 amendment membership was increased to 25 members who serve a four-year term. The members of parliament are elected from among the citizens according to a proportional representation system. The president of parliament is the highest representative of the people. The official opening of parliament is made either by the prince himself or by a person delegated by him. Parliament makes the laws and the state treaties; it has sovereign decision rights in the field of finance, and it controls the government and the administration of the country. According to the Constitution of 2003 the right to initiate legislation belongs to the prince, but parliament and the communes have an equal right to initiate legislation through the mechanisms of popular initiative and direct democracy. The government can also initiate laws but only after discussing its initiatives with the prince.

JUDICIARY

Liechtenstein has a modern judiciary system. A peculiarity of the judicial system of Liechtenstein consists in the fact that it comprises both Austrian and Swiss citizens. The Constitution of 2003 stipulates that jurisdiction is exercised in the first instance by the Princely Court (Fürstliche Landgericht) in Vaduz, where the judges work full-time and are usually Austrian and Swiss citizens in order to ensure impartiality. They are appointed until their retirement age, either by a permanent contract or a temporary but renewable one. The second instance is the High Court of Appeals (Fürstliche Obergericht) in Vaduz that has, under the new constitution, three Senates, instead of two, in order to better deal with the increased work provided by the financial sector. The president of the Court of Appeals is a Swiss citizen, while his deputy is Austrian. The third instance is the Supreme Court (Fürstlichen Obersten Gerichtshof) formed by judges who work part-time and whose president is an Austrian citizen, aided by an assistant who is a Swiss national. Both the High Court of Appeal and the Supreme Court are collegial judicial bodies.

The judicial system of Liechtenstein also comprises two other courts: the Administrative Court, which plays an important role in public life by judging all the decisions of the government, and the State Court, which makes sure that the rights of citizens guaranteed by the constitution are respected and that the decisions of parliament are in accordance with the constitution. The State Court is a disciplinary body for government members and can play the role of an electoral tribunal.

REGIONAL AND LOCAL GOVERNMENT

The Principality of Liechtenstein consists of two regions (Oberland and Unterland) and of 11 communes with independent administrative bodies: Vaduz, Balzers, Eschen, Gamprin, Mauren, Planken, Ruggell, Schaan,

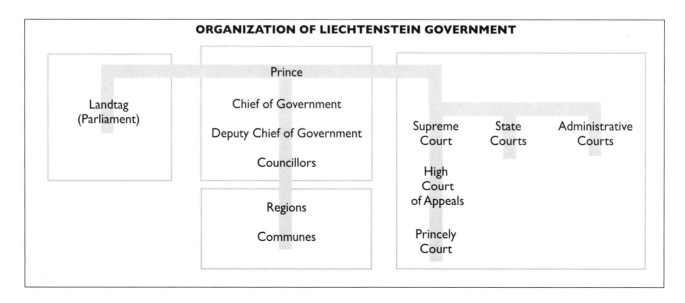

ORGANIZATION OF LIECHTENSTEIN GOVERNMENT

Prince

Landtag (Parliament)

Chief of Government
Deputy Chief of Government
Councillors

Regions
Communes

Supreme Court　State Courts　Administrative Courts

High Court of Appeals

Princely Court

Schellenberg, Triesenberg, and Triesen. Vaduz, the capital of the principality, is situated in the region of Oberland; it is the residence of the reigning prince and the headquarters of both the government and parliament. The communes of Triesenberg and Planken were founded approximately 700 years ago by emigrants coming from the Swiss Valley; with a population of almost 400 inhabitants, the commune of Planken is the smallest commune of all. The autonomy of the communes is guaranteed by the constitution. The voters of each commune elect the council of the commune, which is run by a mayor. The citizens (one-sixth of the electorate of a commune) may propose or contest the decision of the council by a referendum. The mayors are elected with absolute majority vote to serve a four-year mandate; they can work either part-time or full-time. The councilors' election is subject to a proportional representation vote. Law forbids the relatives of those who are members of the council to run for the position of mayor of the commune.

The communes are responsible for administering local affairs and imposing additional taxes. The communes are also the beneficiaries of state financial endowments used to facilitate the accomplishment of particular tasks. To exercise full citizenship rights, all citizens of Liechtenstein must also be citizens of a commune.

The Electoral System

Suffrage is universal for all citizens of Liechtenstein aged 18 and over. Parliament has 25 members elected by proportional representation in two constituencies. Voters may also directly participate in the legislative process through the use of the initiative and referendum.

In the 2005 elections the Progressive Citizens' Party (Fortschrittliche Bürgerpartei, FBP) won the elections with 48.7 and 12 seats in the Landtag; the Fatherland Union (Vaterländische Union, VU) got 38.2 percent of the vote and 10 seats; the Free List (Freie List, FL) got 13 percent and three seats. Otmar Hasler of the FBP, who had been prime minister since 2001, formed a new coalition government following the 2005 elections.

The Party System

The political spectrum of the Principality of Liechtenstein is formed by two main political parties, the Fatherland Union (VU) and the Progressive Citizens'

Party (FBP); three small parties, the Free List (FL), the Christian Social Party (CSP), and the Liechtenstein Non-Party List (ULL); and pressure groups. Starting in 1984 all political parties that get at least 3 percent of the votes of the electorate receive yearly financial support from the state to the amount of 180,000 Swiss francs. Political parties are also allowed to receive financial support from donations and membership fees, which actually constitute their main source of revenues.

Major Political Parties

PROGRESSIVE CITIZENS' PARTY
(Fortschrittliche Bürgerpartei; FBP)

The Progressive Citizens' Party (FBP) was created in 1918 by the supporters of the existing political and social order, mainly from the communes that had economic relations with Austria. It also has at its origins a newspaper, the *Liechtensteiner Volksblatt*, that was first published in 1878 under clerical auspices. The main political goals of the FBP were opposite to those of the VU, whose aims were perceived by the FBP as a threat to the monarchy and to the independence of the country itself. Although these two political parties are rival parties labeling each other "Reds" (VU) and "Blacks" (FBP), the difference between the two is not fundamental in ideology. Both are Catholic and conservative-based parties, which make both parties members of the same party at the European Union level, the Christian Democrat and Conservative European Democratic Union (EDU).

FATHERLAND UNION
(Vaterländische Union; VU)

The Fatherland Union (VU) was founded by Wilhelm Beck, a lawyer from Triesenberg educated in Switzerland and influenced by the Swiss in both democracy and political conservatism. He founded a newspaper, the "Upper Rhine News" (*Oberrheinische Nachrichten*) espousing the institutional and economic progress of Liechtenstein. In 1918, he founded the Christian-Social People's Party (Christlich-Soziale Volkspartei) whose political aims were to occupy official posts with native Liechtenstein citizens and to have citizens elect the parliament of Liechtenstein. The main supporters of the VU were the southern communes that had different ties with Switzerland and the citizens of Liechtenstein who were working in Switzerland.

Minor Political Parties

FREE LIST

(Freie Liste; FL)

Free List (FL), called also "the Whites," originated in the Art Museum ("Kunsthaus") initiative and in the campaign for women suffrage. It was constituted as an alternative to the FBP and the VU, and it has participated in elections since 1986. It usually gets either one or two seats, but in the 2005 elections the FL obtained three seats.

CHRISTIAN SOCIAL PARTY

(Christlich-Soziale Partei; CSP)

The Christian Social Party (CSP) was founded in the 1970s as an alternative to the main political parties, the FBP and the VU, but it never succeeded in getting any parliamentary seat, neither when the threshold was 18 percent nor when it was 8 percent, mainly because the CSP did not have a distinct political platform.

LIECHTENSTEIN NON-PARTY LIST

(Liechtenstein Überparteiliche Liste; ULL)

Liechtenstein Non-Party List (ULL) competed in national elections for the first time in 1989. It has many points in common with the FL, from origins in the Art Museum initiative to political views, but they still consider each other political rivals.

Other Political Forces

The process of decision making in Liechtenstein is shaped by a large number of organized civic associa-tions, given the size of the country, that are consulted on a wide range of issues regarding the national well-being. These organizations focus on different areas of lobbying and have a more or less long tradition, such as the Liechtenstein Loyal Union (1939), the Liechtenstein Forum (1994), the Democracy Secretariat (1991), the Dual Liechtenstein Citizens' Movement (2002), and the Constitution Peace Initiative (2002).

National Prospects

Liechtenstein is the fourth smallest country in Europe but has developed a highly industrialized, free-enterprise economy with a financial service sector and living standards on a par with its large European neighbors. The nation's GDP derives to a large extent from the revenues of its citizens working abroad. Although the principality's primary economic partners are its neighbors in Western Europe, Liechtenstein also has significant economic relations with the North American countries.

Further Reading

Banks, Arthur S., Alan J. Day, and Thomas C. Muller, eds. *Political Handbook of the World.* New York: CSA, 1995-96.

Beattie, David. *Liechtenstein—A Modern History.* Trieste: Frank P. van Eck Publishers, 2004.

Europa World Yearbook. *Liechtenstein.* London: Europa, 1996.

Liechtenstein in Figures 2003. Vaduz: Office of Economic Affairs, 2003.

Liechtenstein—Principauté au coeur de l'Europe. Vaduz: Office de Presse et d'Information, 2000.

REPUBLIK OF LITHUANIA
(Lietuvos Respublika)

By Jeffrey K. Hass, Ph.D.

The System of Government

Formally Lithuania is a republic. The national government is composed of three branches—executive, legislative, and judiciary. Lithuania has a stronger presidency than the other Baltic countries and is referred to as a "presidential democracy" that has come to resemble the French system, where the president presides over policymaking and the parliament (Seimas) is weakened by divisions between several parties and factions; however, this strength may be illusory for institutional reasons.

EXECUTIVE

Lithuania did not initially have a president after independence from the Soviet Union; instead, the country had a prime minister and a speaker of parliament. Before 1993 the prime minister ran the government—essentially heading the bureaucracy and implementing policy—and was joined by the speaker of parliament (Vytautis Landsbergis in 1991–93) as head of state. However, Landsbergis felt himself to be a captive of parliament, which was particularly troublesome when the majority Sajudis coalition began to fragment. To free the figurative head of state from parliament, Landsbergis campaigned for a strong presidency that would head the executive branch, effectively taking the place of the prime minister. A presidential position was created in the 1992 constitution, passed by a national referendum.

The president's powers are, however, weak. As in other Eastern European countries, the president is a figurehead, representing Lithuania in the international arena. Along with this responsibility are the president's powers to appoint and dismiss diplomatic personnel. However, the president is not as weak as in Estonia or Latvia, and presidential powers do extend somewhat beyond diplomacy. When a new government must be created, the president selects the prime minister for approval in the Seimas. The president has the use of a weak veto to send legislation back either to the Seimas for reconsideration or to the Constitutional Court to check the constitutionality of laws; only with an absolute majority can parliament override the veto. Further, the president has the power to dissolve the Seimas in two situations: when the Seimas refuses to approve the governmental budget within a 60-day period, and when parliament passes a vote of no confidence in the prime minister and his government. Such power of threat over parliament is a double-edged sword, however, for parliament also holds the right to call early presidential elections, and a parliament following in the footsteps of one dissolved by the president may decide to call early elections as punishment.

Formally the president is picked by popular election, except in 1993, when the Seimas chose the president. (This is the opposite of Estonia.) A president may serve only two terms in office. To be elected, a candidate must win more than 50 percent of votes cast, and

50 percent of registered voters must participate in the election. If fewer than 50 percent of voters cast ballots, then the candidate with the most votes (plurality) wins, unless the number of votes received is less than one-third of votes cast. If no candidate wins a majority (or more than one-third for a weak voter turnout), the two candidates who garnered the most votes move on to a second round held within two weeks, where the winner needs to receive only a plurality.

While the president is an important figure, he is also not, strictly speaking, the head of the executive. While he performs executive duties, he is almost above politics. The head of the executive branch (meaning the head of the state bureaucracy of police, ministries, and representatives of the federal government) is the prime minister, who is formally the head of the government. The prime minister is assisted in policy and administration by his deputy ministers and heads of ministries, who together make up the Council of Ministers.

LEGISLATURE

The legislative branch is headed by parliament (Seimas), a unicameral body that holds the majority of political power. As in the other two Baltic countries, parliament is the most important governmental body. Parliament holds the most power of all three branches of government, it has the final say on legislative matters, and it both wields greater responsibilities than the executive and holds the power of accountability over the executive to a much greater degree than in most Eastern European countries.

The Seimas is made up of 141 seats, which come up for election every four years. Of these seats, 70 are reserved for party lists and 71 for single-member voting. That is, 71 deputies are chosen in single-mandate elections (where individuals campaign against each other and are chosen by local voters), and 70 are chosen on the basis of votes cast for political parties. For the single-mandate positions, a candidate must win more than 50 percent of votes cast; otherwise, a runoff between the top two is held.

For the party lists, a party must receive 5 percent or more of the total votes cast (except for the 1992 elections, when the barrier was 4 percent); the barrier is 7 percent for coalitions of parties running together. Those parties or coalitions that do not overcome this barrier do not receive any of the 70 party-specified places; a party or coalition that *does* overcome the barrier receives a proportion of seats equal to the proportion of votes it received out of votes cast for parties that overcame the barrier. (This means that if some parties do not overcome the barrier, a successful party's seats will be a percentage of 70 greater than its percentage of total votes received; consequently, a vote cast for a party that does not overcome the barrier is a wasted vote.) Finally, parties representing ethnic minorities do not need to overcome the 5 percent barrier.

JUDICIARY

Lithuania's judiciary follows the civil law tradition of continental Europe; precedent does not play an important role in judicial review or in defining laws and policies. Instead, court decisions are made for individual cases of conflict or contestation. The three levels of courts, which are local, district, and the Court of Appeals, are the stages through which conflict between

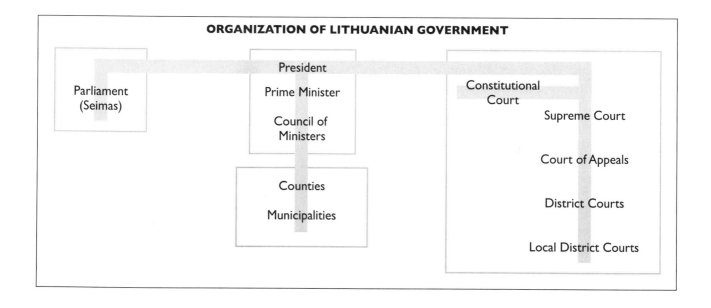

ORGANIZATION OF LITHUANIAN GOVERNMENT

President

Parliament (Seimas)

Prime Minister

Council of Ministers

Counties

Municipalities

Constitutional Court

Supreme Court

Court of Appeals

District Courts

Local District Courts

parties or prosecution of criminals moves. Local courts are the first stage, and appeals move up the judicial ladder. Above the Court of Appeals is the Supreme Court, whose decisions either on criminal cases or on arbitration between conflicting parties is the final judgment.

In general, only the Constitutional Court has the power to review legislation. Expressly created for this purpose and separate from the other courts, the Constitutional Court is based on the American model of the Supreme Court. In Lithuania, the Constitutional Court acts as a watchdog for rights and freedoms from a vantage point beyond the everyday political process. Other courts neither review nor interpret legislation. Courts act as arbitrators in cases of legal conflict, applying the law to individual cases (there is no precedent, as in Anglo-American common law), and mete out justice in the case of criminal trials.

Three of the nine members of the Constitutional Court and all members of the Supreme Court are nominated by the president and must be confirmed by the Seimas. According to the constitution, members of the Constitutional Court serve for a nine-year period, and every three years three judges must come up for reappointment.

REGIONAL AND LOCAL GOVERNMENT

Lithuania consists of 10 counties and 60 municipalities; the latter have directly elected councils. These councils sit for a term of two years and upon convocation select an executive board, which acts as the head of the local-level executive—responsible for implementation of local policies and of national laws and policies handed down by the Seimas. Recently, local authorities have battled with the central authorities for more autonomy in decision making. Reminiscent of the Soviet era, the central government in Vilnius had increased its presence in localities, even with the prime minister appointing governors. Also, local officials have been unhappy with the Lithuanian tax system (which gives collection power to the central government) and with the dearth of funding coming the locals' way from Vilnius; because of the way taxes are collected, the lion's share goes to Vilnius and then is redistributed to the regions.

The Electoral System

Before the 1992 elections the important political players were the Lithuanian Communist Party and

its successor, the Lithuanian Democratic Labor Party (LDLP), and Sajudis, the nationalist movement for liberation of Lithuania from Soviet domination. At the top of politics (in the Supreme Soviet), Sajudis, which is not a party but a movement of several nationalist partiers, was the most powerful, while the LDLP controlled political offices at the local level. Sajudis was headed by Vytautis Landsbergis, whose nationalist defiance of Mikhail Gorbachev set the tone for Lithuanian politics up to the failed August 1991 coup in the USSR.

Landsbergis and Sajudis attempted to pass a law denying office to any who had held some position within the Communist Party. Landsbergis's confrontational tactics, however, backfired; Sajudis suffered a surprising defeat in the 1992 parliamentary elections, and the LDLP went on to become the party of power in Lithuania. This change in power occurred for several reasons: because of Landsbergis's anti-Communist virulence; because the LDLP had a stronger presence in the localities; because conflicts within the movement had led to political paralysis and conflict in the Seimas; because of the negative effects of economic reform; and because the LDLP, while preferring more gradualist economic reforms and compromise and moderation with Russia, remained committed to Lithuanian independence and held a more moderate rhetorical line. A vote for LDLP was not a vote for return to the pre-1991 status quo but rather for a kinder, gentler Lithuania.

In 1992 the LDLP received 42.6 percent of votes and 73 seats in the Seimas, to only 30 seats for anti-Communist Sajudis. However, LDDP was less than competent with economic reforms, and a severe banking crisis in 1995 led to their defeat in 1996. In that year the right-leaning faction of Sajudis returned in a new form, the Homeland Union/Conservatives of Lithuania coalition (Tevynes Sajunga/Lietuvos Konservatoriai, TS-LK). Homeland Union had a stable ruling government until 1998, when policy differences created tensions between Prime Minister Gediminas Vagnorius and newly elected president Valdas Adamkus. Vagnorius resigned in 1998 and was replaced by Vilnius mayor Rolandas Paksas, who resigned five months later after a scandal over the sale of an oil firm. While Homeland enjoyed some stability, their austerity policies bred popular backlash. In the 2000 elections the Social Democratic coalition, uniting four leftist parties and led by the LDLP, appeared to be triumphant. However, a centrist coalition led by the Lithuanian Liberal Union and New Union managed to scrape up just enough votes for a majority in parliament and the chance to form a new government. However, this ruling coalition lasted only eight months, and it collapsed from internal discord over energy privatization. New Union joined with the new Lithuanian Social Democratic Party to form the new government. Meanwhile, Homeland Union's fortunes continued to fade: in contrast to its dominance in 1996, when it had 70 seats, after 2000 the party had only nine.

In the 2004 elections no party won a majority of seats in parliament, although a new party, the Labor Party (Darbo Partija; DP), emerged with the most number of seats, 39. The DP joined a new coalition government led by the Social Democrats. Algirdas Brazauskas, who had been prime minister since 2001, carried on in the position following the 2004 elections. Valdus Adamkus won the presidential election.

Voting for a party does not mean voting for a particular ideology or policy. This leads to the interpretation that Lithuanians do not vote for political programs but rather for appealing personalities. (Some observers claim that all Baltic peoples have been antiparty since independence in the 1990s, ignoring party appeals and platforms.) As in the other two Baltic nations, parties in Lithuania are connected more to the personalities of those leading them.

The Party System

Lithuania's parties fall on a typical spectrum from left to right, although there remains instability, with parties likely to go into sudden decline.

Major Political Parties

LITHUANIAN SOCIAL DEMOCRATIC COALITION

(Lietuvos Socialdemokratu Koalicija)

This coalition was formed for the 2000 elections. Bringing together the most important left-wing parties under Prime Minister Algirdas Brazauskas's leadership, this bloc gained the most votes and seats, although they did not manage to form a majority coalition. Key players are the Lithuanian Social Democratic Party (Lietuvos Socialdemokratu Partija, LSDP), the Lithuanian Democratic Labor Party (Lietuvos Demokratine Darbo Partija, LDDP), and the leftist New Democratic Party and the Lithuanian

Russian Union. LDDP is the Communist party, but as in other post-Socialist countries changed its name and ideology. Their initial appeal came from promises of security in the context of economic collapse in the early 1990s, but their policies when in power did little to help the country. Recently the party has taken a pro-market role, supporting an export-oriented economy and privatization, although agriculture should receive state aid. While precise data are unavailable, LDDP has the largest popular base and grassroots structure of all Lithuania's parties. In the 2004 elections the coalition 20.7 percent of the vote and 20 seats in parliament, coming in third behind the DP and the Homeland Union. However, Brazauskas was able to retain the prime ministership at the head of a governing coalition.

LABOR PARTY

(Darbo Partija; DP)

This party was formed in 2003 by Russian-born business tycoon Viktor Uspaskich. In the 2004 elections the party won the most seats in parliament, 39, and joined the coalition government led by Brazauskas. Uspaskich became the new ecnomics minister, but he was forced to resign in 2005 when a state inspector ruled that his business ties to Russia represented a conflict of interest. However, the party remained part of the governing coalition.

HOMELAND UNION

(Tevynes Sajunga)

The quintessential and original party on Lithuania's right is Homeland Union. The heir to Sajudis, Homeland ideology was anti-Communist and championed returning to prewar owners property confiscated after the Soviet invasion. However, Homeland Union gained a populist streak, seen in their advocacy of agricultural subsidies, increasing pensions, and raising state officials' salaries. In the 2004 elections the party won 14.6 percent of the vote and 25 seats.

FOR ORDER AND JUSTICE

(Uz Tvarka Ir Teisinguma)

This coalition was formed prior to the 2004 elections and includes the Liberal Democrats and the Lithuanian People's Union, an offshoot of the Lithuanian Liberal Union. In the 2004 elections it won 11.4 percent of the vote and 11 seats in parliament.

LIBERAL AND CENTER UNION

(Liberalu Ir Centro Sajunga)

This party was formed in 2003 from the merger of the Lithuanian Liberal Union, the Center Union of Lithuania, and the Modern Christian-Democratic Union. In the 2004 elections the party won 9.1 percent of the vote and 18 seats in parliament.

UNION OF FARMERS AND NEW DEMOCRACY

(Valstieciu Ir Naujosios Demokratijos partiju Sajungos)

This conservative party is led by former prime minister Kazimiera Prunskiene. In the 2004 elections it won 6.6 percent of the vote and 10 seats in parliament.

Minor Political Parties

Among the other smaller political parties in Lithuania are the Social Union of Christian Conservatives and the Young Lithuania and New Nationalists.

Other Political Forces

Lithuania's entry into the European Union (EU) in 2004 will likely play a large role in the country's political process in coming years. Internally, the military does not interfere in the political process. Following a 2002 agreement labor unions gained important rights related to collective bargaining. The three major trade unions are the Confederation of Lithuanian Trade Unions, the Lithuanian Trade Union "Solidarity" (the former Workers' Union), and the Lithuanian Work Federation.

National Prospects

The first Soviet republic to challenge Soviet domination, Lithuania has undergone a bumpy transition to a democracy and capitalism, although the transition here has been smoother than in other former Soviet republics. While former Communists enjoyed a brief return to power (as in other Eastern European nations), they have since lost power to more nationalist promarket forces.

The Lithuanian government has pushed strong reform in privatization (industry and most housing) and fiscal discipline (reducing inflation). Lithuania relies on imports for its raw materials and fuel and has focused on creating an export economy. Prior to EU membership in 2004 the country experienced strong economic growth and low inflation. The entrance into the EU and NATO promises to offer Lithuania continuing economic development and some security vis-à-vis Russia.

Further Reading

Bremmer, Bremmer, and Ray Taras, eds. *New States, New Politics: Building the Post-Soviet Nations.* Cambridge: Cambridge University Press, 1997.

Iwaskiw, Walter R., ed. *Estonia, Latvia, and Lithuania.* Country Studies. Washington, D.C.: Federal Research Division, Library of Congress, 1995.

Pavlovaite, I. "Being European by Joining Europe: Accession and Identity Politics in Lithuania." *Cambridge Review of International Affairs* 16, no. 2 (July 2003): 239–55.

GRAND DUCHY OF LUXEMBOURG
(Grand-Duché de Luxembourg)

By William G. Andrews, Ph.D.
Revised by Tom Michael

Situated in northwestern Europe, Luxembourg is one of the smallest countries in the world. With an area of less than 1,000 square miles, it has a population of approximately 468,000 (2005 est.). Though the majority of the population is made up of native Luxemburgers, there are significant minorities of other Europeans, notably from Portugal, Italy, and Belgium.

The System of Government

Luxembourg is a constitutional monarchy with a parliamentary form of government. The Grand Duchy was created in 1815 with the Dutch king as the first grand duke. Following Belgium's secession from the Netherlands (1830), part of the duchy became autonomous (1839), while the rest became the Belgian county of Luxembourg. Full independence came in 1867, and the present constitution dates from 1868. The present grand ducal family, the House of Nassau, ascended the throne in 1890.

EXECUTIVE

The position of grand duke is hereditary and its powers primarily formal. As chief of state, the grand duke appoints the prime minister. Real executive power, however, lies with the prime minister and cabinet, who are responsible to the Chamber of Deputies.

LEGISLATURE

The 60-member Chamber of Deputies is the unicameral legislature. However, the constitution requires that it reaffirm legislation after three months, unless the Administrative Council of State waives that rule. In practice, the vast majority of bills are exempted from the second reading. The Council of State, 21 members appointed for life by the grand duke, gives advisory opinions on all bills before they go to the Chamber and on any subsequent amendments. Also, the Chamber must consult one of six corporatist "chambers" on all bills that affect directly a trade or profession.

JUDICIARY

The highest court is the Superior Court of Justice. Its 16 full members are appointed for life by the grand duke on advice of the Superior Court itself. The Superior Court also nominates judges for the lower courts, whose members can be removed only by the Superior Court. The Superior Court, when sitting as a court of review, has jurisdiction over questions of law, but no general power to disallow legislation. Below the Superior Court are the Court of Assizes, district courts, and justices of the peace.

REGIONAL AND LOCAL GOVERNMENT

Luxembourg is divided into three main districts that are subdivided into 12 administrative units (cantons).

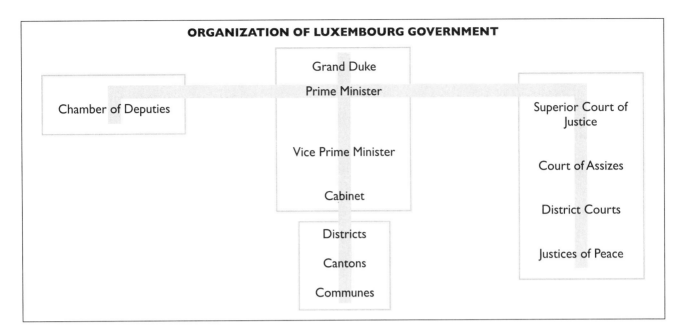

ORGANIZATION OF LUXEMBOURG GOVERNMENT

Grand Duke
Prime Minister

Chamber of Deputies

Vice Prime Minister

Cabinet

Superior Court of Justice

Court of Assizes

District Courts

Justices of Peace

Districts

Cantons

Communes

Below them are about 118 municipalities (communes) with councils elected for six-year terms and mayors (burgomasters) appointed by the councils. Politically, the larger communes are miniatures of the nation, with elections based on proportional representation and party lists. As a result, interparty cooperation and coalition are essential. In smaller communes, council members are elected by simple majorities and personality is usually more significant than party affiliation.

ELECTIONS TO THE CHAMBER OF DEPUTIES (1994–2004)

	1994		1999		2004	
	%		%		%	
CSV	31.4	21	29.8	19	36.1	24
LSAP	24.8	17	23.8	13	23.4	14
DP	18.9	12	21.6	15	16.1	10
Greens	10.9	5	9.1	5	11.6	7
ADR	8.2	5	10.4	6	10.0	5
Others	5.8	—	5.3	2	2.8	—

The Electoral System

The Chamber of Deputies has a five-year term but may be dissolved early if the prime minister chooses or if the government loses the confidence of the Chamber. However, no special election has been held early since World War II. Seats are allocated from party lists in four electoral districts using proportional representation. Voting is compulsory for all citizens age 18 or older. Each voter has as many votes as that district has seats and may cast them all for a single party list or distribute them among candidates from several parties. The latter option, known as *panachage*, affects the representation of parties and the ranking of candidates on the party lists. This "personalization" benefits well-known politicians, thereby aiding bourgeois parties at the expense of the left.

The Party System

ORIGINS OF THE PARTIES

The modern party system dates from the formation of the Socialist Workers' Party (LSAP) in 1902. Under electoral pressure from the LSAP, the previously unstructured personalist coalitions of bourgeois interests coalesced into the Party of the Right in 1914, and the oldest political formation in Luxembourg, the Liberals, followed suit.

THE PARTIES IN LAW

The parties are not specifically mentioned in the constitution, although they are safeguarded by its general provisions. A series of electoral laws, beginning with the adoption of proportional representation in 1919, determines in detail the conduct and form of elections, especially the presentation of party lists. Otherwise, the parties are free concerning their internal organization and financing.

PARTY ORGANIZATION

Parties are organized at both the communal and the national levels. Party congresses (usually annual) constitute the primary authority. The strength of cantonal politics means that even the smaller parties are active locally. However, party membership is never very large, so activists tend to determine party policy. The parties' relationships with nonparty organizations—the Catholic Church and trade unions (separate confessional, secular, and salaried employee associations)—are very important.

CAMPAIGNING

Despite the coalition basis of politics, campaigns are hard fought. Partly, given the electoral system, competition is a matter of personality, but left and right have sharp ideological differences. Party newspapers play a significant part in campaigns.

INDEPENDENT VOTERS

The influence of the Catholic Church and the organized labor movement ensures that party identification is high. However, because the voting system permits voters to cross party lines, they tend to give some votes to attractive candidates of parties not sharply opposed to their preferred party.

Major Political Parties

CHRISTIAN SOCIAL PEOPLE'S PARTY

(Chrëschtlich Sozial Vollekspartei; CSV)

Founded as the Party of the Right (Partei der Rechten) in 1914, the CSV took its present name in 1944. It has been the "natural" party of government for many years. It has been represented in every government since 1919 and has supplied every prime minister since 1945, except for a stint in the opposition in 1974–79. The LSAP and the Democratic Party (DP) alternate as junior coalition partners.

In an overwhelmingly Catholic country (95 percent), the CSV enjoys widespread support, fairly evenly distributed among all ages and classes throughout the country, although the party is affected adversely by urban encroachment and the declining importance of agriculture. Party membership (9,500) is higher than for the other parties. CSV finance depends partly on membership dues, but it also gets help from such organizations as the Christian trade union movement and benefits from its close association with the Catholic Church and from the support of the country's leading daily newspaper.

For decades, the party was dominated by Pierre Werner (prime minister 1959–74, 1979–84). He retired after the 1984 elections and was succeeded by Jacques Santer, who had been finance minister under Werner. When Santer became president of the European Commission in 1995, Jean-Claude Juncker, born in 1955, his finance minister, took over. He led a coalition government from 1999 (with DP) and from 2004 (with LSAP).

The CSV's proven record in office and its unswerving anti-Socialist policy helped, in the more conservative decades at the end of the 20th century, to counter a long-term decline in the social bases of its support. The CSV president is François Biltgen.

DEMOCRATIC PARTY

(Demokratesch Partei; DP)

The Democratic Party was founded in 1945, based partly on the anti-German resistance movement. It was characterized by a strong anticlericalism that it inherited from its forerunner, the prewar Liberal Party. The DP is fully in the mainstream of European progressive liberalism and joined with the LSAP in 1974–79 to implement a program of social reform. The party appears to have a secure electoral base in the middle classes and among white-collar employees, especially in Luxembourg City. The party is also attractive to floating voters who make use of *panachage*. Party membership is only about 3,500, so finance from this source is low.

The party favors free enterprise and, in the liberal tradition, stands close to industry. The DP publishes its own daily newspaper. The DP leader until 1980 was the widely popular Gaston Thorn, born in 1928, prime minister from 1974 to 1979. In 1981 he became president of the European Commission. His successor as DP leader was Colette Flesch, born 1937. The current president is Lydie Polfer. By its character and its location on the political spectrum, the DP has become a sort of "party of government." In 1979 it switched alliances from the Socialists to the Christian Democrats and remained in the ministry. In 1984 it defied unsuccessfully the Luxembourg convention relegating to opposition parties that loose seats in an election. In any case, a DP-LSAP combination rarely has an overall majority in the assembly. A DP-CSV coalition was crafted following the 1999 elections. The DP was unable to duplicate its 1999 success in the 2004 elections.

LUXEMBOURG SOCIALIST WORKERS' PARTY

(Letzeburger Sozialistisch Arbrechterpartei; LSAP)

Founded in 1902, the LSAP is determinedly "working class," with little sign of ideological weakening. The party has very close links with the trade union movement, especially the Independent Trade Union Federation of Luxembourg (Onofhängege Gewerkscheftsbond Lëtzebuerg), the left wing of a union movement that is deeply divided ideologically and between Catholic and secular organizations. During the 1974–79 coalition, the LSAP promoted programs to increase the authority and unity of the trade union movement. Despite that stance, the LSAP has joined several coalition governments with the CSV, both before and after its 1974–79 partnership with the DP—not surprising given the affiliation of the Christian unions to the CSV. The party has overtaken the CSV in share of the vote only once (1964) but came within 1.3 percentage points in 1984. In the 1999 elections the LSAP was eclipsed by the DP but regained the lost ground with the 2004 elections.

Party support and membership comes largely from trade unionists, especially manual occupations. The LSAP has approximately 6,000 members. Party finance relies on membership dues and trade union support. The LSAP publishes a daily newspaper with a relatively large circulation. Unlike the CSV and the DP, the LSAP lacks a significant personality as leader, reflecting the nature of the party. Its present leader is Jacques F. Poos, foreign minister and a banker. The party president is Jean Asselborn.

Minor Political Parties

THE GREENS

(Déi Gréng)

Environmental parties appeared on the Luxembourg scene in the late 1970s. The "Alternative List," a loose coalition favoring the "new politics" of environmental and antinuclear concerns, attracted only about

1 percent of the vote in 1979 but increased to 5.2 percent and two deputies in 1984. The Greens survived a fractious period between the mid-1980s and mid-1990s. By 1994 they had 10.9 percent and five seats. The Greens constitute the more moderate wing of the movement, advocating grassroots democracy, social concerns, and increased foreign development aid, along with environmentalism.

ACTION COMMITTEE FOR DEMOCRACY AND PENSION JUSTICE

(Aktiounskomitee fir Demokratie a Rentegerechtegkeet; ADR)

The ADR was founded in 1987 as a special-interest party to campaign for improved pensions for private-sector employees. Since then it has broadened its policy concerns somewhat but continues to place heavy emphasis on economic equity for pensioners. In its first national electoral appearance, it polled 7.1 percent of the vote and won four seats in the 1989 parliamentary elections. Its share rose to 8.2 percent and five seats in 1994, and it emerged under the Juncker government as the most active opposition party. Rohy Mehlen has been national president since 1991, and Fernand Greisen is general secretary. Both are also ADR members of parliament.

THE LEFT

(Déi Lénk)

In 1999 the Left was formed by former adherents of the Communist Party. It promotes a far-left, "post-Communist" platform, advocating, among other planks, the complete redistribution of wealth. Luxembourg also has had some ephemeral, special-interest minor parties. The Conscriptees movement ran a common list with independent Socialists in 1979 that won 7 percent of the vote. However, its only MP defected to the CSP before the 1984 elections, and the party disappeared. It was an interest group for persons forcibly recruited into the German army during World War II.

Other Political Forces

Luxembourg maintains an active military force of less than 1,000 troops, made up entirely of an army; it has no air force or navy. Compulsory military service was abandoned in 1967. The country uses less than 1 percent of its GNP to fund its military. Luxembourgers contribute to international peacekeeping missions, notably through the Eurocorps for the European Union and NATO.

Labor relations are generally good, which help to attract foreign investment. The largest trade unions are the Luxembourg Confederation of Independent Trade Unions (Onofhängege Gewerkschafts-Bond Lëtzebuerg) and the Luxembourg Confederation of Christian Trade Unions (Lëtzebuerger Chrëschtleche Gewerkschafts-Bond). In the early 21st century these trade unions claimed about 57,000 and 38,000 members, respectively. They have strong links with the Christian Social People's Party (CSV) and the Luxembourg Socialist Workers' Party (LSAP). At one time the Federation of Private Sector White-Collar Employees (Fédération des Employés Privés) was seen as an alternative to the two main groups, but it has since fallen into decline.

In 2003 a new trade union alliance was formed from four smaller "white-collar" trade unions, anchored by the Luxembourg Association of Bank Staffs (Association luxembourgeoise des employés de banque, ALEBA). Claiming political independence, ALEBA joined forces with the Union of Private Sector White-Collar Employees (Union des employés privés), the Neutral Union of Luxembourg Workers (Neutral Gewerkschaft Luxembourg), and the National Union of Private Sector White-Collar Employees (Syndicat national des employés privés-Rénovateurs). In total, the federation has a membership of 20,000. The main employers' association is the Fédération des Industriels Luxembourgeois. It is made up of about 450 companies in two dozen business sectors.

National Prospects

Luxembourgers pride themselves on their stable, consensual politics. Governments rarely fall between elections, and all major parties are potential coalition partners. The general economic slump precipitated by the oil crises has been followed by unprecedented prosperity, making Luxembourg the wealthiest country in Europe per capita. However, the low unemployment and relative prosperity attracted an influx of immigrants, who now constitute about two-fifths of the population. Perhaps the biggest question confronting nativists in the Grand Duchy is whether, with so many foreigners in residence, it will remain true to the national motto, "We want to be what we are."

Further Reading

Flesch, Colette. *The Luxembourg Chamber of Deputies: A Microcosmic Image of a Small Country*. Luxembourg: European Parliament, 1974.

Hey, Jeanne A. K. "Luxembourg's Foreign Policy: Does Small Size Help or Hinder?" *Innovation: The European Journal of Social Science Research* 15, no. 3 (September 1, 2002): 211–25.

Majerus, Pierre. *The Institutions of the Grand Duchy of Luxembourg*. Rev. ed. Luxembourg: Grand Duchy of Luxembourg, 1995.

Weil, G. L. *The Benelux Nations: The Politics of Small Country Democracies*. New York: Holt, Rinehart and Winston, 1970.

REPUBLIC OF MACEDONIA
(Republika Makedonija)

By Stephen Markovich, Ph.D.
Revised by Auron Dodi

Macedonia is a small, landlocked country situated in the central part of the Balkan Peninsula. Bordered by the Serbian part of Serbia and Montenegro, Bulgaria, Greece, and Albania, it covers 25,713 square kilometers and has about 2 million people (2005 est.). Some three-fifths of the population are ethnic Macedonians; about one-fourth are Albanians, and there are smaller percentages of Turks and Roma (Gypsies). More than one-half the population are Serbian (Macedonian) Orthodox, but Sunni Muslims make up about one-third of the population.

Macedonia became an independent democratic republic in 1991, though the development of democracy has been a difficult process. Internal ethnic, political, and economic differences have hampered the firm establishment of a fundamental consensus in the country; externally, problems with all of its neighbors—Yugoslavia (since 2003, Serbia and Montenegro), Bulgaria, Greece, and Albania—have also slowed progressive development. (Even the awkward international name of the country, Former Yugoslav Republic of Macedonia, resulted in Greek objections to the use of *Macedonia*.)

Macedonia's moderate policies eased relations with its neighbors in the 1990s, but in March 1999, when NATO forces began the bombing campaign against Yugoslavia because of that country's treatment of the Albanians of Kosovo, tensions also rose in Macedonia. The Macedonian government opened its border to hundreds of thousands of Albanian refugees expelled from their houses in Kosovo. The Kosovo refugees left Macedonia a few months later, when Yugoslavia signed an international peace accord. But the armed struggle of the Albanians of Kosovo taught other Albanians that fundamental rights can be achieved even by waging a war. Other Albanians of the region also became familiar with the "war business."

OHRID FRAMEWORK AGREEMENT

As long as the Yugoslav Federation existed, Albanians of Macedonia had enjoyed a better treatment by the Macedonian state than the Albanians of Kosovo by Serbia. But after the secession of Macedonia from the Yugoslav Federation, the relationships between Slav Macedonians and ethnic Albanians became problematic. The Albanians opposed the new constitution in 1991, and, in a nonofficial referendum in 1992, they demanded territorial autonomy. Different Albanian parties joined the government coalitions of Macedonia, but many Albanians thought that they did not have enough power to achieve equal treatment because the state was set up in their disfavor. They complained that they were underrepresented in the government structures and that they were forbidden to display their national symbols in public life. In 1996 in Tetovo, Albanians demanded official recognition of the Albanian language at the city's university.

Growing tensions in February 2001 led to armed clashes involving both ethnic Albanian rebels and the government forces. Armed Albanians, through the

National Liberation Army, clamored for constitutional reforms and reorganization of the Macedonian state in order to have greater rights as a minority. The uprising, which lasted several months, led the country to the verge of civil war. Non-Albanians, discontented with what they considered a soft attitude toward the Albanian rebels, attacked the parliament. However, the demands of the rebels had achieved international political support, especially after they declared that they supported the maintenance of Macedonian state integrity.

The Albanian uprising ended through international mediation in August 2001, when a peace agreement was signed in Ohrid. The main political parties of Macedonia promised to promote the position of minorities, especially of the Albanian minority, and in exchange the armed rebels agreed to hand over about thousands of weapons to NATO forces. As a result of the agreement, a NATO peacekeeping mission was established in September 2001. The Government of National Unity led by Prime Minister Ljubco Georgevski declared an amnesty to former members of the National Liberation Army, which then disbanded. Most of its members joined the new Albanian political party Democratic Union for Integration (DUI), which joined the government coalition after parliamentary elections in September 2002.

To implement the Ohrid Peace Agreement, the Macedonian parliament made important amendments to the constitution. The new constitution recognized the Albanian language as an official language and increased access for ethnic Albanians in administration, police, and other areas. The implementation of the laws based on the constitutional amendments was carried out generally without problems. But in August 2004 the parliament passed the "Law about the Territorial Organization" of the country, a critical final element from the Ohrid Framework Agreement. According to this law, the total number of municipalities would have decreased from 123 to 84 and have redrawn municipal boundaries to increase the number of municipalities inhabited by an Albanian majority. The government agreed to test acceptance of the law with a referendum, for which the World Macedonian Congress collected signatures. The referendum was held in November 2004. The attempt to overturn the new law failed due to low turnout—slightly more than a quarter of voters cast ballots, far shy of the required 50 percent minimum needed to make the vote valid— and because of clear international warnings that rejection of the law would lead to negative consequences for Macedonia, especially as far as its future integration to

important international organizations was concerned. Macedonia aimed at joining the European Union (EU), after signing an Agreement of Stabilization-Association in April 2001.

The System of Government

Macedonia is a parliamentary democracy with a unicameral legislature.

EXECUTIVE

Macedonia has a dual executive consisting of a president and a prime minister. The president is elected by the people for a term of five years, and the prime minister is the head of the party or coalition of parties that has a majority in parliament. Constitutionally, the president is the head of state and the prime minister is the head of government.

The constitution states that the president represents the republic, signs bills into law, nominates the prime minister, appoints several governmental and judicial offices—usually in consultation with the government and with approval by parliament—grants decorations and honors, and serves as commander in chief. In signing bills into law, the president may veto a bill and send it back to the Assembly for reconsideration; if the Assembly reconsiders the bill and passes it by an absolute majority, then the president is obliged to sign it. Apart from this discretion on bills and possibly the role as commander in chief, the presidential powers collectively, as they are presented in the constitution, provide that the president act more as a formal head of state than as a political leader of the country.

In practice, however, in the early years of the new Macedonia, the first president, Kiro Gligorov, was active in leading the country and therefore served as something more than simply a formal head of state. An experienced politician with a strong sense of leadership, he achieved a revered status in Macedonia as the father of the new Macedonia and the symbol of political reform. This status enabled him to win the parliamentary election for president in 1991 and the popular election for that office in 1994.

The stability of Gligorov's leadership was particularly significant in light of the latent instability in the coalition governments that ran the country. The first coalition government, headed by Prime Minister

Nikola Kljusev, lost a vote of confidence in 1992 and had to resign after a little more than a year in office. The second coalition government, headed by Branko Crvenkovski, survived a vote of confidence after several months in office and went on to run the country for several years. Still, to stay in office Crvenkovski had to manage broad coalitions that were fragile partnerships, and he needed both to balance his ministerial assignments among three or four parties and placate the Albanian elements in his coalitions. By 1998 his coalition could not withstand the vigorous challenge by the opposition, forcing Crvenkovski to resign as prime minister. He was replaced by Ljubco Georgievski, who formed an inclusive coalition government that included Albanian parties, but he had to reshuffle his cabinet often. Following the Albanian uprising in the country, Georgievski set up in May 2001 a broad government of national unity. In subsequent parliamentary elections in 2002, Georgievski's coalition lost, and Crvenkovski returned to office (in 2004 Crvenkovski became president of Macedonia). The role of the president of the state proved to be of special importance for Macedonia even after the Gligorov era, especially during the time when ethnic tensions flared up. President Boris Trajkovski (elected in December 1999, killed in a plane crash in February 2004) led the peace process in Macedonia, despite opposition in the country. He played a decisive role in efforts to control the interethnic tensions during a dangerous time for Macedonia. In general, his moderating role had an impact on the functioning of the country's institutions and on prospects for Macedonia's integration into Europe.

Now, as long as a prime minister can maintain a stable cabinet, he and his cabinet are in a strong position to govern, as the constitution gives them sufficient powers. Article 91 states that the government determines policies, introduces laws, proposes the budget, establishes relations with foreign nations, and appoints a series of officials including diplomatic officers and public prosecutors. For the government proposals to be enacted, they have to be passed by the Assembly, but this is usually pro forma in a parliamentary system when a majority party or coalition controls the legislature. While Macedonian governments have more often than not managed to maintain themselves in power, they have frequently had to do considerable maneuvering to retain this control and sustain the support of the Assembly.

LEGISLATURE

The Macedonian legislature is a unicameral parliament called the Assembly (or Sobranie) and consists of 120 representatives elected to four-year terms. Representatives who accept ministerial posts in the government must resign their legislative seats.

According to Article 68 of the constitution, the Assembly can enact laws, adopt the budget, elect the government, elect judges and other officials, amend the constitution, ratify international agreements, and decide on war and peace. It can also reject the government through a vote of no confidence. So far the Assembly has forced one government to resign and forced another to defend itself against legislative challenges. Until the parliamentary elections in 2002, the Assembly complicated the passing of law packages resulting from the Ohrid Framework Agreement. In general the Assembly has taken all of its legislative powers seriously and has vigorously exercised them,

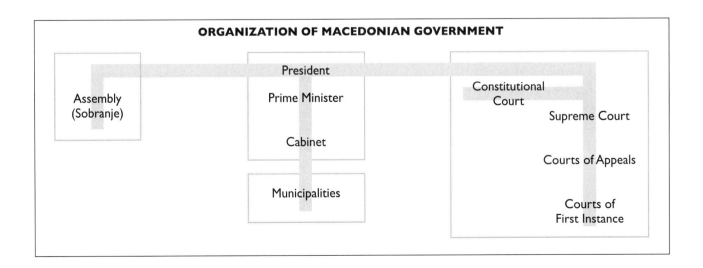

ORGANIZATION OF MACEDONIAN GOVERNMENT

Assembly (Sobranje)

President
Prime Minister
Cabinet
Municipalities

Constitutional Court
Supreme Court
Courts of Appeals
Courts of First Instance

and has consequently acted as a viable branch in the political system.

JUDICIARY

For regular judicial matters, the legislature has established 27 courts of first instance, three courts of appeals, and a Supreme Court. These courts cover all civil and criminal matters, the lower courts hearing original cases and the upper courts hearing appeals; in addition to considering appeals, the Supreme Court also monitors the uniform application of laws. A special Constitutional Court of Macedonia decides on the constitutionality of laws, on jurisdictional disputes between the branches of government, on conflicts between national and local governments, and on cases involving individual freedoms.

Judges for the regular courts are nominated for life terms by the Republican Judicial Council, a seven-member board of prestigious legal experts, and confirmed by a majority of the Assembly. The nine judges on the Constitutional Court are elected by the Assembly for nine-year terms and cannot be reelected.

REGIONAL AND LOCAL GOVERNMENT

The provisions for local government are laid out in section V of the constitution and in the Law for Local Self-Government enacted in 1995. This law was partially amended in 1996. These provisions allow municipalities to be governed by elected mayors and councils, but their governing jurisdictions are limited to local matters and are subject to supervision by the national government. Until the 1995 law was passed, there was considerable tension between the national government and the municipal councils, particularly between national bodies and Albanian municipalities. What generated this tension were disputes over which languages could be officially used in municipal transactions. In January 2002 the Assembly decided to give more powers to local government, and in August 2004 it passed the law on territorial reorganization, compiled to replace the law of 1996. The proposed law, which would have redrawn municipal boundaries, reduced the number of municipalities and provided local government institutions with new powers. However, the implementation of the new law was impeded for many months, and the law was put to a referendum vote in November 2004. The referendum failed to reach the minimum turnout required to make the vote valid, thus allowing the new law to be implemented.

The Electoral System

All citizens at least age 18 are entitled to vote. On the national level this vote may be exercised in elections for president and parliament. In the 1990 parliamentary elections, the first free elections held in Macedonia prior to independence, more than four-fifths of eligible voters turned out to cast their ballots for more than 20 parties. In 1994 turnout stood at about four-fifths of the electorate in the first round but only three-fifths in the second—a drop attributed to the boycott of the second round by some parties. Subsequent national elections saw turnout of about 70 to 75 percent.

Under the new constitution the president of the republic is elected directly by the people for a five-year term. There are, potentially, two rounds of voting. For a candidate to be elected in the first round, he or she must win a majority of the votes; if no candidate wins a majority on this ballot, then a second ballot or runoff between the top two candidates is held two weeks later. In the presidential elections of October 1994, there was no need for a second ballot as the popular Kiro Gligorov, the incumbent president, garnered 78 percent of the votes cast. In 1999 and 2004, however, a second ballot was required. Elections in 1994 for the 120 seats in the Assembly also employed the double ballot system, and winning one of the seats in the first round proved to be a rarity—only 10 candidates escaped a second-round runoff. Despite some irregularities in the electoral process and despite the advantages that the incumbent government had with the media, international observers judged that the elections overall were free and fair and that they contributed significantly to democratic development in Macedonia.

The elections in 1998 were also considered free and fair, though they had to be repeated in seven districts due to irregularities, but both the electoral system and the results were different from 1994. Legislation had altered the electoral system, providing that 35 seats would be allocated based on proportional representation, while the other 85 seats (still conducted in a double-ballot fashion) would be individual districts represented by a single member of the Assembly. To achieve representation for the 35 proportional seats, a party had to surpass a 5 percent threshold. The parliamentary elections of 2002 were the first after the end of the armed conflict. Brutal incidents, threats, and accusations were part of the electoral campaign of different political forces. However, international observers judged that the elections were conducted largely in accordance with international standards for democratic elections. In spite of some isolated incidents,

Macedonians successfully passed their first test after the end of interethnic conflict. For the 2002 elections the electoral system was altered again. This time, the country was split into six constituencies, each electing 20 MPs, and the seats were apportioned based on the percentage of votes that a party received.

The Party System

Once the one-party Communist monopoly ended in Macedonia, multiparty elections were scheduled in late 1990. Numerous parties were formed—though many did not even last long enough to register as official parties. By the time the first round of balloting took place, there were 20 parties registered, and 16 of these participated in the elections; when the elections were over, only 10 parties or party coalitions had gained legislative seats and only 4 of these had seats in double figures. In the 1994 elections only 9 of 31 registered parties won any representation and only 3 of them won in double figures; and for the 1998 elections 39 parties were registered, 17 parties/coalitions participated, and 5 won some seats—again only 3 in double figures. In the elections of 2002, 38 parties/coalitions and independent candidates were registered. Of these only 19 parties and party coalitions took part in the elections. Based on the 2002 elections, major political parties of Macedonia may be considered the Social Democrat Union of Macedonia (SDUM), the Internal Macedonian Revolutionary Organization–Democratic Party of Macedonian National Unity (IMRO-DPMU), and the Liberal Democratic Party (LDP). As for the Albanian political parties, the major players currently are Democratic Union for Integration (DUI), Democratic Party of Albanians (DPA), and Party for Democratic Prosperity (PDP).

Major Political Parties

SOCIAL DEMOCRATIC UNION OF MACEDONIA (SDUM)

(Socijaldemokratski Sojuz Makedonije)

The Social Democrats are the successors to the reform Communists of Macedonia. In 1989, when Yugoslavia was still intact, they established their party as the League of Communists of Macedonia–Party of Democratic Transformation but later changed it to Social Democratic Union. As reform Communists they had to convince the people that they did in fact favor fundamental political and economic changes rather than cosmetic touch-ups of Titoism. To be convincing, therefore, they made firm commitments to democratic pluralism and a market economy, and then lived up to these commitments.

Though Kiro Gligorov was one of the original reform Communists, in his role as president he rose above party politics. As pluralism began to emerge in Macedonia, Gligorov began to drift from partisan positions and leave party politics to others. The first leader of the reform Communists was Peter Gosev, but he was supplanted by Branko Crvenkovski, who became leader of the party in 1991 and prime minister of the country in 1992. While Crvenkovski's Social Democrats were not able to win a majority on their own, they were able to sustain themselves as the major centrist party and as the senior partner in the coalition governments that ruled Macedonia from 1992 to 1998. The party has enjoyed success, attracted more than 100,000 members to its local organizations throughout the country and convincing voters and observers that their transformation from Yugoslav Communists to Macedonian democrats was complete. By 1998, however, the voters wanted a change and consequently voted the Social Democrats out of office. The Social Democrats decided to join the Government of National Unity under Ljubco Georgievski, but they later left the government. Together with other parties, the Social Democrats signed the Ohrid Framework Agreement, and in 2002 the party led a coalition that won that year's parliamentary elections. It got 43 seats in parliament and its coalition won 60 seats. The party leader, Crvenovski, was prime minister until the early presidential elections of April 2004, when he was elected president of the state.

INTERNAL MACEDONIAN REVOLUTIONARY ORGANIZATION– DEMOCRATIC PARTY OF MACEDONIAN NATIONAL UNITY (IMRO-DPMNU)

(Vnatresno-Makedonska Revolucionerna Organizacija–Demokratska Partija za Makedonsko Nacionalno Edinstvo)

The Internal Macedonian Revolutionary Organization (IMRO) was first founded in 1983 to promote Macedonian nationalism and became a legendary organization among Macedonians for its role in establishing a Macedonian identity. In promoting its goals, IMRO resorted to terrorist activities so frequently that it was often referred to as a terrorist group. When today's IMRO-DPMNU was founded in 1990, its leaders assumed the goals of the original IMRO but not the means; that is, they established a legitimate party that eschewed terrorist means yet remained stridently nationalistic.

The strident nationalism and legendary name of the party paid dividends in the 1990 elections but not in the 1994 elections. The success of the party in 1990 was surprising to everyone, including its own leaders, when it led all political parties with 38 seats. In 1994, however, the IMRO-DPMNU faltered. The party was ineffective in the first round of voting and pulled out of the second round because of alleged electoral irregularities. Moreover, its party leader, Ljubco Georgievski, gained only 22 percent of the vote to Gligorov's 78 percent. After pulling out of the political arena, the IMRO-DPMNU was forced to convey its views and criticisms through public speeches and press releases, which proved a less effective way to further party interests. Nevertheless, since it had a solid organization and over 100,000 members, the party survived its self-imposed isolation and rebounded dramatically in the 1998 elections, winning 62 seats with its electoral partner, the Democratic Alternative (DA), and becoming the dominant partner in the new coalition government. Its success was due partly to its large membership and core support and partly to its shift to moderation and inclusiveness, an inclusiveness that accepted the Albanians in their government. In 1999 Boris Trajkovski, the successor of President Gligorov, was nominated president by this party. IMRO-DPMNU together with other parties signed the Ohrid Framework Agreement. In the 2002 elections it formed an electoral coalition with LPM (Liberal Party of Macedonia), winning 29 seats in parliament (33 together with LPM). After its failure, Georgievski resigned as party leader.

DEMOCRATIC UNION FOR INTEGRATION

(Demokratska Unija za Integracija— Bashkimi Demokratik për Integrim)

The Democratic Union for Integration is an Albanian Party founded after the end of the interethnic armed conflict. Although the party was formed only a few months before the general elections of 2002, it succeeded in getting most of the votes from the Albanian population and won 16 seats in the Assembly, joining the coalition government led by SDUM. Former fighters of the National Liberation Army, following its disbandment, founded DUI. It is estimated that about half the members of the party fought in the armed conflict. The others are former members of different Albanian parties and people who had not been members of other parties before. This specific membership spectrum has brought about frequent internal discussions over party policy. Nevertheless, the position of this party and of its leader (the former commander of the National Liberation Army, Ali Ahmeti) has remained moderate and can be defined as closer to social democracy.

The program of DUI includes the quick implementation of the obligations of the Ohrid Framework Agreement: interethnic reconciliation and the economic development of the country. DUI supports the integration of Macedonia in international structures, such as the European Union and NATO. Despite the fact that the government of Georgievski accused the DUI leader of terrorism, wanted to arrest him, and would not let him participate in the electoral campaign for the 2002 general elections, the former rebel Ahmeti declared that his party will always respect the Macedonian constitution and that there is no alternative but to implement the Ohrid Framework Agreement.

LIBERAL DEMOCRATIC PARTY (LDP)

(Liberalno Demokratska Partija)

The Liberal Democratic Party was formed in 1997 through the merger of the Liberal Party and the Democratic Party in an attempt to stay the faltering fortunes of the once-successful Liberal Party. After the Liberal Party itself was created in 1991, it did very well as a small but influential party. Although it numbered about 10,000 adherents, most of these members were successful businesspeople who strongly supported the transformation to a market economy and heavily promoted privatization in the country. Their influence in the economic sector was nearly matched by their role in the government; as partners in coalition governments from 1992 to 1996, members of the party held important posts in both the cabinet and the legislature, posts which allowed them some say in the policy-making process.

One of the important posts, president of the Assembly, was held by a party leader, Stojan Andov, from 1991 to 1996. From this post Andov could affect governmental policies and decisions and, concomitantly, because of his governmental power, manage his party in a disciplined and authoritarian manner. Much of this power vanished when differences between Andov and Crvenkovski came to a head in 1996. Because of these differences Andov had to resign his position as Assembly president, and his Liberal colleagues lost their ministerial posts in a cabinet reshuffle engineered by Crvenkovski. Once they were removed from ruling posts, the Liberal's influence and support dropped precipitously. Whereas they won 24 percent of the popular vote and 29 parliamentary seats as the single Liberal Party in 1994, they won only 7 percent of the vote and four seats as the united Liberal Democratic Party in 1998. The new party will have to generate a dramatic comeback to repeat the earlier Liberal successes or, more pointedly, even to survive as a viable party. In the parliamentary elections of 2002 it was second among the Macedonian parties, winning 11 seats and joining the governing coalition.

ALBANIAN DEMOCRATIC PARTY

(Demokratska Partija na Albancite—Partia Demokratike Shqiptare)

DPA seceded in 1994 from the Party for Democratic Prosperity (1990) of the Albanians in Macedonia. It gained a political profile and sympathy among Albanians by defending their national and cultural demands especially in 1995–96. In the parliamentary elections of 1998 it won the greatest number of votes from the Albanians and joined the Macedonian government coalition headed by IMRO-DPMNU. During this time the Albanian votes for the first time became decisive for the election of the president of the state. The coalition of this party with IMRO-DPMNU—parties where the nationalistic tones were present—eventually created conditions thatradicalized the situation in Macedonia. During the armed conflict in 2001 DPA did not officially support the National Liberation Army (NLA), but many members of this party joined the NLA. DPA with other parties signed the Ohrid Framework Agreement. In the parliamentary elections of 2002 this was the only party that openly insisted on the independence of Kosovo, considering it as a precondition for the stability of Macedonia. Though it only won seven seats in the Assembly in 2002, most of the leaders of municipalities with an Albanian majority are members of this party. The party has sought to place Macedonia under an international protectorate.

Minor Political Parties

In 1995 the Assembly passed a law that required a party to have 500 citizens signed as members before it could be registered. This law served to reduce the number of parties from about 60 proclaimed parties to 38 registered parties.

The Party for Democratic Prosperity (PDP) is a party of the Albanian minority that won two seats in the 2002 elections. This party signed the Ohrid Framework Agreement. The National Democratic Party (NDP) is a small Albanian party that has one seat in parliament. The Democratic Party of Turks (DPTM) has two seats in the new parliament, while the Democratic League of Bosniaks (DLBM), the Democratic Party of Serbs (DPSM), and the OPRM (United Party of Romas in Macedonia) each have one seat in parliament.

There are many other parties that have registered, but their support in elections is diminishing rather than increasing, and consequently their prospects are not encouraging.

Other Political Forces

Macedonia, as a small post-Communist country, has something in common with other post-Communist Balkan countries: other political forces, besides political parties, are still weak and do not have much influence on everyday life. The army remains very weak. There exist nongovernmental organizations and organized labor (in 2004 a "parliament of nongovernmental bodies" was constituted), but everything is very new and no distinguished role has emerged for any of these bodies. Outside influences, particularly the European Union and NATO, are particularly important in Macedonia.

National Prospects

Ten years after the secession from Yugoslavia and the declaration of independence, Macedonia was threatened by an armed interethnic conflict. The outbreak of the civil war between the ethnic Macedonian majority and the ethnic Albanian minority was prevented only by a timely and coordinated intervention of the United States, the European Union, and NATO. Together with the parties in conflict, they outlined, in the Ohrid Peace Agreement, a political compromise that, it was hoped, would guarantee the future of the Macedonian state. This agreement was also supported through deployment of peace-keeping missions by NATO and the European Union. The Ohrid Framework Agreement, the constitutional reform, and new laws deriving from it have so far proved a successful instrument for the preservation of peace in the country.

However, the question of decentralization and territorial organization increased tensions during the last months of 2004 and became another test for the Peace Agreement and the stability of the country. A referendum to reverse the decentralization law in November 2004 failed due to low voter turnout and as a result of clear international warnings of consequences for Macedonia, especially concerning its future integration to important international organizations.

The interethnic issue remains explosive, and it is the gravest problem for Macedonia at the moment: the gap between different ethnicities (the Macedonians, Albanians, Serbs, Turks, and others) has become larger since the end of the armed conflict. Voices from the opposition and the minorities increasingly announce the failure of the multiethnic state and demand a division of the country. In 2005 the Assembly passed legislation enabling the flying of the Albanian flag in areas where Albanians predominate; the future effects of this law—whether it will reduce or increase ethnic tensions—will play an important role in determining the country's future.

The party system is undergoing a process of change after the split of the largest opposition party IMRO-DPMNU, the changes at the leadership of the SDUM, and the foundation of the new minority parties. As far as Macedonia's neighbors are concerned, during the armed conflict they respected or supported the official line of the United States, NATO, and the EU for maintenance of the territorial integrity of Macedonia. Although some problems with neighbors still exist, relationships with them have been continually improving. At present there are ongoing negotiations with Greece to finally clarify the name-question for Macedonia. Aiming to support the consolidation of the Macedonian state, in November 2004 the United States and the German Bundestag (parliament) decided to refer to the Former Yugoslav Republic of Macedonia simply as the "Republic of Macedonia." These positions were later moderated, leaving this question to the United Nations; the intention of the international community, however, remains clear.

International diplomacy is helping to further stabilize Macedonia either by concrete steps or by promising to facilitate the country's membership in organizations such as NATO and the European Union. Through their diplomats in Skopje, they observe political developments and alert the government if they notice deviations from the international agenda that calls for the stabilization of the country. Indeed, the European Commission was so impressed with Macedonia's efforts that in November 2005 it recommended that the country become a candidate for membership in the European Union.

Economic questions still pose a problem for the country, but political forces are at the moment little involved in discussions of these issues. In this area, progress has been slow, and it has almost stopped because of the ethnic conflict. Although economic reforms remain a priority of the government program, the economic status quo might be transformed into a destabilizing factor for the country.

Finally, it can be said that progress has been made after the end of the armed conflict, and therefore there is some hope for the future. If the political actors are successful in reconciling hostile ethnicities, and if the economic problems are taken seriously, then Macedonia will have a good chance to survive as a state in its present form.

Further Reading

Cohen, Lenard J. *Broken Bonds: Yugoslavia's Disintegration and Balkan Politics in* Transition. 2d ed. Boulder, Colo.: Westview Press, 1995.

Danforth, Loring M. *The Macedonian Conflict.* Princeton, N.J.: Princeton University Press, 1995.

Glenny, Misha. *The Balkans: Nationalism, War and the Great Powers, 1804-1999.* New York: Penguin Books, 2001.

Lampe, John R. *Yugoslavia as History: Twice There Was a Country.* New York: Cambridge University Press, 1996.

Mazower, Mark. *The Balkans: A Short History.* New York: Modern Library, 2002.

Phillips, John. *Macedonia: Warlords and Rebels in the Balkans.* New Haven, Conn.: Yale University Press, 2004.

Poulton, Hugh. *Who Are the Macedonians?* London: Hurst, 1994.

Pribichevich, Stojan. *Macedonia: Its People and History.* University Park: Pennsylvania State University Press, 1982.

Singleton, Fred. *A Short History of the Yugoslav Peoples.* New York: Cambridge University Press, 1985.

REPUBLIC OF MADAGASCAR

(Repoblikan'i Madagasikara)

(République de Madagascar)

By B. David Meyers, Ph.D.

The Republic of Madagascar is an island country in the southwestern Indian Ocean. The population of more than 18 million people (2005 est.) is divided between the *Merina*, persons of Malayo-Indonesian descent who make up about one-fourth of the population, and the *cotiers*, coastal people of African descent who make up the majority. Malagasy, a language that resembles Malay and Indonesian, is spoken throughout the country.

During the late 19th century *Merina* kings, who controlled the entire island, lost a series of wars to the French, and in 1896 Madagascar became a French colony. On June 26, 1960, the country regained independence as the Malagasy Republic. Philibert Tsiranana, who played a leading role in securing independence for Madagascar, became its first president, serving in office until 1972.

In May 1972 the First Republic ended as popular discontent with inflation and continued French influence caused Tsiranana to resign in favor of a military government. The new, leftist government nationalized French holdings, closed French military bases and an American space-tracking station, and accepted foreign aid from a number of Communist states. The highly authoritarian, Socialist, military government expelled foreigners, suppressed strikes, and arrested its opponents. In June 1975 Didier Ratsiraka, a naval officer of *cotier* background, became the fourth in a series of military leaders to head the government. Both in and out of power, he remained Madagascar's dominant political figure for the next 25 years.

In a June 1975 referendum 95 percent of the voters favored changing the name of the country to Madagascar, adopting a new constitution that proclaiming the Second Republic, and confirming Ratsiraka as president. In 1977 Ratsiraka allowed parliamentary elections, and, in 1982 and 1989 presidential elections were held that Ratsiraka won—though opposition parties were banned for these elections. During these years Ratsiraka's unsuccessful attempts to bring about a socialist revolution further damaged the country's already-troubled economy.

During 1990–91 Madagascar suffered widespread civil unrest. After failing to quell the unrest by force, Ratsiraka agreed to surrender some of his powers. In August 1992 a new constitution, which created the Third Republic, was quickly written and then endorsed by a national referendum. This constitution replaced Madagascar's presidential government with a parliamentary system. Under the constitution, the presidency, still held by Ratsiraka, became a largely ceremonial position, with governing power being exercised by a prime minister chosen by the National Assembly. In another liberalizing change there was a return to multiparty politics.

In national elections held in 1993, Ratsiraka's rule temporarily ended, as Albert Zafy was elected president. Hopes that Madagascar was on the path to becoming a successful parliamentary democracy were soon dashed as the new president got into a series of clashes with the National Assembly and the prime minister. In September 1995 Zafy called for—and won—a national referendum on a constitutional amendment that again allowed the president to appoint the prime minister, essentially returning the political system to presidential rule.

Zafy's actions angered members of the National Assembly who had previously supported him. In 1996 he was impeached by the legislature and removed from office by the Constitutional Court. New presidential elections then became necessary.

Fifteen candidates, including both Ratsiraka and Zafy, filed for the vacant office. The first round of presidential elections, held on November 3, 1996, failed to achieve the required absolute majority but led to the elimination of 13 of the candidates. In the second polling, an aged and infirm Ratsiraka narrowly defeated Zafy and was returned to power.

The Madagascan political system was again altered in 1998 when the public once again approved a new constitution, proposed by Ratsiraka. This created a federal system with a strong president and a weak legislature. Ratsiraka's position was further strengthened when his supporters won the majority of seats in the National Assembly.

By 2001 Ratsiraka had again become unpopular in many parts of the country. The presidential elections that began in December 2001 developed into a political crisis that included bloodshed, threats of secession, efforts at foreign mediation, and, finally, intervention by the Constitutional High Court. From February 2002 until July, when Ratsiraka fled the country, Madagascar had two governments, with Ratsiraka controlling most of the countryside and his ultimately successful rival, Marc Ravalomanana, the capital and most of the other urban areas. In sharp contrast, National Assembly elections held a few months later, and municipal elections in November 2003, were quiet and peaceful. While in exile in France in 2003, Ratsiraka was convicted of embezzling public funds and sentenced to 10 years hard labor.

The System of Government

Madagascar is a federal republic with a bicameral legislature.

EXECUTIVE

The 1998 constitution essentially provides a legal basis for the strong presidential regimes that had, in fact, already been the rule. The prime minister and cabinet members, who carry out the day-to-day management of the government, are chosen by, and responsible to, the president. According to the constitution the president is elected popularly for a five-year term. If no candidate obtains a majority of the overall vote, a second round of voting takes place within 30 days of the publication of the results of the first ballot.

The tumultuous 2001 presidential election initially drew six candidates. Following the first round of balloting, both major candidates claimed to have crossed the 50 percent threshold. The government declared Ratsiraka the winner, but Ravalomanana contested the results. In February 2002 both were separately sworn in and violence flared as their supporters ignored calls for a second round of balloting. By summer Ravalomanana's forces controlled most of the island and the High Constitutional Court announced that, according to a recount, he had gained 51.5 percent of the vote and had been elected as president. Shortly thereafter, Ratsiraka's prime minister was arrested and Jacques Sylla was appointed to that position.

LEGISLATURE

Madagascar's legislature has undergone frequent changes. The National Assembly, until recently the only house of parliament, has, since 1990, twice been increased in size, and its composition has been changed from a system where all of the members were chosen by proportional representation to one that includes both single-member and two-member constituencies. In 2002 the legislature became bicameral with the addition of a Senate consisting of 90 senators, two-thirds chosen by regional legislators and one-third appointed.

Despite changes in its structure and composition, Madagascar's parliament has, with only one exception, remained unimportant. The exception was its impeachment of then-president Zafy in 1996. The impeachment vote aside, the Madagascan tradition of authoritarian presidents and fractious parties left the National Assembly powerless. Its debates dramatize problems but seldom accomplish much toward their solution.

The 1998 Assembly elections had assured President Ratsiraka a comfortable majority in parliament as his party (AREMA) captured 63 seats, while allied parties, most importantly Leader-Fanilo, which held 16 seats, and a number of supportive independents won enough to assure control.

The National Assembly elections held in 2001 produced an overwhelming victory for the parties that supported Ravalomanana (i.e., his own TIM [I Love Madagascar] and its allies FP and RPSD) and a defeat for those who had been associated with Ratsiraka (i.e., AREMA and Leader-Fanilo).

MADAGASCAR NATIONAL ASSEMBLY: SEATS BY PARTY, 2002

Party	Seats
Tiako I Madagasikara (TIM)	103
Firaisankinam-Pirenena (FP)	22
Rénaissance du Parti Social-Démocratique (RPSD)	5
AREMA	3
LEADER-Fanilo	2
other parties	3
independents	22
Total	160

JUDICIARY

The apex of Madagascar's legal system is a Constitutional High Court comprised of seven judges who are elected by the National Assembly. The Court has the power of judicial review, in that it interprets the Madagascan constitution and rules on the constitutionality of new laws. Often it has served as the final arbiter of political differences, including electoral disputes and conflicts between central and local authorities. The Court supported and, in effect, finalized Zafy's impeachment in 1996, certified Ratsiraka's extremely narrow comeback victory in 1997, and endorsed Ravalomanana's claim to power in 2002.

In addition to the Constitutional Court, there is a Supreme Court, a Court of Appeals, and a large number of local lower courts, some of which have highly specialized jurisdiction. The legal system is largely based on French legal codes and practices with the addition of some practices from traditional Malagasy law.

REGIONAL AND LOCAL GOVERNMENT

Madagascar's poor communications and transportation infrastructures have made it difficult for any regime to effectively link the capital to the outlying areas. A popular federalist movement received renewed momentum when, during the 1996 presidential elections, Ratsiraka promised that a national referendum on federalism would be held in the near future. In March 1998 a federal system was adopted as part of the new constitution. There are six autonomous provinces, each with an elected governor and legislative council. The provinces have great financial autonomy.

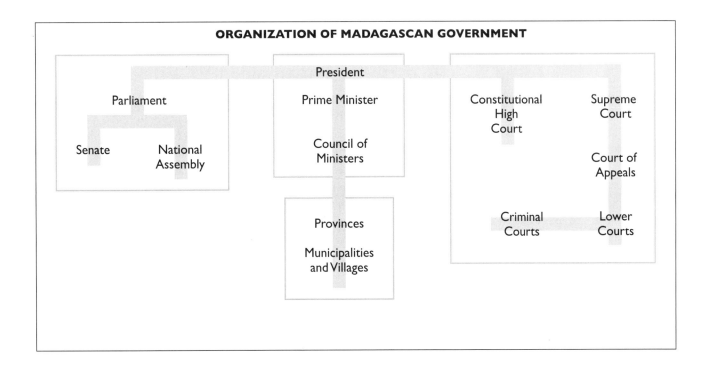

ORGANIZATION OF MADAGASCAN GOVERNMENT

President

Parliament — Senate, National Assembly

Prime Minister, Council of Ministers — Provinces, Municipalities and Villages

Constitutional High Court, Supreme Court, Court of Appeals, Criminal Courts, Lower Courts

Local government in Madagascar has been based on traditional village assemblies (*fokonolona*) and elected urban district councils (*fokontany*) headed by mayors.

The Electoral System

There is universal suffrage in Madagascar for those aged 18 or older. National elections are held for the office of the presidency and members National Assembly, and there are elections for provincial and local leaders, recall elections, and constitutional referendums. As illiteracy is widespread, ballots have usually been marked with party symbols and colors. Elections are often accompanied by claims of fraud. In May 1997 the National Assembly passed a law making an identity card necessary to register on voting lists and take part in elections.

Presidential candidates file with a deposit that is returned to candidates who receive at least 10 percent of the vote. If no candidate receives a majority on the first ballot, the two highest finishers compete in a runoff a month after the first-round results are officially announced.

Members of the National Assembly are chosen in elections that are separate from the presidential balloting. Members are chosen from either single- or two-member constituencies.

The Party System

Political parties in colonial Madagascar were originally developed in the mid-1940s but were suppressed by the French following widespread violence in 1947. Parties reemerged in preparation for elections in 1958. As was typical in French Africa, most were affiliates of parties found within France. The most important of these parties was the Social Democratic Party (PSD) of Philibert Tsiranana, the country's first president. PSD remained the governing party throughout the First Republic. Its major opposition was the Congress Party for the Independence of Madagascar (AKFM), which wanted complete independence rather than internal self-government within the French Community. In general, PSD support came from the coastal tribes, AKFM's from the *Merina*.

As one of the new, "revolutionary" institutions of the Second Republic, Ratsiraka created his own party, the Vanguard of the Malagasy Revolution (AREMA). AREMA formed the nucleus of a fractious coalition called the National Front for the Defense of the Revolution (FNDR). Under the constitution, the FNDR was the only legal political organization. All political parties had to be within the Front, which offered a single list of candidates to the voters. Ratsiraka's efforts to create a viable one-party system were, however, thwarted by conflicts among the groups and individuals supposedly united within the Front.

In March 1990 the Ratsiraka government, recognizing the disintegration of the Front and faced with popular demands for democratic change, agreed to the resumption of multiparty politics. The lifting of the ban was codified in the constitution, which guarantees freedom of political organization in political parties and associations. In an effort to avoid communal-based politics that might threaten national unity, parties that advocate ethnic, tribal, or religious segregation were prohibited.

Since then, parties have abounded as new ones formed and older ones were reconstituted. Over 120 parties contested the 1993 Assembly elections, and more than 150 participated in 1998 and 2002. Only a few of these parties run candidates throughout the country and most lack any permanent organization or officials. Not surprisingly, few have ever captured a single seat. The larger and more successful parties are only relatively more organized and stable. Party members move from one party to another and allegiance to a local leader is often stronger than party affiliation.

With a few exceptions, Madagascan parties frequently fracture and combine, change names, and disappear only to reappear again. In general, the parties have tended to form broad, fluid coalitions that either support or oppose the nation's president.

CAMPAIGNING

Political and economic programs are often largely absent or meaninglessly vague in political campaigns. Candidates appeal to popular dissent and clamors for radical change. Many of Madagascar's voters have little party loyalty but rather appear increasingly inclined to defeat incumbents. Ratsiraka's electoral success in 1996 may have had less to do with his previous experience or his extensive personal campaigning than it did with popular dissatisfaction with President Zafy, under whom the economy had worsened. Voters again turned out incumbents in the 2001 presidential and 2002 National Assembly elections. Ravalomanana promised reforms, claimed to have a much-needed antipoverty program, and had the support of other big-city mayors, but, probably most importantly, was seen as "a new face."

Major Political Parties

The strength of political parties can change greatly from election to election; those discussed below are, or recently have been, the most significant. Parties are not usually distinguished on the basis of ideology or policy issues but, rather, whether they support or oppose the president.

I LOVE MADAGASCAR

(Tiako I Madagasikara; TIM)

TIM was created in 1999 to support businessman Marc Ravalomanana's candidacy for mayor of Antananarivo. The party supported him in the 2001 presidential election. In 2002 TIM presented Assembly candidates in all six provinces, winning 34 percent of the popular vote and 103 of the 160 seats.

Somewhat stronger in the urban areas and among the *Merina* people, the party has had, despite some talk of political reform and economic development, no clear ideology or purpose other than support for Ravalomanana.

NATIONAL SOLIDARITY

(Firaisankinam-Pirenena; FP)

The FP was created in 2002 and was supportive of Ravalomanana. In the 2002 elections it won 22 seats in the National Assembly and joined the governing coalition.

VANGUARD OF THE MALAGASY REVOLUTION

(Avant-Garde de la Révolution Malagasy; AREMA)

AREMA was established by then-president Ratsiraka as one of the new revolutionary institutions of the Second Republic. It formed the core group of the FNDR and served as the electoral instrument for the president, most members of the National Assembly, and the majority of elected local government officials. It included youth and women's groups and was closely tied to organized labor. Its ability to coordinate and govern was, however, continually compromised by internal factions. Its members held differing images of Socialism, disagreed strongly about its application, and had varying reactions to the president's slide from Socialist revolutionary toward reluctant free marketeer.

The party was temporarily dissolved following Ratsiraka's defeat in the February 1993 presidential elections. AREMA did not participate in the June 1993 elections to the National Assembly. By the mid-1990s AREMA was reconstituted by Ratsiraka, and the party served as his vehicle in the successful 1996 presidential elections. The party's national strength was demonstrated in the 1998 National Assembly elections when it fielded candidates in every constituency and won four times as many seats as its closest rival.

The party was badly weakened, but not destroyed, when Ratsiraka and many of his major political supporters chose exile in 2002. Before 2002 National Assembly elections the party split, one faction calling for a boycott while another fielded 94 candidates. In the elections the AREMA candidates won slightly less than 5 percent of the popular vote, the most of any opposition party, and captured three seats.

TORCH

(Leader-Fanilo)

Leader-Fanilo was organized in 1992 as a party of "nonpoliticians." Its founder and was Herizo Razafimahaleo, a businessman who had previously served as an adviser to Ratsiraka. In the 1993 National Assembly elections it captured 13 seats. The party was one of the more powerful members of the coalition of parties that regularly opposed then-president Zafy.

The party maintained close ties to Ratsiraka. In 1996, for example, Razafimahaleo received 15 percent of the vote in the first round of the 1996 presidential balloting, and in the second round he asked his supporters to back Ratsiraka. Razafimahaleo was subsequently chosen as a deputy prime minister, and three other party members received cabinet portfolios.

In 1998 Leader-Fanilo was the only party other than AREMA to contest all of the National Assembly seats. It won 16 seats, making it the second largest in the Assembly. The party opposes Ravalomanana and, like its ally AREMA, has seen its appeal decline precipitously. In the 2001 presidential election Razafimahaleo received only 4 percent of the popular vote. In the 2002 National Assembly elections it fielded only 74 candidates and captured only two seats.

REBIRTH OF THE SOCIAL DEMOCRATIC PARTY

(Rénaissance du I Parti Social-Démocratique; RPSD)

Formerly known as the Rally for Social Democracy, the RPSD, which has roots going back to the former president Philibert Tsiranana's PSD, was established in 1993. A social democratic party, often critical of Ratsiraka, it was supportive of President Ravalomanana. The RPSD won 8 seats in 1993, 11 in 1998, and 5 in 2002.

NATIONAL UNION FOR DEVELOPMENT AND DEMOCRACY

(Union Nationale pour le Developpement et la Démocratie; UNDD)

The UNDD was created by Albert Zafy in 1991 to oppose the Ratsiraka regime, which it denounced as despotic and corrupt. Its electoral slogan was simple: "Ratsiraka out." With support from Catholic and Protestant church groups, it promised to effect a peaceful democratic revolution.

The UNDD became a core member of the anti-Ratsiraka Coalition of Living Forces. In May 1993, following his election as Madagascar's president, Zafy resigned as UNDD's president but accepted the title of "honorary president" and remained the party's leader.

Zafy's impeachment and subsequent loss in the presidential elections and the party's unsuccessful opposition to the 1998 constitution left the party's future, at best, uncertain. The UNDD boycotted the 1998 National Assembly elections. In 2001 Zafy received only 5 percent of the popular vote, and in 2002 the party captured no Assembly seats.

Minor Political Parties

Madagascar has had as many as 150 different parties active at the same time. Usually less than a dozen of these offer candidates in more than one province. Asa Vita Ifampitsanara (Work Finished by Solidarity, AVI), a moderate party founded by former prime minister Norbert Ratsirhonana, provides a good example of the rapid rise and decline of parties in Madagascar. The party was created in 1998 and won 14 seats in that year's elections to the National Assembly. By 2002, however, most of its supporters had moved elsewhere: the party fielded candidates in only two provinces, won no seats, and retained a core of members only in the city of Antananarivo.

Toamasina Tonga Saina (TTS) is organized only in Toamasina Province and, even there, is found almost exclusively in the city of the same name. This small party, which successfully elected two members to the National Assembly in the 2002 elections, is notable

primarily because its leader, Roland Ratsiraka, the mayor of the city of Toamasina, is the nephew of the exiled former president and is sometimes considered as his in-country spokesman.

Other Political Forces

CHRISTIAN CHURCHES

Many of Madagascar's churches are organized in the politically active, staunchly democratic National Council of Christian Churches. During the early 1990s they supported Zafy and the movement for democratic reform. In 1998 they opposed the new constitution, which they claimed would create a presidential dictatorship. Their opposition is believed by many observers to be the major reason why the new constitution was adopted by only the slimmest majority of voters.

MILITARY

Madagascar's military, including the regular army, gendarmes, and a presidential guard, have long been highly politicized. The military overthrew the First Republic and installed its own leaders, including Ratsiraka as president. During these years the military was responsible for internal security and frequently turned its guns on political protesters. More recently, the military's role has been less overt, but if strife breaks out, it could again become the final political arbiter.

FEDERALIST MOVEMENT

A movement that has long been in existence to devolve some government powers to provincial and local authorities apparently has the support of President Ravalomanana.

NEWSPAPERS

Press censorship has often been the rule in Madagascar. During the Third Republic, however, Madagascar has enjoyed a free press. Unfortunately, illiteracy, poverty, and the isolation of many communities have limited its readership.

National Prospects

It is difficult to predict Madagascar's prospects. The tumultuous nature of Madagascar's politics reached the point of violence following the most recent presidential election. Since then, however, National

Assembly and local elections have been peaceful. TIM's ability to field candidates, and win Assembly and local contests throughout the country, is another positive sign. The economy may be the primary determinant of Madagascar's future. Ravalomanana is continuing his predecessor's efforts to diversify the economy and to obtain international aid and debt forgiveness. He achieved important successes in his first term as president. For example, in 2004 the World Bank and International Monetary Fund agreed to write off about half of the country's $4 billion external debt, and the United States in 2005 made Madagascar the first recipient of a program aimed at providing assistance to countries pursuing democratic and market reforms.

Further Reading

Allen, Philip M. *Madagascar: Conflicts of Authority in the Great Island.* San Francisco: Westview Press, 1995.

Sandbrook, Richard. "Transitions without Consolidation: Democratization in Six African Cases." *Third World Journal* 71, 1 (1996): 69–88.

REPUBLIC OF MALAWI
(Dziko ia Malai)

By Christopher J. Lee, M.A., Ph.D.

Malawi is a country of some 12 million people (2005 est.). In the late 19th century the territory that is now Malawi became a British protectorate, alternatively named the Nyasaland Districts Protectorate, British Central Africa Protectorate, and Nyasaland (1907–53). In 1953 Malawi became part of the British-ruled Federation of Rhodesia (present-day Zimbabwe and Zambia) and Nyasaland. After a period of active African opposition to both the federation and colonial power, the former was dissolved in 1963. Malawi formerly achieved independence the following year, on July 6, 1964.

In 1966 Malawi became a one-party republic under President Dr. Hastings Banda, who was named president for life in 1971. The political system was dominated by Banda and his Malawi Congress Party (MCP) until 1994, when internal pressures forced the regime to hold multiparty elections and adopt a new constitution. The rule of the Banda regime finally came to an end when Bakili Muluzi won the presidency by defeating Banda in 1994.

The System of Government

Malawi is a multiparty democratic republic with a unicameral legislature.

EXECUTIVE

Executive power is exercised by the president. The president is both head of state and head of the government and is elected for a five-year term by universal adult suffrage. The government consists of the president, two vice presidents, and a cabinet comprising several dozen members. In 2004 Bingu wa Mutharika of the ruling United Democratic Front (UDF) was elected president, though some observers considered the election unfair.

LEGISLATURE

Parliament comprises the unicameral National Assembly, which has 193 members elected for five-year terms. The speaker is chosen from among the members of the Assembly. The Assembly also has the power to change the constitution with a two-thirds vote. In the mid-1990s there were plans to establish an upper legislative house, but these plans were scrapped in 2001.

The president has the right to refuse the assent of any bill in the Assembly. In the event that a bill is resubmitted and passed within a six-month period, the president has the right to dissolve the legislature and call new elections. Both constitutionally and in the view of the party system, the legislature is dominated by the executive branch.

JUDICIARY

The court system in Malawi includes the Supreme Court of Appeal, the High Court, and magistrate's courts. Formally, the highest court is the Supreme Court, which hears appeals against decisions of the High Court. It is headed by the chief justice, who is a presidential appointee. The High Court has full jurisdiction over civil and criminal cases. It consists of a

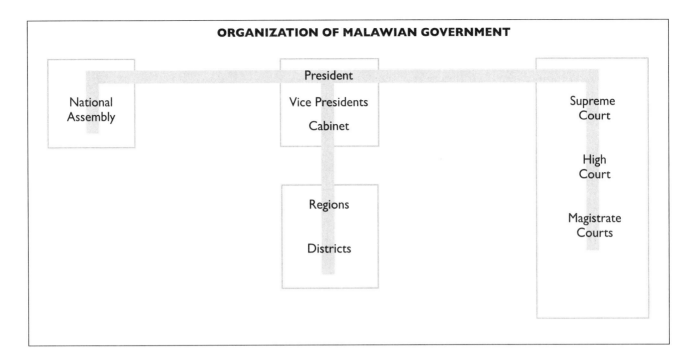

ORGANIZATION OF MALAWIAN GOVERNMENT

chief justice and five puisne judges. Magistrate's courts handle criminal and civil matters at the regional and local levels. Traditional courts were established in 1970 by the Banda regime and were presided over by local chiefs. These were abolished by the 1994 constitution.

REGIONAL AND LOCAL GOVERNMENT

Malawi is divided into three major areas, the Southern, the Central, and the Northern Regions. Each is represented in the national cabinet by an appointed regional minister. The regions, in turn, are divided into a total of 27 districts that include the cities of Blantyre and Lilongwe, the municipality of Zomba, and several towns. While local councils are elected, all are supervised by the Ministry of Local Government, which also controls the allocations of money to all levels.

Elections since 1994 have revealed regional and ethnic differences in the support of the major political parties. The UDF has had its strongest showing in the heavily populated south, whereas former President Banda's MCP maintains support in the center, and the Alliance for Democracy (AFORD) holds the north.

The Electoral System

Deputies to the National Assembly are directly elected in single-member districts. The ballot is secret, although the high level of illiteracy requires voters to show their preferences by placing slips of paper in a separate box for each candidate. Eligibility for voting is universal for those age 18 or older.

Elections in 1971 and 1976 were uncontested, but in 1978, 47 of 87 electoral districts were contested. Although all candidates were from the MCP, no fewer than 31 sitting MPs were replaced. President Banda stated that he would use the election to reshuffle his cabinet and was pleased with the defeat of so many MPs. The 1978 elections was Malawi's first experiment with electoral competition. However, it was regarded with skepticism by Western observers and opposition parties, since it provided Malawians a choice among competing personalities, not policies.

Elections held in 1981 and 1987 followed a similar pattern. In 1981, 75 of 101 seats were contested, and, in 1987, 69 of 112 seats. Again, all candidates were MCP members. In 1983 and 1984 Banda appointed a number of additional members to the National Assembly, bringing the total to 124 seats. In 1992 elections took place for an enlarged legislature that now consisted of 141 seats; 91 were contested as 62 former members lost their seats. Banda also nominated 10 members. The government claimed a voter turnout of 80 percent, but other observers gave much lower figures.

The most significant election in recent history was the national referendum on multiparty democracy in 1993. Although the government tried to disrupt the process and the activities of opposition groups, the measure passed with over 63 percent of the vote. Banda opposed the immediate creation of a government of national unity but agreed to establish a multiparty national executive council to oversee the transition to multiparty democracy and to draft a new constitution. Legislative elections were scheduled to take place in 1994. It is widely believed that the Banda regime agreed to the referendum after international donors cut economic aid in response to the government's human rights violations.

The country's first multiparty elections were held in May 1994. The elections brought almost 3 million Malawians to the polls and resulted in the election of Bakili Muluzi (UDF) as president with 1.4 million votes (47 percent). His party also captured 84 seats in parliament. Dr. Hastings Banda and the MCP came in second with 1 million votes (33.5 percent) and 55 parliamentary seats, while Chakufwa Chihana (AFORD) came in third with 550,000 votes (18.6 percent) and 36 parliamentary seats. Elections in two of the legislative districts were invalidated but were later repeated to give the UDF and MCP one additional seat each. Turnout in elections in the early 21st century has been modest, with usually slightly more than half the electorate participating.

The Party System

Dr. Hastings Banda and the Malawi Congress Party ruled Malawi from 1964 to 1994, making both Banda and his party one of the most enduring political institutions in Africa. Between 1963 and 1993 all opposition parties to the MCP were banned. But since 1993, when opposition parties were legalized, several parties have been formed. In addition to the MCP, there are two other major political parties in Malawi: the Alliance for Democracy (AFORD) and the United Democratic Front (UDF). The UDF emerged victorious in the 1994 elections and held power continuously into the early 21st century.

Despite recent political changes in the country, it is important to place the political future of the country in the historical context of the autocratic rule of Dr. Hastings Banda and the Malawi Congress Party.

Major Political Parties
MALAWI CONGRESS PARTY (MCP)

HISTORY

The MCP was established in 1959 under Banda's leadership to fight for the end of the federation with Rhodesia and for independence from British colonial rule. The party's early success stemmed from Banda's ability to secure independence and create successful programs of economic development. From 1965 until the mid-1990s political opposition was virtually nonexistent. The party suffered losses following the legalization of opposition parties, but in the 2004 parliamentary elections it emerged as the largest party in the National Assembly.

ORGANIZATION

The party was more of an organization for promoting support for the regime than a forum for debating policy issues. Officially, party policy was made by the annual party convention composed of party officials from national, regional, and district levels, members of parliament, some traditional chiefs, chairmen of the district councils, and representatives of other organizations.

In the past, the convention's role was at best advisory and at worst ceremonial. But, given the party's poor electoral showing in the mid-1990s and the passing of Banda, the party has been reorganized in a more democratic fashion.

POLICY

Banda was responsible for setting MCP policy while alive. In foreign affairs, Malawi was distinguished from other sub-Saharan Africa states by its willingness to remain on good terms with South Africa during that country's apartheid era.

Despite its relationship to South Africa, Malawi joined the South African Development Co-ordination Conference (SADCC) in 1980 to decrease its economic dependence on South Africa. Internally, Banda sought to encourage the growth of private industry, especially commercial agriculture and small-scale industrial development. These ventures were financed and promoted through foreign investment and by the Malawi Development Corporation (MDC), a state-owned development organization.

MEMBERSHIP

All Malawi adults were required to join the MCP, but few took an active part. It was a strictly disciplined organization that was reorganized several times to exclude threats to party integrity. Although recent political changes have reduced the size of the party, it remains a major political force and maintains a large following. No membership figures are available.

UNITED DEMOCRATIC FRONT (UDF)

HISTORY
The UDF was formed in September 1992 as an opposition group to the Banda government. The party was organized by Bakili Muluzi and other former MCP members who favored political and economic reforms. Together with the Alliance for Democracy (AFORD), the UDF was instrumental in promoting the referendum on multiparty democracy and constitutional reform in 1993 and the multiparty elections that followed in 1994.

ORGANIZATION
The UDF is well financed and organized, advantages that derive from the fact that much of the party leadership consists of business leaders and former MCP government officials. The MCP links helped the party to establish an instant national foothold that carried it to victory in 1994. The party is especially strong in the south, but superior party organization and financing have also given it a solid presence in the traditional MCP stronghold of the Central Region.

POLICY
One of the party's principal issues has been the promotion of democratic and political reforms. In this respect it differs little from AFORD. But since the party does have closer links to commercial interests, there is a greater emphasis on the role that the private sector plays in this process. The UDF has sought political and financial support from numerous European nations and solicited international organizations to help liberalize the economy. The party is fully in support of IMF policies of privatization, tariff cuts, and currency devaluations.

MEMBERSHIP
Party membership consists largely of individuals who formerly supported the MCP. As Banda's grip on the government and economy created intolerable conditions in the country, many MCP members moved to support the newly created UDF in 1992. Many of the party's members are younger people who felt that democratic reforms were the only alternative to the autocratic rule that was quickly coming to an end in Malawi and the rest of Africa. The UDF's support of economic liberalization has also made it popular among the business class, including most of the country's Asian population. No membership figures are available.

FINANCING
The party derives much of its financial support from its members, who include many prominent Malawians in commerce and government. The party's strong political position and its promotion of internal reforms have also brought it international financial support from governments and institutions that are in sympathy with these policy positions.

LEADERSHIP
In the early 21st century the party was led by President Bingu wa Mutharika. But cracks began to emerge in the party, and soon after being elected president in 2004, he embarked upon a campaign to stamp out corruption. Three officials in the party were convicted of treason for carrying guns to a meeting with the president (they were later pardoned), and in 2005 Mutharika resigned from the party, claiming that his reform policies were being met with opposition from within the party. He formed a new party, the Democratic Progressive Party. Mutharika's defection casts doubt on his own political future as well as that of the UDF.

ALLIANCE FOR DEMOCRACY (AFORD)

HISTORY
AFORD was formed in September 1992 under the leadership of Chakufwa Chihana shortly before the organization of the UDF. Together with the UDF it pressured the Banda regime into the political reforms that came to fruition in 1994. After the formation of the party in 1992, it absorbed the membership of the Malawi Freedom Movement (MAFREMO), another outspoken political opposition group.

ORGANIZATION
The party, as organized by Chihana, sought to be truly national in scope, attracting support from the country's different regions. Although its strength lies mainly in the north, AFORD has brought many of its key members from the Central and Southern Regions. Despite these efforts, the party still suffers considerable organizational weakness due to financial and institutional deficiencies.

POLICY
AFORD was originally organized around a platform that sought to implement multiparty democracy with a mixed economy. During the elections of 1994, the party also identified itself with moral issues such as

human rights and political freedom. While AFORD supports IMF liberalization and donor aid programs, it retains stronger links to labor movements and hence a more social democratic vision of democracy than either of its rivals.

One of the important positions of the party with respect to the democratization process is that it sees itself as the true representative of democracy in Malawi. Unlike the MCP or the UDF, AFORD's members have always operated in opposition to the Malawian political system. This distinction led Chihana to attack the UDF as "recycled politicians" and members of the "Malawi Congress Party B" during election campaigns. This legacy also led to Chihana's refusal to unite with the UDF in a broad political coalition against the MCP. Yet, after a vitriolic campaign and the UDF victory in 1994, AFORD joined the ruling party to resolve the country's many socioeconomic and political problems. Nevertheless, in the 1999 election AFORD ran on a joint slate with the MCP to defeat the UDF.

MEMBERSHIP

AFORD is distinct from the UDF and the MCP in that it has drawn its leadership from outside the Malawian political system. Its membership also reflects this, in that it appeals to those citizens who have been peripheral to the national political and economic system. As such, much of the party's membership is based on ethnic and regional affiliation with the more isolated north. Moreover, given Chihana's career as a trade union leader and the party's strident positions on human rights and political freedom, it has been popular in urban areas among workers, religious groups, students, intellectuals, and journalists. No membership figures are available.

FINANCING

Without strong links to the political and economic institutions of the country, AFORD has had greater difficulty in raising money than its competitors. Much of the party's funds seem to come from loyal supporters.

Minor Political Parties

There were eight political parties authorized to participate in the 1994 elections. The impact of the smaller parties has generally been negligible, though in the 2004 elections the National Democratic Alliance outpaced AFORD, winning eight seats to AFORD's six, and a coalition of several parties captured 27 of the National Assembly's 193 seats.

Other Political Forces

Internal forces outside of organized political movements have had a minimal role in shaping the nation's political system. The military has remained subservient to the state. Although the country contains several ethnic groups, the only conflict to arise occurred when the capital was moved from Zombe to Lilongwe in 1975. This caused resentment among ethnic groups in the more prosperous Southern Region of the country. They saw the decision to move the capital to the center of the country as bias toward the Chewa people, whose language has become dominant throughout the country. The role of labor and religious factions in political matters has had some impact, particularly during the transition of the mid-1990s, though party politics has frequently taken precedent over these elements of civil society. External influences, particularly international donor agencies, have had an impact on the country.

National Prospects

Despite the claims of its opponents, the Banda regime was responsible for creating economic and political stability during its period of rule. For this reason it maintained fairly high levels of popular support. More recently, however, internal and external factors have significantly altered Malawi's political and socioeconomic situation. Political change in South Africa affected Malawi's economic and security status in southern Africa. As the charismatic Hastings Banda began to fade from the political scene, the creation of a competitive multiparty system became a logical next step.

The election of 1994 signalled a major watershed in Malawi's political history. The victory of Bakili Muluzi as a freely elected president marked the beginning of a new era in Malawi in which the country has struggled to create a new identity and direction after decades of one-party rule. Despite the massive political changes, the internal obstacles to political and socioeconomic transformation remain tremendous. Lack of infrastructure and natural resources and massive poverty will undoubtedly plague future regimes, and corruption—being combated by Mutharika—has been rife. The government continues to face the daunting task of rebuilding political and social institutions, many of which have collapsed or still operate under the distortions and corruption created by decades of Banda's influence. HIV/AIDS—which has helped reduce life expectancy to under 40 and prompted the government in 2004 to announce a program to provide free anti-viral drugs to AIDS patients—and widespread poverty also persist as significant social issues.

Further Reading

Englund, H., ed. *A Democracy of Chameleons: Politics and Culture in the New Malawi*. Uppsala, Sweden: Nordiska Afrikainstitutet, 2002.

Pachai, B. *Malawi: History of a Nation*. London: Longman, 1973.

Short, Philip. *The Rise of Nationalism in Central Africa*. London: Oxford University Press, 1974.

Williams, T. David. *Malawi: The Politics of Despair*. Ithaca, N.Y.: Cornell University Press, 1978.

FEDERATION OF MALAYSIA
(Persekutuan Tanan Malaysia)

By Peter Dawson
Revised by Carlo Bonura, Jr.
Further revision by Joel Selway

Malaysia comprises the 11 states of the Malay Peninsula and the states of Sabah and Sarawak on the island of Borneo, along with a federal territory with three components: Kuala Lumpur, the capital, Labuan Island, and Putrajay. The country has a population of some 24 million (2005 est.), of whom some three-fifths are Malay and other indigenous, one-fourth Chinese, and about one-fourteenth Indian. It achieved independence from British colonial rule on August 31, 1957, as the Malayan Federation, then consisting of the states of the peninsula only. In September 1963 Sabah, Sarawak, and Singapore joined the federation, but Singapore seceded on August 9, 1965. The federal territory of Kuala Lumpur was created in 1974.

The System of Government

Malaysia is a federal constitutional monarchy. The present constitution has been effective from 1957, with only limited subsequent alterations. It provides for a parliamentary and cabinet system closely modeled on that of the United Kingdom.

EXECUTIVE

The head of state is the Yang di-Pertuan Agong (or king), who serves for a term of five years. The office rotates according to precedence among the royal rulers of nine of the 13 states of the federation, but accession to the office is confirmed by election among these nine rulers. The office thus constitutes a unique combination of monarchic, rotation, and elective principles. Although formally the head of government, the king is in practice a constitutional monarch with only very limited discretionary power.

The effective head of government is the Perdana Mentri (prime minister), working with and through the Juma'ah Mentri (cabinet). The king appoints as prime minister the member of the Dewan Rakyat (House of Representatives) likely to command the confidence of a majority in the House, normally the leader of the majority party. Members of the cabinet are appointed by the king from either of the two houses of Parliament on the advice of the prime minister. The cabinet is required by the constitution to be collectively responsible to parliament. In June 2002 Asia's longest serving prime minister, Mahathir bin Mohamad, announced he was stepping down as head of the largest party in the ruling coalition, UMNO. After 22 years under Mahathir, the population—including members of the ruling party, UMNO—was shocked at the announcement. UMNO party elders persuaded Mahathir to continue until the following year. In October 2003 Abdullah Badawi was sworn in as Malaysia's fifth prime minister since independence.

LEGISLATURE

The legislature consists of the king and the two *majlis* (councils): the Dewan Negara (Senate) and the

ORGANIZATION OF MALAYSIAN GOVERNMENT

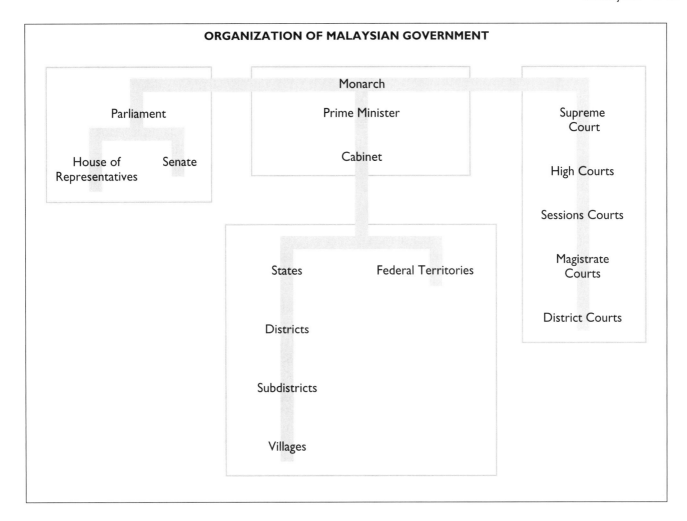

Dewan Rakyat (House of Representatives). The king, however, takes no active part in the proceedings of parliament. The Senate, which is the less powerful of the two houses, has some 70 members. Each of the 13 state legislatures elects two members, while the king, acting on advice from the prime minister, appoints an additional 44, including two to represent the federal territory.

Senators serve for three year-terms (they may serve a maximum of two terms), their term being unaffected by a dissolution of the House of Representatives. Senators tend to be prominent older figures in public life, representative of occupational and ethnic groupings, although in recent years Senate seats have sometimes been used to groom younger, rising politicians. Despite the minority group of territorial representatives, the Senate has never been active in promoting states' rights against those of the federation.

The House of Representatives, which changes in size, had at the 2004 elections 219 members directly elected from single-member constituencies by simple majorities. The minimum qualifying age for member-

ship is 21. Dual membership of the two federal houses is forbidden as is simultaneous representation of two federal constituencies, but several federal legislators also hold seats or office in their state assemblies. The maximum life of the House of Representatives is five years, but it may be dissolved at any time by the king acting upon the request of the prime minister. The king does have the power, never used so far, to refuse such a request.

A simple majority in both houses is sufficient to carry legislation. The Senate has a delaying power of one month over money bills and of one year over other bills. Most constitutional amendments require a two-thirds majority, while certain articles of the constitution cannot be amended without the consent of the Majlis Raja Raja (Conference of Rulers). The Majlis Raja Raja, which meets three or four times a year, comprises the 13 rulers of the states of the federation, including the nine hereditary royal rulers and the governors of Penang, Malacca, Sabah, and Sarawak. It acts as a third house of parliament on amendments to certain sections of the constitution (especially Article

153, which protects the position of Malays), the extension of Islamic religious practices, and the making of certain major state appointments (such as judges of the Supreme Court), as well as on legislation affecting the position of rulers and the boundaries of states. The nine royal rulers, sitting within the Conference of Rulers, are responsible also for the election of the king and his deputy.

Since independence, the government coalition, the National Front, dominated by the United Malays National Organization, has always held an absolute majority of the seats in the House of Representatives. Opposition groups have achieved only limited success

JUDICIARY

The Supreme Court is the highest judicial authority in Malaysia. It has the power to interpret the constitution and to adjudicate in disputes between states or between any state and the federal government. It is also the highest court of appeal in criminal cases for the federation. Beneath the Supreme Court are two High Courts, one for West and one for East Malaysia, which have original jurisdiction in their areas in both civil and criminal cases as well as appeal from subordinate courts. The lord president, who heads the Supreme Court, is appointed by the king, who must act on the advice of the prime minister after consulting the Conference of Rulers. Other senior judges are similarly appointed with the lord president also being consulted. The independence of the judiciary is maintained by this means as well as by the stipulation of legal qualifications, a high security of tenure and remuneration, and restrictions on discussion of judicial conduct in the legislatures. In numerous cases, the judiciary has displayed a very high standard of independence from political influence. The legal system is largely based on English common law.

REGIONAL AND LOCAL GOVERNMENT

Each of Malaysia's 13 states is governed by a *mentri besar* (chief minister) responsible to a unicameral legislative assembly whose members are directly elected, except in Sabah, which retains a limited number of nominated members. The relations among the state ruler or governor, the chief minister, and the assembly are broadly similar to those that prevail at the federal level among the king, the prime minister, and parliament. But the powers of states are limited, being confined principally to land and natural-resource management and the oversight of local government. Sabah and Sarawak, however, enjoy some powers not available to the states of West Malaysia. The federal government is the main taxing authority and controls the borrowing powers of states so that apart from land revenue, states enjoy no significant sources of income. Since state legislatures are now dominated by political parties that are members of the governing coalition at the federal level, a further degree of state and federal harmonization is achieved.

The Electoral System

All members of the House of Representatives are directly elected by a simple majority within each of the 219 single-member constituencies. Of the 70 members of the Senate, 26 are elected by their state legislatures with 44 members appointed. All citizens age 21 or older (other than those detained as being of "unsound mind" or serving a prison sentence or who have been sentenced to death or imprisonment of more than 12 months) are eligible to vote by secret ballot in elections for the House of Representatives or legislative assemblies. Malaysia has adopted a simple plurality system more commonly known as first-past-the-post. Candidates with more votes than any other are elected in a series of single-member constituencies. For administrative purposes, each parliamentary constituency represents a registration area. Each registration area is broken up into smaller units known as polling districts, which are subsequently broken up into subunits known as localities.

The Election Commission conducts elections and prepares and annually revises electoral rolls. It is also responsible every 8 to 10 years for reviewing and recommending changes to the boundaries of state and national constituencies. Registration of voters is neither automatic nor compulsory. The ballot paper in each constituency lists all the candidates and their party symbols; voters indicate their choice by marking an X. Votes are counted centrally within each constituency in the presence of candidates and their agents. Turnout is usually above 60 percent. The system is in the main fair and equitable, although various technical factors relating to voter registration and constituency delimitation together with the effects of the simple-majority method have produced, in all national elections, a highly disproportionate number of seats for the governing coalition.

The Party System

ORIGINS OF THE PARTIES

The most distinctive feature of Malaysian political parties is that they are communally based, but a second major feature is a tendency toward consolidation and coalition. The communal divisions not only are racial but are also reinforced by language, religion, culture, and, to a considerable extent, economic role. With Malays constituting more than half of the total population, Chinese approximately one-quarter, and people of Indian descent about one-fourteenth, parties that represent the interests of these groups are assured of substantial support. The three major communally based parties—the United Malays National Organization, Malayan Chinese Association, and Malayan Indian Congress (UMNO, MCA, and MIC)—all came into existence in the late 1940s specifically to defend their respective ethnic communities against threats perceived in the various constitutional proposals advanced by the colonial government. A coalition they had formed well before independence in 1957 was formally registered as the Alliance Party in 1958. The Alliance collapsed in the wake of communal rioting after the 1969 election, which had shown a growth in support for non-Alliance parties and thus an erosion of the claim by the Alliance to represent a national interest.

After a period of emergency rule, during which electoral and parliamentary activity was suspended, the coalition was reconstituted in 1971 as the National Front (Barisan Nasional; BN). At the same time, it was broadened to include several smaller parties, previously in opposition, so that the Malay and Chinese communities were now represented by more than one party within the front. The United Malays National Organization (UMNO) has always been the dominant participant. With intercommunal harmony the overriding aim of government throughout Malaysia's history, the BN has achieved this aim by private interparty compromise. However, resentment among some sections of the population against this process of elite adjustment has sustained support for several opposition parties.

THE PARTIES IN LAW

The constitution makes no reference to political parties, but under separate legislation (the Societies Act of 1966) all organizations seeking to contest elections must be formally registered. On a few occasions, the refusal of registration has effectively suppressed the activities of some smaller opposition parties. A 1981 amendment to the Societies Act requires all clubs, societies, and associations to register as either political or nonpolitical. This has been seen as limiting the capacity of pressure groups to campaign and lobby to secure changes in government policy. From time to time, security and sedition laws have been used to detain members of opposition parties either because of suspected communist links or because their activities were deemed to be subversive. Parties receive no direct, formal state support. Any qualified election candidate whose nomination has been properly made can be included on the ballot whether or not he or she is a representative of a political party.

PARTY ORGANIZATION

Malaysian parties are too numerous, too different in size, and in several cases too limited to particular regions for many substantial generalizations to be possible. The parties are permanent associations sustained by membership dues and private donations. Most maintain a three-tiered organization at the constituency, state, and national levels. They are identifiable principally by communal characteristics, although different parties drawing their membership from the same community may be distinguished by socioeconomic and, to a limited degree, ideological differences. The major support for the Democratic Action Party, for example, comes from the poorer stratum of Chinese, while the Malayan Chinese Association is more substantially supported by the more affluent. The participation of the major parties in the National Front and the dependence of all—except the United Malays National Organization—on that membership for access to Cabinet office and the consequent benefits to their communities necessitate keeping close central control over subordinate levels. A major instrument of this control for parties within the National Front is the patronage exercised by the chief ministers of states. Although the principal parties hold annual conferences at which major policy issues are determined and national officers are chosen, these processes are usually closely and successfully regulated. Nevertheless, despite this consistent pattern of central and elite domination, some opportunity remains for local leaders to develop local support. For the wealthier, especially within Chinese and urban Malay communities, contributions to community projects, such as schools and places of worship, may generate prestige and power. For all aspirants to party office or candidacy, the role of broker representing constituents' interests within the multiple and many-layered processes of governmental bureaucracy is universally expected. Thus, education and experience of working within bureaucracies are important factors determining election at the local level.

CAMPAIGNING

A fear of threats to public order has led the government, in recent elections, to ban large public rallies by any party. The preferred method of campaigning has been to hold meetings within private houses at which a largely invited audience participates in a process akin to a seminar, with an address by a speaker followed by questions and discussion. This method, where it is used, permits issues to be presented in a way that is specific to particular areas or occupational groups. In addition, door-to-door canvassing occurs, and pamphlets and posters are widely distributed and displayed although their influence, if any, is difficult to assess. The press has an important role. Seven newspapers, published in local languages as well as in English, have an influence that is generally felt to be substantial, their effect being usually to enhance support for candidates representing the ruling National Front.

It is difficult to determine accurately the full expenditure of parties during election campaigns. Local party branches are in all cases dependent on central party funds derived either from voluntary contributions or from levies on holders of well-paid posts that have been secured by party intervention. The larger parties, most of which are in the National Front, are by far the richer and can thus readily afford the costs of publicity, transport for party workers, and other necessary expenses.

There is usually no close national party control of local campaigns. With the larger parties, preexisting party cohesion encourages a uniformity of approach, although the fact that state assembly elections are held at the same time as those for the national legislature will often ensure that wholly local issues may be promoted in a manner that conflicts with the national party's line.

INDEPENDENT VOTERS

The existence of the National Front as an electoral, as well as a governing, coalition may present some voters with a dilemma when the National Front-endorsed candidate is not from their own ethnic community. In that event, if a candidate from their own community is standing for an opposition party, a conflict arises between the desire to vote for the coalition that almost inevitably enjoys a national majority and is regarded as the source of many material benefits and the wish to

assert communal solidarity. There has been some evidence of differential voting for national and for state assemblymen.

Major Political Parties

NATIONAL FRONT

(Barisan Nasional; BN)

This interparty organization is broadly known by its Malay title, Barisan Nasional, or BN. Although registered for legal purposes as a political party, the BN is an electoral and governing coalition comprising more than a dozen and has no organizational structure of its own. In the early 21st century its constituent parties were (in general order of strength) the United Malays National Organization, Malaysian Chinese Association, United Traditional Bumiputra Party, Gerakan, Malaysian Indian Congress, Sarawak Dayak People's Party, Sarawak United People's Party, United Sabah Party, Sarawak Progressive Democrat Party, United Pasokmomogun Kadazandusun Murut Organization, Sabah Progressive Party, People's Progressive Party, the Sabah People's Union, and the Liberal Democrat Party. Most—but not all—of the parties have representation in the legislature. The BN, in some ways, acts like a government body. Parties regularly join and leave the organization in such a manner that the BN seems responsive to voters' demands. Nowhere is this more apparent than in Sabah. Prior to 1985 the Sabah People's Union (PBRS), part of the BN machinery, was the most dominant party in Sabah. Following a split where an ex-PBRS politician set up his own party—the United Sabah Party—the BN began to lose seats in both state and general elections in Sabah. Consequently, the BN soon brought the PBS on board, thus maintaining its power on Sabah. Today, the once fiercely contending Sabahnese parties are both members of the encompassing BN organization.

UNITED MALAYS NATIONAL ORGANIZATION

(Pertubohan Kebangsaan Melayu Bersatu; UMNO)

HISTORY

The UMNO was founded in May 1946 by Dato Onn bin Ja'afar, a leader in the effort in the country's independence movement, to resist the introduction by the British colonial administration of a unitary form of government throughout peninsular Malaya. The British efforts were seen by Malays and especially by their hereditary rulers as detrimental to Malay interests. The UMNO was not formally registered as a political party until April 1950. Throughout Malaysia's history, it has been the largest national party and the dominant party of government. All four of Malaysia's prime ministers since 1957 have been the leaders of UMNO. Onn's attempts in 1950 to widen UMNO membership to include non-Malays and to introduce other reforms were strongly opposed and led to his resignation and replacement as party president in 1951 by Tunku Abdul Rahman. An ad hoc coalition between UMNO and the MCA to fight the Kuala Lumpur municipal Malaysian Chinese Association elections in 1952 led to the establishment a year later of the Alliance coalition that also included the MIC. Tunku Abdul Rahman became Malaysian Indian Congress prime minister following the first general election in 1955 and led the country to independence in 1957, becoming independent Malaya's first prime minister. Throughout the 1960s his attempts to hold the Alliance together and placate ultranationalist Malays in his own Alliance Party weakened his position. The decline in support for both UMNO and the Alliance revealed by the 1969 election results and the communal rioting that followed led to Rahman's resignation, both as prime minister and as party president, and his replacement by Tun Abdul Razak.

After a period of emergency rule during which parliament was suspended, Razak was able to put together a wider governing coalition of nine parties, including some that had previously been in opposition. This Barisan Nasional was registered as a political party on June 1, 1974. In the parliamentary elections that followed, the front won 135 out of the 154 seats. Other major measures taken during the emergency period included the introduction of the New Economic Policy (NEP), which sought to promote substantially the economic advancement of the Malay population, and the passing of a constitutional amendment that declared seditious any questioning of Malay privileges, the status of Malay as the national language, and such issues as citizenship and the position of traditional rulers. Important controversies were thus barred from public debate, even in parliament, and the grounds on which opposition parties might base their criticisms were denied to them.

The death of Tun Abdul Razak in 1976 and the succession of Hussein Onn were followed by a brief period of factional fighting within UMNO. In part, the conflict was between older members of the party, who had been associates of Tunku Abdul Rahman, and younger members, technocratically inclined, who had been brought to prominence by Tun Abdul Razak. The outcome involved the arrest of several of the latter group for alleged Communist activities, although much of the evidence, including their confessions, appeared fragile. At the same time, others of Tun Abdul Razak's protégés, untainted by any Communist association, survived. Of this group, Dr. Mahathir bin Mohamad, who in 1970 had been expelled from the party's supreme council, was appointed to the deputy premiership over the heads of more senior men. A major casualty of this period was Datuk Harun, the chief minister of Selangor. His control over the massive patronage of his state and his support in the youth wing of the party constituted a threat to the leadership of Razak and then of Datuk Hussein Onn. He was charged with corruption in late 1975. Over the next two years, he was successively stripped of office, expelled from the party, and tried and sentenced to a term of imprisonment, thus demonstrating Hussein Onn's growing control of the party. But in August 1982 he was granted a royal pardon and resumed party activity.

In July 1981 Hussein Onn was succeeded as prime minister by Mahathir, who within a year led his party into a general election, the results of which reemphasized UMNO's continuing dominance in the political life of Malaysia. The UMNO general assembly reelected him five successive times as party president, and he remained prime minister of Mahathir until 2003. Despite Mahathir's long tenure, his leadership of UMNO did not go uncontested. His largest threat came from within the party in 1986 and 1987. The beginnings of UMNO's "split" arose in the general assembly of 1984 when, as minister of education, Dutak Musa Hitam successfully defeated Tengku Razaleigh for the position of party deputy president. In late 1985 Mahathir chose to offer Tengku Tazaleigh the powerful position of minister of finance within the prime minister's cabinet. Dutak Musa Hitam resisted the move and saw it as a direct affront to his status within UMNO. As the crisis progressed, both Dutak Musa Hitam and Tengku Razaleigh resigned their positions in the cabinet to cooperate in opposing the reelection bid of the UMNO president, Mahathir, and his new selection for deputy president, Gafar Baba, at the 1986 general assembly. Mahathir and Baba successfully won the hotly contested election. This victory resulted in a legal challenge brought against UMNO by Musa and Razaleigh. In a surprising outcome, a judge sided in their favor and declared UMNO to be an illegal society under the Societies Act, which regulates the activities of all political parties. Old UMNO leadership's response was to reconstitute the party under the name New UMNO

(UMNO Baru). In the wake of UMNO's quick recovery from its decertification as a party, Razaleigh three years later would form the party Semangat 46 and organize an oppositional coalition against the BN in the 1991 general elections.

During this time Anwar Ibrahim, the finance minister, began to gain considerable respect and power within UMNO. Recruited by the UMNO president, Mahathir, in 1982 to join the party, Anwar left his activist leadership position in the Angkatan Belia Islam Malaysia (Malaysian Islamic Youth Movement). During the 1980s Anwar's status within UMNO increased with considerable speed to the amazement of many and the dismay of some (such as Dutak Musa Hitam). After the 1995 election the position of deputy prime minister was added to Anwar's finance portfolio. But in 1998, during the East Asian financial crisis, the once-buoyant Malaysian economy contracted by an estimated 7 percent. Anwar and Mahathir had a bitter falling out over economic policy, with Anwar supporting a more open-market approach. In September, Mahathir dismissed Anwar from both his posts, provoking public demonstrations of support for Anwar. Anwar was then arrested under the Internal Security Act, released, and almost immediately brought up on charges of corruption and sodomy, to which he pleaded complete innocence.

In 1999 Anwar was sentenced to six years incarceration for corruption in a highly controversial trial. In 2000 another nine years was added to this term for sodomy. Anwar maintained his innocence throughout the trial, and his supporters were thrown into disarray. To prevent any further disruption in the party, Mahathir had several supporters arrested over the next year, a move that led to mass, but peaceful, demonstrations in April 2001. For now, the party wounds seem healed, even if but artificially.

In 2002 Mahathir, Asia's longest serving leader, announced he would resign from his position as prime minister. The reins were handed over to a more moderate leader, Abdullah Badawi, who was sworn in as party leader in October 2003. His first task was to gain support within UMNO and the BN coalition. The mild-mannered man Abdullah is affectionately called *Pak Lah* (roughly meaning "Uncle Abdullah). He immediately set a different tone from his predecessor Mahathir. Preferring quiet public appearances, Abdullah focused on the needs of the poorer segments of society. He moved in the opposite direction from the mega-projects of Mahathir, and promised to tackle corruption, develop small businesses and agriculture, and prioritize rural development. The Malaysian public responded by giving Abdullah a strong mandate

(BN won over 90 percent of the seats in Parliament). In September 2004, reflecting a new political climate, Malaysia's highest court overturned the sodomy charges against Anwar Ibrahim and promptly released him. It is already evident that both UMNO and Malaysia have entered a new era.

ORGANIZATION

The UMNO is a cadre party, exclusively Malay in membership, which has succeeded through its extensive organization in every state and penetration to the village level in uniting Malay interests across region and class. As an exclusively Malay party, UMNO enjoys a high degree of homogeneity. It is distinguished also by being the only party with branches throughout the federation, including Sabah and Sarawak. It is relatively highly structured with a president, deputy president, and several vice presidents. The heads of the party's youth wing and its women's wing (Wanita UMNO) are automatically vice presidents, the remaining three being elected by the party's general assembly. Together with other appointed and elected members, including a secretary-general, treasurer, and publicity chief, they constitute the principal power center of the party.

The dual roles of party president and prime minister have been employed in a mutually enhancing manner by all four incumbents, whose positions have usually been supported by the senior party officers, who are also cabinet ministers. The youth and women's wings enjoy a semi-autonomous status, at times acting as pressure groups within the party. They have both performed vitally important functions during elections in organizing campaigns at the local level.

POLICY

The principal objectives of UMNO policy have consistently been UMNO dominance and Malay unity. The one is seen as reinforcing the other. These aims are secured by maintaining tight central control of the party while securing the widest possible electoral and governing coalition with Malay and non-Malay parties. These two strategies have at times been felt to conflict, leading to strains within the party, notably in 1969. Since 1991 the party has promoted the New Development Policy (NDP), successor to the New Economic Policy of 1971–91, which uses active discriminatory measures to advance the material well-being of Malays. This policy has coincided with a more strident assertion of economic nationalism that has led the government to buy its way into many of the large expatriate corporations, especially in the mining and plantation industries.

The NDP has been enacted in conjunction with Vision 2020 (*Wawasan 2020*), a development strategy that promises to achieve full development by the year 2020. Determinedly anticommunist both at home and abroad, the party's and government's foreign policy has been characterized by active membership in the Association of Southeast Asian Nations, an increasing concern to promote cooperation among Islamic countries, very cautious relations with China, the assertion of ostensibly anti-British sentiment coupled with a more markedly amenable attitude toward Japan, and lately a more critical and outspoken diplomatic stance against the United States.

UMNO policy has taken a new direction under Abdullah Badawi. Political prisoners have been released; focus is turning to the ordinary people, and ethnic relations are improving. In an early speech as prime minister, Abdullah announced that he was one-quarter Chinese—just like Malaysia. This marks a sharp turn around from Mahathir's ethnonationalistic policy. Abdullah has repeatedly stated that Malaysia is as much for Chinese and Indians as it is for Malays. Furthermore, foreign relations have improved. A rapprochement has begun with its closest neighbor Singapore after years of mudslinging by Mahathir. Much of Mahathir's economic policy is still in place, however, as Malaysia is vying to become the top outsourcing country for Western firms.

MEMBERSHIP AND CONSTITUENCY

No information is available on the size of the membership of UMNO. The party's supporters include most of the Malays of West Malaysia and many in Sabah and Sarawak. Only those Malays whose political views are most influenced by their Islamic faith support other parties in any appreciable number.

PROSPECTS

While the party's leadership remains acutely sensitive to any threat to its hegemony, especially from rival Malay parties, it is extremely difficult to envisage displacement of UMNO as the governing party.

MALAYAN CHINESE ASSOCIATION (MCA)

The MCA was founded in 1949 to protect the interests of the Chinese people living in Malaya, in the face of what were regarded as markedly pro-Malay policies of the British colonial government. Officially registered as a party in 1952, the MCA cooperated with UMNO at an electoral level and, in 1953, became a member, together with the MIC, of the Alliance coalition. The MCA is again a member of the front, but the inclusion as well of Gerakan, a rival Chinese party, has reduced the MCA's standing, since it can no longer claim to be the sole representative of Chinese interests in the government. While it has a widespread organization throughout Malaysia, it does not control any state assembly—unlike Gerakan, which controls Penang. Although from its inception it attempted to be a mass-membership party, it is seen as representing the interests of the better-off among the Chinese community and is vulnerable to the more populist appeal of some of the opposition parties among the poorer Chinese. These difficulties as well as the party's overall dependence on UMNO leadership were reflected in a sharp factional struggle through the 1970s and 1980s between some of the older founding members of the party and younger and more radical elements. With 31 seats in the federal Parliament as of the 2004 election, it is the second largest coalition partner, but its freedom to formulate policy is powerfully circumscribed by its membership in the front. In order to protect its position and that of its members, it must acquiesce in policies, especially with regard to Malay advancement, that cannot always be regarded as being in the immediate interest of its members.

Organizationally, the MCA is very similar to UMNO, with a powerful central committee comprising members elected by a general assembly or nominated by the party president. It has a strong state-level organization with subordinate levels down toward branches.

UNITED TRADITIONAL BUMIPUTRA PARTY

(Parti Pesaka Bumiputra Bersaut; PBB)

The PBB is a Sarawak-based party established in 1973 within the front. It obtained 11 seats in the 2004 federal election, making it the most powerful of BN parties in Sarawak. Its appeal is to the Malay and Melanau population of that state. In terms of current parliamentary seats, it is the third largest party in the BN coalition.

MALAYAN INDIAN CONGRESS (MIC)

From its inception in 1946, the MIC has been faced by the difficulty of sustaining unity in the face of divisions within the Indian community, which constitutes less than 10 percent of the population and is clustered in geographically scattered locations or thinly spread in urban centers. A member of the Alliance Party and subsequently of the Barisan Nasional, it commands support from the Indian population, but because the Indian population accounts for no more than 25 percent of the voters in any constituency, without the constituencies and seats allocated to it by the front it could not hope to survive politically as a significant group. It won nine seats in the federal parliament in 2004.

MALAYSIAN PEOPLE'S MOVEMENT (GERAKAN)

(Parti Gerakan Rakyat Malaysia)

The party is universally known as Gerakan, but its full name can be loosely translated as Malaysian People's Movement. It was founded in 1968 by Dr. Lim Chong Eu and is pledged to a program of noncommunalism, moderate Socialism, and democracy. It entered the BN in 1972. Despite the presence of Malays on the party committee, it is still seen as a Chinese party. Its power base is in Penang, where it controls the state government with the patronage that entails, but it also has a few branches elsewhere. It won 10 parliamentary seats in the 2004 election.

SARAWAK UNITED PEOPLE'S PARTY (SUPP)

The oldest Sarawak party in the front was founded in 1959. Its Barisan Nasional support is predominantly from the Chinese population. It has six seats in the federal parliament.

SARAWAK DAYAK PEOPLE'S PARTY

(Parti Bansa Dayak Sarawak; PBDS)

Formed in July 1983 by federal MPs who had broken away from the Sarawak National Action Party, it successfully won six seats in 2004. Prior to the 1986 general election the PBDS left the BN to contest Sarawak's elections independently. In 1991, however, after it failed to win a majority of votes in the Sarawak state assembly, the party reentered the BN. Its major objective is to represent the interests of the indigenous Dayak community.

PEOPLE'S PROGRESSIVE PARTY OF MALAYSIA (PPP)

Originally founded in 1953 as the Perak Progressive Party, it changed to its present name in 1956. Its appeal is restricted mainly to non-Malays in the Ipoh area. It survives as a party within the Perak state assembly, where its appeal to poorer Chinese offsets some of the advantage that might otherwise accrue to the DAP, one of the two Democratic Action Party opposition parties in that state. The PPP won one federal parliamentary seat in 2004.

SABAH PEOPLE'S UNION

(Bersatu Rakyat Jelata Sabah; Berjaya)

Berjaya was founded in 1975 and from 1976 until its defeat in 1985 held an overwhelming majority of seats in the state assembly. In the wake of this defeat, which significantly changed the makeup of Sabah state politics, the party has lost considerable political power. It was regarded as one of the few multicommunal parties in Malaysia, but its 1985 defeat was largely the result of the belief, on the part of the majority Christian Kadazan population, that it had become more markedly pro-Muslim in its policies. Berjaya remains a member of the BN, but picked up only one seat at the 2004 general elections.

UNITED SABAH PARTY

(Parti Bersatu Sabah; PBS)

Parti Bersatu Sabah (PBS) was registered as a political party on March 5, 1985, by Datuk Seri Panglima Joseph Pairin Kitingan who was forced out of the ruling Berjaya Party. In the April 1985 state election, PBS won 26 of the 48 Legislative Assembly seats. It formed the new state government with Datuk Seri Panglima Pairin as chief minister. PBS subsequently won 34 and 36 seats in the 1986 and 1990 state elections. It won a fourth term in office in 1994, but this time by only a close margin of 25 to BN's 23. Two weeks later, with some questionably undemocratic maneuverings, PBS was forced out of office by Barisan Nasional. A majority of PBS assemblymen defected to BN parties. In the 1995 general parliamentary election, PBS won eight 8 of the 20 parliamentary seats in Sabah. PBS's power has waned due to the internal problems that came about in 1994. Ten years later, in 2004, PBS won only half the parliamentary seats it won in 1995. Its state seats had also declined. The PBS first entered the BN in 1986, but left in 1990 after the government detained several PBS leaders under the Internal Security Act. PBS returned to the BN fold at the end of 2002.

UNITED PASOKMOMOGUN KADAZANDUSUN MURUT ORGANISATION (UPKO)

UPKO was formed in May 1964 when two political parties, the United Kadazan National Organization

(UNKO) and the United Pasok Momogun Organization (PASOK), combined. UPKO seeks to represent and protect the rights of the native Kadazandusun Murut of Sabah.

SABAH PROGRESSIVE PARTY (SAPP)

The SAPP was formed on January 22, 1994. Its founder was Datuk Yong, a former PBS politician who had left the party just days earlier upon the PBS leadership announcing the dissolution of the State Assembly for the fourth time in five years. The SAPP is made up of ex-PBS Chinese leaders although it claims to represent the interests of all races in Sabah.

Minor Political Parties

Smaller parties in the BN are the Liberal Democratic Party (LDP) and the Sarawak Progressive Democratic Party. The LDP failed to win any seats in the 2004 elections. While the SPDP won four seats, very little is known about this organization.

OPPOSITION PARTIES

DEMOCRATIC ACTION PARTY (DAP)

Founded in 1966 in the wake of Singapore's secession from the federation, the DAP was the Malayan version of the People's Action Party, Lee Kuan Yew's Singapore-based party. DAP's objective was and is to establish a democratic and socialist society in Malaysia. It analyzes Malaysian society in class rather than communal terms, and while its support comes mainly from urban, working-class Chinese, it retains an appeal for many disaffected non-Malays, including some of the intelligentsia. Although it is efficiently organized, the competition from rival Chinese parties, MCA and Gerakan, and its inability to secure any substantial Malayan Chinese Association support in rural areas have denied it control of any state assembly and thus substantially limited its capacity to secure federal parliamentary seats. The DAP won 12 seats in the 2004 elections, making it the largest opposition party.

PAN-MALAYSIAN ISLAMIC PARTY (PARTAI ISLAM SE MALAYSIA; PAS)

Known variously by its English (PMIP) or Malay/Arabic acronym, the PAS originated in the early 1950s as an Islamic promotional group within UMNO. In 1951, alienated by UMNO concessions to non-Malays, it was established as a separate party. A Malay nationalist party, its primary appeal is to poorer, especially rural, Malays. It seeks to combine Islamic traditions with a modernizing thrust and some elements of Socialism. Islam is regarded as a force for national unity. Religious teachers are active in its campaigning, and religious themes are interwoven with political assertions. PAS may represent the only significant potential threat to UMNO's dominance, partly because the rural poor as a whole have derived the least benefit from the substantial economic changes since independence, partly because PAS may be ready to accommodate the interests of other racial groups, and partly because its appeal echoes the success of radical Islamic movements elsewhere. In 1973 PAS entered the BN for four years until it left again in 1977. Since 1982 the role of the Islamic "theocratic" element in the party has been greatly strengthened. Attacks by fundamentalist elements on the party's president, Datuk Haji Mohamed Asri bin Haji Muda, led to his resignation in 1983. Four of the five federal MPs resigned with him to form a new party, Hamim. In 1991 it won a major victory in both the Kelantan state assembly and in national parliamentary elections. Under the leadership of Nik Aziz, PAS used its victory to consolidate its power and embark on a new policy of Islamicization. This statewide program included the introduction of Islamic legal codes into the Kelantan state court system. Subsequently, the BN has made a substantial effort to regain its lost influence in the state. In the 1995 general election PAS lost some seats at both the state and the federal levels, but in the 1999 elections PAS made big gains. It increased its seats in parliament to 27 from 8, largely as a result of support from Malays who had previously voted for the UMNO. However, 2004 saw a reversal of fortunes for PAS. First, the country became strongly skeptical of anything resembling a fundamentalist Islamic party in the wake of the terrorist attacks on the United States and the resulting moderate Islam rhetoric by Mahathir. Second, PAS suffered from the popularity of the new prime minister, Abdullah Badwai, particularly as he attempted to address the problems of the rural electorate—the PAS strongholds. PAS lost 20 seats in 2004, leaving it with a mere seven seats, a shock that will cause the party leadership to do some serious rethinking.

NATIONAL JUSTICE PARTY
(Parti Keadilan Nasional; ADIL)

The National Justice Party was founded by Anwar Ibrahim, just after his fall from grace in UMNO. Following Ibrahim's arrest and subsequent imprisonment, his wife, Wan Azizah Wan Ismail, took over the party. With Ibrahim's release, Keadilan will most likely be built up as a multiracial opposition party with a moderate Muslim core. However, the release of Ibrahim may have done more for Abdullah's image than it will for the future of Keadilan.

Other Political Forces

Formal groups other than political parties are not of significance in Malaysian politics. The principal parties are capable of articulating within themselves and within the governing coalition many of the demands and pressures that would elsewhere find separate institutional expression. Traditional social structures within the main communal groups provide a further channel for meeting demands, while extensive networks of patronage and clientelism within and outside the public sector perform the same function. Another important factor inhibiting the rise of other political organizations has been the 1981 amendment to the Societies Act, which forbids political activity to groups not registered as political. This has severely inhibited overt political activities on the part of all nonparty groups. A similar tool for limiting oppositional activities exists in the Internal Security Act, which allows for detention without charge. In 1987 the Malaysian government carried out Operation Lalang, resulting in the detention of more than 100 party leaders, academics, religious leaders, and political activists. The ISA has been used over time to remove central figures within oppositional movements.

ORGANIZED LABOR

Trade unions provide only a very limited exception to these generalizations. Their membership is drawn principally from the Chinese and Indian communities. Subject to strict government control, not affiliated with any political party, and with the joint holding of union and political party office forbidden, unions have had their role restricted to localized place-of-work bargaining with employers. They have no impact on national political activity.

Ethnic occupational groups also exist, such as the Chinese Chambers of Commerce or the United Chinese School Teachers' Association, but a largely overlapping membership with the Malayan Chinese Association ensures that collective interests are promoted within and through the party.

Briefly, during the early to mid-1970s, student organizations, notably the University of Malaya Students Union, were active in making political assertions, especially on behalf of poor peasant communities, but separate legislation making political activity on university campuses a punishable offense and the more general restraints referred to above have served to preempt any further student role in national or local parties.

National Prospects

Since 1969 Malaysia's political system has been remarkably stable and relatively peaceful, even though its party system is predominantly based on ethnic differences. The government and the unique political arrangement of the National Front have worked to maintain communal peace by any means necessary. The drastic impact of the global financial crisis and the destabilizing effects of Anwar Ibrahim's removal from office, his trial, and the resulting protest movement seemed to have robbed Malaysia of potentially positive prospects for the future. However, with the change of guard in 2003 and release of Ibrahim a year later, Malaysia seems to be heading on a course toward a more open and democratic system. Nevertheless, the overwhelming dominance of the BN and especially UMNO cannot be understated. It will be some time before such a formidable power structure can be dismantled. Another problem that continues to beset Malaysia is the ethnic mixture of the country. The year 2001 saw Malaysia's worst civic clashes between ethnic Malays and Indians. For Malaysia to achieve unhindered progress, it must successfully incorporate all ethnic groups into the political process. Abdullah has made it a part of his image to be more accepting of other ethnic groups, but there are significant institutionalized barriers to success for non-Malays that must be rethought if true harmony is to be achieved. The signs are positive for the new millennium. Malaysia's economy continues to surge ahead, and with Abdullah's commitment to rural development and the needy, Malaysia may become the role model for Southeast Asian nations.

Further Reading

Abdul Razak Abdullah Baginda. *Malaysia in Transition: Politics and Society.* London: Asean Academic Press, 2003.

Barlow, Colin, and Francis Loh Kok Wah, eds. *Malaysian Economics and Politics in the New Century.* Northampton, Mass.: Edward Elgar, 2003.

Crouch, Harold A. *Government and Society in Malaysia.* Ithaca, N.Y.: Cornell University Press, 1996.

Hooker, Virginia, and Norani Othman, eds. *Malaysia: Islam, Society and Politics.* Singapore: Institute of Southeast Asian Studies, 2003.

Kahn, J. S., and L. K. F. Wah, eds. *Fragmented Vision.* Honolulu: University of Hawaii Press, 1992.

Khoo, Boo Teik. *Paradoxes of Mahathirism: An Intellectual Biography of Mahathir Mohamad.* New York: Oxford University Press, 1995.

Lee, R. L. M. "The State, Religious Nationalism, and Ethnic Rationalization in Malaysia." *Ethnic and Racial Studies* 13, no. 4 (1990): 482–501.

Means, G. P. *Malaysian Politics: The Second Generation.* Oxford: Oxford University Press, 1991.

Nagata, Judith A. *The Reflowering of Malaysian Islam: Modern Religious Radicals and Their Roots.* Vancouver: University of British Columbia Press, 1984.

Oo, Yu Hock. *Ethnic Chameleon: Multiracial Politics in Malaysia.* Petaling Jaya, Selangor Darul Ehsan, Malaysia: Pelanduk, 1991.

REPUBLIC OF MALDIVES
(Divehi Raajjeyge Jumhuriyya)

By Robert J. Griffiths, Ph.D.

The Republic of Maldives is a string of some 1,300 small islands and sandbanks stretching for more than 500 miles in a north to south orientation southwest of India and Sri Lanka. The some 200 inhabited islands have an estimated population of some 350,000 people (2005) and are divided for administrative purposes into 19 atolls. Islam is the state religion and most of the inhabitants of the Maldives' are Sunni Muslims. The government, although constitutional, has been dominated in recent decades by a small elite. The Maldives became independent in 1965, and its first constitution was approved in 1968. The constitution has undergone several changes, and the most recent constitution dates from 1998.

The System of Government

The Maldives is a federal republic with a unicameral legislature.

EXECUTIVE

Executive power is vested in the president (who serves as both the head of government and head of state), who is designated by the Majlis and approved by popular referendum for a renewable five-year term. The president appoints major government officials including those with the responsibility for overseeing the legal system. The president governs with the assistance of a cabinet responsible to the Majlis. Since the country's first constitution was adopted, the Maldives has had only two presidents, Ibrahim Nasir (1968–78) and Maumoon Abdul Gayoom (1978–present), who has won election six times (most recently in 2003).

LEGISLATURE

Legislative authority rests in a 50-member legislature, the Citizen's Council (Majlis). Forty-two members are directly elected, and eight are selected by the president. Each of the country's 20 atolls elected two members, as does Male island. Their term of office is five years.

JUDICIARY

The Maldives legal system is based on Islamic law. The most important court is the High Court. The president appoints all judges.

REGIONAL AND LOCAL GOVERNMENT

The country is divided into 19 administrative districts, corresponding to the main atolls, plus the capital. Each atoll is administered by a presidentially appointed chief (*verin*) advised by an elected committee. Each island is administered by a headman (*kateeb*), a number of assistants, and a mosque representative.

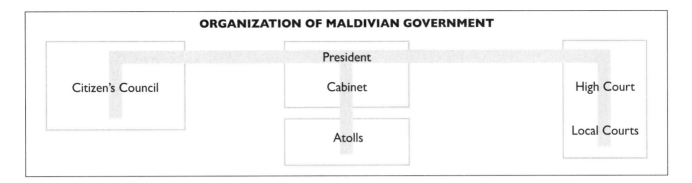

ORGANIZATION OF MALDIVIAN GOVERNMENT

Citizen's Council

President
Cabinet

Atolls

High Court

Local Courts

The Electoral System

The president is nominated by the Majlis and approved by popular referendum for a five-year term. Members of the unicameral legislature also serve five-year terms. Until 2005 parties were prohibited, and as a result all candidates ran as independents. All citizens age 21 or older are eligible to vote.

The long-serving Gayoom provided the country with stability, though he survived various coup attempts and a serious challenge, in 1993, to his presidency by his brother-in-law and minister of atolls administration, Ilyas Ibrahim.

In 1994 President Gayoom outlined further reforms including greater responsibility and autonomy for cabinet officials, greater accountability for civil servants, democratic elections for island development and atoll committees, and formation of a law commission to reform the judicial system. The possibility of multiple candidate presidential elections and constitutional reforms was discussed, but no action was taken. Optimism regarding political reform increased in 1995 when the president told the Majlis that he would introduce legislation to increase public confidence in the electoral system. Prompted by reports that the conservative Muslim Wahabi sect was gaining adherents, the government also promised measures to combat religious extremism. In 1996 the president reshuffled his cabinet and reorganized government bodies, which included the establishment of a Supreme Council for Islamic Affairs to advise the president.

In October 1998 President Gayoom was reelected to a fifth term in office with 90.9 percent of the vote. This was the country's first election under its new constitution, adopted earlier in the year. In his inaugural speech, Gayoom emphasized the importance of strengthening national unity and identity, reinforcing family values, preserving social harmony and cultural traditions, and empowering women. He also announced plans to address the need for building better housing, ensuring safe drinking water, deepening the country's ports, and diversifying the economy. Gayoom was elected to a sixth term in 2003 with 90.3 percent of the vote, defeating three candidates.

The Party System

From independence until the early 21st century political parties were prohibited. In 2001 an effort to register a political party, the Maldivian Democratic Party (MDP), was blocked by the Majlis. The MDP, prevented from operating at home, set up operations in Sri Lanka and continued to voice its displeasure with the government. Political unrest broke out in February 2004 when the government arrested eight democracy activists planning to hold a demonstration to demand press freedom, the release of political prisoners, prison reform, and to call attention to the government's human rights record. In August 2004 a state of emergency was declared, and some 100 democracy activists were arrested and authorities used tear gas to break up an antigovernment demonstration. The government charged that the protests were aimed at toppling the government. Seven members of a constitutional reform committee were arrested for joining the demonstration.

In June 2004 President Gayoom offered changes in the constitution that would limit the president's powers and restrict the president to two terms in office, allow political parties to operate freely, and create the post of prime minister. In 2005 the Majlis voted unanimously to legalize political parties.

Major Political Parties

Despite the prohibition on political parties, the Maldivian Democratic Party endorsed candidates, and in the

2005 Majlis election (postponed because of the 2004 tsunami), its candidates won 31 percent of the vote and 18 of the 42 contested seats. It was officially registered as a party in June 2005. Other political parties that are registered include Maldivian Peoples Party, the Islamic Democratic Party and the Adhaalath Party.

Minor Political Parties

Because of the recent legalization of political parties, the relative importance of political parties and their success will be established over time.

Other Political Forces

Given the lack of political parties for much of the country's history, political activity in the Maldives has often taken the form of protest, though such pro-democracy and antigovernment protests were sometimes met with a harsh crackdown and arrests. For example, a prison protest over the death of an inmate in September 2003 brought a violent response from government forces resulting in two more inmate deaths. This set off large protests against the government, the first time this had occurred during Gayoom's 26-year rule. Amnesty International was particularly vocal in its criticism of political repression by the government.

National Prospects

Tourism has become the islands' largest source of foreign exchange, and infrastructure projects are under way to improve the islands' facilities. Political unrest may have a substantial impact on the country's economy because of the Maldives heavy reliance on tourism. The Indian Ocean tsunami of 2004 devastated the economy and forced the delay of legislative elections. Given that the low-lying islands are situated at or only slight above sea level, the country is particularly susceptible to such occurrences, and there have been fears that if the ocean levels rise that the country could be wiped away. The country has been in the forefront of a movement of island nations, the Alliance of Small Island States (ASIS), concerned with rising sea levels attributed to global warming. In 1994 President Gayoom called for action to address what he termed a global problem. This issue remains an important one in the Republic of the Maldives.

Further Reading

Background Notes, Maldives. Washington, D.C.: U.S. Department of State, Bureau of Public Affairs, Office of Public Communication, 1996.

Forbes, Andrew. *Maldives: Kingdom of a Thousand Isles*. Hong Kong: Odyssey, 2002.

REPUBLIC OF MALI
(République du Mali)

By Pascal James Imperato
Revised by Emmanuel Nwagboso

Mali, a landlocked country of 12.2 million people in the heart of West Africa, is one of the poorest nations in the world. At 1.25 million square kilometers, 65 percent of which is desert or semidesert, Mali is a predominantly Muslim country.

Mali's first fully democratic elections in over 30 years were held in early 1992. These elections effectively ended a 23-year military dictatorship and represented an important step in Mali's development of a democratic government following the ouster of General Moussa Traoré on March 26, 1991. Traoré came to power through a coup d'état on November 19, 1968 (eight years after the country gained its independence from France), which ousted Mali's then one-party Marxist president, Modibo Keita.

Traoré initially ruled Mali with military colleagues through a Military Committee of National Liberation (CMLN). In 1979 this committee was dissolved, and Traoré ruled through a political party, the Democratic Union of Malian People (UDPM), in which the military held important posts. Although legislative elections were regularly held, the military continued to hold onto power through ministerial posts and the central committee of the UDPM.

During 1990 and 1991, pro-democracy groups in Mali placed increasing pressure on Traoré for multiparty democracy. He rejected their demands and insisted on the expression of politically diverse views within the context of the UDPM. Pro-democracy groups were then joined by students, trade unionists, and the unemployed in a series of violent demonstrations that culminated in an opportunistic coup d'état against Traoré by Lieutenant Colonel Amadou Toumani Touré and his military associates. Touré and his clique formed a Military Council of National Reconciliation (CRN). However, under pressure from pro-democracy groups and external donors, they quickly stepped aside and established a 25-member Transition Committee for the Health of the People (CTSP). This joint civilian-military committee guided Mali to multiparty elections in early 1992. Touré returned to power by winning the presidential election of 2002.

The System of Government

Mali is a multiparty state with a civilian government. The government functions under the constitution of the Third Republic, which was adopted through a referendum held on January 12, 1992. This provides for a president elected by universal adult suffrage, a prime minister appointed by the president, a unicameral National Assembly with 147 deputies, and an independent judiciary.

EXECUTIVE

Under Mali's constitution, the president is both head of state and commander in chief of the armed forces.

ORGANIZATION OF MALIAN GOVERNMENT

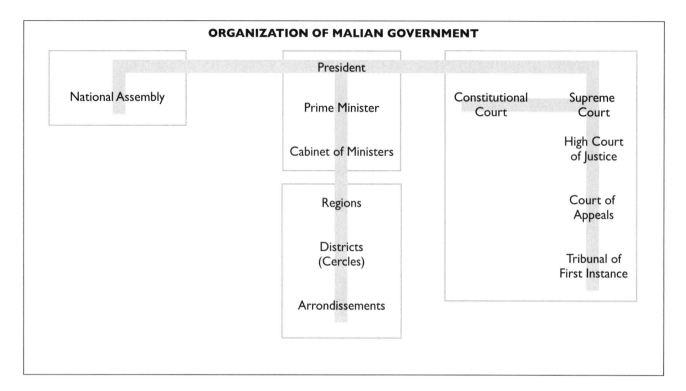

The president is elected to a five-year term and can serve no more than two terms. The first president under the new constitution was Alpha Konaré, who served between 1992 and 2002. In the latter year Amadou Touré was elected president.

LEGISLATURE

Parliament consists of the unicameral National Assembly, which has 147 members who are elected to five-year terms. From 1992 until 2002 the leading party in the National Assembly was the Alliance for Democracy in Mali (ADEMA). In 1997 ADEMA captured an overwhelming number of seats (130), but the elections were marred by irregularities and boycotted by several opposition parties. All parties participated in the 2002 elections, during which ADEMA lost its parliamentary majority to the Rally for Mali Party (RPM) and its Hope 2002 coalition. The coalition won 66 seats to ADEMA's 51.

JUDICIARY

The 1992 constitution provides for an independent judiciary consisting of a Supreme Court, a Constitutional Court, a High Court of Justice, a Court of Appeals, and lower courts. The Supreme Court consists of three sections: judicial, administrative, and accounts. The Constitutional Court, comprised of nine members,

rules on the constitutionality of laws. The High Court of Justice judges the president and ministers accused before the National Assembly of treason, crimes, or offenses committed in the course of discharging their responsibilities.

REGIONAL AND LOCAL GOVERNMENT

Mali is divided into eight regions and the District of Bamako surrounding the capital. The regions in turn are divided into *cercles* (districts) comprised of smaller units known as *arrondissements*. Larger towns have elected councils and mayors while the *cercles* and *arrondissements* are headed by central government appointees. Each region is headed by a governor who reports to the minister of territorial administration and internal security. *Cercles* are administered by commandants and *arrondissements* by chiefs.

The Electoral System

Candidates for local and national government positions are selected by individual political parties. The selection process varies greatly among these various political parties.

The Party System

Political parties were first organized in Mali in the immediate post–World War II era. The strongly anti-colonial and Marxist Sudanese Union (Union Soudanaise-Rassemblement Démocratique Africain; US-RDA) was founded in 1946 by Mamadou Konaté and Modibo Keita. Its chief opponent was the Sudanese Progressive Party (Parti Progressiste Soudanais; PPS) established by Fily Dabo Sissoko the same year. It drew much of its support from traders and merchants. Faced with overwhelming popular support for the US-RDA, Sissoko and the PPS merged with the former in 1959. Following independence in 1960, the US-RDA was the only political party in the country. Under Modibo Keita, it pushed forward with radical Marxist domestic and foreign policies. In 1962 Keita moved to eliminate Sissoko by charging him with treason and attempting a coup during a July 20 riot in Bamako, the capital, by merchants protesting Mali's new nonconvertible currency. Sissoko was arrested, tried by a "popular tribunal," and later shot in a remote northern district of the country. Keita launched a cultural revolution in 1967 during which he purged many party and government leaders and activated a Popular Militia that terrorized the population.

The 1968 military coup by Moussa Traoré and his associates essentially ended all political activity in the country. The military initially ruled through a committee. However, in 1979, Traoré formally established a new political party, the Democratic Union of the Malian People (Union Démocratique du Peuple Malien; UDPM). The UDPM was structured along Marxist-Leninist lines. Although the party was organized down to the grassroots level, the military controlled it and the one-party National Assembly. The UDPM effectively served to give legitimacy to Traoré's military rule. While he used the party apparatus and the National Assembly to build consensus with regard to policy formulation, he and his military supporters remained firmly in control.

Ex-government employees, students, and graduates without hope of future government or private-sector employment and pro-democracy groups galvanized in 1990 to put increasing pressure on Traoré and the UDPM for political reform and an end to gross corruption. Continuous bloody demonstrations in March 1991 led to a military coup d'état and the disbanding of the UDPM. Traoré was sentenced to death for blood crimes and for embezzling 2 billion dollars, an amount equal to Mali's external debt. The sentence was not carried out. The 1992 constitution provides for a multi-party democracy; parties based on ethnic, religious, geographical, or gender lines are illegal. Currently, there are eight political parties represented in the National Assembly although two parties (ADEMA and RPM) hold 117 of a possible 147 seats. Several minor political parties are predominantly active on a local level.

Major Political Parties

ALLIANCE FOR DEMOCRACY IN MALI–AFRICAN PARTY FOR SOLIDARITY AND JUSTICE

(Alliance Pour La Démocratie au Mali–Parti Africain Pour La Solidarité et La Justice; ADEMA)

This party was originally founded in 1990 as a pro-democracy movement by Alpha Oumar Konaré, who had also established Jamana, a cultural cooperative. ADEMA drew its political support from civil servants and the rural population and its financial support from groups in France. Konaré was elected president in 1992 and again in 1997. Diouncenda Traoré subsequently headed the party, which has a vocal left wing.

RALLY FOR MALI

(Rassemblement Pour le Mali; RPM)

This party was established by Ibrahim Keita, who remained party chairman into 2005. It captured the majority in the National Assembly in the 2002 elections by forming a coalition known as Hope 2002.

Minor Political Parties

Other parties in Mali include the Block of Alternative for the Renewal of Africa, led by Yoro Diakite; the Democratic and Social Convention, led by Mamadou Sangare; the Movement for the Independence, Renaissance and Integration of Africa, led by Mohamed Traoré and Mouhamedou Dicko; the National Congress for Democratic Initiative, led by Mountaga Tall; the Party for Democracy and Progress, led by Me Traoré; the Party for National Renewal, led by Yoro Diakite and Tiebile Drame; the Rally for Democracy and Labor, led by Ali Gnangado; the Rally for Democracy and Progress, led by Almamy Sylla; the Sudanese Union/African Democratic Rally, led by Mamadou Touré; the Union of Democratic

Forces for Progress, led by Youssouf Touré, and the Union for Democracy and Development, led by Moussa Coulibaly.

Other Political Forces

MILITARY

Mali's army is equipped primarily with Soviet arms. There were several attempted military coups during the Traoré regime, in 1969, 1976, 1978, and 1981, and finally a successful one in 1991. Hard-line officers opposed to the transition to multiparty rule and the loss of their special privileges organized a successful coup on July 15, 1991. The threats posed by strong internal popular opposition and external repercussions from donors have since served to hinder the military from launching coups.

ORGANIZED LABOR

Unions are federated in the National Union of Malian Workers (Union Nationale des Travailleurs Maliens; UNTM). The UNTM was sequentially controlled by the US-RDA and then later by the UDPM. Since the advent of multiparty democracy, the UNTM is completely independent of any party control.

STUDENTS

Since the late 1970s, student groups have emerged in Mali as an independent and fairly powerful political force. Students were first politically galvanized when the Traoré government intervened to stem the upward flow of students into higher levels by giving tougher examinations. Although students rallied around slogans praising scientific socialism, the real issue was future guaranteed government employment.

Student protests in 1979–81 were organized by an independent union, the National Union of Students and Pupils of Mali (Union Nationale des Etudiants et des Elèves du Mali; UNEEM). Although proscribed by the government, the union effectively boycotted classes and organized demonstrations. The union was finally broken in 1981 through concessions and hard-line retaliation.

In 1990 students banded together in another independent union, the Association of Pupils and Students of Mali (Association des Elèves et Etudiants du Mali; AEEM). Their leader, Oumar Mariko, an ardent Marxist, mobilized large numbers around the issue of perceived inadequate student entitlements and

the government's refusal to agree to guarantee future employment. During 1990 and early 1991, AEEM along with pro-democracy groups and the unemployed organized a number of demonstrations that eventually led to the fall of the Traoré regime.

The Konaré government also had to deal with violent student protests. In March and April 1993, serious clashes took place as students rebelled over the government's austerity measures with regard to their stipends. They burned public buildings and attacked the state radio station. A month later, even more violent clashes took place as they attempted to burn the National Assembly building, the headquarters of ADEMA, and other government buildings. In this case, they were protesting the government's alleged attempt to impose a new leader on their union. This protest led to the resignation of Prime Minister Abdoulaye Sékou Sow. In the final analysis, AEEM succeeded in forcing the resignation of Konaré's first government. Student protests continued throughout 1994–96, during which government and foreign diplomatic facilities were attacked.

Malian student demands for government stipends and guaranteed state employment cannot be met by any government. Concessions around the periphery of these issues have served to defuse them for the short term. However, until Mali develops a free-market economy full of employment opportunities, students will continue to look to the government to guarantee their welfare. The prospects for greater private-sector employment are poor. Thus, students will continue to press their case and confront the government through violent means.

ETHNIC GROUPS

Until recently, there was little ethnic rivalry among Mali's several ethnic groups. The Bambara, Dogon, Malinké, Minianka, Senufo, and Songhay are farmers; the Bozo and Sorko fishermen; the Peul and Tuareg herdsmen; and the Sarakolé merchants. Population growth and a stagnant economy have led to a breakdown in longstanding harmonious and complementary economic relationships. As increasing numbers of people compete for limited resources, they move into economic spheres once the traditional reserve of specific ethnic groups. Thus, the increased ethnic rivalry occurring in Mali is in many ways an expression of economic competition.

Mali's population is 90 percent Muslim. However, syncretic practices combining older indigenous religious beliefs and Islam are common. Indigenous religions have been in steady retreat before Islam for many decades. There are fewer than 100,000 Christians, of whom 20 percent belong to various Protestant groups and 80 percent are Roman Catholic. Christians are actively discriminated against by the Muslim majority, especially in towns and the capital, Bamako.

The Berber Tuareg of the north have been the victims of government policies that have denied them access to education, health services, and development. Both the Keita and Traoré governments also persecuted the Tuareg in a variety of ways. Their livestock were often confiscated, and they were actively encouraged to migrate into Algeria during periods of drought. Government officials have often been vocal and public in claiming that a "white race" such as the Tuareg have no place in a black African state. This position has been strongly denounced by pro-democracy groups in the country. The Tuareg see themselves as the victims of racist government policies. Their armed rebellion of the 1990s forced the government to reverse longstanding policies and meet many of their demands.

National Prospects

By the end of 1998 Mali had made a remarkable political transition from three decades of one-party dictatorial rule to a multiparty democracy. President Alpha Oumar Konaré, respected for his integrity and honesty, successfully built political consensus both within his own party and by reaching out to radical opposition groups. The peaceful transition of power in 2002 to newly elected Amadou Touré further solidified the country's democratic institutions and its international reputation. The country's major problems remain a weak economy highly dependent on agriculture and insecurity in the north where Tuareg splinter groups continue their military operations.

Agricultural output has grown in recent years, largely due to development schemes such as Mali Sud and Opération Haute-Vallée. However, annual production levels depend on rainfall. During the past two decades, weather cycles have included periods of severe drought that greatly affect food and cash crop production. Declines in food crops have also been influenced by conversion to cotton production in certain areas. In

2004 a locust plague depleted the cereal harvest by 45 percent, resulting in extreme food shortages.

Official corruption was rampant during the years of the Traoré regime. This problem, while still present to some degree, has been vigorously addressed by Touré's government, which is widely perceived as being honest. Like Konaré before him, Touré has shown flexibility in following the requirements of major aid donors. He has held the line on public-sector employment and encouraged the development of a free-market economy as had his predecessor.

Manufacturing activity contributes about 8 percent to the gross domestic product. Most manufacturing meets national demands. Although there has been much investment in gold mining by foreign concerns in recent years, overall production is insufficient to alter Mali's basic dependence on agriculture and livestock raising. The construction of hydroelectric dams at Selingué and at Manantali during the 1980s has provided Mali with cheap electricity that could be harnessed in the future to support industrial development.

The country has worked closely with the International Monetary Fund to restructure the country's debt and to modernize the tax system. In September 2002 France agreed to forgive 40 percent of the debts owed to it by Mali, resulting in a reprieve of roughly $79 million. In 2003, as part of an international effort to provide debt relief to developing nations, Mali was able to begin applying debt payments to antipoverty programs. The survival of multiparty democracy in Mali is very much dependent on the government's ability to build political consensus concerning major issues and to successfully address some of the country's pressing economic problems.

Further Reading

Bingen, R. J., D. Robinson, and J. Staatz. *Democracy and Development in Mali.* East Lansing: Michigan State University Press, 2000.

Imperato, Pascal James. *Historical Dictionary of Mali.* 3d ed. Lanham, Md.: Scarecrow Press, 1996.

———. *Mali: A Search for Direction.* Boulder, Colo.: Westview Press, 1989.

REPUBLIC OF MALTA
(Repubblika ta' Malta)

By Kenneth E. Bauzon, Ph.D.
Revised by Piotr Mikuli, Ph.D.

Malta is an island country in the Mediterranean consisting of the inhabited islands of Malta, Gozo, and Comino as well as the tiny uninhabited islands of Cominotto and Filfla. It is one of the most densely populated countries in the world with a population of 398,000 (2005 est.) and a total land area of 122 square miles. Its population is predominantly of Carthaginian and Phoenician background, and its culture is a mix of Arab, Italian, French, and English traditions. This population mix reflects Maltese history in which the country has been, throughout the centuries, under the control of the Roman and Byzantine Empires (212 B.C.E. and 870 C.E., respectively), the Normans (1020), the Knights of Malta (1523), the French (1798), and the British (1814). The major religion is Roman Catholicism, subscribed to by 98 percent of the Maltese population. Official languages are Maltese and English, although Italian is also widely spoken. The seat of government is in the port city of Valletta, located on the island of Malta.

Until its political independence from Great Britain in September 1964, Malta was a constitutional monarchy with the queen of England as its titular head. In December 1964 the Malta independence constitution was proclaimed, transforming Malta into an autonomous liberal parliamentary democracy within the British Commonwealth. While maintaining the centralized character of the government, this new constitution provided safeguards for the human rights of citizens, guaranteed a degree of power separation among the branches of government, and ensured periodic elections based on universal suffrage. Under this constitution, the governor-general retained his power to appoint the prime minister and the Cabinet from among members of parliament. In 1974 this constitution was revised to transform Malta into an independent republic. The amendment retained the Westminster model of government, which provided for the president—of Maltese citizenship—as the constitutional head of state, with a term of five years, to be indirectly elected through parliament. The office of the president replaced the office of the governor-general, who, up to that time, represented the British royal crown as de jure head of state. In 1987 the constitution was once again amended to modify the electoral law so that the party garnering the majority in a popular election would have a parliamentary majority by being awarded additional parliamentary seats, if necessary.

After the country officially joined the European Union (EU) in May 2004, the parliament of Malta ratified the EU constitution in July 2005.

The System of Government

Malta is a parliamentary republic with a unicameral legislature.

EXECUTIVE

Under the current constitution, the president is elected to a five-year term by parliament. The president wields formal executive authority and assents to bills, prorogues and dissolves parliament, and acts on the advice of the prime minister. The president can be removed from office by Resolution of the House of Representatives on the ground of inability to perform the functions of the office or for misbehavior. Dr. Edward Fenech Adami currently holds the office of president. He was elected to office on March 29, 2004.

The prime minister is both the effective head of government and chief executive officer. The prime minister, as leader of the majority party in parliament, exercises prerogative in filling ministry positions in the cabinet, although the president formally appoints this body. The government consists of ministers who must be nominated from among the members of the House of Representatives. The office of the minister becomes vacant if he or she ceases to be a member of parliament. After Adami retired from the post of prime minister to campaign for president, Lawrence Gonzi was appointed in replacement as leader of the National Party, which won a majority of seats in the legislative elections held on April 12, 2003.

The cabinet is responsible for the general direction and control of the government of Malta and is collectively responsible to parliament. The president may remove the prime minister from office if a majority of the House of Representatives passes a vote of no confidence.

LEGISLATURE

Under the constitution the legislature formally consists of the president of the Republic and a House of Representatives, analogous to the British concept of "King in the Parliament." Members of the House are elected by universal suffrage for a maximum of five years on the basis of proportional representation. The majority party forms a government consisting of the prime minister and a cabinet formally appointed by the president. The party with a majority of popular votes may be awarded additional seats in the House to ensure a legislative majority.

Parliament may make laws in conformity with full respect for human rights, generally accepted principles of international law, and Malta's international and regional obligations—in particular those assumed by the treaty of accession to the EU signed in Athens on April 16, 2003, and those dictated by the EU constitution ratified in July 2005.

Members of parliament are elected from electoral divisions. Each division is represented by at least five but not more than seven members, as determined from time to time by parliament, to ensure equal and proportional representation of the divisions. The Speaker of the House is elected from among its members.

In the Maltese parliament the office of the leader of the Opposition is formally appointed by the president of the Republic.

JUDICIARY

The Maltese judicial system is basically a two-tier system. The superior courts are the Court of Appeals and its subsidiary, the Court of Criminal Appeal, and the Constitutional Court. The heads of all three courts are appointed by the president based on the recommendation of the prime minister. The Court of Appeals and the Court of Criminal Appeal review the judgments of

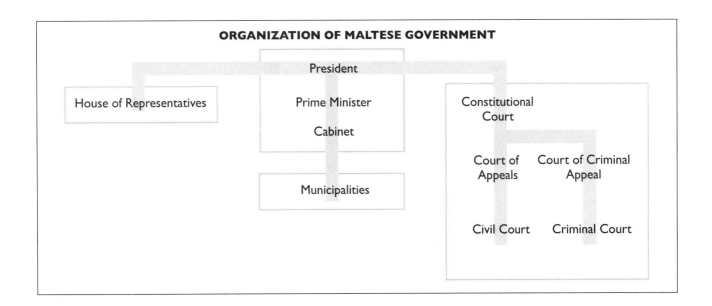

ORGANIZATION OF MALTESE GOVERNMENT

President
Prime Minister
Cabinet
Municipalities
House of Representatives
Constitutional Court
Court of Appeals
Court of Criminal Appeal
Civil Court
Criminal Court

lower courts in civil and criminal cases, respectively. The Constitutional Court considers cases involving alleged violations of human rights, the interpretation of the Constitution, and the invalidity of laws. It also has jurisdiction to decide questions as to membership in the House of Representatives and any electoral issues related to that body.

The Commission for the Administration of Justice is designed to be an independent body. It supervises the work of both the superior courts and the lower courts; formulates recommendations to be submitted to the minister of justice related to the operation, administration, and organization of the courts; provides advice to the president on appointments; draws up a code of ethics to govern the behavior of members of the judiciary, legal practitioners, and procurators; and draws attention to any judge or magistrate whose performance may be hampering the efficient and proper functioning of his office. This commission is headed by the president of the Republic and is composed of nine other members including the chief justice, the attorney general, two members elected by the judges of the Superior Courts for a period of four years, two members elected by the magistrates of the lower courts for a period of four years, one member appointed by the prime minister for a period of four years, and another member nominated by the leader of the opposition as well as the president of the Chamber of Advocates.

REGIONAL AND LOCAL GOVERNMENT

Prior to 1993 there were no local governments per se in Malta, with the exception of the island of Gozo, which was governed by a civic council. In 1993, however, through an act of parliament, municipal councils in various localities throughout the country were created. According to the amendment of the Constitution of April 24, 2001, the State shall be divided into such number of localities as may by law be from time to time determined. Each locality has to be administered by a local council elected by the residents of the locality. Elections of local councilors are held every three years by means of the system of proportional representation using the single transferable vote. Today, there are 68 such councils elected popularly, serving as local governments charged with the administration of the local police, post office, medical facilities, and other government programs. They also assist in the administration and enforcement of national laws. Ultimately, however, they are advisory in nature and depend for their budgetary allocation on, and are answerable to, the central government.

The Electoral System

Malta's unusual electoral system, adopted in 1921, is based on the method called single transferable vote. Ireland is the only other country that uses this system.

The method seems complex but is not. At election time, voters, who must be at least 18 years of age and registered, are asked to rank numerically the candidates, regardless of political party affiliation, whose names appear on the ballot. To qualify for a parliamentary seat, a candidate must fill a specified "quota" in the electoral division or district in which he or she is a candidate. This quota is determined on the basis of the total number of valid votes cast divided by the number of seats allotted for that district, plus one. If in a particular district, for instance, five parliamentary seats are open to competition, and 12,000 votes have been cast (assuming they are all valid), then the quota of votes that a candidate must fill would be 12,000 divided by 6 (i.e., 5 + 1), or 2,000 votes.

Any candidate who meets the quota after the initial vote count is declared a winner. If that winning candidate has received votes in excess of the required minimum needed to meet the quota, as frequently happens, these excess votes are then transferred and added on to the votes of the next-highest-ranked candidate indicated by the voters. It is in this context that the method is called "transferable" because the excess or, more appropriately, the "surplus" votes are used to help the next-highest-preferred candidate attain the quota instead of being discarded.

The Party System

Malta's political party system has evolved from that of a multiparty one to that of a dominant two-party system. The two main parties have their origins in a dispute over the use of English in schools. Those who favored the use of English and acquired the distinction as liberals later formed the Malta Labour Party. On the other hand, those who supported the retention of Italian earned the label of conservatives and eventually formed the core of the Nationalist Party.

Although these two parties dominate political life, Malta is still a multiparty state. Political party competition in Malta is characterized by intense and vigorous partisanship. Their strong party loyalty and allegiance distinguish voters themselves. Even though the electoral system allows them to cross party lines, they rarely do so. Thus, crossover votes tend to constitute a very small portion of the overall votes cast during any given election (or since the 1971 elections).

Despite sharp differences on issues, however, all political parties are agreed on the democratic premises of the Maltese constitution, primary of which is the parliamentary means to political power through competitive elections. There is no underground revolutionary movement seeking the overthrow of the political system.

Major Political Parties

MALTA LABOUR PARTY

(Partit Laburista)

Paul Boffa established the Malta Labour Party officially in 1921. Its unique structure explains in large measure its durability and cohesiveness. At the village level, it maintains a network of village committees. Members of these committees are elected annually by dues-paying party members. Each village committee in turn elects one representative to the district committee. The district committee is responsible for preparing campaign materials as well as organizing and mobilizing support for the national party within the district. At the national level sits an executive committee consisting of representatives from the various districts as well as from the Labour Youth League, incumbent members of parliament who are party members, and representatives from the national party conference, which convenes annually. The national conference is composed of delegates from village committees nationwide.

The party platform of the Malta Labour Party envisions a Socialist future. Throughout the years it has been in power, the Malta Labour Party has adopted policies oriented toward the equalization of social wealth. A key component of this orientation is the nationalization of key sectors of the Maltese economy, including banking, insurance, and shipping. With the assertion of the public sector in the economy, particularly through governmental and quasi-governmental corporations, it has increased the number of those employed in governmental departments and governmental-controlled corporations to nearly 40 percent of the overall labor force. It also has adopted progressive social policies with regard to social freedom, employment, and education. It has frequently complained about church intrusion into state affairs and has pushed for greater appropriation of church property.

The Malta Labour Party was opposed to Malta's membership in the EU. Its leaders argued that membership of the EU would weaken national autonomy and would violate Malta's neutrality status. In 1996 the party's leader, Alfred Sant, who at the time was the country's prime minister, stopped the country's application for EU membership. Although the membership application was later successfully restarted, the party long maintained that free trade agreements with the EU would better have served Malta's interests than accession.

At the 2003 general elections the Malta Labour Party lost power to the Nationalist Party, obtaining 30 of the 65 seats in the Maltese House of Representatives, with a 47.5 percent share of the vote.

NATIONALIST PARTY

(Partit Nazzjonalista)

The Nationalist Party, unlike the Malta Labour Party, has a loose national organization. It relies largely on the semi-autonomous organizations organized by its candidates, members, and supporters at the local level; these are usually prominent local personalities (mainly religious leaders, business entrepreneurs, or white-collar professionals) who have built up extensive networks of supporting clients in their respective municipalities or districts. While the national party organization does not generally maintain permanent local committees, these are supplemented by the local or district networks of clients that designate representatives to form a sort of executive body at the national level; this body, in turn, serves to formulate policies and strategies for adoption by the party as a whole.

The party platform of the Nationalist Party may be described as conservative. It favors the retention of traditional Roman Catholic values in Maltese religious and social life. It is protective of the church's preeminent role in the country by deferring to its influence in the policy-making process, particularly in the area of education and in the matter of church property. While standing for liberal democratic beliefs of the Western European variety, it has particularly advocated electoral reforms that would achieve both "proportionality and ability to govern" in obvious response to the 1981 election in which the Nationalist Party garnered more popular votes than the Malta Labour Party but failed to secure a majority of parliamentary seats. In this reform effort, it succeeded only in achieving the proportionality segment of the reform package because Labour Party parliamentarians contended that inclusion of the "ability to govern" segment would have allowed one-party dictatorship in government.

In economic matters, the Nationalist Party has always stood for the principle of free enterprise. In pursuit of this principle, it has dedicated efforts and resources to attract foreign investors into the country. It has promoted an investment code, officially adopted in October 1987, liberalizing rules on tariffs and repatriation of profits by foreign companies. These companies currently invest and generate employment in such areas as light engineering, footwear and clothing, automotive spare parts, electrical goods and devices, medical and health care-related products, among others. The long-term goal was to transform Malta into a center for overseas banking, insurance, and financial services; it also sought to make Malta a shipping capital in the Mediterranean. To help accomplish this, the Nationalist-led government retained the services of a U.S.-based financial institution, the Chase Manhattan Bank Corporation, in late 1987 as a consultant in the formulation of appropriate legislation.

The leaders of the party have always been strong supporters of European integration. After returning to power in 1998, the party revived the application to enter the EU. When the EU initiative finally reached voters in 2003, it passed with a slight majority—only 53 percent of vote. The party also won the elections in 2003 and as of 2005 held 35 seats in the 65-member House of Representatives.

Minor Political Parties

DEMOCRATIC ALTERNATIVE

(Alternattiva Demokratika)

Founded only shortly prior to the 1992 elections, the Democratic Alternative advocates environmentalism. It managed to get a 1.7 percent share of the popular vote in the 1992 balloting but gained no parliamentary seat. In the 2003 elections it won less than 1 percent of the popular vote.

COMMUNIST PARTY OF MALTA

(Partit Komunista Malti)

The Communist Party of Malta is a legal, aboveground Marxist-oriented political party. It adopted a pro-Soviet stance in the context of the cold war. Instead of fielding its own candidates to run in the elections of 1987 and 1992, it deferred to Malta Labour Party candidates,

presumably so as not to take away votes from the latter. In the 1996 elections it did field a candidate who managed to get only a little over 100 votes altogether. Consequently, it has never secured any legislative seat. The party did not participate in the 2003 elections.

MALTA DEMOCRATIC PARTY

The Malta Democratic Party was founded in 1986 on the basis of the principles of environmentalism, administrative decentralization, and political pluralism. Although it has fielded candidates since the 1987 elections, it has never had significant grassroots support or any parliamentary representation.

EUROPEAN EMPIRE

(Imperium Europa)

Founded in 2000 by Norman Lowell, this party is a controversial far-right political group that received less than 0.6 percent of the vote during the 2003 elections. The party espouses a pro-environmental, pro-libertarian, patriotic, and nationalistic platform, and it also strongly opposes the immigration of non-whites and seeks to reduce the number of African immigrants allowed to enter the country.

Other Political Forces

In Malta there are various interests groups that aim to have influence over political and public issues. Among the most important such groups are the General Workers' Union, the Malta Employers' Association, and the Chamber of Commerce and Enterprise.

The General Workers' Union (GWU) was formed in 1943. It is now the largest trade union in Malta. It should be mentioned that the General Workers' Union has played a crucial role in the country's political life. GWU took part in a national strike against the British colonial government in 1958. The Malta Employers' Association (MEA), in turn, was set up in 1965 following a merger between the Association of Employers and the Malta Employers' Confederation. MEA represents interests of entrepreneurs in many types of businesses. The parallel organization, the Chamber of Commerce and Enterprise, was founded as a voluntary constituted body and was officially recognized in 1948. Its main object is to promote and protect interests of commerce, industry, shipping, insurance, tourism and other types of businesses in Malta.

The interest groups in Malta regularly cooperate with political parties. In particular, the General Workers' Association is strongly connected with the Malta Labour Party, whereas the Malta Employers' Association collaborates with the Nationalist Party.

Due to a 98 percent Catholic population, the Roman Catholic Church is also highly influential in Malta.

National Prospects

Malta's dominant-two-party system is well entrenched. Despite the appearance of third parties in recent years, these have not been significant enough to pose a serious challenge to the hegemony of the Malta Labour Party and the Nationalist Party on the national political scene. The current political arrangement in Malta and the consolidation of political control between the Malta Labour Party and the Nationalist Party has had a stabilizing effect on the country's political system.

The Maltese parliament, has demonstrated the capacity to persist and survive. The two major political parties are aware of this parliamentary function and, thus, would be unlikely to initiate a political agenda that would veer too far in any direction from the center. This is especially true given the country's recent entrance into the EU.

Further Reading

Flanz, Gisbert H., ed. *Constitutions of the Countries of the World: Malta Supplement*. Dobbs Ferry, N.Y.: Oceana, May 1995.

Frendo, Henry. *Malta's Quest for Independence*. Valletta: Valletta Publishing, 1989.

———, ed. *Maltese Political Development 1798-1964: Selected Readings*. Valletta: Ministry of Education and Human Resources, 1993.

Grofman, Bernard Norman, and Shaun Bowler, eds. *Elections in Australia, Ireland, and Malta under the Single Transferable Vote: Reflections on an Embedded Institution*. Ann Arbor: University of Michigan Press, 2000.

Pace, Roderick. *The EU's Mediterranean Enlargement: Cyprus and Malta*. London: Frank Cass, 2004.

Political Handbook of the World 1995-1996. Binghamton, N.Y.: CSA, 1996.

Thackrah, Richard. *Malta*. London: Oxford University Press, 1985.

REPUBLIC OF THE MARSHALL ISLANDS

(Aolepān Aorōkin Ṃajeḷ)

By Eugene Ogan, Ph.D.

The Republic of the Marshall Islands (RMI) was one of the Pacific Island nations created in 1986 from what had been the United Nations Trust Territory of the Pacific (TTPI). It comprises 29 coral atolls and five islands (some of which are uninhabited),. These form two roughly parallel chains, called *Ratak* (Sunrise) and *Ralik* (Sunset). Though the Marshall Islands spread over 1.95 million square kilometers of eastern Pacific Ocean, the combined land mass is 181.3 square kilometers. The population is 59,000 (2005 est.), almost all of whom are ethnically Micronesian.

The islands have a long colonial history. Beginning in 1885, they were successively administered by the Spanish, Germans, and Japanese; the last ruled under a mandate of the League of Nations. World War II had a terrible impact on the islands as fighting killed many Marshallese while bombing devastated the landscape. After establishing military control in 1944, the United States regarded the islands as having strategic importance (the government used various atolls as nuclear test sites). This perspective shaped American administration when the United States became trustee of TTPI and continues to affect political developments in the modern republic.

The Compact of Free Association that produced RMI was the result of long negotiation with Marshallese and others in the trust territory. In these negotiations, Marshallese chose by referendum to be a nation separate from the other TTPI groups. Although the Compact became effective in 1986, it is still subject to interpretation. This fact has not prevented the Marshallese from establishing their own political institutions.

The System of Government

The Marshall Islands is governed by a mixed parliamentary-presidential system.

EXECUTIVE

The executive branch is made up of the president and the cabinet, but true executive authority lies with the cabinet. The members of the legislature, which is known as the Nitijela, elect the president from among their ranks, and he in turn appoints from 6 to 10 Nitijela members as cabinet ministers. In contrast to a true presidential system, the Marshallese president cannot veto bills passed by the legislature. His only power in case of serious disagreement is to dissolve the Nitijela, forcing a general election. The president, however, is both head of state *and* head of government.

LEGISLATURE

The Nitijela is the key political institution. This chamber at present consists of 33 members who are elected to four-year terms. The members are elected by 24 electoral districts that correspond approximately to each atoll. The Nitijela elect the president from among their

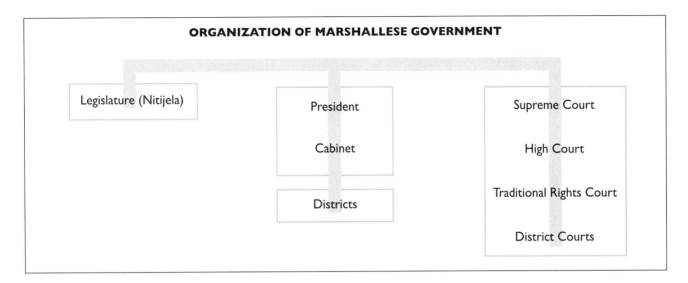

ORGANIZATION OF MARSHALLESE GOVERNMENT

Legislature (Nitijela)

President

Cabinet

Districts

Supreme Court

High Court

Traditional Rights Court

District Courts

number; he then vacates his legislative seat, which is filled by special election.

Traditional Marshallese society was built around tribal chiefs (*iroij*), some of whom were recognized as paramount in their islands (*iroijlaplap*). Their status is institutionalized in the Council of Iroij, which is considered the upper house of the Marshall Islands bicameral parliament (the Nitijela is the elected lower house). The Council is technically an advisory body with special concern for Marshallese culture, and although the council has no veto power, every bill passed by the Nitijela must be sent for its consideration. The council is composed of 12 "eligible persons," five from the Ralik chain of islands, seven from the Ratak chain. Eligible persons are *iroij*, or equivalent, eligible to vote in general elections but not members of the Nitijela.

JUDICIARY

The constitution provides that the judiciary is independent of the executive and legislative branches. There is a Supreme Court, High Court, Traditional Rights Court, and a system of subordinate courts. The High Court is both a trial court and an appellate court for cases from lower courts; appeals from its decisions go to the Supreme Court, which may take appeals from lower courts. Judges of both courts are appointed by the cabinet, acting on recommendation of the Judicial Service Commission and with Nitijela approval. Despite its name, the Traditional Rights Court does not have jurisdiction over such issues as composition of the Council of Iroij or the declaration of customary law and may be regarded as a body ancillary to the rest of the system.

REGIONAL AND LOCAL GOVERNMENT

Four of the twenty-four districts (those that are the most populated) are run by a mayor and a locally elected council.

The Electoral System

Suffrage is universal for Marshallese over the age of 18. However, candidates for the Nitijela must be 21 or older.

The Party System

Traditionally, there have been no formal political parties in the Marshall Islands. However, two groupings are now generally recognized as parties: Ailin Kein Ad (Our Islands) and the United Democratic Party.

Major Political Parties

UNITED DEMOCRATIC PARTY (UDP)

The UDP is the dominant political party and is led by Kessai Note, who won the 1999 presidential elections and was reelected in 2003. He is the first commoner to lead the country.

Minor Political Parties

Another political party is the Our Islands Party.

Other Political Forces

There are no other political forces in the Marshall Islands, although the country depends heavily on financial support from the United States.

National Prospects

The election of Kessai Note as president in 1999 and his reelection to a second term in November 2003 marked a major change in Marshall Islands leadership. Note is the first president who is not an *iroij*. Indeed, his election brought an end to the domination of the Kabua family, two members of that family having served as president since the republic's inception. A member of the United Democratic Party, Note specifically campaigned on a reform platform that raised questions about corruption and nepotism. The successful renegotiation of the Compact of Free Association under Note's leadership insures continued American financial support for the Marshall Islands.

The Marshall Islands, however, faces major environmental issues; many studies predict that the entire nation will be underwater by the year 2030 as a result of climate change and subsequently rising sea levels. While the RMI has taken part in the United Nations Framework Convention on Climate Change, its future as a nation is uncertain.

Further Reading

Patterson, Don. *Selected Constitutions of the South Pacific.* Suva, Fiji: (Institute of Justice and Applied Legal Studies, University of the South Pacific, Suva), 2000.

ISLAMIC REPUBLIC OF MAURITANIA

(al Jumhūrīyât al-Islāmīyâ al-Mūrītānīyâ)

By Isla MacLean
Revised by Deborah A. Kaple, Ph.D.
Further Revision by Soeren Kern

Mauritania, which borders the Atlantic Ocean, the disputed area of Western Sahara, Algeria, Mali, and Senegal, is a link between the Arab Maghreb (a group of predominantly Muslim countries in Africa) and western sub-Saharan Africa. A largely desert country, Mauritania is very poor and heavily dependent on food and financial aid from other countries. It is predominantly Muslim, and its main languages are Arabic and French.

Mauritania's nearly 3.1 million people (2005 est.) are spread out across a vast and empty country the size of France and Spain combined; many of its people are nomads. Its population consists of two communities: one, in the north, is Arabic-speaking, with two components: the Baidhans (white Moors) and the Harattin (black Moors), who are descendants of former slaves of the Arabs but culturally and religiously completely Arabized. The south is black African, also essentially Muslim, and includes three ethic groupings (Fulani, Soninke, and Wolof). The three basic communities are roughly equal in number, with a slight advantage to the Harattin. Tensions between the groups continue to surface, with allegations of "Arabization" efforts and black slavery. Although Mauritania officially banned slavery in 1981, international human rights groups say the practice continues.

Mauritania became a French protectorate in 1903 and a French colony (within the former French West Africa, a federation of eight French territories) in 1920. In 1958 Mauritania became an autonomous republic within the French Community. It became independent on November 28, 1960. Moktar Ould Daddah, who led the independence fight, set up one-party rule and governed for 18 years. In 1964 all political parties merged into the Ould Daddah's party to form the now-defunct Party of the People of Mauritania (PPM). In 1978, after the Ould Daddah regime seized the southern part of Western Sahara, he was ousted in a bloodless coup by Lieutenant Colonel Mustapha Ould Salek. Ould Salek was replaced by Colonel Mohamed Khouna Ould Haidallah, who then was ousted in 1984 by Colonel Maaouiya Sid'Ahmed Ould Taya in a bloodless coup.

In June 2003 Ould Taya, a pro-Western strongman, faced the most serious challenge to his rule since 1984, when an attempted coup was put down after heavy fighting between loyal troops and rebel soldiers. The nine coup leaders were current or former army officers leading an armed rebel movement called the "Knights of Change" that advocated the overthrow of the Ould Taya regime. More than 125 soldiers were detained in connection with the coup attempt. Among those arrested were three leading opposition figures, including former president Ould Haidallah, who was also the main challenger to the head of state in the presidential election held in November 2003.

On August 3, 2005, when President Taya was out of the country, troops seized government buildings in a largely bloodless coup led by Colonel Ely Ould Mohamed Vall (who took on the presidential role) and the Military Council for Justice and Democracy. The council then appointed Sidy Mohamed Ould Boubacar as prime minister. The council, which said it acted to end a "totalitarian" regime, has promised to hold presidential elections within two years. Many Mauritanians welcomed the coup, citing decades of repression under Taya's tenure.

The System of Government

Mauritania is formally a republic with a bicameral legislature, although it has been under military control for most of the period since independence.

EXECUTIVE

Mauritania is a highly centralized Islamic republic dominated by a strong presidency. According to the 1991 constitution, the president is elected by the people for a six-year term. There are no term limits, but elections have been suspended until 2007 (at the earliest) as a result of the 2005 coup. The president presides over the Council of Ministers. He is also the supreme chief of the armed forces and presides over the Superior National Defense Councils and Committees. The president is assisted by a High Islamic Council composed of five persons whom he appoints and whose role is vague. According to the 1991 constitution, the High Islamic Council "formulates opinions concerning the questions about which it has been consulted by the President of the Republic."

The head of government is the prime minister, who is also appointed by the president. Under the authority of the president, he defines the policy of the government and directs and coordinates the business of the government. He is responsible for dividing tasks among ministers.

LEGISLATURE

The parliament has two chambers. The National Assembly (Al Jamiya al-Wataniyah/Assemblée Nationale) has 81 members who are popularly elected for a five-year term in single-seat constituencies. The Senate (Majlis al-Shuyukh/Sénat) has 56 members, 53 of whom are elected for six-year terms by municipal leaders. Among these, 17 are up for election every two years. Mauritanians abroad elect three members.

Parliament meets in regular session twice a year during the first two weeks of November and again during the first two weeks of May. The length of each ordinary session may not exceed two months.

JUDICIARY

Islamic Law (sharia) was introduced in 1980, and the Islamic Court of Justice was founded to try crimes against people and adjudicate in family matters. The first application of the sharia (a public execution and three hand amputations) was in September of that year. In June 1983 it was decided to apply the

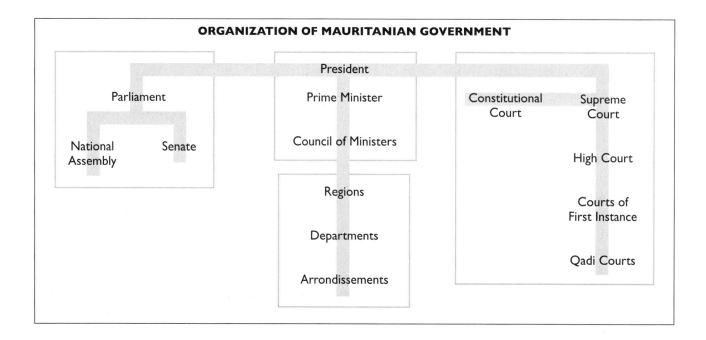

ORGANIZATION OF MAURITANIAN GOVERNMENT

President

Parliament — National Assembly — Senate

Prime Minister — Council of Ministers

Regions — Departments — Arrondissements

Constitutional Court — Supreme Court — High Court — Courts of First Instance — Qadi Courts

sharia in all domains. The Special (Military) Court of Justice was set up in 1980 to investigate and try cases that threaten the security of the government and state. In 1985 the court was reorganized to include civilian magistrates and the right of appeal in civilian and commercial cases. This court was abolished in 1991.

The main courts include a Constitutional Court, the Supreme Court, a High Court, and courts of first instance. There are also traditional (Qadi) courts.

REGIONAL AND LOCAL GOVERNMENT

Mauritania is divided into 12 regions administered by governors who are appointed by the central government. Nouakchott, the capital, is administered directly by the central government. Within these regions, there are 53 departments and 216 prefectures with elected mayors.

Municipalities have taken on greater responsibility within the context of the government-promoted decentralization process. In January and February 1994, Mauritania had its first multiparty municipal elections, in which Ould Taya's political party, the Democratic and Social Republc Party (PRDS), took 172 of the 208 districts. Since then, the PRDS has dominated local governments.

The Electoral System

All Mauritanians 18 years or older may vote. Equal voting rights for civilians and military personnel were introduced in 2000. A second round of voting is required if no candidate wins more than 50 percent of the vote in the first round.

The Party System

The 1991 constitution guarantees "freedom of association" in Mauritania, and subsequent legislation provides for the formation of opposition political parties. Of the 31 authorized parties, only five are of significance in the political arena. In reality, however, Mauritania remains a one-party state. The governing PRDS controls both chambers of parliament by wide margins, and in the last presidential election, held in November 2003, the PRDS garnered 67 percent of the vote.

Major Political Parties

DEMOCRATIC AND SOCIAL REPUBLIC PARTY

(Parti Républican Démocratique et Social; PRDS)

The PRDS is a coalition of conservative political forces and the direct heir of the pre-1990 military state of emergency regime. After the new constitution was promulgated in 1991, the PRDS was one of the first parties to be accorded official status. The PRDS is the official government party and has been criticized by opposition groups for its close relationship with the state apparatus.

The PRDS is the only party so far to have structured its organization at a national level, and it more or less controls the media in Mauritania. It is supported by two other parties in the government coalition: the center-right Rally for Democracy and Unity (RDU) and the right-wing and economically liberal Union for Democracy and Progress (UDP).

Minor Political Parties

Despite the legalization of political parties in 1991, opposition parties in Mauritania have been largely ineffectual in elections or campaigns. Historically, the military coup has been the only method effective in the transfer of political power.,

Of the 81 seats in the National Assembly, 64 are held by the governing party, the PRDS, and 17 by the opposition parties. In the Senate, all but two of the 56 seats belong to the governing PRDS.

RALLY FOR DEMOCRACY

(Rassemblement des Forces Démocratiques; RFD)

The center-right nationalist RFD is the successor party to the Union of Democratic Forces–New Era (Union des Forces Démocratiques; UFD/EN). It is supported by the Arab bourgeoisie who are economically liberal. The UFD was legalized in 1991 and used to be the most important opposition party. The UFD had been highly critical of the government. It was banned in October 2000 for "damaging the country's reputation and interests" and for "incitement to intolerance and violence." It comprised a diverse cross section of political groupings that were all united in the goal of ousting the Ould Taya regime. Ould Daddah obtained over 30 percent of the vote in the 1992 election but boycotted the 1997 poll. However, his chances in 2003 were undermined by the fact that 23 prominent members of his party, critical of his leadership style, defected to support former president Ould Haidallah.

UNION OF PROGRESS FORCES

(Union des Forces du Progrès; UFP)

The UFP was established in July 1998 after splitting with the principal opposition party, the UFD/EN (now the RFD), of which it was the left wing. Supported largely by formerly Marxist-Maoist elements, the UFP now caters to a multiethnic democratic revolutionary left. The UFP is the only opposition party to have secured elected representatives by direct election in single-member constituencies outside the major cities in which proportional representation was used for the first time.

RALLY FOR DEMOCRACY AND UNITY

(Rassemblement pour la Démocratie et l'Unité; RDU)

The RDU is a pro-presidential party aligned with the ruling PRDS.

UNION FOR DEMOCRACY AND PROGRESS

(Union pour la Démocratie et le Progrès; UDP)

The UDP is a pro-presidential party aligned with the ruling PRDS. The UDP is chaired by a woman, Naha Bent Meknass.

POPULAR FRONT

(Front Populaire Mauritanien; FP)

The centrist FP was established in early 1998 after splitting with the Rally for Democracy and Unity (RDU). FP leader Mohamed Lemine Shbih Ould Cheikh Melainine was held in detention between April 2001 and August 2003. Ould Shbih was sentenced to five years imprisonment in June 2001 for "setting up a criminal association" in constitutionally questionable proceedings. Shbih was released early by presidential decree in August 2003, partly because of the political pressure exerted by foreign governments and international human rights organizations.

ACTION FOR CHANGE

(Action pour le Changement; AC)

The AC was granted full legal status in 1995, after splitting with the UFD/EN, but it was banned by the government in January 2002 because the party's allegedly racist and extremist language was said to be a threat to national unity. A left-wing nationalist party, the AC includes some of the most militant parts of the black-Moorish and Negro Mauritanian population. The party's leader is Messoud Ould Boulkheir, who now heads the Arab Nationalist Popular Progressive Alliance (APP), a coalition of nine opposition groups. He has presented himself as a candidate of the poor. Ould Boulkheir has been one of the most vocal critics of the U.S. military intervention in Iraq.

Other Political Forces

BA'THISTS

Since the dissolution of diplomatic relations with Iraq and the establishment of full diplomatic relations with Israel in 1999, the government has attempted to suppress opposition from Mauritanian Ba'thists. The Ba'thist Taliaa Party and its student associations have been banned since November 1999, but Mauritania's outspoken support of the U.S.-led war on Iraq has further antagonized remaining Ba'thist factions within the Arab-Berber elite.

ETHNIC GROUPS

About 70 percent of Mauritanians are Arabic-speaking Moors of mixed Arab, Berber, and black Berber African stock. They are divided into numerous tribal groups and into the White Moors, the dominant class, and the Black Moors, the ex-slaves also known as Harattin. Some 30 percent of the population is black African. The dominant position occupied by White Moors in the past is being eroded, and Black Moors now constitute a sizable portion of the free labor force and urban shantytown dwellers. The black African population is growing at a faster rate than the Moorish population. Black demands for greater representation and protests at the "Arabization" of education have erupted into violence. Periodically, organizations have been formed in the south to seek an independent black state.

The fragile unity of the country is maintained through a common adherence to Islam and, more importantly, an intricate power-balancing process. The government includes representatives of the various ethnic groups, although White Moors still predominate.

HUMAN RIGHTS GROUPS

There are three Mauritanian organizations concerned with human rights issues. The oldest is the Mauritanian League for Human Rights (LMDH), an independent, government-recognized body. A second organization, the Mauritanian Association for Human Rights (AMDH), is not officially recognized. While not affiliated with the opposition, the AMDH had many opposition members, and the AMDH has been more critical of the government than the LMDH. The International Study and Research Group on Democracy and Economic and Social Development in Africa (GERDDES-Africa) is not officially recognized either. The government position is that these organizations are illegal because they are ethnically based; however, the unrecognized organizations carry out their activities unimpeded.

MILITARY

Undoubtedly the most powerful of the non-traditional political forces, the military has been responsible for several coups since the country's independence in 1960 and has been the only organization responsible for marked political change.

RELIGIOUS LEADERS

Although 100 percent of the country's population is reportedly Muslim, the constitution proscribes religious political parties and the use of mosques for political activity of any kind. However, most Mauritanians, black and Moor, are followers of one or another marabout (traditional religious figures who gain their position partly by inheritance and partly by their reputations for wisdom and piety) and frequently consult that marabout on all matters. Given their dominant role in society, the marabouts are essentially a conservative political force. They favored introduction of the sharia, and many opposed the abolition of slavery on the grounds that the practice is sanctioned in the Koran.

National Prospects

Mauritania has faced extreme economic difficulties for many years, their per capita GNP is estimated at $430 (2003, World Bank). In February 2000 Mauritania qualified for $1.1 billion in debt relief under the World Bank's Heavily Indebted Poor Countries (HIPC) initiative. In December 2001 a number of Paris Club creditors promised debt relief beyond that provided under the HIPC initiative.

Poor management of state enterprises had led to Mauritania being heavily indebted. A new investment code was approved in December 2001 and improved the opportunities for direct foreign investment. Ongoing negotiations with the International Monetary Fund (IMF) involve problems of economic reforms and fiscal discipline. Structural measures in the form of price liberalization; the privatization, liquidation, or restructuring of several public enterprises; and agricultural sector reforms have been undertaken in an attempt to reduce debts.

Mauritania has extensive deposits of iron ore, which account for nearly 40 percent of total exports. The decline in world demand for this ore, however, has led to cutbacks in production. The country's coastal waters are among the richest fishing areas in the world, but overexploitation threatens this key source of revenue. Moreover, a devastating invasion by locusts in 2004 destroyed half of all crops and much of the pasture used by nomads to graze their animals. Destitute farmers drifted away from their villages to join the mass of urban unemployed living in slums around the country's main towns.

The government has also initiated a number of public works projects to create jobs. New projects include dams, roads, water supply, electricity plants, and 53 public libraries. A new $36 million terminal for offloading oil products at the port of Nouakchott and a new tank farm have tripled the size of its oil storage facilities. These new facilities should help to relieve Mauritania's chronic fuel shortages as the country joins the ranks of Africa's new oil exporters.

The government is pinning its hopes on two offshore oil tracts. The Chinguetti field is the first to come on stream, producing around 75,000 barrels per day for export by 2006; it is expected to yield some 120 million barrels of oil and gas reserves of several trillion cubic feet. Oil exports are expected to add about US$100 million to Mauritanian government revenues by 2008. Mauritania is one of four West African countries with an operating refinery.

Ultimately, the country's future as a republic rests on the promise of the current government leaders. Whether they will step down and allow elections to resume in 2007 remains to be seen.

Further Reading

Amnesty International. *Mauritania: A Future Free from Slavery?* New York: Amnesty International, November 7, 2002.

Mauritania Country Report: December 2004. London: Economist Intelligence Unit, 2004.

Pazzanita, Anthony G. *Historical Dictionary of Mauritania.* 2d ed. Lanham, Md.: Scarecrow Press, 1996.

U.S. Department of State. *Country Reports on Human Rights Practices 2004: Mauritania.* Washington, D.C.: U.S. Department of State.

World Trade Organization. *Mauritania: Trade Policy Review.* Geneva: World Trade Organization, September 13, 2002.

REPUBLIC OF MAURITIUS
(République de Maurice)

By B. David Meyers, Ph.D.

Most of Mauritius's 1.2 million citizens live on the Indian Ocean island of that name, while 35,000 reside, some 300 miles away, on the much smaller island of Rodrigues. Mauritius also claims Tromelin, an island held by France, and Diego Garcia, a strategically important, mid-ocean atoll, administered by the United Kingdom.

This former French and, more recently, British, colony is an ethnically diverse society of religious, color, caste, class, and linguistic differences. A majority of the population is Hindu, descendants of persons brought from India to work the sugar plantations. Other ethnic communities include white Franco-Mauritians, Creoles (persons of mixed, white and African, descent), Africans, Muslims, and Chinese.

Since gaining its independence from Britain, Mauritius has successfully maintained a stable government and economy. Elections have been held regularly, and power has been transferred peacefully. In contrast with this stability, the multiparty system, which reflects the complexity of Mauritian society, demonstrates an ever-shifting pattern of consolidation, fragmentation, and reassembly.

The System of Government

Mauritius is a parliamentary democracy with a unicameral legislature.

EXECUTIVE

The head of state is a ceremonial president, elected for a five-year term by a simple majority of the National Assembly. The vice-president is also elected in this manner. Executive power is vested in a prime minister, who leads the majority party or coalition in the legislature. Other members of the governing Council of Ministers are appointed by the president on the recommendation of the prime minister. The Council of Ministers is responsible to the National Assembly.

In 2000 the winning electoral coalition of the Mauritian Militant Movement (MMM) and the Mauritian Socialist Movement (MSM) included an agreement between party leaders Sir Aneerood Jugnanth (MSM) and Paul Berenger (MMM) that, at mid-term, one would replace the other as prime minister. Accordingly, in September 2003 Berenger replaced Jugnanth as prime minister. A month later, Jugnanth became the nation's president. While Jugnanth remains president, the prime minister who replaced Berenger, Navin Ramgoolam, was elected to office in 2005. He had already served as the country's prime minister between 1995 and 2000.

LEGISLATURE

Legislative authority is vested in a unicameral National Assembly presided over by a Speaker. Ordinary legislation requires a majority vote, constitutional amendments require the approval of three-quarters of the deputies.

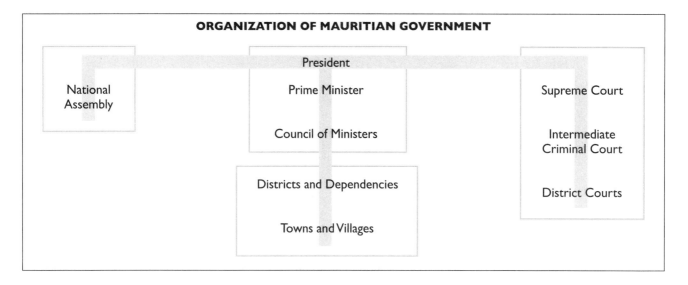

Sixty members of the Assembly are elected by receiving the three highest vote totals in 20 three-member districts, two additional members are elected from Rodrigues, and four to eight additional seats are allotted to "best losers."

In 2005 the Alliance Sociale (which is a partnership between the Mauritian Labour Party [MLP] and the Mauritian Party of Xavier Duval [PMXD]) won 38 seats. The MSM/MMM/Mauritian Social Democratic Party (PMSD) coalition won 22 seats. The two remaining seats for Rodrigues were won by Organization of the People of Rodrigues (OPR) candidates. With the remaining seats awarded to "best losers," an additional four seats went to the Alliance Sociale, two seats went to the MSM/MMM/PMSD, and two more seats went to the OPR.

JUDICIARY

The legal system is based on French civil law together with some elements of English common law. There is a Supreme Court whose judges preside additionally in lower courts. The Supreme Court, which has the authority to find legislation unconstitutional, has been a powerful, independent institution.

REGIONAL AND LOCAL GOVERNMENT

There are nine administrative districts on Mauritius and a resident commissioner for Rodrigues. There are elected town councils in the urban areas and district and village councils in the rural areas.

The Electoral System

The Mauritian electoral system is complicated and unique but it has continued to serve the country well. Two independent supervising bodies, an Electoral Boundaries Commission and an Electoral Supervisory Committee, define the districts, supervise voter registration, and oversee polling. Elections are scheduled every five years but can be called earlier by the government. Voter turnout is high and the polling results and the decisions of the independent supervising bodies are accepted by everyone.

Mauritius is divided into 20 Assembly districts wherein the three highest vote-getters receive seats. The island of Rodrigues is a single two-seat district. Following the polling, the Electoral Supervisory Commission does a statistical analysis of the votes and awards seats to between four and eight "best losers" to balance ethnic and political minorities.

The elections attract participation by numerous political parties and independent candidates, most of whom have no chance of victory. Elections boil down to contests between two competing alliances struck by the three or four major, centrist, parties.

The Party System

Political parties in Mauritius go back to 1947, 21 years before independence, with the founding of the MLP by Sir Seewoosagur Ramgoolam. The MLP was overwhelmingly a party of the Indo-Mauritian community; other communal-based parties, one for Indo-Mauritian Muslims and another for Franco-Mauritians and Creoles, were organized shortly thereafter. As the number of parties proliferated, still others were formed on the basis of class, region, ideology, and individual personalities. In recent years the major parties have become increasingly pragmatic, more centrist, and less based in either a particular ethnic community or economic class. None of the major parties is organized in all of the Assembly districts.

Campaigns are vibrant with massive rallies and streets covered with party pennants and posters. The campaigning is extensively covered by local newspapers and radio. All candidates receive free time on the government-owned television station.

As ethnicity and class have become less important political factors, Mauritian voters have increasingly been inclined to switch party allegiances every five years and to vote out the governing coalition.

Major Political Parties

MAURITIAN LABOUR PARTY

(Parti Travailliste; MLP)

Over the years, the MLP has been Mauritius's most successful political party. Alone, or in coalition, it controlled the government from independence in 1968 until 1982, from 1995 to 2000, and took control again in 2005. The party still gets most of its support from the Hindu community. Once strictly a supporter of free-market economic policy, it now promotes a mixed economy with widespread social welfare benefits. It is led by Navinchandra Ramgoolam, the son of the party founder and the nation's first prime minister. In coalition with the Mauritian Militant Movement, it won all 60 contested Mauritian Assembly seats in 1995 and formed the government. In 2000, this time in alliance with the Mauritian Party of Xavier Duval (PMXD), it captured only six seats. In 2005, maintaining the PMXD cooperative under the Alliance Sociale, the party won a total of 42 seats, once again becoming the assembly majority.

MAURITIAN MILITANT MOVEMENT

(Mouvement Militant Mauricien; MMM)

The MMM was founded in 1969 by Paul Berenger (the country's former prime minister), who remains its leader. Its constituency was based on Franco-Mauritian and Creole urbanites and trade union members. Over the years its Socialist ideology has been increasingly moderated. For the 2000 elections it allied with the Mauritian Socialist Movement and captured slightly over 52 percent of the vote, winning 54 of the contested seats. In 2005 the combined parties won only 24 seats.

MAURITIAN SOCIALIST MOVEMENT

(Mouvement Socialist Mauricien; MSM)

Still led by its founder, Sir Anerood Jugnauth (the current president), the MSM originated as a moderate splinter party from the MMM. Its ideology is social democratic. In 2000 it was part of the winning electoral coalition.

Minor Political Parties

ORGANIZATION OF THE PEOPLE OF RODRIGUES

(Organisation du People Rodriguais; OPR)

This is the most successful regionalist party as it usually wins the island's two Assembly seats. It then often joins the governing coalition and tries to represent the special interests of the island's inhabitants.

MAURITIAN PARTY OF XAVIER DUVAL

(Parti Mauricien Xavier-Luc Duval; PMXD)

The PMXD is a conservative party that allied with MLP for the 2000 and 2005 elections. Its leader is Charles Duval, son of Xavier Duval the party's founder and namesake. Originally known as the Social Democratic Party its declining support has traditionally come from Creoles and whites concerned with perceived Hindu political dominance.

MAURITIAN SOCIAL DEMOCRATIC PARTY

(Parti Mauricien Social-Démocrate; PMSD)

The PMSD predominantly represents the interests of the Franco-Mauritian and Creole landowning class. Once affiliated with the MLP it has now joined forces with the MSM and MMM.

HIZBULLAH

A Muslim party, Hizbullah alone has fielded a full electoral slate in every Assembly constituency. Although Muslims make up 17 percent of the population, most have not supported the party, which won only a single contested seat in 1995 and none in 2000 or 2005. The party is led by Cecil Mohamed Fakeemeeah.

Other Political Forces

The Mauritian press, subject to state censorship during the early 1970s, is now free and robust. Labor unions and communal groups are often politically active.

National Prospects

The Mauritian political system has remained stable and democratic while the economy has been transformed from one dependent solely on sugar plantations to a successful mix of agriculture, tourism, finance, and manufacturing. This country has been, and will probably remain, one of the developing world's success stories.

Further Reading

Bowman, Larry W. *Mauritius: Democracy and Development in the Indian Ocean.* Boulder, Colo.: Westview Press, 1991.
Srebrnik, Henry. "Full of Sound and Fury: Three Decades of Parliamentary Politics in Mauritius." *Journal of Southern African Studies* 28, no. 2 (June 2002): 277–91.

UNITED MEXICAN STATES

(Estados Unidos Mexicanos)

By Dale Story, Ph.D.
Revised by David M. Goldberg, Ph.D.

Mexico occupies just over 1.25 million square miles connecting the land mass of North America to Central America. Mexico shares a nearly 2,000 mile-long border with the United States to the north and borders Belize and Guatemala to the south. With nearly 106 million people Mexico is the third most populous country in the hemisphere. The people of Mexico are majority mestizo or mixed race made up of a combination of Amerindian and European descendants. Nearly all of the population speaks Spanish although indigenous languages remain prevalent among some groups. The population remains overwhelmingly Roman Catholic although some Protestant denominations have recently made significant gains. The country is characterized by profound geographic diversity with deserts, rain forests, volcanoes, and fertile valleys.

Throughout its history Mexico has been dominated by strongly personalistic leaders called caudillos. From the rule of dictator Porfirio Díaz (1876–1911) to the presidents that dominated throughout the 20th century, Mexican politics has been shaped by the power and personalities of its strong leaders. In addition, the majority of the 20th century was dominated by a single party, the Institutional Ruling Party (Partido Institucional Revolucionario; PRI). From 1929 to 2000 the PRI never lost a presidential election and controlled most governors and state legislatures. Opposition parties did not win a gubernatorial election until 1989. No opposition party held a Senate seat until 1988. Incumbent presidents informally chose their successors usually based on experience, training, and their service to the PRI. The constitution guarantees federal government control over most areas of social and economic policy. The result was that the PRI dominated Mexican political life at all levels for seven decades.

In July 2000 Vicente Fox of the center-right National Action Party (PAN), surprised Mexico and international observers by upsetting the PRI candidate, Francisco Labastida, and won the presidency by more than 2.4 million votes. While the election was a shock domestically and internationally, the outcome was the result of a series of PRI defeats at the state and congressional levels and indicated the presence of growing party competition in Mexico.

In the lower house, the Chamber of Deputies, the PRI lost 31 seats in the 2000 election, Fox's Alliance for Change coalition increased its representation by nearly 8 percent to 205 seats. The leftist coalition led by Cárdenas and the PRD won 68 seats denying the PRI a majority.

EXPLAINING THE PRI DEFEAT

Fox's victory and the PRI's loss of the presidency were not singular events but the outcome of more than 12 years of national discontent with Mexican politics. The PRI had several ideological factions, some of which were unhappy with the direction of the party and called for internal reform. In 1985, after a failed attempt to democratize the PRI's candidate selection process, Lázaro Cárdenas left the party and challenged its dominance in the 1988 presidential election. In that election the Cárdenas lead alliance officially won 32 percent of the vote while the PRI candidate Carlos Salinas won 51 percent. Plagued by irregularities and the appearance of fraud, supporters of Cárdenas accused the PRI of stealing the election. The impact was a confirmation of what many Mexicans already believed, namely, that the PRI would use whatever tactics necessary to remain in power. The Cárdenas lead alliance would go on to form the Party of the Democratic Revolution and win several governorships and a consistent, sizable minority standing in the Chamber of Deputies and the Senate. Cárdenas went on to become mayor of Mexico City while the PRD's fortunes declined due to infighting and the rise of the PAN.

In 1993 and 1996, partly in response to allegations of voter fraud, Presidents Carlos Salinas and Ernesto Zedillo initiated broad electoral reforms designed to create greater transparency in the electoral process and increase minority party representation. The Senate was expanded to 128 seats with each state getting two members and the remaining seats allocated based on proportional representation and the granting of some seats to minority parties. The most significant immediate reform was the creation of the independent Federal Electoral Institute (Instituto Federal Electoral; IFE). In 1994 the North American Free Trade Agreement was enacted while Mexico continued to undergo significant economic reform. In response to the lack of democracy and growing economic inequality, a new guerrilla uprising began in the southern state of Chiapas on January 1, 1994. The Zapatistas criticized PRI hegemony and called for legitimate political reform and an end to economic policies that they charged had created a two-tiered system of economic development.

On March 23, 1994, the PRI's presidential candidate, Luis Donaldo Colosio was assassinated under murky circumstances. Rumors of drug cartel involvement or an internal PRI conspiracy with conservative hard-liners behind the plot circulated with little closure on the matter a decade later. Colosio's campaign manager and former education minister Ernesto Zedillo was appointed the new candidate and won the election with 49 percent of the vote. The general perception among observers was that the election met accepted international standards and the Salinas reforms were viewed as effective.

The results of the 1997 legislative elections continued the trend of declining PRI dominance. In the Senate the PRI lost its two-thirds majority and its share of all seats declined from 74.2 percent in 1994 to 60.9 percent. In the Chamber of Deputies the PRI lost its majority and the share of total seats was reduced from 64 percent in 1991 to 47.8 percent in 1997. For the first time in the PRI's history divided government was a reality.

In 1997 Vicente Fox began his campaign as the PAN nominee for the presidency. Fox was a former governor of the state of Guanajuato and had risen through the ranks of the Coca-Cola Company to become the executive for Mexico and Central America. Along the way Fox developed a persona and politics that sharply contrasted with both the ruling PRI and the leftist ideology of Cárdenas and the PRD. He promoted free-market policies but was much less driven by ideology than others in his party. His reformist bent put him at odds with the PAN leadership. As governor of Guanajuato he created and broadened his personal base of support across the country, in part at the expense of building the PAN. Trade missions to the United States, Asia, Europe, and Latin America increased his visibility and popularity at home and abroad. Through his informal style, his ability to raise money and support outside the party, and his growing international presence Vicente Fox was poised to challenge the PRI in the upcoming elections.

The 2000 defeat was the result of growing dissatisfaction with PRI rule across broad sectors of the Mexican population. This dissatisfaction manifested itself with widespread criticism of the results of the 1988 presidential election, PRI defeats in legislative midterm elections, and the rise of Fox and the PAN as a viable alternative. Ironically, the viability of alternatives to the PRI was partly facilitated by the electoral reforms instituted by PRI presidents in the 1990s.

THE MEXICAN REVOLUTION AND ITS AFTERMATH

In order to understand the Mexican political landscape it is necessary to recognize the significance of the Mexican Revolution. The events of 1910 are symbolic beyond Mexico. The revolution was the first of its kind in the 20th century and reverberated throughout the hemisphere and ultimately the world. Prior to the revolution, General Porfirio Díaz had ruled Mexico as a repressive dictator from 1876 to 1911. The army and police maintained order through force. Díaz took land from political opponents and peasant villages, concentrating large farm-ranch-plantations (called haciendas) among a ruling elite. A few hundred hacienda owners controlled half of the nation's arable area. Some 90 percent of the rural population spent their lives working on the haciendas at marginal pay, perennially in debt to their employers, virtually under feudal conditions.

The revolution began in November 1910 as a reaction to the political and economic dominance of Díaz. Over the following 10 years more than a million lives were sacrificed—almost one-tenth of the population. Francisco Madero, the first revolutionary president (1911–13), stressed a political agenda of "effective suffrage and no reelection." The peasant leader Emiliano Zapata emphasized the socioeconomic goals of "land and liberty." Venustiano Carranza spearheaded the writing of the 1917 constitution, which codified the aims of the revolution (including the secularization of education, nationalization of subsoil rights and other assets, agrarian reform, and extensive labor rights). The 1920s consolidated the power of the "Revolutionary Family," which was institutionalized in the creation of the precursor to the PRI in 1929. The rest of the century has seen the continued dominance of the ruling party through the continual election of its presidential candidates to six-year terms.

The "no reelection" clause limits the president to one six-year term, with no second term ever, and prohibits members of Congress, state legislatures, and municipal councils from serving two consecutive terms. After an intervening term, these lesser officials can run again for the same office. Thus the Mexican political structure is a "musical chairs" system under which PRI leaders rotate horizontally as well as vertically from one government position to another.

Between 1930 and 1994 14 Mexican presidential elections were won by the PRI. This continuity provided a tremendous amount of political stability in Mexico at a time when many of its neighbors were racked with instability. Political stability, however, came at the cost of a pluralistic, democratic political system.

The System of Government

According to the 1917 constitution, upon which the current government is founded, Mexico is a federal republic with a bicameral legislature. The country is comprised of 31 states and a federal district.

EXECUTIVE

Executive power is vested in the president as the head of government and head of state. Informally, the president has been the most important actor in Mexican politics since 1930. The president must be a native-born Mexican of native-born parents and at least 35 years of age. The president is limited to one six-year term in office and any and all reelection is prohibited by the constitution.

Formally and informally the president has a great deal of power that, under PRI rule, allowed for the dominance of both the executive and the legislative branches. The president can initiate legislation in both houses of the legislature and set legislative priorities. The president is dominant in the making and implementation of foreign policy. In the period since the PRI defeat in 2000 President Fox has experienced much greater difficulty in enacting his agenda than his predecessors.

The president can veto legislation. The president appoints the cabinet ministers, diplomats, high-ranking officers of the armed forces, and all federal judges, with Senate confirmation. The president can pardon anyone convicted of any felony, and chief executives have used this right freely in political matters to co-opt former opponents.

The constitution grants the chief executive the power to issue decree laws in most areas of public life. For example, the income tax was created by presidential decree, followed years later by congressional action. Presidential decrees have created cabinet ministers, government corporations, major public works projects, significant budget changes, and public policies ranging from family planning to nuclear energy, followed later by congressional legislation.

Under the PRI, the senior cabinet officer was the *Secretaría de Gobernación* (minister of internal affairs), who controls federal-state-municipal relations, liaison with Congress, elections, voter and party registration, immigration and emigration, motion picture production and theaters, television and radio noncommercial air time, the federal police, and federal prisons. More recently the economic ministries of planning and budget, finance, and commerce and industrial development have risen to the forefront due to the primacy of economic policy. Ranking next is the minister of foreign relations, who helps the president conduct foreign policy. Preceding their presidencies, many of Mexico's former leaders served in ministerial positions.

LEGISLATURE

The Mexican legislature is divided into an upper house (Senate) and a lower house (Chamber of Deputies). The Senate has 128 members each serving a six-year term. Members are prohibited from running for immediate reelection but can run again after an interim term has transpired. The senators are chosen through a mixed electoral system. Three senators are elected from each state and the Federal District. Two are chosen through a plurality rule (the party that received the most votes) and the third seat is given to the party receiving the second highest vote total. The remaining 32 seats are chosen through proportional representation in a single national district.

The Chamber of Deputies has 500 members who serve three-year terms. Like the Senate, members may not seek immediate reelection but may run again after an intermediate term has expired. A total of 300 seats are elected from districts based on population in plurality elections. The remaining 200 seats are chosen through proportional representation. The table below illustrates the representation of the major parties since 1997. The most striking result is the PRI decline between 1997 and 2000 and the comparative resurgence in the 2003 elections.

Up until 1997 the PRI dominated Congress regardless of slight shifts in the number of minority-party deputy seats. Since the legislative branch debated the form rather than the substance of new laws, changes in bills received from the executive branch were generally cosmetic rather than substantive. Both houses put legislation in final form in committee hearings that follow the guidelines set down by the appropriate cabinet ministry. Floor debate serves as an escape valve for frustration but has had little effect on legislation.

Both houses of the legislature must hold two sessions per year. The first begins on September 1 and runs until December 15. The second begins on March 15 and ends April 30. In the interim a Standing Commission is formed, made up of 37 members from both houses. The Commission has the power to call the Congress back into session and approve presidential appointees but cannot pass legislation. Lacking the ability to serve in consecutive terms, members are appointed to committees based on length of service to the party rather than seniority in Congress.

Mexico's post-2000 experiment with divided government has yielded mixed results at best. As a result of the 2003 elections the PRI has been able to exert control over the legislative agenda and the president's priorities. The PRD's initial unwillingness to work with President Fox hurt both sides.

JUDICIARY

Mexico's federal court system has exclusive authority for all important civil litigation, leaving to the court

CHAMBER OF DEPUTIES PARTY REPRESENTATION 1997–2003 (IN PERCENTAGES)

Year	PRI	PAN	PRD*	Other
1997	47.6	24.2	25.2	3.0
2000	37.8	39.2	19.1*	3.9
2003	44.4	30.2	19.0	5.6

*In the 2000 elections the PRD lead the Alliance for Mexico coalition. While the PRD share of seats remained fairly constant, the share of seats for smaller leftist candidates with whom the PRD has allied increased. The impact was in increase in representation for leftist parties.

Sources: Andreas Schedler, "Mexico's Victory: The Democratic Revelation," Journal of Democracy 11, no. 4 (2000): 5–19; And Instituto Federal Electoral.

system of each state civil jurisdiction over minor sums of money and divorce cases. Suits involving contracts, finance and banking, labor-management relations, corporations, and interstate and intrastate commerce are handled by federal courts. In criminal law, federal courts handle bank robberies, kidnappings, and most major felonies. Murder cases, however, are heard in state courts.

The one major restraint on presidential power is judicial, specifically the writ of *amparo* (relief), which can be issued by any federal judge on behalf of a citizen claiming his constitutional rights have been violated by a government official. The *amparo* can be directed against a government official at any level but can be obtained only from a federal court. This writ stays the disputed governmental action until an appeal can be heard by the federal Supreme Court. The *amparo* combines some of the judicial powers found in the Anglo-Saxon writs of injunction, mandamus, and habeas corpus. It may halt official action, compel officials to carry out constitutional obligations, or force judges to tell a defendant the specific charges against him in a criminal case. Political disputes over elections and campaigns are excluded from the authority of *amparos*.

From 1917 to 1980 some 5,000 writs of *amparo* involved the president and his cabinet ministers as defendants. In one-third of these cases, private citizens or groups won their Supreme Court appeal over presidential action. However, the court has never issued such a writ when political rights or economic policies were involved.

Reforms in 1994 reduced the size of the federal Supreme Court from 26 to 11 members and precluded individuals who have just left political office from being appointed to the court. Supreme Court justices must be native-born Mexicans and be at least 35 years old. The president appoints them with Senate confirmation. Ministers to the court serve 15-year terms. A justice must retire at age 65 or at any time after age 60 if he or she has completed 10 years of service. Since 1929 every justice has been a member of the PRI.

The intermediate federal judicial level is comprised by circuit courts of appeals, of which there are six. The Supreme Court selects appellate judges from among federal district court judges to serve four-year terms. The president can grant an appellate tenure until age 65. Each of the 31 states has a state supreme court (Supremo Tribunal de Justicia), ranging in size from three to eight justices. The governor selects these justices for six-year terms.

REGIONAL AND LOCAL GOVERNMENT

In each of the 31 states, a governor is popularly elected for a six-year term and can never serve a second term. From 1929 until 1989 every governor was a member of the PRI. Despite the formality of state party conventions, the dominant party's inner circle in Mexico City has selected the candidate most likely to carry out the national administration's wishes. Except in six states, gubernatorial terms do not coincide with the presidential term. Under Article 76 of the constitution, the president can have the Senate remove the governor of any state in which law and order cannot be maintained. The chief executive then designates an interim governor to finish the term. From 1917 to 1964 presidents have removed an average of one governor per year. Since 1964 presidents have averaged only one removal per presidential term. However, each chief executive has pressured one to three other governors to voluntarily resign when political crises have gotten out of control.

Each state has a one-chamber legislature, with members elected for three-year terms, every other election coinciding with the election of the governor. State constitutions reserve most of the powers for the governor, making the legislature a rubber-stamp committee formalizing details of his programs. Legislatures vary from 9 to 25 members. In each state the legislature must approve all municipal budgets, which the governor's finance director coordinates. Mexico has 2,359 municipalities (*municipios*), which

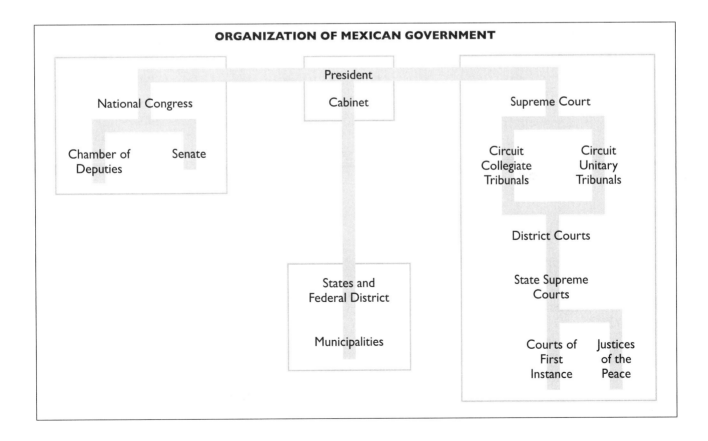

ORGANIZATION OF MEXICAN GOVERNMENT

are like counties in the United States. Every town and city within the *municipio* is governed by the municipal council (*ayuntamiento*). Councils range in size from 5 to 11 members who serve three-year terms. Mayors (*presidente municipal*) have the constitutional powers to dominate the councils.

The Electoral System

Elections at all levels of government are popular and direct and provide representation by a simple majority winner, except for the 200 seats in the federal Chamber of Deputies and 32 seats in the federal Senate, which are chosen by a system of proportional representation. Federal Chamber of Deputies districts and state legislative districts each have a single representative. For each senator and deputy, as well as state legislators and municipal council members, a substitute is also elected. This allows each party to reward its workers with nominations as substitutes. In the event of a vacancy between elections, the substitute immediately fills the post, obviating the need for an interim election.

With the PRI having dominated so many elections, voter apathy characterized most elections. Half of the eligible voters historically do not go to the polls in presidential elections (however, the 1994 election saw a record turnout of 78 percent); in congressional or municipal races with strong minority-party candidates, the turnout may reach 70 percent of the registered voters. PRI leaders encourage PRI voter turnout with promises of continuing welfare programs and patronage. Voter turnout in the 2000 presidential election approached 64 percent and in the 2003 legislative election was just over 62 percent. The rise of competitive multiparty elections appears to have a positive effect on voter turnout. Interestingly, universal suffrage is compulsory, but not enforced.

The Party System

ORIGINS OF THE PARTIES

After Mexico achieved independence from Spain in 1821, its party system consisted of several small parties, each a personalistic group following a strong leader. The real impetus for the institutionalization of parties and the end of more personalistic movements was the desire by the revolutionary leaders of the 1920s (particularly Plutarco Calles) to consolidate the victory of the revolutionary government in the context of an umbrella

party—first known as the National Revolutionary Party (Partido Nacional Revolucionario; PNR).

THE PARTIES IN LAW

The federal Law of Political Organizations and Electoral Processes (Ley Federal de Organizaciones Politicas y Procesos Electorales, or LOPPE) gives Congress the authority to set requirements for a party to qualify for a place on the ballot. The LOPPE has required a party to have a minimal number of members and to win a similarly minimal percentage of the total national vote to retain its legal status. The standards have been interpreted loosely in order to promote the image of a multiparty system. Typically, as many as eight minority parties have participated as registered parties.

PARTY ORGANIZATION

The LOPPE requires each party to maintain a permanent national headquarters and a national executive committee. At least six months before an election, a party must hold a national convention to publicly announce its candidates for all offices it intends to contest. In practice, the standard procedure has been for each party's inner circle to choose its candidates. National officers of each party dominate state and local committees.

CAMPAIGNING

Electoral reforms through the 1980s and 1990s were directed at creating a more independent Federal Electoral Institute and providing a more level playing field for all parties to contest elections. The Federal Electoral Institute has increased in prominence and importance in recent elections. While considerable progress has been made in equalizing the resources available to parties, the PRI undoubtedly maintains a distinct advantage through its years of domination of the political system. For example, the PRI continues to garner a disproportionate share of media attention. A variety of factors contribute to the PRI's dominance of both television and print coverage. The ruling party enjoys a symbiotic relationship with the major networks and several newspapers. Even in cases of journalistic independence, the fact that the PRI dominates events that make the news explains its overwhelming lead in coverage.

SPECTRUM OF MEXICAN POLITICAL PARTIES

In 2003 the Federal Electoral Institute recognized 11 national political parties. Six parties registered and received the necessary number of votes to participate in the federal legislative elections. Recognition is given to the parties that effectively win greater than 2 percent of the vote. Historically, parties have been divided into the right (PAN), center (PRI), and left (PRD). Increasingly the parties span the political spectrum and smaller parties, while still comparatively weak, have increased their share of seats in the last two elections.

Major Political Parties
INSTITUTIONAL REVOLUTIONARY PARTY
(Partido Revolucionario Institucional; PRI)

HISTORY
The dominant party of Mexico, the PRI, was originally founded as National Revolutionary Party (Partido Nacional Revolucionario; PNR) by the former Mexican president Plutarco Calles on March 4, 1929, in Querétaro. At this point in history, Calles can be credited for making two influential decisions. First, he announced in his state of the union address that he would not seek another term in office—thereby solidifying the concept of no reelection. Second, he outlined and enacted the plan to create a new national party to encompass all the revolutionary factions and to institutionalize the succession of power. After three "puppet" presidents between 1928 and 1933, Calles endorsed Lázaro Cárdenas as the presidential candidate of the PNR for the 1934 election. The decision proved as pivotal as that of creating the party. Cárdenas immediately began to shape the landscape of Mexican politics for decades to come. The new president demonstrated the powers of the office, declaring his independence from previous administrations and even sending Calles into exile in the United States. Fulfilling many of the aims of the revolution, Cárdenas redistributed land to peasants at levels unparalleled before or after his administration, organized more of the working class than ever before, and nationalized the petroleum and railroad industries. Finally, Cárdenas solidified the concept of the six-year presidential term, the unilateral selection of the next presidential candidate by the incumbent, and also the recognized independence and autonomy of the succeeding president.

The party's national assembly changed the name to the Institutional Revolutionary Party in 1946 to emphasize the continuing social and economic reforms to which it is committed. The renamed PRI was also organized along the corporate lines of economic sectoral representation. In this case, the PRI focused on bringing together three major sectors: labor, the peasantry, and the middle class. The umbrellas for both organized labor, the Confederation of Mexican Workers (Confederación de Trajabadores de México; CTM), and the peasantry, the National Peasant Confederation (Confederación Nacional Campesina; CNC), were already in place by the 1940s. President Manuel Avila Camacho in 1943 created the National Federation of Popular Organizations (Confederación Nacional de Organizaciones Populares; CNOP) as the sector for bureaucrats, professionals, housewives, merchants, and others of the growing middle class. These three groups became the institutional and organizational backbone of the party, with the CNOP subsequently becoming a dominant force in the party, overshadowing the labor and agrarian sectors in policymaking.

In a significant initiative in 1963, the party created an Institute of Political, Economic, and Social Studies (Instituto de Estudios Políticos, Económicos, y Sociales; IEPES) to research national needs and policy priorities. The IEPES coordinates PRI and government policy formulation. In 1964 the PRI elected as its president an attorney, Carlos Madrazo, former governor of Tabasco. He convinced the PRI to adopt a policy of party primaries to open nominations for state and local offices to those not tied to political cliques. Madrazo arranged party primaries in two states, Baja California Norte and Chihuahua. However, since its 1929 founding, the PRI has relied on an elite inner circle to select nominees. The inner circle, therefore, got the party's national executive committee to cancel the policy of primaries and forced Madrazo to resign in a major defeat to internal party reform efforts. While many other aspects of the political scene have been liberalized and reformed, the PRI has continued to use a closed system of selecting nominees.

ORGANIZATION
At the apex of the PRI's organization is the national executive committee (Comité Ejecutivo Nacional; CEN). The "inner circle" of the CEN includes the party president; the secretary-general; secretaries for agrarian, labor, and popular action; and two secretaries of political action (always one federal deputy and one senator). The CEN has 13 additional secretaries, who are designated by the inner circle. The next level is the national council, which has at least 60 representatives from each of the agrarian, labor, and popular sectors, plus the heads of the state committees from the 31 states and the Federal District. The CEN dominates the

council. The council guides state and municipal PRI assemblies and reports on them to four staff officers of the CEN: the director of administrative services, the director of adjudication, the director of electoral action, and the director of social activities. The lowest nationwide entity is the national assembly, in which about 2,000 representatives chosen from both the sectoral and the regional divisions of the party represent the general PRI membership. National assemblies meet every three or four years and merely ratify CEN policies. In addition, the PRI convenes a national convention every six years to formally ratify the presidential candidate whom the CEN already has announced.

As mentioned earlier, the agrarian sector is dominated by the National Confederation of Peasants, which grew from state-organized peasant leagues. The labor sector includes eight confederations, seven federations, and 19 independent unions, all under the umbrella of the Congress of Labor. The largest and most influential of these labor groups is the Mexican Confederation of Labor. The popular sector is headed by the National Confederation of Popular Organizations, with government employees being the dominant force.

POLICY

PRI's domestic policy stresses "no reelection," the revolutionary ban on continuation in one office. The party supports (some would say controls) the right to strike, even for those working for the government in essential services (except for the military). PRI economic policies have initiated many important social programs: minimum wages for all trades and for unskilled labor, social security, basic health care for the poor, public housing for workers, communal or individual farms for peasants, and profit sharing for private-sector workers. Yet the party has done much to placate the private sector, particularly in creating a stable economic environment and courting business confidence. PRI's foreign policy stresses Mexico's independence from the United States, the Soviet Union, and Europe. It favors cooperation with the Organization of American States to promote Latin American regional common markets and has consistently sympathized with left-of-center and even revolutionary Latin American governments.

A key to the success of the PRI has been its ability to maintain a sense of balance and equilibrium. Presidential administrations oscillate between leftist and rightist perspectives to mollify various constituencies. A perceived pro-business domestic bent in economic policy has been balanced with a perceived leftist favoritism in foreign policy.

MEMBERSHIP AND CONSTITUENCY

PRI members have held all executive government posts from minister down through middle-level bureaucrats, all federal judgeships, and most governorships, Senate seats, and congressional district deputy seats. Civil service merit systems are only token, with the PRI's political patronage being the rule in public life. Government jobs are filled on the basis of the political clique (camarilla) system. A successful PRI politician's entourage is horizontal among peers who were classmates in school and vertical among rising administrators and their trusted assistants. Since a camarilla is based on close friendships and loyalty, as a camarilla leader rises in the PRI and in government, he has his associates promoted into higher-level offices. Among rank-and-file PRI members, extended family relationships form clusters within the party, based on lifelong friendships within each age group, class, and community.

FINANCING

Bureaucrats pay party dues equal to three days' pay a year. Other members pay token dues or are given credit for dues by performing various services for the party. Prominent politicians fund banquets and entertainment within their own cities and states, and, at every level of government, unaudited government contingency funds have long been suspected as financing for PRI activities.

PROSPECTS

The PRI has run the government since 1929 and dominates most facets of public life. In the 1960s and the 1970s communist guerrilla kidnappings and killings did selective damage to the PRI in a few cities. The most serious challenge to the PRI in this period came in 1968 when student demonstrators protested political repression, hoping to force the government to cancel the Olympics. Such a cancellation might have discredited the PRI enough to drive it from power, but the demonstrators were repressed violently by the government in the infamous Tlatelolco Massacre.

The late 1980s, however, saw the onset of a steady erosion of PRI electoral and popular support. Economic decline forced the PRI to yield ground in terms of political liberalization and also to lose political support to opposition parties. As described above, in presidential elections in 1988 and 1994 and in national congressional elections (particularly those of 1997), the ruling party's margin of victory has steadily declined to below 50 percent. Gains in the legislative elections of 2003, however, coupled with the loss of seats by the PAN, have made PRI consent necessary for nearly every presidential initiative.

NATIONAL ACTION PARTY
(Partido de Acción Nacional; PAN)

HISTORY

The political party seen as the chief opposition to the PRI in the postwar years has been the conservative National Action Party. The PAN was founded on September 14, 1939, by Manuel Gómez Morín, on a platform of Catholic social principles within the framework of the institutionalized revolution. Gómez Morín (1897–1972) was dean of the law school of the National University of Mexico and university president. The party's roots can be traced to a number of earlier political and social movements, although its initial leaders were primarily motivated by reactions against the anticlericalism of the 1920s and the perceived radicalism of the Cárdenas regime in the 1930s. The early *panistas* wanted to restore to the church many of its prerevolutionary powers, especially in the areas of religious education and political participation. When the PAN ran its first candidate in 1940, it marked the first time since 1914 that a conservative party could fully participate in revolutionary Mexico. In 1946 the PAN won four deputy seats in Congress and its first two municipal governments. In 1947 the PAN won its first seat in a state legislature in Michoacan. The national vote for the PAN has steadily increased from around 8 percent in the early 1950s to 15 percent in the 1980s and rose dramatically to 43 percent in the 2000 presidential election.

ORGANIZATION

The party president and secretary-general direct the national executive committee, which has secretaries for political action, public relations, finance, recruitment, and campaigning. The committee guides state and municipal chairmen. In 1958 PAN presidential candidate Luis H. Alvarez introduced into Mexico the first open party convention—an obvious contrast to the PRI's inner-circle selection of candidates. PAN's subsequent conventions also have been open contests. In 1976 the necessary 80 percent of delegates could not agree to nominate Pablo Emilio Madero, nephew of the father of the 1910 revolution, Francisco Madero. The party then voted not to offer a 1976 presidential candidate.

POLICY

On economic and social issues the PAN in recent years has not perfectly fit the model of a conservative party favoring free enterprise over economic justice and growth over equity. Certainly the party's philosophy has been pro-business and oriented toward private ownership. But at least since the 1960s the PAN has also stressed social consciousness. In an important document issued at the close of the party's 20th national convention in 1969, the PAN advocated a third path of development between capitalism and socialism: *solidarismo*, or, as described by one author, "political humanism." Private property is viewed as positive provided that it also contributes to the society at large.

MEMBERSHIP AND CONSTITUENCY

The PAN has claimed upwards of 500,000 members, a majority undoubtedly coming from the middle class and upper class. A base of strength has always been northern Mexico, where an independent and conservative spirit has served as a fertile base for the PAN. However, the PAN has achieved successes in other regions of Mexico as well. Key early victories came in 1967 when the PAN took over local government in two state capitals, Hermosillo in Sonora and Mérida in Yucatán. As of 2004, the PAN controlled 9 governorships, 46 senators, 151 federal deputies and a host of state deputies and municipal mayors.

FINANCING

Three-fourths of the members pay voluntary, locally set dues. Political officeholders often contribute a portion of their salaries to the party. Catholic Action groups make contributions, as do many wealth entrepreneurs. The party holds fund-raising raffles, dances, and concerts to enhance its financial coffers and is well known for its past refusal to accept government financing as a sign of its fierce independence.

PROSPECTS

Fox's victory in the 2000 elections is undoubtedly the largest victory in the history of the PAN. In the 2003 legislative elections the PAN lost 9 percent of its seats creating a situation where the PRI was again the dominant force in the Mexican legislature. To the extent that the PAN's electoral fortunes are contingent on the success of President Fox the party's short-term electoral future looks negative.

PARTY OF THE DEMOCRATIC REVOLUTION
(Partido de la Revolución Democrática; PRD)

HISTORY

The political left in Mexico has had a long and torturous history of divide-and-rule control exercised by the

PRI. Only in the last decade, with the onset of the PRD (essentially as a splinter from the PRI), has the left achieved any considerable electoral success.

The history of today's PRD begins with the creation of the Communist Party of Mexico (Partido Comunista de México; PCM). Francisco Cervantes López, publisher of a weekly socialist newspaper, and Manabendra N. Roy, a Marxist from India, founded the PCM at a Mexico City socialist conference in September 1919. In 1920 the PCM began publishing its official organ, *Vida Nueva*, twice a month. In 1921 the party launched its communist youth of Mexico group, sent delegates to the third Comintern congress in Moscow, and held its own first party congress.

In 1922 the famous painters Diego Rivera and David Siqueiros joined the PCM and began its magazine, *El Machete*. However, from 1930 to 1935, the party was outlawed for its violence against the government. The Hitler-Stalin nonaggression pact in 1939 cost the PCM many members; and, in 1940, the PCM helped the French Stalinist Jacques Mornard assassinate Soviet dissident Leon Trotsky in Mexico City. In 1978 the PCM applied for conditional registration after 30 years of being denied legal status. Allied with three small parties, the PCM gained legal registration after the 1979 elections in which it won 5.4 percent of the vote and 18 proportional representation seats in the Chamber of Deputies. At a national party convention in November of 1981, the PCM officially dissolved itself; and a few days later the Unified Socialist Party of Mexico (Partido Socialista Unificado de México; PSUM) was created by the union of the old PCM and the other smaller parties. However, the PSUM did not fare any better in the 1982 presidential election, receiving less than 5 percent of the national vote.

Frustrated with the economic decline and the slow pace of political reform, in late 1985 a group of dissident *priista* leaders began to foment change, particularly in terms of a more open process of selecting nominees within the PRI. This group became known as the "Democratic Current" and was led by the key PRI leaders Cuauhtémoc Cárdenas and Porfirio Muñoz Ledo. The split within the PRI escalated throughout 1986 and 1987, culminating with Cárdenas and Muñoz Ledo leaving the PRI and Cárdenas accepting the presidential banner of a small opposition party. In January 1988, the National Democratic Front (FDN) was constituted as a coalition of leftist parties to support the *Cardenista* candidacy. While Cárdenas struck a very popular chord throughout Mexico, the PRI candidate (Carlos Salinas) won the presidency in July with just over 50 percent of the vote. The following year,

the FDN dissolved—replaced by the PRD as the leading political party on the left. The PRD ran Cárdenas again for president in 1994 and won considerable electoral gains in the congressional (and Mexico City mayoralty) elections of 1997. Cárdenas's term as mayor of Mexico City was beset by crime and economic problems and was not generally viewed as a success for him or the party. He ran as the PRD's candidate in the 2000 election winning 17 percent of the vote, down considerably from his 1988 high of 32 percent but consistent with his 1994 share of the vote. After the 2003 legislative elections the PRD controlled 97 seats in the Chamber of Deputies, 16 in the senate, four governorships, and a variety of seats in state and local government.

ORGANIZATION

The PRD defines itself as a union of three political movements: the "Democratic Current" splinter from the PRI; the "Socialist Left" descending from the Mexican Socialist Party (PMS), the Mexican Worker's Party (PMT), the PSUM, the PCM, the Coalition of the Left, and the Movement of Popular Action; and the "Social Left" composed of independent worker, peasant, and civic action groups

The PRD was formed in and has been chiefly directed by national party congresses, of which there have been three (in 1990, 1993, and 1995).

POLICY

The traditional domestic policy of the PCM called for expropriation of all privately owned businesses, industries, and services under a Marxist government; party ownership of all media; and abolition of nonsocialist schools. Its foreign policy was anti–United States and pro–Soviet Union—supporting Cuba, the Sandinista government in Nicaragua, and the Democratic Revolutionary Front in El Salvador. The new reincarnation under the format of the PRD, however, has produced a much more moderate left, which has led to more successful electoral outcomes. While the party openly sympathizes with revolutionary movements, such as the Zapatistas, its domestic policies principally focus on moderate reforms, exemplified by efforts to reduce the value-added tax.

MEMBERSHIP AND CONSTITUENCY

Somewhat akin to the dilemma of the PAN, the Mexican left has been challenged to find a significant electoral base in the Mexican political spectrum. With the PRI monopolizing the imagery of the Mexican Revolution and dominating the organizational bases of both labor and peasants, the left has had little room in which to operate. However, with the economic decline of the 1980s and the resulting political misfortunes of the PRI, the more moderate leftist split from the PRI has come together in the PRD to represent a formidable alternative and challenge to the PRI. The remarkable increases in congressional representation in 1997 and the election of Cárdenas as mayor of Mexico City marked an apex in electoral success for leftists in Mexican history.

PROSPECTS

In part, the PRD is a victim of its own success. The party came into existence as an electoral and ideological challenge to PRI dominance. With the defeat of the PRI and the perception of a poor performance by Cárdenas as the first elected mayor of Mexico City, the party's standing has been hurt. The PRD has maintained its standing as the third largest party in both the Chamber of Deputies and the Senate but its future remains unclear.

Minor Political Parties

GREEN ECOLOGICAL PARTY OF MEXICO

(Partido Verde Ecologista de México; PVEM)

The Green Ecological Party or PVEM was founded in 1986 by Jorge González Torres. González was a former PRI loyalist who broke away from the party. The PVEM was registered and received recognition in February 1991. Given the many benefits afforded political parties and members of the legislature some suggested the party was created as a personal political base for González. Since his retirement from public life in 1991 the party has been ruled by his son Jorge Emilio González Martínez, affectionately known as *El Niño Verde* or the Green Kid.

After the 1988 election the PRI began to allow the formation of party alternatives in response to growing criticism against corruption and the party's rule. It was against this backdrop that the PVEM was created and managed to fashion a small niche for itself in Mexican electoral politics. The PVEM and several other smaller parties played the role of "loyal opposition," challenging PRI dominance more in form than substance by giving the appearance of a multiparty political system without demanding substantive reform.

The PVEM does have well-articulated policies on a variety of environmental and economic issues, but its recent past and future have been clouded by accusations of bribery, scandal, and impropriety. In February 2004 Emilio González Martínez was filmed negotiating a two million dollar bribe with developers in that PVEM-controlled municipality of Quintana Roo, where numerous towns and cities catering to foreign tourists are located.

In October 2003 the IFE levied a multimillion dollar fine on PVEM for violations of Mexican campaign finance law. In order for the PVEM to be a viable party in the future it needs to break away from the appearance of belonging to the González family and develop a legitimate party organization throughout the nation based on its principles.

In 2000 the PVEM formed an alliance with the PAN that contributed to the election of Fox. Since that time the alliance has collapsed and the PVEM is more closely allied with the PRI. After the 2003 elections the PVEM controlled 17 federal deputies, five senators, and several seats in state and local government.

LABOR PARTY

(Partido del Trabajo; PT)

The Labor Party was created in 1990 and registered with the IFE in February 2001. Ideologically, the party is similar to the PRD. It was formed by leaders with the some former ties to Maoist parties but this does not appear to exert a significant influence on the party's current activities. Critics allege that the PT was formed with the help of then- president Zedillo and the PRI for the purpose of weakening and dividing support for the PRD and other leftist parties in the 1994 presidential election. During PRI rule the PT was considered among the "loyal opposition" supporting the governments' initiatives more often than not.

The PT currently has six federal deputies and one Senate seat. Its commitment to building democracy and promoting economic equality may resonate with the Mexican public in future elections but there are other larger parties, which are better organized, that have a similar message.

CONVERGENCE OF CIVIL SOCIETY FOR DEMOCRACY

(Convergencia de Organismos Civiles por la Democracia; CD)

Convergence was created in 1990 as an umbrella network including over 121 different civil groups. The grouping includes organizations concerned with human rights, economic development, democracy promotion, public health indigenous rights, and the environment, among others. A central goal is strengthening democracy through the inclusion of broad-based actors across the Mexican political landscape.

Convergence currently holds five federal deputy seats and has some representation at the state and local level.

ZAPATISTA NATIONAL LIBERATION ARMY

(Ejército Zapatista de Liberación Nacional; EZLN)

While the Zapatistas do not hold any seats in the federal government they are an important actor that merits some attention. The Zapatistas came forward on January 1, 1994 (the same day that NAFTA went into effect), in the southern state of Chiapas to call for a broad range of reforms. Although they do have a militant wing and have engaged in brief encounters with the Mexican army, it is not their stated intention to take over power by force. Instead, they are primarily concerned with the profound economic inequality between the industrialized north and the largely rural, agricultural, indigenous southern part of Mexico. They were very critical of PRI dominance and called for legitimate democratic reforms. Various peace plans between the Zapatistas and the government have failed outright or stalled. While they do not command the attention and support they did during the 1990s many of the social and economic issues they first addressed have not received the necessary attention from the federal government. Like the PRD, the Zapatista message has in part been overshadowed by the electoral defeat of the PRI in 2000.

Other Political Forces

ORGANIZED MANAGEMENT

Under a 1941 law, every retail store or commercial company must join the local chamber of commerce. These chambers in turn must unite in the Confederation of National Chambers of Commerce (Confederación de Cámaras Nacionales de Comercio; CONCANACO). It has an executive council, holds annual general assemblies, and assesses dues on a scale based on annual sales.

Under the 1941 law, every manufacturer, wholesaler, and distributor within a nationwide industry must belong to that industry's national chamber. For example, every shoe manufacturer must belong to the National Chamber of the Shoe Industry; every radio and television station must belong to the National Chamber of Broadcasters, and so on. These industrywide chambers in turn must unite in the Confederation of Industrial Chambers (Confederación de Cámaras Industriales; CONCAMIN). It, too, has an executive council, holds an annual general assembly, and assesses dues on a scale based on annual sales.

Neither CONCANACO nor CONCAMIN are part of the PRI, but individual business and industrial executives may join the PRI. CONCAMIN and CONCANACO have full-time staffs of economists, lawyers, and other specialists who draft suggested policies, regulations, and procedures. They then lobby directly with the highest appropriate level of government concerned. These private-sector groups are widely recognized as the most autonomous and potentially the most powerful political organizations in Mexico.

ORGANIZED BUREAUCRACY

All federal government employees below the top five levels of administrators belong to unions. Thirty-one unions have members throughout the agencies and departments of the executive branch and among staff employees of the judicial and legislative branches. Since 1936 these unions have been united in the Federation of Unions of Workers in the Service of the State (Federación de Sindicatos de los Trabajadores en el Servicio del Estado; FSTSE). It has 1 million members.

The FSTSE dominates the popular sector of the PRI and helps formulate major government policies. Its well-disciplined members turn out for political rallies, campaign speeches, and elections. The FSTSE has its own Social Security Institute, which provides better pensions and health services than the social security system for workers in the private sector.

ORGANIZED LABOR

The largest group of unions is the Confederation of Mexican Workers (CTM), which helps formulate labor policy for the PRI and the government. Other federations less politically powerful have been the Revolutionary Federation of Workers and Peasants (Confederación Revolucionario de Obreros y Campesinos; CROC) and the National Workers Federation (Confederación Nacional Trabajadores; CNT). The Railroad Workers, Petroleum Workers, and Telephone Workers

Unions are semi-autonomous, having loose links to the CTM but operating independently. All federations and autonomous unions meet annually in the Congress of Labor, whose key committees articulate organized labor's needs and goals.

National Prospects

The presidential elections of 2000 ushered in a new era for Mexican politics. A country so rich in natural resources, diversity, and population is well positioned to increase its role as a regional power and to make great strides in domestic political and economic development. Indeed, Mexico stands at a unique place in its often tumultuous history. Due to PRI dominance for most of the past century the government formally and informally still mirrors that past. While the defeat was a tremendous victory for democracy in Mexico the aftermath has been more complicated.

President Fox's approval ratings have fallen substantially. His party lost a sizable number of seats in the 2003 elections, usually an indicator of discontent with the incumbent president. His efforts at economic and social reform have become mired in controversy or have failed outright. Upon coming to office he promised he would calm the Zapatistas right away but little progress has been made. The economy has drifted in large part due to greater dependence on the United States, which has been in a recession for most of Fox's term. Relations with the United States, which had initially seemed so optimistic, have moved at a glacial pace as the aftermath of September 11, 2001, and disagreements over immigration reform and the death penalty have soured much of the original good feeling.

In the past few years, gang wars related to narcotics trafficking have escalated to record levels and there is no foreseeable end to the violence. A general rise in crime has also occurred; the rate at which kidnappings take place is one of the highest in the world. Although Mexico is in a position to make great strides, it is also in a position to suffer great setbacks.

Further Reading

Baer, Delal M. "Mexico at an Impasse." *Foreign Affairs* 83, no. 1 (2004): 101–9.

Gonzales, J. Michael. *The Mexican Revolution 1910–1920.* Albuquerque: University of New Mexico Press, 2002.

Handelman, Howard. *Mexican Politics: The Dynamics of Change.* New York: St. Martin's Press, 1997.

Lawson, Chappell. "Fox's Mexico at Midterm." *Journal of Democracy* 15, no. 1 (2004): 139–53.

Levy, Daniel, and Kathleen Bruhn. *Mexico: The Struggle for Democratic Development.* Los Angeles: University of California Press, 2001.

Pastor, Robert. "Exiting the Labyrinth." *Journal of Democracy* 11, no. 4 (2000): 20–24.

Schedler, Andreas. "Mexico's Victory: The Democratic Revelation." *Journal of Democracy* 11, no. 4 (2000): 5–19.

Shirk, David. "Vicente Fox and the Rise of the Pan." *Journal of Democracy* 11, no. 4 (2000): 25–32.

FEDERATED STATES OF MICRONESIA

By Eugene Ogan, Ph.D.
Revised by Leon Newton, Ph.D.

The Federated States of Micronesia (FSM) is an island republic that developed out of the former United Nations Trust Territory of the Pacific. It was administered by the United States from 1947 to 1982, when a Compact of Free Association was signed between the two nations. FSM is made up of some 607 islands, including a number of tiny coral atolls, which were charted on the map as the Caroline Islands. (Another Caroline Island group now constitutes the Republic of Palau.) The total land area of 270.8 square miles contains a population estimated in 2005 at 108,000.

The Caroline Islands had a complicated colonial history, as they were administered successively by Spain, Germany, and Japan before the United States become trustee. During the long series of negotiations that reconstituted the UN Trust Territory as separate nations, four island groups decided to remain in a confederation to form the FSM. These are the present states of Kosrae, Pohnpei, Yap, and Chuuk. This history, combined with the islanders' general distrust of centralized authority, has produced a distinctive structure for a polity of such small size.

The System of Government

The FSM is a republic with a unicameral legislature.

EXECUTIVE

The FSM has a national government headed by a president who is both chief executive and head of state. He and his vice president must be from different states within the federation. They are chosen from the at-large members of congress by majority vote of that body; they must then resign their congressional seats, which are subsequently filled by special election. They cannot serve more than two consecutive terms of four years each. President Joseph Urusemal was elected in 2003. The next executive election is slated for 2007.

LEGISLATURE

The congress is unicameral, but the constitution provides for two kinds of members with different terms of office. Four at-large members are elected from each state for a four-year term. The 10 remaining members are elected for two-year terms from congressional districts within each state. Districts are based on population and each state must be assigned at least one district. Congress must reapportion districts at least every 10 years in order to accommodate for population fluctuations.

Members of congress must be at least 30 years old. Elections for four-year term seats will next be held in 2007; elections for two-year term seats were held March 2005 will be held again in 2007.

JUDICIARY

National judicial authority is vested in a Supreme Court, with both trial and appellate divisions. The chief justice and no more than five associate justices

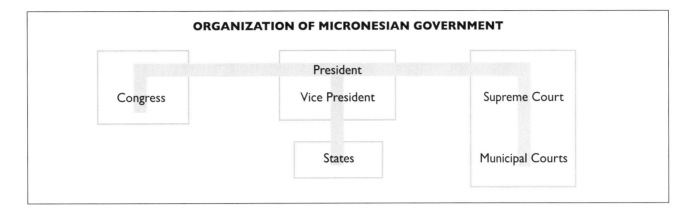

ORGANIZATION OF MICRONESIAN GOVERNMENT

Congress

President
Vice President

Supreme Court

States

Municipal Courts

are appointed by the president with the approval of two-thirds of Congress.

REGIONAL AND LOCAL GOVERNMENT

Each state has its own constitution, designating executive, legislative, and judicial powers. While the states differ in some detail from the others constitutionally, all states place executive authority in a popularly elected governor who serves for a four-year term. State legislatures vary in form, though all try to deal with the problem of balancing representation according to population numbers with appropriate attention to geographic and social configurations.

Only Chuuk's legislature is bicameral, and Yap is the only state with constitutionally established councils of traditional leaders. These councils have the power to veto legislation; otherwise, they are primarily advisory bodies. State judiciaries also vary. Unique to Yap are municipal courts in which presiding judges are the traditional leaders.

The Electoral System

Suffrage is universal to all those over 18 years of age. Presidential elections are held every four years. Congressional elections are held every four years and every two years depending on the length of term of the members being chosen.

The Party System

There are no formal political parties in the FSM. Political parties, however, are not banned. Political lines run along myriad nuanced tribal, family, and island-based affiliations.

Major Political Parties

There are no political parties in the FSM.

Minor Political Parties

There are no political parties in the FSM.

Other Political Forces

There are no other political forces that affect the direct elections or political climate.

National Prospects

The Compact of Free Association between the FSM and the United States was amended and renewed for an additional 20 years in 2003. However, financial support provided by the United States has not continued at the levels operating during its trusteeship. It remains to be seen if an economy based largely on gardening and fishing, in which the government is almost the sole employer paying monetary wages, will sustain the present political system. The burgeoning tourist industry offers some hope, but growth has been limited due to the country's geographical remoteness and weak infrastructure (supplies of electricity and potable water are limited and unreliable). Under the Compact of Free Association, citizens of the FSM can live and work in the United States without being subject to the usual immigration procedures. It is possible that increasing numbers will take advantage of this opportunity and, like migrants from other Pacific Island nations, maintain a system of monetary remittances to support those who remain at home.

Further Reading

Levy, Neil M. *Micronesia Handbook.* 4th ed. Chico, Calif.: Moon, 1996.

Hanlon, D. L. *Remaking Micronesia: Discourses over Development in a Pacific Territory, 1944–1982.* Honolulu: University of Hawaii Press, 1998.

REPUBLIC OF MOLDOVA
(Republica Moldova)

By William Crowther, Ph.D.
Revised by Tom Michael

The Republic of Moldova, which was established on August 27, 1991, is a relatively small country, with a territory of approximately 13,000 square miles and a population of about 4.4 million (2005 est.). Located in southeastern Europe, it is bordered on the north, east, and south by Ukraine, and on the west by Romania.

Moldova's political circumstances are largely consistent with those found in other former Soviet republics. Paralleling developments in the Baltic republics, Moldavian nationalists participated in the campaign for election to the Soviet Congress of People's Deputies of the USSR in 1989 and formed the nationalist-oriented Moldavian Popular Front. The Soviet Republic of Moldavia's first partly democratic elections for the Supreme Soviet, in February 1990, produced a majority of delegates aligned with the Popular Front. Competitive national elections have been held since independence: for the president of the republic since 1991 and for an entirely new post-Soviet parliament, beginning in 1994.

Among the key factors complicating the republic's current situation is its ethnic diversity. Many political parties that emerged following independence drew upon these ethnic differences. Ethnic Moldovans make up the largest group, comprising about three-quarters of the population. In 2004 the minority percentages were divided among Ukrainians (8.4 percent); Russians (5.8 percent); Bulgarians (1.9 percent); Romanians (2.1 percent); and the Turkic-Christian Gagauz community (4.4 percent).

Furthermore, Moldova's sovereignty was challenged by two active separatist movements initiated by Gagauzia and Transnistria. The so-called Gagauz Republic attempted to break away from southern Moldova, but the dispute was largely resolved in the mid-1990s through negotiation. The political situation of Transnistria, or Transdniester, was resolved in 2005 when parliament officially granted the region full autonomy (it is basically a country unto itself in all but name). As a result of this concession, Russian troops stationed in Transnistria for the purpose of keeping the peace have been ordered to withdraw.

The System of Government

The government of Moldova is a parliamentary republic with a unicameral legislature.

EXECUTIVE

The head of state of Moldova is the president of the republic. Under constitutional arrangements prevailing at the time of the 1990 national elections, the president was elected by the members of parliament. New provisions were introduced in 1991 calling for direct presidential elections. A constitutional amendment in 2000 returned the election of the president to members of parliament.

The president is elected for a term of four years. His election is validated by the Constitutional Court. He is charged with guaranteeing the independence and unity of the republic and overseeing the efficient functioning of public authorities. The president may be impeached by vote of two-thirds of the total number of deputies elected to parliament. His case is then heard by the Supreme Court of Justice. The president can take part in meetings of the government and presides when he does so. He also can take part in the work of parliament and is called upon to deliver to parliament messages concerning issues of national concern. He names the prime minister following consultation with the parliamentary majority and names the government on the basis of a vote of confidence by parliament. The president can dissolve parliament for a period of 60 days if it fails to form a government. This can be done only once in one year, not during the last six months of the life of a parliament, and not during a state of emergency or war.

The government (or cabinet) of Moldova is made up of a prime minister, two deputy prime ministers, and approximately 20 ministers. This leadership directs the activities of 20 functionally organized ministries and seven departments of state. Members of the government are nominated by the president but must be confirmed by parliament before taking office. Once selected by the president, the prime minister selects a government and establishes a program that is then submitted to parliament for a vote of confidence. The government must submit to parliamentary questioning, if requested. Parliament is given the power to dismiss the government or an individual member thereof through a vote of no confidence by a majority vote of the members.

Moldova's first president was Mircea Snegur. He gained the position at the time of the transition to independence with the support of the Popular Front delegates in parliament. He retained it by winning the first popular election to the post in 1991, which he contested unopposed.

In 1996 President Snegur faced a reelection challenge from two prominent leaders with power bases in the legislative branch: the Socialist Party leader, Petru Luchinschi (president of parliament), and the Agrarian Democrat Andrei Sangheli (prime minister). Despite earlier cooperation with the Agrarians and the Socialist Party, Snegur found himself at a disadvantage to his former partners in vying for the support of moderate Moldovans and Russian-speakers in presidential elections. Forming his own political organization, the Party of Revival and Conciliation in Moldova, Snegur courted the pro-Romanian nationalist support formerly directed to the Popular Front but failed to achieve widespread appeal. Parliamentary speaker Luchinschi, benefiting from a combination of left-wing parties, eventually won the election with 54 percent of the vote over Snegur's 47 percent.

As president, Luchinschi sought a constitutional referendum to introduce greater presidential powers. He faced resistance from parliament, which in 2000 passed an amendment calling for Moldova to abandon its semipresidential system to become a parliamentary republic. Luchinschi responded by vetoing the law, but his veto was overturned. Under the new law, parliament was able to mount presidential elections but, when voting in them proved inconclusive, Luchinschi dissolved parliament. When in early 2001, general elections were finally held, unreformed Communists were returned to power—a first for any former Soviet republic. Communist leader Vladimir Voronin became the next president. He was reelected by parliament for an additional term in 2005.

LEGISLATURE

Moldova's legislative branch is a unicameral body referred to as the Parliament of Moldova (Parlamentul Moldovei). It is described in the constitution as the supreme representative body of the republic and is made up of 101 deputies elected to four-year terms by means of direct universal vote. It elects a president of the parliament by secret majority vote of the deputies and may remove him by a two-thirds vote. Leadership of parliament is vested in the president of parliament, two vice presidents, and a standing bureau of nine members (the preceding three officers are ex officio members). Parliament meets in four-month sessions, twice a year, and may be called into extraordinary session by the president of the republic, the president of parliament, or a two-thirds vote of the deputies. The parliament passes laws, may call for referenda, and exercises control over the executive as called for in the constitution. Permanent commissions consider legislation in the following areas: legal affairs and immunity; economy, industry, and privatization; budget and finance; state security and public order; foreign relations; human rights and national minorities; culture, science, education, and mass media; social and health protection and ecology; control and petitions.

Results of the 1994 legislative election marked a sharp reversal from the politics of the early post-Soviet transition. Turnout for the election was 79.3 percent. A total of 13 electoral blocs, political parties, and social political formations, as well as 20 independent candidates, contended for 104 legislative positions (in 2001 the number of seats were reduced to 101). The greatest beneficiaries of the election were the Agrarian Democrats, who won

43.2 percent of the vote and 56 of the 104 seats, providing them with an absolute majority. Another 28 seats were won by the Socialist Bloc, allies of the Agrarians, which captured 22 percent of the vote. The nationalist pro-Romanian parties suffered a massive defeat, while more moderate pro-Romanian parties fared somewhat better. The other two parties that won seats were the Bloc of Peasants and Intellectuals (9.2 percent, 11 seats) and the Popular Front Alliance (7.5 percent, 9 seats). None of the other nine parties and blocs that campaigned surpassed the threshold required for participation in the national legislature.

A second round of legislative elections in 1998 pitted a reconstituted Communist Party against parties on the political center and the right. In this contest, three parties and one electoral alliance, the Democratic Convention of Moldova, bringing together the former president Mircea Snegur's Party of Revival and Accord in Moldova and the Christian Democratic Popular Front, surpassed the 5 percent threshold for entry into parliament. The Communist Party of Moldova emerged with a substantial plurality: 30.1 percent of the national vote and 40 out of 104 parliamentary seats. The Bloc for a Democratic and Prosperous Moldova, strongest of the center parties, polled 18.1 percent of the vote and garnered 24 seats in Parliament. On the political right, the Democratic Convention of Moldova won 19.4 percent of the vote and 26 parliamentary seats. Finally, Valeriu Matei's center-right Party of Democratic Forces attracted 8.8 percent of the vote and won 11 seats in the legislature. Strikingly, the Agrarian Democratic Party, which overwhelmingly dominated the previous election, could attract only 3.6 percent of the vote and was not able to enter parliament.

The 2001 elections were a resounding victory for the Communist Party, which picked up 71 parliamentary seats after gaining 50.1 percent of the vote. Twelve seats and 13.4 percent of the vote were won by the center-left bloc Braghis Alliance, edging out the right-wing Christian Democratic Peoples Party, which captured 11 seats and 8.2 percent of the vote. The seven remaining seats (of 101 total) were divided among independents.

In 2005 the Communist Party retained the majority, albeit by a smaller margin; garnering 46.1 percent of the vote, they were awarded 56 seats. The Christian Democratic Peoples Party earned 9.1 percent of the vote and earned 11 seats. The most interesting change, however, is that the Democratic Moldova Bloc, which is made up of the Democratic Party of Moldova, the Our Moldova Alliance, and the Social Liberal Party, earned 28.4 percent of the votes and 34 seats.

JUDICIARY

The Moldovan judicial system consists of a Supreme Court of Justice, a Court of Appeals, subordinate tribunals, the Superior Council of the Magistracy, the Procuracy, and a Constitutional Court. The Superior Council of the Magistracy is made up of judges chosen by Parliament for five-year terms and is responsible for discipline in the judicial system. The Constitutional Court comprises nine deputies, three chosen by the president and six by parliament. It is named as the sole authority with constitutional jurisdiction in the republic and is described as entirely independent, subordinated only to the constitution itself. The Procuracy, which is headed by a procurator and a collegium, directs investigations, orders arrests, and administers the prosecution of criminal cases. It is also charged with administration of the justice system and insuring the legality of government actions. Below the national

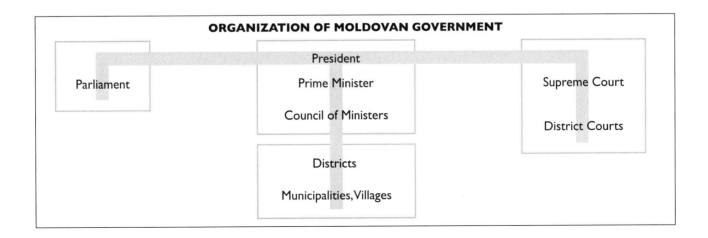

ORGANIZATION OF MOLDOVAN GOVERNMENT

Parliament

President
Prime Minister
Council of Ministers

Supreme Court

District Courts

Districts
Municipalities, Villages

level the judicial system is based on a network of local courts and higher-level appeals courts.

REGIONAL AND LOCAL GOVERNMENT

After independence, Moldova retained a regional system of government not unlike the Soviet system: below the central government, there were 40 administrative districts, each of which was governed by a locally elected council. With the local elections of 1999, however, regional government was reformed and concentrated into nine provinces with two autonomous regions (Transnistria and Gagauzia). Further reform in 2003—harkening back to the Soviet system—replaced the provinces with 33 districts (*rayons*) and one municipality.

The Electoral System

The law on Moldovan legislative elections was passed on October 19, 1993. It called for the formation of a new national parliament that differed significantly from its initial legislature. In a key shift, it was decided that Moldova's first entirely post-Soviet legislature would comprise 104 delegates. After years of deadlock, republican leaders hoped that this smaller body would be more manageable than the 380-member Soviet institution, in which it was often difficult even to achieve a quorum. (By the 14th legislature, it was further reduced to 101 delegates.) Rules governing the electoral mechanism were also fundamentally altered. Under the new system, delegates were elected on the basis of proportional representation from closed party lists. A 4 percent threshold for participation in the legislature was established in order to avoid excessive fragmentation. In a move that distinguished it from the vast majority of proportional representation systems, the Moldovans adopted a single national electoral district for the 1994 elections. While not ensuring participation in the separatist region, this mechanism allowed elections to go forward, selecting a body of delegates whose constituency was the entire republic, regardless of their individual places of residence. Transnistrian leaders refused to allow voting in their region but did agree to permit those who wished to cross over into Moldovan territory in order to participate in the elections. Some 6,000 people took advantage of this opportunity to cross the Dniester and vote in specially established west bank polling places.

The president is chosen by agreement of at least three-fifths of the legislature. If no candidate achieves such a majority, a runoff between the top two candidates determines the outcome in the second round.

The Party System

The Communist Party of Moldavia (CPM) dominated the political life of the republic from its inception in 1944 until 1990. During that period CPM officials monopolized all politically significant positions. However, the party's power disintegrated with remarkable swiftness once democratic elections were held. The Communist Party was formally abolished in 1991, following the abortive August 1991 coup attempt in Moscow. But the CPM continued to dominate in Transnistria, which initially refused to recognize the legitimacy of the government of Moldova.

The character of party politics in Moldova after independence reflected the relatively recent emergence of competitive politics in the republic, the legacy of communism, and the existence of deeply divisive ethnic and linguistic issues. Party competition has focused on pro-reform/antireform and pro-CIS/pro-Romania orientations.

Major Political Parties
COMMUNIST PARTY OF THE REPUBLIC OF MOLDOVA
(Partidul Communist Republica Moldovei; PCRM)

The Communist Party of the Republic of Moldova is a direct successor of the Soviet-era Communist Party. It was outlawed until late 1994 and thus did not compete in the February 1994 parliamentary elections. After the party reentered political activity, it formed a parliamentary faction from among deputies who migrated to it from other left-wing party factions. It has since established itself as a powerful electoral force in the country, winning the majority of seats in parliament in 2001. It has strong support among industrial workers and Russian-speakers. It favors alliances with the Commonwealth of Independent States and a compromise with the leadership of Transnistria. The party is led by Vladimir Voronin.

CHRISTIAN DEMOCRATIC PEOPLE'S PARTY

(Partidul Popular Crestin Democrat; PPCD)

The Christian Democratic People's Party was formed in 1989 as the Popular Front of Moldova. The Popular Front emerged as an advocate of increased autonomy from the Soviet Union and of the rights of the ethnically Moldovan population of the republic. Following the Popular Front's success in the 1990 elections, delegates were able to dominate proceedings in the national legislature and secure government support of its agenda. The Popular Front is well organized nationally but is strongest in the capital and in the areas of the country most heavily populated by Moldovans. At its third congress, in February 1992, the Popular Front became explicitly committed to unification with Romania and changed its name to the Christian Democratic Popular Front. Popular reaction against the party's increasingly nationalist orientation led to defections of moderate party leaders and significant decline in popular support in the period leading up to the 1994 legislative elections.

For the 1998 elections, the party consolidated into a successful, right-wing, electoral bloc called the Democratic Convention of Moldova. In 1999 it took on its present name, and, in the 2001 elections, it again won parliamentary seats. The Christian Democrats emphasize Romanian alliances over Russian ones, pursue democratic reforms, and seek to curb the heightened power of the ruling Communist Party. In fact, the government temporarily suspended the Christian Democratic People's Party following their protests in opposition to the government in 2002. The party is led by Iurie Rosca.

DEMOCRATIC PARTY OF MOLDOVA

(Partidul Democrat din Moldova; PDM)

This centrist party was formed in 1997 as the Movement for a Democratic and Prosperous Moldova. It was created by members of parliament who supported the legislative agenda of President Petru Luchinschi. It favored European integration and market reforms. After modest victories in the 1998 elections, it participated in the government. In 2000 it was reconstituted under its present name, and later entered into an agreement with the opposition sides of the Social Liberal Party and the Braghis Alliance known as "Our Moldova." The party leader is Dumitru Diacov.

As of the 2005 elections the party has become a significant political force, holding a third of the parliamentary seats.

SOCIALIST UNITY/EDINSTVO

(Unitatea Sociulisla/Edinstvo)

Edinstvo was formed in 1989 as one of the "interfront" organizations that emerged among workers in many of the former Soviet republics in order to oppose the anti-Soviet independence movements. In the early transition it was politically conservative in the sense of supporting the status quo of the pre-1990 period and strongly pro-Russian and sympathetic to Transnistria. Edinstvo's main base of support is found in the ethnic Russian urban population. It is positively inclined toward the Commonwealth of Independent States (CIS). Its president is Petr Shornikov.

SOCIAL LIBERAL PARTY

(Partidul Social-Liberal; PSL)

This progressive party was formed in 2001, drawing from the Christian-Democratic Women's League, the National Youth League of Moldova, and other minority associations. In 2002 it drew in the Party of Democratic Forces, which had been formed in 1995 from the United Democratic Congress and was led by Valeriu Matei. In 2004 the Social Liberal Party entered the anticommunist "Our Moldova" electoral bloc along with the Democratic Party and the Braghis Alliance. The leader of the Social Liberals is Oleg Serebrean.

DEMOCRATIC AGRARIAN PARTY OF MOLDOVA

(Partidul Democrat Agrar din Moldova)

The democratic Agrarian Party was originally formed by deputies in the transition legislature elected in 1990. The Agrarians were able to maintain a remarkable degree of cohesion throughout the disruption that occurred within Parliament from 1990 through 1993, and they emerged as a powerful electoral force. They peaked with the 1994 elections, in which they earned 56 seats in Parliament. Their success was due in part to the close relationship of agribusiness with the Agrarian deputies, such as village mayors or collective farm managers, who also held cautious views on land reform. The party maintained a strong electoral base among rural Moldovans and many held common ideological views, as reform Communists. The Agrarian Party fell into swift decline in the late 1990s, however, particularly in the wake of their defeat in the 1998 general elections, in which they failed to win a parliamentary seat. For the 1999 local elections, the party formed a bloc with the

Communist Party and the Socialist Party, but in the parliamentary elections of 2001, the Agrarians campaigned alone and again did not cross the threshold of representation. The party is led by Anatol Popusoi.

PARTY FOR REVIVAL AND ACCORD OF MOLDOVA

(Partidul Pentru Renastere si Conciliere din Moldova)

The Party of Renaissance and Accord of Moldova was formed in July 1995 as an electoral vehicle through which the then incumbent president, Mircea Snegur, sought a second term in office in November 1996. Its original leadership was drawn from defectors of the Democratic Agrarian Party in Parliament. It sought the support of former constituents of the Christian Democratic Popular Front, which had fallen into decline by the mid-1990s. The platform of the Party for Revival and Accord was pro-Romanian and pro-reform.

For the 1998 elections the party joined an electoral bloc with the Democratic Party of Moldova and in 2002 it ceased to exist when it merged with others to create the Liberal Party. By 2004 the Liberals had entered into the "Our Moldova" Alliance.

Minor Political Parties

Since its inception, the new Moldova has seen the formation of several minor political parties. These include Alianta Civica "Furnica" (Civic Alliance "Ant"), Gagauz People's Party, League of Christian Democratic Women, National Liberal Party, National Peasant Party, National Christian Party, National Youth League, New Forces Movement, Party of Social and Economic Rights, Popular Democratic Party, the United Liberal Party of Moldova, the Congress of the Intellectuals, the Party of Democratic Forces, and the United Social Democratic Party of Moldova.

Other Political Forces

The country entered into a partnership and cooperation agreement with the European Union in 1998, and this agreement may eventually evolve into full membership; the process of negotiation and cooperation with the EU also will exert a strong influence in coming years.

National Prospects

The political party environment has been volatile in Moldova since independence. The interaction of ethnic conflict and pro-reform versus antireform political cleavages has complicated the process of party formation. A second negative factor has been the disjunction between elite political competition and mass-level politics. Individual leaders have both repeatedly abandoned their party affiliation and formed parties as vehicles for the pursuit of their individual ambitions. Both of these practices decrease the ability of the electorate to vote on the basis of stable expectations concerning leaders' behavior, and have hence undermined party institutionalization.

On the positive side, some parties, particularly those on the center-left, have remained stable despite these conditions. Moldova has carried out a series of competitive elections that have exhibited the peaceful change in power in both the legislative and executive branches. While substantial fragmentation remains, the Republic of Moldova thus appears to be moving in the direction of stable competitive politics, with the institutionalization of some parties.

Further Reading

Crowther, William. "The Construction of Moldovan National Consciousness." In *Beyond Borders: Remaking Cultural Identities in the New Eastern and Central Europe.* Ed. Laszlo Kurti and Juliet Langman. Boulder, Colo.: Westview Press, 1997.
———. "Nationalism and Political Transformation in Moldova." In *Studies in Moldavian: The History, Culture, Language and Contemporary Politics of the People of Moldova.* Ed. Donald Dryer. Boulder, Colo.: East European Monographs, 1996.
———. "The Politics of Democratization in Postcommunist Moldova." In *Democratic Changes and Authoritarian Reactions in Russia, Ukraine, Belarus, and Moldova.* Ed. Karen Dawisha and Bruce Parrott. London: Cambridge University Press, 1997.
Dima, Nicholas. *From Moldavia to Moldova: The Soviet Romanian Territorial Dispute.* Boulder, Colo.: East European Monographs, 1991.
Roper, Steven D. "Regionalism in Moldova: The Case of Transnistria and Gagauzia." *Regional and Federal Studies* 11, no. 3 (fall 2001): 101–22.
Way, L. A. "Weak States and Pluralism: The Case of Moldova." *East European Politics and Society* 17, no. 3 (August 2003): 454–82.

PRINCIPALITY OF MONACO
(Principauté de Monaco)

By Kenneth E. Bauzon, Ph.D.
Revised by Tom Michael

The sovereign country of Monaco is situated in western Europe, facing the Mediterranean Sea to the south. It is bordered on its other three sides by France, specifically the *département* of Alpes-Maritimes. It has a population of 32,000 (2005 est.) and occupies a land area of no more than three-quarters of a square mile. It is home to French, Italians, Swiss, and Belgians, as well as native Monegasques. The French make up the largest portion of the population, nearly half, while the native Monegasque comprise one-sixth and speak their own language, Monegasque, a cross between Italian and French. Roman Catholicism is the official religion, adhered to by nine-tenths of the population.

The System of Government

Monaco's government is a constitutional monarchy with a unicameral legislature.

EXECUTIVE

The prince of Monaco holds the title chief of state along with at least 20 other titles. Actual political power rests with the prince, and all powers vested with the legislature and the judiciary are derived from him. Executive authority is exercised jointly by the prince and the four-member Council of Government, which consists of three state councilors and the minister of state, who is head of the Council. The Council of Government derives its authority from the prince and is answerable to the prince. Further, two other bodies—the Council of State and the Council of the Crown—are also established for the purpose of providing advice to the prince.

LEGISLATURE

Legislative authority rests with a unicameral body, the National Council, which consists of 24 members who each serve a term of five years. These legislators are elected through a competitive electoral process based on universal adult suffrage. Sixteen of the 24 members are elected by list majority system, while the other eight are elected via proportional representation. Eligibility for election to this body requires Monegasque citizenship and at least 25 years in age.

JUDICIARY

The judicial branch consists of the Supreme Court (or Supreme Tribunal), the Criminal Court, the High Court of Appeals, the Court of Appeals, the Criminal Court, and the Courts of First Instance. Two other courts were established in 1946 and 1948, namely, the Industrial Court and the Higher Court of Arbitration of Collective Labor Disputes, respectively.

REGIONAL AND LOCAL GOVERNMENT

Due to the small size of the country, there is no regional or local government.

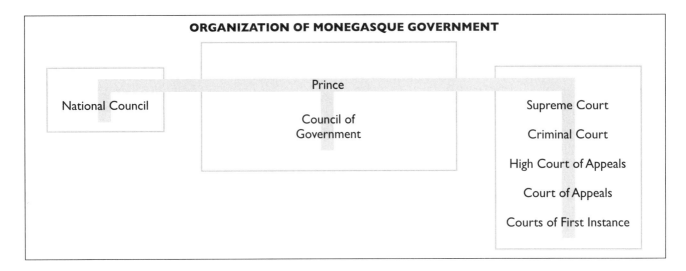

ORGANIZATION OF MONEGASQUE GOVERNMENT

Prince

National Council

Council of
Government

Supreme Court

Criminal Court

High Court of Appeals

Court of Appeals

Courts of First Instance

The Electoral System

Monaco's electoral system is currently based on universal direct adult suffrage at age 21, and women have had the right to vote since 1963.

The Party System

The political party system in Monaco is generally classified as a dominant-party system much like that of Mexico during the latter half of the twentieth century.

Major Political Parties

The National Democratic Union (Union Nationale et Démocratique; UND) has dominated the political scene for decades, but its control is not absolute and it has been successfully challenged on occasion by minority parties. For a long time, the UND existed mainly to articulate and support the wishes of the monarchy and the prince.

Minor Political Parties

In 1973 two seats in the National Council were shared between two minor political parties, and again, in the January 31, 1993, elections, three seats were shared. Another minor political party, the Monegasque Socialist Party (Parti Socialiste Monegasque; PSM) has been in existence but has never succeeded in electing a candidate to the National Council.

There was a great upheaval in the 2003 elections when an opposition party, Union for Monaco (UNAM), led by Stéphane Valéri, captured 58.5 percent of the vote and came into power with 21 of the 24 seats. Voters turned out in high numbers—about 80 percent of all eligible voters participated—because of their interest in the key issue of the election; the UNAM, as well as Prince Rainier III, advocated Monaco's entrance into the Council of Europe, while the ruling UND resisted the effort. The UND, with only 41.5 percent of the vote, was left with only three seats.

The most important functions of Monaco's political party system have been to secure and maintain the country's political stability and to validate and legitimize the monarchy. Prior to the 2003 elections, with the UND safely in control, most people did not engage in political activity, and although the party system gave the semblance of democratic choice, the perception of a foreordained outcome deterred many from voting. Some dissenting political parties, particularly those of Marxist orientation, have had little luck in Monaco. Visitors and citizens alike are always reminded of the ubiquitous presence of the police and how it safeguards the tiny principality from any disorder and the royal house from any criticism.

Other Political Forces

There are no other political forces.

National Prospects

The economic prosperity and political stability of Monaco may be attributed generally to the strict discipline and the conservative style with which the principality have been ruled. Propitious international conditions may also be credited, in particular, its protected status with France, which obviated the necessity of raising an army. According to a 1918 treaty, France can annex Monaco if the longtime ruling clan, the Grimaldi family, is unable to field an heir. Its conscious efforts to promote the principality as a tax haven have attracted significant businesses, for example, perfumes, pharmaceuticals, and ceramics, enough to transform it into an international business center. Also, the entire principality is a free trade zone without actually becoming a member of the European Union. In 2002 it abandoned the French franc for the common currency of the euro. Although long known for its gambling casinos, raceways, and pleasure-seeking visitors, Monaco has striven to diversify its image and enhance its international status. In addition to tourism, the economy relies upon banking and financial services, as well as light manufacturing.

The domestic political and administrative institutions show no sign of weakening or discontinuity. The ruling Grimaldi family celebrated 700 years of reign in Monaco in 1997. Barring the extinction of the Grimaldi clan or, unlikely, a radical shift in both domestic and international conditions, the Grimaldi family may yet lead the principality for another 700 years. This is especially likely due to the 2002 change in the constitution which allows for the throne to pass to a female Grimaldi when there are no male heirs.

Also, as of the 2002 a new treaty with France prevents Monaco from becoming a French principality. Under the previous 1918 treaty it was subject to French rule following the end of the male Grimaldi bloodline. These changes are timely given Prince Albert II's ascension to the throne after the death of his father Prince Rainier III on April 6, 2005. Prince Albert has no male heirs.

Further Reading

Bibliography of Monaco. New York: St. Martin's Press, 1971.

Conniff, Richard. "Monaco." *National Geographic* 189 (May 5, 1996): 80, 82–94.

MONGOLIA
(Mongol Uls)

By Paul Hyer, Ph.D.
Revised by Christopher P. Atwood, Ph.D.

The state of Mongolia, formerly the Mongolian People's Republic (MPR) until 1992, is a nation of 2.7 million people (2005 est.). A Communist state until the collapse of the Soviet Union, it made a rapid transition to democracy and a free-market system after 1990. The Mongolian economy was traditionally based on nomadic herding. In the early 2000s the country's main exports are animal products, such as cashmere and leather, textiles, and minerals, including semi-processed copper, molybdenum, zinc ores, fluorspar, gold, and crude oil. For 70 years Mongolia was characterized as a satellite of the Soviet Union; indeed, it was the prototype of the satellite system that later emerged in the Soviet bloc in Eastern Europe. Now it is the first Communist state in Asia to move toward democracy.

Mongolia was under the control of China's Manchu-Ching dynasty from 1691 to 1911, when it declared itself an independent monarchy under a traditionally powerful "reincarnated" Buddhist lama. Mongolia's Soviet-supported revolution (1921) was the first in Asia when it revolted against a continuing Chinese threat. Mongolia declared itself a People's Republic in 1924. From that time most Mongols believed that their independence from China required a strong link to the Soviet Union.

Mongolian politics were historically characterized by fragmented political power in the hands of a hereditary nobility paralleled and complemented by a powerful monastic clergy of lamas (Tibetan Buddhist monks). These elites dominated politics, and commoners had no active role.

The move toward independence in 1911 was followed by a decade of nationalistic fervor and continued political turbulence. In January 1920 radical Mongolian nationalists, encouraged by the victory of the Bolsheviks in Russia, organized the vanguard of a revolutionary party (Mongolian People's Revolutionary Party; MPRP). Support from the Soviet political cadre and the Red Army consolidated the party's dominance.

After gaining power in 1921, this party controlled Mongolia's political life for the next 70 years. It looked to the Soviet Union for direction and institutions to revolutionize the nation. As a satellite of the Soviet Union, its political control was ensured by Moscow.

During the 1920s there were great internal divisions among left-wing radicals, moderates, and conservatives. The nobility and clergy were neutralized if not liquidated, and covert competition for personal power continued within the party for many years. The late 1920s and the 1930s saw violent purges and an abortive attempt at collectivization of the countryside.

In 1936 Khorloogin Choibalsan, a dominating personality with a Stalinist approach to politics, emerged as the strongman. He ran the government with virtually no consultation with formal government bodies. Yumjaagiin Tsedenbal succeeded Choibalsan on his death in 1952. His administrative style, while still repressive, was much more staid and conventional; Tsedenbal remained in power until 1984, the eve of reforms. Collectivization of the countryside was completed in 1960 and urbanization accelerated in the 1970s and 1980s.

As a prelude to the cataclysmic changes of the 1990s, Mongolia saw the rise of a younger, nationalistic generation, anathema to Moscow and a worry to Marxist governmental leadership. There were occasional purges—no executions but simply removal from office. Despite this, there was considerable stability in government structure, dynamics, and personnel, accompanied by a fair amount of mobility or "changing of the guard." All this made the bloodless revolution of the 1990s a much less painful process.

With the breakup of the Soviet block in 1989, Mongolia's Communist rulers faced huge demonstrations for democracy and real independence. The leaders resigned, multiparty elections were held, and a younger generation of MPRP leaders led their party to a solid electoral victory. Several new parties, however, won seats in the new legislature. Decollectivization of the countryside and privatization of all but the largest state-owned businesses followed, despite a severe economic downturn from 1990 to 1995. Since the ratification of a new democratic constitution in 1992, the MPRP and a shifting coalition of more libertarian democratic parties have alternated in power. While the new reformist MPRP holds a more culturally conservative and economically statist stance, differences between it and the democratic opposition are not fundamental, and a reversion to authoritarian government or Socialist economics seems most unlikely.

The System of Government

The government of Mongolia is a mixed presidential/parliamentary system with a unicameral legislature.

EXECUTIVE

Mongolia's president is the head of state, the commander in chief of the armed forces, and the head of the National Security Council. Previously the president was elected by the State Great Hural (the nation's parliamentary body), which was manipulated by the Communist Party. Now he is popularly elected by a majority, for a four-year term and is limited to two terms. He is empowered to nominate a prime minister who must be confirmed by the parliament. The president may initiate legislation and veto all or part of the same. He may issue decrees and call for the government's dissolution. He directs foreign affairs and national defense and maintains public order through

the police. In the absence, incapacity, or resignation of the president, the chairman of the State Great Hural exercises presidential power until the inauguration of a newly elected president.

The office of the president includes the following services in suboffices: organization, correspondence, information services, an economic adviser, a legal adviser, a National Defense Council secretary, and an adviser on public order.

The prime minister is nominated by the president and confirmed by the parliament for a four-year term. He chooses a cabinet, also subject to parliamentary approval. Decrees issued by parliament become effective when signed by the president. In 1994 Prime Minister Puntsagiyn Jasray moved to combine or abolish many ministries in a radical change to reduce governmental expenses and bureaucratic agencies. This move had long been discussed and was supported by many groups, including independent economists.

After the upset victory of the Democratic Coalition in the 1996 elections, a constitutional controversy helped prevent a stable government. While previously the prime minister and government ministers had not been members of parliament, in the new government, a reshuffling of the coalition leadership in 1998 led to a proposed government with members of parliament as ministers, on the model of parliamentary government elsewhere. The Mongolian president, Natsagiin Bagabandi, refused to form such a government, citing both constitutional issues as well as ongoing investigations of corruption against the proposed prime minister. Not until after the defeat of the Democratic Coalition in 2000 and the formation of a new MPRP government was an amendment to the constitution approved explicitly authorizing parliamentary government.

LEGISLATURE

The State Great Hural, or parliament, is the supreme state authority. It is a democratic body organized in 1992 as a new unicameral legislature. Before 1990 there was a bicameral assembly that simply rubber-stamped Communist Party policy and decisions. Seventy-six members are popularly elected for a four-year term. Meeting twice annually this assembly elects a chairman and a vice chairman to serve four-year terms. Its constitutional role is to enact and amend laws, determine domestic and foreign policy, ratify international agreements, and declare a state of emergency if necessary. The State Great Hural can override a presidential veto by a two-thirds majority vote. It may issue decrees that become effective with the president's

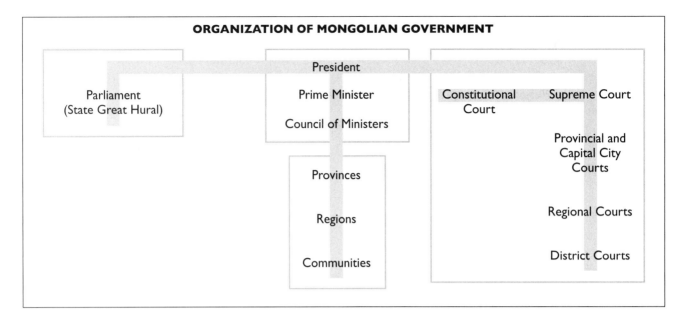

ORGANIZATION OF MONGOLIAN GOVERNMENT

President
Prime Minister
Council of Ministers

Parliament
(State Great Hural)

Constitutional Court   Supreme Court

Provincial and Capital City Courts

Provinces

Regions

Communities

Regional Courts

District Courts

signature. A dissolution of the government occurs if the prime minister resigns, if half the cabinet resigns, or if it votes to dissolve itself.

JUDICIARY

The constitution inaugurated in January 1992 marked a new historical era for the country; it is more an expression of hope and aspiration than a reflection of the political realities of the country. Moreover, it resulted from some two years of intense debate over the issues and means of transforming the country from a Communist Party dictatorship to a pluralistic democracy and from a command economy to a free-market system. In addition to establishing Mongolia as an independent, sovereign republic the constitution guarantees a number of rights and freedoms. The new political structure of Mongolia mirrors Western democracies.

For some 70 years Mongolia's legal system was a blend of Mongolian, Russian, and Chinese elements and there was no provision for an independent judicial review of legislation. Now the 1992 constitution provides for an independent judiciary on the model of those found in democratic societies. The highest judiciary body is the Supreme Court. A General Council of Courts is empowered to nominate justices, who are then confirmed by the State Great Hural.

The Supreme Court is mandated to examine all lower court decisions upon appeal, and it is empowered by the constitution to interpret all laws except the constitution. This last function is reserved to a special Constitutional Court of nine members, including a

chairman, appointed for terms of six years. Its sole function is to interpret the constitution.

REGIONAL AND LOCAL GOVERNMENT

Mongolia is divided administratively into 21 provinces and a capital city. The provinces are subdivided into regions, and the regions into communities. The capital city, Ulaanbaatar, is divided into districts, and the districts into neighborhoods. There are 380 local authorities, who elect their own councils in order to address problems and promote economic advancement.

The Electoral System

Until 1990 the Communist Party controlled elections to the Great State Hural; voting was usually by single candidate election lists. But now there is a plurality of parties and free, open elections. Suffrage is universal for all over 18 years of age. In the 2004 legislative elections 82 percent of the electorate was reported to have voted.

The Party System

In the 1990 democratic transition, three new political parties, all with broadly libertarian programs, arose: the Democratic Party, the Social Democrats, and the National Progress Party. Due to factional quarreling, these parties were unable to present a common program when the MPRP leaders resigned and the ruling party suddenly agreed to free elections.

The first multiparty elections in Mongolia's history were held on July 26, 1990, and the MPRP, with the advantages of solid organization and sufficient time to prepare, gained 85 percent of the seats in the State Great Hural and took the presidency. But representatives of the major opposition parties were appointed to top positions in the new government.

Free parliamentary elections were held in June 1992 with a 92.7 percent turnout and a Communist Party landslide. It won 72 of 76 seats in the new parliament. One reason given for this rout is that the people had lost confidence in the opposition leaders due to their lack of experience and poor performance. It should be emphasized, however, that the "Communists" elected were *not* old party "hard-liners" but those of a younger generation.

President Punsalmaagiyn Ochirbat, elected in the 1993 presidential election, had switched from the former MPRP/Communist Party and ran as a candidate for the opposition. This was the first defeat for the Mongolian People's Revolutionary Party.

In preparation for the 1996 election the Democratic Party and National Progress party merged as the National Democrats, and a coalition was formed with the Social Democrats. This united opposition won an upset victory against the MPRP on a program of faster privatization, and more economic openness. The government's slow response to destructive forest fires also helped the opposition. The Democratic Coalition pushed through a popular privatization of state-owned apartments, but after 1998 was paralyzed by internecine quarrels, constitutional controversies, and accusations of corruption. The *zud* (harsh weather leading to livestock deaths) during the winter of 1999–2000 added to their difficulties and the coalition forces again suffered a massive defeat in the 2000 election. The MPRP won 72 of 76 seats and most of the rest were held by small splinter parties.

From 2000 to 2004 the economic revival begun in 1995 and interrupted by the *zud*s of 2000 and 2001 resumed. The new MPRP administration of Nambaryn Enkhbayar completed privatization of farm and residential land in 2003 and sent troops to join U.S. forces in Iraq. By 2004 the country enjoyed a growth rate of 5 percent. Nevertheless, voters, reacting to perceived clumsy campaigning and a sense that the MPRP was too dominant, split the parliamentary vote that year almost exactly between the MPRP and the new Motherland-Democratic Coalition. This, of course, resulted in a political stalemate and it took several weeks for the parliament to appoint

Prime Minister Tsakhia Elbegdorj (a member of the Democratic Coalition), who had previously been prime minister in 1998. The appointment was made with the agreement to reappoint a new prime minister in 2006.

Major Political Parties

MONGOLIAN PEOPLE'S REVOLUTIONARY PARTY (MPRP)

The Mongolian People's Revolutionary Party was Mongolia's only political party from 1920 to 1990, and since 1990 it has retained its position as the majority party. The MPRP was founded in 1920 as the Mongolian People's Party and was installed in power in Mongolia in 1921. In 1925 the party's name was changed to the Mongolian People's Revolutionary Party. From 1940 to 1990 the MPRP was a Soviet-oriented Communist-style party exercising one-party rule in Mongolia. Membership expanded from less than 8,000 in 1934 to over 89,500 in 1989. Since the democratic transition in 1990, the MPRP has faced electoral opposition from the Democratic Party.

At present, the MPRP's program supports multiparty democracy, pluralism, and a market economy. Its electoral campaigns have stressed competence and a more statist version of democratic governance. Compared to the opposing Democratic Party, the MPRP has stronger support in the rural areas, especially in the west of the country, among the elderly, and among Buddhists. The MPRP is a member of the Socialist International, the world league of social democratic, Socialist, and labor parties. Membership in 2004 was estimated at over 100,000.

DEMOCRATIC PARTY

The Mongolian Democratic Party has been the main opposition party and the center of a number of opposition coalitions in Mongolia since the democratic transition of 1989–90.

The Mongolian Democratic Party was created in March 1990 on the basis of the Mongolian Democratic Association, which had been formed in December 1989 to lead the demonstrations against the one-party Communist-style rule of the MPRP. A number of other smaller parties also formed at the same time. In 1996 the Democratic Party merged with the smaller National Progress Party to form the Mongolian National Democratic Party (MNDP). The MNDP-led "Democratic Coalition" won the 1996 parliamentary elections. The coalition broke up before the 2000 elections and the MNDP was swept out of power by the MPRP. In December of that year, the MNDP renamed itself the Mongolian Democratic Party. The party in 2004 led the "Motherland-Democratic Coalition" to win exactly half of the parliamentary seats in the 2004 election.

The Democratic Party has strong support among youth, urban dwellers, private businessmen, and religious and ethnic minorities (Christians, Kazakhs). It has a more libertarian program and a populist, anti-elitist image. In 2003 the Democratic Party counted a membership of about 160,000.

Minor Political Parties

Other political parties include the Civic Courage and the Mongolian New Socialist Party, which are members of the Motherland-Democratic Coalition, and the Republican Party, which counts one MP who generally votes with the MPRP.

Other Political Forces

MONGOLIA BETWEEN CHINA AND RUSSIA

Seventy years of dependence on the USSR, until the recent collapse of the Soviet empire, was crucial in both internal politics and foreign policy. Policy for decades was anti-Chinese but has now moderated, and Soviet troops stationed in Mongolia along the border with China have been withdrawn.

Mongolia now pursues an independent, nonaligned foreign policy. Previously, policy decisions made in Moscow were invariably echoed in Ulaanbaatar. Mongolia frequently reminds itself and others that, due to its land-locked position, it is essential to have good relations with both of its large neighbors. Long-term, fairly cooperative relations with Russia continue. Relations with China are more complex and are now of prime importance. During the period of Sino-Soviet confrontation Mongolia initially tried to maintain a neutral position. But in 1966, with the onset of China's Cultural Revolution and the dangers it posed, Mongolia signed agreements introducing large-scale Soviet ground forces in a buildup on the Mongolia-China frontier. As relations worsened, Mongolia began expelling the 7,000 ethnic Chinese contracted in the 1950s as construction workers.

The above moves were motivated by Mongolia's historical enmity for the Chinese; Chinese statements suggesting a desire to reannex Mongolia; continued border tension in spite of the 1964 demarcation agreements; Mongolia's heavy dependence on Soviet economic aid; and Russia's historical role in counterbalancing Chinese influence.

With the demise of the Soviet Union, Mongolia is particularly concerned with its relations with China, because its strategic trade access to the sea is via China and China is now the prime destination for Mongolian exports of minerals and animal products. With its new options in the late 1980s Mongolia reached consular agreements with China and cross-border trade is expanding. In 1989 Mongolia and China exchanged foreign minister visits. In 1990 Mongolia's head of state visited China, and in 1991 China's president, Yang Shangkun, visited Ulaanbaatar. Regular high-level visits have continued since then. Contacts have been established between a number of Mongolian and Chinese ministries, local areas, and private firms and their Chinese counterparts. Soviet troop withdrawals from Mongolia's China border began in 1987 and were completed in 1992.

Meanwhile, Mongolia has maintained close relations with Russia, including agreements for bilateral trade and cooperation, exemption of Mongolian exports from Russian customs duties, and the establishment of a commission to speed up important trade exchanges. The government of Vladimir Putin has emphasized rebuilding Russia's influence in Mongolia. Putin visited Mongolia in November 2000, the first visit by a Russian head of state since 1974. Russia still retains a significant share of Mongolia's imports and Mongolia's debt was settled on favorable terms in 2003. In 2004 Mongolia joined the Shanghai Cooperation Organization, formed by China and Russia, as an observer.

National Prospects

Of all former Soviet satellites Mongolia made the smoothest transition to new, more democratic institutions, and there is good cause to be optimistic for its political development in the future. The United States and Japan have worked closely with international organizations to assist Mongolia's transition. Numerous donor group meetings coordinated considerable financial and development assistance.

The Mongolian people face the great challenges of an inhospitable environment. The summer droughts of 2000, 2001, and 2002 significantly stunted the country's economic growth. Their agenda to change to an industrial and agricultural society has proceeded rapidly but is by no means complete. The majority of the people are less than a generation removed from a pastoral-nomadic society.

A positive pattern has emerged in recent decades during which have a major increase in the percentage of the population has become involved in the political life of the country. It is the consensus of specialists that a higher percentage of the Mongolian people were represented in the power structure of Mongolia than in any other Communist nation—or indeed in most other Asian nations. This trend increased with the current move to democratization. Progress is due in part not only to Mongolia's sparse and relatively homogeneous population but also to improvements in education, communications, and transportation—developments that are essential in Mongolia's institutionalization of democracy, the rule of law, and the modernization of the nation.

Further Reading

Atwood, Christopher. *Encyclopedia of Mongolia and the Mongol Empire*. New York: Facts On File, 2004.

Batbayar, Tsedendambyn. *Modern Mongolia: A Concise History*. Ulaanbaatar: Mongolian Center for Scientific and Technical Information, 1996.

Bawden, Charles R. *The Modern History of Mongolia*. New York: Praeger, 1968.

Jagchid, Sechin, and Paul Hyer. *Mongolia's Culture and Society*. Boulder, Colo.: Westview Press, 1980.

Kotkin, Stephen, and Bruce A. Elleman. *Mongolia in the Twentieth Century: Landlocked Cosmopolitan*. Armonk, N.Y.: M.E. Sharpe, 1999.

Lawless, Jill. *Wild East; Travels in the New Mongolia*. Toronto: ECW Press, 2000.

Rupen, Robert A. *How Mongolia Is Really Ruled*. Stanford, Calif.: Hoover Institution Press, Stanford University, 1979.

Sanders, Alan J. K. *Historical Dictionary of Mongolia*. 2d ed. Lanham, Md.: Scarecrow Press, 2003.

———. "Mongolia 1990: A New Dawn." *Asian Affairs* 22, no. 2 (June 1991): 158–66.

Shirendev, B., and M. Sanjdorj. *History of the Mongolian People's Republic*. Translated and annotated by William A. Brown and Urgunge Onon. Cambridge, Mass.: Harvard University Press, 1977.

KINGDOM OF MOROCCO
(Al-Mamlakâ al-Magribīyā)

By David Seddon, Ph.D.
Revised by Deborah A. Kaple, Ph.D.
Further revision by Florina Laura Neculai

The Kingdom of Morocco, in northern Africa, borders the North Atlantic Ocean and the Mediterranean Sea and lies between Algeria and Western Sahara. With a population of nearly 32.7 million (2005 est.), it is a constitutional monarchy, with the crown being hereditary and passed to the eldest son of the reigning king. Although all three of Morocco's postindependence constitutions (adopted in 1962, 1970, and 1972) enhanced rather than limited the king's power, the 1992 and 1996 constitutional revisions gave the prime minister more power, broadened the authority of the legislature, and established new constitutional councils.

Morocco has often come under the sway of various occupying powers in its history, but not until the seventh century when Islam made its appearance did any of them have an impact on Morocco's population. Since that time, both Arab and Berber peoples have united around Islam. Morocco was independent until 1912, when France and Spain made it a "protectorate," by the Treaty of Fez (1912). During this time, the foreign "protectors" endowed the sultan with enhanced powers so as to better control and rule through him. When they left in 1956, giving Morocco its independence, the sultan emerged as the sovereign figure in Moroccan politics. This created a tension that still exists today between the monarchy and political parties. In 1957 the country changed its name to the "Kingdom of Morocco."

In the 1990s King Hassan II attempted to liberalize Morocco. The king released many political prisoners, reduced censorship and curbed the power of the security services, initiated a new constitution, helped to force Morocco's 17 political parties into three main blocks, and called new elections for November and December 1997.

The center-left government that took over in March 1998 has been praised for setting the foundations of a civil society. The press has been a critical force, an active opposition has been allowed, and there have even been revelations about extrajudicial killings. In a year of political surprises, the king shocked everyone by choosing Abderrahmane Youssoufi, a well-known opposition Socialist and a former political prisoner, to be prime minister. Youssoufi's party, the Socialist Union of Popular Forces (USFP), controlled about a third of the parliamentary seats, and the seven-party coalition Cabinet was seen as fragile, though hopeful.

In 1999 Muhammad VI succeeded King Hassan II upon the latter's death. The 2002 parliamentary elections were considered to be free and transparent elections and were won by the Socialist Union of Popular Forces (USFP), which received a narrow victory. After the elections of 2002, the multiparty government was led by Driss Jettou, the prime minister appointed by the king.

The System of Government

The Morroccan system of government is a constitutional monarchy.

MONARCHY

The pivotal role of the monarch is spelled out in the 1996 amended constitution: "The King, Commander of the Faithful, shall be the Supreme Representative of the nation and the Symbol of its unity thereof. As defender of the Faith, he shall ensure respect for the Constitution." While the latest version of the constitution rather obliquely mentions the word "faith" and the previous ones mentioned that the king "ensures the observance of Islam and the Constitution," Article 6 states that "Islam shall be the state religion."

The constitutional powers of the king are wide-ranging. He appoints and dismisses the prime minister and the other ministers. He has the right to address the parliament: "The messages shall be read out before both Houses and shall not be subject to any debate." He is commander in chief of the armed forces and appoints the senior military officers. He controls the judiciary by virtue of his powers to appoint the judges and preside over the Supreme Council of Magistracy.

The king has the right to dissolve the two houses of parliament by decree and exercise its legislative powers until new elections, which must be held within three months. However, by virtue of Article 35 of the constitution, the king may declare a state of exception under which he may rule by decree for an indefinite period. Hassan II first invoked this right in 1965. The state of exception lasted almost five years, until the promulgation of the 1970 constitution. Hassan II was able once again to rule by decree without any elected legislative body between 1972 and 1977 simply by refusing to call general elections after the adoption of the 1972 constitution.

Constitutional revision, which can be initiated by the king without reference to the parliament, requires approval in a referendum, but the constitution specifies that "Neither the state system of monarchy nor the prescriptions related to the religion of Islam may be subject to a constitutional revision."

The king claims a divine right to rule, as *Amir al-Muminin*, or Commander of the Faithful; and it is this presumption to both the spiritual and temporal leadership of his subjects that sanctions his claim to ultimate control over the nation's political life. A rule of primogeniture is established in the constitution. If the king dies or abdicates before his successor reaches the age of 16, the king's powers are exercised by a regency council, composed primarily of royal appointees. Until the heir reaches his 20th birthday, it acts as a consultative body.

EXECUTIVE

The king retains primary executive power as the head of state, while the prime minister (appointed by the king) serves as the head of government. The cabinet is formed of ministers appointed by the monarch. The government is responsible to both the king and the parliament. The king is advised by a small, influential royal cabinet, a group of four or five royal counselors headed by a director-general, who are among the king's most trusted political allies.

LEGISLATURE

From 1977, when the first parliamentary elections were held under the 1972 constitution, until the constitutional revisions of 1996, Morocco had a unicameral legislature, known as the Chamber of Representatives (Majlis al-Nuwab). The 1996 constitution established a bicameral legislature, which was effected by adding a lower house, the Chamber of Councilors (Majlis al-Mustasharin).

Members of the Chamber of Representatives are elected for six-year terms by direct, universal suffrage; there are 325 members. For three-fifths of its 270 seats, members of the Chamber of Councilors are elected in each region by electoral colleges made up of elected members of local councils, and two-fifths of them are elected by the people. The parliament meets for two sessions a year. The first session begins on the second Friday of October and is presided over by the king. The second session starts on the second Friday of April. Parliament can also meet in special sessions that have a defined agenda and must end with a decree. The meetings of the two chambers of parliament are open to the public, but they can also be held as private meetings at the request of one-third of its members or at the request of the prime minister.

The parliament's legislative competence is relatively narrow. The constitution bars the legislature from adopting bills or amendments that reduce the state's revenue or raise public expenditure. If, by December 31, parliament has not approved the following year's budget, the government can simply proceed as if the budget had been approved. The deputies have the right to vote on the development plan but cannot amend it. With regard to the broad objectives of economic, social, and cultural policy, parliament can pass *lois cadres* (framework laws), but the details of such laws and all other subjects not specified as falling within the legislature's competence are considered to come under the government's administrative authority. The government is entitled to reject any legislative proposal passed by parliament that it deems to be outside its legislative competence. In the event of a disagreement between parliament and the government in such a case, a ruling is made by the Constitutional Council of the Supreme Court.

JUDICIARY

Although formally independent of the executive and the legislature, the judiciary is under the strong influence of the king, who appoints the judges and presides over the Supreme Council of Magistry, which supervises the judicial system. In political trials, sentences often appear to be predetermined by the Ministry of Justice; and Amnesty International has claimed that political prisoners frequently are not given a fair trial, often subjected to torture, and may be held incommunicado for months or years.

The court system includes communal and district courts for minor offenses, 30 tribunals of first instance, nine courts of appeals, a Supreme Court (with criminal, civil, administrative, social, and constitutional chambers), social courts for labor cases, the High Court for crimes committed by ministers in the exercise of their public functions, the Special Court of Justice for crimes committed by civil servants, and the Court of Justice, which judges serious state security and political cases.

However, Morocco's commitment to promote human rights materialized in the 1990s in the creation of a series of institutions such as the Consultative Council of Human Rights (1990), the Constitutional Council (1992), the High Commission for Disabled Persons (1994), and the "Integration of Woman in Development" Unit. There are also associations that deal only with human rights issues: Moroccan Human Rights League (1972), Moroccan Human Rights Associations (1979), Moroccan Human Rights Organization (1988), and Committee for the Defense of Human Rights (1992).

REGIONAL AND LOCAL GOVERNMENT

According to the constitution, local government consists of 37 provinces and two *wilayas*, with further subdivision into regions and rural communes. (A 1997 decentralization law created 16 new regions.) In each of these, local assemblies are democratically elected, and it is these assemblies that are responsible for managing the region. However, the governors, who "shall carry out decisions by provincial, prefectoral and regional assemblies in accordance with the conditions set by the law," also represent the state and "see to it that the law

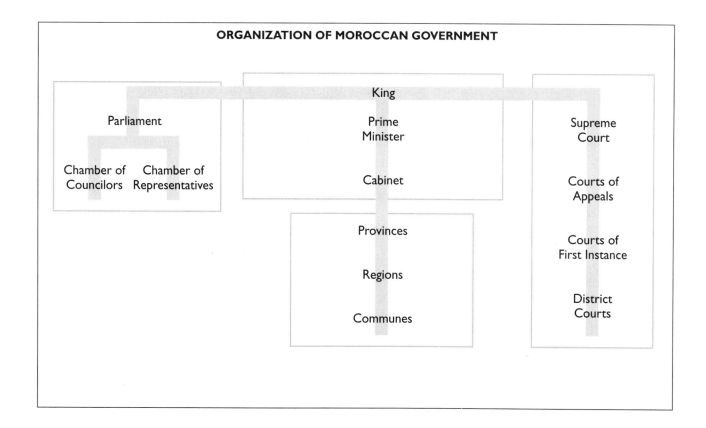

ORGANIZATION OF MOROCCAN GOVERNMENT

ELECTIONS TO THE CHAMBER OF REPRESENTATIVES, SEPTEMBER 2002

Party	Seats
Socialist Union of Popular Forces (USFP)	50
Independence Party (IP)	48
Justice and Development Party (PJD)	42
National Assembly of Independents (RNI)	41
Popular Movement (MP)	27
National Popular Movement (MNP)	18
Constitutional Union (UC)	16
National Democratic Party (PND)	12
Front of the Democratic Forces (FFD)	12
Progress and Socialist Party (PPS)	11
Democratic Union (UD)	10
Other	38

is enforced" and that government decisions are implemented. The king appoints all of the governors.

The Electoral System

Suffrage is universal for Moroccan citizens age 18 and over. Suffrage was once granted at the age of 21, but this requirement was changed in 2003. The parliament, made up of two houses, the Chamber of Representatives and the Chamber of Councilors, holds various elections at which citizens may vote. Elections for the 325 members of the Chamber of Representatives are held every five years. The Chamber of Councilors's 270 members are elected for nine-year terms. One-third of the Chamber of Councilors is renewed every three years. Three-fifths of the councilors are elected by local councils, and two-fifths of them by the people.

The Party System

Parties first emerged in Morocco as a consequence of the nationalist struggle against French and Spanish rule, which began under the leadership of French-educated intellectuals and religious reformists (*Salafis*) and reached a mass scale in the late 1930s. In 1943, Ahmed Balafrej and other nationalists founded the Independence Party (Istiqlal), which was to spearhead the struggle for independence under the leadership of Allal el-Fassi.

The Istiqlal Party formed a close alliance with Sultan Mohammed V, whose Alawite dynasty had been forced to accept a Franco-Spanish "protectorate" in 1912. After about 1946, he refused to cooperate with the French authorities, who retaliated by exiling him to Madagascar in 1953. This step only fanned the flames of nationalist revolt. An Army of Liberation began guerrilla attacks in 1955, and France, which was already facing a rebellion in Algeria, decided to come to terms with the Moroccan nationalists. Mohammed V returned to Morocco as a national hero, and, in 1956, France and Spain ended their protectorate.

In granting Morocco independence, France and Spain returned full sovereignty to the sultan, who acquired the title of king. A struggle for primacy then ensued between the monarch and the more radical factions of the nationalist movement. The king retained

ELECTIONS TO THE CHAMBER OF COUNCILORS, DECEMBER 1997

Democratic Bloc	
Socialist Union of Popular Forces (USFP)	16
Independence Party (IP)	21
Party of Renewal and Progress (PRP)	7
Organization of Democratic and Popular Action (OADP)	—
National Entente	
Popular Movement (MP)	27
Constitutional Union (UC)	28
National Democratic Party (PND)	21
Center	
National Assembly of Independents (RNI)	42
Democratic and Social Movement (MDS)	33
National Popular Movement (MNP)	15
Other	60

all legislative powers and refused to hold elections or allow a constitution to be drafted. He also encouraged the emergence of royalist political movements. The king's enormous prestige stood him in good stead in this contest, as did the practical support of France, which helped to build up the king's Royal Armed Forces (FAR) and provided many of his government's civil servants for several years. Between 1956 and 1959, the irregulars of the Army of Liberation were gradually forced to hand over their arms, join the FAR, or disband. Though the Istiqlal Party was included in the postindependence government, the king tried to weaken it by giving cabinet posts to royalist independents and the small Democratic Independence Party (Parti Démocratique de l'Indépendance; PDI) and by encouraging the Berber-based MP after its creation in 1957. As little more than a loose alliance of factions united in support of independence, the Istiqlal Party was unable to check Mohammed V's tightening grip on power. In 1959 the party split, the more radical nationalists setting up the National Union of Popular Forces (Union Nationale des Forces Populaires; UNFP). By the time of Hassan II's ascent to the throne, in 1961, upon Mohammed V's death, the monarchy was well entrenched in power.

Multipartism is an essential characteristic of the current Moroccan political system. Today there are several political parties, most of which belong to one of the major groupings: the Democratic Bloc (Bloc Démocratique), the National Entente (Entente Nationale), and Center.

Major Political Parties

DEMOCRATIC BLOC

(Bloc Démocratique)

Founded in May 1992 to promote democracy within the framework of a constitutional monarchy, the Democratic Bloc currently includes the Socialist Union of Popular Forces (Union Socialistes des Forces Populaires; USFP), the Independence Party (Istiqlal; IP), the Party of Renewal and Progress (Parti du Renouveau et du Progrès; PRP), and the Organization of Democratic and Popular Action (Organisation de l'Action pour Démocratie et Peuple; OADP). Since its formation, it has tried to ensure that all political actions are legal and that elections are free and fair. In the 2002 Chamber of Representatives elections, the Democratic Bloc won 30 percent of the seats (98 of 325 available seats);

in the 1997 Chamber of Councilors elections they won 16 percent of the seats (44 of 270 seats).

SOCIALIST UNION OF POPULAR FORCES

(Union Socialiste des Forces Populaires; USFP)

Founded in 1974, the USFP emerged from a split in the National Union of Popular Forces (UNFP) in 1972. The UNFP had itself split from the Istiqlal Party in 1959. Led by the more radical Istiqlal leaders, among them Mehdi Ben Barka, the UNFP was immediately harassed by the palace—first by its expulsion from the government in 1960, then by the mass trial of UNFP leaders in 1963. Two years later, Ben Barka was assassinated.

The loss of the party's most radical leaders led to the emergence of a more compromise-prone leadership, while the uneasy relations between the UNFP and Moroccan Union of Labor (UMT) leaders led to a party split in 1972. One faction, led by Abderrahim Bouabid, broke ranks with a rival faction led by Abdallah Irbahim and the UMT's leader, Mahjoub Ben Seddik. Bouabid's "Rabat wing" of the UNFP was briefly banned in 1973 and 1974 but was relegalized as a result of the liberalization initiated by the king in 1974 changing its name to the Union Socialiste des Forces Populaires the same year. The party accused the government of fixing many of the results in the 1977 elections and has since remained in opposition. It was severely repressed after the June 1981 Casablanca riots and massacre. Its newspapers were immediately suppressed and had still not been allowed to restart publication a year later. Some 200 leaders of the party and its allied Democratic Labor Confederation (Confédération Démocratique du Travail; CDT) were jailed. Abderrahim Bouabid and two other members of the party's political bureau were imprisoned between September 1981 and March 1982. In May 1983 the king pardoned 22 of the imprisoned USFP and CDT members, and the USFP decided to participate in the local and national elections. In November 1983 Abderrahmin Bouabid, leader of the party, was included in the government as a minister of state.

Although it won a sizable number of seats in the 1993 legislative elections, USFP ultimately rejected the king's invitation to participate in a coalition government. In April 1995 the king again tried to convince leftist groups to join the government, but USFP declined. In the 1997 parliamentary elections USFP garnered 57 seats, the largest number of seats of any party, in the Chamber of Representatives, and 16 seats in the Chamber of Councilors. In March 1998 the king appointed the prominent socialist USFP member Abderrahmane Youssoufi to be prime minister. In the 2002 Chamber of Representatives parliamentary elections USFP got 50 seats and Driss Jetton was appointed prime minister.

The USFP's political outlook is, broadly speaking, social democratic. It advocates reform of the constitution, civil liberties, and the liberation of political prisoners. It calls for the nationalization of the principal means of production, transport, exchange, and credit; land reform on the basis of "land to the tiller"; large-scale housing programs and the control of urban rents and property speculation; anticorruption measures; and wage increases.

Primarily urban-based, the USFP draws most of its members from the educated middle class. It is particularly strong among students, teachers, and lower-level civil servants, but it also recruits through the trade unions affiliated with the CDT, which it controls. In elections, it enjoys wide support in the cities from workers, the unemployed poor, students, and the middle class. The USFP has been liberally supported by its wealthier adherents. Its leaders include Noubir el-Amaoui, Mohamed el Yazghi, and Abdelwaheb Radi. Fathallah Oulaalou is the party's first secretary.

As the major left-wing party, the USFP seems to be growing in strength and influence. Although the repression it suffered off and on since June 1981 seriously handicapped the party and prevented it from capitalizing effectively on its political opportunities, it still has managed to garner an impressive number of seats in the current Parliament. Now, with the appointment of USFP's Driss Jetton as prime minister, the party's stock will certainly rise.

INDEPENDENCE PARTY (IP)

(Istiqlal)

Founded in 1943, the Istiqlal Party led the struggle for independence, in close alliance with Sultan Mohammed V. As a broad alliance united in pursuit of independence, it enjoyed overwhelming popular support, but it had no agreed program of policies for independent Morocco. It was unable to offer effective resistance to the consolidation of political power in the hands of the monarch. The party was greatly weakened by the split with the National Union of Popular Forces (Union Nationale des Forces Populaires; UNFP) in 1959, as well as by the palace's encouragement of ultraloyalist factions. In 1963 it was forced out of the government, in which it had participated since 1956, and it remained in opposition until 1977, when it reentered the government with eight Cabinet posts. It continued to maintain an important involvement in government after November 1983, when the new Cabinet was formed, although its strength has been somewhat reduced.

In the 1993 elections it was already allied with the Socialist Union of Popular Forces (USFP) into the newly formed Democratic Bloc. The bloc, a coalition of center-left opposition groups, garnered 99 parliamentary seats. In the 1997 elections, Istiqlal won 32 of 325 Chamber of Representatives seats and 21 of 270 Chamber of Councilors seats. In the 2002 Chamber of Representatives parliamentary elections Istiqlal won 48 of the 325 seats.

Between party congresses, which are held every two or three years with over 5,000 delegates attending, the party is headed by a 510-member national council. Day-to-day leadership is provided by the much smaller executive committee. The party publishes two daily newspapers, *Al-Alam* in Arabic and *L'Opinion* in French.

Party policy is strongly nationalist. In the immediate postindependence years, it championed the idea of "Greater Morocco"—the incorporation into Morocco of Western Sahara, Ifni, Mauritania, the Algerian Sahara, and northwestern Mali. The party objected strongly to King Hassan's recognition of Mauritania and to the de facto border with Algeria in 1969 to 1972. Istiqlal would be the most resistant to concessions to the Polisario Front in Western Sahara. The party has been noted for supporting full Arabization of education, strict adherence to Islamic principles, rejection of birth control, and denigration of "foreign ideologies" like Marxism.

Once pro-royalist, the party now is more reformist and only supports the king on a few issues. In fact, it has challenged the monarchy on human rights abuses and has begun to rally for improving living standards in Morocco.

The party is primarily urban and middle class and enjoys the support of much of the country's religious officialdom. It is weak among students and unionized workers, though it has a very small student organization and a labor organization.

Istiglal's funding traditionally has come from prominent bourgeois families. This support, however, has declined significantly since the early 1960s. Mohamed Douri is the party leader, and Mohamed Boucetta is the secretary-general.

Because of its participation in the Democratic Bloc, Istiqlal has changed its focus to one of reform and therefore garnered a sizable support. Its biggest challenge may be the tensions within the party between the aging members and the younger, more reform-minded members.

NATIONAL ENTENTE
(Entente Nationale)

The National Entente is made up of the Popular Movement (Mouvement Populaire), the Constitutional Union (Union Constitutionelle), and the National Democratic Party (Parti National-Démocrate). It is a center-right coalition whose parties had leading roles in the government in the 1985 to 1992 period. In 1993 when King Hassan tried (and failed) to entice other, more left-leaning parties to participate in the government, Entente parties were named to form the cabinet in 1995.

POPULAR MOVEMENT
(Mouvement Populaire; MP)

Created in 1957 and legalized in 1959, the MP exploited local rural grievances that lay behind rural rebellions in 1957 to 1959. It presented itself in the Berber-populated mountainous regions as a Berber alternative to the Arab-dominated, urban-based Istiqlal Party. It received encouragement from the palace, which saw the movement as a useful counterweight to the urban parties. It gave loyal support to the king and joined the FDIC in the 1960s. It received four posts in the government after the 1977 elections and was third-ranked after the 1984 and 1993 elections.

The MP's distinctive features are its royalism and Berberism. In 1986 an extraordinary party congress removed its founder and then secretary-general, Mahjoubi Aherdane (born 1921).

CONSTITUTIONAL UNION
(Union Constitutionnelle; UC)

This party was founded in April 1983 under the leadership of former prime minister M. Maati Bouabid after extensive preparation during the preceding three months. Between January and April 1983, M. Bouabid toured the country and held innumerable meetings with local officials, dignitaries, and other influential persons, with a view to constructing a broad-based, popular, yet conservative and loyalist, political alliance. The new alliance received support from the palace and

was able to command very considerable electoral support both in the local elections of June 1983 and in the national elections of September–October 1984. In electoral terms it was the most popular party of all—in all stages of the elections—garnering more seats, both in the rural and the municipal commune councils and in the Chamber of Representatives, than any other party. In the 1997 parliamentary elections, as part of the National Entente, the UC garnered 50 Chamber of Representatives seats and 28 Chamber of Councilors seats. In the 2002 parliamentary election the UC got 16 of the 325 seats.

The UC declares that it is faithful to the country's constitutional traditions and to the monarchy. It seeks to mobilize a new alliance centered around a program "quite distinct from the demagogy of imported ideologies and destructive forces." Its major stated concern is to move beyond the politics of the immediate postindependence period and to develop a new "centrist" grouping. It is weak on specific economic and social policy.

Party members are drawn generally from the wealthy and middle classes, both urban and rural; landowners, industrialists, and business interests are represented, as are the professional middle classes. The electoral base is predominantly, but by no means exclusively, rural.

The financial support of its broad constituency covers the UC expenses. It may also receive support from the palace. The founder, Maati Bouabid, former prime minister, died in 1996. Current leaders are Abdellatif Semlali and Jalal Essaid.

As the major conservative, loyalist political grouping, with evident electoral support and the approval of the palace, the UC is no longer as popular and powerful as it once was. The death of founder Maati Bouabid in 1996 appears to have weakened the party's former internal unity.

NATIONAL DEMOCRATIC PARTY
(Parti National-Démocrate; PND)

Registered as a parliamentary group in April 1981 and as a political party a few weeks later, the National Democratic Party is a breakaway from the National Assembly of Independents (Rassemblement National des Indépendents; RNI). In the November 1981 Cabinet reshuffle, it increased its number of ministerial posts from three to five, while the RNI rump left the government. In the Cabinet of November 1983 its number of ministerial posts was back to three, while the RNI also obtained a ministerial presence. The PND continues to attract electoral support, although to a significantly lesser extent than does the RNI. In the 1997 parliamentary elections, as part of the National Entente, the PND won only 10 Chamber of Representatives seats and 21 Chamber of Councilors seats. In the 2002 parliamentary elections the PND got 12 seats of the total of 325.

Like the RNI, the PND is strongly pro-royalist. It is anti-Socialist, pro-Western in foreign policy, and supportive of private business. But whereas the RNI rump tends to represent the interests of industry and commerce, the PND is supported by many of the large landowners and therefore supports policies favorable to the development of large-scale commercial farming. Nevertheless, it presents itself as the defender of the interests of the small farmer and peasant, claims to be progressive, and condemns those political tendencies and ideologies that encourage the division into left and right.

The leaders of the PND are generally wealthy and are often large landowners. Their electoral base is overwhelmingly rural. The financial support of its wealthy constituency covers most expenses. Abdelhamid Kassimi is the party leader, and Arsalane el-Jadidi is the party's secretary-general.

Although for a while, between 1981 and 1983, it seemed as though the PND would emerge as the favored conservative, loyalist grouping, its position has been seriously undermined by the Constitutional Union. The PND has as its mandate to remain loyal to the monarchy, yet to be a counterweight to the "old" parties. It is probable that its strongly rural base will weaken its claim to be a broad and unifying party.

CENTER
(Center)

Center consists of the National Assembly of Independents (Rassemblement National des Indépendents; RNI), the Democratic and Social Movement (Mouvement Démocratique et Social; MDS), and the National Popular Movement (Mouvement Nationale Populaire; MNP).

NATIONAL ASSEMBLY OF INDEPENDENTS
(Rassemblement National des Indépendents; RNI)

Founded in October 1978, the RNI was initially a loose coalition of the royalist "independents" who won the 1977 general elections. It had much in common with the earlier FDIC, the bloc of pro-royalist forces that held half the seats in the 1963–65 Parliament, although, unlike the FDIC, it did not include the MP. Like the FDIC, the RNI was soon beset by internal squabbles. Two rival factions emerged in 1980; and, in April 1981, 59 of the RNI's deputies announced that they were forming a new parliamentary group, known as the Democrat Independents. The RNI rump then suffered a serious setback when its six members in the government lost their ministerial posts in a cabinet reshuffle in November 1981. The Cabinet formed in November 1983, however, once again contained RNI ministers. However, its parliamentary representation fell to 41 in 1993.

The RNI is strongly pro-royalist. It is supportive of private business, strongly antisocialist, and pro-Western in foreign policy.

The party's top leaders come mainly from the wealthiest strata of Moroccan society. Many have important commercial or industrial interests or have served as senior technocrats in successive governments. The party enjoys support from members of the chambers of commerce and industry and such bodies as the employer's General Economic Confederation of Morocco (Confédération Generale Economique du Maroc; CGEM). Its electoral support is primarily rural.

The RNI is supported by the personal funds of its leading members. Ahmed Osman is the RNI's president. He is a brother-in-law of King Hassan and was prime minister from 1973 to 1979.

Despite continuing difficulties, the party maintains a presence in the government and commands considerable support among the electors. It is rumored that deep divisions exist in the RNI and that a new generation of party leaders is rising to challenge the charismatic Osnan.

Minor Political Parties

Among the smaller parties that have representation in parliament are the Front of the Democratic Forces, the Progress and Socialist Party, and the Democratic Union. However, the party that made the biggest gains in the 2002 elections was the Justice and Development Party (PJD), the only Islamic party allowed to compete in the elections. It won 42 seats in the Chamber of Representatives, even though it fielded candidates only in 56 of the 91 legislative districts.

Other Political Forces

OPPOSITION PARTIES

Morocco's multipartyism has traditionally not extended to include Islamist parties, which have no legal basis for existing. Justice and Welfare (Adl wal Ihsan), founded in 1980, is the country's leading Islamic fundamentalist organization. Its leader, Abd Assalam Yasine, has served several prison sentences, has been placed under house arrest, and has been under police protection since the 1970s. Other Islamist parties include Movement for Reform and Renewal, To the Future, and Islamic Youth.

These Islamist organizations denounce what they see as a decline in moral values and Morocco's deviation from the Muslim faith. They have not advocated violence, but their presence is a reminder to the king that his religious authority could be challenged.

ORGANIZED LABOR

Though French unions had had affiliates in Morocco for some years, the first Moroccan labor federation, the Moroccan Union of Labor (Union Marocaine du Travail; UMT) was founded in 1955 by supporters of the Istiqlal Party. Under Mahjoub Ben Seddik, the federation supported the UNFP's split from the party in 1959; but, from 1962, relations between the UMT and the UNFP were strained. The UMT, which was subsidized by the government, was generally unwilling to back the UNFP's political campaigns and concentrated on narrow trade union matters.

After the split in the UNFP in 1972, Ben Seddik retained links with the rump led by Abdallah Ibrahim. In consequence, the larger faction, which went on to form the USFP in 1974, set about building a rival trade union movement. From the beginning it had the support of the National Education Union (Syndicat National de l'Enseignement; SNE), which had been independent of the UMT since its creation in 1965, and the postal workers' union, which had split from the UMT in 1963. In 1978, eight USFP-led unions, representing teachers, phosphate workers, postal workers, health employees, sugar and tea workers, water and electricity workers, petroleum and gas workers, and some railwaymen, founded the Democratic Labor Confederation (Confédération Démocratique du Travail; CDT). By 1979 there were three more affiliates, representing workers in the tobacco industry, agriculture, and municipal administration; and although the UMT retained some of its traditional strength in basic industries, notably the railway and the electricity-generating industries, the CDT had become the more powerful of the two federations by 1981.

Morocco owes its profusion of trade unions to its pluralism of political parties. However, according to some observers, trade unions are still linked to the regime or to political parties, which means that patronage, clientelism, and power sharing still exist, thus undermining their power and role in society.

National Prospects

The 1990s in Morocco were a time of drastic change for this traditional monarchy-led Muslim country. Beginning with the political reforms that have led to the latest coalition government in March 1997, Morocco appears on its way to democratizing and reforming. However, critics quickly pointed out that King Hassan II still maintained supreme power in his country's political and economic matters.

Indeed, one of the country's main selling points is stability in a largely unstable Middle East. On the economic front, beginning in December 1989, Morocco dropped its state-centrist economic policy in favor of privatization. Now the country has begun to call for more reliance on private entrepreneurship and investment as tools for future economic growth. A new Moroccan middle class has appeared, and the privatization program has attracted foreign investment. In 2004 Morocco signed free trade agreements with the United States and the European Union.

However, Morocco is a developing country with 19 percent of the population living under the poverty line (1999 estimate) and an unemployment rate of 12.1 percent (2004 estimate). The majority of the labor forces are concentrated in the services sector (45 percent); 40 percent work in agriculture and 15 percent in the industry sector (2003 estimate). Morocco mainly exports to France (25.9 percent) and Spain (14 percent), but also to the United Kingdom (7.8 percent), Germany (5.7 percent), Italy (5.5 percent), and the United States (4.7 percent) (2002 estimate).

With all the political and economic reforms, however, the king still has the political legitimacy of descending from a dynasty and the religious legitimacy of descending from a prophet. As long as he is able to hold on to these status claims and, at the same time, oversee even limited economic and political reform, Morocco will be a bright spot of stability in the Middle East.

Further Reading

Bendourou, Omar. "Power and Opposition in Morocco." *Journal of Democracy* 7, no. 3 (1996).

Hammoudi, Abdellah. *Master and Disciple: The Cultural Foundations of Moroccan Authoritarianism.* Chicago: University of Chicago Press, 1997.

Henry, Clement M. *The Mediterranean Debt Crescent: Money and Power in Algeria, Egypt, Morocco, Tunisia, and Turkey.* Gainesville: University Press of Florida, 1996.

Hoisington, William A., Jr. *Lyautey and the French Conquest of Morocco.* New York: St. Martin's Press, 1995.

Islam, Roumeen. "Growing Faster, Finding Jobs: Choices for Morocco." World Bank Middle East and North Africa Economic Studies. Washington, D.C.: World Bank, 1996.

Joffé, George. "Elections and Reform in Morocco." In *Mediterranean Politics*, vol. 1. Ed. Richard Gillespie. Cranbury, N.J.: Association of University Presses, 1994.

Ketterer, J. P. "From One Chamber to Two: The Case of Morocco." *Journal of Legislative Studies* 7, no. 1 (spring 2001): 135–50.

Khosrowshahi, Cameron. "Privatization in Morocco: The Politics of Development." *Middle East Journal* 51, no. 2 (spring 1997).

Park, Thomas Kerlin. *Historical Dictionary of Morocco.* New York: Scarecrow Press, 1996.

Pazzanita, Anthony G. *Western Sahara.* World Bibliographical Series, vol. 190. Santa Barbara, Calif.: ABC-Clio, 1996.

Shahin, Emad Eldin. "Under the Shadow of the Imam." *Middle East Insight* 11, no. 2 (January–February 1995). Washington, D.C.: International Insight, Inc., 1995.

Waltz, Susan Eileen. *Human Rights and Reform: Changing the Face of North African Politics.* Berkeley: University of California Press, 1995.

REPUBLIC OF MOZAMBIQUE
(República de Moçambique)

By Robert J. Griffiths, Ph.D.

The Republic of Mozambique is located on the southeast coast of Africa with a population of 19,406,703 (2005 est.). After 17 years of single-party rule, Mozambique became a multiparty democracy with the October 1994 elections. The current president is Armando Guebuza.

Mozambique became independent on June 25, 1975, following more than a decade of guerrilla war against Portuguese colonial rule. The independence war was waged by the Front for the Liberation of Mozambique (Frelimo). The revolution in Portugal in 1974 led to a cease-fire and independence agreement on September 7. The agreement transferred power to a transitional government led by the then prime minister, Joaquim Chissano, and composed of Portuguese officers and representatives of Frelimo. The country became fully independent on June 25, 1975. After independence, Mozambique adopted a presidential system of government with Samora Machel as president and Chissano as foreign minister.

In 1977 the country was proclaimed a people's republic, with Marxism-Leninism as its official ideology and Frelimo as the only legal party. After achieving independence, Frelimo shifted its focus onto Mozambique's pressing economic and social problems. Frelimo's efforts to improve the nation's economy were complicated by its support for the nationalist movement in Rhodesia. In 1976 Mozambique closed its borders with Rhodesia in response to the international boycott of the Ian Smith regime. This boycott was extremely costly to Mozambique. The United Nations estimated that between 1976 and 1980 Mozambique lost $550 million in trade. In addition, the Rhodesians had trained and financed a counterrevolutionary movement, the Mozambican National Resistance (MNR, more popularly known as Renamo).

By 1980 Mozambique faced two major problems: a serious drought, which extended from Ethiopia to South Africa, and increased tension within South Africa. After independence, Frelimo was left with an economy that had been almost completely destroyed by the war and the attendant loss of the middle class. Also, the Mozambican economy was still dependent on income from migrant workers in South Africa and fees from South African goods exported from the Mozambican ports of Maputo and Beira. Drought compounded the country's difficulties. Second, rising conflict within South Africa led Pretoria to implement a destabilization campaign against neighboring countries from which antiapartheid forces were operating. Part of this campaign involved increased support for guerrilla groups in bordering countries. Although Renamo had lost its foreign support with the fall of the Smith regime and the independence of Zimbabwe in 1980, it began to receive aid from South Africa and waged a campaign of economic destruction, kidnapping, and killing of the civilian population.

Renamo activities increasingly escalated after 1980. No longer able to sustain the economic and human losses, Machel concluded the Nkomati Accords with South Africa on March 16, 1984. The Accords were a nonaggression treaty in which Mozambique agreed to bar the African National Congress (ANC) from its territory and South Africa agreed to end its support for Renamo. The Nkomati Accords were controversial. The treaty was widely criticized as a concession to the white South African government. Machel's optimism about Mozambique's ability to make accommodations with South Africa proved to be ill-founded. By December 1984, ANC operations were no longer conducted from Mozambique, but Renamo operations had, in fact, increased and were receiving support from South African army personnel.

In October 1985 Mozambique conducted a joint military operation with Zimbabwe against Renamo. The government was able to overrun the rebel headquarters, and captured documents revealed that South Africa had continued to support Renamo in violation of the Nkomati Accords. Relations between Mozambique and South Africa worsened with President Samora Machel's death in an October 1986 plane crash. There was speculation that South Africa was involved, although this was never confirmed. Frelimo appointed the foreign minister, Joaquim Chissano, Machel's successor as president.

Relations between South Africa and Mozambique improved in 1987 with an agreement to jointly investigate a massacre allegedly carried out by Renamo. In 1988 the two countries agreed to revive the Nkomati Accords and reestablish the Joint Security Commission. Meetings between Chissano and the then South African president, P. W. Botha, produced further cooperation between Maputo and Pretoria.

In July 1989 Frelimo renounced its exclusive commitment to Marxism-Leninism, opened party membership to all citizens of the country, and adopted more pragmatic policies. In 1990 the government announced that it would present a new constitution to the Popular Assembly, and the document was adopted in November.

In the meantime, fighting between the government and Renamo continued. Efforts to find a negotiated settlement began with face-to-face talks in Rome in July 1990. The talks continued in December when a Joint Verification Commission was established and a partial cease-fire took effect. Several more rounds of talks took place before a General Peace Agreement (GPA) was finally signed on October 4, 1992. The agreement called for a cease-fire, demobilization of soldiers on both sides, and multiparty elections.

The United Nations sent approximately 8,000 peacekeepers to oversee the agreement. The UN operation (UNOMOZ) faced the difficult task of demobilizing soldiers on each side prior to elections. This was essential to avoid a repeat of the situation in Angola, another former Portuguese colony, where failure to demobilize the warring factions led to renewed fighting.

By mid-1995 nearly 1.7 million refugees who had fled Mozambique during the conflicts had returned to the country, and the ensuing period of political stability has contributed greatly to the country's development.

The System of Government

Mozambique is a republic with a unicameral legislature.

EXECUTIVE

The 1990 constitution provides for a popularly elected president who can serve a maximum of two consecutive five-year terms. The president is the head of government

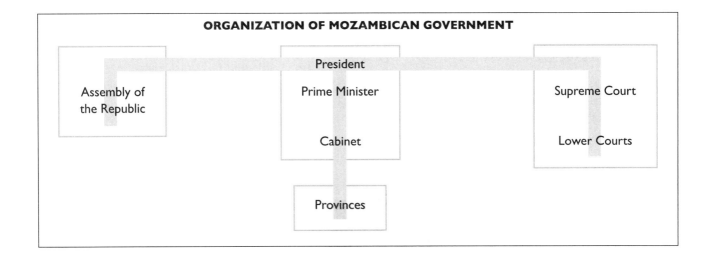

ORGANIZATION OF MOZAMBICAN GOVERNMENT

President

Assembly of the Republic

Prime Minister

Cabinet

Supreme Court

Lower Courts

Provinces

and the state, as well as commander in chief of the armed forces. The Council of Ministers is headed by the prime minister, who is selected by the president. The prime minister assists and advises the president and puts forth the government's budget and programs to the legislature.

LEGISLATURE

The national legislature, the Assembly of the Republic, consists of 250 deputies elected on a multiparty basis according to a system of proportional representation. The deputies are elected for a five-year term, but the assembly can be dissolved by the president before its term expires. The assembly meets for two sessions each year.

JUDICIARY

Under the terms of the 1990 constitution, Mozambique has an independent judiciary. The Supreme Court is at the top of the system of courts provided for by the law on the judiciary. Some Supreme Court judges are elected by the assembly; the remainder is appointed by the president. The courts are subordinate to the Assembly of the Republic.

REGIONAL AND LOCAL GOVERNMENT

Mozambique is divided into 11 provinces. The capital, Maputo, has provincial status and, unlike the other provinces, is administered by a city council chairman. The other 10 provinces are presided over by a provincial governor, appointed by the president. Local assemblies are directly elected (a system that began in 1998) and choose representatives to district assemblies, which, in turn, select members of the provincial assemblies. Decisions of these bodies may be annulled by the president.

The Electoral System

The president is elected by popular vote and the assembly is elected by proportional representation. All elections are made by universal suffrage. Democratic elections in Mozambique were originally scheduled to take place within a year of the General Peace Accord. The run-up to Mozambique's first multiparty elections was long and complicated, and the election date had to be postponed. Troop demobilization was delayed as both sides tried to maintain a military advantage in case of a breakdown in the peace accord. Renamo

stalled while it tried to transform itself from a guerrilla movement into a political party and sought to gain assurances that it would play a role in governing the country, whatever the outcome of elections.

THE 1994 ELECTIONS

Elections were finally scheduled for October 27–28, 1994. Renamo's leader, Afonso Dhlakama, threatened to boycott the elections just one day before they began, but international pressure forced Renamo to reconsider. Western diplomats also encouraged Mozambique's president, Joachim Chissano, to form a government of national unity with Renamo in order to avoid the winner-take-all formula that contributed to electoral failure in Angola, but President Chissano resisted this pressure.

The elections marked the culmination of the two-year process that began with the General Peace Accord of 1992. The UN-monitored process cost an estimated $1 billion and elections were judged to be substantially free and fair with over 80 percent voter turnout. Renamo received a surprising 38 percent of the popular vote, giving it 112 seats in the 250-seat Parliament. Its greatest strength was in the central and northern regions. Frelimo got 48 percent of the popular vote and 129 seats in Parliament. The remaining nine seats went to the Democratic Union party. Renamo also won a majority of the popular vote in five of the 11 provinces in the country. Renamo's leader, Afonso Dhlakama, was less successful in the presidential poll, receiving only 34 percent, compared with President Joachim Chissano's 53 percent. On the strength of Frelimo's electoral victory, Chissano appointed a government made up entirely of his Frelimo supporters, assuring continued political divisions.

THE 1999 ELECTIONS

Disputes between Frelimo and Renamo over local elections in June 1998 set the stage for Mozambique's second round of legislative and presidential elections in December 1999. In those elections Frelimo's Joachim Chissano defeated Renamo's Afonso Dhlakama with 52.3 percent of the vote. Frelimo also won 133 of the 250 seats in the Assembly of the Republic. Renamo-UE, an electoral coalition consisting of 11 opposition parties, won the remaining 117 seats. Renamo rejected the results of the election charging fraud. International observers judged the balloting to be free and fair and the Mozambique Supreme Court, performing the function of the Constitutional Council, rejected Renamo's appeal of the outcome. Nevertheless, Renamo supporters continued to protest the results and in a demonstration in November 2000 41 were killed in clashes between Frelimo and Renamo supporters. Renamo also charged the government with responsibility in the deaths of 83 people arrested at the demonstrations. Although the government denied responsibility, a Mozambique Human Rights Association report supported the charge. Amid tensions between the two parties, Chissano and Dhlakama held their first talks since the elections in December 2000 to try to resolve differences between the parties. A second meeting was held in January 2001 but did not produce much progress.

In May 2001 Chissano announced that he would not run as Frelimo's candidate in the next elections. At a Renamo party congress in October 2001 Dhlakama was reelected party president and Joaquim Vaz was elected secretary-general. A 10-member political committee was also formed indicating Renamo's intentions to become a full-fledged political party. At the eighth Frelimo party congress in June 2002, Armando Guebuza was elected secretary-general and also became the party's candidate in the next presidential elections. The next month, Renamo's Dhlakama dismissed Vaz as secretary-general and dissolved the Political Committee. The turmoil within Renamo seemed to diminish with the appointment of Viana Magalhães as secretary-general in November but the party was soon embroiled in another controversy over the seating of five Renamo legislators who had resigned or been expelled from the party. Renamo also announced that it was going to contest the 2003 municipal elections alone. The remaining 10 opposition parties that had been part of the Renamo-UE founded a new coalition, the União Eleitoral. Frelimo won the municipal elections securing a majority in 29 municipalities and the mayorship in 28. Renamo won a majority in only four municipalities and claimed mayorships in five. A split emerged within Frelimo between supporters of Secretary-General Guebuza and Chissano supporters. In February 2004 the Frelimo government named Luisa Diogo prime minister. Diogo will also retain her portfolio as finance minister.

By June 2004 Frelimo and Renamo were at odds once again over changes to draft constitutional amendments drawn up by an ad hoc commission of the Assembly of the Republic charged with revising the 1990 constitution. National elections were scheduled for December 2004.

THE 2004 ELECTIONS

During the 2004 elections the power of the Frelimo party increased. Frelimo candidate Armando Guebuza took presidential office in February 2005 with 63.7 percent of the vote. In addition, Frelimo captured 160 assembly seats with 62 percent of the vote while Renamo was awarded the 90 remaining seats with 29.7 percent of the vote. Although the Renamo party once again contested the elections, their claims were dismissed by election monitors.

The Party System

The major parties in Mozambique, Frelimo and Renamo, were both born out of armed rebellions and have been in conflict with one another since the 1970s. Despite the transition from military group to political party that marked each organization after the General Peace Agreement in 1992, tensions have remained.

Major Political Parties
FRONT FOR THE LIBERATION OF MOZAMBIQUE
(Frente de Liberacão de Mozambique; Frelimo)

Frelimo was created on June 25, 1962, when Dr. Eduardo Mondlane unified three different movements headquartered in Dar es Salaam: Udenamo (National Democratic Union of Mozambique), Manu (Mozambican-Makonde Union), and Unami (National African Union of Independent Mozambique). He was then chosen as president of the umbrella group Frelimo but was subsequently assassinated in 1969. Frelimo pursued a Marxist-Leninist ideology in 1977 but retreated from this philosophy at its 1989 party congress, adopting a more pragmatic, free-market orientation.

MOZAMBIQUE NATIONAL RESISTANCE
(Resistencia Nacional Mocambicana; MNR, Renamo)

Renamo was established in the early 1970s by the Rhodesian government as an intelligence network to keep track of its opponents operating out of Mozambique. With the independence of Zimbabwe in 1980, South Africa took over as Renamo's patron and the organization engaged in a bloody, widespread guerrilla war against the Frelimo government. Locked into a stalemate with the government and under increasing pressure to negotiate with the government, Renamo finally agreed to the General Peace Accord in October 1992. Renamo then set about to recast itself as a political party in order to contest the 1994 elections. The party remains in a state of some disarray.

Minor Political Parties

There are some 38 other parties active in Mozambique, but their support is limited.

Other Political Forces

ARMED FORCES

A critical component of the peace process was the demobilization of combatants and the creation of new armed forces. According to the General Peace Accord (GPA), troops from both sides were to assemble at separate designated areas. Those who wanted to enlist in the new armed forces were evaluated and processed while those who wished to return to civilian life were demobilized. The new army was to be composed of equal numbers of soldiers from both sides for a total troop population of 30,000. A commission was established consisting of representatives of Frelimo, Renamo, and the UN to oversee the creation of the new military. Demobilization and the formation of the Forcas Armadas de Defesa de Mocambique (FADM) was slow because of delays in deploying UN personnel, dissatisfaction on both sides over conditions in the camps, and mutual suspicion. The FADM came into existence in August 1994, but at well below the 30,000 troops envisioned. Although the GPA called for each side to contribute 15,000 troops, by the time the Cease-Fire Commission issued its final report in December 1994, a combined total of only 11,579 troops had enlisted in the FADM. In 1995 the government announced that it would introduce legislation to increase troop strength by 4,500 and that government policy, not the figure specified in the GPA, would determine troop strength. The armed forces are also contending with reduced budgets and continued dissatisfaction in the ranks. Current troop strength stands at 8,200 active members of the armed forces.

National Prospects

Despite the success of Mozambique's multiparty, democratic elections, the country continues to face formi-

dable obstacles. In 1993 the per capita GNP was only $80, making Mozambique one of the poorest countries in the world. The 16-year civil war decimated the economy and infrastructure. Mozambique has also been plagued by substantial external debt, high inflation, lack of a coherent economic policy, and corruption in the bureaucracy. Although the 1987 Economic and Social Rehabilitation Program supported by the IMF and the World Bank helped reduce the deficit and curb inflation, the country still depends heavily on foreign aid. The lack of economic opportunity, particularly for demobilized soldiers, and the presence of large numbers of weapons left over from the war contributed to rising crime rates.

There are major legacies of the civil war to be overcome. By 1992 there had been approximately 1 million casualties Repatriation of refugees was both slow and expensive. A further legacy of the long civil war is the presence of an estimated 2 million land mines scattered throughout the country that threaten civilians and complicate vital agricultural production.

Mozambique emerged from the war as one of the poorest countries in the world; since then it has experienced substantial growth. In April 2000 Mozambique qualified for debt relief under the Highly Indebted Poor Countries (HIPC) initiative. Subsequently, the country was approved for the Enhanced HIPC program and, as a result, Paris Club members agreed to reduce outstanding bilateral debt. The country's average growth rate between 1993 and 1999 was a healthy 6.7 percent and between 1997 and 1999 it averaged over 10 percent. Severe flooding in 2000 slowed growth and set the country's recovery back, but it recovered with a growth rate of 14.8 percent in 2001 and 8.3 percent in 2002. Extensive economic reforms have been carried out, including the privatization of state-owned enterprises, and investors have responded by pumping some $6 billion into the country's economy over the past two years. According to Prime Minister Diogo, who also holds the finance minister portfolio, Mozambique has become one of the top three investment destinations on the African continent.

Further Reading

Alden, C. *Mozambique and the Construction of the New African State: From Negotiations to Nation Building.* New York: Palgrave, 2001.

Finnegan, William. *A Complicated War: The Harrowing of Mozambique.* Berkeley: University of California Press, 1992.

Haines, Richard, and Geoffrey Wood. "The 1994 Election and Mozambique's Democratic Transition." *Democratization* 2, no. 3 (autumn 1995): 362–76.

Issacs, Dan. "Fulfilling a Dream." *Africa Report* 40, no. 1 (January–February 1995): 13–21.

Pitcher, M. A. *Transforming Mozambique: The Politics of Privatization, 1975-2000.* Cambridge, U.K.: Cambridge University Press, 2002.

Vines, Alex. *Angola and Mozambique: The Aftermath of Conflict.* London: Research Institute for the Study of Conflict and Terrorism, 1995.

———. *Renamo: Terrorism in Mozambique.* London: Centre for Southern African Studies, 1991.

Wurst, Jim. "Mozambique: Peace and More." *World Policy Journal* 11, no. 3 (fall 1994): 79–83.

UNION OF MYANMAR
(Pyihtaungsu Myanmar Naingngandaw)

By Mary P. Callahan, Ph.D.
Revised by Kristin Marsh, Ph.D.

The largest country in mainland Southeast Asia, Myanmar encompasses 261,228 square miles and shares 4,016 miles of land borders with Thailand, Laos, China, India, and Bangladesh. Its coastline in the south rests along the Bay of Bengal and the Andaman Sea. The people of Myanmar are ethnically diverse, with minority groups estimated to make up at least one-third of Myanmar's total population of nearly 43 million. The Burmans, who reside mainly in the central agricultural valleys and in the southern coastal and delta regions, comprise the major ethnic group. Although an accurate census of the minority regions has not been attempted since 1931, most government and scholarly sources estimate that the ethnic makeup is as follows: 68 percent Burman, 9 percent Shan, 7 percent Karen, 4 percent Rakhine, 3 percent Chinese, 2 percent Mon, 2 percent Indian, along with small numbers of Assamese and Chin minority peoples. The official language of the state is Burmese, although other languages such as Karen, Chin, Shan, and Kachin are spoken in ethnic-minority regions. Theravada Buddhism is practiced by 89 percent of the population. Within Myanmar, there are also Christians (4 percent of the population), Muslims (4 percent), animists (1 percent), and other (2 percent).

The Union of Myanmar has been ruled by a military junta since the September 18, 1988, coup d'état, which brought a definitive end to 26 years of military-dominated, socialist rule. This junta, now called the State Peace and Development Council (Naingngandaw Ayechanthayaye Nint Phwinphyotothetye Counci)

(SPDC), is made up of 19 senior military officers, most of whom also serve as members of the government's cabinet. Soon after taking power, the junta changed the name of the country from "Burma" to "Myanmar."

The territory that came to be known as "Burma" with the advent of British rule had never before been fully integrated or controlled by a single, central state. It was not until the late 18th century that a Burman king, Alaungpaya, was able to establish authority reaching out to many parts of the land.

In the 19th century, Britain began a gradual, three-stage takeover of all territory today considered part of Myanmar. The conquest was complete in 1886, when the last Burman king was deposed and Burma became a province of India. The colonial regime divided the country into two administrative zones. The central area was called "Ministerial Burma" and was home to most of the ethnic majority Burmans, while the "Frontier Areas" were located in the territory along the newly drawn borders and were populated mainly by other ethnic groups. The Frontier Areas were left largely untouched by the British rulers. In Ministerial Burma, the more intrusive, direct colonial rule sparked the emergence of an ethnic Burman-dominated nationalist movement (the Dobama Asiayone) in the 1920s and 1930s, demanding complete independence from Britain. The agitation by nationalist leaders, including Aung San, along with the wartime collapse of the British regime eventually led to the granting of independence on January 4, 1948.

From independence until 1958 and again from 1960 to 1962, the Union of Burma experienced civilian rule with a parliamentary form of government. Former nationalist leader U Nu served as prime minister during most of this period. Political life was dominated by one party: the Anti-Fascist People's Freedom League (AFPFL). The early years of independence were characterized by a number of serious threats to survival, including internal ones (Communist and separatist ethnic rebellions) and external ones (the U.S.-backed Kuomintang incursions into Burma, where they prepared to stage an assault to retake mainland China from the Chinese Communists). Due to AFPFL infighting that threatened to aggravate the civil war and also due to poor economic performance, the military (in Burmese, the *tatmadaw*) stepped in to govern as a caretaker government in 1958, and then more permanently in March 1962 when the army again took power. Under the leadership of its commander in chief, General Ne Win, the coup group formed a Revolutionary Council of military officers to replace the cabinet and parliament. The Council suspended the 1947 constitution, established the Leninist-style Burma Socialist Program Party (BSPP), and outlawed all other political parties. Under its "Burmese Way to Socialism," the BSPP attempted to impose a central, command economy and to eliminate foreign control over business in Burma.

In 1974 a new constitution provided for a highly centralized, civilian, single-party form of government. The constitution vested state power in the unicameral People's Assembly, the State Council, the Council of Ministers, and the Council of People's Justice. At the national, state, township, and village levels, government administration was greatly influenced by the BSPP, which stepped up its efforts to build a mass following across the country. Most party and government leadership positions came to be occupied by the same military officers who had held them before 1974. As chairman of the State Council and party chairman, General Ne Win continued his hold on power into the 1980s.

In September 1987, following a series of unexpected demonetization measures that devastated the economy, student demonstrations erupted in Rangoon and continued sporadically into the following year. The police used harsh tactics to put down the demonstrations, one incident led to the suffocation deaths of 41 students in a police van. Public outcry over the incident led to further demonstrations, some of which began attracting participants from other walks of life. This led to the convening of an extraordinary BSPP congress in July, during which Ne Win and San Yu resigned from the party leadership. Nationwide demonstrations continued until September 18, when the army leadership took power directly and established the State Law and Order Restoration Council

(SLORC) under the chairmanship of the army commander and Ne Win follower General Saw Maung.

The SLORC suspended the 1974 constitution and abolished the presidency, State Council, Council of Ministers, and People's Assembly. Under SLORC's orders, the crack troops of the armed forces put an abrupt end to the popular pro-democracy demonstrations, killing thousands of unarmed civilians in the process. The SLORC distributed cabinet portfolios to senior military officers, with General Saw Maung assuming the responsibility of prime minister and defense minister. Saw Maung was replaced in April 1992 in a palace coup by the SLORC vice chair, General Than Shwe. In November 1997 the junta renamed itself the State Peace and Development Council.

The System of Government

Myanmar is governed by a military junta.

EXECUTIVE

After suspending the 1974 constitution, the SLORC took over executive authority in Myanmar in September 1988. Executive power is vested in the chief of state and head of government, Chairman of the SPDC Senior General Than Shwe (since April 23, 1992). Than Shwe also serves as commander in chief of the defense services and defense minister, and initially he also served as prime minister. In August 2003 General Knin Nyunt was appointed prime minister, only to be dismissed abruptly in October 2004. General Soe Win is currently the appointed prime minister. At present, there are no legal provisions that limit executive power. As the ruling junta, the SPDC consists of 19 members, including commanders of the service branches and regional military commands. SPDC members wield considerable power. Many, though not all, of the members also held ministerial positions. Beginning in 1992, the junta began appointing some civilians to the cabinet; in 1997, 27 portfolios were held by military officers, eight by civilians. Below the cabinet level, the executive is dominated by military or recently retired military officers who hold numerous director general and subordinate posts as well as crucial positions in economic ministries.

With apparently unlimited power, SPDC rules with an authoritarian fist in its pursuit of what it calls the "three main causes": nondisintegration of the Union, nondisintegration of the national solidarity, and perpetuation of national sovereignty.

Upon assuming the chairmanship of the junta in 1992, Than Shwe called for a national convention to meet and draw up a new constitution. Opening on January 9, 1993, the National Convention (Amyotha Nyilagkan) consisted of 702 handpicked delegates. Although the National Convention witnessed sporadic dissension in its ranks, the discussions were tightly controlled by the regime and the proposed constitution that emerged continued to shore up the power of the military. The gathering produced a number of principles. It promised "a genuine multiparty democracy" but stressed the "basic principle" that the military would be guaranteed a "leading role" in national politics. The president would be chosen by an electoral college but would be required to have military as well as political experience. The military was to be represented at every level of the executive. Progress on the constitution stalled until May 2004, when the government convened a second constitutional convention. Meetings were once again tightly controlled and sporadic; breaking after two months, they are scheduled to begin again early in 2005.

LEGISLATURE

Under the present regime, there is no legislative branch of government. After abolishing the People's Assembly in September 1988, SLORC continued to allow political parties to prepare for the coming May 1990 elections, although the government banned all public gatherings of more than four individuals. Nonetheless, 223 parties were legalized and registered in 1989, the most significant of which were the National League for

Democracy (led by Daw Aung San Suu Kyi, daughter of the national martyr Aung San) and the National Unity Party (the pro-government successor to the BSPP). In the remarkably free and fair election for the legislative assembly held on May 27, 1990, the NLD secured 392 of the 485 seats available (more than 80 percent of the vote), while the junta's NUP gained a miniscule 10 seats (2.1 percent). Since that election, SLORC set aside the results and disqualified, arrested, or drove into exile many of the elected candidates.

JUDICIARY

The judiciary in Myanmar functions as an appendage to the executive junta. SPDC appoints justices to the Supreme Court, and they in turn appoint lower court judges with the approval of SPDC. Courts are located at the national, state, division, and township levels of government. Although there are remnants of the British colonial-era legal system formally in place, in actual practice there is pervasive corruption that undermines the impartiality of the judiciary. Court trial procedures vary greatly according to whether a case is criminal or political. Due process protections are more likely to be upheld in criminal cases. More sensitive political cases are tried in private to avoid public scrutiny, and junta officials frequently dictate the outcome. In November 1994 the SPDC announced the release of nearly 4,000 political prisoners, including leaders of the NLD and student leader Min Ko Naing. While welcoming the release, the oppositional coalition government (NCGUB) called for broader steps toward reconciliation.

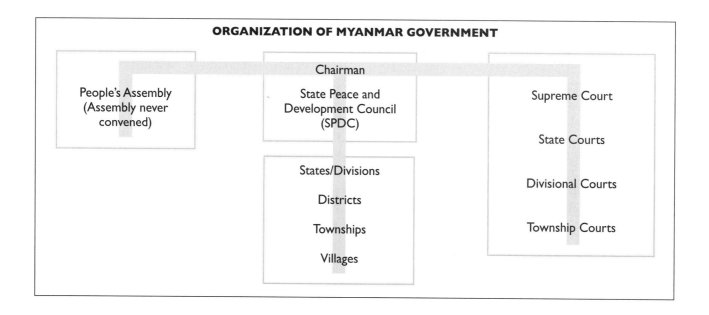

ORGANIZATION OF MYANMAR GOVERNMENT

People's Assembly (Assembly never convened)

Chairman
State Peace and Development Council (SPDC)

States/Divisions
Districts
Townships
Villages

Supreme Court
State Courts
Divisional Courts
Township Courts

REGIONAL AND LOCAL GOVERNMENT

The regional configuration of states and divisions established under the 1974 constitution has been maintained under SPDC. There are seven states and seven divisions; the term "state" refers to an ethnic minority region, whereas "division" refers to a region in central Myanmar largely populated by ethnic Burmans. Each regional unit is governed by a state or division Peace and Development Council (PDC), which is dominated by locally based, senior military officers. Below the state level, there are district, township, and village PDCs—also under the leadership of active-duty or recently retired military officers—that administer local affairs. In most cases, the PDCs at all subnational levels simply were grafted onto the administrative structures left behind by the BSPP; in fact, in many cases, the same military officers who ran local-level BSPP administrative bodies or local party councils were reassigned to the PDCs of that same locality or region.

The Electoral System

No elections have been held in Myanmar since May 1990, and the results of that election were never realized. Because of the suspension of the 1974 constitution, there is neither an "electoral system" nor a "party system" enshrined in a constitution, government decree, or law. These aspects of the draft constitution have not been revealed at this writing.

The Party System

Despite the noninstitutionalized nature of party and electoral politics, two political organizations dominate the political landscape of Myanmar.

Major Political Parties

UNION SOLIDARITY DEVELOPMENT ASSOCIATION (USDA)

(Pyihtaungsu Kyankhainyeh Pwinphyotothetyeh Athin)

Although not registered as a political party, the Union Solidarity Development Association (Pyi-htaungsu Kyankhainyeh Pwinphyotothetyeh Athin) has emerged as the government's heir apparent to the collapsed BSPP and the NUP (repudiated in the May 1990 election). According to the junta, the USDA was formed on September 15, 1993, to help the army fight against threats to the nation. In 1999 the government claimed 11.8 million members. Geared toward the mobilization of youths throughout the country, the USDA resembles a scout organization, stressing patriotism and good character. Additionally, the USDA has vast economic holdings throughout the country. But its most prominent characteristic is its mobilization of huge public rallies numbering in the hundreds of thousands, held to support government policies. While there is strong evidence that attendance at these rallies is coerced by local PDC officials, it is clear that the regime is preparing to develop a political party for the postjunta era.

NATIONAL LEAGUE FOR DEMOCRACY (NLD)

(Amyotha Democracy Apwehgyoke)

Founded in September 1988, the National League for Democracy (Amyotha Democracy Apwehgyoke) is the only viable opposition political party in Myanmar. The party is led by Aung San Suu Kyi (general secretary and spokeswoman), Brigadier General (ret.) Aung Shwe (chairman), and General (ret.) Tin Oo. Despite the disqualification and detention of its two national leaders (Suu Kyi and Tin Oo) and many of the local leadership as well, the NLD won a landslide electoral victory in the May 1990 legislative elections. After the release of Tin Oo (March 1995) and Suu Kyi (July 1995), the NLD attempted unsuccessfully to force the junta into a dialogue on future political arrangements. Frustrated with the conduct of the National Convention, the NLD boycotted the constitution-writing assembly in November 1995, and the government subsequently banned all its representatives from any future participation in the Convention. The NLD continues to attract support in Rangoon and other parts of the country, despite ongoing attempts by the regime to harass and frustrate the party leadership. The current constitutional convention convened without the participation of Suu Kyi or the NLD. The NLD has offered to take part when the convention resumes meetings in February 2005, but only under the conditions that Suu Kyi is freed and NLD offices are allowed to reopen.

Minor Political Parties

The National Unity Party (NUP) is the main progovernment political party. Replacing the Burma Socialist Program Party (BSPP) for the 1990 elections, the NUP was overwhelmingly defeated. Other opposition parties that participated in the 1990 elections and have representation on the CRPP include the Shan Nationalities League for Democracy (SNLD), the Arakon League for Democracy (ALD), the Mon National Democratic Front (MNDF), and the Zomi National Congress (ZNC).

Other Political Forces

In the 1990s rebel activity throughout Myanmar greatly diminished, in part because of the 1989 collapse of the Communist Party of Burma and in part because of the effort of the regime to reach cease-fire agreements with ethnic minority insurgent groups. By 1997 the regime had attained such agreements with 17 of the 21 largest armed opposition movements in the country. The remaining rebel groups do not pose a serious threat to the regime. Nevertheless, as many observers have noted, the cease-fires have broken down in a number of regions. Additionally, the agreements have provided ethnic groups with the authority to hold onto their arms, to police their territory, and to use their former rebel armies as private security forces to protect both legal and illegal business operations. This authority, however, is due to run out when the junta's handpicked National Convention completes its new constitution. At that point, it is difficult to imagine that SPDC will be able to convince ethnic warlords to turn in their weapons peacefully.

After the September 1988 and post–1990 election crackdowns on the popular pro-democracy movement, many of the participants fled to the Thai border region where they linked up with the ethnic minority groups who had set up rebel headquarters in the region. This alliance led to the formation of a parallel government, the National Coalition Government Union of Burma (NCGUB) and its governing body, the Committee Representing People's Parliament (CRPP). The CRPP's 18 current members include representatives from various political and civil rights organizations. U Aung Shwe (NLD) is the current chairman; U Aye Tha Aung and U Than Tun serve as secretaries. The NCGUB has campaigned in international arenas to bring pressure upon SPDC to respect the results of the 1990 election and to transfer power to elected officials.

National Prospects

The costs of over 17 years of oppressive military rule have been mounting, and the people of Myanmar find themselves facing continuing human rights abuses, environmental degradation, a growing AIDS problem associated with heroin use, and an economy largely dependent on international trade in heroin. International isolation, including economic and military sanctions, has had a mixed impact on social conditions. First, the international community has not been uniform in withholding economic and military support; second, while sanctions have been effective in putting pressure on the SPDC, international observers such as the Free Burma Coalition point out the damage that such sanctions inflict on both social and political conditions in Myanmar. And although Myanmar is reported to have escaped the high death rates of nearby countries from the December 2004 tsunami, the damage was considerable in the coastal areas, and this crisis will not find easy resolution.

The opposition, led by the charismatic Aung San Suu Kyi, continues to attract widespread popular support both within and outside the country. The military officers in SPDC show little inclination to step out of the political realm and back to their barracks or to discuss a possible transfer-of-power scenario with the NLD. Furthermore, the military's extensive involvement in the economy is an added incentive to hold onto the political power that can protect their economic holdings. Nevertheless, efforts toward potential dialogue between opposition groups and the SPDC persist, as work continues on the constitution and civil groups begin to express the need for compromise.

Further Reading

Maung Maung. *Burmese Nationalist Movements: 1940-1948.* Honolulu: University of Hawaii Press, 1990.

Rotberg, Robert I., ed. *Burma: Prospects for a Democratic Future.* 2d ed. Washington, D.C.: Brookings Institution Press, 1998.

Silverstein, Josef. *The Political Legacy of Aung San.* 2d ed. Ithaca, N.Y.: Cornell Southeast Asia Program, 1993.

Smith, Martin. *Burma: Insurgency and the Politics of Ethnicity.* London: Zed, 1991.

Steinberg, David I. *Burma, the State of Myanmar.* Washington, D.C.: Georgetown University Press, 2001.

Taylor, Robert. *Burma: Political Economy under Military Rule.* New York: Palgrave MacMillan, 2001.

———. *Ethnic Groups in Burma: Development, Democracy and Human Rights.* London: Anti-Slavery International, 1994.

REPUBLIC OF NAMIBIA

By Richard Dale, Ph.D.
Revised by Robert J. Griffiths, Ph.D.

The current political system of Namibia is the product of nearly a quarter century of a war of independence (1966–89) that pitted the government of the Republic of South Africa against the internal and external wings of the South West Africa People's Organization of Namibia (SWAPO). Originally the country had been a German colony (1885–1915) conquered primarily by South African forces (and to a lesser extent by Southern Rhodesian forces in the northeast) during the early part of the First World War.

From 1920 until 1966 Namibia was a League of Nations Mandate, administered by South Africa, whose political leaders refused to accede to numerous international requests to transform the Mandate into a United Nations Trusteeship Territory. The UN General Assembly and the Security Council asked the International Court of Justice on several occasions to determine the international standing of the territory. In 1966 the General Assembly declared the anomalous League Mandate to be ended, and the United Nations itself became the administrator of the territory, a position South Africa challenged.

Both the South African regime and its SWAPO opponents (often relying upon the United Nations Council for Namibia) claimed to be the sole legitimate authority in the territory. The legitimacy gap was characterized by the different names for the country, with the African nationalists terming it "Namibia" and the South Africans calling it "South West Africa." The South Africans employed both their police and defense forces in the bush war against the People's Liberation Army of Namibia (PLAN), which was SWAPO's army, and armed confrontations usually took place in the northern reaches of the territory and even in the southern parts of neighboring Angola, which served as a sanctuary for PLAN after the 1974 Portuguese coup d'état.

This war was fought on diplomatic, economic, and military battlefields and had a noticeable impact upon the domestic politics of South Africa. There was a small, albeit important, fallout among the English-speaking whites in South Africa, a number of whom took up the cause of conscientious objection with respect to the South African Defense Force (SADF). In the final stages of the war, concern about the number of white SADF casualties in Namibia was an important consideration, as was the dire combat state of the South African Air Force, which bore the brunt of international arms sanctions. The war became increasingly localized by the use of South West African units, known as the South West Africa Territorial Force (SWATF), as well as internationalized when PLAN was able to take advantage of Cuban forces and aircraft and Soviet and Eastern-bloc military advisers. International negotiations involving the Cubans, the Angolans, and the South Africans, under the aegis of the United States (and to a much smaller extent the Soviet Union), brought the hostilities to an end, with the Cuban forces vacating Angola and the SADF leaving Namibia. Military and civilian components of the United Nations oversaw and legitimated the 1989–90 phase of international decolonization ending in independence on March 21, 1990.

SWAPO won the first two national elections, handily sweeping independence leader Shafilsona Samuel "Sam" Nujoma to the presidency. After Nujoma's reelection as party president in 1997, SWAPO pushed through a constitutional amendment that would allow him to run for a third term as Namibia's president. The opposition criticized this idea, but the amendment was approved in October 1998. In the 1999 presidential and legislative elections Nujoma again won a resounding victory, capturing 76.8 percent of the vote. Ben Ulenga of the Congress of Democrats (CoD) got 10.5 percent and the Democratic Turnhalle Alliance's (DTA) Katuutire Kaura received 9.6 percent of the vote. SWAPO secured 55 seats in the National Assembly, while the CoD and the DTA each won seven seats.

President Nujoma announced in November 2001 that he would not run for a fourth term as president but that he would continue to serve as party president until 2007. As party president, Nujoma engineered the nomination of SWAPO's vice president, Land Minister Hifikepunye Pohamba, as the party's presidential candidate for the 2004 elections, although the party rejected his effort to restrict the field to a single candidate for the nomination. Other candidates for the nomination included Foreign Minister Hidipo Hamutenya and Higher Education Minister Nahas Angula. At the May 2004 SWAPO party congress Nujoma undermined Pohamba's main challenger, Hamutenya, by dismissing him as foreign minister and charging him with encouraging disunity. Pohamba easily won the election for SWAPO's presidential nomination and faced the CoD's Ben Ulenga and the DTA's Katuutire Kaura in elections held in November 2004. Pohamba won in a landslide, garnering 76 percent of the vote.

The System of Government

Namibia is a democratic republic with a bicameral legislature.

EXECUTIVE

The executive branch in Namibia includes the head of state (the president), the head of government (the prime minister), the cabinet, and the civil service. The president is no mere figurehead, as sometimes occurs in nations with a dual executive. The president serves a five-year term and is limited to two terms. The duties of the president include the appointment of the prime minister and cabinet ministers as well as six special, nonvoting members of the National Assembly, and the president serves as commander in chief of the Namibian Defense Force (NDF). In addition the president enjoys a veto power with respect to legislation and can use certain circumscribed powers in a declared national emergency. There is, however, a constitutional provision for the impeachment of the president.

LEGISLATURE

Effectively Namibia has a unicameral system embodied in a National Assembly, although in early 1993 a second chamber, known as the National Council, became operational. The 26 National Council members, who have six-year terms, represent the 13 different elected regional councils, and hence its members are indirectly elected. The Council can be seen as an institutional mechanism to reflect loyal diversity without adopting a federal system. The National Assembly, which includes 72 elected and six nonvoting members appointed by the president, is the senior legislative body, with the National Council playing a secondary role, although it can turn down a bill passed by the National Assembly. It did so for the first time in 1996. As in the Westminster (British) model the National Assembly, whose members enjoy five-year terms, has the customary question period and provides a forum for the criticism (and defense) of government policies through departmental budget debates and various types of motions. Parliamentary debates are conducted in English, the official language.

JUDICIARY

The president of Namibia is responsible for appointing judges and the ombudsman pursuant to the recommendations of a Judicial Service Commission. The judicial system includes both a Supreme Court and a High Court, along with lower courts, such as traditional courts and magistrates' courts. There is demonstrable concern for human rights in the Namibian political system that reflects not only many Namibians' revulsion against the authoritarian aspects of the preindependence regime, which were exacerbated during the war of independence, but also international concern about the treatment of individuals once majority rule took effect. Observers

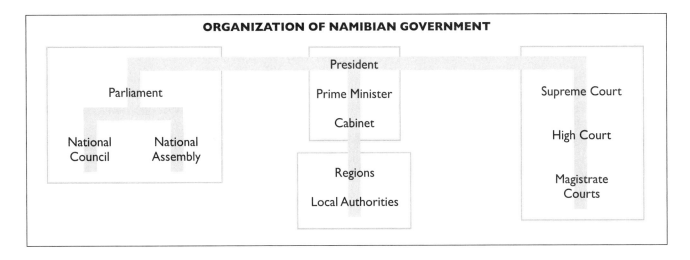

ORGANIZATION OF NAMIBIAN GOVERNMENT

Parliament

National Council   National Assembly

President

Prime Minister

Cabinet

Regions

Local Authorities

Supreme Court

High Court

Magistrate Courts

have generally been satisfied with the quality of the constitution and of its implementation.

REGIONAL AND LOCAL GOVERNMENT

Namibia has a unitary system of government, which is a reflection of the African nationalists' desire for a unified, rather than a fragmented, state. These nationalists were reacting to the earlier German and South African policies of dividing the country into African and non-African areas and controlling the movement of Africans into what was called the Police Zone (that is, the area occupied by the white inhabitants in the central and southern part of Namibia). Under the system of apartheid (practiced in fact by the Germans and in law by the South Africans) there were exclusive African areas, particularly in the north, which served as catchment areas for African migrant workers for the white-owned farms and mines in the central and southern portions of Namibia. As apartheid came to be applied more systematically in the 1960s under the Odendaal Plan, some of these areas, especially in the north, were granted self-government in the name of separate development, and they became employment havens for civil servants, many of whom were posted to the country from metropolitan South Africa.

The bicameral legislature with its regionally oriented 26-member National Council has become an institutional device for taking into consideration the geographic and ethnic diversity of this generally thinly settled land without adopting a federal system. Ethnic balancing and arithmetic come into play in the Namibian cabinet, as they also do, for instance, in the cabinet (rather than in the parliament) of the Canadian federal system.

The Electoral System

Elections in Namibia are held for local, regional, and national offices. In 1992 elections were held on the first two levels, and in 1994 the postindependence national elections took place, with international monitors as in the 1989 Constituent Assembly elections. In the elections for the National Assembly the system of party lists is combined with a system of proportional representation. In 1996 a select committee of the National Assembly proposed that the state underwrite the political parties, which would benefit both SWAPO and the DTA, but not the smaller political parties. This recommendation reflected distaste for foreign bank-rolling of political parties. Suffrage is universal for all citizens age 18 and older.

The Party System

The political party system can be dated to the early period of the League of Nations Mandate system, when the Pretoria government (following the German precedent) granted the white inhabitants of the territory a limited system of self-government. The principal lines of cleavage were between the German-speaking inhabitants (who were granted South African citizenship) and the South African (primarily Afrikaans-speaking) inhabitants; the former looked to Berlin for civic protection and the latter to Pretoria for cultural comfort and public goods. During World War II many German-speakers were placed in South African internment camps, and once the war ended, some were slated for deportation to Germany.

Following the accession of the National Party to power in the 1948 South African general elections, the

Afrikaner government of Dr. Daniel F. Malan demonstrated its concern for these Germans because of their fundamental anglophobia, dating back to the 1899–1902 Anglo-Boer War. Thereafter the Germans in the territory aligned themselves with the local National Party, which held a hegemonic position in the Legislative Assembly in Windhoek.

Political parties catering to African, rather than to white, needs developed much later. A political protoparty organization termed the Ovamboland People's Congress (OPC) was formed by expatriate Namibian workers and students in Cape Town in 1958. The next year the OPC changed its name to the Ovamboland People's Organization (OPO). Also in 1959 the South West Africa National Union (SWANU) began. Some of SWANU's founding members also had been involved in the OPC. By 1960 OPO had evolved into yet another political grouping called the South West Africa People's Organization (SWAPO), which served as the foremost mobilizing agent for the majority African population. It was able to capitalize on the Africans' grievances against the migrant labor system, which had its greatest and most deleterious impact upon the Ovambo people, the largest single ethnic cluster in the country.

Major Political Parties

SOUTH WEST AFRICA PEOPLE'S ORGANIZATION OF NAMIBIA (SWAPO)

In many postcolonial nations the premier nationalist party attempts to wrap itself in the mantle of legitimacy and to portray itself as the herald and protector of independence. Such behavior is characteristic of SWAPO, which was able to secure recognition from the United Nations General Assembly (but not the Security Council) as the authentic, as well as sole, representative of the Namibian people, a status it was loath to lose. As part of the international understanding worked out between South Africa and the Western Contact Group (composed of diplomats from Canada, France, the Federal Republic of Germany, the United Kingdom, and the United States), SWAPO forfeited its position of nationalist and symbolic hegemony and its access to UN funding in the United Nations–monitored 1989 elections for the Constituent Assembly. This assembly, whose members drafted the constitution of Namibia, was reconstituted as the National Assembly. In the 1989 election SWAPO won 57.3 percent of the votes (and 41 of the 72 legislative seats) but failed to achieve the two-thirds majority that would have permitted it to write its own version of the constitution.

One reason SWAPO did not secure electoral paramountcy had to do with unanswered allegations that it had mistreated quite a number of Namibians who fled to SWAPO enclaves in Angola. This maltreatment stemmed from wartime fears that South African spies and agents had infiltrated refugee groups, and SWAPO was concerned about its own security and vulnerability. These charges were ventilated both in the 1989 electoral campaign and in the National Assembly, where passions ran high on the issue. Nevertheless, SWAPO has dominated the political landscape since independence. In the 2004 legislative elections it won 55 of the 72 National Assembly seats.

Minor Political Parties

Other political parties with representation in the National Assembly include the Congress of Democrats (CoD) with five seats, the Democratic Turnhalle Alliance (DTA) with four seats, the United Democratic Front (UDF) with three seats, and the Monitor Action Group (MAG) with one seat. There are also several minor parties without representation in the National Assembly. The Caprivi National Union, the political arm of the Caprivi Liberation Army (CLA), operates from Denmark.

Other Political Forces

As is the case with Botswana, transnational mining corporations are influential political players in the political economy of Namibia. Foreign public aid donors, especially Germany and the Scandinavian states, are significant, the former because of its historic links with its erstwhile colony and the latter because of their support for SWAPO during the war for independence. Since independence the government has actively courted foreign private investors, signing agreements with the United States, Switzerland, and Germany to create an attractive investment climate. Job creation in the private sector is vital, and some argue that the public sector is demonstrably overstaffed. The NDF, which the country created with British military assistance, is an amalgam of former enemies in PLAN and the SWATF. As yet it is not an intrusive force in Namibian politics, but it might become one in future, as have the armed forces in neighboring states.

National Prospects

Namibia has struggled with a secessionist movement in the Caprivi Strip. In August 1999 a group calling itself the Caprivi Liberation Army (CLA) launched an attack against the regional capital of Katima Mulilo, leading President Nujoma to declare a state of emergency in the area. Instability continued, exacerbated by the conflicts in the Democratic Republic of Congo (DRC) and Angola. There was speculation that the National Union for the Total Independence of Angola (UNITA) supported the Caprivi rebels as a way to divert Namibia's support for the Kabila government in the DRC. Namibia deployed up to 2,000 troops in support of Kabila, who was also supported by Angola, which hoped that the DRC would deny UNITA a base from which to launch attacks. Stability in the region improved after the cease-fire agreement between the Angolan government and UNITA in mid-2002. Namibia withdrew all its troops from the DRC by the end of 2002. In August 2004 the government opened its case against 120 people charged with trying to overthrow the government for their part in the 1999 Caprivi attack.

A key issue in Namibia is land reform. White commercial farmers control the majority of the good farmland. The government has pursued a "willing seller, willing buyer" program to purchase land and redistribute it to black farmers. However, critics complain that the pace of reform has been too slow. In July 2003 the National Assembly passed a law giving the government the authority to acquire agricultural land "in the public interest for resettlement purposes." This power has not been used yet, but there are growing concerns that the government may be on the verge of expropriating land. There have been threats from the farm workers' union to begin seizing land, and Prime Minister Theo-Ben Gurirab said in February 2004 that the government would begin seizing land from white farmers. The government has issued some expropriation notices and encouraged farmers to set a price for their land. If the government and the farmers cannot agree on a price, the government will proceed with expropriation, paying the landowners what it considers a just price. There is concern that this will lead to a disastrous land reform policy similar to the one that plunged Zimbabwe into a crisis.

Namibia is seeking investment from abroad and has a well-developed infrastructure and resources upon which to expand its economy. Its political stability makes it an attractive investment opportunity, provided the new direction of the land redistribution program does not scare off investors.

Further Reading

Carpenter, Gretchen. "The Namibian Constitution: *Ex Africa Aliquid Novi* after All?" *South African Journal of International Law* 15 (1989–90): 22–64.

Cliffe, Lionel, with Ray Bush et al. *The Transition to Independence in Namibia.* Boulder, Colo.: Lynne Rienner, 1994.

Diescho, Joseph. *The Namibian Constitution in Perspective.* Windhoek: Gamsberg Macmillan, 1994.

Dreyer, Ronald. *Namibia and Southern Africa: Regional Dynamics of Decolonization, 1945-90.* New York: Kegan Paul, 1994.

du Pisani, André. *SWA/Namibia: The Politics of Continuity and Change.* Johannesburg: Jonathan Ball, 1985.

Groth, Siegfried. *Namibia, the Wall of Silence: The Dark Days of the Liberation Struggle.* Trans. Hugh Meyer. Wuppertal, Germany: Peter Hammer, 1995, distributed by David Philip, Claremont, South Africa.

Grotpeter, John. *Historical Dictionary of Namibia.* African Historical Dictionaries, no. 57. Metuchen, N.J.: Scarecrow Press, 1994.

Kaela, Laurent C. W. *The Question of Namibia.* New York: St. Martin's Press, 1996.

Leys, Colin, and John Saul, with contributions by Susan Brown et al. *Namibia's Liberation Struggle: The Two-Edged Sword.* Athens: Ohio University Press, 1995.

Lush, David. *Last Steps to Uhuru: An Eye-Witness Account of Namibia's Transition to Independence.* Windhoek: New Namibia, 1993.

Saul, John, and Colin Leys. "Lubango and After: 'Forgotten History' as Politics in Contemporary Namibia." *Journal of Southern African Studies* 29, no. 2 (June 2003): 333–353.

Sparks, Donald L., and December Green. *Namibia: The Nation after Independence.* Boulder, Colo.: Westview Press, 1992.

Tötemeyer, Gerhard. "The Regional Reconstruction of the State: The Namibian Case." *Politikon* (Florida, South Africa) 19, no. 1 (December 1991): 66–82.

REPUBLIC OF NAURU
(Republik Naoero)

By Eugene Ogan, Ph.D.

The island republic of Nauru is a single raised atoll with an area of 8 square miles. Nauruans are ethnically Micronesian, but it is difficult to establish accurate population figures for the nation. Of some 13,000 island residents, more than 2,000 are there temporarily as contract officers and laborers. These include Europeans, Filipinos, Indians, and other Pacific Islanders. At the same time, the wealth enjoyed by indigenous Nauruans permits them to migrate and travel widely.

Nauru gained its independence in January 1968. Because of its rich phosphate deposits the island had been governed by outsiders for the preceding 80 years. Initially annexed by Germany, Nauru came under the joint administration of Australia, New Zealand, and Britain as a League of Nations Mandate after the First World War. It became a United Nations Trusteeship, administered by Australia on behalf of the other two trust powers, after World War II.

The System of Government

Nauru is a parliamentary republic with a unicameral legislature.

EXECUTIVE

At independence Nauru's constitution established the nation as a republic with a parliamentary system of government. The president is de facto head of state as well as head of government. He is elected by Parliament from among its elected members and is the most important authority in the system, since legislation tends over time to vest more power in that office. He appoints and removes the four or five ministers who make up the cabinet. The cabinet is collectively responsible to Parliament, which can remove them along with the president by a no-confidence vote of at least half its members. If it fails to choose a new president within seven days, Parliament itself is dissolved.

LEGISLATURE

The unicameral Parliament consists of 18 members. They are elected from eight constituencies for three-year terms, unless Parliament is dissolved earlier. Seven of the constituencies elect two members each, except Ubenide, which is made up of four smaller districts and elects four members. Parliament elects one of its members to preside as Speaker; the Speaker cannot at the same time be a member of the cabinet.

JUDICIARY

Judicial authority is vested in a Supreme Court with a chief justice (and other judges, if any) appointed by the president. A Supreme Court judge must have been entitled to practice as a barrister or solicitor in Nauru for at least five years and

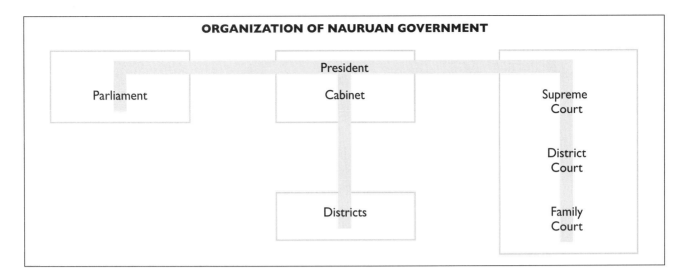

ORGANIZATION OF NAURUAN GOVERNMENT

President
Cabinet

Parliament

Supreme Court

District Court

Districts

Family Court

must retire at the age of 65. The Courts Act also establishes a District Court headed by a resident magistrate with the same qualifications as a Supreme Court judge. He too is appointed by the president, after consultation with the chief justice. A family court also operates.

REGIONAL AND LOCAL GOVERNMENT

The Nauru Local Government Council was originally responsible for matters relating to land ownership and the provision of public services. However, after independence it took over ownership and control of many of the country's numerous enterprises and investments, including a national airline and extensive real estate holdings in Australia and Hawaii. The Local Government Council was abolished in 1992, and the Nauru Island Council was formed to handle these functions.

The Electoral System

Voting is compulsory for all Nauruan citizens over the age of 20.

The Party System

There is a very loose party system, and the parties that exist are informally organized. In the 2004 legislative elections the 18 members elected to Parliament were all independents.

Major Political Parties

The main political parties are the Democratic Party, the Nauru Party, and the Nauru First Party.

Minor Political Parties

There are no minor political parties in Nauru.

National Prospects

Based on control of phosphate revenues, Nauru once enjoyed the highest per capita income of any Pacific Island nation and one of the highest in the world, estimated in 1985 at more than $8,000 for every Nauruan. However, in large part because of the "revolving door" presidency—three different presidents in 2003 alone—the once-prosperous country has gone bankrupt. One current estimate is of more than $2 billion wasted on ill-advised investments, including a short-lived London play based on the love life of Leonardo da Vinci.

Corruption has also taken a toll. The U.S. Treasury has forbidden American banks to do business with their Nauruan counterparts because the latter have laundered Russian mafia money. Phosphate revenues are almost exhausted, and creditors have begun to foreclose on Nauru's extensive property holdings in Australia.

Ludwig Scotty succeeded René Harris as president on the latter's death in June 2004, but observers see little reason for optimism that new leadership can restore Nauru's once-secure economic position.

Further Reading

Crisp, Jeff. "Refugees and the Global Politics of Asylum." *Political Quarterly* 74, no. 1 (August 2003): 75.

Macdonald, Barrie. *In Pursuit of the Sacred Trust: Trusteeship and Independence in Nauru.* Wellington: New Zealand Institute of International Affairs, 1988.

KINGDOM OF NEPAL
(Nēpāl Adhirājya)

By Kanak Mani Dixit, M.A.
Revised by N. Koirala
Further Revision by Deborah A. Kaple, Ph.D.
Further Revision by Leon Newton, Ph.D.

Nepal, a nation of 27.6 million people (2005 est.) in the Himalaya Mountains north of India, has been a monarchy since the country was unified two centuries ago. There have been extended periods when the king was merely a figurehead while the country was ruled by various oligarchs, the last of whom was ousted in 1951. King Mahendra initiated a brief experiment in parliamentary democracy in 1959 but terminated it in December 1960. In 1990 several political parties and coalitions exerted pressure on the government to introduce multiparty elections and to end its age-old system of government. After a very rocky few years the king accepted the draft of a new basic law that provided for multiparty elections. Since November 9, 1990, Nepal has been a parliamentary democracy with a constitutional monarchy.

HISTORY

In 1961 King Mahendra developed the *panchayat* system of guided "partyless democracy" to facilitate his direct involvement in national politics. The *panchayat* system was based on the king's vehement objections to party politics. Parties were said to foster factionalism, and their internecine feuds were thought to distract the national consciousness from the tasks of development. The *panchayat* system was initially a four-tiered structure (later reduced to three) leading up from village assemblies to a national legislature of indirectly elected and appointed members representing localities, the king, and class and professional organizations (of women,

peasants, and ex-servicemen). Party alignments of any form were prohibited. In 1975 the system was further restricted when the class and professional organizations were disbanded and all candidates for the national legislature were selected by a government body.

In May 1979 King Birendra, Mahendra's son, who had ascended the throne in 1972, announced a national plebiscite that gave the people a choice between a "suitably reformed" *panchayat* system and a multiparty system of government. The announcement followed large-scale agitation in Katmandu, the capital, and in other towns. In 1980 the majority (54.7 percent) of the 6 million eligible voters opted for the *panchayat* system. The monarchy's close association with the *panchayat* system to a large extent explains the outcome of the plebiscite. Despite his bold step in announcing the exercise, King Birendra failed to disassociate himself from the issues. As a result the "multiparty" proponents were pitted not only against the *panchayat* status quo but also against kingship.

In February 1990 thousands of Nepalese took to the streets to demand an end to the *panchayat* system. Later that year the king announced a new constitution that basically replaced the *panchayat* system with a mostly elected bicameral legislature and a multiparty system of government. In the 1991 general elections, the country's first multiparty general election since 1959, the Nepalese Congress Party (NCP) won control of the House of Representatives with 110 seats. The other main political party, the Communisty Party of Nepal–Unified Marxist Leninists (UML), which was a merger of the Communist Party of Nepal–Marxist and the Communist Party of Nepal–Leninists, won 69 seats. Girija Prasad Koirala was elected prime minister.

Since 1991 there have been tensions between the two leading political parties, as the Communists constantly suspect the government of colluding with the NCP in order to keep Communists out. The radical left continues to hold strikes and protests in Katmandu against price rises, water shortages, and corruption. In response the NCP has become more authoritarian in its internal party politics and has helped facilitate the government's rehabilitation of old *panchayat* officials. In the 1999 elections the Communists garnered 69 seats, while the NCP received 113. The coalition governments that have formed and re-formed since this election have been troubled by the seemingly inescapable ideological differences between these two major parties.

King Gyanendra was proclaimed king in June 2001, following the assassination of his brother, King Birendra, and Queen Aishwarya and several other royals by Crown Prince Dipendra, who then killed himself. In October 2002 Gyanendra removed Prime Minister Sher Bahadur Deuba and assumed executive power, citing Deuba's failure in dealing with the country's Maoist insurgency. The entire Council of Ministers was dissolved, as was the House of Representatives. Gyanendra reappointed Deuba in 2004 but removed him and again assumed executive power in 2005. In September 2005 Gyanendra and the Maoist rebels announced a cease-fire, and in November the rebels and the main opposition parties agreed to a tentative program to restore democracy to Nepal.

The System of Government

Nepal is a constitutional monarchy with a bicameral legislature.

EXECUTIVE

The 1990 constitution vested executive power of the Kingdom of Nepal in the monarch and the Council of Ministers. The powers of the king are theoretically exercised upon the recommendation and advice and with the consent of the Council of Ministers. Such recommendation, advice, and consent are submitted through the prime minister. The king appoints the leader of the party that commands a majority in the House of Representatives as the prime minister, and he chairs the Council of Ministers. In addition the king, on the recommendation of the prime minister, appoints state ministers from among the members of parliament.

LEGISLATURE

The constitution provides for a parliament (Sansad) that has two chambers. The House of Representatives (Pratinidhi Sabha) has 205 members, who are elected by popular vote for five-year terms in single-seat constituencies. The House of States (Rashtriya Sabha) has 60 members, 35 of whom are elected by the House of Representatives, 15 of whom are elected by an electoral college, and 10 of whom are appointed by the king. One-third of the members are elected every two years to serve six-year terms.

The king must summon a session of Parliament within one month after the elections to the House of Representatives are held. Thereafter he can summon other sessions as he sees fit, provided that the interval between two consecutive sessions is not more than six months. The king may also dissolve the House of Representatives on the recommendation of the prime minister. If the king dissolves the House, then he must specify a date within six months for new elections to the House of Representatives.

In the most recent parliamentary elections, which took place in May 1999, the UML and the NCP took the majority of the seats. King Gyanendra dissolved Parliament in 2002. There is no legislature in Nepal as of 2005.

JUDICIARY

According to the 1990 constitution, courts in the Kingdom of Nepal consist of the following three tiers: the Supreme Court, the Appellate Court, and the District Court.

The Supreme Court is the highest court in the judicial hierarchy. All other courts and judicial institutions of Nepal, other than the Military Court, are under the Supreme Court. The Supreme Court may inspect, supervise, and give directives to its subordinate courts and other judicial institutions. The Supreme Court also functions as a Court of Record. It may initiate proceedings and impose punishment in accordance with law for contempt of itself and of its subordinate courts or judicial institutions. In addition to the chief justice, there is a maximum of 14 other judges.

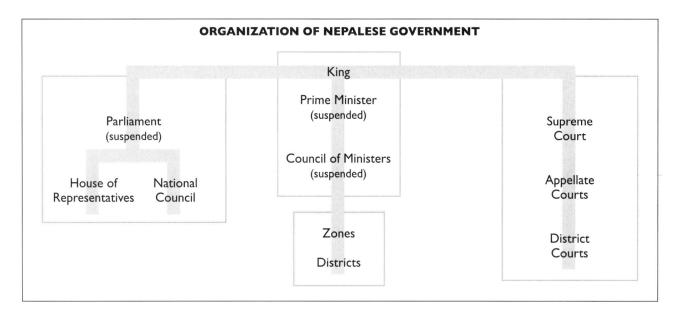

ORGANIZATION OF NEPALESE GOVERNMENT

King

Prime Minister (suspended)

Council of Ministers (suspended)

Parliament (suspended)

House of Representatives   National Council

Zones

Districts

Supreme Court

Appellate Courts

District Courts

The king appoints the chief justice of Nepal on the recommendation of the Constitutional Council and appoints other judges of the Supreme Court on the recommendation of the Judicial Council. (This council makes recommendations and gives advice concerning appointment of, transfer of, disciplinary action against, and dismissal of judges and concerning other matters related to judicial administration.)

The tenure of office of the chief justice is seven years from the date of appointment. On the recommendation of the Judicial Council, the king also appoints any chief judge and judges of the appellate courts and any judges of the district courts of the Judicial Council.

REGIONAL AND LOCAL GOVERNMENT

Nepal is divided into 14 zones and subdivided into 75 districts. Zonal commissioners are appointed by the king and serve as executive heads within the zones. Central district officers, who are assigned from the Home Ministry of Katmandu, handle individual districts. In 2002 King Gyanendra authorized district administrators to punish offenders outside courts of law.

The Electoral System

According to the constitution, elections to the national legislature are direct and based on universal adult (age 18) suffrage. The Election Commission, which conducts, supervises, directs, and controls the elections to Parliament and local elections in villages, towns, and districts, consists of a chief election commissioner and others. The chief election commissioner, who is the chairman of the Election Commission, is appointed by the king. The term of office of the chief election commissioner and other election commissioners is six years from the date of appointment.

In the 1994 national parliamentary elections 61.9 percent of the electorate turned out to vote. Elections have been suspended since 2002.

The Party System

Political parties made their debut in the late 1940s and early 1950s and were strongly influenced in policy and structure by the parties of neighboring India, which gained independence from the British in 1947. While the Indian parties were preoccupied with shedding colonialism, the Nepali parties were engaged in ousting the Rana family, whose oligarchy finally collapsed in 1951.

Prior to the royal coup of 1960 a host of minor parties existed, primarily as personal vehicles for ambitious individuals. With the banning of parties these groups disappeared as the leaders began to bargain individually with the king for ministerial positions. The exceptions were the Congress Party and the Communist Party, which continued to maintain a shadowy existence as their leaders went either underground or into exile in India. These two constitute major parties today.

Major Political Parties

COMMUNIST PARTY OF NEPAL–UNIFIED MARXIST LENINISTS (UML)

Formed in January 1991 as a merger of Communist Party of Nepal-Marxist and Communist Party of Nepal-Leninists, this party is an amalgamation of various Communist and Socialist parties. In May 1991 Man Mohan Adhikari, the party leader was elected to Parliament and became the leader of the opposition, but he resigned in September 1994. In November 1994 he was reelected parliamentary leader but was obliged to resign in September 1995 after losing a no-confidence vote.

In the 1999 parliamentary elections UML garnered 69 of the 205 seats. Despite its name, the UML advocates social democracy and had called for an end to the absolute monarchy in Nepal. The Communists are committed to economic liberalization and advocate land reform to break up large landholdings.

NEPALESE CONGRESS PARTY (NCP)

The Nepalese Congress Party originated in the late 1940s as a movement against the feudalistic Rana oligarchs in Nepal. The party won an absolute majority in the first general elections of 1959. With the dissolution of parliamentary democracy in December 1960, Congress activists were prosecuted under the *panchayat* system as they provided the most potent threat to the newly established *panchayat* regime.

The party weathered several decades underground or in exile and the defection and the co-option of some of its leaders to emerge as a still-viable entity. It abandoned its confrontationist policy with the king when its leader, B. P. Koirala, called for national reconciliation and returned to Nepal from exile in India. Although constitutionally banned, the party was allowed to function in a semilegal fashion. In the 1999 parliamentary elections this party garnered 113 seats of the 205.

Minor Political Parties

In the 1999 parliamentary elections five minor parties earned seats: the National Democratic Party earned 11; the National People's Front, 5; the Nepal Goodwill Party, 5; the Workers and Peasants Party, 1; and the United People's Front, 1.

Other Political Forces

No political party in Nepal has held power for more than two consecutive years since 1991. Some critics argued that government reforms did not improve the situation because the new government was extremely corrupt. In 1996 one of the Maoist parties, the Maoist United People's Front, started a bid to replace the parliamentary system with a Socialist republic using a "revolutionary" strategy called a people's war. A civil war resulted and continued into 2005, when the rebels and King Gyanendra announced a cease-fire. During the early 2000s Gyanendra tried to exert more control over the rebels by declaring martial law, dissolving the government, and sending the military after the insurgents. This violent insurgency has affected most of the country and has resulted in over 10,000 deaths. As of 2005 the rebels controlled two-thirds of the countryside and had in effect set up a shadow government. In November 2005 the rebels agreed with the country's main opposition parties on a tentative plan to restore democracy to Nepal.

National Prospects

Nepal is one of the poorest and least-developed countries in the world. Its economy is largely agricultural, engaging about 80 percent of the Nepalese population. Around 60 percent of the population lives below the poverty line. Although the government in the 1990s had been trying to encourage foreign investment and trade to bolster its economy, Nepal's landlocked and remote location and its susceptibility to natural disasters do not bode well for foreign investment and economic reform.

Nepal made the transition from constitutional to parliamentary democracy in the 1990s. However, the Maoist insurgency and the unilateral actions by King Gyanendra to control the government have erased that progress. Plagued by governmental instability and a violent civil war, the country has much work to do to regain its democratic footing.

Further Reading

Blaike, Piers, John Cameron, and David Seddon. *Nepal in Crisis.* London: Oxford University Press, 1980.

Crossette, Barbara. *So Close to Heaven: The Vanishing Buddhist Kingdoms of the Himalayas.* New York: Vintage, 1995.

Gurung, Harka. "The Sociology of Elections in Nepal, 1951–1981." *Asian Survey* 22, no. 3 (March 1982).

Hutt, Michael, ed. *Nepal in the Nineties.* SOAS Studies on South Asia. New Delhi: Oxford University Press, 1993.

Laksman, Bahadur K. C. *Recent Nepal.* Niral Series-24. New Delhi: Nirala, 1993.

KINGDOM OF THE NETHERLANDS
(Koninkrijk der Nederlanden)

By William G. Andrews, Ph.D.
Revised by Chris Palazzolo

The Netherlands (population about 16.4 million in 2005) as a unified state dates to the late sixteenth century, especially with the institutionalization of the States General in 1579. That system was replaced in 1815 with the adoption of a new constitution and the accession to the throne of William of Orange-Nassau as monarch of the north and south Netherlands. The fragile union was broken when the south seceded and became the independent state of Belgium in 1831.

The king ruled as a constitutional monarch through representation by estates until direct, but limited, suffrage was introduced in 1849. Adult suffrage became universal in 1919. Until very recently Dutch politics and government were based very solidly on a system of four highly articulated subcultures: Catholic, Protestant, socialist, and liberal. Most Netherlanders carried out all social activities within organizations, institutions, and enterprises of one of those groups, and making public policy was largely a carefully modulated balancing act among them. However, that so-called pillarization has declined significantly in recent years, and the cultures no longer monopolize Dutch political life.

The System of Government

The Netherlands is a constitutional monarchy with a bicameral legislature.

EXECUTIVE

The House of Orange is a hereditary monarchy in a unitary state. Since 1890 three successive queens have reigned, Wilhemina (1890–1948), Juliana (1948–80), and Beatrix (1980–). Following the Napoleonic tradition of strong central administration, the Netherlands emphasizes executive authority. Until 1849 the king was the dominant executive. Thereafter the principle of representative government gained recognition and the scope for active intervention by the monarch gradually diminished. Effective executive authority now resides with the prime minister and cabinet, though the monarch still plays a key role in the process of forming a government and sometimes exerts effective influence over cabinet policy in private. The prime minister is more a cabinet coordinator than a true chief executive.

The government is formally responsible to both houses of the bicameral States General (Staten-Generaal), but in practice only the directly elected lower house, the Second Chamber, wields that authority. Once a government is formed, it becomes distinct from the legislature, and ministers must relinquish their seats in the States General on appointment. Also, government ministers may be nonpolitical experts or public officials, although over the years parliamentary recruitment has become paramount. Dutch government is distinctive by the degree to which it incorporates interest-group representatives into the policy-making and implementing processes—an extreme form of "corporatism."

After an election the monarch appoints an *informateur* to identify the combination of parties that can provide the basis for a governing majority in the Second Chamber. Those parties negotiate a formal policy agreement as a sort of governmental contract. After the government is formed, the agreement becomes its policy program. Such accords have become increasingly long and detailed, resulting in longer periods of governmental paralysis but greater cabinet stability. Between 1971 and 1982 three prime ministers headed six governments with six different sets of coalition partners, but from 1982 to 1994 only one prime minister led three governments with two different coalitions. The prime minister (Wim Kok) and government that took office in August 1994 was still there through 1998. From 1998 to 2002 there were no major changes in the executive save for brief period when the D66 (Democrats 66) left the so-called "purple coalition," only to return later. The inclusion of the Lijst Pim Fortuyn (LPF) in a governing coalition in 2002 engendered some significant instability, and a new election in 2003 eventually led to a more stable cabinet without the LPF. This tradition of stability was accentuated until 1994 by the presence in every government since 1917 of one party (Catholic), which had also provided most prime ministers.

LEGISLATURE

Legislative power is shared between the First and Second Chambers, but the popularly elected Second Chamber, with 150 members, has primary authority. The First Chamber, with 75 members, has general veto power but cannot initiate legislation or propose amendments. Its principal function is to review bills for constitutionality and proper legislative form. Also, only the Second Chamber exercises significant administrative oversight.

The government initiates most legislation, which it submits to the Second Chamber after review by the independent administrative Council of State for consistency and compatibility with existing law. Normally the government's legislative program prevails. The deputies adhere closely to party discipline in voting on bills, though recent years have seen a marked increase in the number of private member's bills and amendments to government bills. Nevertheless, disagreements are much more likely among government parties than within them. For proposed constitutional changes to be adopted, elections must be held for the Second Chamber and the revisions passed thereafter by

a two-thirds majority in both houses. A 1995 amendment permits popular referendums to reverse parliamentary laws.

The two chambers can disagree but rarely do, since their party composition is similar. The First Chamber is chosen for four-year-terms by an electoral college composed of all members of the provincial assemblies voting by proportional representation. The Second Chamber is elected for four years by direct, universal adult suffrage but may be dissolved early. Second Chamber members are full-time, meeting in plenary session Tuesdays, Wednesdays, and Thursdays, whereas the First Chamber is a part-time institution, meeting only on Tuesdays.

ELECTIONS TO THE SECOND CHAMBER OF THE STATES GENERAL (NETHERLANDS)

	Percent of Popular Vote (Seats)		
	1998	2002	2003
Christian Democratic Appeal (CDA)	18.4 (29)	28.0 (43)	28.6 (44)
Center Democrats (CU)	0.6 (0)	2.5 (4)	2.1 (3)
Democrats 66 (D66)	9.0 (14)	5.1 (7)	4.1 (6)
Green Left (GL)	7.3 (11)	7.0 (10)	5.1 (8)
Liberal Party (VVD)	24.7 (38)	15.4 (24)	17.9 (28)
Liveable Netherlands (LN)	—	1.6 (2)	0.4 (0)
Pim Fortuyn List (LPF)	—	17.0 (26)	5.7 (8)
Labor Party (PvdA)	29.0 (45)	15.1 (23)	27.3 (42)
State Reform Party (SGP)	1.8 (3)	1.7 (2)	1.6 (2)
Socialist Party (SP)	3.5 (5)	5.9 (9)	6.3 (9)
Reformational Political Federation (RPF)	2.0 (3)	—	—
Reformed Political Union (GPV)	1.3 (2)	—	—
General Union of the Elderly (AOV)	0.5 (0)	—	—
Others	1.9 (0)	0.7 (0)	0.9 (0)

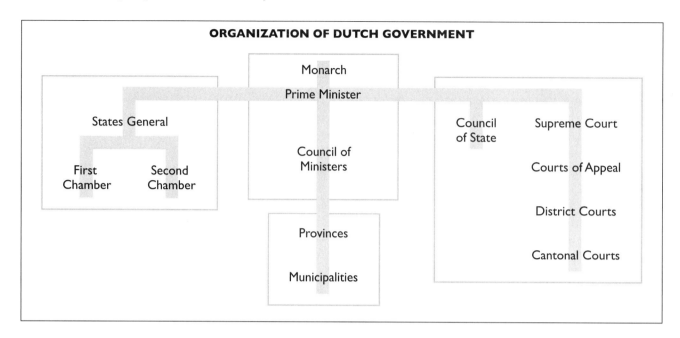

ORGANIZATION OF DUTCH GOVERNMENT

Monarch
Prime Minister

States General

First Chamber   Second Chamber

Council of Ministers

Provinces

Municipalities

Council of State

Supreme Court

Courts of Appeal

District Courts

Cantonal Courts

JUDICIARY

The Supreme Court, with 20 judges appointed for life (in practice, the retirement age is 70), is the ultimate court of appeal. It cannot review a law or treaty for constitutionality. This limitation places the onus for protecting basic rights on the States General and the government, with the judiciary concerned solely with correct application of the law. Lower courts include five courts of appeal, 19 district courts of justice, and 62 cantonal courts. A separate court system handles administrative litigation.

REGIONAL AND LOCAL GOVERNMENT

Dutch local government consists of 12 provinces and about 636 municipalities, the latter grouped into 62 "cooperation districts." The municipal level is the more important, though both may be controlled closely by the national executive. Provinces and municipalities have elective councils serving four-year terms. Both types of council elect executive committees from among their members. Commissioners for provinces and mayors for municipalities are appointed by the central government to preside over both the executives and the councils at both levels.

Mayors are career officials serving more or less permanently. However, in making appointments the central government gives due weight to local factors—especially religious and political-party considerations. Local party collaboration is fairly close, for one party

rarely has an absolute majority on a council and executive committees are usually coalitions. Moreover, the mayors lack formal political attachment, helping to ensure partisan neutrality.

The Electoral System

The Dutch electoral system is one of the "purest" examples of proportional representation, as each party obtains precisely the same share of seats in the Second Chamber as it received of popular votes. Exact proportionality is achieved by treating the country as a single constituency, so that a party's representation depends entirely on its aggregated national vote. The electoral quotient—the number of votes needed to win a seat—is calculated by dividing the number of votes cast in the election by the number of seats in the Second Chamber (150). Thus each party that polls at least 0.67 percent of the national vote (about 60,000 votes) is represented. The Netherlands does not require parties to reach a threshold (say, 5 percent of the total vote) to qualify for parliamentary seats. As a result minor parties always win seats and multipartism is a permanent feature of Dutch political life.

Voting is entirely by party lists, whose preparation is controlled closely by the party leaders. Voters may change the presented order but rarely do. The country forms 19 electoral districts. Parties offer lists in as many districts as they wish, and the nominees may vary by district. However, such variations do not affect the principle of national proportionality. Seats are first allocated on a regional level and then nationally. A 1995 constitutional amendment provided that half the members are elected on regional lists and half on national lists. Seats that are unallocated in the first distribution are allotted on the basis of the "highest average," that is, to the parties with the highest averages of votes to seats already won.

One consequence of the Dutch electoral system is that deputies represent the nation at large, rather than being attached to regional or local interests. Interest in elections is considerable, with turnout exceeding 70 percent, a decline from the level before compulsory voting was abolished in 1970.

The Party System

ORIGINS OF THE PARTIES

Before the franchise was expanded in 1887, only about 3 percent of the population could vote, Conservatives and Liberals held political power, and parties were very loosely organized. The modern party system began emerging in the 1880s, taking shape around the complex, especially religious, cleavages in Dutch society. One line of separation lay between Protestants (Calvinists) and Roman Catholics, and another divided the religious from the secular forces in society. The latter in turn were split between the anticlerical, bourgeois liberals, and the organized working-class movement.

Various factors prevented the system from fragmenting. One was the absence of a single state church, so that religious pluralism fostered political pluralism. A second reason was the 1917 fundamental compromise on the "schools issue": denominational schools thereafter received state subsidies, removing a contentious issue for the religious parties. A third reason was that no single political grouping constituted a majority, requiring alliances and accommodation. This conciliatory impulse has remained a hallmark of Dutch political life.

Five parties were dominant from 1919 until recently, providing the pattern of governing coalitions and accounting for up to 90 percent of the popular vote. Three were religious parties; the others were the Liberals (later the People's Party for Freedom and Democracy—Volkspartij voor Vrijheid en Democratie; VVD) and the Social Democrats (now the Labor Party—Partij ven de Arbeid; PvdA). Despite the number of parties—no fewer than 54 parties contested the 1933

election—the inherent stability of Dutch parliamentary democracy was never in doubt.

Two changes have become evident since the 1960s. One is the long-term decline of the religious parties, a development that led to the amalgamation of the three major ones in 1980. A second, possibly related change has been the growth of parties that oppose the lack of electoral influence on the formation of the government. The direction of voting frequently has little influence on the composition of the governing coalition that ultimately results. Parties that lose voting strength often increase their governmental strength.

THE PARTIES IN LAW

Very little restricts the formation and operation of Dutch parties. The electoral law is the main regulator by penalizing very small parties: those that fail to win 75 percent of the national electoral quotient lose their deposits. During election campaigns the parties have access to the public broadcasting media; the parliamentary blocs in the States General receive assistance for their parliamentary work. The executive has an important restrictive power in that it can ban extremist parties without involving the Supreme Court, though it has been more tolerant than the parliamentary majority.

PARTY ORGANIZATION

The large number and range in the size of the parties have produced wide variations in organization. At the local level all major parties have district associations that are active for local, provincial, and parliamentary elections. Typically an annual delegate congress is the supreme party organ to which an executive committee is responsible, and a party council exercises the authority of the congress between its sessions. Dutch parties are membership parties, but their size has declined since the mid-1960s. The larger ones number fewer than 100,000 members, while the smaller ones represented in the States General count perhaps 10,000. On average the ratio of members to voters is rather low and declining. However, an important contribution to the vitality of the parties is made by a political "infrastructure" of social organizations: the churches, church-related organizations, and the trade unions.

All parties represented in the States General receive government subsidies proportionate to their respective shares of the popular vote. Most parties also rely heavily on membership dues and contributions and assessments on party members who hold salaried public office. The Liberals receive substantial income from gifts, but the other parties do not. Research and educational foundations affiliated with parties receive modest subsidies from the government. Declining membership has inevitably given the parties major financial problems.

CAMPAIGNING

Election campaigns in the Netherlands are relatively short, since polling takes place 43 days after the nomination of candidates. Television and radio broadcasting is relied on heavily, and the leaders of the larger parties are the major contestants. Most parties can also rely on the support of at least one national daily newspaper, although official party publications are weeklies or magazines and journals. Campaigning concentrates on mobilizing support among adherents, since structural and historical factors determine party loyalties and these are not weakened in the course of a single campaign. Moreover, elections are primarily about the choice of parties rather than a choice of government. As a result party leaders are regarded primarily as party representatives rather than potential national leaders. This emphasis may be changing, since even if recent elections have been indeterminate in their outcome, increasingly the parties have been forced to spell out their coalition preferences during the election campaign.

INDEPENDENT VOTERS

The best single predictor of voting behavior remains religion, and practicing members of the Protestant and Catholic churches tend to support one or another of the religious parties. But since the end of "pillarization" in the 1960s such connections have declined significantly. In 1956, for instance, 95 percent of practicing Catholic voters cast their ballots for the Catholic party, but the corresponding figure in 1989 was only 72. The scale of the decline of the main confessional parties—from about 50 percent of the vote in the 1950s to 30–35 percent in the 1970s and 1980s and 23 percent in 1998—indicates that party identification has weakened considerably. Nor is it safe to rely on social-class variables, since parties tend to be interclass in their appeal. Thus, while the Labor Party attracts about half the working-class vote, the Christian Democratic Appeal takes about a third. A third variable, urban-rural differences, also reveals less than might be supposed, for although the religious parties tend to fare better in rural communities and the Liberals and Labor in the cities and suburbs, all the major parties are strongly competitive in all types of communities.

These factors all point to considerable flux in electoral behavior now that the formerly strong segmentation of Dutch society with its "spiritual families" is in decay. Evidence of the growing volatility has been seen in the rise of "protest" parties, such as Democrats 66. They are particularly attractive to younger voters and draw support from all sections of the electorate.

Major Political Parties

CHRISTIAN DEMOCRATIC APPEAL
(Christen Democratisch Appel; CDA)

HISTORY

The CDA was formed as a unified party in 1980. It amalgamated the three main religious parties—the Catholic People's Party (KVP) and two Protestant groups, the Anti-Revolutionary Party (ARP) and the Christian-Historical Union (CHU). The ARP, founded in 1879, was the oldest Dutch party; the CHU was formed in 1908; and the Catholic party was based on the League of Roman Catholic Voters' Clubs established in 1904. The KVP, the largest of the three, was formed in 1946 as the successor to the more exclusive Roman Catholic State Party (founded in 1926). It was consistently the strongest single party in the States General until the 1970s, when the three parties all experienced a downturn in membership and in their electoral appeal. The first moves to create the CDA began in the early 1970s, and the three parties fought the 1977 election as a loose federation.

ORGANIZATION

After the full merger in 1980 the constituent parties gradually harmonized their structures, which are now fully integrated. The basic units (municipal, district, or village departments) may be organized by any 10 CDA members and exist in almost every municipality. The departments are grouped in 12 areas, corresponding to the provinces. The sovereign body at the national level is the party congress, which meets at least biennially. Its authority is exercised in the interim by the party council, which meets twice a year. A 30-member party executive manages the political and organizational activities and delegates 11 of its members as an executive board, responsible for day-to-day management. An "Informal Management Bureau," consisting of the president, the two vice presidents, the secretary-treasurer, and the director, meets weekly. The party's affiliated organizations include women's and youth groups, an association of local councilors, a research institute and educational institute, and a foreign outreach foundation.

POLICY

The CDA is a center party, advocating the application of Christian principles to political life and professing that its "political creed is established in a constant dialogue with the Bible." Its basic concepts are legal and social justice; domestic and international solidarity; differentiated responsibility to give individuals, families, and organizations specific duties; and personal stewardship. The party favors orthodox financial and economic management and economic austerity, especially curbs on social security expenditures. The CDA supports NATO and has been a leader in the construction of the European Union.

MEMBERSHIP AND CONSTITUENCY

The CDA is the largest party in the Netherlands. Its most loyal supporters are professed Christians who are independent tradespeople and farmers, but it draws nearly equal support from all social classes. The CDA is strongest in smaller towns and rural areas.

FINANCING

The party depends on membership dues for 90 percent of its income.

PROSPECTS

Ruud Lubbers's dynamic leadership from 1982 to 1994 reinvigorated the CDA and made him the most popular politician in the country. The party's solid organization and basis of support in the religious communities were other valuable assets, despite the declining intensity of religious commitment in the Dutch population. However, in 1994 and 1998 the party suffered several severe losses, losing over half of the peak vote share it had achieved in 1989. Much of this decline resulted from the party's very unpopular proposals to reform the pension system. The outcome of 1994 election also marked the first time that the CDA (or any of its Catholic predecessors) had not been a member of the governing coalition since 1917. Between 1998 and 2002 the party regained some support in provincial and European elections, partly due to softening its conservative attitude on several social issues. The increase in support in the provincial councils substantially impacted the standing of ruling government in the First Chamber (since the provincial elections help to determine the constitution of the First Chamber). In the 2002 general elections the CDA made a significant comeback under the leadership of Jan-Peter Balkenende. The CDA formed a coalition with the VVD, along with the extreme-right LPF. The CDA maintained its support and control of the premiership in 2003 after the dissolution of the unstable CDA-VVD-LPF coalition.

DEMOCRATS 66
(Democraten 66; D66)

HISTORY

A long tradition of "free-thinking democratic" political organizations led to the formation of D66 in 1966 as a constitutional reform party. As a pragmatic, modernizing, reformist party it contributed significantly to the decline of "pillarization." After initial successes the party lost momentum but grew again in three successive elections from 1986 to a peak of 15.5 percent of the vote in 1994, before declining again in 1998 and the early 2000s.

ORGANIZATION

The party structure is very open and democratic. All members can attend the annual national congress and vote on all issues. Elected officials and local units are not bound by those decisions so long as their positions conform to the party's basic policy program. Between congresses the party is run by a chairman and a 21-member national board elected for two-year terms by the congress. The executive, formed by nine board members, is responsible for day-to-day management. The other 12 represent the board to the regions. The party chairman has organizational but not political responsibilities.

POLICY

A liberal-radical party, D66 finds a natural ally in the PvdA. The party argues that the political system fails to alter governments to reflect the wishes of the voters. It advocates the abolition of proportional representation and the direct election of the prime minister. It also wants the parties to set forth their coalition commitments before elections so the voters can choose clearly among potential governments. The party also actively promotes an environmental protection program. The party's social policies are progressive, but its economic policies fit with the CDA's better than with the Labor Party's.

MEMBERSHIP AND CONSTITUENCY

D66 is predominantly an urban party with a strong base in Amsterdam. Its staunchest supporters tend to be younger than average, upwardly mobile, and relatively well educated.

FINANCING

With its small membership D66 is financially hard-pressed and depends more on small contributions and volunteer effort than most parties.

PROSPECTS

D66's overall support has waned rather severely since 1994 when its charismatic leader, Hans van Mierlo, stepped down. However, its pivotal place on the political spectrum and its electoral growth enable it to arbitrate among its larger rivals and maximize its influence. In particular the party has been able to influence policy to some degree by acting as a junior member of both PvdA and CDA-led coalitions.

LABOR PARTY

(Partij ven de Arbeid; PvdA)

HISTORY

The PvdA was founded in 1946, succeeding the Social Democratic Workers' Party, which had begun in 1894 as an orthodox Marxist organization. During the interwar period it became reformist, and it reorganized under its present name as a more broadly based movement to include progressive Christians and members of resistance groups. The PvdA served in various coalitions, always with the KVP until 1994, and has provided prime ministers Willem Drees (1948-58), Joop Den Uyl (1973-77), and Wim Kok (1994-2002). The PvdA benefited from the gradual weakening of the religious parties, becoming the largest single party in the Second Chamber in 1971. Elections since then have given the party approximate parity with the CDA. After the 2003 elections it held 42 seats in the Second Chamber, behind only the CDA's 44.

ORGANIZATION

Although unusually susceptible to schisms, the PvdA is the best-organized Dutch party, with some 500 local committees and the full panoply of regional and national organizations. The annual congress decides policy, formulates the party's election platform, selects the parliamentary candidates, and elects biennially the 23-member national board executive, which oversees party management between congresses.

POLICY

The PvdA advocates a "personal socialism" that emphasizes religious and humanist commitments to socialism. Between 1966 and 1986 the party was strongly influenced by a New Left movement that turned it sharply to the left. Some of the moderate old guard left to form the Democratic Socialists in 1970. Since 1986 it has become more moderate, seeking to create a new, modern form of social democracy without the ideological baggage of the past. The PvdA stresses a search for solutions within the free-market system to the persistent unemployment and advocates reform and protection of the social security system. Internationally it has supported European integration but wants more emphasis on social cohesion and less on purely economic matters. It promotes a strong United Nations and increased international development aid. It has switched from main critic to supporter of economic austerity programs, combined with extra measures to improve the Dutch infrastructure, environmental protection, and suppression of crime. Under the leadership of Wouter Bos the PvdA has been moving somewhat more to the left, particularly in relation to economic and public-sector issues such as healthcare.

MEMBERSHIP AND CONSTITUENCY

The party's supporters come from all sectors of the population, but its most faithful members tend to be urban working-class people without religious ties and middle-class professionals. It also draws heavily on white-collar workers. Support for the party is fairly evenly spread through all age groups.

FINANCING

The party is considerably better financed than the others. Most of its income derives from government subsidies and income-based membership dues of a maximum of 2 percent of gross annual income.

PROSPECTS

The PvdA is at a disadvantage in comparison with other European Socialist parties in that the structure of Dutch politics and parties, particularly the religious ones, operates against a purely class-based party, so that the PvdA lags in growth despite the disappearance of the Communist Party. At the same time, the party, with its natural alliance partners, D66 and the VVD, does not produce a parliamentary majority. Therefore, until 1994 the PvdA could only come to office in coalition with the CDA, a combination not likely to produce the legislation the PvdA most wanted to see enacted. From 1994 to 2002 the PvdA led the "purple coalition" along with the VVD and D66. The coalition supported rather tight fiscal policies, reducing public expenditures in many key areas. With stable growth in 1998 the purple coalition was able to renew its mandate. However, in 2002 the PvdA suffered a severe setback, losing almost half of its seats in the Second Chamber. The reasons behind this setback were multiple: (1) growing opposition from key supporters of its neglect of its traditional social issues program, (2) a slower economy that hurt its support of tight fiscal policies, (3) the publication of a report that blamed the Dutch government for not preventing the massacre of over 7,000 Muslims in the Bosnian city of Srebenica (the entire Council of Ministers resigned after the report), and (4) the rise of the immigration issue as accentuated by the rise of Pim Fortuyn. However, the PvdA regained significant support in 2003 under the charismatic new leadership of Wouter Bos, who was able to sway working-class voters back from the disintegrating LPF. The PvdA was poised to join the CDA as a coalition partner after the 2003 election, but disagreements over support for the U.S.-led military campaign against Iraq and over fiscal spending cuts to boost the economy have led the PvdA to remain in the opposition.

Nevertheless, the party's solid organization and membership base are likely to ensure that it will continue to claim nearly a third of the vote and will remain a major force in the States General.

PEOPLE'S PARTY FOR FREEDOM AND DEMOCRACY

(Volkspartij voor Vrijheid en Democratie; VVD)

HISTORY
The Liberals dominated Dutch politics from the 1848 beginning of constitutional rule until the 1917 extension of the franchise and adoption of proportional representation. Then they went into partial eclipse. The original Liberal movement, loosely organized in several parties, was decidedly anticlerical. In 1948 a single Liberal party emerged and took its present name. Until 1972 the party hovered around 10 percent of the vote. Under Hans Wiegel's leadership it shed its anticlerical image, became more progressive while remaining middle-class, and reemerged as a major party, usually drawing votes in the 15–20 percent range. It was the largest party in the 1995 local elections with 27 percent of the vote and second-largest in the 1998 parliamentary elections with 25 percent. In 2003 it garnered 18 percent of the vote, third behind the CDA and PvdA.

ORGANIZATION
The VVD is fairly decentralized, especially for candidate selection, over which the party congress has some say. The party is also notable for limiting the influence of parliamentary deputies on the party executive. Otherwise the VVD's organization is similar to that of the other parties. The general assembly is the supreme authority, but the smaller national executive committee elected by the assembly has more practical day-to-day influence on the party executive.

POLICY
On many counts the VVD is the most conservative Dutch party. However, it advocates worker participation in profits and management. It supports the social security programs in principle but advocates cutting benefits to help get control of the budget. The VVD represents a moderately polarizing force in the Dutch context, particularly in its attachment to free enterprise and to a restrictive view of government economic intervention. Its secular orientation has not prevented the VVD from cooperating with the religious parties in governing coalitions. Although generally supportive of the European Union and the single currency, the VVD has expressed some criticisms of the growing European federal structure. In recent years the VVD also has begun to espouse a more anti-immigrant policy.

MEMBERSHIP AND CONSTITUENCY
The VVD's primary appeal is to the upper and middle classes, but it also draws support from white-collar workers. Like the PvdA, the party attracts the support of those with no religious attachment.

FINANCING
To a greater extent than any other party the VVD can depend on substantial contributions from business and industry and therefore does not rely as much on government subsidies and membership dues.

PROSPECTS
The decline of the religious parties over the years has probably contributed to the VVD's success. That trend is likely to continue, though perhaps at a slower pace than recently. For many years the party's conservative policies made it unacceptable as a coalition partner to the PvdA, but the latter's evolution toward the center made possible the 1994 coalition. The CDA is ambivalent toward it. Its electoral strength and central location on the political spectrum give it a continuing role in most Dutch governments.

The VVD suffered great losses in 2002 with the rise of the LPF, which advocated harsher immigration policies and fiscal policies. It regained some of these seats in 2003 and is again a coalition partner with the CDA and D66.

Minor Political Parties

LIST PIM FORTUYN

(Lijst Pim Fortuyn; LPF)

The LPF, primarily a protest party with a xenophobic focus, was created in 2002 under the leadership of a radical sociology professor, Pim Fortuyn, known as a harsh critic of the government. Prior to the establishment of the List, Fortuyn had been fired as the head candidate on the ticket of the Leefbar Nederland (Liveable Netherlands), another protest party. Fortuyn was assassinated nine days before the May 2002 elections by a radical animal-rights and environmentalist activist. The party subsequently surprised most commentators by taking 17 percent of the popular vote and 26 seats in the election. Along with the CDA and the VVD, the LPF formed a coalition government.

It soon became rather evident that the party had been built primarily around Pim Fortuyn. Significant conflict and scandals soon erupted among the party's new leaders (many of whom had little if any prior political experience). Due to the instability posed by their coalition partner, the CDA and PvdA agreed to call for new elections less than three months after the initial election. In January 2003 new elections were held and the LPF lost 18 of its 26 seats as well as its status as a coalition partner. As of 2005 the party was viewed as a lingering protest party whose support has been steadily waning. The LPF's platform primarily centers on toughening immigration policies and crime laws and reducing public spending. In particular, the party (at least under its original incarnation with Fortuyn as leader) called for tougher policies toward those immigrants who did not assimilate into Dutch culture and for a quota to prevent Muslims from entering the Netherlands.

GREEN LEFT

(Groen Links)

Four leftist parties that had suffered declining influence in the preceding elections—the Communist Party of the Netherlands (CPN), the Evangelical People's Party (EPP), the Radical Political Party (RPP), and the Pacifist Socialist Party (PSP)—merged in 1989 as the Green Left. The CPN was a traditional Marxist-Leninist party that had broken away from the predecessor of the PvdA and adopted a more moderate Euro-Communist stance in the 1960s. The EPP was formed by the merger in 1980 of leftist dissidents of the major Christian parties. The RPP were young, activist, anti-nuclear Catholics who defected from the KVP during the widespread student disorders in 1968. The PSP was formed in 1957 by radical, pacifist leftists who objected to the moderate positions of the PvdA. Green Left won 11 seats in 1998, 10 seats in 2002, and eight seats in 2003. A change in leadership has recently taken place, potentially giving the party a more radical edge. It is the leading environmentalist party in the Netherlands, takes leftist positions on most social issues, and is the only Dutch party to oppose privatization.

SOCIALIST PARTY

(Socialistische Partij; SP)

The SP was founded in 1972 by social democrats opposed to the leftward drift of the PvdA. Although a small party for many years, the SP has become the fourth-largest party in the Netherlands (even beating D66). The party has been particularly critical of the conservative VVD. It won nine seats in the 2003 elections.

REFORMATIONAL POLITICAL FEDERATION

(Reformatorische Politieke Federatie; RPF)

The RPF is the newest of the three very small Calvinist parties represented in the States General. It was formed in 1975 by the National Evangelical Association, largely as a splinter off the Anti-Revolutionary Party, arguing that Calvinist teachings should be more directly applied to political and social problems. It three seats in the 1994 and the 1998 elections but failed to win any in 2002 and 2003.

REFORMED POLITICAL UNION

(Gereformeerd Politiek Verbond; GPV)

The GPV, founded in 1948, is a fundamentalist religious party that looks back to the national Calvinism of the seventeenth century for its political doctrine, holding that the Anti-Revolutionary Party diluted these ideas with liberalism and socialism. It favors severe governmental restrictions on immoral social behavior, supports NATO and a strong defense policy, but opposes supranationalism. The GPV has a small but consistent following and is usually represented in the Second Chamber with two seats. However, the party won no seats in either 2002 or 2003.

STATE REFORM PARTY

(Staatkundig Gereformeerde Partij; SGP)

The SGP is the oldest and largest of the Calvinist parties and like the others was a split (in 1918) from the Anti-Revolutionary Party. The SGP is ultraconservative in outlook, drawing its support mainly from fundamentalist members of the Dutch Reformed Church. It has the distinction of having banned female members in 1993. The party consistently wins about 2 percent of the vote and two or three seats in the States General.

GENERAL UNION OF THE ELDERLY

(Algemeen Ouderen Verbond; AOV)

(Unie 55+)

These are really interest groups for the elderly that formed to protest governmental proposals to freeze state pensions. They first appeared in national elections in 1994 but had split into three squabbling groups by 1997. The AOV won six seats and Unie 55+ one in 1994, but they lost them all in 1998.

Other Political Forces

Trade unions and other labor organizations continue to be important players in Dutch politics. The so-called polder model has been the traditional means of negotiating economic change in the Netherlands. Very similar to the corporatist model, it typically involves consensus-building negotiations among government, trade unions, and employers. This model had been rather successful in the 1980s and 1990s. However, such agreements have broken down somewhat in recent years due to slow economic growth. The current Christian Democrat–led coalition has attempted to push through welfare reforms and increased labor-market liberalization. Such reform efforts have led to a much more tenuous relationship between trade unions and the government.

National Prospects

The Dutch party and political systems can best be described as being "in transition." The "pillarization" of society has been giving way to secularization. This change became especially evident in the negotiations following the 1994 elections, in which the three leading parties (Labor, Liberal, and D66) excluded the CDA

from the government for the first time since 1917 by forming a "purple," or secular, coalition. This development suggested, also, that the "clubbiness" of the past may have broken down definitively.

The disjunction between voting shifts and the eventual makeup of coalition governments shows clearly in the difficulties surrounding coalition building in recent elections. It has become normal that the voting results give no clear guide to the coalition outcome and that interparty negotiations take several months. In fact it was not until the middle of 2003 that the official governing coalition emerged from the January 2003 elections. Although such an impasse is serious, it also serves to underline the stability of Dutch politics: In spite of serious problems with government cohesion, a high degree of tolerance and social consensus holds the system together and diffuses political tension.

Several specific problems have plagued the Dutch political scene in recent years. Immigration and crime have been key issues. The quick rise (and rapid demise) of the LPF took many of the mainstream parties by surprise. The PvdA in particular suffered from the movement of working-class voters to the LPF. With the LPF's decline the PvdA and CDA have been forced to more significantly address such contentious issues. General economic policies (public spending, unemployment, and the deficit) and health care continue to be important issues for the Dutch electorate. In terms of the European Union, there seems to be a growing skepticism, and in June 2005 the public rejected the proposed European Constitution in a referendum.

Further Reading

Andweg, Rudy B., and Galen Irwin. *Governance and Politics in the Netherlands.* New York: Palgrave, 2002.

Bryant, Christopher G. A., and Edmund Mokrzycki, eds. *Democracy, Civil Society, and Pluralism in Comparative Perspective: Poland, Great Britain, and the Netherlands.* Warsaw: IFIS, 1995.

Daalder, Hans, and Galen A. Irwin, eds. *Politics in the Netherlands: How Much Change?* Totowa, N.J.: F. Cass, 1989.

Deth, Jan W. van. *Dutch Parliamentary Election Studies Data Source Book 1971-1989.* Amsterdam: Steinmetz Archive/ SWIDOC, 1993.

Gladdish, Ken. *Governing from the Center: Politics and Policy-Making in the Netherlands.* DeKalb: Northern Illinois University Press, 1991.

Green-Pedersen, Christoffer. *The Politics of Justification: Party Competition and Welfare State Retrenchment in Denmark and the Netherlands from 1982 to 1998.* Amsterdam: Amsterdam University Press, 2002.

Lijphart, J. *The Politics of Accommodation: Pluralism and Democracy in the Netherlands.* Berkeley: University of California Press, 1975.

Middendorp, C. P. *Ideology in Dutch Politics: The Democratic System Reconsidered, 1970–1985.* Assen/Maastricth: Van Gorcum, 1991.

Rochon, Thomas R. *The Netherlands: Negotiating Sovereignty in an Interdependent World.* Boulder, Colo.: Westview, 1999.

Snellen, I. Th. M. *Limits of Government: Dutch Experiences.* Amsterdam: Kobra, 1985.

Tash, Robert C. *Dutch Pluralism: A Model in Tolerance for Developing Countries.* New York: P. Lang, 1991.

Timmermans, Arco L. *High Politics in the Low Countries: An Empirical Study of Coalition Agreements in Belgium and the Netherlands.* Burlington, Vt.: Ashgate. 2003.

NEW ZEALAND
(Aotearoa)

By Peter Aimer, Ph.D.

New Zealand is a small, South Pacific unitary state with a population in 2005 of 4 million people. Of these, more than half a million claim descent from the indigenous population, the Maori. Much smaller non-European minorities reflect patterns of immigration by different Pacific Island peoples since 1950, and more recently from Asia. Most European settlement dates from the nineteenth century, and Britain claimed New Zealand as a colony after a negotiated treaty with a number of Maori chiefs in 1840.

The System of Government

New Zealand is a constitutional monarchy with a unicameral legislature. The core of the constitution is contained in the Constitution Act of 1986, which codifies the basic institutions and practices associated with a Westminster model of parliamentary democracy. New Zealand's colonial status gave way to dominion status in 1907, and complete autonomy was achieved in 1947. New Zealand is currently one of the community of sovereign states making up the Commonwealth of Nations.

EXECUTIVE

The formal head of state is the British monarch, represented by a governor-general appointed by the monarch on the advice of the New Zealand government, usually for a term of five years. All governors-general since the 1970s have been resident New Zealanders. Among them, the first Maori to hold office was Sir Paul Reeves (1985–90) and the first woman was Dame Catherine Tizard (1990–96). The governor-general's constitutional duties include assenting to bills, appointing and dismissing judges and cabinet ministers, dissolving or opening Parliament, and attending meetings of the Executive Council, consisting of cabinet ministers. The governors-general perform these duties on the advice of ministers. The head of state's reserve powers over the appointment and dismissal of ministers and the dissolution of Parliament remain vague and unused.

Effective executive power resides in a single or multiparty cabinet headed by the prime minister. The cabinet functions according to the convention of collective responsibility. Only elected members of Parliament may hold portfolios in the cabinet of 15 to 20 or outer ministry of five or six. A government remains in office as long as it has the confidence of a majority of elected members of Parliament and can secure the passage through Parliament of the necessary supply (money) bills. The business of government is conducted by public servants organized in departments of state headed by nonpartisan chief executive officers appointed by the State Services Commission.

LEGISLATURE

Parliament has been unicameral since the abolition of the appointed Legislative Council in 1950. The 120-member

House of Representatives is elected for a maximum term of three years. The prime minister may advise the calling of an election at any time. It is usual, however, for Parliaments to run their full term, with elections normally being held in October or November.

Parliament's principal presiding officer is the speaker, usually, though not necessarily, elected from one of the governing parties. Once elected, the speaker is expected to be nonpartisan. Cabinet ministers continue to sit as elected members of Parliament. MPs sit in party blocks, with government ministers and senior opposition spokespersons occupying their respective parties' front benches.

Parliament is required to meet within six weeks of the return of the writs following a general election. The parliamentary year normally runs from February to December, with sittings usually on three days a week (Tuesday through Thursday) for three weeks out of four. Regular cabinet meetings are scheduled for Mondays, and party caucuses customarily meet on Tuesday mornings, when Parliament is in session.

Most legislation is introduced by ministers as part of government business. Provision is also made for a limited number of members' bills to be introduced. Passage of these and other nongovernmental bills depends, however, on the leave of a majority of members of Parliament. As well as being debated in detail, bills are sent to select committees, enabling public submissions and possible amendment of the original bill. Since the passage of the Bill of Rights Act in 1990 all draft legislation must be scrutinized for consistency with the basic civil and political rights of citizens specified in that act.

Legislative power, while formally located in the plenary sessions of Parliament, effectively flows from the cabinet and from the parliamentary select committees. Cabinet collective responsibility, combined with strict party discipline, normally ensures the passage of government-sponsored legislation, with minimal legislative influence by opposition parties.

Elections since 1987 have been marked by a weakening of the two-party system and the growing share of the vote dispersed among minor parties. This trend was accelerated by the adoption of proportional representation in 1996. The single-party, National or Labour, majority governments manufactured by the plurality electoral system gave way under proportional representation to coalition or minority government. Another result of the introduction of proportional representation was an increase in the representation of women and Maori.

Since 1993 citizens have been able to initiate referenda on submission of a petition to Parliament supported by at least 10 percent of eligible electors. The result of such a referendum, however, is not binding on the government.

JUDICIARY

The judicial branch of government is derived from the British system. Most civil matters involving interpretation of the law are handled at the level of the lowest tier of the judiciary, the district court and associated specialist courts—the family court, youth court, environment court, Maori land court, and employment court. More serious cases, including appeals from the district courts, are determined in the High Court.

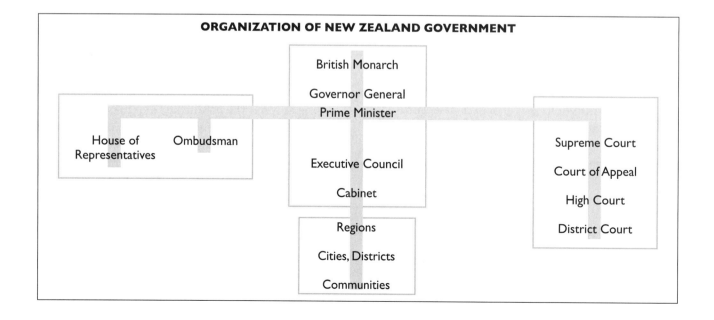

ORGANIZATION OF NEW ZEALAND GOVERNMENT

British Monarch

Governor General

Prime Minister

House of Representatives   Ombudsman

Executive Council

Cabinet

Regions

Cities, Districts

Communities

Supreme Court

Court of Appeal

High Court

District Court

Appeals against the High Court are dealt with by the Court of Appeal, with final recourse to the Supreme Court, established in 2004 to replace appeals to the Judicial Committee of the Privy Council in England.

Appointments to the judiciary are formally made by the executive, after a process of consultation. Such appointments are not regarded as being influenced by partisan considerations, and judges may be removed only by a directive to the governor-general from Parliament.

Since 1962 ombudsmen have been appointed as officers of Parliament, independent of the executive. The ombudsmen function as intermediaries between citizens and the various branches of government administration, offering citizens the possibility of redress of grievances and making procedural recommendations. The office of the ombudsmen receives on average about 6,000 complaints a year. The success of the institution has led to the establishment of private-sector ombudsmen in the consumer-sensitive areas of banking and insurance.

Other quasi-judicial watchdog bodies dealing with the rights of citizens are the Human Rights Commission, which includes a separate privacy commissioner and race relations conciliator, and a parliamentary commissioner for the environment. All are independent of the executive and report annually to Parliament.

A distinctive and highly significant statutory body is the Waitangi tribunal, which takes its name from the Treaty of Waitangi (1840), the founding document of modern New Zealand history. The Waitangi tribunal was enacted in 1975 to hear and recommend on grievances relating to Maori land and resources. The Treaty of Waitangi broadly ceded sovereignty to the British Crown in return for a guarantee to the Maori of the retention and use of their land and legal equality between Maori and immigrant settlers. Subsequently, however, much land was alienated from the Maori by illegal and often violent means. The tribunal has significant power in relation to state land and assets on the land and has been an important catalyst in the negotiation of settlements of several major grievances between the state and the Maori. The Waitangi tribunal has established itself as a central institution in the politics of race relations in New Zealand.

REGIONAL AND LOCAL GOVERNMENT

New Zealand is constitutionally a unitary state. Subnational units of government exist on the basis of statutes passed by the central government. Since 1989 there are three categories of local government—region, city and district, and community. All three categories are directly elected by citizens on the general electoral roll and residents within the boundaries of the authority concerned. Terms of office are for three years, and mayors of the city and district authorities are elected directly and separately from councillors.

Political parties may stand tickets of candidates, but the partisan patterns and allegiances of national politics are only loosely if at all replicated in the arena of local government. Participation rates in local elections fall well below those in national elections, leading some local authorities to introduce postal voting in elections. City and district authorities perform a wide range of regulatory and service functions close to the daily life of citizens, levying rates on property in order to finance the supply and maintenance of such basic utilities as local roads, water supply, sewerage, libraries, and recreational facilities.

Regional councils are primarily concerned with the planning and management of natural resources over larger geographic areas. Community boards have little power and function as channels for parochial interests, linking citizens with their larger elected territorial authority.

The Electoral System

In 1996, after more than 80 years of first-past-the-post (winner-take-all) elections, New Zealand switched to a form of proportional representation modeled on the German system and known in New Zealand as mixed-member proportional (MMP). MMP had been recommended by a royal commission in 1986 and after much controversy was affirmed by 54 percent of the voters in a referendum in 1993.

MMP combines single-member electorate representation with party list representation. The total number of members of Parliament is fixed at 120. The country is divided into general territorial electorates, and also into a smaller number of Maori territorial electorates, guaranteeing representation of New Zealand's indigenous ethnic minority. Each territorial electorate returns one representative to Parliament. From 2002 there were a total of 68 territorial electorates (seven of which were Maori electorates) and 52 list seats. An increase in the number of either general or Maori electorates results in a similar decrease in the number of list MPs. Under MMP registered electors have two votes, one for an electorate MP, the second for a political party on the nationwide list of parties.

Electors vote by attending a designated polling place in their local community on election day, traditionally a Saturday, and ticking a circle opposite the chosen candidate or party. Provision is made for electors who cannot visit a polling place to cast a special vote.

Electorate MPs are elected by first-past-the-post contests in each electorate. Proportional representation in Parliament is achieved by calculating the total number of parliamentary seats each party is eligible for on the basis of its nationwide party vote, using the St. Lague formula for this purpose. Party candidates who have won electorate contests are automatically elected to Parliament. If necessary this number is then topped up from candidates on the parties' ranked lists until each party's rightful share is reached. If a party has won more electorate seats than its party vote entitles it, the party retains the seats and Parliament is temporarily increased in numbers.

To qualify for a proportional allocation of seats in Parliament a party is required to win either one electorate or 5 percent of the total party vote. Only registered political parties are eligible to compete for party votes. To register, a party must satisfy the Electoral Commission, the overseeing body, that it has at least 500 financial members. Independent (nonparty) and unregistered party candidates may contest electorates only.

The age of eligibility to vote in general and local elections is 18. Registration is required by law, though it is not rigorously enforced. Rather, publicity campaigns are used to encourage newly eligible citizens to register. Maori (being defined as people of Maori descent who identify as Maori) may choose to register on either the general roll or the separate Maori roll. This Maori option is revised every five years. Since 1993 the number of Maori electorates, formerly fixed at four, has been determined by the number of Maori registering on the Maori roll.

Electorate boundaries are redrawn after every fifth-yearly census to take account of changes in population distribution. This is the task of a seven-member, largely nonpartisan Representation Commission. Boundaries are drawn, having regard for specified community, geographic, and demographic criteria, and the maximum permissible population variance among electorates is 5 percent. The number of South Island electorates is pegged at 16. The population of the South Island is divided by 16 to identify the population quota for general electorates. Following the 2001 census the population quota for general electorates was 54,296.

Turnout in general elections is between 80 and 90 percent of registered electors. The trend, however, is one of decline. Election campaigns are normally four to six weeks in duration. Legal limitations on the parties' electoral expenses are, however, calculated over a period of three months before election day. The maximum expenditure permitted for registered parties is $1 million plus an additional $20,000 for every electorate candidate nominated by the party. While there is no direct state funding of political parties, broadcasting time and money are allocated on the basis of defined criteria, the object being to provide greater equality of access to powerful mass media.

The Party System
ORIGINS OF THE PARTIES

The left-right dimension remains the predominant organizing principle of the party system, reflecting the historical cleavage between advocates of an active versus a diminishing economic and social role for the state. Rural sectionalism has for long been absorbed into a broad coalition of the right. Religious cleavages have not contributed significantly to party divisions. Since the 1970s this rather simple pattern of conflict has been only slightly blurred by the emergence of a postmaterialist dimension in the form of environmentalism and by the development of a clearer ethnic cleavage based on Maori political interests. The main influence on political thinking and practice since the 1970s has been the upsurge of neoliberal doctrines.

Labour and National, the traditional adversaries of the left and right, remain the main political actors under MMP and the anchors of the left and right blocks, respectively. The two parties converge in terms of ideology and political objectives, competing for the so-called moderate center ground of New Zealand politics. Both parties experience internal tensions between those who favor a central tendency and those who advocate either a stronger pursuit of free-market policies (in National) or social democratic policies (in Labour). Both parties suffered splits in the transition to proportional representation, as MPs weighed their future prospects under the restructured electorate boundaries and reassessed their relations with their parties in the light of their own ideological leanings.

State funding of parties has been recommended, but since it has been resisted by some parties and is widely unpopular, no state funding formula has yet been adopted. Instead all parties rely on internal sources of finance and donations from sympathetic interest groups, some of which donate to more than one party. The law requires public disclosure of national donations of more than $10,000 and single electorate donations of more than $1,000.

PARTY ORGANIZATION

All parties broadly follow the same principles of organization, with a loosely defined membership organized into local branches and electorate or regional structures lying between the grassroots and the central party executives. Party membership has tended to decline over the years. To register and compete for a proportional share of the seats in Parliament, however, a party must provide evidence to the Electoral Commission that it has at least 500 financial members. Parties are also expected to select and rank their lists of candidates in a manner compatible with democratic practices, and to avoid conflict and damaging publicity, it is in their interests to do so. This means that candidates must be either selected by the party membership directly or by selection committees that themselves have been democratically selected by members.

Among all parties the most representative and constitutionally authoritative unit of organization is the annual conference. As the conferences have tended to become the public showpieces for the parties, so their agendas and proceedings have become more structured and managed by the party leadership. Nevertheless, the conferences remain vital arenas for the interaction of the party hierarchies with their grass roots and of the members of Parliament with the active members of the organization. Conferences set the direction of party policies, thus binding the party leadership to varying degrees, but the linkage between party policy and conference remits has loosened, especially in the Labour Party in recent years. Party conferences also have the important function of electing the powerful party executives and the officers of the organization. Organizational leaders are not precluded from also being MPs, but such role duplication is rare. Parliamentary leaders are chosen by and from the respective party caucuses.

The main parties all have a central office serviced by a small body of paid clerical staff answerable to the chief executive or general secretary. The larger parties also maintain regional offices and, depending on the state of their finances, employ a small number of field staff or organizers. In addition, parties represented in Parliament qualify for state-funded research staff and clerical assistance, as well as printing and postage entitlements.

CAMPAIGNING

Party campaigns are fought at both the electorate and the national levels. Electorate campaigns are organized locally by active party members or personal supporters of the candidate and consist of public meetings, door-to-door canvassing, the distribution of leaflets to households, and other candidate-centered activities. Except in the case of unusual contests little media attention is given to individual electorates. The main media focus is on the national level of the campaign, centered on the party leaders. To the extent that the parties' resources permit, their campaign themes and tactics are adjusted to the results of public-opinion polls, private party polling, or focus group research and the advice of professional agencies. One or two televised leaders' debates have become a normal feature of campaigns and may have a significant influence on the fortunes of individual party leaders and parties. Under MMP, party resources focus more on the national campaigns, with less concentration on the few key marginal electorates, which determined election outcomes under the previous winner-take-all electoral system. However, the strength of the leading parties' local organizations in the marginal electorates act as a check on the centralization of the campaign and ensure that some local contests continue to be vigorously fought.

In survey research around 40 percent of electors decline to identify themselves as "usually" aligned to one party or another. Nevertheless, people vote for parties and party candidates. Independent candidates contesting electorates usually attract less than 1 percent of the total electorate votes.

Major Political Parties
LABOUR PARTY

HISTORY
The New Zealand Labour Party (NZLP) was formed in 1916 at a conference of delegates from trade unions and radical and moderately reformist political groups. It contested its first general election in 1919. By 1922 it had captured a large share of the urban wage earners' vote and that of miners and timber workers in more rural electorates. A more moderate image and program under the leadership of Michael Joseph Savage after 1933 and the widespread effects of the world depression brought the Labour Party to power in 1935. The first Labour government greatly expanded the welfare

state with innovative policies in housing, public works, social welfare, public health, and price support for farm commodities. Labour retained its electoral popularity in 1938 but lost votes and seats in the 1940s, its problems compounded by the death of the popular Savage and bitter internal conflict. Amid a mood of rejection of continued wartime state controls and restrictions, Peter Fraser lost the 1949 election, which was the beginning of a long period of National political dominance in New Zealand politics.

In 1957 the second Labour government, under Walter Nash, was elected, but with only a one-seat majority. Faced with a severe balance-of-payments crisis, the government introduced the infamous "Black Budget," which raised taxes on beer and cigarettes and deeply antagonized many Labour supporters. The Nash government was voted out in 1960. The third Labour government (1972–75), led by Norman Kirk, similarly faced severe economic problems associated with the world oil crisis. It was further destabilized by Kirk's sudden death in 1974 and by the highly effective attack mounted by the pugnacious leader of the opposition National Party, Robert Muldoon. Labour was heavily defeated in 1975. Although it recovered to receive more votes than National in 1978 and 1981, under the first-past-the-post electoral system it failed to attain a parliamentary majority. In 1984, however, in a rare snap election, a largely new generation of tertiary-educated and professional Labour politicians, led by David Lange, won in a landslide rejection of the National government. Lange's Labour government stunned its traditional supporters by commencing a program of radical economic reform involving financial deregulation, increased competition, a removal of rural subsidies, public-service restructuring, and micropolitical reforms more consistent with a neoliberal than a social democratic agenda. Although Labour was returned in 1987, its natural constituency was already eroding and rapidly declined further in the face of a deep split in the cabinet between supporters of the treasurer, Roger Douglas, who wished to continue the program of economic reform, and Lange, who advocated a slowing of the pace. The party split extended through caucus and into the party organization. In 1989 Lange resigned as party leader and PM. He was replaced by his deputy, Geoffrey Palmer, who in turn stepped down in 1990 in favor of Mike Moore. The change of leadership could not save the government, which was swept from office in the 1990 election.

The party slowly recovered electoral ground in the 1990s and in 1999 recaptured government office in coalition with the small left-wing Alliance Party.

Labour was again returned to government in 2002, in a minority coalition with the Progressives (a splinter from the Alliance), supported on essential supply and confidence votes by the centrist United Future Party. Following new elections in 2005 Labour once again led a coalition government with the Progressives. In office Labour has led governments that have combined fiscal caution with mildly redistributive and socially liberal policies.

ORGANIZATION

The formal structure of the party is based on branches, defined as at least 10 eligible persons. Reflecting the party's historical origins, unions may affiliate with the party. The resulting voting power of union affiliates, formerly a contentious issue, has lessened in recent years owing to declining union membership and disaffiliation of some unions. Besides general branches there is provision for special branches associated with women, youth, Maori, Pacific Islanders, and the universities. Branches appoint delegates to electorate committees, which coordinate election campaigns at the local level. Groups of electorates may be designated as a region, and regions may combine to hold conferences whose policy remits are channeled to the party's central annual conference. The supreme governing body, with formal jurisdiction over constitutional and policy matters, is the annual conference of delegates representing all constituent sections of the party. Executive power within the party is held by the New Zealand Council of 17 members. Another powerful group is the policy council, which prepares policies for inclusion in the party's election manifesto. Elected members of Parliament are influential at all levels of organization, have speaking and voting rights at the annual conference, and are represented on the New Zealand Council and the policy committee.

MEMBERSHIP AND CONSTITUENCY

Party membership is secret. The long-term trend has been toward a decline in both affiliated and dues-paying members. Numbers fluctuate according to the party's political circumstances, dropping after periods of unpopular government, as in 1957–60 and 1987–90, and rising again as the party's political fortunes revive. Although historical patterns of class voting have blurred in the postwar period, Labour retains its electoral base among manual occupations and also receives disproportionate support among state-sector white-collar occupations, Maori and Pacific Island voters, welfare beneficiaries, and low-income earners.

POLICY

Official party policy is contained in the election manifesto. The manifesto evolves within an elaborate framework of policy committees, the policy council, and the annual conference. Labour governments are expected to make progress on implementing the manifesto. Departures from policy are reported by the policy council to the annual conference. Although party policy is presented in the name of democratic socialist principles, this must be interpreted in practice in the context of a modern, competitive, capitalist, largely deregulated, and globally influenced economy. The party not only eschews socialism but is now associated with the radical neoliberal reforms of the fourth Labour government. As a self-designated center-left party it proposes a moderately more redistributive tax policy than center-right and right parties, greater expenditure on health, housing, education, and welfare, and employment policies offering more protection to the wage earner, along with a stronger commitment to achieving gender equality in the workforce. Labour's distinctive antinuclear policy has been adopted by other parties. Its post–cold war foreign policy stresses regional alignments, especially with Australia, in the South Pacific and Southeast Asia, participation in multilateral peacekeeping roles, a continued liberalization of international trade and investment, and a more vigorous pursuit of international environmental protection programs.

FINANCING

Like membership, the party's finances are secret. Intraparty and union sources have declined as a share of the total party income. Also like membership, income fluctuates with the political environment. In 1987, for example, the private financial sector gave generously in acknowledgment of the fourth Labour government's deregulative and generally pro-business policies. By 1990 both these and party sources had contracted again, leaving the party in debt after the election.

LEADERSHIP

The party president is elected by the annual conference. Caucus elects the parliamentary party leader and deputy leader, usually with some regard to a North Island–South Island spread of leadership. After narrowly losing the 1993 election, Mike Moore was successfully challenged by his deputy, Helen Clark, the party's first woman leader, a graduate in political science and former university lecturer who represents an Auckland electorate. Her deputy, Dr. Michael Cullen, also a former academic, represented a Dunedin (South Island) electorate before moving north to stand as a list member only.

PROSPECTS

During the transition to proportional representation and the lead-up to the 1996 election Labour's electoral status according to opinion polls fell to a historic low, due largely to internal tensions following the change of leadership. Labour's dominance of the center-left was at this time under challenge by the Alliance and New Zealand First Parties. The 1996 election turned both the party's and the leader's fortunes around. Labour is guaranteed to be the dominant center-left party in the new MMP-based multiparty system for the foreseeable future. Nevertheless, its governing prospects are contingent on the aggregate strength of the center-left block, leading to either a Labour-led coalition or Labour minority government, supported by one or more small parties.

NATIONAL PARTY

HISTORY

After Labour's electoral success in 1935 the two non-Labour parliamentary opposition parties—Reform and United—merged to form the National Party in 1936. They were joined by a newer grouping, the Democrats, to create the foundations of a single conservative party spanning rural and wealthier city interests. The formation of National marked also the beginning of a long period of two-party dominance in parliamentary politics, which, although weakening after the 1970s, lasted effectively until the transition to proportional representation after 1993.

National remained in opposition under its first leader, Adam Hamilton, but began to make electoral advances under S. G. Holland in the 1940s, first winning back the rural electorates it had lost to Labour in 1935 and 1938 and finally attaining a parliamentary majority in 1949. By 1999 National had governed alone or in coalition for nearly 40 of the last 50 years. This parliamentary dominance owed much to the first-past-the-post electoral system, which enabled the party to achieve clear parliamentary majorities despite only once, in 1951, winning a majority of votes. A second reason for National's disproportionate tenure of office was its pragmatic moderation in government, administering a regulated mixed economy strongly tied to the protected British commodity market until the 1970s and maintaining the welfare state developed by the first Labour government. Thirdly, National benefited from the stable, effective leadership associated with Sir

Keith Holyoake (1957–72) and Sir Robert Muldoon (1974–84).

Out of office for only two separate single terms, 1957–60 and 1972–75, National's dominance was finally undermined not only by the Labour opposition but from within the party by those who had begun to subscribe to the free-market, small-state thinking in the late twentieth century. Attacked from the right and the left, National was defeated in 1984, only to return in a landslide win in 1990. Since then it has proceeded along the path of economic reform and restructuring initiated by the fourth Labour government. After the first MMP election in 1996 National continued to govern in a majority coalition with New Zealand First. The coalition proved both unstable and unpopular. National's defeat in 1999 was followed by a period of internal strife, a change of leadership, and a disastrous electoral collapse in 2002. After another change of leadership National has recovered its historical place as one of the two major parties in a two-party dominant system. In 2005 National made a strong showing in the elections, winning 48 seats—an increase of 21 seats over 2002—to the Labour Party's 50 seats.

ORGANIZATION

Members, defined as those eligible to vote who pay a subscription to the party, are organized in geographical branches of at least 20 members within electorates. The electorate committees, consisting of representatives of branches, are, however, the basic effective units of the grassroots level of organization. National's regional organization is more developed and influential than Labour's. National's five regional divisions model the overall party organization, holding annual conferences, electing officers, dealing with policy matters, and since 1996 ranking list candidates from within the region. The activities of the divisions are initiated and coordinated by elected divisional councils and executives. The party's annual conference comprises representatives of the electorate and divisional levels of organization. The conference elects the officers of the party, considers selected policy remits, and ratifies any constitutional changes. It is not as influential in policy matters as Labour's conference. Provision is made within the party for separate structures for youth, women, Maori, and Pacific people.

After National's disastrous election in 2002, constitutional changes were made to strengthen central control of the party, to some extent at the expense of the regions. The central governing body of the party is a powerful nine-member board of directors, consisting the party leader, a second representative of the parliamentary caucus, and seven members elected by the annual conference. The party's annual conference comprises representatives of electorates, the regional chairs, the board of directors, and representatives of the youth branch. The conference elects the majority of board members, considers policy remits, and ratifies constitutional changes. It is not as influential in policy matters as Labour's conference. Policy formulation is the responsibility of the policy consultation committee, assisted by a number of advisory groups. Final approval of policy is in the hands of the board of directors.

MEMBERSHIP AND CONSTITUENCY

National has been more successful than Labour in mobilizing and maintaining a mass membership. As with Labour, however, the long-term trend is one of erratic decline, from a high of 246,000 to fewer than 40,000. National's constituency is strongest in rural regions and among the self-employed, higher-income groups, private-sector employees, and churchgoers and is slightly stronger among men than women.

POLICY

In its revised constitution (2003) National lists "values" central to the party's purpose. These include: "national and personal security; equal citizenship and equal opportunity; individual freedom and choice; personal responsibility; competitive enterprise and rewards for achievement; limited government; strong families and caring communities; sustainable development of the environment." At the rhetorical level there is little in these to distinguish National from Labour. In opposition National has taken strong stands against policies which might benefit Maori on the basis of ethnicity rather than need, advocates a more punitive approach to law and order; and resists labour laws sympathetic to trade unionism. In government National would move toward a flatter income tax regime and keep a tight reign on welfare costs and benefit levels. Although National aspires to a closer defense relationship with the United States and Australia, in practice there is little difference between National's and Labour's pro-Western foreign policies or their pro–free trade policies. Once heavily influenced by a powerful rural lobby, National is now more closely aligned with business interests.

FINANCING

Sources and amounts are secret. However, National has usually been the wealthier of the two major parties, sustained by personal contributions and fund-raising among its substantial membership, along with donations from business and wealthy supporters.

LEADERSHIP

The party leader is elected by the National members of Parliament from among their ranks. The party's record of stable leadership during its postwar period of electoral dominance changed in the mid-1990s. Since then electoral setbacks have triggered a series of leadership changes. In 1997 the prime minister, Jim Bolger, was replaced by Jenny Shipley, who thus became National's first woman leader and New Zealand's first woman prime minister. After losing to Labour in 1999 Shipley was ousted by her deputy, Bill English, who in turn suffered a major electoral defeat in 2002. He was successfully challenged soon after by Dr. Don Brash, a first-term list member of Parliament and a former governor of the Reserve Bank. The party president, who heads the extraparliamentary organization, is elected by the annual conference.

PROSPECTS

National has survived the transition to proportional representation to become the dominant party of the center-right block, but with its future governing status dependent on the parliamentary strength of potential coalition partners or parties prepared to support a minority National government. Its electoral and parliamentary presence is contingent also on its ability to check the development of an assertive free-market party to its right while at the same time maintaining the support of its more moderate, pragmatic constituency.

Minor Political Parties

ALLIANCE

The Alliance originated in 1989 as a splinter party, called New Labour, formed and led by a Labour MP, Jim Anderton, in protest at the neoliberal direction of the Labour government's policies. New Labour formed a coalition with four other minor parties on the left to become the Alliance Party. The grouping was forged before the 1993 election in an attempt to surmount the disadvantages of small parties under the first-past-the-post electoral system. Reaching 18 percent of the vote in 1993, the Alliance aspired to replace Labour as the main opposition party to National. More realistically the Alliance's place in the political spectrum was as Labour's coalition partner or support party. It fulfilled this role in the Labour-led coalition of 1999–2002. The

experience of sharing government proved disastrous. Overshadowed by Labour, falling in the opinion polls, frustrated at its failure to achieve significant progress on its policy aims, and divided over the government's decision to send troops to Afghanistan, the Alliance split. The party was virtually destroyed in the 2002 election, losing all its members of Parliament.

GREENS

The Green Party originated in 1972 as the Values Party. It was re-formed as the Aotearoa Green Party to contest the 1990 election, when it attained nearly 7 percent of the vote. It contested the 1993 and 1996 elections as one of the five constituent parties making up the Alliance. Three of the 13 Alliance MPs elected in 1996 were members of the Green Party. In November 1997 the party withdrew from the Alliance, judging that under the new proportional electoral system (MMP) it stood a good chance of attaining the 5 percent of the national vote needed for representation in its own right. The move paid off. In 1999 the Green vote entitled it to seven seats in parliament, rising to nine in 2002 but falling back to six in 2005. The Greens have taken strong stands on environmental, energy, transport, defense, and Maori issues. They have led opposition to the release of genetically modified organisms into the environment. Too uncompromising to be an easy coalition partner for Labour, the Greens still play a significant role on the left of the political spectrum, backing Labour-led governments against parties of the right.

NEW ZEALAND FIRST

The party is synonymous with its founder and leader, Winston Peters, a Maori and a former National MP who, after a short stormy period as minister of Maori affairs, was dismissed from the cabinet in 1991 and expelled from the caucus in 1992; he finally split from his party in 1993 by resigning from Parliament and forcing a by-election in his seat of Tauranga. Peters, whom polls identified as the country's most popular politician, easily won the by-election and founded his own party, New Zealand First, in July 1993. The party won 8.4 percent of the vote in the general election a few months later, and Peters was again returned to Parliament. In the unstable transition to MMP between 1993 and 1996 Peters capitalized on his continuing personal standing, his espousal of populist issues, and a widespread sense of discontent with the major parties to place his party electorally in a pivotal balance-of-power position between Labour and National. New

Zealand First won 13.4 percent of the vote in 1996. In a historic realignment of Maori partisanship New Zealand First candidates won all five Maori electorates. After prolonged negotiations with both Labour and National, Peters entered into a majority coalition with National, securing for himself the roles of treasurer and deputy prime minister and a further eight ministerial positions for his party. Within months his and the party's ratings had slumped to very low levels. Although New Zealand First was able to slow the pace of National's economic liberalization program, a majority of New Zealand First voters had expected Peters to help end the National government, not join it. The image of New Zealand First was also damaged by the inexperience of its ministerial members and the aggressive performance of the Maori MPs.

In 1998 the coalition with National was dissolved and half the New Zealand First MPs left the party. In 1999 the party suffered a major electoral setback. All Maori electorates returned to Labour, and the party fell below the threshold of 5 percent of the national vote. However, Peters narrowly retained his Tauranga seat, qualifying the party for proportional representation under the rules of MMP. In 2002 New Zealand First recovered lost ground, increasing its parliamentary representation from 5 to 13 MPs, the third largest parliamentary grouping. But in 2005 the party lost six seats to put its total at seven. The party continues to play a centrist role, critical of parties on both the left and right. But the forthright and uncompromising style of Peters tends to reduce the party's coalition potential despite its pivotal place in the party spectrum.

UNITED FUTURE NEW ZEALAND

In the transition to MMP some saw a need for a party of the center to mediate between Labour and National. In 1995 three Labour or ex-Labour and five National MPs left their parties to form the United Party. It was a dismal failure, winning less than 1 percent of the vote in 1996. One member, however, Peter Dunne, retained his electorate seat and thus became the party's sole MP. His firm grip on his electorate seat was a valuable resource under the rules of MMP, which did not go unnoticed. In 2000 Dunne was approached by leaders of the Future New Zealand Party, a descendant of the now-defunct 1996 Christian Democrats. A merger of the two parties was negotiated, and United was renamed United Future New Zealand. It contested the 2002 election as a center party, stressing "common sense" in politics, but also finding sympathy for its emphasis on "family values." Dunne, an experienced

politician and assured of his own seat, campaigned effectively, attracting support among a socially conservative, often Christian, section of the electorate. The outcome was a surprise to most people. United Future secured nearly 7 percent of the vote, and Dunne was joined in Parliament by another seven MPs. While holding a strategic pivotal position Dunne acknowledged Labour as the overall winner of the election and undertook to secure the minority Labour-Progressive coalition in the interest of governmental stability. In 2005, however, the party's total dropped to three seats. The party is frequently critical of government policies, however, and depending on election results is equally prepared underpin a government of the right. United Future's electoral position remains insecure, and very dependent on Dunne's electorate seat to maintain a parliamentary presence.

ACT NEW ZEALAND

ACT is evidence of the deep impact on the partisan structure of New Zealand politics of neoliberal thinking and the move to proportional representation. ACT began as a lobby group advocating further market liberalization and small state politics. Roger Douglas, the reforming treasurer of the fourth Labour government, was a founding member. He was joined by people from both Labour and National backgrounds, including Richard Prebble, a former Labour cabinet minister who led the party from 1996 to 2004, and Derek Quigley, a former National minister forced from the cabinet for his free-market advocacy in 1982. Generously funded from business sources, ACT has consistently secured 6–8 percent of the vote to maintain a parliamentary presence since 1996. Located on the right of the political spectrum, ACT provides a potential coalition partner or support party for National. In 2004, however, the National Party, on the basis of its new leadership and stronger stands on ethnic issues, social conservatism, and law and order, was attracting sufficient electoral support away from ACT to cast doubt on its future. In the 2005 elections the party saw its number of seats dwindle to two.

PROGRESSIVE PARTY

The Progressive Party has its origin in the rancorous breakup of the Alliance in 2002. One faction of the Alliance remained loyal to the party's founding leader, Jim Anderton, and contested the election under a new party banner—Jim Anderton's Progressive Coalition, since shortened to Progressive Party. Anderton, the deputy prime minister in the Labour-Alliance coalition, and the Progressives remained loyal to the continuing coalition with Labour. While the new party attracted less than 2 percent of the overall vote, Anderton was secure in his own electorate seat, and under the rules of MMP brought one other MP into Parliament on the Progressive list. The two MPs promptly joined Labour in a minority center-left coalition, where they were little more than an appendage of the dominant Labour Party. In 2005 the party won seat but remained part of the governing coalition with Labour.

MAORI PARTY

In 2003 an issue arose over the ownership of the foreshore and seabed. The Court of Appeal judged that the Maori Land Court was competent to hear claims of ownership by Maori applicants. The government, concerned at the scale of a possible backlash by non-Maori citizens proposed legislation that would effectively place the seabed and foreshores in public ownership. Maori opposition was widespread and prolonged. By 2004 Maori Labour MPs faced great pressure to oppose the legislation. One of the MPs, Tariana Turia, an associate minister outside cabinet, and known for her radical views, resigned from Parliament to successfully contest her seat in a by-election under the banner of the new Maori Party, of which she became the coleader. The party became a threat to Labour's traditional grip on the Maori territorial electorates, and in fact in 2005 the party won four seats in Parliament.

Other Political Forces

Parties and governments in New Zealand function in a pluralistic, secular, democratic environment comprising a great variety of interest groups, an influential bureaucracy, and media independent of any political party. Interest groups and ideologically committed promotional groups extend across the political spectrum. The most powerful, in terms of their influence on public policy, are the long-established peak organizations representing the various sectors of a capitalist economy, such as the Council of Trade Unions, Business New Zealand, Federated Farmers, and the Bankers' Association. Also influential in molding the climate of opinion in which public policy is formulated are well-funded "think tanks" such as the Business Roundtable (neoliberal economics), the Maxim Institute (Christian conservatism), and the New Zealand Institute (unaligned pragmatism). Vigorous in articulating their concerns are associations speaking for various occupational groups, such as the Law Society, the Medical Association, the Nurses Organization, and the several teachers' unions. Other groups have organized around ethnic and gender interests, pensioners, various branches of sport and leisure, and environmental issues.

With the exception of Labour's provision for trade unions to affiliate with the party, the relationship between groups and parties is informal. Ideological affinity and overlapping memberships may align different parties more closely to some groups rather than to others—business and farmer groups with the National Party, for example, or environmental groups with the Greens. The Labour case notwithstanding, no significant political party functions as the political arm of a pressure group or groups. While membership in blue- or white-collar unions still figures more frequently in the background of Labour politicians than those of the political right, the historical links between the Labour Party and the trade unions have weakened to the extent that the party is no longer commonly perceived as the instrument of organized labor.

The traditional churches generally stand aside from partisan politics, only rarely entering directly into political debate when issues such as poverty, gay rights, abortion, and divorce raise emotion-laden moral concerns. Newer, more fundamentalist church groups, however, are less constrained in their advocacy of moral conservatism.

No branch of the media is either under state direction or directly affiliated to a political party. Yet the media collectively, far from being a neutral element in the conduct of politics, catering for a variety of prejudices, have become overt political actors through a trend to a more opinionated style of print journalism, paralleled in the electronic media by talk radio, and celebrity-based television news presentation. In this way the media influence the style and tenor of political debate, cultivating intense, short-term, personality-based perspectives on current issues, which contribute to the electorally volatile, politically cynical climate within which the parties compete.

National Prospects

Despite the switch to proportional representation in 1996 the contours of the two-party-dominant, Labour-National party system remain strong. MMP, as expected, greatly enhanced the electoral and parliamentary prospects of the small parties. Their participation in coalition politics, however, has so far proved destructive of their cohesion and electoral bases, and they are vulnerable to resurgent major parties. Consequently there is still considerable electoral instability among the aspiring small parties. The prospects for a revitalized left, either from a reconstituted Alliance or invigorated Progressive Party, appear slight. Within the party spectrum the Greens have filled the space on the left. On the political right ACT is sorely challenged to surmount the 5 percent threshold for representation in Parliament. Ethnic issues have gained in salience, and a new Maori Party has threatened the long-standing loyalty of Maori voters to Labour. Consequently Labour's grip on the Maori electorates, already overturned once, in 1996–99, by New Zealand First, appears less certain. Yet the very existence of separate Maori electorates, which were established in 1867, is being challenged by New Zealand First, National, and ACT. Although a parliamentary review of the MMP electoral system in 2002 recommended no significant changes, it is still not fully supported by National, whose leadership prefers a less proportional allocation of list seats and advocates opening up the issue again through referendum.

Further Reading

Bush, Graham. *Local Government and Politics in New Zealand.* 2d ed. Auckland: Auckland University Press, 1995.

Jackson, Keith, and Alan McRobie. *New Zealand Adopts Proportional Representation.* Aldershot: Ashgate, 1998.

Miller, Raymond, ed. *New Zealand Government and Politics.* Melbourne: Oxford University Press, 2003.

———. *Party Politics in New Zealand.* Melbourne: Oxford University Press, 2005.

Mulgan, Richard. *Politics in New Zealand.* 3d ed. Auckland: Auckland University Press, 2004.

Palmer, Geoffrey, and Matthew Palmer. *Bridled Power: New Zealand Government under MMP.* Auckland: Oxford University Press, 1997.

Rudd, Chris, and G. A.Wood. *The Politics and Government of New Zealand.* Dunedin: University of Otago Press, 2004.

Vowles, Jack, et al., eds. *Voters' Veto: The 2002 Election in New Zealand and the Consolidation of Minority Government.* Auckland: Auckland University Press, 2004.

REPUBLIC OF NICARAGUA
(República de Nicaragua)

By John A. Booth, Ph.D.

The Republic of Nicaragua (2005 population approximately 5.5 million) spans the Central American isthmus between Honduras and Costa Rica. From the 1970s through the early 1990s Nicaragua experienced repeated economic crises, two civil wars, and a massive foreign intervention as it passed from rightist dictatorship through Marxist-led revolution to electoral democracy. The Somoza dynasty (1936–79) ruled Nicaragua using the National Guard and the Liberal Nationalist Party (PLN) as its instruments of control. A violent 1978–79 insurrection toppled the Somozas and brought to power a revolutionary coalition dominated by the Sandinista National Liberation Front (Frente Sandinista de Liberación Nacional; FSLN). The Marxist-Leninist FSLN, led by its National Directorate, dominated the new regime and revolution and promoted extensive sociopolitical change. Opposition grew and some FSLN allies broke with the revolution. Various forces encouraged and backed by the United States rebelled against the regime. In the 1980s civil war disrupted the economy and polarized Nicaraguans as the Sandinista government mobilized to defend the revolution against these counterrevolutionary ("contra") forces.

Until 1984 the FSLN governed de facto through a multimember junta guided by the FSLN National Directorate. Despite Sandinista dominance of public policy, other parties participated in the junta, cabinet, and bureaucracy. Opposition parties existed openly. In 1984 the revolutionary government held a national election in which FSLN candidate Daniel Ortega Saavedra won the presidency and the FSLN captured about 60 percent of the new National Assembly. The Assembly drafted a new constitution, effective in 1987. It established a republican, presidential government with a strong executive but with some checks and balances.

The counterrevolutionary war, the antagonism of the Reagan and Bush administrations (including an economic embargo and diplomatic opposition), economic problems aggravated by the war, embargo, and revolutionary policies, and restrictions on civil liberties deepened polarization and discontent. Pursuant to the 1987 Central American Peace Accord the government forged a cease-fire with the contras in 1989. It also imposed draconian economic stabilization measures in the late 1980s, but to little avail. In the 1990 election 20 opposition parties formed the U.S.-backed Nicaraguan Opposition Union (Unión Nicaragüense Opositora; UNO) coalition that nominated Violeta Barrios de Chamorro for the presidency. Winning 54 percent of the vote, Chamorro defeated incumbent Ortega, and the Sandinistas relinquished power.

Chamorro settled the war, demobilized the contras, and dramatically trimmed the armed forces. Her government liberalized the economy and shrank the public sector to curtail inflation, but conflict over property confiscated during the revolution blocked economic recovery. The UNO coalition in the National Assembly collapsed, leaving President Chamorro to legislate by forging transitory alliances with other parties, often including the FLSN.

In the 1996 election the Liberal Alliance (AL), led by the former Managua mayor Arnoldo Alemán

Lacayo, won the presidency with 51 percent of the vote, handing Daniel Ortega of the Sandinistas his second successive defeat. Nicaragua's third national election since the overthrow of the Somozas and second peaceful exchange of power from an incumbent to the opposition definitively signaled the end of the Sandinista revolution. In 2001, despite a major corruption scandal in the Alemán administration, Liberal Alliance candidate Enrique Bolaños Geyer captured the presidency with 56 percent of the vote, with the FSLN's Ortega again defeated.

The System of Government

Nicaragua is a democratic republic with a strong presidential system and a unicameral legislature.

EXECUTIVE

The 1987 constitution vested great executive authority in a reelectable presidency with a six-tear term. The president had a virtual monopoly on budgeting and enjoyed decree authority. Combined with the strong FSLN majority in the National Assembly, these powers weakened formal constitutional checks upon executive authority. The FSLN's defeat in 1990 triggered a struggle to curtail presidential power. Reform efforts, resisted by President Chamorro, sparked a protracted legislative-constitutional crisis. Legislation and constitutional amendments trimming executive authority finally passed in 1996.

Nicaragua's president now serves for five years, may not seek immediate reelection, and has a two-term maximum. The president appoints cabinet ministers and ambassadors and shares with the National Assembly both the appointment of the Supreme Court and Supreme Electoral Council and budgeting and fiscal authority. The 1996 reforms divide presidential military and decree powers with the National Assembly, which also won new powers to hold executive officials accountable.

Restructured by the revolution in the 1980s and again by UNO in the 1990s, the Nicaraguan executive branch has experienced dramatic alterations in its size and mission. The revolution expanded government's size and scope with new economic and welfare functions. Neoliberal reforms, begun in the late 1980s and extended by subsequent government, radically retrenched the public sector, curtailing services, state economic regulation and ownership, and the government's budget and payroll. The government slashed spending, privatized hundreds of state-owned firms, and ended its banking monopoly. The military and police, dominated by the FSLN during the revolution, were depoliticized. The police were civilianized and the army's forces cut by 80 percent.

LEGISLATURE

Nicaragua's legislature is the unicameral National Assembly (Asamblea Nacional). In 1996 the Assembly's term of office increased to five years. The body has 90 regular seats for deputies (*diputados*) plus one additional seat for the runner-up in the last presidential race and one seat for previous president. The Assembly in 2002 lifted the legislative immunity from prosecution of former president Arnoldo Alemán. The courts convicted Alemán of corruption in 2003, and he was imprisoned.

Nicaraguans elect deputies from two lists: the 20-seat national list is allocated among the parties in proportion to their share of the national list vote; 70 regular departmental seats are elected from party slates from each of the 15 departments and two autonomous regions, apportioned by population. Distribution of winning seats within each department/region is in proportion to party vote share.

The National Assembly is presided over by a president, secretary, and other officers elected by the membership. Subject-area committees handle legislation; their makeup is distributed in rough proportion to parties' shares of deputies. The larger parties' caucuses shape legislation through committee action and maintaining voting discipline. The FLSN caucus has sometimes boycotted Assembly sessions to block a quorum and thus prevent legislation.

The Assembly's partisan makeup has changed since 1990. President Alemán assembled a broad anti-Sandinista coalition in the 1996–2001 Assembly, but in 1999 Alemán's PLC and the Sandinistas led by Daniel Ortega forged a broad pact to reform the constitution and electoral law. The Alemán-Ortega pact strengthened both party leaders within their own parties and especially advantaged the PLC and FSLN at the expense of smaller parties and political movements. One impact was to decrease sharply the number of small-party deputies elected to the 2001–2006 Assembly.

The executive-legislative power balance was tilted away from the Assembly under the 1987 constitution until 1996, when a fractious temporary coalition seeking to curtail presidential authority prompted a political crisis. This conflict crippled the Chamorro administration and required international mediation, which brought the Assembly enhanced authority in budgetary matters. After leaving the presidency in 2001, Arnoldo Alemán had the AL fraction elect him president of the Assembly. In 2002, however, the Liberal bench split as a growing corruption scandal deeply implicated the former president. Alemán lost control of the Assembly, which voted to lift his legislative immunity from prosecution. He was convicted of fraud and imprisoned in 2003.

Because the Assembly may amend the constitution by a 60 percent vote, the legislative-executive balance of power (indeed constitutional provisions in general) may remain unstable.

SEATS IN THE NICARAGUAN NATIONAL ASSEMBLY, 1990–2006

Party[a]	1990–1996	1996–2001	2001–2006
FSLN	39	36	38
UNO	51	—	—
AL	42	53	—
CC	—	4	—
PCN	—	3	1
PN	—	2	—
Others	2	6	—
Total Seats	92	93[b]	92[b]

Sources: Consejo Supremo Electoral; Latin American Studies Association, The Electoral Process in Nicaragua: Domestic and International Influences (Austin, Tex.: November 19, 1984), table 3; Latin American Studies Association, Electoral Democracy Under International Pressure (Pittsburgh: March 15, 1990), table 4; and "How Nicaraguans Voted," Envío 15, nos. 185–186 (December–January 1996–97): 40 (with corrections by the author), and "Split Down the Middle," Barricada Internacional, no. 403 (December 1996): 8–9.

[a]*Party names: FSLN = Sandinista National Liberation Front; PDC = Democratic Conservative Party; PLI = Independent Liberal Party; PPSC = Popular Social Christian Party; UNO = Nicaraguan Opposition Union; AL = Liberal Alliance; PCN = Conservative Party of Nicaragua; CC = Christian Way; PN = National Project.*

[b]*Total seats for 1996–2001 include an extra seat each for losing 1996 presidential candidates of the FSLN, CC, and PCN. Total seats for 2001–2006 include an extra seat for losing FSLN candidate Ortega and for former AL president Alemán, who later lost his seat after conviction in 2003 on corruption charges.*

JUDICIARY

Nicaragua's legal system follows the civil law tradition, based upon legislated codes. The judiciary established under the 1987 constitution includes a Supreme Court (Tribunal Supremo) and civil and criminal lower courts. The Supreme Court's 16 magistrates (appointed by the National Assembly) sit as members of four specialized benches (criminal, civil, constitutional, and administrative). Under the 1987 constitution the president submitted a list of candidates from which the Assembly had to choose, but reforms in 1996 freed the Assembly to appoint magistrates not among the president's nominees. The Assembly also won the power to remove judges for diverse motives, including vaguely defined inappropriate moral or political conduct. The reforms also extended magistrates' terms of office from five to seven years, gave the Court jurisdiction over disputes among the branches of government, and doubled the judiciary's share of the national budget to 4 percent. The president of Nicaragua formerly designated the Court's president, but since 1996 the magistrates themselves annually elect their president.

Prior to 1996 critics viewed the Court as too subservient to the presidency and the FSLN, largely unchecked by the legislature, and underfunded. The reforms rectified those problems, but now the Court's dependency upon the National Assembly raises concerns over legislative manipulation of the courts. The Alemán-Ortega pact of 1999 enlarged the Supreme Court to 16 from 12 magistrates, a measure intended to dilute the influence of FSLN-appointed judges and place more Liberals on the Court.

Below the Supreme Court are courts of appeals, district courts, and municipal courts.

REGIONAL AND LOCAL GOVERNMENT

Nicaragua's political subdivisions consist of 15 departments and two autonomous regions. Departments per se have very limited functions, serving mainly as subdivisions for the election of the 70 departmental list members of the National Assembly and fulfilling some administrative responsibilities for the national government. The autonomous regions of the Atlantic coast, formed during the revolution, have more functions than the departments do. Responding to disaffection among ethnic and racial groups of the Atlantic zone, the revolutionary government gave the autonomous regions quasi-federal status. Each has an elected regional council with certain legislative and

ORGANIZATION OF NICARAGUAN GOVERNMENT

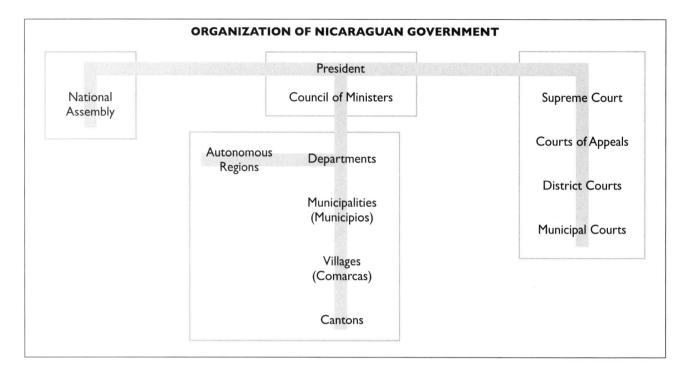

administrative authority and resources beyond those of the departments.

Departments are subdivided into 145 municipalities (*municipios*—analogous to counties), each headed by an elected mayor (*alcalde*) and councils. Municipal councils vary in size according to local population, ranging from Managua's 16 members down to four members for municipalities of under 30,000. The mayor, elected separately, chairs the municipal council. The 1966 electoral reforms set municipal office terms at four years.

Municipalities have local authority, including modest powers to tax, regulate, and promote development. Traditionally underfunded because of limited taxing authority, municipalities receive additional funding from the national government.

The Electoral System

Nicaragua employs direct elections for all offices. The voting age is 16. The presidential–vice presidential ticket requires a 40 percent plurality to avoid a runoff between the top two candidates (this threshold was lowered from 45 percent by electoral-law changes enacted following the Alemán-Ortega pact of 1999). Mayors win by simple plurality votes. Seats in the National Assembly (both national and departmental lists), the Central American Parliament, and on all municipal councils are distributed among the contend-

ing parties by proportional representation. Citizens vote for slates of candidates nominated by parties on both Assembly and municipal ballots.

Nicaragua has a fourth governmental branch that administers elections. Established in 1984, the five-member Supreme Electoral Council (Consejo Supremo Electoral; CSE) is appointed by the National Assembly. The CSE handles voter registration, election organization and administration, and resolution of electoral disputes.

In the early 1990s the CSE began developing national civil registry functions, including issuing to all citizens a national identity card (*cédula*) that doubles as a voter registration document. Unable to complete this process prior to the 1996 general election, the CSE employed two ad hoc strategies to register voters. Despite multiple systems the CSE successfully registered voters and delivered documents.

Until 1995 a majority of CSE magistrates and staff came from FSLN ranks. Despite its partisan cadres the CSE earned a reputation for technical competence and nonpartisanship during the 1984 and 1990 elections. Reforms undertaken by the National Assembly in 1996, however, reorganized the CSE and caused numerous flaws in the 1996 general election:

- New elections for the National Assembly list, Central American Parliament, and mayors were added to those for president, Assembly, and municipal councils, doubling the number of ballots.

- Electoral regions for the Assembly changed from regions to the departments and autonomous regions.
- The CSE lost the power to name departmental and local electoral staff, which shifted to the parties. This change politicized the electoral apparatus and increased local staff inexperience. Delays in naming local electoral officials snarled the electoral apparatus.
- The number of polling places (*juntas receptoras de votos*) doubled to almost 9,000.
- The National Assembly funded the 1996 election at the 1990 level despite having a much larger staff and greater ballot complexity, prompting the resignation of the longtime president of the CSE.

Many problems ensued in the 1996 vote, including improper handling of 5 percent of the ballot materials at the national collection venue in Managua. The mishandled and discarded ballots were too few to have changed the national outcome, so parties and observers noted the flaws but recognized Alemán's victory.

The 2000 municipal elections and 2001 presidential and National Assembly elections took place under new rules designed by the 1999 Alemán-Ortega pact to help the big parties and minimize the number of parties competing. The CSE was expanded from 5 to 7 magistrates, postelection party recertification would require a party to win 3 percent of the total vote, and no nonpartisan slates could contest municipal elections. In both elections the CSE considerably improved its performance over the 1996 election, especially in logistics and ballot handling. Both domestic and international observers found the 2001 election's conduct satisfactory.

The Party System

ORIGINS OF THE PARTIES

Nicaragua's party system retains traits that originated in the late colonial era. Factions of promonarchy Conservatives from around Granada and proindependence Liberals from the León area evolved into extended clans with regional bases that survive today. Independence from Spain (1821) and inclusion into the Central American Republic (1823) eventually pitted Liberals and Conservatives in a nearly continuous violent competition that hardened regional partisan identification and cyclical political violence. By the early twentieth century most Liberal-Conservative ideological differences had vanished, but violent civil clashes persisted.

The United States intervened heavily in Nicaraguan politics after 1909 to protect its transisthmian canal monopoly in Panama. U.S. Marines occupied Nicaragua for most of the period from 1909 to 1925 in support of Conservative governments. A Liberal revolt in 1926 led to another U.S. occupation and a truce between the combatants that let the Liberals assume power in 1932. One Liberal general, the anti-interventionist revolutionary Augusto Sandino, rejected the truce and waged a six-year guerrilla struggle against the U.S.-trained Nicaraguan National Guard. Without defeating Sandino, the United States withdrew its troops in 1933.

The legacy of U.S. occupation included weakened political institutions, anti-American resentment, and the National Guard. At the head of the Guard was Anastasio Somoza García, a Liberal who had Sandino assassinated in 1933 and in 1936 seized ruling power. Somoza García took over the Liberal Party (renamed Liberal Nationalist Party; PLN) as a tool to control government and distribute graft. He employed the Guard to repress opponents and manipulated U.S. ties to bolster his power. Beginning in 1948 Somoza García countered prodemocracy sentiment by co-opting Conservatives into the government with a share of offices and spoils. These arrangements continued after his 1956 assassination; his sons Luis and Anastasio Somoza Debayle succeeded him in control of the presidency, National Guard, and PLN.

Several parties arose to protest Somocista National Liberalism and collaborationist Conservatism; others were ideological movements. The Independent Liberal Party (Partido Liberal Independiente; PLI) split from the PLN in the 1940s. The pro-Soviet Nicaraguan Socialist Party (Partido Socialista Nicaragüense; PSN) appeared in the 1940s, and the Christian democratic-aligned Social Christian Party (Partido Social Cristiano Nicaragüense; PSCN) arose in the 1950s, each developing a significant base in the labor movement.

The twentieth century's most important new political movement was the Sandinista National Liberation Front, formed in 1961 as a Marxist guerrilla group drawing members from the disaffected of other parties and anti-Somoza movements. FSLN rule dramatically altered the party spectrum. The Sandinista party dominated politics during the 1980s and has survived its electoral defeats of 1990, 1996, and 2001 able to marshal a large minority vote.

The revolution shattered the old party system. It outlawed the PLN and collaborationist Conservative splinters but permitted other political parties to develop and contend for power. Older anti-Somocista parties like the PLI, Social Christians, and some Conservatives took part in the FSLN-led coalition government of 1979–84, as did several new parties—the latter typically personalistic rather than ideological. Outside of Nicaragua, ex-PLN and National Guard figures, dissident Sandinistas, and alienated former FSLN collaborators from others parties formed new parties or revived old ones in opposition to the FSLN. One expression of this anti-Sandinism was the U.S.-backed contras, who emphasized guerrilla insurgency. The contras (several coalitions of divergent interests and personalities) failed to form a coherent political movement after the 1989 cease-fire and had fragmented into and among various parties by the 1990 election.

The other major anti-Sandinista movement was the several new internal opposition parties that appeared in the late 1980s. Many received support from the United States or from social democratic, liberal, and Christian democratic party international organizations. In the 1990 vote the United States labored assiduously to defeat the FLSN. It encouraged 20 ideologically diverse parties, old and new, to form the Nicaraguan Opposition Union (Unión Nicaragüense Opositora; UNO) and nominate Violeta Barrios de Chamorro for president. Although victorious, Chamorro's UNO coalition soon fragmented.

The 1990 election law provided for disbanding unsuccessful parties, but liberal rules governing party formation permitted a multiplication of groups by the 1996 election, eventually contested by over 40 parties and coalitions. The FSLN retained about 38 percent of the national vote. The reformist splinter Sandinista Renovation Movement (Movimiento de Renovación Sandinista; MRS) fared poorly, as did Conservatives. The big news was the resurgence of the Liberals behind Arnoldo Alemán. A coalition of Alemán's Liberal Constitutionalists and other groups, the Liberal Alliance attracted back to Nicaragua many exiled Liberals, including personalities once associated with the Somozas' PLN.

In 2001 the Liberal candidate Enrique Bolaños easily won the presidency over the FSLN's perennial presidential nominee, Daniel Ortega. The Liberal Alliance won 53 of 92 legislative seats, with the FSLN taking 38 seats. Election-law revisions made by the PLC-FSLN pact of 1999 made it much harder for parties to survive a poor election performance and sharply cut the number of parties allowed to contest future elections.

PARTY ORGANIZATION

Great organizational differences exist between the FSLN and other parties. The FSLN is a mass-based, ideological party with an elaborate bureaucratic structure. During the revolution it had large ancillary organizations among women, youth, communities, labor, and peasants. Since the FSLN's 1990 electoral defeat it has effectively lost most such groups. Long dominated by its original revolutionary directorate, the FLSN added new members to this directoral body in the early 1990s. Despite reforms, various moderates, led by the former vice president Sergio Ramírez Mercado, defected to form the MRS, which failed to woo many votes away from the FSLN in 1996. Out of power the FSLN not only lost midlevel leadership to the MRS and to disenchantment but also developed funding problems. Sandinista hard-liners won greater control of the party with the 2001 election, solidifying Daniel Ortega as the undisputed FSLN *caudillo*.

Except for the Liberals and Conservatives, other parties tend to be small and formed around an ideology (Socialists, Social Christians, Independent Liberals), interest group, or personality. From this amalgam, two big anti-Sandinista coalitions have arisen to dominate postrevolutionary politics. In 1990 UNO rallied behind the unifying personality of Violeta Chamorro, a Conservative by background but nominally and recently a member of the new Social Democratic Party. Chamorro headed an extended clan that ran all of Nicaragua's main newspapers: the FSLN's *Barricada*, pro-FSLN *El Nuevo Diario*, and the opposition *La Prensa*. In 1996 Arnoldo Alemán pulled several Liberal factions, some unions, and some Conservatives into the AL.

The PLC under Alemán appeared likely to be dominated by the ex-president and a coalition of elites from rural areas and the agro-export sector. The investigation of Alemán in 2001, however, split the party, with a more progressive elite sector supporting president Bolaños while the many of the former president's supporters remained loyal to Alemán. The future of the PLC and the Liberal Alliance remains questionable with this schism ongoing. In 2001 the Conservatives virtually disappeared as an electoral alternative in Nicaragua, fully supplanted as the second party by the FSLN, and their legal future lay imperiled by their tiny vote share and their holding but a single Assembly seat.

CAMPAIGNING

Before 1979 campaigns were ritualistic; the regime so manipulated results that it was unaffected by campaigns.

When the opposition campaigned effectively, the National Guard usually disrupted the activity. Since the 1980s, with outcomes more in doubt, campaigning by the FSLN and its major opponents has become more open, civil, organized, and modern.

Nicaragua's 1984, 1990, 1996, and 2001 elections were among the most highly and systematically monitored votes ever conducted anywhere. In 1984 the revolutionary government invited hundreds of journalists, scholars, and foreign governmental representatives as election observers in hopes of improving the regime's legitimacy. Registered, legally participating parties campaigned without problems, but progovernment crowds disrupted events of the Democratic Coordinating Committee, an anti-Sandinista, U.S.-backed coalition that did not contest but sought to disrupt the election. Outside observers characterized the election as flawed by the weakness of the FSLN's opponents and by U.S. efforts to disrupt the vote but fair in terms of the opposition's freedom to campaign and media access.

In 1990, with even more external observation, the FSLN confronted a stronger, better-financed, and more unified opponent, UNO. Campaigning was open and intense. External observer missions of the United Nations, Organization of American States, and Carter Center facilitated the campaign and mediated disputes. Parties had access to subsidized mass media, and both the FSLN and UNO received considerable external funding and technical advice. Both UNO and the Sandinistas used public-opinion polling and sophisticated advertising. External observers helped cool the acrimonious environment. The opposition's win bore witness to the fairness of the 1990 campaign and election.

In 1996 and 2001 a reduced external observer contingent took part, but several thousand domestic observers from nongovernmental organizations and tens of thousands of party poll watchers scrutinized the processes. Compared with 1984 and 1990, 1996 and 2001 were less tense (the war having ended and partisan acrimony marginally diminished). Larger parties and the press polled extensively. The FSLN and the AL smeared each other enthusiastically by referring to ugly aspects of prior regimes, but otherwise interparty relations were generally civil.

Three other forces have played significant roles in recent Nicaraguan election campaigns—the Catholic Church, foreign political parties, and foreign governments. The church has often expressed its distaste for the Sandinistas. For example, during the final days of the 1996 campaign Cardinal Miguel Obando y Bravo,

a harsh critic of the FSLN both during and after the revolution, held a televised mass that encouraged citizens to vote against the FSLN.

Foreign political parties have supported ideologically similar Nicaraguan parties with funding and technical assistance during recent campaigns.

Foreign governments have played diverse roles. Spain and the Nordic countries have provided technical assistance to the Supreme Electoral Council to facilitate the conduct of the election. U.S. intervention has varied according to whether the FSLN held power and the prospects of the Sandinistas' opponents. In 1984 the United States denounced the CSE and tried to disrupt the election. In 1990 the United States criticized both the CSE and the campaign as unfair while heavily backing UNO. In 1996 the United States provided extensive technical assistance to the CSE, a new role. The U.S. embassy in Managua proclaimed formal neutrality in 1996 and 2001, but the State Department in Washington made clear it hoped the FSLN would lose.

INDEPENDENT VOTERS

Identifying independent voters in Nicaragua is difficult given the instability of voting patterns since 1984. The FSLN's share of the vote fell from 67 percent in 1984 to 38 percent in 1996 but recovered to 42 percent in 2001. The party system and allegiances are fragmented and personalistic, somewhat masking patterns of support for parties other than the FSLN. A large shift in party support occurred from 1990 to 1996 and again from 1996 to 2001, and UNO and AL consisted of different party coalitions.

In addition to the numerous loyal FSLN identifiers there are contingents (of size unknown) of strong identifiers with other parties—especially Liberals and small nuclei of Conservatives, Independent Liberals, Social Christians, and Socialists. Outside these core identifiers, however, a substantial but indeterminate portion of Nicaraguans appeared to vote in 1990, 1996, and 2001 on the basis of candidate personality, ideology, or policy preference. Opinion polling so far offers scant insight into the phenomenon because of the recent great shifts in party support. Ultimately, shifting party identification and voting per se constitute voter independence.

LIBERAL PARTIES

A cluster of parties arising from the Liberal clans, led by the PLC under the leadership of Arnoldo Alemán, successfully challenged all others as the Sandinistas' most effective opponent in the late 1990s. This success augured the Liberals' return to near-hegemonic power, but the corruption scandal and the ex-president's imprisonment split the party and clouded its future.

The Neo-Liberal Party (Partido Neo-Liberal; PALI) formed in 1989, as did the Liberal Party of National Unity (Partido Liberal de Unidad Nacional; PLIUN). A handful of Liberals took up the Liberal Nationalist (PLN) label again in 1994. All three joined the Liberal Alliance in 1996; their prospects as independent parties appear dim. The Liberal Salvation Movement (Movimiento de Salvación Liberal; MSL) and the Liberal Nationalists won certification to take part in the 2004 municipal elections.

CONSERVATIVE PARTIES

Another cluster of parties arose from the Conservative clans. The Conservative Party of Nicaragua (Partido Conservador de Nicaragua) dominated Nicaraguan politics for most of the nineteenth century but was displaced by the Liberals in 1890. U.S. military intervention (1909–28) put in power Conservatives willing to guarantee the U.S. canal monopoly in Panama, but Conservatives lost ascendancy in the 1930s in a U.S.-brokered pact. Afterward Conservatives took two approaches to the Somoza Liberals: earnest opposition and co-opted collaboration. While the latter discredited the movement, the principled opposition of Conservatives like Fernando Agüero Rocha and martyred *La Prensa* publisher Pedro Joaquín Chamorro earned them repression and exile. Their example inspired many to oppose the dictatorship, and numerous Sandinista leaders came from Conservative backgrounds. Many Conservatives have tended toward class reconciliation and support government social welfare responsibilities. The Conservatives fragmented in the late 1970s and 1980s over questions of social welfare, the revolution, whether to seek exile, and personalities. Conservative parties fared disastrously in the national elections of 2001, falling below the 3 percent vote threshold for survival and thus losing certification to compete in elections for four years. By the end of the twentieth century the failing Conservative movement was supplanted in the Nicaraguan tradition of two dominant parties, replaced as the second strongest party by the FSLN. The Conservative movement regrouped under the banner of the Conservative Party in 2000 but faced daunting prospects for survival as a national political force as the twenty-first century began.

Major Political Parties

SANDINISTA NATIONAL LIBERATION FRONT

(Frente Sandinista de Liberación Nacional; FSLN)

Carlos Fonseca Amador founded the FSLN in 1961 to pursue a revolutionary guerrilla struggle against the Somoza regime. A Marxist-Leninist, he had abandoned the Nicaraguan Socialist Party because it rejected armed struggle. Fonseca's cofounders were Tomás Borge Martínez, a former Independent Liberal activist, and Silvio Mayorga—both also Marxists. All three were from Matagalpa (a region once loyal to Sandino), had been student activists at the National University, and had suffered imprisonment for their antiregime efforts.

Until the mid-1970s the Sandinistas operated as a rural guerrilla force and grew very slowly. Limited support from Cuba and urban and university groups developed despite major military reversals in 1963 and 1967. In the mid-1970s growing public opposition to the Somoza regime evoked escalating repression, which drove disaffected elites, repressed civil society, and many ordinary citizens into the arms of the FSLN, the only armed challenger of the regime. The FSLN divided into three "tendencies" over tactics in the mid-1970s, a schism resolved by the spontaneous popular uprisings of 1978. The FSLN grew rapidly in late 1978 and 1979, drawing civil society into an anti-Somoza coalition and recruiting as many as 5,000 troops. After its final offensive defeated the National Guard, the FSLN assumed leadership of the rebel coalition that took power on July 19, 1979. Within months the Sandinistas consolidated control of the revolutionary government.

ORGANIZATION

The FSLN developed a complex nationwide structure supported by ancillary organizations of students, women, peasants, workers, and neighborhood organizations. Until the 1990s a nine-member National Directorate (Dirección Nacional; DN) of top military commanders from the insurrection headed the party. DN members served on the junta through 1984 and held key cabinet and military portfolios until 1990. Throughout the revolutionary era the armed forces and police were fused with the FSLN. FSLN cadres penetrated the government bureaucracy.

By the late 1980s hard times had eroded or alienated the FSLN's ancillary organizations. The electoral defeat of 1990 dealt the party several further blows. The FSLN lost control of the police. The military (albeit retaining Sandinista officers) was dramatically downsized and its party links severed. The Chamorro administration reversed revolutionary policies. Feeling its way as an opposition party in the National Assembly, the FSLN struggled to salvage its policy legacy. The party debated its political errors and sought a strategy for the long term. Party congresses in 1991 and 1994 sought to regroup and revise its charter. The 1991 congress reorganized the party, but the DN blocked important democratization initiatives. The party congress became the FSLN's highest authority. An elected (by secret ballot among members) party assembly would govern between congresses. A new party secretary-generalship was established, to which the congress elected the old guard's Daniel Ortega.

Major fissures appeared in the FSLN's leadership, in part because harder-line, old-guard leaders resisted certain intellectuals' reform proposals. Social democratic "renovationists" led by the former vice president Sergio Ramírez Mercado pushed for further reforms. The Sandinista bench in the National Assembly split, most of the deputies aligning with the renovationists. Rebuffed and punished by the 1994 congress, key reformers bolted the party and established the splinter Sandinista Renovation Movement. However, the "democratic left" old guard remained united behind Ortega. The 1994 congress enacted deeper reforms: new members on the DN (including the first women), the election of party leaders, primary elections for party nominees for public office, and assigning women 30 percent of legislative slates. Despite such efforts Ortega's leadership of the party became more powerfully entrenched in the late 1990s and remained so in the early 2000s. Party rank and file rallied around him in 1998 when his stepdaughter publicly accused him of sexually molesting her when she was an adolescent.

POLICY

Although Marxist-Leninist, the FSLN experimented widely and pragmatically with its goals and policies. Early objectives included eliminating the Somoza dictatorship, improving popular living standards and participation in decision making, progressive socialization of the economy, and reducing U.S. influence over Nicaragua. Once in power the FSLN openly pursued many of these policies. It greatly expanded government participation in the economy, redistributed agricultural land and firms owned by the Somozas and their allies to cooperatives of peasants and workers, and established a panoply of new health, education, and welfare services.

The FSLN's pragmatism stood out in several arenas: In concession to its geopolitical context and the dominant U.S. regional role the revolutionary regime retained a private sector, permitted opposition parties and independent media and civil society, held elections, and remained formally unaligned with the Soviet bloc.

Economic and geopolitical strains forced the FSLN to improvise and change just to salvage the revolution during the mid- and late 1980s. Capital flight, a U.S. economic embargo, revolutionary policy blunders, and the contra war demolished the economy. To finance military mobilization and the war, the government curtailed public services. Political and civil liberties decreased when the contra war intensified, and increased around elections.

The 1990 electoral defeat and the demise of Soviet-bloc economic support forced further FSLN policy changes. The outgoing FSLN-dominated National Assembly in 1990 approved a widespread distribution of government and confiscated private property to party leaders and members. This shameful "piñata," as it came to be called, embarrassed the party and exacerbated the byzantine complexity of property ownership disputes generated by the revolution. After 1990 the FSLN generally embraced the role of loyal opposition but never definitively renounced recourse to violence. In effect the party behaved moderately, oscillating between two tactics: (1) using its remaining mobilizational capacity to challenge rollbacks of revolutionary policies, and (2) using its National Assembly votes to cooperate with the legislative majority in exchange for concessions. In 1999 this deal-making orientation took the form of the pact between President Alemán and Daniel Ortega, which included legal and constitutional reforms that enhanced both *caudillos* within their parties, strengthened both of their parties vis-à-vis smaller ones, reduced the national comptroller's independent oversight over the president, and packed the Supreme Court with new justices. The pact indicated to many observers that the FSLN had abandoned its revolutionary idealism for personalistic ambition and jockeying for narrowly defined electoral advantage.

MEMBERSHIP AND CONSTITUENCY

The FSLN drew its first members from the insurgent forces of the 1960s and 1970s. During the revolution it brought in tens of thousands of new members by recruiting from support groups and the armed forces. After losing power the FSLN became an even more broadly based membership organization, claiming 350,000 members in 1996 despite the defection of the MRS. Current FSLN support comes disproportionately from León, Estelí, and Managua and from the middle class.

LEADERSHIP

Major Sandinista leaders come primarily from middle-class backgrounds, many recruited out of Liberal and Conservative families into the armed struggle through student opposition to the Somozas or as victims of repression. National Directorate membership remained unchanged until 1991, consisting exclusively of the nine men on the body in 1979. New members have been added and some removed since 1991. Among the key DN members since 1979 have been:

- **Tomás Borge Martínez**, born in 1930 of middle-class parents affiliated with the Independent Liberals. He studied law and owned a bookstore before cofounding the FSLN in 1961. The only surviving FSLN founder, he was imprisoned twice and tortured during the Somoza regime, and the National Guard also killed his wife. From 1979 through 1990 Borge served as minister of interior.
- **Daniel Ortega Saavedra** was born in 1945 in Chontales to a middle-class family and quit the university for the FLSN. He spent several years in guerrilla combat and several more in prison for subversion. He represented the DN on the revolutionary junta from 1979 through 1984 and in 1984 was elected president of Nicaragua. Although defeated in his 1990, 1996, and 2001 reelection bids, he became party secretary-general in 1991. Long regarded as a policy pragmatist, in defense of a harder party line he fended off the reformist challenge of 1994–95. Supported by loyalist hard-liners, Ortega continued in the FSLN's top post following his 2001 electoral defeat.
- **Humberto Ortega Saavedra**, younger brother of Daniel, lost his right hand in combat. A student of politics and guerrilla tactics, he was the insurrection's main strategist. As commander in chief of the Sandinista Popular Army (later the Nicaraguan Army) from 1979 until his retirement from that post in 1995, Humberto Ortega was the architect of Nicaragua's successful military strategy during the contra war. He resigned from the DN in 1990 to retain his military command. In 1996 he resigned his command of the armed forces.
- **Jaime Wheelock Román**, born in 1946 in Managua to an upper-class family, is an intellectual, theorist, and author of two books on Nicaraguan political economy. Although without combat experience, he served as minister of agrarian reform and agriculture (1979–90).

The FSLN's 1990 and subsequent election defeats, internecine organizational and leadership debates, and the increasing dominance of Daniel Ortega and his allies raised problems for the party. Many loyal and experienced middle-level FSLN leaders and intellectuals quit over the party's increasing personalism and lack of ideological change. While the party retained a substantial base of loyal followers and voters, its pool of talented middle-level leaders (many veterans of the insurrection and years in power) had diminished sharply by the late 1990s.

PROSPECTS

Popular early on, the FSLN easily won its first election, but a deteriorated economy, the contra war, repression, and conflict with the United States eventually alienated many supporters. The FSLN remains strong, but its prospects for recapturing power—even with its large base—appear limited for several reasons: Its depleted leadership ranks and its persistent demonization by other actors for its policy failures, Marxism, repression, Daniel Ortega's domination of the party, and the "piñata" undermine the Sandinistas' image. The end of the cold war and loss of socialist-bloc support limit resources, especially given the old guard's refusal to fully renounce violent methods. Perhaps most important, most other parties and many voters tend to form a working anti-Sandinista coalition for elections.

LIBERAL CONSTITUTIONALIST PARTY

(Partido Liberal Constitucionalista; PLC)

The PLC first surfaced within the Somocista PLN in the late 1960s as a mildly reformist faction known as the Liberal Constitutionalist Movement (MLC). The movement distanced itself from Somoza and reconstituted itself as a party. The PLC stayed for the civic struggle within Nicaragua during the revolution and took part in government. Its economic policies follow rightist classical liberalism (favoring a small state, private property, and unfettered markets). With U.S. support and progressively antagonistic toward the FSLN and revolutionary economic policies, the PLC joined the Democratic Coordinator (Coordinadora Democrática; CD) that boycotted the 1984 election.

In 1990 the PLC joined UNO, and attorney Arnoldo Alemán Lacayo won the mayorship of Managua. Alemán adopted a mixture of urban populism and fierce anti-Sandinism. He leveraged the Managua municipality's patronage power, development projects, his confrontational style, and intense criticism of President Chamorro's cooperation with the FSLN to become a leading presidential contender for 1996. Having partly relegitimized Liberalism, Alemán and the PLC attracted support from the wealthy Liberal exile community in the United States. During the early 1990s the party organized nationwide, eventually claiming 150,000 members. The PLC forged the Liberal Alliance in 1995 with two other small Liberal splinter parties, some former PLN elements, a PLI splinter, some ex-contras, and anti-Sandinista unions. Also pulled into the AL was a powerful private-sector organization known as the Superior Council of Private Enterprise (COSEP), whose former president Enrique Bolaños became the AL's vice presidential candidate. The AL campaigned for neoliberal economic policies similar to Chamorro's, judicial reform, and a reopening of the contentious property conflicts stemming from the revolution.

The AL held together for the 2001 election, with Bolaños winning the presidency. He subsequently had the government bring charges against Alemán for fraud and money laundering, and the latter was convicted and sent to jail. Some PLC deputies supported the efforts of Bolaños to reduce the incarcerated former president Alemán's power within the party, but many others did not. The resulting conflict roiled the party in its preparation for the 2006 national election.

INDEPENDENT LIBERAL PARTY

(Partido Liberal Independiente; PLI)

A liberal splinter established in 1944, the PLI struggled against the Somozas and allied with the FLSN in the insurrection and the revolutionary government until 1984. Led since the late 1970s by Virgilio Godoy Reyes, a former labor minister (1979–84), the PLI entered formal opposition to the Sandinistas when it contested the 1984 election.

The PLI joined UNO in 1990, winning Godoy the vice presidency, but the party quickly broke with UNO and the Chamorro government and thereafter decried the UNO-FSLN cooperation of the mid-1990s. Originally social democratic in ideology, the PLI's image in later revolutionary years revolved around an intense anti-Sandinism. The PLI eschewed the AL in 1996 and finished catastrophically with no seats in the National Assembly. By 2004 the PLI had recovered sufficiently to win certification to contest the 2004 municipal elections.

CONSERVATIVE PARTY OF NICARAGUA

(Partido Conservador de Nicaragua; PCN)

This party formed in 1992 when the Democratic Conservative Party, National Conservative Party, and Social Conservative Party merged. It reclaimed the traditional Conservative Party name. Fernando Agüero Rocha became its leader. Demonstrating some residual Conservative voter loyalty despite years of fragmentation, the PCN won three seats in the National Assembly in 1996. The PCN elected only one Assembly deputy in 2001, failed to meet the 3 percent of the vote required for party survival, and lost its legal standing.

CONSERVATIVE PARTY

(Partido Conservador; PC)

A new Conservative Party, reborn from the remnants of the old Conservative parties, was established and received Supreme Electoral Council certification to compete in the municipal election of 2000. The PC won 13 percent of the 2000 municipal vote and captured five mayoralties in southern and central Nicaragua. The PC won certification to contest the 2004 municipal elections.

Minor Political Parties

CHRISTIAN WAY

(Camino Cristiano; CC)

This new party arose from the Assemblies of God congregations of Nicaragua in the 1996 election. Its presidential candidate, Guillermo Osorno, is an Assembly of God pastor. He won 4 percent of the 1996 presidential vote. Osorno and three other CC deputies served in the 1996–2001 National Assembly. The CC won 4 percent of the 2000 municipal elections. It captured no mayorships but retained its legal standing to compete in the 2004 municipal elections.

NATIONAL PROJECT

(Proyecto Nacional; PN)

Founded around 1995 by Antonio Lacayo, son-in-law and minister of the presidency to President Violeta Chamorro, the centrist PN originally appeared to be a vehicle for Lacayo's presidential candidacy. Other parties reformed the constitution with antinepotism rules that blocked his bid in 1996. The PN won two seats in the National Assembly. Despite having two Assembly seats, the PN as a national party effectively vanished with the blocked presidential aspirations of Antonio Lacayo and did not survive the party recertification process following the PLC-FSLN pact of 1999.

NICARAGUAN RESISTANCE PARTY

(Partido de Resistencia Nicaragüense; PRN)

Consisting of elements from the counterrevolutionary groups who fought the Sandinista revolution, the PRN has retained sufficient support in the Atlantic coast region and central Nicaragua to survive the tough party thresholds imposed after 1999. The PRN contested the Atlantic autonomous region election of 2002 and qualified for the 2004 municipal election.

SOCIAL CHRISTIAN PARTIES

The Social Christian Party (Partido Social Cristiano Nicaragüense; PSCN) was founded in 1957, led the 1960s electoral movement against the Somoza dynasty, and introduced Christian democratic politics to Nicaragua. It established Christian labor unions and participated actively in university student politics in the 1960s. The more left-leaning Popular Social Christian Party (Partido Popular Social Cristiano; PPSC) broke away from the PSCN during the 1970s. During the revolution the PPSC supported the FSLN early on but contested the presidency in 1984 and won six seats in the National Assembly. Meanwhile the more conservative PSCN increasingly identified with the opposition. The PPSC joined UNO in 1990, but the PSCN ran separately and won only one Assembly seat. By 1990 both the PPSC and PSCN had faded badly. Neither the PPSC and PSCN survived the party survival thresholds imposed after 1999.

ETHNIC AND REGIONAL PARTIES

Several small parties obtained certification to contest the elections of the municipalities and regional governments of the Atlantic autonomous regions in 2002 (autonomous regions) and in the 2000 and 2004 municipal elections. These include the Multiethnic Indigenous Party (Partido Indígena Multiétnico; PIM), the United Coastal Movement Party (Partido Movimiento de Unidad Costeño; PAMUC) and the ethnically Miskito YATAMA Party (Partido Yapti Tasba Masraka Nanih Aslatakanka).

MISCELLANEOUS ALLIANCES

The electoral law allows alliances among parties to contest elections jointly if the required threshold of signatures can be reached. Two new electoral alliances secured the required number of signatures to qualify for participation in the 2004 municipal elections: the Alliance for the Republic (Alianza para la República) and the Christian Alternative (Alternativa Cristiana).

Other Political Forces

MILITARY

The National Guard (Guardia Nacional; GN) was the Somozas' main instrument of political control. The FSLN's guerrilla army destroyed the Guard in 1979, though GN remnants formed the early nucleus of the contras. FSLN forces were reorganized into a new Sandinista Popular Army (Ejército Popular Sandinista; EPS), air force, and militia and the Sandinista Police (Policía Sandinista). Top FLSN leaders commanded these forces, and officers were FSLN cadre.

After the cease-fire with the contras in 1989, the 1990 election defeat of the FLSN, and the negotiated end of the contra war, the military underwent drastic changes. President Chamorro retained General Humberto Ortega as defense minister until 1995 to allay Sandinista fears of persecution of the party, although he relinquished his DN post. Troop strength was slashed by 80 percent, the draft abolished, and militias disbanded. Party identification of the police and military with the FSLN was dropped, after which the army was renamed the Army of Nicaragua (Ejército de Nicaragua), and the police became the National Police (Policía Nacional). Critics feared military disloyalty to the regime after 1990, but both army and police have enforced order against labor and popular protesters and against re-armed former contra and Sandinista/ EPS combatants alike.

ORGANIZED LABOR

Freed from Somocista repression, the labor movement expanded greatly to encompass 250,000 workers by 1990. Before 1979 myriad unions and labor confederations existed: the General Workers Confederation (Confederación General de Trabajadores; CGT), the Independent General Workers Confederation (Confederación General de Trabajadores-Independiente; CGTI), the Social Christian Nicaraguan Workers

Confederation (Confederación de Trabajadores de Nicaragua; CTN), and the AFL-CIO-linked Council for Union Action and Unity (Consejo de Acción y Unidad Sindical; CAUS). There were various associations of public employees. During the revolution independent labor lost ground to the rapidly growing FSLN-linked Sandinista Workers Confederation (Central Sandinista de Trabajadores; CST).

During the late 1980s the CST restrained workers in support of the FSLN government's harsh austerity programs, but this opened FSLN-CST fissures. After 1990 the FLSN lost much of its influence over the CST, which struck frequently despite party wishes and formed new labor alliances such as the National Workers Front (Frente Nacional de Trabajadores; FNT). These strikes protested Chamorro and Alemán administration reversals of revolutionary policy gains, public-sector layoffs, and public-sector privatization. Labor confrontation won some concessions (shares for workers in privatized firms), but despite labor efforts public payrolls shrank and wages eroded.

The Association of Rural Workers (Asociación de Trabajadores del Campo; ATC), an FSLN-linked peasant union, arose in the 1970s. The union helped shape agrarian policy in the 1980s, winning land for many peasants and giving rise to the small-landowners group UNAG (see below). Government austerity programs eventually undermined ATC loyalty to the FSLN, and the ATC in the 1990s struggled to defend peasants' shares and rights during agrarian reprivatization.

As of the early 2000s the FSLN-linked umbrella organization the National Workers Front (Frente Nacional de Trabajadores; FNT) included the farm workers of the ATC, health workers, professionals, teachers, clerical workers, journalists, the farm owners of UNAG, and the CST. The non-Sandinista labor umbrella organization the Permanent Congress of Workers (Congreso Permanente de Trabajadores; CPT) included the CTN-A (Autonomous CTN), the Confederation of Labor Unification (Confederación de Unificación Sindical; CUS), the CGT-I, and CAUS. The CTN remained independent from both confederations.

BUSINESS GROUPS

Private-sector interests find expression through several national chambers (e.g., commerce, industry) and through the Superior Council of Private Enterprise (Consejo Superior de la Empresa Privada; COSEP). COSEP and other business groups eventually opposed the Somozas in the late 1970s, then held some influence in the early revolutionary government (especially cabinet positions). Most capitalists and such groups as COSEP soon broke with the revolution. Many joined the CD opposition coalition in 1984. By 1990 these business groups were deeply committed to UNO but found themselves frustrated with the Chamorro administration's economic policies, especially the failure to resolve property claims in favor of former owners. Business interests hoped for better from the AL in 1996 because former COSEP leader Enrique Bolaños was Alemán's vice president.

One private-sector group that sprang from the revolution was the National Farmers and Cattleman's Association (Unión Nacional de Agricultores y Ganaderos; UNAG). The Sandinistas' ATC began as a rural labor union but gradually came to include small property holders, especially those created by agrarian reform. The interests of landless peasants and smallholders diverged enough that UNAG separated from ATC. UNAG became an important voice for rural smallholders and increasingly independent of the FSLN. After 1990 UNAG worked to assist and to reconcile former Sandinista and contra combatants who received land in the demobilization.

ATLANTIC COASTAL ZONE AND ETHNIC MINORITIES

Once isolated in the Atlantic coastal zone, a heterogenous population of indigenous peoples (Miskito, Sumu, Rama) and English-speaking blacks (together 10 percent of Nicaragua's population) was thrust into national politics by the revolution. When the Sandinista regime attempted to integrate them into the revolution and to isolate the indigenous from the contras operating from nearby Honduras, many Miskitos joined the counterrevolutionaries.

After several years of war the government in 1987 passed laws and constitutional provisions that conceded limited autonomy to the peoples of the region. This dampened Miskito resistance, and the area's refugees began to return. Autonomy established two 45-member elected regional councils: the Northern Atlantic Autonomous Region (Región Autónoma del Atlántico Norte; RAAN) and the Southern Atlantic Autonomous Region (Región Autónoma del Atlántico Sur; RAAS). YATAMA, a Miskito opposition group originating among contra elements, has contested RAAN and RAAS elections with the FSLN, UNO, and the Liberals. Strong at first, in successive elections YATAMA has lost ground to national parties and coalitions and other multiethnic alliances.

RELIGIOUS GROUPS

The Roman Catholic hierarchy, influenced by social Christian doctrines and activist clergy, opposed the Somoza regime during the 1970s. Many Catholics and some clergy joined or assisted the revolutionary forces and after the insurrection collaborated with the revolution. The hierarchy, however, soon swung right and opposed the FSLN-led regime. Headed by Archbishop (later Cardinal) Miguel Obando y Bravo and increasingly supported by the Vatican, the Nicaraguan church often collaborated with the revolution's domestic and armed foreign opponents. Despite a pretense of political neutrality, the church rather openly sided with UNO in the 1990 election and with the Liberal Alliance in 1996 and 2001. Since 1990 the church has supported conservative shifts in national social, family, and education policy. In 2004 Archbishop Obando seemingly sided with the Alemán wing of the PLC when he advocated releasing ex-president Alemán from prison early for medical reasons.

Much of the small Protestant community, growing quickly since the 1980s, supported the Sandinista insurrection and the revolution. Over time Protestant support for the revolution became divided. The Assembly of God–based Christian Way Party, a newcomer to national politics, won four seats in the National Assembly in 1996 but no seats in 2001.

National Prospects

With its 1996 election Nicaragua took another step beyond its divisive, economically devastating revolution and civil wars. The Liberal government enjoyed prospects for good U.S. relations and a chance to resolve outstanding property claims. These could have stimulated economic recovery by attracting back flight capital and by encouraging foreign investment and assistance. The Alemán administration, marred by serious corruption, the PLC pact with the FSLN to suppress party pluralism, and considerable repression of critical civil society organizations, failed to live up to its potential. Economic recovery lagged. In late 1998 Hurricane Mitch devastated parts of Nicaragua, destroying lives, homes, jobs, roads, and crops. Despite extensive international relief efforts the impact of the hurricane aggravated economic problems.

After the election of Enrique Bolaños in 2001 and the arrest and prosecution of the former president, divisions within the PLC widened between critics and supporters of Alemán. During the Bolaños adminis-

tration economic development and growth improved modestly, but prospects for the second-poorest economy of the hemisphere remained clouded as unemployment exceeded 20 percent and underemployment was much higher, several banks failed, and continuing fiscal deficits blocked international debt relief efforts.

Despite its reservations about the 1996 election and despite another presidential defeat in 2001, the FSLN remained in its role of loyal opposition. The prospects for gradual consolidation of Nicaraguan democracy appeared to grow with the FSLN's willingness to continue in this mode. The polity remained polarized, with the FSLN holding the loyalty of around 40 percent of the electorate and the PLC somewhat more. The numerous small parties and alliances, their survival more difficult after the PLC-FLSN pact of 1999, scrambled for other votes but remained generally anti-Sandinista in general elections. Prospects for the FSLN to win a national election seem limited while its revolutionary-era old guard, headed by Daniel Ortega, leads the party.

Further Reading

Arnove, Robert F. *Education as Contested Terrain: Nicaragua, 1979-1993.* Boulder, Colo.: Westview Press, 1994.

Booth, John A. *The End and the Beginning: The Nicaraguan Revolution.* Boulder, Colo.: Westview Press, 1985.

Booth, John A., and Patricia Bayer Richard. "The Nicaraguan Elections of October 1996." *Electoral Studies* 16 (September 1997): 386–393.

Booth, John A., and Thomas W. Walker. *Understanding Central America.* Boulder, Colo.: Westview Press, 1999.

Close, David, and Kalowatie Deonandan, eds. *Undoing Democracy: The Politics of Electoral Caudillismo.* Lanham, Md.: Lexington, 2004.

Everingham, Mark. *Revolution and the Multiclass Coalition in Nicaragua.* Pittsburgh: University of Pittsburgh Press, 1996.

Jones, Adam. *Beyond the Barricades: Nicaragua and the Struggle for the Sandinista Press, 1979-1998.* Athens: Ohio University Press, 2002.

Latin American Studies Association. *Electoral Democracy under International Pressure.* Pittsburgh, March 15, 1990.

———. *The Electoral Process in Nicaragua: Domestic and International Influences.* Austin, Tex., November 19, 1984.

Merrill, Tim L., ed. *Nicaragua: A Country Study.* Washington, D.C: Federal Research Division, Library of Congress, 1994.

Prevost, Gary, and Harry E. Vanden, eds. *The Undermining of the Sandinista Revolution.* New York: St. Martin's Press, 1997.

Spalding, Rose J. *Capitalists and Revolution in Nicaragua: Opposition and Accommodation, 1979-1993.* Chapel Hill: University of North Carolina Press, 1994.

Walker, Thomas W. *Nicaragua: The Land of Sandino.* Boulder, Colo.: Westview Press, 1991.

Walker, Thomas W., ed. *Nicaragua in Revolution.* New York: Praeger, 1981.

———. *Nicaragua: The First Five Years.* New York: Praeger, 1985.

———. *Nicaragua without Illusions: Regime Transition and Structural Adjustment in the 1990s.* Wilmington, Del.: Scholarly Resources, 1997.

REPUBLIC OF NIGER
(République du Niger)

By Christopher J. Lee, Ph.D.

Previously a part of French West Africa, Niger achieved independence on August 3, 1960. It is the largest country in West Africa, covering an area of approximately 1,267,000 square kilometers. Proportionately, its population is relatively small at 11.6 million (2005 est.), primarily due to arid conditions. Two-thirds of Niger's territory is Saharan desert. Hausas form the largest demographic group at 56 percent, with the Djerma Songhai at 22 percent, Peuhls at 10 percent, and Tuaregs at 8 percent. Islam is practiced by an estimated 80 percent of the population. Roughly 0.5 percent practice Christianity and the rest traditional beliefs. Niger's capital is Niamey.

Since independence executive power has experienced significant fluctuations. Hamani Diori, leader of the Niger Progressive Party (PPN), was the first to have executive authority and followed a policy of maintaining close links with France. In April 1974 Diori was overthrown by a military coup on the basis of corruption charges. A Supreme Military Council (Conseil Militaire Supreme; CMS) was set up, headed by Lieutenant Colonel Seyni Kountché. Political parties were outlawed.

Nevertheless, political activism existed, and tensions within the CMS existed as well. In 1981 Kountché began to increase civilian representation in the CMS. In January 1984 a commission was established to write a "national charter." A draft was completed in 1986 and approved by a national referendum in June 1987 by 99.6 percent of the voters. This charter provided for nonelected, consultative bodies at local and national levels. Kountché died in November 1987.

The military chief of staff, Colonel Ali Saïbou, succeeded Kountché as head of state. A national referendum in 1989 approved a constitutional motion to support continued military involvement in the government. The new government was to be referred to as the Second Republic. In December 1989 Saïbou was elected to a seven-year term as president. The position of prime minister was abolished. Economic unrest in 1990 prompted an announcement of further political reform along the lines of a more pluralist system.

In July 1991 a national conference was convened to address Niger's political problems. The constitution was suspended and the government dissolved. Saïbou remained in office for an interim period, though his position was largely ceremonial. Amadou Cheiffou was appointed prime minister in October. A 15-member interim legislature was convened as well. In December 1992 a new constitution was approved by a national referendum. A presidential election followed, consisting of two rounds. In March 1993 Mahamane Ousmane, leader of the Democratic and Social Convention-Rahama (CDS-Rahama), won the election with 55.4 percent of the vote (approximately 35 percent of the total electorate voted).

Ousmane's succession brought the Third Republic. Further labor unrest developed during his administration. Moreover, a political challenge came from the National Movement for a Society of Development Nassara (MNSD-Nassara). A lack of confidence also developed within the National Assembly, and Ousmane eventually dissolved this body in October 1994. This action provoked further criticism and unrest. New elections in January 1995 resulted in a MNSD-Nassara majority. Ousmane initially rejected the MNSD-Nassara's choice for prime minister, Hama Amadou, but later relented. In July 1995 tensions between the president and prime minister reached a new peak with foreign mediation from Mali, Benin, and Togo. This tension was only temporarily resolved. Labor unrest and student protest further exacerbated political conditions.

A military coup ended the Third Republic on January 27, 1996. Led by Colonel Ibrahim Baré Maïnassara, the Council of National Health (CSN), consisting of 12 members, was formed. The constitution was suspended, and the National Assembly was dissolved. Political parties were banned as well. The CSN aimed to reform the government and to improve economic conditions. Boukary Adji was appointed the prime minister of a transitional government. A national forum for government reform was convened in April 1996. A plan was outlined with greater power being conferred on the president. Constitutional reforms were approved by a referendum held on May 12, 1996. A presidential election was held on July 7, 1996. Political rivalries among the five candidates instigated controversy during the election.

Maïnassara won with 52.2 percent of the vote. The Fourth Republic was ushered in on August 7, 1996. Legislative elections were held in November 1996 with opposition parties, despite having wide support, boycotting the elections. Maïnassara supporters gained control of 52 out of 83 seats. In December 1996 the CSN was dissolved and a new government established.

Since 1996 tensions between Maïnassara and opposition forces, collectively existing as the Front for the Restoration and Defense of Democracy (DRDD), have continued. Social protests by various unions have taken place, as well as an attempted coup in January 1998 and a military mutiny in February 1998. Maïnassara was assassinated in April 1999 by members of the presidential guard. Following a period of transition and constitutional change, Tandja of the MNSD-Nassara was elected.

The System of Government

Niger is a unitary republic maintaining a constitutional government within a multiparty political system.

EXECUTIVE

Executive authority is vested exclusively in the president as dictated by the constitution promulgated on 18 July 1999. National policy emanates from this authority. The prime minister is presidentially promoted and has the responsibility of implementing the president's agenda. Since December 1999 the president has been Mamadou Tandja. The prime minister is Hama Amadou.

ORGANIZATION OF NIGERIEN GOVERNMENT

President

National Assembly

Prime Minister

Cabinet

Departments

Arrondissements

Communes

High Court of Justice   Supreme Court   Court of State Security

Court of Appeals

Courts of First Insurance

LEGISLATURE

Legislative authority is vested in a National Assembly consisting of 113 members elected for five-year terms. Elections to this body are conducted on the basis of universal adult suffrage within a multiparty system.

JUDICIARY

The judicial system consists of several levels of courts. The Supreme Court provides a forum for matters of national importance. The High Court of Justice was created with the sole function of indicting political officials, including the president, for matters such as treason. The Court of State Security serves as a court for martial law. Below these courts is a national court of appeal, and below this, criminal courts, courts of first instance, and labor courts handle matters at the local level.

REGIONAL AND LOCAL GOVERNMENT

Niger is divided into seven departments, which are further divided into arrondissements and communes.

The Electoral System

Candidates for legislative and presidential elections are chosen by universal adult suffrage; the voting age is 18. In the presidential election held in 2004 Mamadou Tandja won a second and final term, easily defeating Mahamadou Issoufou. Several parties participated in the 2004 legislative elections, with the National Movement for a Developing Society–Victory (MNSD-Nassara) securing the most seats with 47.

The Party System

Niger has a history of instability regarding its party system. This history has been characterized primarily by tensions between military leaders and opposition parties rather than conflicts solely on the basis of expressed ideological differences. The party system remains in jeopardy to this day.

Beginning in 1959 Niger was a one-party state with the Niger Progressive Party (PPN). In 1974 legislation was enacted that further abolished alternate political groups. In August 1988 this ban on other political organizations was slightly lifted with Saïbou forming a new party, the National Movement for a Developing Society (MNSD; later it would become MNSD-Nassara). However, Saïbou was against establishing immediately a multiparty

system. In July 1991 a national conference attended by 1,200 delegates was convened to address Niger's political problems. The constitution was suspended.

In December 1992 a new constitution was approved by a national referendum, and in February 1993 elections for a new 83-member national assembly were held. The MNSD-Nassara, the previously ruling party, won the most seats at 29, but a coalition of other parties, the Alliance of Forces of Change (AFC), took a majority with 50 seats. The AFC consisted of six parties, though its main members were the Democratic and Social Convention–Rahama (CDS-Rahama), the Nigerien Party for Democracy and Social Progress–Tarayya (PNDS-Tarayya), and the Nigerien Alliance for Democracy and Social Progress–Zaman Lahiya (ANDPS–Zaman Lahiya).

Following the military coup of January 1996, political parties were suspended. After a new constitution was approved in May 1996, political parties were reinstated. Shortly after Maïnassara's election an opposition coalition formed consisting of eight parties, notably the MNSD-Nassara, CDS-Rahama, and the PNDS-Tarayya. This coalition was named the Front for the Restoration and Defense of Democracy (FRDD). In reaction a coalition in support of Maïnassara was formed, called the Front for Democracy and Progress. Since Maïnassara's assassination multiparty politics has reemerged, with the MNSD-Nassara accruing power once again.

Major Political Parties

NATIONAL MOVEMENT FOR A DEVELOPING SOCIETY–VICTORY

(Mouvement National de la Societé de Développement–Nassara; MNSD-Nassara)

This party has dominated the political scene since the mid-1990s. In the 2004 elections its presidential candidate, Mamadou Tandja, easily won a second term. In the legislative elections of 2004 the party won 47 of 113 seats in the National Assembly.

NIGERIEN PARTY FOR DEMOCRACY AND SOCIALISM

(Parti Nigerien pour la Democratie et le Socialisme; PNDS)

In the 2004 elections this party won 17 legislative seats, second only to the MNSD-Nassara's 47. It led an electoral coalition of several other parties. It's presidential candidate, Mahamadou Issoufou, finished second in the voting behind Tandja.

DEMOCRATIC AND SOCIAL CONVENTION

(Convention démocratique et sociale-Rahama; CDS)

This party won 22 legislative seats in the 2004 elections. It's presidential candidate, Mahamane Ousmane, came in third in the first round of presidential voting and was thus ineligible to compete in the second round.

Minor Political Parties

Other parties that won seats in the 2004 elections include the Niger Progressive Party–African Democratic Rally (PPN-RDA); the Social Democratic Rally-Gaskiya; the Rally for Democracy and Progress; the Nigerien Alliance for Democracy and Progress; and the Niger Social-Democratic Party.

Other Political Forces

THE TUAREGS

In the late 1980s an influx of Tuareg nomads arrived from Libya and Algeria. They were primarily returnees, having left Niger approximately a decade earlier because of drought conditions. Nevertheless, their large numbers caused tensions to develop in the North.

In May 1990 a Tuareg attack in Tchin Tabaraden, based on political grievances, met a violent military response that attracted international attention. The governments of Niger, Mali, and Algeria met to try to resolve the problem by agreeing to expedite the return of persons to their places of origin. In 1991 further Tuareg attacks occurred. In 1992 the government recognized formally a rebellion in the North consisting of a Tuareg movement, the Liberation Front of Aïr and Azaouad (FLAA). The FLAA was led by Rissa Ag Boula. It sought not independence but a federal system of government in which it would be able to practice a form of self-administration.

A truce was agreed to in 1992 but soon broken, with each side blaming the other. A major government military offensive was launched in August 1992. In November a government commission recommended a plan of decentralizing authority to the local level as

a compromise with the FLAA's federalist plan. Still, the Tuaregs launched further attacks in early 1993. In March a temporary truce was reached. A more formal accord, signed in June in Paris, called for demilitarizing the North and further political negotiations. France pledged financial help for Tuareg resettlement.

Tuareg resistance to this agreement developed, however. A new Tuareg group, the Revolutionary Army of Liberation of Northern Niger (ARLN) rejected the accord. The FLAA split into factions, with the Liberation Front of Tamoust (FLT) supporting the truce while Boula and his supporters rejected it. Shortly thereafter the ARLN, FLAA, and FLT formed a negotiating body known as the Coordination of Armed Resistance (CRA) to deal with future negotiations. However, negotiation failed to take place. The French withdrew from their mediating role. Incidents of violence originating from both sides began anew.

In January 1994 a new Tuareg movement was organized, the Patriotic Front of Liberation of the Sahara (FPLS). With the CRA they demanded regional autonomy along with greater participation in the national government and military. The Niger government meanwhile sought a more general program of political decentralization. In June an agreement was reached in Paris for the establishment of a regional system of government for local ethnic groups, though greater Tuareg participation at the national level was not decided upon. Further unrest developed in late summer and early fall.

A new accord was signed on October 9. In early 1995 Boula formed a new group, the Organization of Armed Resistance (ORA), as a protest against the delayed implementation of the October 1994 accord. In April 1995 a more formal agreement was reached with an affirmation of the principles laid out in October. A period of disarmament would take place, with general amnesty being granted to all parties involved in the conflict. Development in the North was to take place along with a process of political decentralization.

However, this agreement met a new set of national problems. Unrest developed between Toubous and Peuhls in the East and South near Lake Chad. Refugees from Chad, primarily Toubou, created insecure border conditions with Chad. Moreover, a movement known as the Democratic Front of Renewal (FDR), formed in October 1994, demanded political autonomy in this region. Implementation of a peace agreement was slow, with incidents of violence continuing to occur. In March 1996 the CRA and FDR both recognized the April 1995 agreement.

Since Maïnassara's election in 1996 efforts at disarmament and repatriation have continued with some success despite occasional incidents of violence. Financing and implementing the peace process are ongoing issues that have necessitated continued international coordination for approaching resolution.

National Prospects

Mamadou Tandja appears to be secure in power following his second consecutive electoral victory. His government has achieved a level of legitimacy within the international community. The government has loosened control over oppositional political activity, and students and workers remain a significant factor within civil society. Whether economic and political reform will succeed in appeasing these and other domestic forces remains to be seen. In July 2005 the United Nations warned that millions of people were faced with malnutrition as crops were devastated by locusts and a lack of rain.

Further Reading

Baier, Stephen. *An Economic History of Central Niger.* Oxford, U.K.: Clarendon Press, 1980.

Boyle, Elizabeth Heger, Barbara J. McMorris, and Mayra Gomez. "Local Conformity to International Norms: The Case of Female Genital Cutting." *International Sociology* 17 (2002): 5–33.

Charlick, Robert. *Niger Personal Rule and Survival in the Sahel.* Boulder, Colo.: Westview Press, 1991.

Charlick, Robert, and James Thompson. *Niger.* Boulder, Colo.: Westview Press, 1986.

Decalo, Samuel. *Historical Dictionary of Niger.* Metuchen, N.J.: Scarecrow Press, 1989.

Miles, William F. S. *Hausaland Divided: Colonialism and Independence in Nigeria and Niger.* Ithaca, N.Y.: Cornell University Press, 1994.

FEDERAL REPUBLIC OF NIGERIA

By Terry M. Mays, Ph.D.

Nigeria is a country of perhaps 128 million people (2005 est.). The exact population of the largest country in Africa is in question. The country obtained its independence from Great Britain on October 1, 1960.

Nigeria emerged at independence with over 200 ethnic groups living in the country's three regions—a western region dominated by the Yoruba; a northern region dominated by the Hausa/Fulani; and an eastern region dominated by the Ibo. The Hausa/Fulani, the largest ethnic group in the country, represented approximately 30 percent of the total population, while the Yoruba were 20 percent and the Ibo 17 percent. Today the country consists of 36 states in an attempt to dilute the political power of these groups.

HISTORY

With independence Abubakar Tafawa Balewa, a northerner, became prime minister and Nnamdi Azikiwe, an easterner became governor general under a British-style parliamentary system of government. Independence intensified the campaign by many Nigerians, particularly among the country's minority ethnic groups, for greater autonomy. On January 15, 1966, the military, led by General Johnson Ironsi, ended the First Republic by means of a coup. Most Nigerians welcomed the demise of a regime hopelessly compromised by corruption, rampant patronage, sectionalism, factionalism, and election fraud. On May 24 the Federal Military Government (FMG) abolished the regions of the country and introduced a unitary state. Because the leader of the FMG was an Ibo, the move was not seen as a step toward national unity but as a device to break the powerful grip of the northerners on the country. Violent protests in the North resulted in great loss of life and property, primarily among Ibos settled there.

On July 26, 1966, a second military coup replaced Ironsi with General Yakubu Gowon. However, southerners were not satisfied with the change. On May 27, 1967, the FMG divided the country into 12 states in an attempt to settle regional divisions. Three days later the former Eastern Region, renamed Biafra, seceded. A bitter 30-month civil war followed, with some 600,000 military and civilian deaths. The defeat of Biafra and the exile of its leader, Lieutenant Colonel Odumegwu Ojukwu, reaffirmed the continuation of a federal system rather than the confederal one Ojukwu had proposed.

General Gowon presided over the relatively enlightened reintegration of the Ibo people into Nigeria. However, he failed to prepare to return the country to civilian rule. He was overthrown on July 29, 1975, by Brigadier Murtala Muhammed. By October Muhammed had appointed the 50-member Constitution Drafting Committee to prepare a constitution to be submitted to a constituent assembly for debate, amendment, and approval before October 1978. Four months later Muhammed decreed the establishment of seven new states, raising the total to 19. He also introduced a plan to move the capital from Lagos, a Yoruba stronghold, to a federal capital territory in the ethnically mixed center of the country. Muhammed, a popular leader among average Nigerians, was assassinated in February 1976, but his transition timetable was carried out by his deputy, Olusegun Obasanjo.

THE SECOND REPUBLIC

On October 1, 1979, the Second Republic came into being under democratically elected civilians led by Shehu Shagari. The civilian government survived one complete term in office but fell early in its second term, on December 31, 1983, to another military coup, which brought into power a mixed military-civilian government headed by General Muhammadu Buhari. General Ibrahim Babangida toppled Buhari's regime on August 27, 1985. Babangida planned a gradual transition to a democracy because of domestic and international pressure. However, his government refused to announce the results of a presidential election, apparently won by Moshood Abiola, on June 12, 1993. Babangida established a civilian government under Chief Ernest Shonekan and stepped down from power on August 26, 1993.

Shonekan's government quickly collapsed following a coup led by General Sani Abacha on November 17, 1993. After assuming power, Abacha dismantled the various elements of the democratic process developed under the Babangida regime and arrested Abiola. Domestic and international pressure forced Abacha to pledge a return to civilian government in 1998. The execution of Ken Saro-Wiwa, the leader of the Movement for the Survival of the Ogoni People, and others on November 10, 1995, led to international condemnation. The British Commonwealth suspended Nigeria's membership, and several Western states recalled their ambassadors for consultation. Various forms of mild international sanctions were also imposed on Nigeria.

General Abacha legalized five new political parties, and each nominated him as its presidential candidate in an obvious sham of a democratization pledge. However, Abacha died suddenly on June 8, 1998, and was replaced by General Abubakar. Many questioned the circumstances behind Abacha's death. Abiola died of a heart attack in prison on July 7, 1998—only one month after Abacha's death. Within months of assuming power General Abubakar, facing considerable internal and external pressure to return the country to civilian rule, announced that he would do so. He legalized political parties and established a transition timetable with local elections set for December 1998, state elections in January 1999, and national elections in February 1999.

Olusegun Obasanjo of the People's Democratic Party (PDP) emerged from the February 1999 elections as Nigeria's first democratically selected president in 16 years. Nigeria successfully held its next presidential election on April 19, 2003. Obasanjo won reelection after receiving 61.9 percent of the vote. Muhammadu Buhari, the general who led the 1983 coup against the democratic government of President Shagari, amassed 31.2 percent of the vote, followed by Chukwuemeka Ojukwu with 3.3 percent and other candidates splitting the remaining 3.6 percent.

The System of Government

Nigeria is a federal republic with a strong president and a bicameral legislature.

EXECUTIVE

The president serves as head of state and government as well as commander in chief of the armed forces. Presidential elections are held every four years and involve direct selection of the chief executive by the people. Presidents are limited to serving two terms, and candidates for the office are selected by registered political parties. The president is assisted by a vice president and a cabinet known as the Federal Executive Council.

LEGISLATURE

Nigeria's national legislature, under the current constitution, is bicameral with a 109-member Senate and a 360-member House of Representatives. Each of Nigeria's 36 states is allocated three seats in the Senate, while the Federal Capital Territory holds one seat. Each member of the House represents a single constituency in the country. Elections for each house are held every four years. Members of the House of Representatives and Senate are not selected on the same day. The combined two houses of the legislature are known as the National Assembly.

The People's Democratic Party dominated both houses following the February 1999 legislative elections. The next legislative elections occurred in April 2003. The PDP again dominated the process and secured majorities in both houses. Seats in the Senate were divided among the PDP with 73, the All Nigeria People's Party (ANPP) with 28, the Alliance for Democracy (AD) with six, and other parties with two.

Seats in the House were held by the PDP (213), ANPP (95), AD (31), and other parties (21).

JUDICIARY

The Supreme Court is the highest court in Nigeria. The president appoints the chief justice at his discretion, while the other judges on the Court, no more than 15, are appointed by the president on the advice of the Judicial Service Commission. The Supreme Court is the final court of appeal and has original jurisdiction in disputes between the federal government and a state or between states. The Supreme Court is duly constituted by five judges in most cases but requires seven judges in cases involving constitutional interpretation or questions of civil or human rights. The Federal Court of Appeals sits below the Supreme Court and hears appeals from the Federal High Court, the High Court of the Federal Capital Territory, state high courts, the Sharia Court of Appeal, the Customary Court of Appeal, and the National Industrial Court. The Federal High Court holds jurisdiction over all civil cases involving customs and excise duties, taxation, banking, and citizenship.

State courts consist of a high court with appellate and supervisory functions as well as original jurisdiction. States with a large Islamic population also have sharia (religious) courts of appeal and/or customary courts of appeal. These courts deal with appeals from lower sharia and customary courts, which handle personal and family matters on the basis of Islamic or traditional law. Judges may be removed only for disability or misconduct. Sentences handed down by these Islamic courts, including death by stoning for adultery, have led to considerable criticism in the West.

REGIONAL AND LOCAL GOVERNMENT

Nigeria emerged at independence with three regions but currently consists of 36 states in a federal system. The original three regions were split into 12 states in 1967, 21 states in 1987, 30 states in 1991, and then 36 states under General Abacha. Nigeria also has a Federal Capital Territory similar to the District of Columbia in the United States or the Federal District in Brazil.

The large number of states reflects an attempt to dilute the power wielded by ethnic groups and local leaders. Most groups support the establishment of additional states. Minority ethnic groups view new and smaller states as offering greater autonomy, while the Nigerian workforce recognizes new states, during periods of civilian rule, as presenting opportunities for additional political offices and government jobs.

A hotly debated issue in Nigerian politics is that of revenue allocation from the federal to the state and local governments. During the Second Republic, after months of debate over the amount to go to the state governments and whether the allocation to local governments should go directly to them or through state

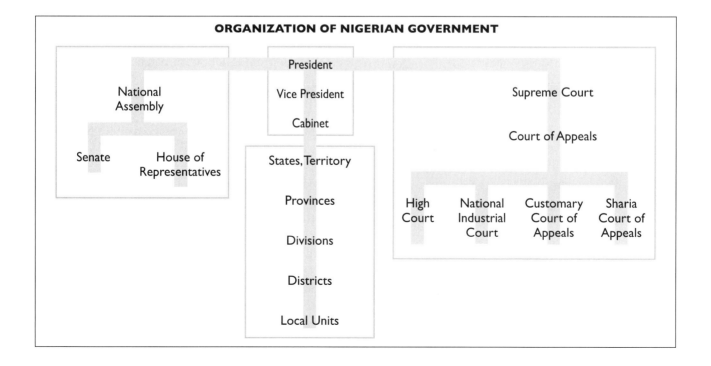

ORGANIZATION OF NIGERIAN GOVERNMENT

President
Vice President
Cabinet

National Assembly
Senate   House of Representatives

States, Territory
Provinces
Divisions
Districts
Local Units

Supreme Court
Court of Appeals
High Court   National Industrial Court   Customary Court of Appeals   Sharia Court of Appeals

offices, the National Assembly finally agreed in 1982 that the federal government would keep 55 percent of the revenues, distribute 35 percent to the states, and pass 10 percent directly to the local governments. The amount of the shares of each state and local government also causes great controversy. A few states, particularly the oil-rich ones, produce large numbers of petroleum-based jobs. However, many individuals within the states argue that they do not receive their fair share of petroleum income from the federal government. Other states are not as wealthy and/or have larger populations. Individuals in these states believe that they should receive increased funds from the federal government as compensation for the lack of lucrative mineral resources.

In the past the Nigerian government has attempted to allocate federal funding of the states based upon population. As a result states have tended to inflate their population reports as a means of increasing their percentage of funds. Due to this factor and the sensitivity of religious differences, census taking has been a heavily criticized activity within the state. For two decades Nigeria operated with a continuing series of estimates added to its 1963 census. The 1973 census count was not trusted by states and ethnic groups. The 1991 census counted over 88 million people, far below the estimated population of over 105 million Some observers attributed the discrepancy to overreporting by states in search of funds, while others viewed the count as inaccurate and an underreporting of the true population.

Southerners fear that the population growth of the Islamic North could increase the latter's influence in a democratic government and share of federal funds. On the other hand, the North would like to keep southerners divided in order to prevent any possible attempt to dominate a democratic government. The Abacha regime temporarily settled the question by annulling the 1991 census count in 1994.

The structure of state government has usually paralleled that of the federal government. Each state has a governor and vice governor of the same party, both elected statewide to four-year terms, as well as a state legislature. Under military rule the states were administered by military governors who held powers at a state level similar to those of the president at the federal level.

Local government represents the only political unit below that of the state. Elections for local government positions were last held on March 27, 2004. Traditional chiefs and religious leaders still carry considerable influence in many local areas.

The Electoral System

The electoral register consists of all Nigerians 18 years of age or over. Some violence occurred prior to the 2003 federal elections. Many international observers pointed to serious incidents of ballot tampering, vote rigging, and the questionable operation of polling stations. Others indicated that the transgressions could have been much worse due to the divisions within the country and were at least satisfied that the polling did not result in massive civil strife. Opposition parties called upon President Obasanjo to negate the results and conduct new elections. The matter was then referred to the Nigerian Court of Appeals. In the end, the results stood.

The Party System
ORIGINS OF THE PARTIES

Political activity by Africans appeared in the South, especially in Lagos, as early as the 1880s. It was largely a consequence of the spread of European-style education brought by Christian missionaries, as well as a natural continuation of southern Nigerian patterns of participation in government. In the North, where the British indirectly ruled a feudal society from which missionaries were banned, popular political activity was rare until the 1950s.

The first political parties were formed to contest limited indirect elections to a southern advisory legislative council in 1922. Herbert Macauly, of Yoruba–Sierra Leonean descent, founded the Nigerian National Democratic Party (NNDP) in Lagos prior to those elections. The NNDP dominated southern politics until 1934 when students founded the Nigerian Youth Movement (NYM). Although based in Lagos and largely Yoruba in membership, the NYM made efforts to be a national party and replaced the NNDP as the dominant political party in 1938.

As World War II drew to a close, political activity became more intense in Nigeria. In 1944 Nnamdi Azikiwe founded the National Council of Nigeria and the Cameroons (NCNC). Azikiwe, an American-educated Ibo, worked for national unity in spite of the fact that the NCNC was largely Ibo in membership. In 1951 Chief Obafemi Awolowo founded the Action Group as an outgrowth of a Yoruba cultural preservation society. Awolowo, in contrast to Azikiwe, argued that the sharp ethnic divisions in Nigeria made it unrealistic to expect the populace to suddenly abandon their ethnic identifications and adopt a vague national one. Instead he advocated that ethnic identities be protected and enhanced as the first step in a process of developing a pluralistic national polity. Also in 1951 the Northern People's Congress (NPC) was founded by Ahmadu Bello, the sardauna of Sokoto, heir apparent to the Fulani sultan of Sokoto, the most important political and religious position in the North.

The first government of independent Nigeria in 1960 emerged as a coalition between the NPC and the NCNC (which in 1961 changed its name to the National Convention of Nigerian Citizens). The Action Group became the formal opposition party. Awolowo and Azikiwe shifted their focus to the national level, with Azikiwe becoming governor-general and later president. The sardauna concentrated his efforts on the Northern Region and became premier of this area. Abubakar Tafawa Balewa, the sardauna's representative in Lagos, became Nigeria's first prime minister.

In 1962 a splinter of the Action Group re-formed the Nigerian National Democratic Party under the leadership of S. L. Akintola. Shortly thereafter Awolowo and many other Action Group leaders were arrested and tried on controversial charges of conspiracy to overthrow the government. Most, including Awolowo, were released in 1966 in the aftermath of the military takeover. The NCNC and the Action Group boycotted the elections of 1964, which were won overwhelmingly by an NPC-NNDP alliance. Azikiwe, as president, tried to force new national elections but failed. New elections were held in the Western Region in October 1965, and after a particularly violent campaign the NNDP won openly rigged elections and Akintola became premier of the region.

When the army took over in January 1966, the constitution was suspended, regional governments were dissolved, and political-party activity was banned. The coup was particularly bloody as evidenced by the murders of Balewa, Akintola, Ahmadu Bello, and other politicians. Ten senior army officers, most of them northerners, were also killed.

When political parties were allowed to re-form on September 21, 1978, most of the new organizations could trace their roots directly to the precoup parties. Azikiwe and Awolowo reappeared as major political party leaders. In an attempt to reduce regional and ethnic loyalties, political parties had to prove they operated offices in at least 13 of Nigeria's 19 states. Candidates for the presidency had to receive at least 25 percent of the vote in at least 13 states to claim

victory. Five political parties participated in the 1979 elections for the new office of president and a national legislature. The parties included the Nigerian People's Congress, Great Nigeria People's Party, United Party of Nigeria (led by Awolowo), People's Redemption Party, and the Nigeria's People's Party (led by Azikiwe).

The Nigerian People's Congress, led by Shehu Shagari, received a majority in the national elections. Shagari became Nigeria's first elected national leader since Balewa in October 1979. The collapse of the national economy and charges of corruption were followed by a military coup on December 31, 1983. When General Buhari assumed power in Nigeria on January 3, 1984, he banned all political parties in the country.

After another military coup General Babangida announced in September 1987 that he planned to guide Nigeria toward democratic elections. University representatives recommended the establishment of only two political parties in an attempt to eliminate regional and ethnic tensions during an election process. The Armed Forces Ruling Council of the Babangida regime accepted the plan and called for the establishment of two national political parties. After May 1989, 50 organizations sought recognition as legal political parties and 13 were able to meet the strict requirements imposed by the government. Of these, six were nominated to the Armed Forces Ruling Council. However, the Babangida government disqualified all 13 parties. In their places Babangida established two new parties, the Social Democratic Party (SDP) and the National Republican Convention (NRC), on October 7, 1989. Both received government funding.

The SDP tended to dominate the election process during local and national balloting. Abiola, the SDP's candidate, won the election for the presidency according to most observers. However, Babangida disqualified both Abiola and his opponent and called for new elections. Following Babangida's departure and Abacha's overthrow of the Shonekan government, political parties were again banned and the government arrested Abiola.

In 1995 General Abacha allowed political parties to form under complicated guidelines that led to only promilitary parties being recognized by the government and able to participate in future elections. After the deaths of Abacha and Abiola, General Abukabar legalized mass political parties, resulting in the establishment of nine organizations in October 1998. Following local elections in December 1998 only three of these parties could garner enough popular support to qualify for state and national elections in 1999. These organizations were the People's Democratic Party, the All People's Party (APP), and the Alliance for Democracy. Since the 1999 election there has been a proliferation of small political parties in Nigeria.

Major Political Parties

PEOPLE'S DEMOCRATIC PARTY (PDP)

The PDP, a coalition of smaller parties chaired by Audu Ogbeh, is the strongest political organization in Nigeria. Consisting of many former opponents of General Abacha, it cuts across ethnic and geographical boundaries and is the closest thing to a national party in Nigeria. Leadership within the PDP includes President Olusegun Obasanjo, a popular figure among many Nigerians for returning the country to democratic rule in 1979, and the former vice president Alex Ekwueme. The party nominated Obasanjo to run for the national presidency in 1999, and he won with 63 percent of the popular vote. In 2003 Obasanjo was reelected with 61.9 percent of the popular vote. The PDP also won 73 seats in the Senate and 213 seats in the House of Representatives in 2003.

ALL NIGERIA PEOPLE'S PARTY (ANPP)

The ANPP, the second-strongest political party in the country, formed in 2002 from an alliance of the United Nigeria People's Party (UNPP) and the All People's Party (APP). A splinter of the southeastern-based UNPP refused to join the coalition with the northern-based APP and ran its own slate of candidates for national office in 2003. The ANPP's presidential candidate, Muhammadu Buhari, a former military chief executive of Nigeria, won 31.2 percent of the popular vote in 2003. The ANPP did not do as well as the PDP in the 2003 elections for the national legislature, securing 28 seats in the Senate and 95 seats in the House of Representatives.

Minor Political Parties

ALLIANCE FOR DEMOCRACY (AD)

The Alliance for Democracy is a Yoruba-based party with its strength in the southwestern part of the country. Led by Adamu Abdulkadir, the AD includes many

former supporters of Abiola. The party won less than 15 percent of the local seats in December 1998 and six gubernatorial seats in January 1999, but it received approximately 25 percent of the seats in both national legislative houses. The AD united with the All People's Party under a single presidential candidate, Olu Falae, to counter the PDP's candidate, Olusegun Obasanjo. Falae received 37 percent of the popular vote in the February 1999 election. In 2003 the AD supported President Obasanjo's bid for reelection and did not field its own candidate. The party did secure a third-place showing in elections for the national legislature, taking six seats in the Senate and 31 seats in the House of Representatives.

ALL PROGRESSIVE GRAND ALLIANCE (APGA)

The APGA emerged following the formation of the All Nigeria People's Party. The APGA's support lies among the Ibo of southeastern Nigeria. Chief Emeka Odumegwu-Ojukwu ran for the national presidency on the APGA ticket in 2003 and won 3.3 percent of the popular vote. The party secured two seats in the national House of Representatives but did not win a seat in the Senate.

Other Political Forces

MILITARY

The Nigerian military, numbering over 78,000 in 2003, can also be seen as a political party/movement due to its history of manipulation and coups since independence. Although all ethnic groups are represented in the military, the Hausa tend to dominate the senior officer ranks.

ORGANIZED LABOR

Labor unions have also participated in the Nigerian political scene. Labor organizations tend to cut across ethnic and regional lines in order to concentrate on basic issues of workers' welfare such as minimum wages, fringe benefits, and a variety of special subsidies. These groups are major champions of the demands of government employees. Oil unions were among the most instrumental in organizing the strikes in support of Abiola following his arrest by the government. The Provisional Ruling Council replaced the union leaders with individuals more sympathetic to the government, thus ending much of the union-based political resistance at the end of the second military period. The National Labour Congress (NLC) is an organization that unites many labor unions. The NLC organized a general strike in July 2003 to protest an increase in fuel prices. The eight-day strike involved gasoline stations, banks, ports, and shops. Police attempting to disrupt the strike killed at least 10 individuals. The NLC ended the strike following a government agreement to slash fuel prices.

STUDENTS

The expansion of Nigeria's system of higher education during the 1970s, which brought a university to every state in the federation, increased the political importance of the students, who have consistently been an invaluable indicator of public opinion in the country. During the Shagari and Buhari administrations students were vociferous in opposition to the government. As educational institutions expanded, these student forces have become important factors on the Nigerian political, economic, and social scene. The government tended to base special riot-control police units near Nigerian universities to provide a quick response to protesting students. Frequently in recent years the government shut down the country's universities for entire semesters to relieve the boiling political tensions on campus. Professionals, journalists, and intellectuals have also emerged to speak for a broad array of public interests. On a national level students are organized under the National Association of Nigerian Students. Student protest remains a potential challenge to any Nigerian local or national government.

ETHNIC GROUPS

The various major ethnic groups that make up modern Nigeria are important forces in the national political arena. Depending on the definitions used, there are between 250 and 350 distinct ethnic groups in Nigeria with different customs, social structures, and languages or dialects. Aside from the three major groups, most of these groups are very small, and most are in the "middle belt," an uneven swath that stretches across the country from Kwara state in the West to Gongola state in the East.

North of the "middle belt" the Hausa-Fulani dominate, although Fulani concentrations can be found in the eastern section of the "belt." Conservative and strictly Islamic, the Fulani are descended from nomadic peoples, partly of Berber origin. Some Fulani still lead a seminomadic life in the Far North. Settled Fulani are the aristocrats of the North, leaders of a stratified feudal society whose emirs wield great political and social authority. That society includes the Hausa, who had established several city-states and the feudal system in the North before the founding of the Sokoto state in the early nineteenth century. Hausa is the lingua franca of the North. The Kanuri are another major people of the North. Nearly all the peoples of the North are Muslim and together make up at least half of Nigeria's population.

The Yoruba of the Southwest are probably the largest single ethnic group. Yoruba society is structured in communal groups based on large extended families. Yorubas profess Islam and Protestant Christianity in nearly equal numbers. The obas, or chiefs, continue to exercise effective social, and often political, control, and the alafin of Oyo is still the preeminent traditional political ruler.

The Ibos of the Southeast are known over much of Africa for their individualism, energy, and personal enterprise. They are largely Roman Catholic, with few vestiges of traditional religion. Among the minority ethnic groups, the Tiv are perhaps the most numerous and live in the North. The Nupe, most of whom are Muslim, are concentrated in the North and exhibit a hierarchic society. The Edo, who predominate in the Midwest, have much in common with the Yoruba, while the Ibibio in the East have been influenced by Ibo culture. The Ijaw of the East are probably of mixed origin, a product of the social disruptions caused by the former slave trade.

National Prospects

Nigeria remains at a political and economic crossroads. President Obasanjo is widely respected for his return of the government to civilian rule in 1999. He is a Yoruba from southwest Nigeria but is trusted by many Hausa-Fulani in the North. As a former general he retains many supporters in the military. Although Obasanjo received an impressive 63 percent of the popular vote in 1999 and nearly 62 percent in 2003, he faces many critics in culturally divided Nigeria. Obasanjo has found it necessary to walk carefully when confronting controversial issues in the various regions of the country. For example, while noting his opposition to stoning adulterers in northern Nigeria, he stopped short of issuing a legal challenge in the national court system. Nigeria's next test will be the 2007 national elections, assuming its democracy survives the ethnic tensions boiling within the country and avoids another military coup. The major political parties will have to select presidential candidates who have national appeal and can secure votes across the entire country. At any point the military could reassert itself into Nigerian politics and overthrow the government.

Nigeria is also facing an economic crisis. Years of rampant corruption and mismanagement have taken a terrible toll on the national economy. Half-completed construction projects lie abandoned across the entire country due to the skimming of funds by officials. The money appropriated for such projects disappears, and the buildings are never completed. The economic growth of the 1970s based on high petroleum prices stagnated with the drop in the cost of oil in the 1980s and 1990s. Rising foreign debt and inflation add to the economic problems facing Nigeria.

Since 1984 successive governments have undertaken self-imposed austerity measures, which included retrenchment of employees in the civil service, floating the national currency, and divestment or closure of a large number of state corporations and agricultural marketing boards. Nigeria's military governments have often refused to abide by International Monetary Fund conditions for the opening of credit facilities and attempted instead to design their own programs for economic resuscitation. The challenges of restructuring the public arena, establishing a strong democratic leadership, and developing effective channels of participation are central to the governability of this large and potentially prosperous country. Steps toward economic stabilization are hence tied to continued political reforms within the state.

Further Reading

Aborisade, Oladimeji, and Robert J. Mundt. *Politics in Nigeria.* New York: Longman, 2002.

Awotokun, Kunle. *Governance and Legislative Control in Nigeria: Lessons from the 2nd and 3rd Republics.* San Francisco: International Scholars Press, 1998.

Beckett, Paul A., and Crawford Young, eds. *Dilemmas in Democracy in Nigeria.* Rochester, N.Y.: University of Rochester Press, 1997.

Diamond, Larry, Anthony Kirk-Greene, and Oyeleye Oyediran, eds. *Transition without End: Nigerian Politics and Civil Society under Babangida.* Boulder, Colo.: Lynne Rienner, 1997.

Dudley, B. J. *Instability and Political Order: Politics and Crisis in Nigeria.* Ibadan: Ibadan University Press, 1973.

———. *An Introduction to Nigerian Government and Politics.* London: Macmillan, 1982.

Graf, William D. *The Nigerian State.* Portsmouth, N.H.: Heinemann, 1988.

Herskovits, Jean. *Nigeria: Power and Democracy in Africa.* Headline Series, no. 257. New York: Foreign Policy Association, 1982.

Kirk-Greene, A. M. H. *Nigeria since 1970: A Political and Economic Outline.* London: Hedder and Stoughton, 1981.

Mwakikasite, Godfrey. *Ethnic Politics in Kenya and Nigeria.* New York: Nova Science, 2001.

Nnoli, Okwudiba. *Ethnic Politics in Nigeria.* Enugu, Nigeria: Fourth Dimension Press, 1978.

Nwachuku, Levi, and G. N. Uzoigwe. *Troubled Journey: Nigeria since the Civil War.* Dallas: University Press of America, 2004.

Nwagwu, Emeka. *Taming the Tiger: Civil-Military Relations Reform in the Search for Political Stability in Nigeria.* Lanham, Md.: University Press of America, 2002.

Ojiako, James O. *Thirteen Years of Military Rule.* Lagos: Daily Times Publications, 1980.

Oluleye, James J. *Military Leadership in Nigeria, 1966-1979.* Ibadan: Ibadan University Press, 1985.

Oyewole, Anthony, and John Lucas. *The Historical Dictionary of Nigeria.* 2d ed. Lanham, Md.: Scarecrow Press, 2000.

Suberu, Rotimi. *Federalism and Ethnic Conflict in Nigeria.* Washington, D.C.: United States Institute of Peace Press, 2001.

KINGDOM OF NORWAY
(Kongeriket Norge)

By John T. S. Madeley, Ph.D.
Revised by Robert S. Kadel
Further Revision by Mary Hendrickson, Ph.D.

The kingdom of Norway, a nation of just over 4.5 million people (2005 est.), adopted its constitution on May 17, 1814, a date on which the Norwegian people declared independence from the Danish Crown, which had ruled them for four centuries. The Norwegian constitution has remained in effect ever since, making it the oldest constitution still in force in Europe. However, Norway remained subject to the Swedish Crown (by cession from Denmark) until 1905.

When Norway finally achieved complete independence, the people decided by referendum to reinstate the ancient Norwegian monarch. Prince Carl Frederick of Denmark was invited to ascend to the Norwegian throne; he assumed the name Haakon VII, and thus began Norway's contemporary monarchy. The official language of Norway is Norwegian with two dialects, Bokmål (Book Standard) and Nynorsk (New Norwegian). The official state religion is Evangelical-Lutheran.

The System of Government

Norway is a parliamentary democracy headed by a constitutional monarchy. The Crown is the chief of state, and the prime minister, with his or her cabinet, is head of government. The constitution also makes provisions for a legislative branch (vested in the Storting, the primary legislative and budgetary authority) and a judiciary power centered in a Supreme Court.

EXECUTIVE

The executive function is vested in the "King in Council," which refers to the king and the government, consisting of the prime minister and the cabinet ministers. The Council of State is formally appointed by the king, who requests the party winning a majority of members in the Storting—or, if there is no majority, a viable coalition—to form a new government and appoint a prime minister. The cabinet ministers are appointed by the king, but only after approval from the majority party (or parties in the case of a coalition government). The king is also the commander in chief of the Norwegian armed forces and the head of the Church of Norway. Prior to 1990 the Crown was hereditary in the male line. The constitution was amended at that time to provide for gender equality in succession rights to the throne. The constitutional amendment affected any heir born after May 1990. The present king is Harald V, who ascended to the throne in 1991.

The main role of the Council of State is to formulate bills and budget proposals for consideration by the Storting. Cabinet ministers implement legislation passed by the Storting.

LEGISLATURE

The Storting is the primary legislative and budgetary authority in Norway. It consists of 169 members elected from the 19 counties in Norway. Elections occur at regular four-year intervals, with no provision in the constitution for dissolving the Storting. A system of alternates, or deputy representatives, ensures immediate replacement for any unoccupied seat. The Storting begins each year's session on the first weekday of October, but there is no formal end of session: The Storting is required to remain in session as long as is deemed necessary and terminates its proceedings only when it has concluded its business.

The entire Storting is elected as a single body. Once elections have taken place, members of the Storting nominate one-fourth of their number to constitute the Lagting, or upper division, the remaining three-fourths constituting the Odelsting, or lower division. The Storting attempts to balance power between the two divisions via the specific members nominated to the Lagting. If a disagreement over legislation does arise between the two divisions, the entire Storting acts to resolve the issue, a two-thirds vote being necessary for a measure to pass. Constitutional amendments also require a two-thirds majority, as well as a general election, before any proposed amendment can be enacted.

A presidium, with the president of the Storting as chair, acts as a steering committee responsible for the smooth operation of the legislature, the order of business, and management of the Storting. Standing committees, which correspond to the government ministries, perform many of the budgetary, legislative, and managerial functions of the government. Caucuses of the political parties in the Storting make

decisions about the membership of the presidium and the standing committees. For the most part the parties function smoothly with one another on the basis of strict rules of internal party discipline and interparty relations. However, albeit very rarely, a government sometimes receives a motion of no confidence—the last time in 2000 when a minority government headed by Prime Minister Kjell Magne Bondevik lost a dispute over an environmental issue. Bondevik and his coalition government regained power in 2001.

The Storting oversees the government. It possesses the authority to wield a vote of no confidence or to launch an investigation into possible impeachment of the prime minister or individual cabinet ministers. More routinely, members of the Storting may voice concerns during the Question Time, at which the prime minister and/or cabinet ministers are held to account for their actions.

JUDICIARY

The Norwegian constitution establishes a court system divided into four sections, with the Hoyesterett (Supreme Court of Justice) at the top. The members of the Hoyesterett are appointed by the king and can be removed only after due process. The courts practice the process of judicial review in constitutional matters and may declare a law unconstitutional. However, the courts generally defer to the Storting in matters

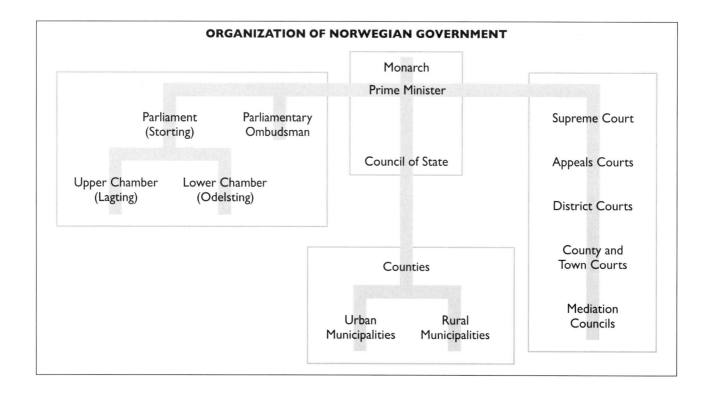

ORGANIZATION OF NORWEGIAN GOVERNMENT

related to the constitution, so it is rare for them to declare unconstitutionality. The Hoyesterett consists of a president and at least four other members. The High Court of the Realm (the Court of Impeachment) is drawn from the permanent members of the Lagting (two-thirds) and the permanently appointed members of the Supreme Court (one-third). Impeachment trials, however, are rare.

REGIONAL AND LOCAL GOVERNMENT

Norway is divided into 19 counties and 434 municipalities. The counties vary in size and range in population from about 73,000 to 517,000. Populations of the municipalities range from a mere 2,100 to around 517,000. Each local body elects its own governing council, the Kommune in the municipalities and the Fylkeskommune in the counties. Elections to these councils are held every four years, although they are staggered so that county elections do not take place at the same time as municipality elections.

There is no hierarchy of control between the two—that is, the municipalities are not subordinate to the counties. Each has its own specific function for its inhabitants. The municipalities are responsible for kindergartens, child care, elementary schools, libraries, various cultural provisions for municipal residents, social welfare, sewer systems and treatment, and primary health services. The counties' primary responsibilities revolve around high schools, hospitals and other special health services, care for substance abusers, county roads and transportation, and large-scale cultural enterprises such as museums.

The Electoral System

The Storting's 169 members are chosen by direct election in multimember constituencies. All citizens who are at least 18 years of age or will reach that age by the end of the election year are eligible to vote. The electoral register is drawn up in the summer months immediately preceding an election; thus voter registration is consistently up-to-date. Each of the 19 counties elects a number of representatives to the Storting in proportion to its population. The largest representation can be found in the counties of Oslo (Oslo) and Hordaland (Bergen), while Finnmark and Aust-Adger Counties have the fewest representatives, all other counties lying somewhere between. Within each constituency each party will offer a list of candidates with at least as many names as there are seats for the county. Thus a voter may vote for none or all from one party. The voter is also allowed to cross out names on one list and write in names from another party list; however, this has had only a minuscule effect on election outcomes in the past. Voter turnout is generally high in Norway, with usually more than 75 percent of the population active in Storting elections and about 60 percent in local elections.

The Party System

Just over a century has elapsed since the introduction of political parties in Norway. Before this time groups existed that had political links to activities in the Norwegian government, but there were no formally organized parties. The year 1884 saw the onset of parliamentarism and, shortly afterward, the creation of the first official political party, the Liberals. Only six months had passed when the opposition to this party formed their own party, the Conservative Party. In 1914 the Labor Party emerged as a major electoral force and was joined shortly after World War I by the Agrarian League. The addition of the Christian People's Party (Kristelig Folkeparti; KrF) in the 1930s completed the basic framework of parties in Norway. Meanwhile smaller parties also emerged, such as the Communist Party in the 1920s and the Socialist People's Party in the 1960s. Members of these groups joined forces in 1973 to form the basis for the Socialist Left Party. On the other side of the political spectrum the right-wing Progress Party also formed in 1973.

The Labor, Conservative, and Agrarian/Center Parties all represent their traditional economic interests: workers, business, and farming, respectively. Formally each party, with the exception of the Labor Party, has adopted a position of neutrality with respect to interest-group organizations. However, voting patterns indicate that there are strong ties between each party and interest groups.

Ideologically the parties fall fairly clearly along the traditional political spectrum: Socialist Left and Labor on the left, Conservative and Progress Party on the right, the Christian People's Liberal and Center Parties in the center, and smaller groups in various positions (e.g., the Communists farther to the left). Pragmatically the split is mostly between the Socialists and non-Socialists and is borne out in the alternation of parliamentary control between these two blocs.

There are other important factors in the party divisions and the vote. In particular, center-periphery, urban-rural, environmental, and religious and cultural divisions exist. Such factors have been particularly important in the development of the Christian People's Party, the Liberal Party, and the Green Party. These parties' identities are not formed necessarily along economic lines but involve other social forces.

Highly articulate system of party discipline and interparty relations ensure that these ideological differences are translated into action by party representatives in the Storting.

PARTY ORGANIZATION

Each of the Norwegian political parties is of the mass-branch type with relatively high levels of dues-paying membership. The Labor Party alone allows for collective membership—e.g., among trade union branches. This exception does not affect the basic fact that all Norwegian parties share the same type of structure; their party constitutions resemble one another to a remarkable degree.

The basic unit in all parties is the local association, which includes all dues-paying members in a particular locality. Associations are joined together at municipal, county, and national levels. An important feature is that the municipal and county party organizations have complete power to nominate candidates for elective office. This means, in particular, that central party organs have no formal power to affect the composition of party lists, even at the level of the Storting. This decentralized structure of power in the matter of nominations is reinforced by the existence of residential qualifications for Storting candidates. The nominating conventions of the constituency organizations usually take pains to include on the party list representatives of a range of groups (whether by locality, sex, or interest group) in order to attract the widest possible support consistent with the (local) party's political line.

The highest governing body in each party is the national conference, usually held every two years. Delegates to the conference are elected by constituency organizations but also include government ministers (where a party has any), members of the Storting, and representatives of the party's women's and youth organizations. The principal business of a conference is usually the discussion and adoption of the party program on the basis of a draft circulated to and debated by local parties in advance. In addition the conference elects party leaders and rules on general matters of organization and discipline. The principal party leader is generally the national chairman, who in most cases is also the leader of the party in the Storting.

The national chairman presides over the national committee, which is elected by the conference and includes members from all constituent organizations. The national chairman also presides over the executive committee, which is in charge of the day-to-day activities of the party. The national committee, which meets much less frequently than the executive committee, possesses the highest authority in the party between conferences. The chairman is assisted by the party general secretary, who heads the party's administrative apparatus.

At the municipal, county, and national levels the party's elected officeholders (Storting deputies and county or municipal council members) frequently meet in caucus with the appropriate level of party leaders. These caucuses ensure a high degree of internal party agreement and discipline. The national or local party membership organizations, through their representatives in conference, are accorded final authority in the party constitutions, but conflicts between them and the caucuses of elected representatives are rare.

CAMPAIGNING

Election campaigns are rarely colorful or exciting affairs because the electoral system generally ensures that the decisive contest lies between disciplined parties rather than between individual candidates. Few newspapers in Norway can be considered nonpartisan, so voters are generally presented with news and views that only confirm their initial predispositions. Since 1960, however, television has tended to supersede the press as the citizens' principal source of information. Although the electronic media generally have exposed the public to a wider spectrum of political debate and have doubtless contributed to the recent increase in electoral volatility, this new element of drama is limited by the absence of political commercials. (There is no commercial advertising on radio or television.) Meanwhile all parties are allotted equal exposure.

INDEPENDENT VOTERS

Party identification in Norway has been an important factor underpinning the remarkable stability of the electorate until recent years. Over the 20 years after 1945 a substantial majority of voters regularly identified with one of the major parties. Until the 1970s the reflection of social and economic cleavages in the party system further reinforced this stability. However, since the issue of Norway's membership in the European Union (EU) became a major concern, the country has experienced a wave of electoral volatility unprecedented since the 1930s. During the stable years it was unusual for individual parties to vary by as much as 3 percent in electoral support from one election to another. Since the post-EU referendum election of 1973, however, a substantial floating vote has made its impact felt in marked changes of electoral strength. These changes have occurred principally among parties that make up the Socialist and non-Socialist blocs themselves. The 1970s and 1980s saw a distinct electoral shift away from the Socialist parties until the late 1980s, when the Labor Party regained power through about 1997. Although briefly restored to power in 2000–2001, the Socialist parties saw their support wane until 2005, when the Labor Party won the September elections and formed a new coalition government with the Center Party and the Socialist Left Party.

Major Political Parties

CENTER PARTY

(Senterpartiet; SP)

HISTORY

The Center Party was founded in 1920 as the Agrarian League. The following year it changed its name to Farmers' Party; the Center Party name was adopted in 1959. From the start it was an agrarian-interest party closely associated with farmers' organizations. In the postwar period it has joined in government coalitions with non-Socialist parties in 1963, 1965–71, 1972–73, 1983–86, 1989–90, and 1997–2000. Looking out for its members' economic interests, the party continues to campaign against membership in the European Union.

ORGANIZATION

The Center Party maintains auxiliary organizations for women and youth and conducts a variety of educational programs, particularly in rural areas. The party reported a membership of 50,000 in 1990, a decline of about 10,000 members over 10 years, and declined further to 33,000 by 2004. A great majority of the membership belongs to the various agrarian-interest associations.

The Center Party's principal aim has been to promote the interests of those engaged in agriculture by securing favorable credit, marketing, and pricing arrangements and to safeguard rural interests in general. Despite its advocacy of government intervention and support in agriculture, the party is firmly non-Socialist.

The party changed its name in 1959 in an attempt to make up for the decline of the agricultural sector by appealing to all centrist voters, regardless of their occupation or residence. The party has adopted a range of "green" environmental and decentralist policies that have modified its traditional political stance.

In foreign policy the party continues its firm stance against membership in the EU, a policy that was largely responsible for the collapse of the center-right coalition in 1971. In other respects the party's foreign policy is orthodox—pro-West, pro-NATO—and favors a strong defense establishment.

PROSPECTS

The Center Party has seen a gradual decline in votes since the 1990s, and in 2005 it won only 6.5 percent and 11 seats. Some of this reduction in popularity is due to a number of Center Party issues being co-opted by the Conservatives. The Center Party became a part of the coalition government with the Labor Party and the Socialist Left Party following the 2005 elections— the first time the Center Party had joined a coalition government with Socialist parties.

CHRISTIAN PEOPLE'S PARTY

(Kristelig Folkeparti; KrF)

HISTORY

The party was founded in 1933 by a group of religious temperance activists after one of their main leaders was dropped from the Liberal Party list for the Storting election that year. It emerged as a national party in 1945 and since then has advanced to become one of the largest parties in the system. It attracts support principally from religious activists both within and outside the state church, in particular from those who are members of the numerous organizations for home and foreign missions. It joined government coalitions with the other non-Socialist parties in 1963, 1965–71, and 1972–73 (when it also provided the prime minister, Lars Korvald), 1986–89, with the Conservative and Center Parties following the 1989 general election, with the Center and Liberal Parties in 1997, and with the Liberal and Conservative Parties in 2001, when it again provided the prime minister, Kjell Magne Bondevik.

ORGANIZATION AND POLICIES

The Christian People's Party maintains auxiliary organizations for women and youth. The party has for most of the postwar period had a relatively weak membership base. This is compensated for by its ability to borrow strength from the religious and temperance organizations despite the fact that the party has no formal connections with them. Its principal stronghold is still in those areas, particularly in the south and west of the country, where these organizations maintain an important, if declining, strength.

From its inception the party has been committed to the promotion and defense of fundamentalist Christian values, including temperance. The party has distinguished itself from all others through its stands on moral and religious issues. Since the late 1960s the most controversial of these stands has been the party's strong opposition to the liberal abortion law espoused and then introduced by the Labor Party. The party's inability to persuade the Conservative Party to adopt an equally strong position led directly to the failure of attempts to form a majority non-Socialist coalition after the 1981 election. When it finally joined the Conservative and Center Parties in government in 1983, it firmly retained its position on this issue.

In economic policy the party is non-Socialist, although in the area of social welfare it has often been closer to Labor than the other non-Socialist parties. In foreign affairs it is strongly pro-NATO, but the EU question in the early 1970s caused severe internal divisions.

For most of the 1970s the main leader of the Christian Democrats was Lars Korvald, who was opposed to EU entry and strongly against any compromise on the abortion issue. The disagreement over these issues led to strong party infighting. Korvald disputed the EU and abortion issues heavily with Kaare Kristiansen, who took over as party leader during the 1980s. However, the disagreements have subsided for the most part. Valgerd Svarstad Haugland is the current party chair.

PROSPECTS

The Christian People's Party reached a peak of popular support in the 1997 election with 13.7 percent of the vote. It received 12.4 percent of the vote in 2001. In 2005 it lost the elections to a "red-green" coalition of the Labor Party, Center Party, and Socialist Left Party. Since 1963 the party has been a coalition partner in all non-Socialist governments.

CONSERVATIVE PARTY

(Høyre; "The Right")

HISTORY

The Conservative Party was founded in 1884 to oppose Liberals' demands that the royal veto should be defied

and the rules of parliamentarism be adopted. For most of this century it has aspired to be the principal national party of all those opposed to Socialism. It constituted a major element in the non-Socialist coalitions of 1963 and 1965 to 1971. Despite being the largest of the non-Socialist parties, in most of the post-1945 period it usually took only about 18 percent of the votes. After 1973, however, it enjoyed a remarkable growth of support, taking as much as 31.7 percent of the vote in 1981. This support has waned in recent elections, although the party joined the Christian People's Party and the Liberal Party to form a government in 2001.

ORGANIZATION

Like the other major parties the Conservative Party has women's and youth wings. In the 1970s the organization was reformed and greatly expanded after a successful membership recruitment drive.

Around the turn of the century the party changed from being the party of the old class of officials, which had administered the state for centuries, to being the party of the rising class of those in business and higher professionals. Because of the survival of the other non-Socialist parties, the party failed to become a national party appealing to all classes and regions, remaining instead a largely urban-based party of high-income earners. The party receives large contributions from private business organizations, although, as in the case of the other parties, exact figures are unknown.

The party's opposition to socialism has been associated with the championship of private enterprise and initiative in the context of a free market. The party supports privatization and lower taxation. Like the other non-Socialist parties, however, it has come to accept the most central aspects of the country's highly developed welfare state. In recent years it has called for the deregulation of the economy, claiming that such a strategy would generate new economic growth and so leave the welfare state intact.

In foreign policy the Conservatives have been strongly pro-NATO and pro-EU. Their support for the EU in the early 1970s, when the country voted by referendum not to join, led to a relative decline in the party's fortune. In the 1980s, a period with less EU concern among Norwegians, the Conservatives attracted growing support for their economic programs. The party continues to support Norwegian membership in the EU.

PROSPECTS

The party's successes in the regional strongholds of the centrist parties and among the young and the better-paid (and more highly taxed) workers support its claim to have become the worthy counterpart and opponent of the long-dominant Labor Party. Together with the Center Party the Conservatives provided a strong challenge to Labor's long-standing rule in the Storting. However, the party was not a part of the coalition government formed when Labor stepped down after the 1997 election. It joined a coalition government with the Liberals and Christian People's Party in 2001 when it received 21.2 percent of the vote. In 2005 it received 14.1 percent of the vote and 23 seats in the Storting. The Conservative Party will continue to argue for deregulation, lower taxes, and membership in the EU, as market forces, it believes, can solve most of the country's problems.

LABOR PARTY
(Det Norske Arbeiderparti; DNA)

HISTORY

Founded in 1887, the Labor Party was from the first closely associated with trade unions, which experienced considerable membership growth in the industrial take-off period immediately before World War I. In 1918 the party was taken over by a radical new leadership that soon brought it into the Communist International, thereby precipitating a number of splits. When the party was reunited in the late 1920s, it immediately established itself as the largest party in the system, a status it has been able to maintain with ease throughout most general and local elections.

In 1935 Labor began a term of office that was to last for 30 years, interrupted only by the German occupation and the two-month non-Socialist coalition of 1963. From 1945 to 1951 it enjoyed an absolute majority in the Storting. In 1971 the party again formed a minority government committed to negotiating Norwegian entry into the EU. When this policy was rejected in the September 1972 referendum, the government resigned. In the 1973 election the party suffered its heaviest loss of votes since 1930 but was able to form a minority government by relying on the support of the Socialist Electoral League (later the Socialist Left Party—Sosialistisk Venstreparti; SV). For eight years thereafter it clung to office on the strength of a single-seat majority for the parties of the Socialist bloc, finally being defeated in the election of 1981. The Labor Party regained its dominance in the late 1980s and has retained its position as the most popular vote-getter, but it was an opposition party between 1997 and 2005, except for a brief period in 2000–2001. After the 2005 elections it led a historic

"red-green" coalition that included the Socialist Left Party and the Center Party. The party's leader, Jens Stoltenberg, regained the prime minister's office in 2005, having previously held it in 2000–2001.

ORGANIZATION AND POLICIES

Like the other major parties, Labor has important women's and youth sections. Its close association with the trade unions is institutionalized in a system of collective membership; i.e., trade union locals are members of the party at the local level. This feature lends the party organization great depth and penetration.

The party has traditionally been supported not only by the industrial working class, which is highly unionized, but also by workers in primary industry and smallholders in agriculture. It is the urban-rural basis of support that accounts for the party's historic strength.

Since the mid-1930s Labor has abandoned its early policies of radical social and economic change, opting instead for gradual reform aimed at maintaining full employment and the development of a welfare state in a mixed economy. In contrast to the non-Socialist parties it is committed to a relatively high degree of government planning and intervention in the economy.

In foreign policy the party adopted a firmly pro-NATO position in the late 1940s. It has generally maintained this stance ever since, but it has opposed the stationing of foreign troops and the installation of nuclear weapons in Norway. During the 1980s the Labor Party committed itself to the introduction of a nuclear-free zone in the Nordic area. From the early 1960s the party was for a decade also strongly pro-EU, but the defeat of the policy in the 1972 referendum led it to abandon this commitment.

Labor's electoral fortunes were undermined in the mid-1970s by tensions between the party's radical and moderate wings. It attempted to accommodate the two sides by dividing the leadership between a moderate prime minister and a more radical chairman. The experiment failed to resolve the tensions, and in early 1981 the two functions were reunited in the person of Grotharlem Brundtland, the country's first female prime minister and one of the most significant Norwegian prime ministers of the latter twentieth century. Despite Conservative rule of the Storting in the 1980s Brundtland returned to the office of prime minister in 1985. She resigned her position in 1989 but returned after one year when the non-Socialist government resigned over internal differences on the European Economic Community. Brundtland has since retired. As of 2005 the party leader was Jens Stoltenberg, who became prime minister following the 2005 elections.

PROSPECTS

The Labor Party remains Norway's strongest electoral party. From about 1935 the party has played a dominant role in government for a preponderance of the time. Through its leadership the nation's strong and comprehensive social welfare programs were instituted. While support for the party has declined, it has made its mark by establishing a direction for the country's policies. The "red-green" coalition government it formed in 2005 was historic for being the first Socialist government to include the Center Party and the firs government of any kind to include the Socialist Left Party.

Minor Political Parties

COMMUNIST PARTY OF NORWAY

(Norges Kommunistiske Parti; NKP)

The Communist Party of Norway was founded by left-wing members of the Labor Party when it disaffiliated from the Third (Communist) International in 1923 after a short period of membership. In the interwar years it declined to the status of an insignificant political sect, but it enjoyed a strong revival (taking almost 12 percent of the vote) in 1945 after a period of active involvement in the resistance to the German occupation. From that high point it again declined, losing its last Storting seat in 1961. In 1973 it joined the Socialist Electoral League (see Socialist Left Party) and shared in the success of that organization as it capitalized on the strong wave of mobilization against the EU. Two years later, however, die-hard elements refused to go along with the decision to merge with other left-Socialist elements in the new Socialist Left Party.

In the years after 1945 the Communist Party purged itself of "bourgeois-nationalist," "Trotskyite," and "Titoist" elements and reverted to being a strict Stalinist, Moscow-aligned party. With the exception of the EU referendum, it has largely remained within this mold and is now again a party of almost no electoral importance.

LIBERAL PARTY

(Venstre; literally, "The Left")

Founded in the early 1880s on the basis of a coalition of peasants and urban intellectuals committed to the introduction of parliamentarism, the Liberal Party's history since then has been very checkered. Until the First World War it remained the predominant party

of government despite two serious splits on the right. In the period since then, however, it was first overtaken by Labor as the principal party of social reform and then lost support to the Farmers' and Christian People's Parties in the center of the political spectrum. Its remaining support was based on an uneasy alliance of diverse groups: temperance, religious, and language activists; secularist libertarians; and low-salaried workers.

Unlike other parties the Liberal Party had no single social or economic constituency and was sustained by little more than a common commitment to rather vague liberal ideas and the party's historic traditions. As such it joined the other non-Socialist parties in the 1963 and 1965–71 coalitions. The EU issue found the party badly divided, however, and it split into two soon after, the faction opposed to the EU retaining the old party label. In 1985 the party declared its willingness to lend support to a Socialist government in exchange for the adoption of its environmentalist policies, but in the election it failed to gain any representation for the first time in its long history. The party returned to regain one Storting seat in the 1993 election. In the 1995 local election the Liberal Party made a stronger showing, taking 4.7 percent of the vote. Finally, in 1997 the Liberals formed a coalition government with the Christian People's Party and the Center Party after Labor relinquished its control of the government. The party received 5.9 percent of the vote in 2005 (up from 3.9 in 2001) and 10 seats in the Storting.

LIBERAL PEOPLE'S PARTY

(Det Liberale Folkepartiet; DLF)

When the Liberal Party split in 1972, the pro-EU faction, which included 9 of the 13 members of the old Liberal Storting group, broke away to form the Liberal People's Party. In the 1973 election it fared even wore than the remaining Liberals, taking only a single seat, which it lost in 1977 and has since been unable to regain. With less than 1 percent of the vote the party is clearly moribund with little or no prospect of resuscitation.

PROGRESS PARTY

(Fremskrittspartiet)

The Progress Party was founded in 1973 under the name Anders Lange's Party for Substantial Reduction in Taxes, Duties, and Governmental Interference. The party received 5 percent of the vote and four seats that year. After the death of Lange, who was a political maverick, the party was torn by internal strife, for which it paid in 1977 with the loss of all Storting representation. Carl I. Hagen, a popular and charismatic leader of the party, has apparently helped to boost its popularity in recent years.

However, the party's anti-immigration and "extreme" right positions have alienated other parties, and it has never joined in a coalition government despite intervals of popular support. Nonetheless, the party was a silent partner with the coalition government of the Conservative, Liberal, and Christian People's Party following the 2001 election. In 2005 it's support jumped to 22.1 percent and 38 seats. In general the party has acted as a watchdog for the right, alert to any slips or sell-outs on the part of, in particular, the Conservative Party.

SOCIALIST LEFT PARTY
(Sosialistisk Venstreparti; SV)

In 1961 a Socialist People's Party was founded by a group of anti-NATO activists who had been expelled from the Labor Party. In the election of the same year the party deprived Labor of its overall Storting majority by taking two seats, which it managed to hold for eight years, to 1969. With the success of the anti-EU referendum campaign in 1972 the party enjoyed a revival that was strengthened by cooperation with other anti-EU and anti-NATO groups in the Socialist Electoral League. In the 1973 election it took 11.2 percent of the vote and 16 seats. Two years later the League was converted into the Socialist Left Party. The process was attended by considerable internal disagreement; the Communist Party die-hards eventually refused to merge into the new party. In the 1980s SV failed to sustain the 1973 level of support for its radical Socialist and neutralist policies. The party's platform has called for improvements in education and social welfare programs, tougher environmental regulation, and opposition to globalization, which the party believes will deepen worldwide inequalities in the distribution of resources. In the 2005 parliamentary elections the party received 8.8 percent of the vote and 15 seats. For the first time in its history, it was invited to join the government, in this case with the "red-green" coalition led by the Labor Party and including the Center Party.

RED ELECTORAL ALLIANCE
(Rød Valgallianse; RV)

In 1973 a Maoist party was formed by the merger of a number of extreme-left splinter groups, the largest of which had split in 1968 from the Socialist People's Party's youth section. The party took the name Workers' Communist Party Marxist-Leninist (Arbeidernes Kommunist parti Marxist-Leninistene; AKPML). Since 1971 the party has fought the Storting elections under the name Red Electoral Alliance, failing to gain representation. Despite internal problems connected with attitudes toward China, the party will doubtless continue to exist, but its prospects for achieving anything but the most marginal electoral support must be meager.

Other Political Forces
ECONOMIC-INTEREST GROUPS

Like neighboring Sweden, Norway has a very highly developed system of interest-group representation that plays an important role within the overall political system. Despite the overwhelming ethnic and confessional homogeneity of the population (the Lapps in the far north account for less than 1 percent, and nearly 90 percent of Norwegians remain members of the Lutheran state church), the earliest voluntary associations to develop were those that articulated emergent cultural differences. In the middle and late nineteenth century movements associated with religious revivalism, temperance or prohibition, and the promotion of an alternative linguistic standard (New Norwegian) based on rural dialects gave rise to organizations that have continued to have a significant political impact. In particular these three "countercultural" movements with their disproportionate strength in the south and west of the country provided the historic basis for the viability of the centrist parties with their opposition to the industrialism and secularism of the Labor and Conservative Parties.

It is the economic-interest organizations—founded around the turn of the century to defend and promote the interests of workers, employers, and farmers—that have had the greatest impact on the style and content of political decision making. Through a system of regular consultation with government in a wide range of ad hoc and regular committees, commissions, and boards, they have provided a second channel of popular representation alongside that of the Storting. The system has been called one of corporate pluralism, and decisions made within it have regularly affected central questions of economic and social policy. The existence of this second tier of decision making or representation helps to explain the high level of policy consensus and general political stability in a system that for 20 years after World War II was dominated by one party, the Labor Party, to the exclusion of all others. The standing of the main interest groups is enhanced by extremely high levels of membership within their respective economic constituencies and a degree of centralization, not least among the trade unions, that has enabled group leaderships to deliver binding agreements.

The major interest-group organizations are the Norwegian Employers' Association (Norsk Arbeidsgiver-forening; NAF), the Norwegian Trades Union Federation (Landsorganisasjonen i Norge; LO), and the Norwegian Farmers' Union (Norges Bondelag). No other groups are nearly so important, but two small groups do have some role; they are the Norwegian Farmers' and Smallholders' Union (Norsk Bonde og Småbrukarlag) and the Norwegian Fishermen's Union (Norges Fiskarlag).

National Prospects

Norway is a relatively prosperous, small, and homogenous country (although a there has been a modest immigration of refugees from war-torn or autocratic nations, resulting in some challenges concerning integration). The economy is strong, depending upon exports of fish, timber, aluminum, oil, and natural gas. Norway ranks among the top nations in the world in per capita GDP, $43,152 in 2004. This success is explained in part by its abundant natural resources. Norway is the third-largest exporter of oil, following Saudi Arabia and Russia. The country's natural resources have permitted it to enact progressive social welfare policies for its citizens, including pensions, medical care, day care, and paid and job-protected parental leave for childbirth and adoption at 80 percent of replacement wages. Levels of unemployment are low.

An egalitarian society, Norway has achieved high levels of gender equity, electing numerous women as political leaders. Nearly one-half of members of the Storting and a high proportion of cabinet members are women. Most of the political parties set aside positions for women to assure gender equity in the proportion of seats held in parliament.

One of the challenges for the new "red-green" coalition that took control of government in 2005 will be to maintain the country's high living standard and innovative policies while also protecting the source of its wealth, the natural resources, against depletion. Of course, there are other issues that could erupt, including reconsideration of EU membership, environmental matters, and the enduring question of the proper role of government versus the private sector.

Further Reading

Arter, David. *The Nordic Parliaments.* New York: St. Martin's Press, 1984.

Berglund, Sten, and Ulf Lindstrom. *The Scandinavian Party System(s).* Lund, Sweden: Studentlitteratur, 1978.

Brundtland, Grotharlem. *Madam Prime Minister: A Life in Power and Politics.* New York: Farrar, Straus and Giroux, 2002.

Cerny, Karl H., ed. *Scandinavia at the Polls.* Washington, D.C.: American Enterprise Institute for Public Policy Research, 1977.

Eckstein, Harry. *Division and Cohesion in Democracy: A Study of Norway.* Princeton, N.J.: Princeton University Press, 1966.

Rokkan, Stein. "Norway, Numerical Democracy, and Corporate Pluralism." In *Political Oppositions in Western Democracies.* Ed. Robert Dahl. New Haven, Conn.: Yale University Press, 1966.

Strom, Kaare, and Lars Svasand, eds. *Challenges to Political Parties: The Case of Norway.* Ann Arbor: University of Michigan Press, 1997.

Storing, James A. *Norwegian Democracy.* Boston: Houghton Mifflin, 1963.

Valen, Henry, and D. Katz. *Political Parties in Norway.* Oslo: Universitetsforlaget, 1964.

Valen, Henry, D. Katz, and Stein Rokkan. "Norway: Conflict Structure and Mass Politics in a European Periphery." In *Electoral Behavior: A Comparative Handbook.* Ed. Richard Rose. New York: Free Press, 1974.